Water

WATER

ASIA'S NEW BATTLEGROUND

Brahma Chellaney

GEORGETOWN UNIVERSITY PRESS
Washington, D.C.

Georgetown University Press, Washington, D.C. www.press.georgetown.edu
© 2011 by Brahma Chellaney. All rights reserved. No part of this book may be reproduced
or utilized in any form or by any means, electronic or mechanical, including photocopying
and recording, or by any information storage and retrieval system, without permission in
writing from the publisher.

Library of Congress Cataloging-in-Publication Data

Chellaney, Brahma.
    Water : Asia's new battleground / Brahma Chellaney.
        p.   cm.
    Includes bibliographical references and index.
    ISBN 978-1-58901-771-9 (cloth: alk. paper)
    1. Water supply—Asia.   2. Water—Government policy—Asia.   3. Water
rights—Asia.   4. Asia—Environmental conditions.   I. Title.
TD299.C47   2011
333.910095—dc22

                                                            2011003841

⊗ This book is printed on acid-free paper meeting the requirements of the
American National Standard for Permanence in Paper for Printed Library
Materials.

15   14   13   12   11   9   8   7   6   5   4   3   2
First printing

Printed in the United States of America

Contents

Illustrations

FIGURES

Acknowledgments

For this multiyear, interdisciplinary study, I received the unstinting support of many experts and institutions. The institutions stretched from Japan and South Korea to Israel and Qatar. The Rome-based Food and Agriculture Organization of the United Nations is a first-rate agency that was the source of valuable insights and data. I am particularly indebted to the Konrad-Adenauer-Stiftung for its support, with Beatrice Gorawantschy and Jörg Wolff lending full backing.

I am thankful to the two anonymous reviewers who read my manuscript with care and acuity to offer constructive suggestions, which by and large have been incorporated. The book also owes much to the expert comments received from many others too numerous to name here, yet they should know that my gratitude goes out to them.

My thanks also go to Georgetown University Press, particularly Don Jacobs, for his interest in my manuscript and for overseeing the peer review process. The Georgetown University Press staff did a great deal to successfully produce this book; they are indeed an excellent team.

Introduction

Water Tensions in Boom Times

Asia faces a daunting water crisis that threatens its economic and political rise and environmental sustainability. Water has emerged as a source of increasing competition and underlying discord between many Asian states striving for greater economic growth. Asia has been booming largely because it enjoys peace and stability. But the recrudescence of Cold War–era territorial disputes—with the renewed revanchism tied to resource interests—has underscored the looming dangers. Various developments are indeed highlighting the linkage between water and peace. Water scarcity is set to become Asia's defining crisis by midcentury, creating obstacles in its path of continued rapid economic growth and stoking new interstate tensions over shared basin resources. Water, of course, is not the only resource that Asia's rapid economic rise has brought under growing pressure. But it is the most critical one, for which there is no substitute.

Asia already is at the center of the global water challenges. Although home to three-fifths of the human population, Asia, the world's fastest-developing continent, has less freshwater per capita than any other continent. To make matters worse, Asia's water efficiency and productivity levels are among the lowest in the world. Yet the uneven availability of water within several Asian nations has given rise to grand but environmentally questionable ideas—from China's Great Western Route to divert river waters from the Tibetan Plateau to its parched north and South Korea's politically divisive four-rivers project, to India's now-stalled proposal to link up its important rivers and Jordan's plan to save the dying Dead Sea by bringing water from the Red Sea through a 178-kilometer-long canal, which is also to serve as a source for desalinated drinking water.

This book, by innovatively looking at water and security issues across Asia, seeks to fill a void in the literature: There are many good studies of subregional water issues in Asia (including in Southeast Asia, China, Central Asia, South Asia, and the Middle East), but none specifically focus on the larger Asian water picture in the context of peace and security. This is the first wide-ranging study of water and peace that examines Asia in its totality and employs this broader framework to thematically focus on critical issues and countries. The book highlights the long-term security

1

implications of the new tensions over the resources of transnational aquifers like al-Disi and international rivers such as the Amu Darya, Syr Darya, Brahmaputra, Mekong, Salween, Indus, Jordan, Tigris-Euphrates, Irtysh-Illy, and Amur. It also brings out the unique triple role of Tibet as Asia's water repository, water supplier, and rainmaker, thereby underscoring the centrality of the Tibetan Plateau on the Asian water map. It offers concrete policy suggestions on how the intensifying competition and discord on transnational water resources in Asia can be prevented from flaring into open confrontation and war. In this sense, it is a pioneering study of Asia's murky water politics and the attendant security challenges.

As an interdisciplinary study written for scholars, policymakers, serving officers, upper-level students, and the educated general public, this book blends materials from geopolitics, sustainable science, hydrology, environmental studies, geology, international law, and international relations to present a holistic picture of the security implications of the growing water stress in Asia, the world's largest and most densely populated continent. By signifying the interconnectedness of the various fields dealing with resource issues, it aims to be useful across a wide range of disciplines in the social sciences, humanities, and natural sciences. In addition to being the first comprehensive study of the larger geostrategic dimensions of Asian water issues, the book seeks to bring out the lessons that other continents can draw from Asia's experiences so as to avert similar resource, environmental, and security challenges.

At a time when water is becoming increasingly tied to security across much of the world, the linkage between water and peace is particularly striking in Asia, where the per capita availability of freshwater is less than half the world average. A number of important Asian economies, especially the fastest growing, are already water stressed. These realities, along with strained inter-riparian relations and the absence of an Asian security architecture, call attention to the risks of water conflicts. Managing interstate and even intrastate water disputes in Asia is likely to become increasingly challenging.

Several disputed or occupied territories at the heart of geopolitical tensions in Asia—ranging from Kashmir and Tibet to the Golan Heights and the West Bank—are strategically valued because of their water wealth and advantageous location. China's newly assertive territorial claim to Arunachal Pradesh (or "Southern Tibet," as it has been called since 2006) has been made with an eye on that remote Indian state's rich water resources. Some other Asian regions that are roiled by separatist unrest—Kyrgyzstan's southern Uzbek-influenced Fergana Valley and Turkey's Kurdish southeast, for example—are also water rich and strategically located.

A number of rivers, including several of Asia's biggest, flow from Chinese-held territory to neighboring countries, where they serve as lifelines. China, in fact, has the distinction of being the source of cross-border river flows to the largest number of countries, ranging from Russia and Kazakhstan to India and Vietnam. No other country in the world matches China's position as a multidirectional, transboundary water provider. But, significantly, the important international rivers in China all originate in ethnic-minority homelands, some of which are racked by separatist movements. The traditional homelands of ethnic minorities, extending from the Tibetan Plateau and Xinjiang to Inner Mongolia and Manchuria, actually span three-fifths of the landmass of the People's Republic of China, although minority communities make up only 9 percent of its total population. Given that the focus of China's dam building and other water diversions is moving from internal rivers to international rivers, megaprojects now are increasingly concentrated in the resource-rich minority homelands, which is triggering new tensions along ethnic fault lines over displacement and submergence issues and is fueling deeper resentment in these poorer regions.

More broadly, as Yemen and Afghanistan illustrate, the battle lines of internal wars tend to follow the lines of watercourses. Intrastate water disputes are endemic in much of Asia, and this book analyzes those situations where domestic discord is grave. The study reveals that, whereas intracountry water conflicts are serious and exact significant costs, the intercountry disputes and geopolitical competition over transboundary basin resources actually pose a greater threat to peace and stability in a continent already troubled by festering territorial and resource disputes.

In Asia, it has usually taken years of efforts to establish water institutions or mechanisms, including the Permanent Indus Commission, the Mekong River Commission, and the Israeli-Palestinian Joint Water Committee for the West Bank. Because water has proven to be a deeply contentious and divisive issue, the tendency is often to defer or delay finding ways to resolve water disputes. The 1996 Ganges Water Treaty, arising from the dispute over the building of India's downstream Farakka Barrage, took nearly as long to emerge as its stated duration— three decades—though it is renewable by joint Bangladeshi and Indian consent. In the Israeli-Palestinian context, the water issue indeed has been put off to the "final status" negotiations, along with other knotty problems like Jerusalem's future, Israeli settlements, and the right of Palestinian refugees to return. And in the Jordan-Israel case, water was taken up so belatedly in the shaping of a peace deal, as the two sides dragged out the negotiations, that the eventual accord on water arrangements was spelled out in Annex II of the 1994 Peace Treaty.

Water increasingly is becoming a precious commodity whose control is at the core of several raging conflicts in Asia. Asia's water woes have been exacerbated by rapidly expanding economies, surging populations, rising per capita consumption levels, and continuing rural-to-urban migration. The water crisis now haunting the continent is the bitter fruit of unsustainable practices and a gross mismanagement of basin resources. And it has been accentuated by the rapid spread of irrigated farming and high water-consuming industries and by a growing middle class that not only uses water-guzzling comforts such as washing machines and dishwashers but is also eating more meat, which is notoriously water-intensive to produce.

The threats to Asia's sustainable water supply are intensifying even as demand for water is soaring. Yet Asia continues to live beyond its means—overexploiting resources while hoping to postpone the day of reckoning. The geostrategic factors that have raised the specter of water wars are being reinforced by the growing water stress arising from the human-induced degradation of watersheds, watercourses, coastal ecosystems, and the broader environment, which is reflected in shrinking forests and wetlands and increasing water pollution. Such developments undermine hydrological and climatic stability and foster a cycle of chronic flooding and droughts.

Indeed, Asia awaits a future made hotter and drier by climate and human-made environmental change. Its unslakable thirst for water now faces the likelihood that an already-limited supply will decrease sharply if climate change projections prove right. Asia is expected to bear the greatest water-related effects of global warming. The Himalayan snowmelt and glacier melt that feed Asia's great rivers are likely to be treacherously accelerated by global warming. And given Asia's vast, densely populated coastal areas, it is expected to become more vulnerable to water-related disasters, whose frequency could increase due to the climate-change-driven rise of ocean levels and surface temperatures. Seawater intrusion, accelerated by recklessly excessive groundwater extraction, is already affecting the availability of freshwater supplies in some coastal cities. The upstream construction of multiple giant dams and other water diversions, for their part, are causing a retreat of Asia's eleven heavily populated megadeltas that are fed and formed by rivers originating on the Tibetan Plateau. These megadeltas—home to megacities like Bangkok, Calcutta, Dhaka, Guangzhou, Karachi, Shanghai, and Tianjin—are, in several cases, also Asia's economic boom zones.

Asia is a huge continent, with a number of different regions and subregions. Although this book covers virtually the whole of Asia, it focuses its in-depth discussions on the most-populous regions, which are the scene of sharpening hydropolitics. These are also the regions where the geopolitical risks of greater conflict are especially serious, with a bearing on the larger Asian and international security and the world economy. This study details the struggle for water in eastern, southern, and southeastern Asia. China and India, for example, are home to 37 percent of the world's population but have to make do with 10.8 percent of its water. These two giants have experienced steep declines in per capita water availability since 1980, although the water situation in India is far more ominous. Actually, the entire contiguous belt from India to Israel—a region that includes Pakistan, Uzbekistan, Iran, Iraq, Syria, Jordan, and Saudi Arabia—has the dubious distinction of being racked by both serious water distress and pressing security challenges.

The book unfolds with Asia's big picture in chapter 1, which examines the continent's unique water challenges in the context of geostrategic trends and power shifts. Those shifts have made Asia the axle of global geopolitical change, with Asian policies and challenges shaping the international security and economic environment. Yet Asia has also morphed into the most likely flashpoint for water wars, a concern underscored by efforts of some countries to exploit their riparian position or dominance.

In chapter 2 the book turns to the securitization of water at a time when Asia is beginning to confront serious constraints on natural resources. The chapter analyzes specific cases—from Singapore's efforts to reduce its dependency on water imports from Malaysia to the grating hydropolitics involving the five former Soviet republics of Central Asia—but its longest sections deal with the manner in which harmful legacies have shaped the water and environmental crises in China and India. With rising grain prices haunting the world, it also discusses the implications of water shortages on Asia's ability to feed itself.

Chapter 3 bares the unique role that the Tibetan Plateau plays in Asia's hydrological and weather cycles, including in supplying river waters, bringing on the annual Asian monsoons, and aiding climatic stability. It then examines the effects of human-made environmental change (through deforestation, the elimination of grasslands, the introduction of Western-style agriculture, and giant hydroengineering projects) and demographic transformation (brought about by a state-sponsored "Go West" Han migration campaign) on this special biogeographic region, which has the world's largest concentration of tall mountains and greatest diversity of ecological zones, extending from arctic to subtropical. Given that China has gerrymandered Tibet by hiving off large parts of it, the terms "Tibet" and "Tibetan" in the book have been used in a broad ethnographic sense to refer to the entire Tibetan Plateau and to the resources and people native to this land. The chapter details the Great South–North Water Transfer Project, the world's biggest hydraulic initiative, and the plans for megaprojects on international rivers originating on the plateau.

Chapter 4 offers an exhaustive case study of the international political and environmental implications of the Chinese plans to divert the Brahmaputra River's waters, including by building the world's biggest dam next to a disputed, heavily militarized border with India. The greatest burden of such a diversion would actually fall on impoverished Bangladesh, which is located farthest downstream. Several factors have whetted China's drive to increasingly tap the resources of the Brahmaputra and other large, fast-flowing international rivers like the Mekong and the Salween, including an officially drawn link between water and national security, the dominance of engineers in the top echelons of power, the rise of water nationalism at a time of increasing water stress, a calculated hydroengineering policy focus on minority homelands because dam building has reached virtual saturation levels in the Han heartland, newly laid infrastructure facilitating greater dam building in the ethnic regions, the country's emergence as the world's largest builder of dams and dominant exporter of hydropower equipment, and the state-run hydropower industry's growing clout.

The next two chapters examine the broader Asian challenges to forestall or manage water conflicts. Whereas chapter 5 deals with intrastate water discord, chapter 6 focuses on intercountry issues, including the links between territorial and resource disputes. The analysis of intrastate conflicts highlights how ambitious supply-side approaches, although intended to mitigate spatial imbalances in resource distribution within countries, can instigate new water disputes between provinces or communities by launching major dam and other diversion projects.

With the help of case studies focused on four very different countries—each with its peculiar internal challenges—the intracountry analysis seeks to subtly underline the imperative to move from purely supply-side approaches to demand-side options that emphasize water conservation and quality as much as quantity. Even on the supply side, it has become necessary to embrace nontraditional measures, from recycling of water to rainwater capture. The examination of intercountry disputes—while highlighting the disputes between China and its neighbors, Israel and its neighbors, and India and its neighbors—underscores the need to invest in institutionalized basinwide cooperation on shared resources to help underpin Asian peace and stability.

The concluding chapter 7 sums up the major test Asia confronts with respect to freshwater—a test whose outcome will shape not only Asia's water future but also its economic and political future. Institutionalized cooperation among basin states needs to be anchored in a careful balance between rights and responsibilities. Appendix A gives a tabular rundown on interstate freshwater agreements in Asia since the start of the decolonization process, and appendix B gives Web links to key Asian water treaties. In a continent where several major territorial disputes rage, the depiction of political boundaries remains a touchy matter. The text and maps in the book reflect boundaries in actual control, and national claims thus are mentioned where necessary.

This book lays out in detail the policy implications of the growing water stress and competition in Asia. Asia's likely emergence as a major food importer, for example, will deepen the international food crisis and squeeze low-income countries, such as those in Africa. Also, given that Asia has the fastest-growing economies and the fastest-rising demand for food, its water shortages will only worsen without major efficiency gains in use. Yet before water efficiency and productivity standards can be raised significantly, the internal challenges in many countries are likely to be exacerbated.

Intrastate water conflicts thus far have proven more damaging and violent than intercountry water disputes in Asia. But as the book brings out, the dangers of greater water conflict between nations are growing. China, with its hold over Asia's greatest transnational water resources, has made the control and manipulation of natural river flows a fulcrum of its power and economic progress, spurring intensifying concern among downstream nations. While China promotes multilateralism on the world stage, it has given the cold shoulder to multilateral cooperation among basin nations—as symbolized, for example, by the Mekong River Commission—and rebuffed efforts by co-riparian states to seek institutionalized water-sharing arrangements with it. The alternative to rules-based riparian cooperation is an arbitrary system as defined and led by it. Sharpening geopolitical competition over water resources also characterizes the situations in Southern and Central Asia, the Near East, and the Arabian Peninsula.

Let me be clear: Even without any shots being fired, transboundary water disputes have become a source of underlying tensions between nations, and they have thus fueled mistrust and soured relationships in Asia. This is a reminder that once water becomes a political and diplomatic battleground, it begins to exact geopolitical costs insidiously, in ways not very different from the legacy of an armed action. Water wars are very damaging to regional stability and cooperation, whether they are waged with or without the resort to force. So make no mistake: There are real and present dangers in Asia.

The book thus stresses the importance of developing cooperative institutional mechanisms between and within states. Three strategies are specifically recommended. The first is to build Asian norms and rules that cover transboundary water resources. The second is to develop inclusive basin organizations encompassing transnational rivers, lakes, and aquifers in order to manage the water competition. And the third is to develop integrated planning to promote sustainable practices, conservation, water quality, and an augmentation of water supplies through nontraditional sources.

Asia needs preventive diplomacy geared toward forestalling water wars. Only regional collaborative mechanisms can help mitigate the risks that arise from the rush to dam transboundary rivers, overexploit aquifers that straddle international borders, or create a hydroengineering infrastructure upstream to support the use of water as an asymmetric political tool. If water is not to draw new battle lines between Asian states, there is no alternative to wise basin resource management that follows institutional norms and means. Water is thus a key test of whether Asian leaders have it within their power and capacity to forge cooperative relations that benefit their peoples, basins, and continent. Much is at stake in Asia, and it also has a bearing on the rest of the world. In fact, what Asia confronts today, the other continents are likely to face tomorrow.

One

Asia

Global Water Crisis Hub

Asia is at the center of the global water security challenges at a time when water is poised to outstrip oil as the world's scarcest vital resource.[1] Water—closely tied to food, energy, and climate change—has gone from being an economic issue to becoming a security issue. Asia stands out because it has experienced the world's most rapid growth in freshwater withdrawals from rivers, lakes, and underground aquifers during the past century.[2] Nothing better illustrates Asia's centrality in the global challenges today than the fact—highlighted by several United Nations agencies—that the world's most-populous and fastest-developing continent has less freshwater per person than any other region in the world.

Indeed, Asia's per capita freshwater availability is less than half the global average.[3] Yet, according to one UN report, Asia continues to draw on tomorrow's water to meet today's needs.[4] Worse still, Asia has one of the lowest levels of water efficiency and productivity in the world. Water scarcity now affects more than two-fifths of the people on Earth, but by 2025, two-thirds of the global population is likely to be living in water-scarce or water-stressed conditions.[5] And the majority of the world's people living in water-related despair will be in Asia.

INTRODUCTION

Water played a central role in the rise and decline of the earliest civilizations. But now history is potentially coming full circle: The rise and fall of powers in Asia could be influenced by water in much the same way that oil in the past century played a key role in determining the ascent or decline of states. The looming struggle over water resources in Asia, home to 60.5 percent of the global population as

8

of 2008, has been underscored by the rapid spread of irrigated farming and water-intensive industries and a growing middle class that is eating more meat (whose production is almost ten times more water intensive than plant-based calories and proteins) and using water-guzzling, energy-hogging home appliances like dishwashers and washing machines.[6]

Some of the world's fastest-growing economies—China, India, South Korea, and Vietnam, for example—are at or near water-stressed conditions. Because aquifers are being drained to dangerously low levels, a number of cities in Asia that rely on groundwater face the specter of running out of water in the coming years. Sanaa, Yemen's capital, and Quetta, in Pakistan, are two of the most prominent such cases, and Beijing must increasingly depend on water transfers from elsewhere. In an ever-deeper search for water, millions of pump-operated wells threaten to suck Asia's subterranean reserves dry, even as the continent confronts river depletion.

Defining Water Shortage, Stress, Scarcity, and Insecurity

The four terms widely used in the international discourse on water—water shortage, water stress, water scarcity, and water insecurity—remain the subject of debate themselves. "Water shortage" refers to an absolute deficiency where the level of available water cannot meet basic societal and economic needs. The actual quantity determining a per capita minimum will vary from place to place, depending on the environment. "Water stress," as a term, was popularized by the Swedish hydrologist, Malin Falkenmark, who in 1989 developed the Water Stress Index, which divided the volume of available freshwater resources in a country with its population. By factoring in water requirements for food self-sufficiency, the index treated countries with 1,666 cubic meters of water availability per capita annually or less as water stressed. Countries with less than 1,000 cubic meters of water per capita were said to be chronically water stressed, or in a state of water scarcity.[7]

In reality, the distinction between water shortage and water stress/scarcity really hinges on national demand as a consequence of the level of agricultural and industrial development: Water shortage is more likely to characterize the situation in an underdeveloped country with low industrial and irrigation utilization, whereas another nation with similar climatic conditions, population size, and water-resources availability but with large-scale irrigation and high industrialization would be faced with water stress or scarcity. One much-respected international agency, the Food and Agriculture Organization of the United Nations, views internal renewable water availability of less than 2,000 cubic meters (m^3) per person per year as an indicator of water scarcity, with a figure below 1,000 m^3 per inhabitant per year signifying acute scarcity and a serious constraint on socioeconomic development and environmental protection.

An aggregated per capita benchmark offers a useful comparative tool, but qualitative determination can be as important as quantitative measurement. After all, the per capita level at which water becomes scarce to cause domestic or trans-boundary conflict will depend on political, economic, and climatic factors. The spatial variability of water resources within countries, seasonal variability, and external-supply dependency ratio also constitute useful determinants in gauging water scarcity or vulnerability. The United Nations, through its principal mechanism, UN-Water, has coined a simple definition of water scarcity: "The point at which the aggregate impact of all users impinges on the supply or quality of water under prevailing institutional arrangements to the extent that the demand by all sectors, including the environment, cannot be satisfied fully."[8] This definition does not differentiate between water stress and water scarcity. "Water security," by contrast, is a term the United Nations Development Program has promoted as part of its human security concept: "In broad terms, water security is about ensuring that every person has reliable access to enough safe water at an affordable price to lead a healthy, dignified and productive life, while maintaining the ecological systems that provide water and also depend on water."[9] A high external-supply dependency ratio, coupled with a growing strain on accessible resources, often spurs water insecurity.

Asia's Resource Challenges

The sharpening Asian geopolitical competition over energy resources has drawn much international attention, but this has helped obscure the other danger: Water shortages in much of Asia are straining inter-riparian relations and becoming a threat to rapid economic modernization and environmental sustainability. Harmonious ties between nations sharing a natural course of water (e.g., a river, aquifer, or lake) depend on the duty of each riparian state to exercise its water rights only in relationship to the rights and duties of its neighbor.[10] And the protection of the sources of water demands that no party withdraw or divert water in such a way as to affect the ecosystems. Yet such a sense of duty is hardly prevalent in Asia. Ecological balances already are being altered through the overexploitation of groundwater and surface-water resources.

Although intrastate water-sharing disputes have become rife in several Asian countries—from India and Pakistan to Southeast Asia and China—the potential intercountry conflict over shared water resources should be of greater concern. The specter of water wars in Asia also is being highlighted by climate change and environmental degradation in the form of shrinking forests and swamps and the overdamming of rivers, which foster a cycle of chronic flooding and droughts. The Himalayan snowmelt that feeds Asia's greatest rivers could be dangerously accelerated by global warming, leading to serious river depletion. The poor management of river basins, environmentally unsustainable irrigation practices, an overuse of groundwater, and the contamination of water sources have all helped aggravate Asian water woes. The overexploitation of subterranean water in large parts of Asia has resulted in a rapidly falling groundwater saturation level—known as the water table. In the Gangetic delta, wells have tapped into naturally occurring arsenic deposits, causing millions of people in Bangladesh and eastern India to be exposed to high levels of poisonous arsenic in drinking water and staple agricultural products like rice. In some Asian coastal areas, the depletion of groundwater has permitted saline seawater to flow in to replace the freshwater that has been extracted.

Asia will continue to have the world's largest number of people without basic or adequate access to water. The Asian water sector is plagued by serious problems, including inadequate infrastructure and poor system maintenance, financially strapped utilities, low-cost recovery, growing pollution, watershed degradation, and unsustainable groundwater extraction. Owing to leaks and system inefficiencies, a sizable portion of the water supply is lost before reaching the consumer.[11] At the same time, water stress in the face of rising demand and poor resource management is sharpening competition between urban and rural areas, between neighboring provinces, and between nations.

As water distress intensifies and global warming accelerates, local, national, and interstate disputes over water are likely to become endemic in Asia, straining efforts to regulate competition through cooperative mechanisms. Access to water already epitomizes the rich/poor divide in Asia. While the poor struggle to get basic access to water for their daily consumption and household chores, the rich rely on bottled drinking water. In this light, the quality and quantity of available freshwater has emerged as a critical component of Asian security-related challenges. Increasingly, dams built on transnational rivers are spurring intercountry friction. If water wars in the future are to be averted over these and other hydroengineering projects, Asian norms and rules on shared resources will need to evolve.

The economic rise of Asia, which has occurred on a scale and speed unparalleled in world history, with some even calling it a miracle, has helped bring key strategic resources like freshwater, food, fossil fuels, timber, and minerals under growing global pressure.[12] Nonrenewable resources such as oil, iron ore, and other mineral wealth as well as renewables like water, cropland, and biomass have come under strain.[13] One factor fueling resource demand is population growth, and Asia's population surge outstripped the rest of the world's growth between 1950 and 2000, a period that witnessed a 260 percent increase in the number of Asians—from 1.40 billion to 3.65 billion.[14] Another factor is consumption growth, a consequence of economic development and rising prosperity. Although Asia's overall population growth has now slowed, its consumption growth is soaring, and thus the average Asian consumes far more water, food, oil, and other resources than before.[15] Today the competing demand for water from agriculture, energy, industry, and cities has brought water resources in many countries under increasing pressure.

Unlike resources such as oil, natural gas, and minerals—which Asia has been importing in fast-growing quantities to keep its economic machines humming— water cannot be bought on the world markets. Water trade between water-rich and water-poor countries is constrained by distance and cost. And though national reliance on oil can be reduced through other sources of energy, there is no such hope with water. Water has no substitute. The only option for water-distressed countries is to sustainably optimize the availability of water resources within their national frontiers and—if they have sufficient and maintainable hard-currency reserves—to import rather than produce water-intensive products, in which "virtual water" is embedded. When agricultural and industrial goods whose production processes consumed water are traded, there is exporting or importing of water in virtual form.[16]

Yet, given that interstate "drainage basins" (i.e., tracts of land that gather water originating as precipitation and drain it into streams, rivers, lakes, reservoirs, or other bodies of water) encompass almost half the Earth's surface area, excluding Antarctica, and account for three-fifths of all freshwater flows in the world,[17] individual countries, according to the United Nations, "have clear incentives to capture and use water before it goes beyond their political control. There is no immediate incentive to conserve or protect supplies for users beyond national borders. Also, partly because in many places a river or lake is the key to a nation's identity, ownership and control over waterways is considered crucial to national interests."[18] That is especially so in Asia, where the extent of shared water resources is particularly wide.

The needs of irrigated farming to help feed large populations, along with rapid urbanization and industrialization, have exacerbated pressures on the quality and quantity of Asian freshwater resources. Even as Asia struggles to expand the access of its poor residents to safe drinking water and sanitation, the Asian demand for freshwater continues to grow at the fastest rate in the world. In a continent where the vagaries of the monsoon affect water supplies, the rapidly expanding Asian economies thirst for more water every year. Virtual-water trade has not been consciously employed by Asian states as an instrument to help improve water productivity and reduce pressures on the environment because few view it as a path to achieving water security. Water is not only getting increasingly tied to national security, but the growing water scarcity or stress also threatens to become a constraint on continued rapid economic growth in Asia.

Indeed, because of its geography as well as its population density, especially in the coastal areas, Asia is likely to bear the brunt of global warming. Nearly two-fifths of the world's population lives within 100 kilometers of a coastline, but a much larger share of Asia's population is concentrated along the coasts, with Asian coastal areas often serving as economic boom zones.[19] Because many of its cities are located along the coast, Asia is highly vulnerable to water-related disasters and the likely effects of climate change, with 62,000 people reported killed in natural calamities just between 2001 and 2005 in the wider Asia-Pacific region.[20] Japan's multiple tsunami-linked calamities in 2011, including the world's worst nuclear accident since Chernobyl, served as a fresh reminder of these dangers. Southeast Asia is particularly vulnerable to the rise of sea levels and to more frequent and severe typhoons, given the fact that it has 3.3 percent of the global landmass but more than 11 percent of the world's coastline.[21] As UN secretary-general Ban Ki-moon warned, "Our planet faces a growing water crisis. But the situation in the Asia-Pacific region is especially troubling. High population growth, unsustainable consumption, pollution, and poor management all threaten the area's clean water sources. Climate change is making a bad situation worse. Glaciers are receding. Floods are getting worse. Droughts are becoming longer and more severe."[22]

Agriculture accounts for 71 percent of all water withdrawals in the world.[23] But in Asia, the farming sector utilizes far more water than the global average. With more than four-fifths of all Asian water withdrawals being channeled to produce food, water literally is food in Asia. This in part explains why per capita water use in Asia is almost twice that of the continent with the highest freshwater availability—South America.[24] However, the fastest increase in water withdrawals in Asia since the 1990s has come not from agriculture but from urban households and the industrial sector, in keeping with the Asian trends of fast urbanization and industrialization. Asia, in fact, leads the world in rapid urbanization. Asian urban populations are projected to increase 60 percent by 2025, even as the number of Asians living in rural areas is expected to remain almost the same between now and then.[25] As Asia continues to rapidly urbanize and industrialize, it can expect to be increasingly strapped for water to grow more food and to meet its other economic and household needs.

Asia has done a relatively good job overall in significantly raising food production since the 1960s through a mix of irrigation expansion, new farm varieties, and fertilizer use. The rapid spread of irrigated farming has been the single most-important factor allowing most Asian states to meet their sharply rising food demand. For example, even as the populations of Asian countries expanded considerably between the 1960s and the 1990s, that increase was more than matched by higher rice yields. As a result of the greater Asian output, global rice production more than doubled, and rice prices plummeted by more than 40 percent.[26]

But Asia now faces growing water and land constraints, which can be mitigated in agriculture only by significantly raising the level of crop yields through improved and more-sustainable techniques and better seed varieties. In fact, the era of cheap and abundant food, as global trends suggest, may be drawing to a close in the face of constraints on the availability of water and arable land, especially in Asia, where population and consumption growth threatens to overtake the output of the staple food grain, rice. The growth of wheat and rice output in Asia actually has slowed since the late 1990s after the dramatic increases of the previous quarter century.

Food is a critical component of national security, with food production closely intertwined with water and energy. Because energy production is itself an important user of water, a business-as-usual outlook on water resources will carry significant risks for investors in the power sector and for the Asian economies at large. Asia's water and energy challenges are compounded by the uncontrolled extraction of groundwater through diesel and electric pumps, and by profligate farming practices and the declining effectiveness of large-scale irrigation projects due to mismanagement, poor maintenance, and inadequate public investment. Changing diets

Rudyard Kipling's "Great Game," played out over the middle to late nineteenth century, has been revived in the twenty-first century with new competitors.[34] Instead of Tsarist Russia taking on Imperial Britain in Central Asia, rising China—hungry for water, energy, land, and raw materials—is shaping the new Great Game across much of Asia. Today, China is involved in water disputes with most of its riparian neighbors—from the countries on the Indochina Peninsula and India to Kazakhstan and Russia. Although China seems intent to aggressively pursue upstream projects on transnational rivers, the forestalling of water wars demands a cooperative Asian framework among river basin states so that they can work toward a common ownership of shared resources and thereby securely share the benefits.

Broadly, water shortages threaten to intensify intrastate and interstate tensions in Asia, besides spurring food insecurity, hindering rapid economic growth, promoting unemployment, and triggering large-scale migrations within and across international borders. According to the FAOSTAT data maintained by the Food and Agriculture Organization of the United Nations, the water stress in Asia holds a direct bearing on economic and human development as well as environmental protection there.[35] A 2009 report from the United Nations Economic and Social Commission for Asia and the Pacific (UNESCAP) captured the Asian crisis through an Index of Water Available for Development—a measure of per capita water availability for human, economic, and ecological uses per year on the basis of each country's internal renewable water resources minus total water used. This index for selected countries, employing 1980 as the benchmark, reveals that there have been steep declines in water availability for development since that year in several Asian nations, including the two giants that make up nearly two-fifths of the global population, China and India.[36] The water situation in India appears the most ominous because of a dramatic decline in water availability for development during the past three decades. The UNESCAP report gave the following warning about the regional water situation: "Water shortfalls on this scale heighten competition for a precious resource and frequently lead to conflicts, which are emerging as new threats to social stability."[37]

The security-related dimensions of water in Asia actually need to be viewed against the larger Asian strategic landscape and the sharpening resource-related competition among Asian economies. At a time when Asia is in flux, and thus the power equations between its major players are still evolving and its security architecture is unclear, water has emerged as a key element on the Asian strategic landscape. Bound in the east by the Pacific Ocean and in the south by the Indian Ocean, Asia extends right up to the Bosphorus and the Suez Canal and thus includes large parts of what is internationally known as the Middle East. Whether Asia is defined that broadly or more narrowly, it confronts a serious water crisis. With freshwater resources coming under strain in Asia, cooperation to manage transnational water resources is set "to become more difficult within and between states."[38] To help prevent a potentially cascading set of resource-related developments from destabilizing Asian peace and stability, it has become imperative to invest in institutionalized cooperation on water issues, especially on shared transboundary resources.

Asia has come a long way since the emergence of two Koreas, two Chinas, two Vietnams, and a partitioned India. The ongoing global power shifts indeed are primarily linked to Asia's phenomenal economic rise. How rapidly Asia has come up can be gauged from Gunnar Myrdal's 1968 book *Asian Drama: An Inquiry into the Poverty of Nations*, in which the Swedish economist, who went on to win the Nobel Prize, bemoaned how impoverishment, population pressures, and resource constraints were weighing down Asia.[39] Today's Asian drama is not about poverty, even though there are still many poor people in Asia and resource constraints there are becoming more pronounced. Rather, today's Asian drama is about high economic growth and a rapidly increasing middle class that is seeking the comforts of everyday life—from using water-intensive household appliances to having potted plants and even a home garden. In the face of fast-rising consumption growth, resource constraints—especially water and energy shortages—potentially threaten the Asian success story.

It should not be overlooked that Asia—the seat of ancient civilizations—is bouncing back after a relatively short period of historical decline, which had been partly precipitated by European colonial interventions during two centuries. However, as the British economic historian Niall Ferguson has pointed out, it was "the decadence of Eastern empires," including the failure to modernize their economic and military systems, "that made European domination possible."[40] Asia's share of the world's economy, in terms of purchasing power parity, totaled 60 percent in 1820, at the advent of the Industrial Revolution, when Western Europe was a distant second, with 23 percent, and the United States—then a young nation—accounted for just 1.8 percent, according to the Asian Development Bank.[41] Asia, after that, went into a sharp decline over the next one and a half centuries. But now Asia is on the march again, having regained its economic momentum.

The events following the 1989 fall of the Berlin Wall transformed Europe's political and military landscape. But no continent benefited more from the end of the Cold War than Asia, as has been epitomized by its dramatic economic rise since then. A key post-1989 development was the shift from the primacy of military power to a greater role for economic power in shaping international geopolitics. This not only helped promote an economic boom in several parts of the world but also led to an eastward movement of global power and influence, with Asia emerging as an important player on the world stage. In a little over fifteen years, Asia's share of global income, in terms of purchasing power parity, grew from 14 percent in 1990 to almost 24 percent in 2006, or just above America's 22 percent contribution.[42]

The nature of power has changed.[43] Global power shifts today are being spurred not by military triumphs or new geopolitical alignments but by a peaceful factor unique to our contemporary world: rapid economic growth. Since 1970, global GDP has grown more than three and a half times, while per capita income has more than doubled. Rapid economic growth, of course, was also witnessed during the Industrial Revolution and in the post–World War II period. But in the post–Cold War period, rapid economic growth by itself has contributed to qualitatively altering global power equations. Consequently, economic power is now playing a unique role in instigating power shifts, even as the United Nations Security Council's permanent membership structure undergirds the continued importance of military power. Today, all states armed with intercontinental-range weaponry hold permanent seats on the Security Council, and all aspirants for new permanent seats have regionally confined military capabilities.

Another defining event in 1989 was the Tiananmen Square massacre of prodemocracy protesters in Beijing. If not for the end of the Cold War, the West would not have let China off the hook over those killings. The Cold War's end, however, facilitated the West's pragmatic approach to shun trade sanctions and help integrate China with global institutions through the liberalizing influence of foreign investment and trade. The limited Western trade sanctions that had been imposed against China after Tiananmen were thus allowed to peter out by 1992. Had the United States and its allies pursued the opposite approach centered on progressively tighter punitive sanctions—as they have done, for instance, against Burma, where the military junta crushed prodemocracy demonstrators ten months before Tiananmen Square—the result would have been a less prosperous, less open, and a potentially destabilizing China.

Therefore, China's spectacular economic success—illustrated by its emergence with the world's biggest trade surplus, largest foreign-currency reserves, and highest steel production, along with a thirteenfold expansion of its economy between 1980 and 2010—owes a lot to the US decision not to sustain the trade sanctions imposed after Tiananmen Square. In fact, there is a long tradition of a China-friendly approach in US policy that dates back to the nineteenth century. In 1905, US president Theodore Roosevelt, who hosted the Japan–Russia peace conference in Portsmouth, New Hampshire, argued for the return of Manchuria to China and for a balance of power to continue in East Asia. The Russo-Japanese War actually ended up making the United States an active participant in China's affairs. In more recent times, US policy aided the integration and then ascension of Communist China, which actually began as an international pariah state. Indeed, there has been a succession of overtly China-friendly US presidents in the past four decades—a significant period that has coincided with China first coming out of international isolation and then embarking on the path of ascension.

In the post-1989 period, without the phenomenal expansion in US-Chinese trade and financial relations, China's economic growth would have been much harder. Having vaulted past Germany to become the world's biggest exporter, China has now displaced Japan as the world's second-largest economy, even as it has emerged as the largest producer of greenhouse gases. With its rapidly swelling foreign-exchange coffers and the role of its state-owned corporate behemoths in frenetically buying foreign firms, technologies, and resources, China is well positioned geopolitically to further expand its international influence.

China's rise, however, is very different from the rises of other powers in modern world history. When Japan, for example, rose to world-power status during the reign of the Meiji emperor in the second half of the nineteenth century, the rest of Asia was in decline, including the Chinese, Indian, and Korean civilizations. After all, by the nineteenth century, much of Asia had been colonized by Europeans. So there was no other Asian power that could rein in Japan, whose rise opened the path to imperial conquests. Today China is rising when other important Asian countries are also rising, including South Korea, Vietnam, India, and Indonesia. Despite the urge of Chinese policymakers to break free "from the confines of their country's history, and thus China's own geography," the expansionist impulses of a rising China are, to some extent, checkmated by the rise of other Asian powers.[44] Militarily, China is in no position to grab the territories it covets. Its power may be vast and rapidly growing, but it lacks the power to compel any rival or enforce its writ on Asia. Still, it is increasingly seeking to use its growing economic clout for political gains.

Japan has been eclipsed by China's rapid rise. Yet for the foreseeable future, Japan—with its $5.5 trillion economy, impressive high-technology skills, Asia's largest naval fleet, and a per capita income almost six times greater than China's, when adjusted for purchasing power parity—is likely to stay a strong nation. As Asia's first modern economic success story, Japan, for a long time, actually inspired other Asian states. Now, with the emergence of new economic tigers and the ascent of China and India, Asia is bouncing back collectively.

However, Japan—after riding high growth and one of the biggest speculative stock and property bubbles of all time in the 1980s, to emerge as "the first Asian nation to challenge the long dominance of the West"—has experienced a reversal of economic fortunes in the post–Cold War period.[45] It has become trapped in still-continuing low growth and deflation, or a debilitating downward spiral of prices, even as it has stayed a global leader in autos, machine tools, flat-panel displays, and other parts of the consumer electronics industry. As a result, its economy remains at virtually the same size as when the Soviet Union collapsed. Still, one of the farthest-reaching but least-noticed developments in Asia in the twenty-first century has been Japan's political resurgence, fueled in part by the rise of an assertive China. Though Japan was long used to practicing passive, checkbook diplomacy, it is now intent on influencing Asia's power balance.

India's rise as a new economic giant was tied to the post-1989 events. India was so much into barter trade with the Soviet Union and its Communist allies in Eastern Europe that when the Eastern Bloc began to unravel, India had to start paying for imports in hard cash. This rapidly depleted its modest foreign-exchange reserves, triggering a severe balance-of-payments crisis in 1991. This financial crisis, in turn, compelled India to embark on radical economic reforms, which laid the foundation for its economic rise. Today, it boasts one of the fastest-growing economies in the world. Indeed, there has not been a strong China, a strong Japan, and a strong India at the same time in history before.

More broadly, the emblematic defeat of Marxism in 1989 allowed developing countries in Asia to overtly pursue capitalist policies. Although China's four-modernization program had begun in the late 1970s under the leadership of Deng Xiaoping, the Chinese Communist Party, after 1989, was able to publicly subordinate ideology to wealth creation, as illustrated by a new aphorism that gained widespread currency, "To get rich is glorious." That example, in turn, had a constructive influence on socialist movements and surviving communist parties in the world.

Geopolitically, too, the post-1989 gains extended far beyond the West. For China, the Soviet Union's sudden collapse came as a great strategic boon, eliminating a menacing empire and opening the way to rapidly increase its strategic space globally. Russia's decline in the 1990s became China's gain. For India, the end of the Cold War triggered a foreign policy crisis by eliminating the country's most reliable partner, the Soviet Union. But as in the economic realm, that crisis had a positive outcome: It led to a revamped Indian foreign policy. The crisis forced India to overcome its didactically quixotic traditions and inject greater realism and pragmatism into its foreign policy. Post–Cold War India began pursuing mutually beneficial strategic partnerships with all the key players in Asia and the wider world. For prime example, the US-India "global strategic partnership"—a defining feature of the twenty-first century—was made possible by post-1989 shifts in Indian policy.

Today Asia's clout is being underlined by its role as the global economic engine, with the continent boasting the world's largest foreign-exchange reserves, highest savings rate, and a growing share of international trade. Significantly, the first Asian economies to rise—Japan, South Korea, Taiwan, Hong Kong, and Singapore—all lacked natural resources and still rely on resource imports to fuel their economic growth. For them and other Asian economies, resource security is a major priority. Also, export-led growth strategies have played a central role in the Asian economic success story; the exception has been India, an import-dependent economy that has relied on domestic consumption for its rapid growth.

Given that aggregate economic growth in Asia has averaged about 7 percent since 2000, that continent's GDP is projected to be double that of the United States in terms of purchasing power parity by 2020, when some Asian states would have achieved middle-income status. And by 2050 Asia's economic ascendancy is likely to become unmistakable, as three of the world's four largest economies (China, India, the United States, and Japan) would be Asian.[46] The Asian economic renaissance, powered by entrepreneurial ingenuity, has been accompanied by a growing international recognition of Asia's soft power, as symbolized by its arts, fashion, and cuisine.

Asia's trajectory suggests it is on track to reclaim the economic preeminence it enjoyed for two thousand years before the Industrial Revolution allowed the West to vault ahead. In the period up to 1820, China and India were the world's largest economies. According to the British economic historian Angus Maddison, India's economy made up 33 percent of world GDP in the year AD 1, compared with China's 26 percent. But by the sixteenth century, China's economy matched India's, before springing into significant lead.[47] As one scholar has put it, "The past two centuries of Western domination of world history are the exception, not the rule, during two thousand years of global history."[48] After all, for two millennia, Asia dominated the world in economy, knowledge, and culture. In this light, the correct characterization of the power developments since the 1990s is Asia's reemergence rather than its rise.

While promoting a greater international distribution of power, Asia's reemergence, however, does not signal the decline of the West. In fact, there is little evidence thus far to suggest that Asia is rising at the West's expense. Asia is seeking to emulate the West rather than supplant the West. It is not that the West is in decline but that the East is on the rise. As the American economist Jeffrey Sachs has said, "Assuming Asia's continued economic success, the twenty-first century could well be a period of unprecedented prosperity and scientific advance, but one in which the United States will have to learn to be one of many successful economies rather than the world's indispensable country."[49] Yet as history attests, tectonic shifts in power are rarely quiet. The shifts in economic and political power actually symbolize the birth pangs of a new world order. The spread of prosperity in the world, however, is likely to create more stakeholders in continued peace and stability. Shared interests will, of course, demand shared responsibilities, making international institutional reforms inescapable.

Even so, Asia faces complex security, developmental, and resource-related challenges in an era of sharper interstate competition. Although Asia may be coalescing economically, as underscored by the number of intra-Asian free trade agreements now in place, it remains deeply divided politically. If anything, with the gulf between its politics and economics widening, Asia is becoming more divided politically. Whereas Europe has built institutions to underpin peace, Asia has yet to begin such a process in earnest. There is neither any security architecture in Asia nor a structural framework for regional security. There are regional consultation mechanisms, but they tend to be weak. Differences persist over whether any security architecture or community should extend across Asia or just be confined to an ill-defined regional construct, East Asia.

One important point is that the bloody wars in the first half of the twentieth century have made war unthinkable today in Europe, but the wars in Asia in the second half of the twentieth century did not resolve matters and only accentuated bitter rivalries. A number of interstate wars have been fought in Asia since 1950, the year both the Korean War and the annexation of Tibet started. Those wars, far from settling or ending disputes, have only kept disputes lingering. China, significantly, has been involved in the largest number of military conflicts.

A Pentagon report cites examples of how China carried out military preemption in 1950, 1962, 1969, and 1979 in the name of strategic defense. The report, released in 2010, states: "The history of modern Chinese warfare provides numerous case studies in which China's leaders have claimed military preemption as a strategically defensive act. For example, China refers to its intervention in the Korean War (1950–53) as the 'War to Resist the United States and Aid Korea.' Similarly, authoritative texts refer to border conflicts against India (1962), the Soviet Union (1969), and Vietnam (1979) as 'Self-Defense Counter Attacks.'"[50] The seizure of the Paracel Islands from Vietnam in 1974 by Chinese forces was another example of offense as defense.

All these cases of preemption occurred when China was weak, poor, and internally torn. So today China's rapidly accumulating power naturally raises legitimate concerns. In fact, a 2010 essay in the *Qiu Shi Journal*, the influential organ of the Chinese Communist Party's Central Committee, declares: "Throughout the history of the new China, peace in China has never been gained by giving in, only through war. Safeguarding national interests is never achieved by mere negotiations, but by war."[51] A stronger, more prosperous China already is beginning to pursue a more muscular foreign policy vis-à-vis its neighbors and assert its territorial and maritime claims, as underlined by several developments since 2010 alone—from its inclusion of the South China Sea in its "core" national interests, an action that threatens to make its claims to the disputed Spratly Islands nonnegotiable, to its presentation of the Yellow Sea as some sort of an exclusive Chinese military operations zone where it wants the United States and South Korea to respect the new Chinese power by forgoing the right to hold further joint naval exercises.

China has also become more insistent in pressing its territorial claims to the Japanese-controlled Senkaku Islands, which it calls the Diaoyu Islands, with Chinese warships making more frequent forays into Japanese waters. Furthermore, Beijing has stepped up military pressure against India along the disputed Himalayan border after resurrecting its long-dormant claim to India's northeastern Arunachal Pradesh state and starting to question Indian sovereignty over the state of Jammu and Kashmir, one-fifth of which China controls. In fact, the largest real estate China covets is not in the South or East China seas but in India: Arunachal Pradesh is almost three times bigger than Taiwan, or more than twice as large as Switzerland. But even against one of the smallest nations in the world—Bhutan—Asia's largest country, China, has aggressively pushed territorial claims through cross-border military incursions.[52]

Respect for boundaries is a prerequisite to peace and stability on any continent. Europe has built its peace on that principle, with a number of European states learning to live with boundaries they do not like. Efforts at the further redrawing of territorial frontiers are an invitation to endemic conflicts in Asia. An overt refusal to accept the territorial status quo only highlights the futility of political negotiations. After all, a major redrawing of frontiers involving the surrender of big chunks of real estate by one disputant to another has never happened at the negotiating table in modern world history. Such a redrawing can only be achieved on the battlefield, as happened in Asia in the second half of the twentieth century. After more than six decades of efforts in that direction, the redrawing of frontiers must come to an end, or else Asia's economic renaissance will stall. This danger has been underscored by the rapidly growing military capabilities in Asia just when territorial and maritime disputes have resurfaced with a vengeance.

It is against this background that the increasing water-security challenges within and between countries in Asia need to be assessed. Water and energy are two key resources whose spiraling demand in Asia carries the greatest strategic significance. With Asia on the front lines of climate change, it cannot be overlooked that those two resources have a close relationship with global warming. Although energy is the main contributor to the buildup of greenhouse gases in the atmosphere, especially the way humanity produces and uses energy, the availability of water will be seriously affected by global warming, thus increasing the risks of water-related conflicts, as the Intergovernmental Panel on Climate Change has warned.[53]

Let us take energy first. With a twenty-first-century version of the Great Game beginning to roil Asia, the specter of resource conflicts has emerged. Competition over oil and gas resources, fueled by rapid economic growth in Asia, constitutes the most important dimension of the new Great Game. Given that some parts of Asia are energy rich and others are poor, the intra-Asian competition to secure oil and gas resources has become increasingly intense. Soaring demand in China, India, and elsewhere in Asia has helped drive up global energy prices during the past two decades, besides encouraging mercantilist attempts to lock up long-term energy supplies. The threat of inadequate energy resources has intensified geopolitical rivalries in the oil-rich regions of Central Asia, the Caspian Sea basin, West Asia, and the East China Sea. Africa's oil wealth is increasing that continent's strategic importance for Asian economies. Resource-hungry Asian states have gone to the extent of employing aid and arms exports as a diplomatic instrument for commodity outreach. Asia's major energy-importing nations are concerned about their vulnerability with respect to resources and thus are determined to find ways to safeguard supplies, in terms of both the security of assured, uninterrupted supplies and the security of vital sea lanes of communication.

The changes occurring in the global energy and materials sectors, with the growth in demand moving from the West to Asian economies, are one key manifestation of the ongoing power shifts in the world. The structural shifts in global energy markets indeed carry important long-term political and economic implications, besides challenging the stability of those markets. Energy prices are going to stay volatile for the foreseeable future, given the rising demand in Asian countries. Despite the total consumption of energy in Asia having grown dramatically since 1990, per capita energy consumption there is still relatively low by Western standards. Not only will per capita consumption grow sharply in Asia in the next two decades, "on the supply side, Asia's strong demand environment for energy and basic materials, coupled with its low labor costs, means that the region will increasingly become a global producer of aluminum, chemicals, paper, and steel"—all water-intensive industries.[54]

Maritime security has emerged as an important issue in Asia in the face of rising concerns over sea-lane safety and the vulnerability of energy supplies to disruption. Much of the global oil trade passes through two constricted Asian passageways—the piracy-plagued Strait of Malacca, which is barely 2.5 kilometers wide at its narrowest point between Indonesia and Singapore, and the 89-kilometer-wide Strait of Hormuz between Iran and Oman. More than 50,000 ships pass through the Malacca Strait alone each year. The security of these main oil arteries is very much tied to the security of energy supplies for the oil-importing countries. Indeed, the security of the two main oil arteries is also linked to the security of the Indian Ocean—the link between the Strait of Hormuz and the Strait of Malacca. But with mercantilist efforts to lock up long-term hydrocarbon supplies and the proliferation of Chinese-aided port-building projects along the great trade arteries, energy has become a key driver of a potentially far-reaching transformation of the Asian security environment.

Water, for its part, could trigger increased conflicts within and between states, and open new (or exacerbate existing) political disputes in Asia. Water shortages, likely to be aggravated by fast-rising use and climate change, pose a potential threat to political stability, economic modernization, public health, food security, and internal cohesion in a number of Asian states. Given that a stable hydrologic process of snowmelt and glacial melt is critical for river runoff in the warmer months when the demand for water in the lowlands reaches its peak, global warming is expected to upset the present Asian melt characteristics. A study of Asia's biggest rivers—the Indus, the Brahmaputra, the Yangtze, the Yellow, and the Ganges—by three Dutch experts has found that the "upstream snow and ice reserves of these basins—important in sustaining seasonal water availability—are likely to be affected substantially by climate change," although the extent of impact will vary from basin to basin.[55]

Such is the deep nexus between water and global warming that the increased frequency of climate-change-driven extreme weather events like hurricanes, droughts, and flooding, along with the projected rise of ocean levels, is likely to spur greater interstate and intrastate migration—especially of the poor and the vulnerable—from delta and coastal regions to the hinterland. As three American scientists have warned in another study about Asia, "It appears that some areas of the most populated region on Earth are likely to 'run out of water' during the dry season if the current warming and glacial melting trends continue for several more decades. This may be the time for long-term planning to see just how the region can cope with this problem."[56] Instead of such cooperative planning, an opposite trend is apparent: The growing interstate Asian competition over water is prompting some countries to build upstream hydroengineering projects on transnational rivers, with little concern for the interests of co-riparian states.

Water security and a stable energy environment are critical to continued Asian prosperity. Yet in Asia, fast-rising national energy demands are compounding the water challenges and affecting inter-riparian relations. The construction of dams on international rivers to generate hydropower is often the principal cause of water-related tensions between neighbors in Asia. China, for example, is now pursuing major interbasin and interriver water transfer projects on the Tibetan Plateau and building a separate cascade of major dams on the Mekong, Salween, Brahmaputra, Arun, and Irtysh-Illy rivers. Having extensively contaminated its own major rivers through unbridled industrialization, China is now threatening the ecological viability of river systems tied to South and Southeast Asia, Kazakhstan, and Russia in its bid to meet its thirst for water and energy. Some of its megaprojects are designed not only for hydropower or irrigation but also for transferring river waters to its parched north. That is best exemplified by its Great South–North Water Transfer Project, which is to divert northward international river waters from the Tibetan Plateau in its third phase, labeled the "Great Western Route."

Another illustrative example is Central Asia, which is blessed with major energy and water resources, although with great spatial variation. Yet water and energy have emerged as the two main issues bedeviling intercountry relations in Central Asia. The geopolitical competition there pits the hydrocarbon-rich Kazakhstan, Uzbekistan, and Turkmenistan against two water-rich but less developed and smaller states, Kyrgyzstan and Tajikistan. The three bigger states are actually rich in a variety of mineral resources, and Kazakhstan is also emerging as an important uranium supplier to help fuel the global nuclear energy resurgence. Tajikistan's move to resume work on the long-stalled, Soviet-era Rogun Dam, which will be the world's tallest and generate 3,600 megawatts of hydropower, and Kyrgyzstan's Kambarata 1 and 2 dams, with a planned combined capacity of 2,260 megawatts, have strained inter-riparian relations in the region, with Uzbekistan vowing to retaliate against diminished transboundary flows.[57] The internal turmoil or unrest racking some of the Central Asian states has only made the regional water-and-energy picture murkier.

China, India, Japan, South Korea, Taiwan, and other Asian economies have been scouring the world for hydrocarbons and minerals to meet their voracious demand for resources. China indeed has taken the lead in turning to foreign trade and investment, including in pariah nations, to help secure the resources it needs for its continued economic growth. But water is one resource that cannot be secured in considerable or adequate quantities through long-distance international trade deals. Yet water is central to development and economic expansion. If the sharpening hydropolitics over transnational drainage basins were to spur greater interstate tensions through reduced water flows to neighboring states, the Asian renaissance could stall in the face of inter-riparian conflicts.

MOUNTING WATER STRESS IN ASIA

Two water-related facts stand out about Asia. The first is that Asia has less fresh-water available per capita—3,920 cubic meters per year—than any other continent, except Antarctica, according to UNESCAP.[58] Antarctica, though it makes up more than 10 percent of the world's landmass, has no permanent residents and its fresh-water, in any case, is largely locked up in the form of permanent ice.[59] Assessments by the Food and Agriculture Organization of the United Nations (FAO) put Asia's water availability even lower: In terms of per capita water resources in each conti-nent, North and South America together have 20,928 cubic meters (m^3) per year; Oceania, 32,366 m^3; Europe, 8,941 m^3; Africa, 4,008, m^3; and Asia, 3,037 m^3.[60]

As table 1.1 shows, when the estimated reserves of rivers, lakes, and aquifers are added up, Asia has marginally less water per inhabitant than Europe, less than one-quarter that of North America, almost one-tenth that of South America, and more than twenty times less than Oceania (Australia, New Zealand, and the Pacific Islands). According to the FAO's calculations, however, Asia has almost one-third of the freshwater resources of Europe per inhabitant, or less than one-tenth those of Oceania. The variation in figures can be explained by differences in computational methods, the reference period employed, the delineation of various regions, and other factors. It is, however, undisputed that, in the face of burgeoning population and consumption growth and the rising water demands of industry, households, and agriculture, per capita availability of water is appreciably declining in Asia, particularly across southern, southwestern, and central Asia and also in semiarid northern China—that is, north of the Yangtze River basin.

TABLE 1.1   Different Continents' Estimated Water Availability (thousands of cubic meters per year)

Continent	Per Square Kilometer of Territory	Per Capita
Europe	277	4.24
North America	324	17.40
Africa	134	5.72
Asia	311	3.92
South America	672	38.30
Oceania	268	83.60

Sources: United Nations, *The State of the Environment in Asia and the Pacific 2005* (Bangkok: United Nations Economic and Social Commission for Asia and the Pacific, 2006); based on "Assessment of Water Resources in Asia and the Pacific in the 21st Century," by Igor A. Shiklomanov (unpublished, 2004).

Statistically, Asia may appear to be endowed with reasonable water resources, considering that the entire continent extending from the Far East to the Caucasus and the Arabian Peninsula receives almost 24 percent of the world's precipitation by volume, with its total annual renewable water resources estimated at 12,393 cubic kilometers, or 28.8 percent of the global total.[61] However, given that Asia is home to three-fifths of the world's population, the amount of freshwater resources available per person is barely half the global average. The FAO, for example, has computed Asia's per capita water availability at 47.6 percent of the global average of 6,380 m³ per year.[62]

The second fact is that many Asian countries already are using too much of their water resources to be able to meet future needs. As a UN report has pointed out, "When it comes to its water resources, Asia seems to live beyond its means. Despite having the lowest water availability per capita of all global regions, Asia uses almost twice as much water per capita as Latin America, which has the highest potential water availability in the world. This situation is partly attributable to the high dependence of Asian countries on irrigated agriculture. At the same time, water use and management are notoriously inefficient in most countries of the region, with the exception of a few countries such as Singapore and Japan."[63] Table 1.2 lays out the total annual renewable water resources of select Asian countries as well as their dependency on waters flowing in from across their national frontiers.

Asia, which is spread over 43.6 million square kilometers, is very diverse. Geographically, it comprises forty-eight separate nations, including Turkey, 3 percent

TABLE 1.2   Annual Renewable Water Resources in Selected Asian Countries

Country	External (million m³)	Total (million m³)	External Dependency Ratio (%)
Bangladesh	1,105,644	1,210,644	91.3
China	17,169	2,840,000	0.9
India	647,220	1,907,760	33.4
Indonesia	0	2,838,000	0.0
Japan	0	430,000	0.0
Malaysia	0	580,000	0.0
Burma (Myanmar)	165,001	1,045,601	15.8
Nepal	12,000	210,200	5.7
Pakistan	170,300	225,300	75.59
Philippines	0	479,000	0
South Korea	4,850	69,700	7.0
Sri Lanka	0	50,000	0
Thailand	199,944	426,744	47.4
Vietnam	524,710	891,210	58.9

Source: Based on FAO's Aquastat online data, 2011, www.fao.org/nr/water/aquastat/main/index.stm.

of which is in Europe.[64] In addition, 72 percent of the Russian Federation is in Asia, although the majority of Russians live in the European part. Asia encompasses very different areas—from the subarctic, mineral-rich Siberian plains to the subtropical Indonesian archipelago; and from oil-rich desert lands to fertile river valleys. In popular perception, however, Asia is seen to cover only the area from the Indian subcontinent to the Korean Peninsula and the Japanese archipelago. Countries like Iran, Iraq, Jordan, Israel, Saudi Arabia, and others, although part of geographical Asia, are viewed as belonging to a separate entity, the Middle East. The problem that scholars face in defining Asia is compounded by the fact that even UN agencies differ in their approach, with some defining Asia more narrowly than others to exclude the Arabian Peninsula, the Caucasus, Iran, and the Near East (Turkey, Israel, Palestinian territories, Jordan, Iraq, Syria, and Lebanon) from their Asian assessments.

How varied Asia is even when it is identified more narrowly can be seen from the fact that it has countries with the highest and lowest population densities in the world—Singapore and Mongolia, respectively. It has some of the wealthiest states in the world, like Japan and Singapore, and also some of the poorest, such as North Korea and Afghanistan. It has tiny Brunei, Bhutan, and the Maldives and demographic titans like China, India, and Indonesia. The least populated Asian country, the Maldives, also happens to be the flattest state in the world. Except where construction has raised the plane, the Maldivian level surface rises up to only 2.3 meters above the ocean level, making the Maldives the most vulnerable to a global-warming-induced rise of the ocean's level. Asia also has exceptionally mountainous nations like Nepal, Bhutan, Afghanistan, and Kyrgyzstan. In fact, all the world's big mountains above 7,000 meters are in Asia, and all peaks above 8,000 meters are located in the Himalayan range.

Similar diversity in Asia exists in climates and hydrological regimes. Asia has some of the most humid climates, with annual precipitation more than 10 meters in some places, and also some of the most arid environments. It has the world's greatest river systems, with summer flooding an annual feature in the Mekong, Brahmaputra, and Ganges basins, and also closed hydrologic systems in arid regions. So it is of little surprise that Asia is characterized by a very uneven distribution of water resources and that its water-use conditions are also extremely varied. The hydrology of much of the Asian region is led by the monsoon climate, which brings on large interseasonal variations in river flows. In fact, with most of the precipitation occurring during the short monsoonal season, "average annual values of river flows are a poor indicator of the amount of water resources available for use" in Asia.[65]

The reality is that Asia is largely a water-stressed continent, with sizable parts dependent on monsoon rains and glacially sourced water reserves, especially of the Himalayas and the Tibetan highlands, where almost all the mighty Asian rivers originate. The water stress is apparent from a key indicator: national per capita

water availability. The riverless Arabian Peninsula has the lowest freshwater availability per inhabitant in the world, with the water scarcity extending to Jordan.
Excluding the Arabian Peninsula and the Near East, per capita water availability
in Asia is the lowest in the Maldives, followed by Singapore, Pakistan, South Korea,
India, Uzbekistan, Iran, and China.[66] Actually, the contiguous Asian belt extending
from Syria through Iran to India is a seriously water-stressed region, with the total
renewable water resources per inhabitant estimated in most areas at below 1,800
cubic meters annually.[67]

The highest per capita water availability in the Asian region, by contrast, is in
Papua New Guinea, followed by Bhutan, Laos, Cambodia, Brunei, Malaysia, and
Burma.[68] Such is the Asian disparity in water resources that, while the per capita
freshwater availability is a copious 113,537 m³ per year in Bhutan, it is well below
the critical threshold of 2,000 m³ in adjacent India, which is home to more than
one-sixth of the world's population. Then there are countries with too much water
at present but that, before long, may have too little to drink. Take the case of
densely populated Bangladesh, whose very future is threatened by saltwater incursion, sea-level rise, and river flooding. The annual summer monsoonal flooding
symbolizes a frustrating paradox for Bangladesh: Although such flooding is essential to maintain soil fertility and fisheries, it often leaves a trail of death and destruction. The overexploitation of coastal aquifers in Bangladesh is inviting saltwater
intrusion, as is also happening in some other Asian areas along the coast.

In addition to the uneven or lopsided water availability in Asia, there has been
an alarming trend of declining per capita availability of water resources on the
continent since 1950 in the face of growing populations, spreading irrigation, new
industries, and spiraling household consumption.[69] The per capita water availability
in Asia is said to be declining at the rate of 1.6 percent a year. In situations where
the average per capita availability already is low, even small declines or annual
variations can exacerbate the vulnerabilities of entire communities by creating
drought-like conditions.

The aggregate rate of freshwater withdrawal as a percentage of internal renewable water resources (IRWR) is another key barometer of a national situation.
There, too, Asian countries betray a disturbing trend of making water withdrawals
in excess of sustainable limits. Asia indeed stands out among all continents for the
highest freshwater withdrawal as a percentage of IRWR, or the long-term average
annual flow of rivers and recharge of aquifers generated from endogenous precipitation. Whereas the IRWR for Africa is 5 percent, the Americas 4 percent, Europe
6 percent, and Oceania 3 percent, it is 19 percent for Asia, with South Asia's and
Iran's withdrawals totaling 52.6 and 72.5 percent of their IRWR, respectively.[70]
This indicates an abnormally intense pressure on indigenous water resources,
which in many countries are supplemented by external inflows.

Even when the total actual renewable water resources, or ARWR—internal
plus external actual inflows—are examined, the picture is not any different: Asia
is conspicuous by its higher freshwater withdrawals than the rest of the world.

The ARWR represents the maximum theoretical yearly amount of water actually available for a country at a given moment. At the root of Asia's water crisis are its excessive water withdrawals for farming. In fact, high agricultural water withdrawals as a percentage of ARWR are indicative of water scarcity or water stress, and the world's largest concentration of areas so affected are in Asia. Uzbekistan, Kyrgyzstan, Tajikistan, Turkmenistan, Pakistan, the entire belt from Iran extending to Israel and the Arabian Peninsula, and the Libya-Egypt-Sudan subregion are the world's worst affected, with their agricultural water withdrawals in excess of the danger point—40 percent of ARWR.[71] India, which extracts 36.21 percent of its ARWR for farming, and Afghanistan, with an agricultural ARWR of 35.14 percent, risk approaching this danger threshold.[72] The risks actually begin when a country reaches an ARWR of more than 20 percent for agriculture—a category that includes Algeria, Kazakhstan, Morocco, Somalia, South Korea, and Spain, the only Western country on the list.[73]

Human Practices That Contribute to Water Paucity

In Asia, water stress and insecurity have been accentuated by unsustainable practices that have upset hydrological cycles and resulted in clean water becoming a precious and scarce resource in many areas. One such practice is the large-scale development and impoundment of water resources for irrigation, energy, and other uses without factoring in long-term environmental considerations. This includes the construction of dams, reservoirs, and irrigation networks to meet domestic demands. Large dams have caused sedimentation, inundation, habitat damage, destruction of fish species, and other environmental and public health problems. The building of dams also affects biotic habitats, as Europe's experience has shown, with the damming of the Danube River, for example, altering "the silica chemistry of the entire Black Sea."[74]

Because dams hold back nutrient-rich sediments through upstream water diversion, they can have a devastating impact on riparian ecology and economy. Such impact actually extends beyond the estuary, because the nutrients and minerals disgorged by rivers are vital to marine life. Dammed rivers result in not only diminished water discharge into the oceans, as has been established in the case of China's Yellow and Yangtze rivers, the Indian subcontinent's Indus, and Southeast Asia's lifeline, the Mekong, but also reduced flows for the lower-basin communities.[75] Equally significant is the fact that heavy damming upsets a river's natural tropical flooding cycle, which is critical to fisheries and the fertilization of soil.

Such effects are best illustrated by China's colossal, $30 billion Three Gorges Dam—the world's biggest—which Beijing likes to trumpet as the greatest architectural feat since the Great Wall was built to denote the edge of the Han Empire's political frontiers. The Three Gorges Dam symbolizes just one part of a much broader water strategy centered on the South–North Water Diversion Project. In addition to the 1.4 million Chinese officially displaced by the Three Gorges Dam, whose construction stretched from 1992 to 2008, another 300,000 local residents or more must now be relocated, according to a Chinese official, to "avoid geographic hazards like landslides caused by the dam" and to stem a growing problem of water contamination in the river system.[76]

The project's mammoth reservoir has triggered hydrological volatility in the Yangtze River system as well as landslides in the surrounding areas that are a threat to the millions who live in its shadow. Even if obliquely, Chinese officials at the local level have started to acknowledge "what geologists, biologists and environmentalists had been warning about for years: Building a massive hydropower dam in an area that is heavily populated, home to threatened animal and plant species, and crossed by geologic fault lines is a recipe for disaster."[77] A government report recorded that "243 dangerous geographic problems occurred around" the reservoir area between 2008 and 2010, affecting 22,355 people.[78] Once a swift-flowing river, the Yangtze has become remarkably tranquil, seriously polluted, and ecologically damaged.

Another disastrous practice in Asia has been the removal of vegetation from river banks and deforestation in watersheds. This has helped trigger more frequent flooding, enhance runoff rates, reduce aquifer recharge, deplete wetlands, and change the natural character of watercourses and estuaries, including increasing the variability of water flows. Across much of Asia, water-related challenges are being exacerbated by environmental degradation. Such unchecked degradation, along with soil erosion and rapid urbanization, has worsened water woes. Add to the picture poorly conceived irrigation projects that have contributed, however inadvertently, to waterlogging and salinity. This has led to cropland losses, especially in arid and semiarid regions where productivity is dependent on efficient irrigation.

Yet another key factor tied to the mounting water woes is that Asia has a far greater percentage of its cultivated land under irrigation than any other continent; whereas the figure for Asia is 36.9 percent, it is 12.5 percent for the Americas, 8.6 percent for the Oceania, 7.7 percent for Europe, and 5.5 percent for Africa.[79] In fact, about 70 percent of the world's 301 million hectares of land equipped for irrigation is in Asia alone.[80] Asia's heavy reliance on irrigation stands in stark contrast to the use of rainwater by the rest of the world as the primary source of water for agriculture. It is thus little surprise that Asia leads the world in the total volume of freshwater withdrawn for agriculture.

By building vast new irrigation systems, Asia more than doubled its total irrigated cropland between 1961 and 2003, with the largest growth in irrigated farming occurring in southern Asia, as figure 1.1 shows. Consequently, today the leonine proportion of the 18 percent of the planet's surface land under irrigation is in Asia, where governments have actively promoted—with state subsidies and other incentives—the maximum possible production of commodity crops (rice, wheat, corn, soybeans, sugar, and oilseeds) from which most supermarket foods are derived.

Figure 1.1   Changes in the Irrigated Area in Asia between 1961 and 2003

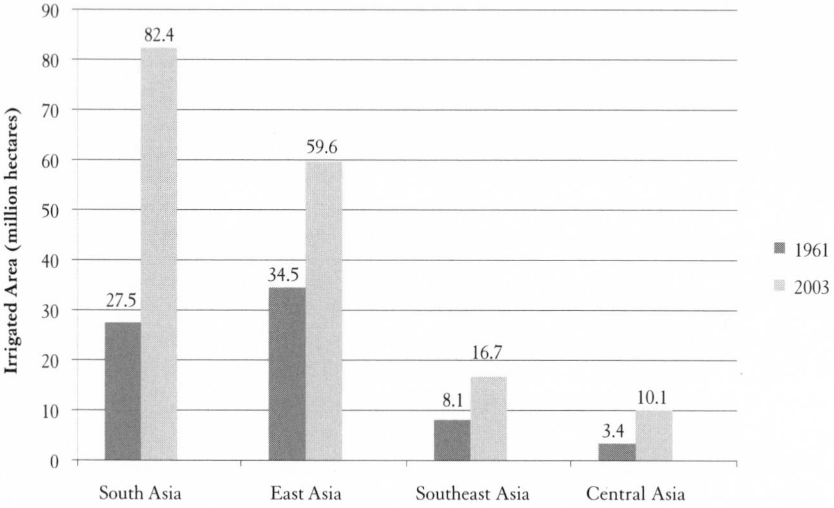

Source: International Water Management Institute and FAO, *Revitalizing Asia's Irrigation: To Sustainably Meet Tomorrow's Food Needs* (Colombo: International Water Management Institute, 2009).

Almost 74 percent of the total global freshwater withdrawals for agriculture by volume are made in Asia alone.[81] As a proportion of its own renewable water resources, Asia's yearly agricultural water withdrawals actually aggregate to 81 percent, or at least 10 percentage points higher than the global average.[82] In comparison, water withdrawals in Asia for industrial purposes account for just 11.4 percent; and for household needs, 7.3 percent. South Asia, for its part, leads the other Asian subregions in terms of water withdrawals for agriculture.[83] As a general rule, a larger share of water is channeled for agriculture in the developing countries than in the West, which on the whole has temperate climates and longer rainy periods each year. Hotter Africa's water withdrawals for the agricultural sector as a percentage of total renewable water resources even surpass Asia's. Asia, however, has the distinction of being the world's irrigation center. In the developed world, other than Australia and New Zealand, it is industry, not agriculture, that ranks as the leading water consumer. Water withdrawals for industry aggregate to 55 percent and for agriculture to 29 percent in Europe, whereas the figures for North America are 48 percent and 38 percent, respectively.[84]

Studies have shown that much higher crop yields can be obtained from irrigation than from rain-fed agriculture—more than double, according to the FAO.[85] But irrigation systems are not only expensive to build and maintain; they often also promote profligate practices and water loss. In fact, more than half of water withdrawals for irrigation are lost in transmission, distribution, and application.[86] Asian irrigation practices actually allow wastage on a prodigal scale, with much of the water trickling away or simply evaporating rather than being put to productive use. In addition to the inefficient application onto fields, much water gets lost through leakage in earthen channels.

Despite being the global irrigation hub, Asia cannot boast high crop yields, other than in Japan, South Korea, and parts of China, Indonesia, and India. In fact, waterlogging or salinization due to excessive irrigation is causing some Asian lands to become less productive.[87] Still, the fact remains that irrigation has played a pivotal role in transforming Asia. The introduction of large-scale irrigated farming since the 1960s has not only helped many Asian countries to achieve higher agricultural productivity and self-sufficiency in basic foods, including rice and wheat, but has also helped reduce rural poverty and set the stage for their economic rise. The substantial gains in food security, per capita income levels, and quality of life gave the countries the confidence to embark on radical economic reforms and to focus on growth in the industrial and services sectors. Food security, in other words, laid the foundation for Asia's rise.

The greatest expansion of Asian irrigation occurred in the thirty-five-year period between the early 1960s and the mid-1990s. Figure 1.2 shows the expansion of irrigated land between 1970 and 2009. Despite the fact that the rate has slowed somewhat, the expansion of irrigation systems in Asia has continued and the region's total land under irrigation dwarfs that of the rest of the world combined. The imperatives to feed large populations and traditions of irrigated cultivation dating back many centuries explain the value attached to irrigation in Asia. With a single-minded focus on raising food production, Asian governments actually made big investments in irrigation and drainage systems and research on new seed varieties, besides providing free water to farmers and subsidies on fertilizers and

FIGURE 1.2   Expansion of the Land under Irrigation, 1970–2009

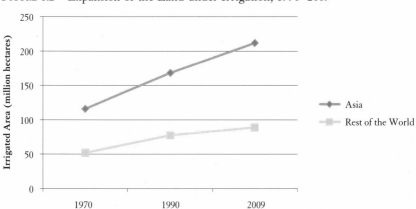

Source: UN FAO Aquastat Database, www.fao.org/nr/water/aquastat/dbase/AquastatWorldDataEng_20100524.pdf.

other agricultural supplies. Often governments also guaranteed to buy food grains at a minimum support price.

The expansion of irrigation, the introduction of genetically modified strains of wheat and rice, the generous use of inputs—from water to fertilizers—and state subsidies were instrumental in bringing about the green revolution in Asia that made a number of Asian economies self-sufficient in food in the 1970s and 1980s, when some even became food exporters. This dramatic growth in food output was largely achieved through much higher yields. But with population, consumption, and developmental pressures now growing and increases in yield gains flattening, Asia needs a second green revolution—for which water will be its single biggest constraint unless it embraces greater water-efficiency practices. In some Asian areas, in fact, there are no additional sources of water to harness to further expand irrigation. Increasing agricultural productivity through better water control has become a priority in Asia to help meet the soaring food demand resulting from a fast-growing middle class. The alleviation of poverty has also spurred the rising food demand.

That rice is Asia's staple food is underlined by the fact that Asians produce and consume more than 90 percent of the world's rice. Four of the world's five largest rice exporters are Asian states (Thailand, Vietnam, Pakistan, and India), but several of the world's leading rice importers are also in Asia (Indonesia, the Philippines, Saudi Arabia, and Bangladesh). China and India alone produce and consume about half of global rice supplies. But the world's highest per capita consumption of rice is in seven other Asian countries—Bangladesh, Burma, Cambodia, Indonesia, Laos, Thailand, and Vietnam—where it averages between 130 and 180 kilograms per year, or 55 to 80 percent of total caloric source.[88] Burma ranks no. 1 in this list.[89]

Rice is integral to Asian cultures. Hindu and Buddhist rites actually use rice as a religious offering. The majority Burman people of Burma trace their country's origin to the dispatch by gods to Burma—one of the world's most fertile lands—of some persons with rice seeds for cultivation. According to a Chinese proverb, "Precious things are not pearls and jade but the five grains, of which rice is the finest." In the Japanese language, the term "eating rice" is actually synonymous with "having a meal."[90] Rice can be mixed with just about anything to make many deliciously different dishes, and the modern Asian experience has shown that per capita rice consumption begins to decline only when countries reach the high- or middle-income category. After all, it is only when people can afford meat, fish, and dairy products that their daily rice intake goes down. Yet to produce just 1 kilogram of meat—the most water-intensive of all food products—between 30,000 to 70,000 liters of water are usually needed.

Rice remains a key political barometer in Asia. To meet its increasing demand for rice—projected to grow by at least 50 percent within the next two decades, despite changing diets—Asia will need to significantly boost its rice output. With water becoming a growing constraint and fertile land being lost to industrialization and urbanization, this will be no easy task. In fact, growth in production has appreciably slowed in the main Asian rice-producing countries that account for the bulk of global output. This has raised a concern that the demand for rice in many parts of Asia could outstrip supply in the coming years—a concern reinforced by the fact that less than 6 percent of continent's rice output is internationally traded. With much of the world's rice thus being consumed in the same countries where it is produced, rice markets are very segmented and protected. Significantly, more than three-quarters of the world's rice production—which totaled 446 million tons in 2009—takes place through irrigation. Rice is the thirstiest grain crop, and thus its production is highly water intensive, with 1,550 to 2,000 liters of water needed on average to grow 1 kilogram of rice. To produce more rice with less water and on less land demands new breakthroughs in rice technology.

Social and political stability in many Asian nations hinges on governments providing affordable rice or, in some places, reasonably priced wheat. Wheat is the staple food in parts of Asia that stretch westward from northern India, where it usually is ground into flour and baked unleavened into breads such as naan and chapatti. With poor families spending as much as 40 percent of their income to buy grains, access to subsidized rice and wheat is important for the most vulnerable sections of society, especially in countries where poverty is still a serious problem. Rural Asia remains home to 700 million people living in poverty, many of them with no access to safe water and sanitation.[91]

Asian countries today face new challenges with respect to food, given the population pressures, changing diets, and the rise in international grain prices, which more than doubled in the first decade of the twenty-first century. They need to produce more rice and wheat so as not to contribute to the international price rise of grains by becoming important importers of grains. But to boost domestic output on existing rain-fed and irrigated land, Asian states need to make more efficient use of available water, land, labor, and energy. In fact, without continued growth in the agricultural sector, it will be difficult to make substantial progress in alleviating poverty in Asia.

Such is the concentration of irrigation in southern, eastern, and southeastern Asia that the aggregate irrigated area in Central Asia, Iran, the Caucasus, the Near East, and the Arabian Peninsula makes up just 18 percent of the Asian continent's irrigated land. South Asia, China, and Southeast Asia by themselves account for about 50 percent of the world's total irrigated land.[92] Pakistan boasts "the largest contiguous irrigation system in the world"—a system that irrigates an area larger than the land size of Uruguay, England, or Greece—thanks to the four-fifths of the waters of the six-river Indus system flowing to it under a generously framed treaty with upper-riparian India.[93]

The irrigation systems in the arid or semiarid belt of Uzbekistan, Tajikistan, Turkmenistan, Iran, and Pakistan actually are the most profligate in the world. The Soviet-era irrigation systems in Uzbekistan, Turkmenistan, and Tajikistan—introduced in the early 1960s under the so-called Aral Sea Plan to transform that region into the Soviet Union's main cotton belt—have been deteriorating because of a lack of investment in maintenance. Cotton remains the main cash crop for Uzbekistan and an important foreign-exchange earner for Tajikistan and Turkmenistan. Not surprisingly, the Central Asian countries have among the world's highest per capita rates of water withdrawal for irrigation, estimated to range from more than 5,000 cubic meters per year in Turkmenistan to more than 2,000 cubic meters annually in Uzbekistan, Kyrgyzstan, Kazakhstan, and Tajikistan; agriculture accounts for 92 percent of all water withdrawals in Central Asia.[94]

An official assessment in Pakistan—the world's third-largest rice exporter and an important cotton producer—has blamed an "overuse of water in many irrigated areas" for growing land erosion due to waterlogging and salinity.[95] After Pakistan's Indus basin irrigation system, the Yellow River basin in northern China represents the next largest contiguous irrigation system in the world, followed by the Ganges basin in India, Nepal, and Bangladesh and the Mekong basin in Southeast Asia. The extent of irrigation has helped turn these regions into Asia's granaries. In terms of the largest cultivated area under irrigation as a percentage of the total national farmland, Pakistan and North Korea top Asia's list, with 80 and 73 percent of their cropland irrigated, respectively, followed by Japan, with 65 percent, and China, with 55 percent.[96]

China and India, given their size, represent three-quarters of the total irrigated cropland in southern, southeastern, and eastern Asia. In China, the Mao-introduced policies helped more than triple the size of irrigated land in the period between 1950 and 1980, with much of the additional acreage that was brought under irrigation located in the arid north and northwest. Leery of import dependency to feed the masses, Mao was determined to make China self-sufficient in food. This resolve, translated into policy, helped turn what had been a land of famine in the north into a breadbasket region. Before, farmers grew only three crops in two years in the northern plains. But official incentives, along with the development of a vast irrigation network and the exploitation of groundwater resources, prompted farmers to plant two or three crops a year, including water-intensive winter cultivation of wheat. The north began producing half the country's wheat.

Today, the north—the center of economic activity and population concentration—makes up 64 percent of China's cultivated land but has only 19 percent of the country's water resources.[97] This has resulted in a strange situation: The north now is beginning to rely on water transfers from the water-rich south via the Great South–North Water Transfer Project, yet it exports water-intensive food products to the south. By creating "a paradox in which huge volumes of water are being transferred from the water-rich south to the water-poor north while substantial volumes of food are being transferred from the food-sufficient north to the food-deficit south," it raises the question of whether such an arrangement is worth the environmental and other costs, and the unambiguous answer—from "a water resources point of view"—is that "this does not make sense."[98] In fact, thanks partly to the water-transfer projects, water quality has badly deteriorated in the south, even as the demand in the thirsty north remains unquenchable.

Asia's irrigation systems face the enormous challenge of meeting the projected 50 percent increase in food demand by 2030. The irrigated areas now produce 60 percent of Asia's rice, wheat, and other staple grains. Given the limits on further expansion of irrigated cropland, this challenge can be met only by significantly boosting farm yields, even as less water is likely to be available for agriculture.

In large parts of Asia, public investment to develop and maintain the irrigation and drainage systems that helped dramatically boost food production has fallen sharply. The FAO indeed believes that whereas further "development of irrigation in India is about to reach its limits and that no *major* extension of irrigated lands" can be expected, China's irrigation expansion potential is now restricted to arid areas, thus demanding "a viable long-term strategy as to how to provide the amount of water necessary to irrigate these lands."[99] Environmental and other problems in China's north already are challenging the sustainability of the large-scale irrigated farming being practiced in arid and semiarid lands. Against this background, making Asia's "existing irrigation systems work more efficiently and, where possible, investing in new irrigation infrastructure will be critical for meeting future food demands. This will not be an easy task, because Asia's natural water resources are already stretched and climate change is likely to bring greater variability in rainfall and runoff, generating uncertainty."[100]

Sustainable agriculture in Asia is coming under threat for multiple reasons, including water shortages and the resulting competition for water resources, water withdrawals that are becoming greater than the renewable capacity of the natural hydrological cycle, soil salinity and erosion, the development of biofuels, and climate change. A number of states, as table 1.3 shows, rely on groundwater to supplement surface-water supplies for irrigation. Yet both sources of irrigation water are coming under growing strain, even as irrigation is becoming more critical than ever to Asian economies. Just as irrigation in the past decades powered Asia's rise in agriculture, it now has a central role to play to help achieve increased food productivity and food security, and to transform the living standards of communities. The growing problem of waterlogging and salinization in Asia, resulting in the land producing less food or becoming unproductive, is a reminder that irrigation needs to be efficiently managed.

Among the reasons for waterlogging and soil salinity are cultivation in saturated fields, poor drainage, and old and inefficient irrigation systems. But the principal reason simply is the overuse of water. Much of the Asian rice production, including in semiarid parts, is based on the "ponded" water culture. In China, for example, less than 5 percent of the farms use drip-feed or sprinkler irrigation for wheat, corn, vegetables, and oilseeds, whose cultivation accounts for the bulk of the agricultural water withdrawals in that country.[101] Despite the example set by Israel—a pioneer in drip-feed irrigation that boosted its food production sevenfold

TABLE 1.3   Irrigated Area Size and Irrigation Water Sources in Selected Asian Countries

Country	Irrigation Area (hectares)	Surface Water (percent)	Groundwater (percent)
Bangladesh	5,050,045	30.8	69.2
China	62,559,200	N.A.	N.A.
India	61,908,000	40.5	53.0
Indonesia	4,427,922	99.0	1.0
Japan	3,128,079	100.0	16.0
Malaysia	362,600	92.0	8.0
Burma (Myanmar)	1,841,400	96.5	3.5
Nepal	1,168,300	73.9	12.4
Pakistan	20,006,000	63.0	37.0
Philippines	1,879,000	90.2	9.8
South Korea	888,795	94.9	5.1
Sri Lanka	570,000	90.2	9.8
Thailand	6,415,720	99.8	0.2
Vietnam	3,000,000	N.A.	N.A.

Note: N.A. = not available.

Sources: Adapted from FAO, *Irrigation in Asia in Figures*, Water Report 18 (Rome: FAO, 1999), and FAO, Aquastat online data, 2011.

between 1975 and 2000 with just a fractional increase in water use—drip or sprinkler irrigation is practiced little across most parts of Asia, including in countries that rely on agricultural exports as a major foreign-exchange earner. Applying water through the low-pressure tubing of micro-irrigation systems helps conserve substantial water and prevent soil salination. By comparison, flooding the field wastes water and contributes to a decline in soil quality.

The Wages of Thirst

The overexploitation of surface waters and groundwater in large parts of Asia has reached alarming proportions. The drying up of the Aral Sea in Central Asia owing to the heavy withdrawals of water for irrigation from its sources, the Amu Darya and Syr Darya rivers, exemplifies the consequences of an unchecked overextraction of water resources. In addition to the widespread problem of river depletion and pollution, some Asian areas have become so dependent on groundwater supply that this resource is being used faster than it can naturally be replenished, which is resulting in a rapidly falling groundwater saturation level. With millions of deep wells and farm pumps in use, the receding water table has resulted in people having to drill even deeper to source water. In some places, water is being drawn from aquifers so deep that these sources cannot be recharged by rainwater seepage. Although pumps have become cheaper, the cost of pumping groundwater has been escalating.

As Asia illustrates, agriculture's appropriation of the bulk of freshwater resources—aided by expansive irrigation systems and even subsidized electricity and fuel in some areas—has created two distinct and major problems. One is that the excessive use of surface waters deprives other areas within and across national frontiers of their rightful share. After all, greater water withdrawals upstream will affect flows downstream. Overpumping of groundwater from areas close to river systems also reduces river flows, as is happening in the basins of the Yellow, the Indus, the Ganges, the Amu Darya, the Syr Darya, and Thailand's Chao Phraya. Water in aquifers in river basins is recharged by rainfall and by seepage from rivers. Overpumping of underground water from near rivers draws additional river waters into aquifers and thus affects downstream flows. The reason why the Indus delta in Pakistan, for example, is drying up is twofold: the heavy damming of the river upstream, and the uncontrolled extraction of groundwater from the basin area by upriver Punjab province. Pakistan's Indus-basin irrigated area, which was 10.75 million hectares at the time of the country's creation in 1947, has nearly doubled since then, putting serious strain on water availability farthest downstream.[102]

The other major problem in Asia is the growing environmental impact. Water withdrawals in excess of the natural hydrological cycle's renewable capacity are affecting ecosystems and degrading water quality. The anthropogenic alteration of ecosystems is an invitation to accelerated global warming. The rampant exploitation of water resources is due not only to the high demands of agriculture and the growing needs of industry and households but also to state policies. Most Asian farmers lack financial resources and knowledge to invest in "more expensive water-saving technologies, like drip irrigation infrastructure or storage," yet state subsidies have helped weaken "price signals, tempting farmers to take too much water from rivers, over-pump groundwater and generally waste freshwater resources."[103] For example, the widespread use of electric and diesel-fuel pumps to extract groundwater, with electricity and diesel fuel supplied to farmers at subsidized rates in several parts of Asia, has helped promote the reckless exploitation of a strategic resource that traditionally has served as a sort of drought insurance.

Using up groundwater means not only the irremediable depletion of a vital resource but also the possible drying up of wetlands, lakes, and streams that depend on the same source. The overpumping of groundwater in coastal areas has facilitated seawater intrusion as a replacement for the lost freshwater. Saline seawater inexorably flows in to supplant the freshwater that has been pumped out. Seawater intrusion into coastal aquifers has affected water supplies to megacities like Manila, Bangkok, Jakarta, Dhaka, and Karachi. Given the fact that Asia has the world's largest concentration of people living within 100 kilometers of the seacoast, the creeping saltwater intrusion into coastal aquifers carries serious long-term socioeconomic implications.

The overexploitation of groundwater due to the scarcity of other water resources remains a widespread problem across Asia. The extension of irrigated farming to arid or semiarid areas in Asia—stretching from Pakistan and Uzbekistan to northern China and North Korea—has promoted the extraction of underground water at rates exceeding the natural ecosystems' ability to stock up on such supplies. A further expansion of cropland watered by large-scale surface irrigation now seems hardly feasible in Asia, especially because surface-water resources are under growing pressure and the poorly maintained infrastructure has actually contributed to a decline in the total area under surface-water irrigation.

Yet the overall irrigated area in Asia continues to incrementally expand through groundwater, in keeping with the spread of the pump culture. The farming boom in China, India, Southeast Asia, Central Asia, and parts of the Near East has been greatly aided by the extensive use of farm pumps to bring subterranean water to the surface for irrigation. "In some pockets of Asia, particularly the Indus basin and river basins of Southeast Asia, much of the groundwater is used in conjunction with surface water, with or without prior planning, but across the rest of South Asia and on the North China Plains, the sole use of groundwater has become the norm. A booming low-cost Chinese pump industry is supporting the explosion of water-scavenging irrigation. The Chinese have pared the weight and cost of pumps to a fraction of their competitors' products and now export some four million each year."[104] In the arid and semiarid areas of Asia, the reliance on groundwater for meeting farming and other daily needs is more than 90 percent.

According to the China Geological Survey Bureau, groundwater usage in that country has doubled nationally since 1970 and now makes up one-fifth of all water use.[105] China continues to grow more than half its wheat and a third of its corn in the water-scarce north, an economic powerhouse that gets limited rainfall and depends heavily on groundwater. But the overexploitation of groundwater, particularly in the Hai basin, and the depletion of surface-water resources, along with increasing water pollution, are contributing to the degradation of water resources and damage to freshwater and coastal ecosystems on the northern plains.

In fact, to compensate for surface-water scarcity and pollution, users in the north increasingly are relying on groundwater, and thereby they are compromising the availability of this resource in the years ahead. China's response to such depletion and degradation has been, at best, haphazard, despite the World Bank's clear warning way back in 2002 that, "without a major concerted successful program to improve water resources management, the damage to the environment and to Chinese natural resources will become irreversible, resulting in huge negative impacts on the quality of life of the Chinese people and on the Chinese economy in the future."[106]

In Pakistan, such is the level of extraction that officials admit that "increasing salinity of groundwater in many areas and declining water levels in others suggest that there is little, if any, further potential for groundwater exploitation."[107] It is India, however, that has the dubious distinction of being the world's largest consumer of underground water. It uses an estimated 230 cubic kilometers of groundwater per year, or more than a quarter of the global total.[108] Environmentally unsustainable irrigation practices and overpumping of groundwater have resulted in a semiarid Indian state like Haryana becoming a major grain producer.

In India, more than 19 million unregulated groundwater pumps supply or supplement water for more than 60 percent of the nation's total irrigated area.[109] Some 85 percent of drinking-water supplies in India also are dependent on groundwater.[110] The groundwater saturation level is receding in parts of northern India by as much as 0.3 meter a year in the face of rampant water extraction, most of it for crop irrigation. According to a satellite-image-based study led by scientists with the Goddard Space Flight Center of the US National Aeronautics and Space Administration, an estimated 109 cubic kilometers of groundwater was drained through such exploitation in the Indian states of Rajasthan, Delhi, Haryana, and Punjab just between 2002 and 2008. The study warned that, "If measures are not taken soon to ensure sustainable groundwater usage, the consequences for the 114 million residents of the region [the four states] may include a reduction of agricultural output and shortages of potable water, leading to extensive socioeconomic stresses."[111]

The extraction of subterranean water for irrigation and other anthropogenic uses at unsustainable rates is a problem that extends to even southern India. In the southernmost Tamil Nadu State, for example, overpumping in certain districts has sunk the water level in many wells by 25 to 30 meters in just one decade. By contrast, in relatively underdeveloped eastern India, which sits on large reserves of groundwater, the extraction levels are relatively low because farmers do not have access to free or cheap electricity as in some other parts of India.[112] They thus must rely on the more-costly-to-operate diesel pumps. According to a World Bank study, at the current rates of national extraction of groundwater, about 60 percent of all aquifers in India will be in a critical condition by 2030, threatening sustainable agriculture, long-term food security, livelihoods, and economic growth. More than a quarter of the country's harvest, consequently, would be at risk.[113]

In several parts of western and central Asia, groundwater has become the primary source of freshwater. Some riverless areas, of course, have no choice but to rely solely on groundwater extraction. For example, there is not a single perennial stream on the large Arabian Peninsula. Fortunately for many of those living in areas with no perennial surface-water source, some of the world's largest aquifers are under desert sands. But the water in these aquifers has accumulated over hundreds of years, and today these key resources are being pumped to the surface at a rate much faster than replenishment by rain. Worse yet, some countries have started exploiting the resources in deep, "fossil" aquifers cut off from any significant recharge.

Saudi Arabia indeed has largely depleted its main fossil aquifer through large-scale irrigated wheat cultivation in its deserts. The heavily subsidized wheat and other food production followed Saudi fears that the Arab oil embargo in 1973–74 could provoke a retaliatory international ban on food exports. The result was that by 1992, in about just two decades, Saudi food production soared from 1.8 million to 7 million tons, with Saudi Arabia emerging as an exporter of wheat, dairy products, eggs, fish, poultry, vegetables, and flowers worth more than $500 million to markets around the world.[114]

The irrigated farming boom in a desert land also helped diversify the largely dates-based diet of the Saudis. But the change of lifestyle and diet—with air-conditioned comfort and fast food replacing the rigor of desert life and a fiber-rich traditional diet—has left Saudi Arabia with among the world's highest rates of obesity and diabetes, including among school-going children and women.[115] In recent years, Saudi Arabia has acknowledged its mistake in depleting fossil-aquifer resources by embarking on a plan to progressively end all wheat cultivation by 2016.

When the overexploitation of groundwater involves transnational aquifers, it raises additional problems, especially because there are no international rules governing the extraction of such waters. If aquifers run dry, the people dependent on them will need to necessarily relocate. As an Asian Development Bank report has pointed out, it is past time to change Asian policies in the water and energy sectors so as to stop the reckless depletion of aquifers. According to the report, "As the groundwater levels decline, more energy is needed to pump the same quantity of water. Because the energy costs for farmers are heavily subsidized, the financial losses of many public electricity boards are continuing to escalate. This has contributed to a vicious cycle of overuse of groundwater, declining aquifer levels, increasing losses to the electricity boards, and increasing adverse environmental impacts (like land subsidence), none of which are sustainable on a long-term basis."[116] To help preserve groundwater resources for future beneficial use, the growing imbalance between human abstraction and natural recharge in Asia must be reversed.

If Asia is to address its serious water challenges, it will need to end the gross mismanagement of its water resources, the result of which is that almost one in five Asians still does not have access to safe water and nearly half the Asian population lacks regular water sanitation facilities. Worse still, some of the nations with the lowest per capita water availability "also have among the worst water qualities in the region."[117] In India, the Ganges has come to symbolize a deeply rooted cultural paradox: A river considered sacred by Hindus across India has been allowed to become polluted.[118] The mismanagement of resources has led to a steadily growing problem of water pollution in large parts of Asia, as exemplified by lax controls on sewage and industrial effluent discharges, urban and agricultural runoff, and saline intrusion.

Levels of suspended solids in Asian rivers quadrupled just between the late 1970s and the mid-1990s, with pollution levels reaching four times the world average and twenty times the average for countries that belong to the Organization for

Economic Cooperation and Development.[119] In addition to suspended solids, other pollutants in water sources in Asia include pathogenic agents, organic chemicals, nutrients, heavy metals, silt, and toxic salts. In contrast to microbial pollutants, which come mainly from domestic sewerage, phosphates, nitrates, toxic chemicals, and heavy metals come largely from agricultural and industrial processes and waste disposal. In keeping with the phenomenal growth of the meat industry in Asia, animal wastes also have been polluting waterways.[120]

With wastewater disposal becoming "a serious social and human health issue" and surface-water and groundwater sources becoming increasingly contaminated, water resources in Asia's many developing countries will demand more intense and costlier treatment before they can be safely used as potable water.[121] In this light, it would be more economical for such states to protect the sources of their water supply from greater contamination than to go in for expensive treatment processes. Wellhead protection programs can be designed to prevent substances from contaminating groundwater, and surface-water protection must cover the watershed.

The Asian focus on controlling industrial pollutants has achieved some success, yet sewerage systems and landfills continue to contaminate underground water. As the United Nations has warned, "While some rehabilitation of polluted surface water systems is possible, pollution of groundwater is, for practical purposes, cumulative and permanent."[122]

To be sure, not all underground water pollution is due to anthropogenic activity. Arsenic contamination of groundwater—a major problem in Asia, including Bangladesh, Burma, Cambodia, China, India, Nepal, Pakistan, Thailand, and Vietnam—is largely caused by water flowing through arsenic-rich rocks. Arsenic is odorless and tasteless in water, and it is a semi-metal element in the periodic table. Arsenic-contaminated water is particularly a serious problem in India's West Bengal state and neighboring parts of Bangladesh, the country that heads the list of Asian nations most affected by arsenic toxicity in underground water.[123] Arsenic gets into the water through the dissolution of minerals and ores.[124]

Arsenic is used commercially, especially in alloying agents and wood preservatives, and thus industrial effluents, according to the World Health Organization and the US Environmental Protection Agency, can cause or augment arsenic contamination in groundwater in some areas.[125] Much of the arsenic-tainted water, however, occurs naturally as a result of complex geochemical phenomena.[126] The overexploitation of underground aquifers in areas with arsenic-rich rocks may exacerbate the problem. In the Gangetic delta, also known as the Bengal delta, the source of the arsenic is natural, although the processes causing the contamination are not well understood, with three hypotheses put forward: Oxidation of arsenian pyrite within aquifers, reductive iron dissolution with release of adsorbed arsenic, and competitive adsorption from phosphate.[127]

The extent of arsenic poisoning in this region was unveiled between the mid-1980s and mid-1990s, but it took local authorities years to recognize it as a serious problem. Drinking arsenic-tainted water causes arsenicosis.[128] Although there are no reliable figures on the number of arsenicosis cases in Asia, UNESCAP has estimated that at least 60 million Asians potentially could be exposed to arsenicosis risks. Studies in countries where communities have had long-term exposure to arsenic-contaminated groundwater indicate that 10 percent of those who drink water containing 500 micrograms of arsenic per liter may eventually die from lung, bladder, skin, and other cancers.[129] The maximum level recommended by the World Health Organization is 10 micrograms per liter, although some countries regard levels up to 50 micrograms per liter as safe.

Another naturally occurring water contaminant is fluoride, with tens of millions of Indians and Chinese exposed to high fluoride content in groundwater.[130] Many communities in the world actually add fluoride to their drinking-water supply to promote dental health. The US Environmental Protection Agency has set an enforceable drinking water standard of 4 milligrams of fluoride per liter, but children under nine should not drink water that has more than 2 milligrams per liter of fluoride. In large parts of Asia, the natural fluoride content in water is significantly higher than the maximum standard for adults set by the Environmental Protection Agency.

Excessive fluoride content is found mostly in calcium-deficient groundwater in many basement aquifers, such as granite and gneiss, and also in geothermal waters and in some sedimentary basins. The entire arc from Iraq and Iran to China through the Indian subcontinent and northern Thailand is one of the best-known high fluoride belts in the world. More than one-third of India has excess fluoride in its groundwater. In fact, such is the extent of the groundwater contamination problem in India that a government statement in Parliament in 2010 revealed that of the 626 districts in the country, the fluoride content in aquifers is higher than the safety level in 224 districts, the iron content in 254 districts, and the arsenic content in 34 districts, with salinity reported beyond tolerance levels in 162 districts.[131] The worst-affected Indian states are Gujarat and Rajasthan in the west and Karnataka in the south. There are continuing gaps, admittedly, in our scientific understanding of how contaminants travel through any groundwater system.

Improving Asia's Water Situation

It is apparent that the water challenges Asia confronts are formidable, with no easy solutions. The continent's water mismanagement has occurred because of multiple factors, the most important being the lack of a policy priority on protection, conservation, and efficiency. Overlapping jurisdictions among government agencies and departments, along with a disconnect between the federal and state governments, engenders a lack of policy coordination on water issues.

Not only does the structure of water governance need to be fixed, but tough decisions also need to be made by Asian governments. For example, it is beyond dispute that groundwater withdrawals across large parts of Asia have surpassed the rate of renewal by natural ecosystems. Yet the water being drawn from aquifers meets such a substantial share of water needs in Asia that the emergence of new users must be discouraged or stopped, even as efforts are made to get existing users to reduce their extraction through the imposition of water fees and other means. Given Asia's exceptionally high water withdrawals for farming, savings will need to come primarily from water conservation and efficiency in agriculture.

What Asia needs is a dramatic increase in agricultural water productivity, which must be a key part of the solution. This can come about only through major investments to overhaul the antediluvian irrigation systems, implement more water-efficient agricultural practices, and develop new grain varieties that are more tolerant of drought. Given that more than half of all agricultural water withdrawals in Asia are for rice cultivation, slashing water use in irrigated paddy fields holds one key to easing water shortages. Without this and other efforts, Asia's water crisis threatens to cause serious food shortages in a region that prides itself for having achieved self-sufficiency.

Not only is population and consumption growth adding to the demand for food, but also the spread of prosperity is changing diets in Asia, with people tending to eat more meat, dairy products, and fruit as they become middle class. Since 1980, China's meat consumption has risen fourfold, and its beef sector has grown from an inconsequential output level to the third largest in the world. Furthermore, Chinese meat consumption is projected to double by 2030. A shift from traditional rice and noodles to a meatier diet already has helped double China's "water footprint" for food production since 1985, given the fact that, as noted above, it takes ten times more water to raise a kilogram of beef than grow a kilogram of rice or wheat.[132] Asian nations also need to face up to the likely effects of climate change on soil moisture, rainfall, groundwater, and river channels.

The critical point on the food front could be reached in several parts of Asia by 2050, according to a computer simulation drawing on the present water-related data and trends.[133] Water scarcity will greatly affect the production of rice, wheat, corn, and meat in particular, compelling a number of currently self-sufficient Asian countries to depend on food imports. Such dependency would also create greater volatility in prices on the world food markets and expose the importing countries to both severe financial risks and political vulnerability.

Given their present water constraints and limited capacity to expand arable land, most Asian states have little choice but to upgrade their old irrigation systems and adopt drip-feed and sprinkler irrigation and other innovations, besides improving and expanding rain-fed agriculture. Agricultural water-productivity measures must seek to increase "crop per drop" through a mix of improved efficiency of water application and net water gains through crop-yield enhancement.[134] Importing large quantities of cereals and meats from other parts of the world that are rich in water may be politically unpalatable for many governments. But it is likely to become inescapable, so that water savings can be channeled to continued economic expansion.

More broadly, Asian countries and communities need to start finding ways to cooperate and collaborate so that the water problems are not exacerbated. The decline in the ecological health of Asian freshwater systems has resulted in a drop in aquatic biodiversity, with vertebrate species declining in numbers most markedly. The Intergovernmental Panel on Climate Change has suggested that, "In some parts of Asia, conversion of cropland to forest, restoration and reestablishment of vegetation, improvement of tree and herb varieties, and selection and cultivation of new drought-resistant varieties [can be] effective measures."[135]

The damage to Asian ecosystems already is affecting the livelihoods of those engaged in freshwater fisheries. Reduced fish catches from rivers, lakes, and wetlands mean less protein for rural communities. As a cheap source of protein for hundreds of millions of poor people, fish is central to the diet of many Asian communities. It is no accident that the highest global consumption levels of fish are in some of the world's poorest states, such as the Maldives and Bangladesh. Among poor communities living along watercourses or the coast, fish consumption usually is way above the global average of 16 kilograms per capita per year.[136]

Given the shrinking endowments of accessible freshwater and the implications of water scarcity for socioeconomic and political stability, Asian governments need to rise to the challenge. Thus they must help efficiently utilize water resources, clean up rivers and other sources, and ease water stress by pursuing a number of measures—including a national regulatory framework; an integrated policy approach; professional water resources planning; a shift from supply-side to demand-side management to deal with the competing demands in the agricultural, industrial, services, and residential sectors; and greater transparency and public accountability. Indeed, national policies on water, energy, food, and the environment ought to be harmonized. Much of the future water demand must be met by achieving greater water efficiency. By plugging losses from leaks in irrigation and city networks and attaining greater water productivity, the water saved can help meet new demand.

Two

Murky Hydropolitics

Asia's rapid economic resurgence has come to symbolize the qualitative reordering of power in the world. In past world history, the competition for a balance of power centered on Europe. Even the Cold War was not really an East/West rivalry but a competition between two blocs over Europe. For the first time, we are facing the task of building power equilibrium across the world—an equilibrium that would be very much influenced by Asian power dynamics and likely bear a distinct Asian imprint. In fact, a stable power balance in Asia has now become critical to international relations. However, Asia's own security situation at present remains in flux, with the baggage of history weighing down all major interstate relationships. If Asia is to shape the new global order and determine the future of globalization, it will need to first build power stability and institutionalized security cooperation among its important states.

The current hyperbole about the dawn of a new Asian age obscures the geostrategic significance of the serious constraints Asia confronts on natural resources, particularly water. Indeed, the greatest potential for water-related conflict in the world exists in Asia, which faces water challenges more weighty than developing economies elsewhere put together. In 1995, the World Bank's then–vice president, Ismail Serageldin, warned: "Many of the wars of this [twentieth] century were about oil, but the wars of the next century will be about water."[1] Similarly, UNESCO director-general Federico Mayor cautioned in 1998: "As [water] becomes increasingly rare, it becomes coveted, capable of unleashing conflicts. More than over petrol or land, it is over water that the most bitter conflicts of the near future may be fought."[2] Nowhere does that prospect look more real than in water-deficient Asia, the world's largest and most densely populated continent that awaits a future made hotter and drier by global warming. Asia's population and consumption growth, its rising resource constraints, and its vulnerability to the effects of climate change underscore the challenge to ensure that water shortages do not retard the continent's rising strength, damage its economic growth, or undermine stability within Asian nations.

47

Water has emerged as a key issue to underpin peace and stability in Asia. After all, the growing water stress carries major political and economic ramifications. As the *Global Trends 2025* report of the US National Intelligence Council—the senior analytic body within the Office of the Director of National Intelligence—has forecasted, "With water becoming scarcer in several regions, cooperation over changing water resources is likely to be increasingly difficult within and between states, straining regional relations. Such regions include the Himalayan region, which feeds the major rivers of China, Pakistan, India, and Bangladesh; Israel-Palestinian Territories; along the Jordan River (Israel-Jordan); and the Fergana Valley of Central Asia. Such dire scenarios are not inevitable even with worse-than-anticipated climate change impacts, however. Economic development, the spread of new technologies, and robust new mechanisms for multilateral cooperation to deal with climate change may foster greater global collaboration."[3]

Global Trends 2025, which represents the US intelligence community's most comprehensive examination of long-term security issues, goes on to say that while strategic rivalries in the twenty-first century probably would center on issues related to trade, investment, technology innovation, and acquisition, "increasing worries about resources—such as energy or even water—could easily put the focus back on territorial disputes or unresolved border issues. Asia is one region where the number of such border issues is particularly noteworthy. . . . As the national power of China, India and others grows, smaller countries in the neighborhood may seek outsiders' protection or intervention in a balancing effort."[4] Resource competition over water and energy is already beginning to rekindle territorial or border disputes.

Sharper resource competition in Asia indeed could escalate conflict over territories that are either the original source of water or through which major rivers flow, such as Tibet, Kashmir, and the Golan Heights. Pakistan, for example, depends on rivers flowing in from Indian-administered Jammu and Kashmir, although only one river (the Jhelum) originates there. India controls the western part, or 45 percent of the original state of Jammu and Kashmir, with Pakistan holding the eastern, 35 percent of the territory and China the remaining 20 percent, including a slice gifted to it by Pakistan in 1963. But from the part India holds, three of the six rivers of the Indus system flow into territories in Pakistan. In the Israeli-Jordanian-Palestinian-Syrian strategic quadrangle, the territories Israel occupies are either the source of major river waters (the Golan Heights) or the source of major supply from underground aquifers (the West Bank).

Water indeed is becoming an important element in shaping internal security and regional security in Asia. At a time when the Asian strategic landscape is qualitatively changing and resource competition is growing, Asia remains a potential flashpoint for water wars—a concern underscored by inter-riparian tensions, especially between China and its neighbors, but also between Pakistan and India. Water rivalry between Israel and its neighbors also is intense, but because of Israel's military preeminence—underlined by its nuclear-weapons monopoly in the region and preemptive conventional force capability—there is no regional challenger to the Israeli control over a dominant share of water resources. It was in the 1967 Israeli-initiated Six-Day War that the water-rich Golan Heights and the aquifer-controlling West Bank were captured by Israel, along with Jordan's Arava (Wadi Araba) aquifer. The war left Israel in control of the Jordan River's headwaters.

The fact that military superiority provides a shield to exploit riparian advantage is also exemplified by the separate cases of Turkey and China. Under its $25 billion Southeastern Anatolia Development Project (referred to as GAP from the Turkish acronym for Güneydoğu Anadolu Projesi), upstream Turkey is building twenty-two dams and nineteen hydropower plants on the Tigris and Euphrates rivers, besides working to bring 1.8 million hectares of additional land under irrigation across nine provinces. But downstream Syria and Iraq are in no position to challenge Turkey's growing appropriation of the Tigris-Euphrates waters. China, with its rapidly accumulating military and economic power, is similarly building upstream megaprojects on international rivers. The scale of its projects simply is beyond compare.

THE SECURITIZATION OF WATER RESOURCES

Except for a few countries—principally Bhutan, Burma, Kyrgyzstan, Laos, and Malaysia—Asia already faces water shortages, especially its more densely populated nations. Large parts of the Indian subcontinent, Central Asia, Southwest Asia, and West Asia are plagued by water scarcity. In Indonesia, the world's most-populous Muslim nation, the annual renewable freshwater resources, estimated at 2,838 cubic kilometers, seem reasonable by Asian standards, yet "the seasonal and spatial variation in the rainfall pattern and lack of adequate storage create competition and conflicts among users."[5] Overexploitation of groundwater in coastal regions, as in Jakarta, has led to critical problems, including saltwater intrusion. In northern China, deteriorating water quality, coupled with a widening gap between supply and demand, is creating a water crisis. Some 400 of China's 660 cities are said to be short of water, with 108 of them facing serious water scarcities, including mega-cities like Beijing and Tianjin.[6]

The growing Asian water-related security concerns undergird the quiet manner in which water has gone from being just an environmental issue to becoming a strategic issue. The "securitization" of water, in one sense, can be helpful to build greater public awareness and to secure national and regional commitments to sustainably manage this vital resource. Security challenges in Asia and elsewhere in the world, after all, have fundamentally changed in the past two decades. Nontraditional security issues—from water security and climate security to transnational terrorism and environmental degradation—have become as important as traditional security issues. Unconventional geostrategic challenges now extend to key aspects of economic security, resource security, food security, environmental security, and human security.

But unlike unconventional challenges such as transnational terrorism, resource insecurity is caused not by hostile forces but by humanity's production and consumption patterns. The same holds true for the climate crisis. Water insecurity cannot be dealt with through the traditional tools of national defense; nor can it be looked at strictly through the environmental prism. As a critical resource whose shortage carries long-term strategic ramifications, water must command attention at the highest policy levels so that an integrated and sustainable approach to resource management can be embraced nationally and regionally.

Water stress or scarcity in the vast majority of Asian states is already a serious problem. Most societies in Asia are agrarian, and the water withdrawals for farming are remarkably high by international standards, as was detailed in chapter 1. In addition, Asia's rapid industrialization and urbanization are boosting demand for water in a significant way. Household water consumption in Asia is rising rapidly, but such is the water paucity that not many Asians can aspire to the lifestyle of Americans, who daily use 580 liters per person, or several times more than the average in Asia. In China the average daily water use per person is 90 liters, but in the more water-stressed Asian countries it is less than 50 liters—the critical threshold defined by the Food and Agriculture Organization of the United Nations.[7]

Add to the picture the likely effects of climate change on soil moisture, rainfall, groundwater, and river channels, and what emerges is a region torn by acute water shortages with a significant bearing on its long-term socioeconomic and political stability. A balanced approach centered on demand- and supply-side measures thus is needed to address the growing "water gap" in which water demand is outstripping supply, making improvements in public health and major advances in poverty alleviation more difficult. The water gap actually threatens to accentuate the already-wide economic and social disparities in many Asian countries.

It is little surprise that water has become an important issue in several important bilateral relationships in Asia, including those between China and India; between China and the other Mekong River basin states; and among states in South Asia, Central Asia, and West Asia. Water is likely to influence Asia's future direction—toward mutually beneficial cooperation or greater interstate competition. That is why it is important for the Asian nations to start discussing options on mitigating the vulnerabilities and risks concerning water through national, bilateral, and regional action.

In terms of its rivers, Asia is unusual. Almost all the major rivers of Asia (excluding its western rim) originate in one area: the Chinese-held Tibetan Plateau. Whether it is the Yangtze or the Yellow that help irrigate the plains of China; or the Mekong, the Salween, and the Irrawaddy that flow into Southeast Asia; or the Brahmaputra, the Indus and the Sutlej that are the lifeblood of parts of the Indian subcontinent—the source of each of these rivers (and several others) is in the Plateau of Tibet. Another Chinese-held homeland of ethnic minorities, Xinjiang, is the starting place of the Irtysh and Illy rivers. Downstream Kazakhstan and Russia have objected to growing Chinese damming activities in the Irtysh-Illy basin. China's control over Asia's riverheads, as is discussed in chapter 3, holds major geostrategic implications, especially for those states located downstream of the international rivers originating in the Tibetan Plateau.

Through its political rule on Tibet, China not only controls the flow of several major river systems that are a lifeline to southern and southeastern Asia, but its current hydroengineering projects and additional construction plans in the Tibetan Plateau also carry the seeds of inter-riparian conflict. China is seeking to deal with its own water problem by means of a bumper solution—massive interbasin and interriver water transfers. Its Great South–North Water Transfer Project is an overly ambitious engineering attempt to take water from the south through human-made canals and tunnels to its arid north and northwest. The diversion of waters from the Tibetan Plateau in this project's third leg is an idea that has been enthusiastically backed by President Hu Jintao, a hydrologist by training whose 1989 martial-law crackdown in Tibet helped facilitate his swift rise in the Communist Party hierarchy.

Globally, water-transfer projects between river basins date back to ancient times. However, it was not until the twentieth century that *large* interbasin water transfer (IBWT) projects were undertaken. Today, at least 155 IBWT projects covering twenty-six countries are in operation, with the vast majority of them on the two water-rich continents, South America and North America. Canada, indeed, boasts the world's largest operating IBWT capacity. Spain, for its part, intends to channel water from its north to its parched south. But China's IBWT plans are unmatched, even if the goals for these projects resemble plans for projects in the United States and the former Soviet Union that failed to take off. In terms of scale, volume, and cost, China has undertaken the most-ambitious water transfer projects in the IBWT history of the world.

Pressure on China's water resources is growing. As Ma Jun, director of the Beijing-based Institute of Public and Environmental Affairs, has brought out in his book *China's Water Crisis*, the decline in the country's water quality and availability, especially in the north, is a problem that has long been in the making due to misguided government policies.[8] Compounding the water situation is the fact that China, hydrologically, is made up of two distinct entities: The arid north, which receives very limited rainfall (concentrated in July and August) and is the region beyond the Yangtze basin; and the humid south, which includes the Yangtze basin and everything south of it. With its long rainy season, plentiful precipitation and winter temperatures above 0 degrees Celsius, the south has rivers with large flows and small seasonal variations in water level. Yet almost two-thirds of China's farmland is in the water-scarce north, where the vegetation is sparse, soil erosion is a serious problem, and rivers freeze in the harsh winter months.

China's overall per capita availability of water is better than India's, although there are major spatial disparities within each country. For example, China's average renewable water resources are 2,112 cubic meters (m³) per person annually,[9] but in its north, the figure is just 700 m³ per year and the amount of exploitable water is much smaller.[10] Much of India is water stressed, but scarcity is acute in the west, northwest, and parts of the south. In response to population and consumption growth and expanding economies, per capita water availability is projected to decline significantly in India and China during the next two decades.

As these two demographic titans gain economic heft, they are increasingly drawing international attention. The two are coming into their own at the same time in history, helping to highlight the ongoing major shifts in global politics and economy. Since the 1990s, "China became factory to the world, the United States became buyer to the world, and India began to become back office to the world."[11] Today, it has become commonplace to speak of India and China in the same breath as two emerging great powers challenging the two-century-old Western domination of the world. As if to underline the eastward movement of power and influence, China and India have been blended together in the "Chindia" concept—an odd synthesis that disregards the rivalry and antagonisms between these giants.[12]

The Weight of Natural Endowments

The future will not belong to China and India merely because they have a huge landmass and together make up more than a third of humanity. Being large in size and population is not necessarily an asset. In history, small, strategically geared states have wielded global power. The colonial powers that emerged starting in the sixteenth century, for example, were led by small Britain and included tiny Portugal and the Netherlands. Japan, between 1895 and 1905, defeated Manchu-ruled China and Tsarist Russia in separate wars. With much of Asia colonized by the Europeans, Russia's military rout at the hands of the Japanese came as a shot in the arm to Asian independence movements.

World history is replete with instances of small states made powerful by far-sighted policies and big states unraveled by weak, unimaginative leaders. If smallness in size does not connote inconsequentiality—as underscored by the manner in which South Korea, Singapore, Dubai, and Bahrain in Asia punch well above their weight—being large in landmass or population does not inevitably portend greatness.[13] The ability to adapt to change has been a key determinant historically. As Charles Darwin put it in his *Origin of Species*, published in 1859, "It is not the strongest of the species that survives, or the most intelligent, but the one most responsive to change."[14]

History rarely moves in a linear fashion. Yet for analysts, it is tempting to make long-term linear projections on the basis of current trends. Such simple extrapolations have hardly ever come right. Remember the popular concerns in the United States in the 1980s that a fast-rising Japan threatened America's industrial might? Just as China is an obsession today, there were Japan mania and even Japan bashing in America in the 1980s, with some castigating Japan as a close-knit, exclusionary society that pursued unfair competition to undercut the United States in international markets.[15] US pressure compelled Japan to accept voluntary export restraints in the automobile industry and to let the value of its currency appreciate.

In fact, economists were forecasting in 1991—in much the same way they are today making predictions about China's future growth—that Japan within two decades would surpass the United States as the world's largest economy. The reality has turned out to be very different: Japan's nearly $5.5 trillion economy has largely stagnated since then, while America's gross domestic product (GDP) has doubled in size to nearly $15 trillion in the same period. In fact, China, whose GDP was just half Japan's in 2005 before ballooning to $5.88 trillion in a five-year period, has claimed the slot of the world's second-largest economy by edging out Japan.

At the beginning of the twenty-first century, agricultural and market specialists declared that cheap food was here to stay. Then, within a few years, soaring food prices and a scarcity of rice and other grains came to haunt several regions, with food riots searing some poor countries. Today, Asia risks slipping into a food supply crisis, which will stoke high inflation, food export restrictions, and sociopolitical unrest, besides sending shock waves through the global grain markets. World food prices, despite reaching record levels in 2011, could continue to climb unless global grain output increases significantly. More fundamentally, the stability of international prices hinges on Asia's ability to feed itself.

Take yet another case: Since at least the 1960s, Brazil has been portrayed by analysts as a land of great potential, with the resources and ambition to become a global power. But Brazil has not lived up to its promise, with many Brazilians themselves tending to echo the view—apocryphally attributed to Charles de Gaulle—that "Brazil is not a serious country." In fact, Brazilians love to restate the familiar locution, "Brazil is the country of the future—and always will be." Brazil today is still hoping to make it—with a land area more than two and a half times the size of India's; a $2 trillion GDP equivalent to Russia's; a population almost equivalent in size to those of Germany, France, and Britain combined; and massive offshore hydrocarbon reserves.

Francis Fukuyama gained intellectual stardom by making the self-righteous claim in a 1989 essay that the conclusion of the Cold War marked the end of ideological evolution, "the end of history," with the "universalization of Western liberal democracy as the final form of human government."[16] Today's Asia, however, demonstrates that Western liberal democratic values and practices are anything but universal. Indeed, singling out China for stepping up Internet censorship, US secretary of state Hillary Clinton warned in 2010 that "a new information curtain is descending across much of the world."[17] Her statement, with its allusion to the Cold War–era Iron Curtain, amounted to an implicit admission that the central assumption guiding US policy on China since the 1990s—that assisting China's economic rise would usher in greater political openness there—has gone awry.

The strategy of using market forces and the Internet to open up a closed political system simply has not worked. The more power China has accumulated, the more adept it has become in extending censorship to cyberspace. If anything, China has proven that a country can blend control, coercion, and patronage to stymie the Internet's politically liberalizing elements. From Latin America to Asia, autocratic states are emulating China's model of "state capitalism."[18] As a result, more than two decades after the end of the Cold War, a bipolar ideological divide has reemerged in the world, with the rise of authoritarian capitalism symbolizing a challenge to liberal democracy.

The reason why linear projections have often come wrong is that statistical probability—the sole tool in forecasting—has little application in strategic analyses. To extrapolate from existing trends is downright dicey because the present is hardly a compass pointing to the future. The straight-line projections on the continued rise of China and India in the coming decades thus may be too one-dimensional. China is projected to overtake the United States as the world's largest economy in the 2020s, with India also forecast to surpass America's output a decade later than China. That could happen, even if it led to a sharper competition for scarce raw materials. After all, in the past half century, the principal sources of international strife—ideology, nationalism, and ethnic or religious identity—have done little to prevent the improvement of living standards.

Although the greatest growth in per capita incomes has been in Asia, living standards in the past five decades went up across the world, including more than three times in the United States. This trend is likely to continue. Economic growth indeed is essential to underpin political and social stability. In China, for example, it is doubtful that the Communist Party's monopoly on power or the government's ability to maintain public order can hold without the present system continuing to deliver high economic growth. But once China and India have plucked most of the low-hanging economic fruit, their GDP growth rates are likely to decline and actually be determined by their ability to develop autonomous and innovative technological capabilities. Only then would a better picture of their long-term economic growth prospects be known.

Sustained rapid economic growth, in any event, hinges on several factors, both endogenous and exogenous. One factor beyond the control of policymakers in India and China that could slow down economic growth and create major policy challenges in the years ahead is climate change, especially its impact on water availability. According to a United Nations study, water shortages have been held responsible for an estimated annual loss of some $28 billion in industrial output in China, while also slowing Indian industrial activity.[19] One American study has warned that agriculture in India is likely to suffer more than any other country due to climate change, with hotter temperatures and other factors possibly diminishing Indian agricultural output by 60 percent in the north and up to 35 percent in the south by the 2080s.[20] Although that assessment did not factor in the favorable effects of carbon fertilization, India's agricultural-productivity losses nonetheless could be serious. In the rosiest scenario, even if climate change did not significantly alter the availability of water resources or affect food production, greater water shortages resulting from population and consumption growth will be a constraining factor for India and China in their goal to maintain high GDP growth rates.

Indeed, when one examines natural endowments—such as arable land, water resources, mineral deposits, hydrocarbons, and wetlands—the picture that emerges is not exactly gratifying for India and China, especially if they are to achieve lasting great-power capacity. Bounteous natural capital is critical for any country to sustain national strength over the long run. It is, of course, not the only factor. After all, in the absence of able leadership and good governance, abundant natural resources can even be a curse. But ample natural capital, powered by able leadership and a high level of autonomous and innovative technological capability, is a key factor in achieving national greatness on the world stage.

India and China together have 37 percent of the global population—or nearly nine times the number of inhabitants of the United States—but just 60 percent more cultivated acreage than America.[21] India's supply of arable land is second only to that of the United States. But India has to support more than one-sixth of the global population, with less than one-twenty-fifth of the world's water resources.[22] China—home to almost one-fifth of the global population—has barely 7 percent of the world's water resources.[23]

Furthermore, China and India suffer from very uneven distribution of water resources within their national territories. Four-fifths of China's water supply is in the south, but the opposite is true of India, where water resources are largely concentrated in the Ganges-Brahmaputra-Meghna basin in the north and east, with serious water deficits plaguing the economically dynamic south, west, and northwest. India's water woes are perceptibly aggravating, while in China, according to a deputy director of the State Environmental Protection Administration, the "central and local governments have all realized that water shortages have become a key constraint to the country's economic and social development."[24] Had their populations been much smaller, the two Asian giants would have had a better balance between population size and available natural resources, including water, food, and energy.

According to Paul Kennedy, the ascendancy of states or empires results from the superiority of their material resources, and the wealth on which this dominance rests is eroded by the huge military expenditures needed to sustain national or imperial power, leading inexorably to its decline and fall.[25] Material resources, of course, can be created through imports of raw materials. Indeed, to help secure its supplies of hydrocarbons, minerals, and other raw materials from overseas, China has been building up its naval capabilities and entering into special strategic arrangements with states located along vital sea lanes of communication.

Water, however, is one resource that cannot be obtained through long-term international trade deals. For most of the fast-growing Asian economies, a critical unsolved problem is growing water stress. In fact, it speaks for itself that, by and large, the developed nations, with their generally temperate environments and relatively favorable land-to-population size equation, have much higher per capita water availability than developing countries. No less ominous is the fact that water scarcity and pollution are most acute in some of the world's poorest and dysfunctional states. Seven of the ten countries that topped the 2010 Failed States Index—Somalia, Chad, Sudan, Zimbabwe, Afghanistan, Iraq, and Pakistan—are also among the world's most water-scarce or water-polluted states.[26]

Acute water distress is a recipe for interminable poverty. If present trends continue, with demand outstripping supply in the countries where water needs are growing at the fastest pace, the world could get divided into two groups—water haves and have-nots—along what would be a dangerous new interstate and intrastate fault line. Such a divide would be most visible in Asia.

The Movement toward the Securitization of Water

The processes of securitization of water have drawn encouragement from the broadening of the concept of security. Paucity of supply due to the degradation and depletion of water resources, along with threats to future supplies, are now widely recognized as important security challenges. When supplies of nonrenewable resources such as oil, minerals, and coal come under strain or become expensive, demand usually drops and new investments search for alternative sources and technologies. But ensuring adequate supplies of a renewable resource like freshwater, paradoxically, poses a greater challenge. Such supplies, after all, are limited by nature's replenishable capacity.

Freshwater scarcity often carries a high price tag. Deficient water resources are not a barrier to economic growth only in city-states such as Singapore, which imports more than 40 percent of its water supply through pipelines from the neighboring country from which it seceded in 1965—Malaysia.[27] But in the Maldives, an archipelago in the Indian Ocean whose geography precludes the possibility of importing water by pipeline from another country, freshwater scarcity exacts serious socioeconomic costs.[28]

Indeed, water-strapped Singapore's dependency on Malaysia also carries costs, which have quietly spurred the securitization of water in Singaporean policy. Disputes over water pricing, coupled with occasional Malaysian attempts to use water as a political card, have prompted Singapore to undertake a costly program to try and become self-reliant through water recycling, rainwater capture, and desalination by 2061—the year of expiration of a 1962 agreement with Malaysia that allows Singapore to draw up to 250 million imperial gallons of water per day (1.14 million m³ a day) from the Johor River and the Linggui Reservoir. A separate accord with Malaysia in 1961 gave Singapore the rights up to 2011 to extract 86 million imperial gallons of water per day—0.39 million m³ a day—from Mount Pulai and the Tebrau and Skudai rivers, with Singapore, in return, agreeing to provide the adjacent Malaysian state of Johor with a daily supply of treated water of up to 12 percent of the raw water drawn by it. The two accords actually predated Singapore's separation, but they were reaffirmed in 1965.[29] Both accords contained a provision for arbitration to resolve any dispute, and also provided for a review of water prices after twenty-five years.

In the years since its expulsion from the Malaysian Federation, Singapore has had a stormy relationship with Malaysia, with the episodic deterioration in bilateral ties over various disputes or disagreements being accompanied by Malaysian threats—veiled or overt—to end the water-supply arrangements. Malaysia over the years has contended that Singapore imports raw water cheaply at 3 Malaysian cents (just under 1 US cent) per thousand imperial gallons (4,546 liters) but makes a handsome profit by selling treated water to Johor State at 50 Malaysian cents (15 US cents) per 1,000 imperial gallons. It has thus demanded a more equitable arrangement, and sought a price on par with what mainland China charges Hong Kong for supplying water to it from Guangdong Province.

Singapore, conversely, has argued: "The water dispute is not about money but Singapore's existence as a sovereign nation. The water agreements are part of the Separation Agreement which guarantees Singapore's existence as an independent nation. If the terms of the water agreements can be changed by Malaysia at will, then Singapore's independence too could be called into question."[30] According to one Singaporean analyst, Malaysian leaders have sought to "periodically exploit" Singapore's water dependency in various ways—from "threatening to terminate the water supply" to seeking to "influence governmental decisions in the city-state," spurring "concerns that Singapore–Malaysia relations may quickly deteriorate, with potentially violent outcomes."[31]

The specter of a Malaysian water-supply cutoff leading to military tensions or conflict has been raised in several studies.[32] After all, Singapore's prime architect, Lee Kuan Yew—once labeled "the little Hitler of Southeast Asia" by an American columnist for establishing a largely one-party state based on the "soft authoritarianism" model also embraced by Malaysia—had cited a water-cutoff scenario to justify building a strong Singaporean military:

> He [then Malaysian Prime Minister Mahathir bin Mohamad] was direct and asked what we were building the SAF [Singapore Armed Forces] for. I replied equally directly that we feared that at some time or other there could be a random act of madness like cutting off our water supplies which they [the Malaysians] had publicly threatened whenever there were differences between us. . . . In [the 1965 Separation] Agreement, the Malaysian government had guaranteed our water supply. If this was breached, we would go to the UN Security Council. If water shortage became urgent, in an emergency, we would have to go in, forcibly if need be, to repair damaged pipes and machinery to restore the water flow. I was putting my cards on the table. He denied that such precipitate action would happen. I said I believed that he would not do this, but we had to be prepared for all contingencies.[33]

In more recent times, Singapore's vulnerability on the water front has led its government to embark on a mission to make the city-state the hydrotechnology hub of Asia. Seeking to emulate the example of Israel—a pioneer in irrigation technology, which has been exporting some $1.5 billion worth of water-related technologies, equipment and services per year—Singapore is setting up a research-and-development base for environment and water solutions that it hopes would generate as many as 11,000 professional and skilled jobs by 2015.[34]

Significantly, through rainwater harvesting, wastewater recycling and desalination, Singapore has been reducing its reliance on imports of Malaysian water. It taps much of its high rainfall, with the effective catchment acreage extending nearly to two-thirds of its total land area. It has built a fifth plant to turn wastewater into high-quality recycled water, and it plans to produce more desalinated water. Such nonconventional water sources now meet more than half of Singapore's needs.

Although clearly more costly than water imports, the nonconventional water supplies offer greater security to Singapore. Besides expanding such alternative sources of supply, Singapore has pursued demand management through greater water productivity and efficiency. By plugging system leaks and inefficiencies and raising the price of domestic water, with the tariff and tax rising steeply after the first 40 m^3 a month, it managed to reduce household water use by about 10 percent since the mid-1990s to about 155 liters per person per day in 2011. That consumption level is nearly four times lower than that of an average American.

Water actually has been a security obsession in Singapore almost since independence, with Lee Kuan Yew reminding citizens that the invading Japanese forces in 1942 blew up the water-supply pipeline before seizing Singapore in just one week of intense fighting in what was the largest surrender of British-led military personnel in history. Israel is another example of a country preoccupied with water security since its inception—a concern that led it to build an elaborate water grid called the National Water Carrier, running from north to south and covering much of the country.

Intended to overcome regional imbalances in water availability within Israel, the completion of the National Water Carrier in 1964 by diverting Jordan River waters served as the trigger for the launch of a rival Arab plan to tap the river's headwaters so as to redirect flows to Syria and Jordan. That, in turn, led to repeated Israeli air strikes on the diversion works in Syria and to the eventual full-fledged Six-Day War in 1967, when Israel seized the Golan Heights, the West Bank, and the Gaza Strip. In terms of both motives and the outcome, 1967 really was a water war that radically altered the political control of regional water resources.

Yet another example of a country fixated on water since its creation is Pakistan, which was carved out of India by the British in 1947 as a homeland for the subcontinent's Muslims. With its main rivers flowing in from India and the headwaters of its largest irrigation canals also located in Indian territory, Pakistan faced an inborn disadvantage, which it tried to correct by seeking to grab the state of Jammu and Kashmir—first in the 1947–48 war, when it seized more than one-third of that region, but not the sources of water; and then in 1965, when its military adventure failed to change the status quo on territory or water resources. Paradoxically, it initiated war in 1965 barely five years after India had agreed by treaty to reserve four-fifths of the total waters of the Indus River system, including the largest three of the six rivers, for Pakistani use. All in all, neither Pakistan's strategy to capture water resources by war nor India's policy to win peace by water munificence has succeeded, and thus the subcontinent is still racked by strategic animosities and water remains as divisive an issue as ever.

The links between water and security have been strong in some other Asian countries, too. The desiccation of the Aral Sea in Central Asia, for example, represents a human-made ecological blow. But the hard times it has brought have made water security a pressing priority for most Central Asian governments. Rising nationalism and competition have not only impeded the development of a regional alternative to the old water resources management system of the Soviet era, but water also has emerged as the most troublesome issue in intercountry relations in Central Asia—a region nearly as large as the Indian subcontinent in land size but with less than 5 percent of the population of the latter. The increasingly sharp hydropolitics in the region since the 1991 independence of the five Soviet republics—the so-called Stans—has been driven by the fact that the weak, upstream states, Kyrgyzstan and Tajikistan, are water suppliers to the larger, hydrocarbon-rich Central Asian countries, which use the bulk of the region's internal renewable water resources, estimated at 263 cubic kilometers per year.[35] Today, in the face of growing water shortages and high dependency on transboundary flows, the "securitization" of water is happening across large parts of Asia.

THE WATER LEGACY OF MAO ZEDONG

China's environmental and water crisis has its origins in the policies that were initiated by the strongman Mao Zedong and carried forward by succeeding leaders. Today, water shortages are severe in the north, promoting the steady depletion of underground water resources. With the groundwater saturation level dropping sharply, northern China—home to nearly half the country's population but with less than one-fifth of the national water resources—risks encountering an ecological disaster. Water scarcity is most acute in the Hai River basin, including Beijing and Tianjin, where per capita water availability has been estimated at only 300 m^3 per year.[36] Indeed, water shortages have become so serious that, in the ominous words of Premier Wen Jiabao, they threaten the very "survival of the Chinese nation."[37]

After the establishment of the People's Republic of China in 1949, the traditional Chinese ideal of "harmony between heaven and humans" gave way to Mao's insistence that "man must conquer nature," leading to what Judith Shapiro has described as the Chinese Communist Party's open war to bend the physical world to human will, with terrible consequences for the natural and human environments.[38] When one-fifth of humanity is made to bend nature to the human will, what will predictably follow is environmental devastation. In fact, it was Mao's quest to subdue nature that precipitated the greatest genocide in modern world history—the "Great Leap Forward," a forced attempt at industrialization and collectivizing agriculture that helped create one of the world's worst famines between 1958 and 1961. Some 36 million people perished (more than three times the number killed in World War I) in the supposed Great Leap Forward, according to the well-researched 2008 book *Tombstone* by longtime Chinese Communist Yang Jisheng.[39]

It was under Mao that the large-scale uprooting of local residents to make way for major water projects began—a trend that not only has persisted to this day, but also has become common. The Chinese government continues to seize land for projects deemed in the "public interest," forcibly evicting residents from their long-time homes and neighborhoods with meager compensation. In fact, the biggest water projects that have been pursued by China in the post-Mao period originally were conceived in the Mao era.

The Great South-to-North Water Diversion Project was visualized by Mao when he reportedly said in 1952: "The south has a lot of water, the north little; . . . . it is okay to lend a little water." Mao's grand ideas to take water from China's flood-prone south to the arid north actually drew inspiration from the dam-building era in the United States, with the mammoth Hoover Dam on the Colorado River serving as a prime example of how water on a massive scale can be diverted to parched areas. Constructed in the late 1920s and 1930s, the Great Depression-era Hoover Dam was designed for multiple purposes in the arid West—from irrigation to hydropower. Mao also was influenced by the mega-projects in the Soviet Union during Joseph Stalin's reign, which lasted from the mid-1920s to the early 1950s.

By launching his own megaprojects, Mao sought to hark back to the glory of imperial China, as symbolized by the Grand Canal and the Great Wall. Monumental projects were Mao's way of presenting himself as the Great Helmsman. Obsessed with taming the Yellow River, whose changing course and devastating floods had earned it the enduring sobriquet "China's Sorrow," Mao took the help of Soviet experts in the post-Stalinist era to build his "biggest monument to man's power over nature" in central China—the 107-meter-high Sanmenxia Dam, which uprooted 400,000 people from their homes but turned out to be an engineering and environmental disaster.[40] Within a few years of its completion, sediment piled up, forcing the authorities to reconstruct large parts of the dam. Yet such are the enduring problems that the mammoth Sanmenxia—which means the "Three Gates Gorge"—has spawned that it is still linked to many of the environmental and social troubles that plague Henan Province and the areas further downstream.

Mao's fixation on big plans found expression in other grand water projects as well, including the 1,225-megawatt Liujiaxia Dam on the upper reaches of the Yellow River in the Tibetan Plateau and the 900-megawatt Danjiangkou Dam on the Hanshui River in Hubei Province. He conceived of several hydro plans that were left to his successors to carry forward, because it took many years of research and planning to finalize them. Finding adequate financial resources to initiate the projects also contributed to their long gestation period. Take the case of the Great South–North Water Transfer Project: Although that plan dates back to the 1950s, it was formally launched only in 2002. Another project with a long, troubled history, the Three Gorges Dam, was also Mao's brainchild.

To be sure, Mao lived in an age when grand engineering ideas were fashionable in the world. The Cold War era's military culture, pivoted on the principle "the bigger the better," subtly influenced developmental projects, with more than 45,000 large dams being built in that period around the world. China was in the lead in dam construction. The worldwide erection of giant dams served as a linchpin of the Green Revolution. Yet such is the negative side to that dam-building spree that the main rivers in China proper now are in poor ecological shape and barely 2 percent of the rivers in the United States run unimpeded,[41] whereas, globally, the flows of more than two-thirds of the rivers have become subject to large-scale diversion and impoundment. Such "thoughtless tampering with nature has left a terrible legacy" in the world,[42] serving as a reminder that it is "not only Communist central planners but capitalists as well who meddle with the flow of rivers,"[43] with often devastating environmental consequences in downstream regions.

China, the world's most "dammed" nation today, still hews to the "bigger the better" notion. Before the Communists came to power in 1949, there were only 22 large dams in China.[44] But the Mao-initiated program to develop massive hydroengineering projects—a program accelerated by the leaders who followed him—resulted in China completing between 22,000 and 24,000 *large* dams by the beginning of the twenty-first century.[45] That number represents at least half of all large dams in the world. A widely accepted definition of a large dam, as drafted by the International Commission on Large Dams, is a structure with "a height of 15 meters from the foundation or, if the height is between 5 to 15 meters, having a reservoir capacity of more than 3 million m^3."[46] If all reservoirs and dams were counted, the number in China total more than 85,100, excluding the small and localized water diversions, check dams, and weirs too numerous to reliably count. According to the Food and Agriculture Organization, these dams and reservoirs in 2005 could store 562.4 cubic kilometers of water, or 20 percent of the country's total renewable water resources (TRWR).[47]

Since then, China has completed more megadams, including the world's biggest at the so-called Three Gorges. As the world's most dam-dotted country, with an unparalleled human-made water diversion infrastructure in place, it is hardly a surprise that China also is the world's largest producer of hydropower, with an installed generating capacity of more than 170 gigawatts.

Yet another significant fact is that China is the global leader in exporting dams. Today it is building more dams overseas than any other country. The Chinese Export-Import Bank and other Chinese financial institutions, state-owned enterprises, and private firms are now involved in more than 100 *major* dam-building projects in different countries, especially in the developing world. Although the Chinese government has released no figures, one American analyst tallied at least

216 dam projects in forty-nine nations that were ongoing in 2010 and had "some form of Chinese involvement," with Chinese companies also in the process of building 19 of the world's 24 largest hydropower plants at home or abroad.[48] In keeping with its penchant to chant a favorite line to justify overseas actions—"it's a win–win for all"—China contends that its role as the world's top dam exporter has created a "win–win" situation for the host countries and its companies. Yet evidence from a number of project sites demonstrates that, with Chinese dam builders still to embrace internationally accepted standards, those dams are imposing serious costs on local communities; the Chinese dam industry, in fact, has "yet to demonstrate that it can be a socially and environmentally responsible partner within China" itself.[49]

Chinese dam-building projects, furthermore, have been embroiled in disputes with local communities in several countries, including Botswana, Burma, Ghana, Pakistan, and Sudan. In Sudan, for example, security forces killed three people and wounded several others in April 2006 to scatter demonstrators protesting the 9.2-kilometer-long Merowe High Dam, and a similar protest against another Chinese dam-building project in that impoverished country, at Kajbar, left four people dead in June 2007.[50] In April 2010, several small bombs went off at the site of Burma's Myitsone Dam, whose construction by a Chinese company in the insurgency-torn, northernmost Kachin state is displacing thousands of subsistence farmers and fishermen by flooding a wide swath of land.[51] Recurring incidents like these show that Chinese state-run enterprises have disregarded the Chinese State Council's nine directives of October 2006 that Chinese overseas businesses, among other things, "pay attention to environmental protection," "support local community and people's livelihood cause," and "preserve China's good image and its good corporate reputation."

The Myitsone Dam, which is located at the confluence of the N'Mai and Mali—the "brother" and "sister" tributaries that form Burma's biggest river, the Irrawaddy—is China's project for China, with the local communities saddled with social and environmental costs but the plant's entire generation of 3,200 megawatts of hydropower earmarked for export.[52] Similarly, the electricity generated elsewhere in northern Burma by a Chinese consortium from its newly built three-dam cascade on the Shweli River is largely for export to China.

Chinese companies also have been erecting dams in an internationally disputed area like the Pakistan-held part of Kashmir, drawing protests from India as well as from local communities that view the projects, including the mammoth 7,000-megawatt Bunji Dam, as benefiting only the dominant Pakistani province of Punjab, located downstream.[53] The Pakistani part of Kashmir stretches from the predominantly Shiite, rebellious Gilgit-Baltistan Region, adjacent to Chinese-held territory, to so-called Azad (or Free) Kashmir in the south. The Washington-based regional security expert Selig Harrison has reported an influx of 7,000 to 11,000 soldiers of the People's Liberation Army into the Gilgit and Baltistan areas (which are closed to the outside world) to work on key projects, including a new railroad, an upgraded highway, dams, and secret tunnels, spurring wider concern that those strategic borderlands could get "overwhelmed, like Tibet, by the Chinese behemoth."[54]

China initially sought dam projects overseas so that its young dam industry could gain sufficient experience in dam building—an objective that led to many Chinese engineers and other technicians being employed at each project site. Today it seeks projects abroad by touting its vast experience and knowledge in dam construction, including its record in having built more dams than any other country. The Chinese practice in overseas projects still is to limit the hiring of local workers and bring in a large workforce from China. The novel twist in recent years is that some batches of laborers dispatched to such sites in several developing nations are made up of convicts "freed" on parole for project-related overseas work, according to a variety of foreign government sources, human rights workers, and media reports.[55]

But just as Beijing has denied the existence (despite evidence to the contrary) of the *laogai* system of forced prison labor within China to make low-cost products for export, it has denied seeking to relieve pressure on its overcrowded prisons by dispatching jail inmates to work on selected projects in countries too poor and weak to protest.[56] As the Nobel Committee bluntly pointed out while awarding the 2010 Nobel Peace Prize to the jailed Chinese dissident Liu Xiaobo, "China is in breach of several international agreements to which it is a signatory, as well as of its own provisions concerning political rights."[57] By the last available official count, China had 1.57 million sentenced prisoners and another 850,000 in "administrative detention"—a total prison population of 2.42 million, which is larger than the national population of Latvia, Namibia, or Slovenia.[58] Moreover, China has since the Mao years operated a vast gulag, sending large but unknown numbers of detainees to notorious camps for "reeducation through labor."[59] It also remains the world's biggest executioner: It executes more people every year than the rest of the world combined, according to Amnesty International.[60] It is against this background that prisoners have been used as laborers on projects abroad.

When it comes to the overseas operations of state-owned Chinese companies, China has failed to enforce its own regulations. For example, on a number of Chinese-run projects in the developing world, the majority of staff is Chinese.[61] According to the Chinese Commerce Ministry, Beijing has sent 4.97 million citizens during the past three decades or more to work abroad, including to Hong Kong before it reverted from Britain to China in 1997. To help boost Chinese exports, Chinese firms overseas also bring in all equipment, steel, cement, and other construction material from China. Such practices run counter to the Chinese Commerce Ministry's August 2006 regulations—promulgated after the death of fifty-one Zambian workers in an explosion at a Chinese-owned copper mine in Zambia triggered a backlash against Chinese businesses—that called for "localization," including hiring local workers, respecting local customs, and adhering to safety norms. Zambia, after all, is not the only African country that has witnessed anti-Chinese protests.

Chinese domestic regulations, however, are sometimes designed simply to blunt external criticism—in the style of the old Soviet Union—and are thus seldom enforced, except when a case attracts international attention. For example, in 2003 China enacted an environmental-impact assessment law, which was followed in 2008 with "provisional measures" to permit public participation in such assessments. Yet Chinese leaders remain more zealous about promoting exports and economic growth than in protecting the country's air and water.[62] Similarly, despite the State Council's 2006 nine good-conduct directives to Chinese overseas businesses, the government and corporate priority is still to aggressively boost exports, even if such a drive engenders environmental and social costs for local communities abroad. As part of the government's "going global" policy, Chinese companies, in fact, are offered major incentives and rewards for bagging overseas contracts and boosting exports.[63]

In its home market, China has put a high premium on building technological capabilities. Since the 1990s, it has used its large and fast-growing market to lure foreign firms to set up technology-sharing joint ventures with state-run Chinese partners, which have subsequently stolen the technology and become strong competitors in the international market, underbidding their onetime collaborators. This has been best illustrated by the manner in which a handful of big Chinese companies led by Sinohydro Corporation have come to dominate the global hydropower market. According to the president of Sinohydro, Fan Jixiang, his company alone now controls half the global hydropower market.

China first got Western hydropower equipment manufacturers to transfer technology as a condition for winning multi-billion-dollar contracts in the early 1990s for supplies to the giant Three Gorges and Ertan dams. To transfer their technology, Western equipment suppliers like ABB, Alstom, General Electric, and Siemens set up joint ventures with Chinese state-owned enterprises. These companies—such as Harbin Power Equipment, Sinohydro Corporation, China Gezhouba Group, and Dongfang Electrical Machinery—were then quick to copy the transferred technology. They started independently building turbines, generators, and other hydropower equipment for the domestic market and for export. Other Chinese companies are now seeking to replicate this growth model in industries ranging from renewable energy and high-speed rail to commercial nuclear power and aerospace.

China's dam builders actually spearheaded the rapid rise of Chinese design, engineering, and construction firms on the international stage, and China's infrastructure companies are today at the vanguard of their country's commercial penetration of the developing world. According to a Western observer of China's hydropower industry, "as in a host of other manufacturing sectors, the Chinese pupils wasted no time copying, underpricing and outpacing their Western masters. . . . In a now familiar approach, the Chinese companies employed vast economies of scale and adapted Western technology to poor-country needs by streamlining production processes—at a substantially lower price. In short, [by] the early years of the twenty-first century, Chinese dam builders began to beat the West at its own game."[64] China's frenetic dam building at home and abroad has further helped reinforce its emergence as the dominant global force in manufacturing and exporting hydropower equipment. Today, "dams are big business in China, and profit-seeking" is driving the push for winning dam-building contracts at home and abroad.[65]

But with profit margins in the home market very tight, Chinese companies hanker after dam projects in other countries. Such projects are aggressively sought by the Chinese government through its export credit arm, the Export-Import Bank, because they underpin the official strategy to earn large profits from exporting hydropower technology and equipment. To bag such lucrative contracts, Beijing usually offers attractive, low-interest loans, as was exemplified by the $519 million Chinese credit for the Merowe Dam on the Nile River in northern Sudan—the largest dam project in Africa after Egypt's Aswan Dam. Low-interest credit packages and other incentives indeed have helped lubricate all Chinese dam-building deals since the 1990s.

In a number of nations, ranging from Burma and Congo to Ecuador and Zambia, Chinese dam construction also helps create "the energy infrastructure for larger resource-extraction projects" to help feed the voracious demand for natural resources in China.[66] Resource imports are at the core of China's more than $100-billion-a-year trade with Africa, where Chinese mining, logging, and infrastructure companies are facing a backlash in several countries over exploitive practices. Similar Chinese practices also are prevalent in resource-rich states in China's immediate neighborhood, such as Laos, Burma, and Cambodia, where Chinese hydropower firms are increasingly active.

The spurt in the number of dam-building projects in which China is involved overseas has been striking from the time the construction of the Merowe Dam began in late 2003. Since then, China has signed dam-construction projects with, among others, Albania, Botswana, Burma, Cambodia, the Democratic Republic of Congo, Ecuador, Ethiopia, Gabon, Ghana, Guinea, Indonesia, Laos, Malaysia, Mozambique, Nepal, Nigeria, Pakistan, Togo, Uzbekistan, Vietnam, and Zambia. In fact, there has been a new wave of dam building within China itself since 2003, following the "corporatization" of the country's hydropower sector, with the State Power Corporation (formerly the Ministry of Electric Power) being split into two power grid companies (including China Southern Power Grid), four hydropower manufacturing and construction companies (including Sinohydro Corporation), and five power-generation companies. The rapid overseas expansion of the Chinese dam industry was aided by such corporate restructuring, which introduced an element of competition between different Chinese entities, and by the government's earlier launch of a package of export and investment initiatives dubbed the "going global" strategy.

In that light, China has no qualms about building dams in disputed territories, such as Pakistan-held Kashmir, in areas torn by ethnic separatism, like northern Burma, or in other human rights–abusing countries. Indeed, China's declaratory policy of "noninterference in domestic affairs" serves as a virtual license to pursue projects that "benefit governments known to repress their citizens."[67] For example, in Sudan, where China has emerged as the principal backer of a regime accused of committing genocide in the arid western region of Darfur, thirteen of the fifteen largest foreign companies operating are Chinese,[68] with Beijing making huge investments in the Sudanese economy—from hydropower to oil. It also has sold hundreds of millions of dollars' worth of weapons, including tanks and fighter jets, to help prop up President Omar Hassan Ahmed Bashir, who is wanted by the International Criminal Court on charges of war crimes in Darfur.

As many as thirty-seven Chinese financial and corporate entities are now involved in dam projects overseas.[69] A few of these entities are very large and have multiple subsidiaries. For instance, Sinohydro Corporation—which is under the supervision of the State-Owned Assets Supervision and Administration Commission of China's State Council, and is made up of ten holdings companies and eighteen wholly owned subsidiaries—boasts fifty-nine overseas branches and representative offices in forty-six countries.

No less significant is the fact that Chinese-built dams in developing countries serve as "highly visible symbols of burgeoning economic cooperation" between China and those nations, just as Chinese construction of parliament, a major sports stadium or some other high-profile building in the capital of a number of Asian, African, and Latin American states helps remind local people of China.[70] But China's more recent use of Chinese convict laborers on dam and other infrastructure projects threatens to create new rifts with local communities overseas. In fact, until Beijing's treatment of its own citizens and those of other countries is guided by respect for basic human rights and the rule of law, China is unlikely to command the respect it seeks on the world stage.

At home, construction of dams and other water works since the Mao years has officially displaced more than 23 million Chinese, as is detailed in chapter 5. With an additional 300,000 residents evicted to deal with the teething problems of the Three Gorges Dam, the total displacement of people caused by what Beijing hails as the world's largest modern engineering feat has officially reached 1.7 million.[71] The Great South–North Water Transfer Project will uproot countless more villagers. It was Mao who went into rhapsodies about a mammoth dam to harness the power of the Yangtze, penning a poem to that idea. The Great Leap Forward and the no-less-cataclysmic Cultural Revolution from the mid-1960s to the early 1970s, however, left Mao with little resources to translate his grand ideas for water plans into reality. Yet thousands of dams for irrigation, hydropower, and flood control were built during the Great Leap Forward, Cultural Revolution, and other state-induced disasters and political witch-hunts, with local peasants often forcibly drafted into construction teams.

It was left to Mao's successors to implement his most-ambitious ideas, including the South–North Water Transfer Project and the Three Gorges Dam. Deng Xiaoping's economic-modernization drive helped transform China, spurring its phenomenal economic rise, but environmental protection took a back seat as Deng and other leaders resuscitated Mao's water-transfer plans. The advent of economic reforms indeed opened the path to the inflow of foreign technology, collaboration with international hydropower companies, and funding for dam projects from multilateral financial institutions, including the World Bank and the Asian Development Bank. The scale of the new dams became bigger, with the primary aim of dam building shifting from irrigation and flood control to energy and river diversion. So it is of little surprise that by 1997, when Deng died of complications from Parkinson's disease and a lung infection at the age of ninety-two, the utilization rate of river-water resources had surpassed 50 percent for the Yellow and Huaihe rivers and neared 90 percent for north China's Haihe River.[72]

Such overdamming of rivers has adversely affected hydrological regimes. For example, by building the Three Gorges Dam to generate 18,300 megawatts of power—almost nine times the total capacity of the seventeen generators at America's Hoover Dam site—the Chinese government has helped radically alter ecosystems of the Yangtze River basin, including contributing to greater fluvial instability, riverbank erosion, reservoir-induced seismicity, and a decline in biodiversity. A reoccurrence of toxic algal blooms in the Yangtze River has decimated some fish species. The dam's environmental effects are likely to get worse in the coming years, especially as downstream flows ebb and reservoir-related landslides recur. Yet for China, the Three Gorges Dam—the world's largest dam and biggest power plant, completed in October 2008—is an exemplar of its engineering prowess. A model of human-made environmental misery has paradoxically become a catalyst for building more giant dams at home and abroad.

The blunt fact is that in the twenty-first century, China is still seeking to subdue nature for economic development, as underlined by its moves to build a separate cascade of megadams on the Mekong, the Salween, and the Brahmaputra—all major international rivers. China has not learned from the mistakes of the Mao era or of the Soviet central planners, who, by introducing cotton cultivation in desert lands, ecologically ruined the Aral Sea in the former Soviet Central Asia. "There is too much emphasis [in China] on big engineering projects," according to Ma Jun, author of *China's Water Crisis*. "Many projects have failed badly. Big engineering projects only make matters worse, causing us to reach the limits of our water resources. It is time to review our water strategy."[73] Yet, as Geremie R. Barmé has pointed out in his book *Shades of Mao*, the Mao cult continues in China, with Mao enjoying a "successful posthumous career."[74] Nowhere is this truer than in the government's approach to water resources. Such is the continuing legacy of Mao that the Chinese leadership still hews to the "modern" paradigm of large-scale water engineering when that model has been abandoned in the developed world in favor of more economical, more secure, and more sustainable options.[75]

In pursuing giant water projects, the post-Mao leaders have simply not paid heed to the lessons of the environmental disasters under Mao. The more recent attempts to control nature without carefully weighing potential environmental effects are reminiscent of the counterproductive initiatives Mao launched extending beyond water resources. One classic example was the 1958 "patriotic extermination campaign" against the sparrow, which Mao declared an enemy of the state for eating grain. Sparrows' nests were demolished, and entire villages collected around trees, clanging pots, pans, and gongs and yelling lustily. As the scared sparrows took to the air, the banging went on and on, and eventually millions of these small, unprepossessing birds—unable to re-alight—dropped dead from sheer exhaustion. Sparrows prey on locusts and other insects, and their near extermination removed a critical link in the food security chain.[76] A plague of locusts followed, ruining many crops and contributing to the deadly famines that became the leitmotif of the so-called Great Leap Forward. Decades later, a slaughter was carried out of civet cats—bred in China as a culinary delicacy—on mere suspicion that the small carnivorous mammals were carriers of the Severe Acute Respiratory Syndrome virus. China's "Maoist past helps explain the speed, thoroughness and aggression with which" that cull was executed.[77]

Just as Mao sold the Sanmenxia Dam to the public as essential to control flooding, generate electricity, and improve river navigation, Deng and the succeeding leaders cited exactly the same reasons for pressing ahead with the Three Gorges Dam. Like the Sanmenxia Dam, the Three Gorges plan was actively championed by the Communist Party elite and People's Liberation Army leadership, with hundreds of thousands of residents being forcibly removed in the first stage of the project itself.[78] The Three Gorges Dam also was built like the Sanmenxia Dam without adequate planning for the potentially negative consequences of the massive impoundment of river waters. As a result, in the same way that Sanmenxia and a series of smaller dams helped upset the hydrological stability of the Yellow River—to the extent that a river traditionally compared by the Chinese to a brass-headed dragon has became sickly—the Three Gorges project is promoting the ecological retardation of the second main river in China proper, the Yangtze.

Today, sedimentation, chronic pollution, and diminished flows seriously afflict the Yellow and the Yangtze, both of which have become part of the environmental emergency that is threatening China's continued rapid economic growth. The heavily polluted and depleted Yellow actually has reemerged as China's sorrow. Yet present-day Chinese leaders chant the same trite line from the Mao era—that the benefits from water megaprojects outweigh the environmental and social costs. So it is of little surprise that Beijing has identified a place on the Brahmaputra River, Motuo, where it plans to build the biggest dam ever conceived in the world to generate 38 gigawatts of power—nearly half as large as Britain's national grid, or more than twice the installed capacity of the Three Gorges Dam.[79]

Actually, China's continuing fixation on megaplans, as illustrated by the Motuo plan and work on the Great South–North Water Transfer Project, is rooted in the fact that most of its political leaders in the past three decades have been engineers, several of them in hydrology, including Hu Jintao, a two-term president up to 2012 who earned a postgraduate degree in "water conservancy engineering" from Qinghua University, which is often called China's Massachusetts Institute of Technology. Hu's putative successor, Xi Jinping, trained in chemical engineering. Wen Jiabao, whose term as premier extends up to 2013, is a geologist and engineer by training.

After Deng Xiaoping emerged as China's paramount leader in late 1978, the shift from Maoist ideology to economic and military modernization helped to gradually bring a succession of technocrats to the upper echelons of government. Mao's death in 1976 triggered a bitter power struggle among rival party factions and leaders. When the less-than-five-feet-tall Deng finally triumphed in the power feud at the age of seventy-four, after cleverly isolating Mao's designated successor, Hua Guofeng, he hardly looked like an agent of reform.[80] But having been purged twice from the Communist Party during the Mao years—including once for proclaiming during the sixties that "it doesn't matter whether a cat is black or white, as long as it catches mice"—Deng was determined to overhaul an organization that still clung to Maoist ideology.

That meant getting rid of the old brass and promoting new faces that would be loyal to him. Deng brought in technocrats, many of them trained in engineering, to replace the old henchmen and cement his grip on power. Although Deng himself had no technical expertise, he took pride in promoting technocrat-protégés. Under his tutelage, the Twelfth Communist Party Congress in 1982 paved the way for a technocratic elite to gain ascendancy when Li Peng, Hu Qili, Jiang Zemin, Hu Jintao, Wu Bangguo, and Wang Zhaoguo were nominated to the party's Central Committee.[81] After this, large numbers of veterans at all leadership levels were forced to resign and their places were filled with much younger technocrats. The massive turnover of leaders facilitated the meteoric rise of engineers in the party hierarchy. Deng eventually became known as China's "last emperor"—that is, its last leader to hold paramount power—although his political supremacy never equaled that of Mao and his reign was much shorter.

Deng and the new generation of leaders he built salvaged the country from the ravages of ideology by putting it on the path of rapid modernization. While opening the country to the influence of Western capitalism and culture, they were still determined to preserve the Communist Party's monopoly on power, ruthlessly crushing student-led, prodemocracy demonstrators at Beijing's Tiananmen Square in 1989. Significantly, the new generation of technocratic leaders shared Mao's passion for water megaprojects to help tame nature. They brought to policy the distinct outlook of professional engineers—the readiness to go in for supply-side solutions, without exploring demand management. In fact, being engineers or other specialists, they authoritatively provided the technical imprimatur to water megaprojects.

For example, during his eleven-year term as prime minister from 1987, Li Peng, a hydro engineer, zealously promoted water megaprojects. It was at the urging of Li, who was trained in hydropower engineering at the Moscow Power Engineering Institute during Stalin's last years, that the Great South–North Water Transfer Project was taken up for research and planning. After Jiang Zemin—who earned a degree in electrical engineering from one of Shanghai's top schools—became the party chief in the wake of the 1989 Tiananmen Square massacre, Li in fact played a crusading role in getting work restarted on the stalled Three Gorges Dam.

The Three Gorges project was one of the first to be approved by the State Council—China's Cabinet—after Deng tightened his grip on the party, government, and army and launched the so-called four modernizations. The construction of the Three Gorges Dam, however, ran into technical and political problems, and the State Council in March 1989—barely three months before the Tiananmen Square killings—formally suspended work on the project for five years. But after the Tiananmen Square crackdown, conservatives in the party gained political ascendancy. It was Li, a known hardliner, who steamrollered the work-resumption decision through the National People's Congress in April 1992—with one-third of the deputies voting "no" or abstaining. When the Yangtze was successfully dammed in 1997 as part of the Three Gorges project, President Jiang Zemin exulted: "This is a major event in China's efforts to achieve modernization and also a remarkable feat in the history of mankind to reshape nature and exploit natural resources. . . . The age-old dream of the Chinese people to develop and utilize the resources of the Three Gorges of the Yangtze River has come closer to becoming true. This proves vividly once again that socialism is superior in being capable of mobilizing resources to do big jobs."[82]

Since then, China's water works have markedly grown in scale. In fact, before he was elevated as premier in 2003, Vice Premier Wen Jiabao declared in 2000: "In the twenty-first century, the construction of large dams will play a key role in exploiting China's water resources, controlling floods and droughts, and pushing the national economy and the country's modernization forward."[83] Historically, as one analyst has noted, the Chinese respected their emperor for undertaking "grandiose projects that no human mind could conceive of," and a succession of China's rulers since 1949—the "new emperors"—have sought to reinforce their legitimacy by embarking on water megaprojects, such as the Sanmenxia Dam, the Three Gorges Dam, and the South–North Water Transfer Project, with the rerouting of the mighty Brahmaputra River next on their list.[84] With every top Communist leader wanting to leave a mark with grandiose projects, China by now has "done more than any country to change the flow of its rivers and to dam so many of its major streams," and there are "many plans to keep on building" more dams.[85] Such is the domination of engineers in the Chinese leadership that in 2011, all nine members except one of the all-powerful Politburo Standing Committee of the Chinese Communist Party were engineers, some of them in hydrology.

China's post-Mao leadership's engineering approach to development, however, has come—as during the Mao era—at the expense of social and environmental solutions. Even as the country has embraced market-oriented policies, with its economy expanding more than thirteenfold over the past three decades, the leadership's temptation to meddle with the flow of rivers has remained as strong as during Mao's time. The grand plan to divert river waters from the Tibetan Plateau to the parched Yellow River symbolizes the leadership's continuing quest to shape China's future through gigantic engineering feats. The Chinese authorities indeed have had their eyes on Tibet's bounteous water resources ever since the People's Republic of China extended its control to that region firmly after the Dalai Lama's 1959 flight to India. Today the plans to increasingly "send western electricity east" indicate how Chinese dam-building activities have moved from the Han provinces to largely the Tibetan Plateau, including the Tibetan parts that have been incorporated into other provinces like Yunnan, Qinghai, and Sichuan.[86] The Tibet Autonomous Region and Yunnan now are at the center of new water megaprojects.

There are at least three main reasons for this. First, dam building has reached saturation levels on the watercourses in the Han provinces. Second, the lack of supporting infrastructure such as roads and the railway that kept major hydroengineering projects away from the Tibetan Plateau has been sought to be remedied on a priority basis in the past two decades. Only a few of the more than 20,000 large dams built between 1950 and 1990 were in the southwest, largely due to the poor infrastructure and difficult terrain. New infrastructure development is now allowing rapid movement of materials and labor, thus opening up greater dam-building options in the sparsely populated minority regions of the Tibet Autonomous Region and Yunnan. Those regions have been at the center of infrastructure development as China has expanded the total length of its national highways from 11,990 kilometers in 2000 to 65,000 kilometers in 2010 and has begun laying about 4,000 kilometers of new rail tracks each year. The new China–Tibet railroad, built at a cost of billions of dollars, is the most striking symbol of how infrastructure development has narrowed the physical space between Han China and the minority regions in the southwest. At each of the new dam-building sites in the southwest, the Chinese authorities have brought in thousands of Han workers from distant provinces.

A third factor is that, with its water usage having more than quintupled since the Communist takeover, China is more desperate for water than ever to keep its economic machine humming. According to one observer, "For three decades, water has been indispensable in sustaining the rollicking economic expansion that has made China a world power. Now, China's galloping, often wasteful style of economic growth is pushing the country toward a water crisis."[87] A fourth factor may also be at play in the continued state emphasis on dam building: The corporatizing of the state-run electric power industry. Both "political motives and profit seeking by politically connected people are almost certainly causing dams to be built," even when a careful cost/benefit analysis would not warrant such construction.[88] The

Chinese state media has reported that shoddy construction, unqualified workers, and embezzlement of funds are threatening dams' safety, with the *China Daily* specifying that some 37,000 reservoirs and dams—or more than 40 percent of the total in China—are in "potential danger" of being breached, including five large newly built dams on the Yellow River in Gansu, on the rim of the Tibetan Plateau.[89] Indeed, in the ten-year period up to 2008, a total of fifty-nine dams were breached in China.[90]

In recent years, China has used the ambitious goals it has set for itself in renewable-energy production to justify its latest dam-building spree. Yet such is China's growing reliance on fossil-fueled energy that not only has it become the world's largest emitter of greenhouse gases since 2006—leading the United States by an ever-widening margin—but its quarterly increases in emissions continue to be the largest by any single country. Indeed, China has also overtaken the United States—which held the top slot for more than a century—to become the world's biggest energy consumer. China's electricity output more than doubled just between 2000 and 2010. An ongoing shift in its economic output—away from light export industries like garment and shoe production and toward energy-intensive heavy industries—has resulted in China's energy consumption growing at a rate much higher than its GDP.[91]

In this light, China's rapid expansion of renewable-energy production, especially through hydropower and wind and solar power, has done little to dispel the threat of its unleashing a carbon tsunami on the world. Coal-burning plants produce about two-thirds of China's electricity, compared with one-half in the United States. The real but modest gains from China's green technology mission, best symbolized by its Solar Valley, have been overwhelmed by the breakneck growth of its mostly coal- and oil-fueled economy. The Solar Valley project, on the outskirts of Dezhou city, was designed to be China's clean technology answer to California's Silicon Valley. Every giant dam China has completed in this century can meet, on average, only a half-percentage-point increase in its energy consumption.

A telling legacy of China's Communist-era strategy to tame nature is the ever-rising sand squalls that blanket Beijing and other northern Chinese cities and threaten to speed up the spread of barren wasteland to the heartland. About 34 percent of China's total landmass, or 3.3 million square kilometers of territory in the country's northwest, north, and northeast (officially called the "three norths"), already has been affected by desertification.[92] The factors responsible for the spreading desertification range from overexploitation of water, forest, and land resources to water pollution and monoculture tree plantations to boost timber production. Provision of heavily subsidized natural resources and other raw materials to the industrial and agricultural sectors has promoted wanton inefficiency and waste. Industries have exacerbated the water problem by dumping vast quantities of untreated wastes into rivers and lakes. Many of the natural forests in China have vanished, with the country's aquatic, wildlife, and plant species also getting decimated in the process. Poorly designed reforestation initiatives, such as the ambitious

Three Norths Shelter Forest System Project, have only contributed to greater environmental degradation by affecting soil moisture, hydrology, and natural vegetation and aiding groundwater depletion.

Misguided government policies have been a principal driver of the damage to ecosystems in the "three norths" and elsewhere in China. The Chinese scholar He Bochuan warned in a 1991 book that the damage to China's environment, including to its water resources, air, soil, and forests, was reaching the "point of no return" because of the government's policy blunders and gross mismanagement of resources.[93] He Bochuan marshaled impressive facts and figures to contend that, despite economic reforms, the country's development strategy still hewed both to Mao's disregard for the protection of the natural environment and to Mao's faith that grand projects would deliver "miracles." But his well-researched and revealing book *China on the Edge*, far from forcing a rethinking in policy circles, was banned by the country's leadership after becoming a best seller, with some 400,000 copies printed. Since then, China's water and environmental challenges have only worsened.

The construction of many dams and reservoirs, for example, has affected the natural flow of rivers, forcing farmers to turn to groundwater to meet irrigation needs. Today, the northern plains are parched, with most of the region's streams or creeks and five-sixths of the wetlands having disappeared.[94] Lake Baiyangdian, the region's largest but now-polluted natural freshwater lake, continues to shrink in size. Droughts have become more frequent. A severe drought that hit in early 2011, for example, damaged the winter wheat crop in parts of the north, and the greatest damage was in Shandong Province, in the heart of the wheat belt. When areas close to Beijing are stricken by a serious drought, breezes lift the bone-dry topsoil from fields and coat houses and trees in the capital with fine dust.

The desert's advance from the arid northwest, reflected in an enlarging dust bowl, has been aided by state-fostered irrigated farming that has helped divert water resources from the area's ecological lifeline—the Shiyang River and its offshoots—and thereby left other land open to desertification. Intensive irrigated farming, river damming, deforestation, livestock overgrazing, and other human activities in the Shiyang basin, which is the most densely populated basin in China and is located in the Hexi Corridor of Gansu Province, have led to the overexploitation of water resources and contributed to a "rapid drop in the water table in the Minqin," an ancient oasis dating back two thousand years that now seems to be disappearing.[95]

The overexploitation of groundwater is exposing aquifers in northern China to growing pollution. Take Beijing, a water-strapped city that is increasingly relying on groundwater supplies for its needs, besides expropriating water from four new reservoirs in nearby drought-prone Hebei Province. Such commandeering of resources is depriving impoverished cultivators of water for their farms. After years of continuous below-average rainfall and breakneck urban expansion, "the city of 17 million people is fast exhausting its water supply," according to a 2008 study, which pointed out that more than two-thirds of Beijing's water supply now gets pumped from subterranean reserves.[96] As a result, the water table is dropping sharply—from 11 meters to 24 meters below sea level in just one decade—prompting the search and exploitation of deeper aquifers.[97] The city has lax enforcement of antipollution measures and no curbs on developers and industries to set up new water-guzzling enterprises. Matters have been made worse by the dumping of wastewater and sewage into Beijing's waterways.

Just as China's rapid economic rise has set a world record, its pollution problem also "has shattered all precedents," with the result that "China is choking on its own success" and its public "health is reeling."[98] The government's push for economic growth at all costs has devastated the country's environment and waterways. The Han heartland's two main rivers, the Yellow and the Yangtze, already have been heavily polluted and their natural hydrology has been seriously compromised. The pollution of China's waterways is so serious that a 2007 official Chinese scientific assessment of the Yellow River found that only 16.1 percent of the water in that river was safe for household use. In fact, according to that survey, conducted by the Yellow River Conservancy Committee, 33.8 percent of the water samples from what is China's second-longest river registered worse than a level 5, meaning that the water was unfit not just for drinking but also for aquaculture, industrial use, and even agriculture, according to the United Nations Environment Program's criteria.[99] Despite government moves to shut down polluting factories located along China's main waterways, chemical contamination of water resources (including from mercury and arsenic) remains a serious issue. For example, potentially cancer-causing chemicals, including benzene, spilled into the Songhua River in November 2005 and then, less than five years later, floods swept thousands of drums containing liquid and other toxic chemicals into the Songhua from a riverside factory.

China's first national pollution census revealed in 2010 that a 2007 estimate of water pollution levels had ignored agricultural waste. The actual water pollution levels, it found, were more than twice the 2007 official assessment.[100] An earlier official survey found that due to unchecked industrial pollution, unscientific waste disposal, and the overexploitation of resources, about 90 percent of the groundwater sources of Chinese cities is contaminated with heavy metals, pesticides, petroleum products, and other toxic chemicals.[101] Furthermore, 70 percent of the water in five of China's seven major river systems is now too contaminated for human use, according to a 2005 report by China's State Environment Protection Agency. In fact, fifty-two urban river stretches in China may be too polluted even for irrigation use.[102] No less significant than water pollution is river depletion due to the overexploitation of resources. As a result, mainland China now is beginning to deal with dry rivers even before it has succeeded in halting chemical contamination or cleaning up its rivers. The parched and polluted Yellow River has become a symbol of China's lurch toward human-made ecological disaster.[103]

Against that background, government plans centered on long-distance water transfers across rivers and basins are unlikely to resolve China's water crisis or stem the overextraction of groundwater. If anything, such projects are likely to exacerbate the threat to groundwater resources. Because of the high cost of transferring surface water to the north, including the added expense of treating such water, many users are likely to rely on the comparatively low-cost groundwater, which typically needs minimal treatment. The transfer projects will also carry costs that are hard to quantify—environmental, social, and international (when transfers from transnational rivers are involved). Balancing the political imperative for continued rapid economic growth—on which the legitimacy of Communist rule now rests—with the increasing need to safeguard the environment and watercourses remains one of the critical unresolved tensions within China.

Dealing with this tension is necessary for China's own future and to help underpin its rising strength. Communist China actually began as an international pariah. Today it is courted by the world, with its rise in one generation as a world power under authoritarian rule coming to epitomize the qualitative reordering of international power. Yet such is the extent of the water crisis now haunting China that, in the frightening words of the country's former minister of water resources, Wang Shucheng, "To fight for every drop of water or die, that is the challenge facing China."[104]

The present situation should serve as a sobering lesson for the Chinese leadership on the need to build harmony between man and nature. The government's approach thus far has been that once a water megaproject is politically approved, it must be implemented, whatever the social and environmental costs, because China's rulers do not like to lose face. In fact, just as China has sought to build world-class capabilities in the economic and military spheres, it has made itself the global leader in water diversions. That approach must change for the country's own ecological well-being. China's interests will be better served by more responsive and responsible policies. Instead of carrying forward Mao's zeal to bend nature, China's current leaders ought to bend more to nature.

THE COSTS OF A FRAGMENTED APPROACH

Asia's other giant, India, serves as a case study of how a disjointed policy approach and lack of vision on managing water resources can exact serious costs by creating water shortages across much of the country. In a sense, India's fragmented approach is exactly the opposite of China's highly centralized, megaprojects-driven approach. In stark contrast to the "man must conquer nature" policies in China since the Mao years, the largest dam projects India has undertaken during the past six decades have been relatively small by international standards. In fact, India's landmark plants—like the 1,000-megawatt Bhakra Nangal Dam on the Sutlej River, the 2,000-megawatt Tehri Dam on the Bhagirathi River, the 1,450-megawatt Narmada Dam (still incomplete after decades of work), and the planned 2,000-megawatt Lower Subansiri Station and 2,700-megawatt Lower Siang plan—pale in comparison to the giant Chinese hydropower projects, such as the 18,300-megawatt Three Gorges Dam and the new dams on the upper Mekong River—the 4,200-megawatt Xiaowan and the 5,850-megawatt Nuozhadu. China's proposed Motuo Dam on the Brahmaputra River, to be built at Tibet's corner with northeastern India, is to produce 38,000 megawatts of power—the equivalent of 25 percent of India's installed electricity-generating capacity from all sources of energy in 2010.

The absence of institutionalized, integrated policymaking in India has blighted water resources management for long. The water situation in India is far worse than in China, including in terms of per capita availability of water. India is home to 17.3 percent of the global population but has only 4.3 percent of the world's water resources and 2.45 percent of the world's total land area.[105] India actually ranked ninth—after Afghanistan, Kyrgyzstan, Iran, Azerbaijan, Tajikistan, Pakistan, and Turkmenistan—in the United Nations Economic and Social Commission for Asia and the Pacific's 2000 water-exploitation index for continental Asia and the Pacific islands.[106] The index represented a measure of intermittent or chronic water scarcity and the diminished ability of natural ecosystems to replenish themselves as a result of national overuse of water resources. The 2030 Water Resources Group—a consortium of private social-sector organizations formed in 2008 to provide insights into worldwide water issues—has a dire warning for India: The country is likely to face a 50 percent deficit between water demand and supply by 2030.[107]

When the Indian Republic was established after World War II, the framers of its Constitution did not visualize water scarcity in the decades ahead, given the relative abundance of water resources then. Therefore, they left water as a state-level subject, rather than making it a federal issue warranting integrated resource management and holistic policymaking. That left state governments in charge of water resources projects, including for irrigation and flood control, with the federal government able to regulate and develop only interprovincial river basins to the extent allowed by Parliament in the public interest.

The federal government's role indeed got largely confined to managing interprovincial water issues, reflected in the enactment of the Inter-State River Water Disputes Act in 1956, the same year that Indian states were reorganized and new ones created along ethnic lines. The Disputes Act was subsequently modified more than once by the national Parliament to help deal with the plethora of interprovincial water disputes that arose over shared water resources.[108] Another law passed by Parliament in 1956 was the River Boards Act, which was intended to set up boards to help promote the regulation and development of interprovincial drainage basins. Although the role of the boards was statutorily limited to an advisory function, the federal government ran into stiff opposition from state governments over the establishment of any such board.

The 1960 Indus Waters Treaty, under which India bigheartedly agreed to the exclusive reservation of the largest three of the six Indus system rivers for Pakistan, was negotiated in a period when water shortages were uncommon in most parts of India. Indian policymakers, at that point, had not envisaged that water resources would come under serious strain due to developmental and population pressures. That led them to sign an extraordinary treaty whose terms commit India to indefinitely reserve four-fifths of the total waters of the Indus system for Pakistan.

In fact, just as the Indian subcontinent was partitioned in 1947 to create the new state of Pakistan, the rivers were partitioned in 1960 through the Indus Treaty. Whereas the British colonial government was the instrument in the land partition, the World Bank served as the agent to partition the rivers, floating the partitioning proposal and signing the treaty as its guarantor.[109] Without the need to redraw the British-set political frontiers, the treaty split the Indus River basin into northern and southern parts by tracing a "fictitious line" from east to west that severely limited the sovereign rights of India on three key upper rivers in order to bestow quasi-exclusive rights to Pakistan over those rivers.[110] India's full sovereignty rights were thus confined by the treaty to the lower three rivers.

It was a unique type of separation which, by parceling out entire rivers, obviated the determination of a quantitative division. Yet the treaty's quantitative aspects are eye-catching. Under the terms of the treaty, India has granted Pakistan virtually exclusive rights to use the waters of the Chenab, the Jhelum, and the main Indus stream—known together as the "western rivers" and constituting the largest three Indus system rivers in terms of discharge. The average replenishable flows of the three western rivers were computed to total 167.2 billion m³ per year. As its own share, India settled for a mere 40.4 billion m³, or the total yearly flows of the three small, so-called eastern rivers—the Sutlej, the Beas, and the Ravi. Four of these six rivers originate in India (three of them in Himachal Pradesh State), and two (the main Indus stream and the Sutlej) originate in Tibet. The largest water collections of the main Indus stream and the Sutlej, however, take place within the present borders of India (table 2.1).

No other water-sharing treaty in modern world history matches this level of generosity on the part of the upper-riparian state for the lower-riparian one. In fact, the volume of waters earmarked for Pakistan from India under the Indus Treaty is more than ninety times greater that what the United States is required to release for Mexico under the 1944 US-Mexico Water Treaty, which stipulates a

TABLE 2.1   Pakistan and India's Shares of the Indus River System Waters

Western Rivers	*Eastern Rivers*	*Total Indus System Flows*
167.2 billion cubic meters (m³)	40.4 billion m³	207.6 billion m³
Pakistan's share of total Indus system waters: 80.52%	India's share of total Indus system waters: 19.48%	100%

Note: Figures represent mean yearly flows.
Source: The 1960 Indus Waters Treaty.

guaranteed minimum transboundary delivery of 1.85 billion m³ of the Colorado River waters yearly.

The Indus sharing formula was heavily weighted in Pakistan's favor because it was influenced by the water-use patterns up to 1947, when the irrigation system under colonial rule was much better developed in the Indus basin area of what became Pakistan. But the treaty was concluded not until 1960, by which time irrigated farming had been introduced extensively in the Indian portion of the Indus basin, thanks to a network of new canals. In any event, past utilization patterns of basin waters is just one of several factors identified by customary international water law for determining an equitable and reasonable sharing of transboundary waters. The other factors spelled out in customary international law include the contribution of water by each basin state and their respective needs, the size of population dependent on the basin waters in each country, future national needs, and possible alternatives to planned or existing uses. In apportioning a reasonable and equitable share, the totality of the circumstances, according to customary international law, needs to be examined, including all the relevant factors as well as the geographic, hydrographic, hydrological, climatic, and ecological characteristics of the basin.[111]

Had such a holistic framework been the basis of the treaty negotiations, a much different sharing formula would likely have emerged. With the upper 400 kilometers of the Indus basin and headwaters of four rivers in India, New Delhi was under no obligation to enter into a legal arrangement that effectively gave away the largest rivers to Pakistan as gifts. It could have asserted its rights as the upper-riparian state in customary international law, as China has sought to do vis-à-vis its co-riparian states. With the lower Mekong states, Russia, Kazakhstan, or India, China indeed is unwilling to enter into any bilateral water-sharing agreement, let alone on generous terms. It is unthinkable that China would countenance the argument that national entitlements to common-river waters should be in proportion to the size of the basin population in each country, the existing water use, or historical entitlement.

But as the chief Indian negotiator, Niranjan Gulhati, candidly admitted in his book *Indus Waters Treaty*, the Indus Treaty was concluded with "no study" having been undertaken in India on the irrigation, energy and other benefits that could be secured for local communities from the western rivers.[112] Even though the western rivers constituted the principal sources of water for India's Jammu and Kashmir State, that territory's long-term interests were overlooked in parceling them out to Pakistan. To be sure, Pakistan had built up tremendous pressure that it would settle for nothing less than the volume of waters that flowed its way when it was carved out of British-ruled India—a pattern of distribution independent India itself had maintained on an ad hoc but continuing basis post-Partition until the Indus Treaty could be concluded and brought into effect. Paradoxically, the magnanimous 80/20 sharing formula enshrined in the treaty failed to fully satisfy Pakistan, and the water issue thus still remains a thorn in bilateral relations.

The treaty actually emerged from complex negotiations through much of the 1950s, the halcyon years of Indian romanticism in foreign policy. The dreams on which Indian diplomacy had subsisted since independence were shattered in 1962, when China invaded India from across the Himalayas—a war that hastened the death of Prime Minister Jawaharlal Nehru, whose idealism and internationalism had become the hallmarks of Indian foreign policy since 1947. The Indus Treaty indeed was signed at a time when Sino-Indian relations were perceptibly deteriorating after the Dalai Lama's 1959 flight to India. India had hoped the water treaty would help improve relations with its other regional rival, Pakistan, and also defuse the Kashmir dispute. However, in a fundamentally competitive world marked by aggressive pursuit of relative gains, Indian diplomacy during Nehru's long seventeen years in office stood out for not learning from mistakes and continuing to operate on ingenuous premises. Despite Pakistan's continuing hostilities against India after its 1947–48 invasion and occupation of more than one-third of the state of Jammu and Kashmir, Nehru personally signed the Indus Treaty that apportioned 80.52 percent of the Indus system waters to Pakistan—a munificent allocation by an upstream country unsurpassed in scale in the annals of international water pacts.

In fact, less than three years after China's invasion and in spite of the water treaty, Pakistan launched its second war against India to grab the rest of Kashmir when India had still not recovered from its humiliating rout in 1962 at the hands of the Chinese. Pakistan, however, failed to realize its war objectives in 1965. In more recent years, Pakistan has ratcheted up tensions on the sensitive water-sharing issue to mobilize domestic and international opinion against India. It has challenged India's treaty-sanctioned right to build run-of-the-river hydropower plants on the western rivers, and it has taken two such projects to the International Court of Arbitration or a neutral outside expert. More than five decades after the vaunted treaty was signed, water has returned as a hot-button issue in the Pakistan–India relationship. At the same time, China's ambitious interriver and interbasin water transfer projects on the Tibetan Plateau have turned water into a contentious issue in Sino-Indian ties.

Today, water shortages have come to haunt India, as it faces a deepening water crisis. In fact, before a climate crisis has hit India, the country already confronts a water crisis. The country has reluctantly come to recognize that its water resources are finite and annual replenishments almost constant while the water demand of its industry, agriculture, and cities continues to spiral. It is apparent that water shortages are going to exact growing economic and social costs in India.[113] Against a current water supply of 740 billion m³, demand in India, according to one international study, will grow to almost 1.5 trillion m³ by 2030; consequently, most of India's river basins are likely to "face severe deficit by 2030 unless concerted action is taken, with some of the most populous—including the Ganges, the Krishna and the Indian portion of the Indus—facing the biggest absolute gap."[114] An Indian government assessment has projected national water demand to soar to 1.09 trillion m³ by 2025 and 1.45 trillion m³ by 2050.[115]

Even as India continues to supply more than four-fifths of the Indus system waters to Pakistan under the terms of the treaty, its own portion of the Indus basin already is reeling under a serious water crisis. Because of inadequate storage and diversion infrastructure, India has not been able to fully utilize the waters of the eastern rivers, which are reserved exclusively for its use. As a result, Pakistan has continued to receive, as an unintended bonus, the waters of the eastern rivers not utilized by India—about 11.1 billion m³ yearly (or six times Mexico's share under its water treaty with the United States), according to the Food and Agriculture Organization, and 10.37 billion m³, according to an official Pakistani report.[116] Yet the present deficit between water supply and demand in India's own Indus basin is a massive 52 percent.[117] A lack of long-term planning, along with poor resource management, have played no mean role in aggravating water shortages in large parts of India.

In the face of mounting water stress, the role of the federal government in water resources management is being redefined in India. The federal authorities are being forced to assume a bigger responsibility in the allocation, protection, and supervision of water resources. The larger role the central government is seeking to play is reflected in its plans to clean up rivers and apply scientific methods to treat water in areas where the resource is either brackish or contains too much fluoride. The National Water Resources Council, with the prime minister as its chair, was set up in 1983 to help frame policy and coordinate action at the federal level. In 2002, the federal government identified access to safe, adequate, and affordable water as a basic right of every citizen, and it thus unveiled a new "National Water Policy" that revised the first one released in 1987. But because water remains a state-level subject in India, the new national water policy directed that, "To achieve the desired objectives, state water policy backed with an operational action plan shall be formulated in a time bound manner, say, in two years."[118]

Few states in India, however, have formulated a state-level water policy. The following 2002 plea of the prime minister to state governments also has gone unheeded:

> I believe that an institutional and legal framework in the form of River Basin Organizations (RBOs) is essential for adopting a holistic and integrated approach to water-resources management. This would provide the states with a forum to discuss the related issues of the conservation, pollution control and development in the basin. I would urge that, realizing the importance of integrated water resources development, the states should come forward themselves and set up these organizations, especially in the river basins falling within one state. Let me assure that the status of these organizations, even [those involving] inter-state rivers, would be decided by the participating states themselves. The central government will play the role of a facilitator, when called upon, and arbiter, where necessary.[119]

The federal government, however, has itself been remiss in discharging its obligations prudently. India today stands out for its lack of a national action plan to build water security, even though water scarcity has become a reality in many parts of the country and, consequently, water has turned into a critical determinant of long-term economic growth and food security. The federal authorities have neither backed up their national water policy with a concrete action plan for integrated resource development and management nor attempted to sort out the constitutional, legal, regulatory, pricing, and investment issues that continue to plague the water sector. Indeed, no specific authority has been set up to implement the policy, including promoting river basin planning through interprovincial institutional mechanisms and establishing a standardized national collection and dissemination system on water-related data.

As a result, the national water policy has been reduced to a declaration of pious intent. Decades after India negotiated a water treaty with Pakistan without adequate assessment of its own long-term needs or the basin dynamics, it has still to plug information gaps relating to its countrywide water resources. Such gaps at the provincial and local levels constrain federal moves to build cooperation between states and among important stakeholders.

The startling fact is that the responsibility for water issues is so fragmented within the federal government that twelve different departments or ministries deal with different segments of water resources. They are the Ministry of Agriculture, Ministry of Rural Development, Ministry of Urban Development, Department of Science and Technology, Department of Space (which is in charge of remote sensing), Department of Atomic Energy (in command of isotope hydrology projects), Ministry of Environment and Forests, Planning Commission, Ministry of New and Renewable Energy (which is responsible for harnessing water for small hydropower projects), Ministry of Power (in charge of large hydropower plans), Ministry of Shipping (in control of waterways), and Ministry of Water Resources.

To some extent, such separation of water issues into multiple parts reflects the multidisciplinary and cross-sectoral nature of water resources management, which involves many academic disciplines and specialists, including hydrologists, biologists, engineers, economists, lawyers, political scientists, geographers, and sociologists. But with such disaggregation of responsibilities at the federal policy level, developing an integrated, holistic approach to water resources is anything but easy. The lack of a clear line of authority promotes a fragmented, piecemeal approach that translates into an absence of urgency and accountability. Such an approach indeed fosters a continued absence of coordination among the stakeholders, management agencies, and political entities, thereby impeding the adoption of a unified, cooperative approach to the cross-sectoral management of a critical resource that is increasingly in short supply in India.

In fact, the present splintered water-management approach has proven not only inadequate and ineffective, but also is compounding the country's water challenges. Nothing can illustrate this better than the way the federal government first began building and then abandoned a 600-megawatt hydropower plant on the Bhagirathi River after having already spent $139 million at the project site and ordered equipment worth $288 million. The project, Loharinag Pala, was the third to be scrapped on environmental grounds on that very river in 2010. It was a similar approach toward preparations to host the 2010 Commonwealth Games in New Delhi—with at least twenty-one governmental or quasi-governmental agencies involved, with each claiming responsibility for pieces of the project yet none responsible for the entire mission—that turned into a serious national embarrassment, with a litany of problems eventually plaguing the games and highlighting ineptitude.

To promote clear responsibility and accountability in national water resources management and to facilitate integrated policymaking, India must end its present fragmented approach on water issues. The results of that approach have been an underfunded and heavily bureaucratized water sector, poor water planning, rising water pollution, and growing water stress. The lack of significant public investments in surface-water-based irrigation, for example, has promoted the unregulated and reckless exploitation of groundwater across much of India. There has been a continuing decline in government spending on irrigation as a percentage of overall expenditures since the late 1970s. Some surface-water irrigation systems are falling into a state of disrepair, resulting in significant water leakage. Groundwater irrigation now accounts for almost two-thirds of total agricultural production, but also for nearly 30 percent of the national consumption of electricity, which is usually supplied to farmers free or at highly subsidized rates, especially in the country's north and west.[120] On the positive side, groundwater, which makes up 38.5 percent of the country's available water resources, has played a key role in helping boost crop yields as part of the green revolution in India, which at independence was still a land of famine and flood.

With water shortages now demanding much higher productivity increases in agriculture, India has started to actively promote the adoption of micro-irrigation systems through its Accelerated Irrigation Benefit Program, which is backed by hundreds of millions of dollars in federal funding. Use of drip-feed irrigation in India can potentially expand tenfold to cover 37 million hectares of farmland by 2030. India has little choice but to aim to achieve net water gains through higher crop yields per unit of irrigation water—that is, increasing "crop per drop." There is also another initiative begging to be launched. Through concrete incentives, the Indian government should encourage "a shift of agricultural output from water-scarce regions to the relatively water-abundant Ganges River basin,"[121] especially in the east. In the process, the disparity in agricultural development between the northern and eastern parts of India would be addressed while simultaneously relieving pressure on water-distressed areas in the north and northwest. Today, water-rich, fertile areas in the east remain agriculturally underdeveloped.

India's central priority is rapid economic modernization to help a quarter of its large population step over the threshold from poverty. That goal demands that India's GDP continue to grow between 6 and 8 percent annually until 2050. But constraints on adequate water availability are going to make continued high economic growth a challenge. That is why water resources management must be integrated with the economic strategy so as to create a long-term blueprint for building a healthy water economy. The current phenomenon of high suicide rates among Indian farmers has been linked to the acute water stress in parts of India, including recurrent drought. To help ameliorate conditions in rural areas and also slow down the rapid urbanization trend, water allocation and regulation policies should give greater weight to the needs of people in the countryside. But most important, given the overuse of water in agriculture and the growing demand from industry, India has to seek water-efficiency gains through agricultural-productivity measures and industrial-efficiency steps.

Addressing water quality must also be a priority, given the extent of contamination of rivers, lakes, and groundwater in India. A review conducted in the late 1990s by India's Central Pollution Control Board found that groundwater was unfit for drinking in all the twenty-two major industrial zones it surveyed.[122] According to an official national assessment released in 2010, contaminants in groundwater were in excess of safety levels in at least two-fifths of the country's 626 districts.[123] It is thus no surprise that waterborne diseases are endemic in India, exacting a heavy social and economic toll.[124] This situation can be remedied only through large public investments in wastewater treatment and the regulation of water quality, including by preventing the discharge of industrial effluents into surface-water sources and controlling the excess use of subsidized fertilizers and pesticides in agriculture. The greater the deterioration in water quality, the more deceptive the overall water-quantity figures will become. After all, if an aquifer gets polluted, its water, to be fit for human consumption, will demand expensive surface treatment.

In India more than in China, "business as usual" is no longer a credible option in the water sector. To arrest the growing water supply/demand gap in India, the institutional and policy impediments need to be eliminated through water-sector reform aimed at ushering in a more prudent management of water resources. While building a holistic policy framework at the federal level, India would do well to set up management agencies at the basin and aquifer levels so as to promote sustainable practices at the grassroots. The water resources base must be managed in a way that the interests of future generations are shielded, including by incentivizing water conservation, efficiency, and recycling. Dam building in India peaked during the 1971–90 period when 2,256 dams were built—the vast majority of them for irrigation—by provincial governments, with western states in the lead.[125]

With a significant expansion of dam-based irrigation not feasible in view of several factors, including environmental concerns and grassroots opposition to the displacement of local residents by new dams, additional water storage can be possible only with rainwater harvesting. The use of harvested rainwater to artificially recharge groundwater, according to an official estimate, can increase India's groundwater availability by about 36 billion m³ a year.[126] For government incentives to promote conservation and rainwater capturing, it is essential to make water resources management a dynamic and participatory process, with both top–down and bottom–up features. Water management and planning at the basin level will facilitate public–private partnerships through the involvement of major stakeholders, with the efforts geared toward augmenting drinking-water supplies, managing demands of agriculture, industry and households, and protecting public health and the environment. Involving local communities in water management not only empowers them but also helps instill social and environmental responsibility, thereby making such mechanisms more useful.

THE LARGER RAMIFICATIONS

One of the greatest effects of growing water shortages would be on Asia's ability to feed itself. Rising caloric intakes and changing dietary preferences are increasing pressures on food production and water resources. Moreover, the rate of increase in grain production in Asia now lags behind the growth in demand. Some Asian countries are already battling growing popular discontent about food price inflation, even as a potential food supply crisis threatens Asia as a whole. The increasing Asian demand for water-intensive food products is best exemplified by the preference for more meat—a trend that strongly influences greater water withdrawals in agriculture because meat production is multiple times more water intensive than growing vegetarian food for direct human consumption. With greater quantities of cereals being fed to livestock, such feed production must compete for water and land resources with food production for humans.

To compound these matters, the gains of the green revolution have begun to ebb in several major Asian countries, including China, Indonesia, India, Japan, Vietnam, and the Philippines. In China, for example, the production of rice, wheat, and corn aggregated 441.4 million tons in 1998 but has not hit that level since. China's wheat harvest actually has suffered a decline of 8 percent, even as it remains the world's largest. Indonesia and the Philippines have stepped up their rice imports, while Japan—Asia's largest wheat importer, along with Indonesia—has seen a rise in grain imports, in spite of its aging population. Like many other Asians, the Japanese are consuming more grain-intensive meat and dairy products, along with Western-style bakery goods and instant noodles made from wheat flour. The world's worst nuclear accident since Chernobyl in the Fukushima Prefecture, an important agricultural area, has hit Japan's food exports and set back its efforts to reduce grain imports. In Asia, only underdeveloped countries like Burma and Cambodia have sufficient water and land resources to significantly boost food production for export.

The Chinese government has sought to encourage farmers to switch back from cash crops to staple foods so that the country does not become a major grain importer. But the continuing problem of water shortages has cast doubt on China's ability to boost the production of cereals.[127] The same holds true for India, where the production of grains more than doubled between 1968 and 1998. But with water scarcity growing, public investment in agriculture shrinking by a third since 1980, and farmers finding it more difficult to access cheap seeds, subsidized chemical fertilizers, or low-interest bank loans, India has had to intermittently turn to the already-stretched international wheat market in recent years to tamp down soaring domestic prices through imports. India is already one of the world's largest importers of vegetable oils and pulses (like lentils and peas, which are the main source of protein for vegetarian Indians, who constitute a sizable share of the national population); its imports of beans, lentils, and cooking oil have risen dramatically in recent years.

China, though largely self-sufficient in grains at present, is the world's largest importer of soybeans, which are oilseeds, not a grain, and mainly serve as animal feed for the fast-growing Chinese meat industry. Since 2008, it has started importing increasing quantities of wheat, although its imports remain small compared with world output. But given that China accounts for one-sixth of global wheat production, a serious drought in some of its wheat-growing provinces can trigger major imports.

India, for its part, faces a crisis in agriculture and a serious threat to its food security. Its population, estimated at 1.2 billion in 2011, is likely to stabilize, according to the National Commission for Integrated Water Resources Development, at between 1.35 billion and 1.58 billion by 2050, when the total food grain requirement is projected to reach more than 450 million tons in a high-demand scenario and 382 million tons in a low-demand one.[128] This would mean that the country would need to substantially increase its grain production from the current level of 234 million tons. To do that, it would have to significantly boost crop yields. After all, China, with less arable land, has consistently outperformed India in agricultural output, producing more than twice as much grain as India. Wheat yields in China, according to 2009 UN data, are 1.7 times as high as those in India. India will have to raise agricultural productivity while embracing water-efficiency measures—a challenge that demands it emulate the example of Israel, which increased its agricultural output sevenfold between 1975 and 2000 with just a fractional increase in the use of water. Efficient irrigation systems cover less than 2 percent of the cultivated land in India, compared with 100 percent in Israel. China, despite its impressive crop yields, also needs to substantially boost its production in the coming decades to meet the rapidly growing demand at home.[129] Farm size, however, is small in both China and India, and farmers' low incomes impede the adoption of modern irrigation and cultivation techniques.

China and India together account for, as table 2.2 shows, 52.8 percent of the world's rice production, 30.1 percent of the wheat, 21 percent of the corn, and 28.5 percent of the total grain. China and India are net food exporters today, although

TABLE 2.2 The World's Top Ten Producers of Corn, Wheat, Rice, and Total Grains

	Corn		Wheat		Rice		Total Grain[a]	
Nation	Nation	Quantity (million tons)	Nation	Quantity (million tons)	Nation	Quantity (million tons)	Nation	Quantity (million tons)
United States	China	332	China	106	China	130	United States	414
China	India	145	India	76	India	94	China	389
Brazil	United States	53	United States	56	Indonesia	34	India	206
Mexico	Russia	23	Russia	49	Bangladesh	28	Russia	79
Argentina	Pakistan	22	Pakistan	23	Vietnam	23	Brazil	68
India	Canada	17	Canada	20	Thailand	19	Canada	48
Canada	Kazakhstan	12	Burma	17	Argentina	43
South Africa	Argentina	11	Philippines	16	Indonesia	41
Ukraine	Turkey	7	Brazil	16	Mexico	33
Indonesia	Iran	7	Japan	15	Pakistan	30
World total	World total	770	World total	605	World total	423	World total	2,084
China and India	China and India	21.0%	China and India	30.1%	China and India	52.8%	China and India	28.5%

[a] Total grain includes barley, corn, millet, mixed grain, oats, rice, rye, sorghum, and wheat.
Source: Earth Policy Institute, March 2008.

to help cushion demand-and-supply fluctuations at home, they import grains moderately or occasionally and cooking oils regularly. But as their economies come under greater water stress, they could turn into major food importers—a development that would drive up international prices and exacerbate the present global food crisis.[130] The continued volatility of domestic staple prices in the world since the 2008 global food price crisis represents additional risks, burdening poor consumers and low-income countries in no position to hedge against such fluctuations.[131] High food prices have has already contributed to political unrest in some countries. Yet global food prices reached a record high by 2011, according to the Food and Agriculture Organization's Food Price Index, which measures the wholesale price of basic foods.

If just China, with its unmatched foreign-exchange reserves, were to become a major food importer, it would destabilize world food markets and reduce the supplies available for low-income countries, particularly in Africa, where agricultural productivity actually has declined since the 1960s even as national populations have soared.[132] After all, a cash-rich China, by buying a lot of food from other countries, would push up world prices, making it harder for poor countries to afford food imports. China is now the world's biggest wheat and rice producer, the grower of one-fifth of the world's corn, and its largest exporter of certain types of fertilizer. It has spent years accumulating very large government reserves of rice and other grains, besides building foreign-exchange holdings that are three times those of Japan, the country with the next largest holdings.

Yet the probability of China becoming an important food importer in the coming years as a consequence of its inability to meet rising consumptive water needs in agriculture is high: "An increased taste for water-intensive food products by a growing population will exceed national production and turn China into a major player on the international food market, with increasing prices as a possible consequence."[133] According to a study by Chinese environmental scientists, water stress and warming climate could reduce key harvests in China by a fifth in the worst-case scenario. The study, led by Shilong Piao of the Center of Climate Research at Beijing University, forecast that rice yields would decrease by 4 to 14 percent, wheat by 2 to 20 percent, and maize by zero to 23 percent by the middle of this century.[134]

Such warning signs on the food front, and the drying up of subsurface aquifers in some areas in India and China, prompted the analyst Sandra Postel to ask, "So, who will export the 'virtual water' in the form of grain that water-stressed countries will need to import in order to feed themselves? And, just as important, at what price? The food riots that erupted in Haiti, Senegal, Mauritania, Bangladesh, and some half dozen other countries as grain prices climbed in 2007 and 2008 are a harbinger of what is to come."[135] Antigovernment demonstrations in some Arab countries in 2011 were actually fueled by soaring food prices, which, along with higher energy prices, contributed to higher inflation. In Asia, sharply higher food prices due to the continent's inability to grow enough food in the face of a deepening water crisis seem a likely scenario in the years ahead, even without taking into account the expected impact of climate change on agriculture.

By 2025, more than half the global population will live in water-stressed or water-scarce countries; the vast majority of them will be in China and India.[136] Constraints on resources are likely to become pronounced as more and more Indians and Chinese gain income to embrace modern comforts in life. Unlike the choices that the old economic giants in Europe had in their path of development—such as the shift from scarce timber to abundant coal in eighteenth-century Germany and Britain—the emerging economic giants can avail themselves of no substitutes for some of the resources whose present demand is beginning to lag availability. Of all the resources, the one with the greatest strategic bearing on the future prospects of Asian countries and their internal stability is freshwater. That is one resource that cannot be secured through international trade deals the way China, India, and other rapidly growing Asian economies scour the world for oil, natural gas, and minerals. According to a global water study by the International Food Policy Research Institute, the magnitude of water stress in China and India already is greater than in the other developing countries put together.[137]

As if things were not bad enough, climate change is likely to have a significant impact on the availability and flow of river waters from the Himalayas and the Tibetan highlands. The Himalayan snow and glacier melt that feeds Asia's great rivers is expected to be accelerated by global warming. That would mean increased river flows in the short to medium terms, but diminished flows in the long run. Although the science of climate change is still too young to reliably gauge the likely impact on the Himalayan hydrologic system, one study has warned that river flows from the Himalayas could decrease 30 percent or more over the long term.[138] Another study by a group of mainly Chinese climate change scientists, while highlighting the retreat of many Himalayan glaciers covering the Tibetan Plateau and the likelihood of 5 percent to 27 percent of China's overall glacial area disappearing by 2050, has said: "Even though the exact timing and magnitude of the 'tipping point' of each glacier is still uncertain, the projected long-term exhaustion of glacial water supply should have a considerable impact on the availability of water for both agricultural and human consumption."[139] Such scenarios and the already-evident water shortages make certain that water increasingly will become a key element in the national security calculus of a number of Asian countries. The Himalayas indeed seem a likely flashpoint.

Although the two demographic titans, China and India, are both water-stressed economies, the gap between the supply and demand of water in 2030 is projected to be much narrower in China than in India. Today China is already better off than India; as home to 19.6 percent of the world's population, China has a 6.5 percent share of global water resources, whereas India, with 17.3 percent of the world's population, must make do with just 4.3 percent of the world's water.[140] But whereas India's water demand by 2030 is forecast to become twice its present supply, China's demand in that year is projected to reach 818 billion m^3 as against a current supply of slightly over 618 billion m^3, although, given the wider extent of water pollution in China, a "quality-adjusted" supply/demand gap would clearly be larger than a quantity-only assessment.[141] The statistics on water pollution in China no doubt are alarming, with roughly 40 percent of the water supply there said to be "unsuitable for drinking, industry or agriculture."[142] Still, China overall is better placed than India on the availability of water resources, even though it too suffers from shortages as well as from splintered responsibility and accountability, "both vertically and horizontally, in the administration of water resources management."[143]

Compounding matters for India is the fact that it lacks adequate surface-water storage infrastructure to moderate the extreme variability of water availability that characterizes its situation across a year. Most of the annual precipitation in India falls in the short monsoon season, when the rain comes in torrents, with about half the yearly precipitation falling in just one month and some 90 percent of the river flows concentrated in the wettest four months of the year.[144] That is followed by meager or no rain in the rest of the year. Yet the country has not built the necessary storage infrastructure to control that variability and ensure reliable year-round supplies. According to the International Commission on Large Dams' database, India's per capita yearly water storage (200 m^3) is not only well below the global average (900 m^3) but is also the lowest relative to other important powers in the world. In China, the per capita storage capacity is eleven times higher, at 2,200 m^3. As a consequence, India's accessible, reliable supply of water—both surface and groundwater—amounts to 744 billion m^3, or just 29.5 percent of its total renewable water resources (TRWR) of 2,518 billion m^3 per year, according to the 2030 Water Resources Group.[145] The Food and Agriculture Organization has a lower estimate of India's TRWR—1,900 billion m^3 per year—while it calculates China's TRWR at 2,840 billion m^3 per year.[146]

The paradox is that despite paying significant socioeconomic costs due to monsoon failures and floods that are tied to intense climatic variability, India has failed to adequately invest in surface reservoirs as "an infrastructural response to the mitigation of flood and drought impacts."[147] The country's limited storage infrastructure seriously constrains its ability to create new supplies of accessible and reliable water. Nature's inconstancies can be buffered only with the aid of reservoirs and other storage capacity to hold back floodwaters in the rainy season for gradual release in the dry season. That kind of infrastructure indeed is expensive, and India has made little public investment in new storage or irrigation systems since the 1970s.

In India and China, the spread of irrigated farming and water-intensive industries and a rising middle class are drawing attention to their serious struggle over water resources.[148] Both countries need to find more water or to significantly boost water productivity and efficiency to deal with the increasing demands of their industries and households and to grow additional food to meet the rising caloric intakes and changing dietary preferences of their populations. Without achieving greater water efficiency and conservation, each will confront a tipping point that could potentially stunt its economic growth. The current water woes have given rise to grand ideas in the two countries—from linking rivers in India to store and convey water across the country to diverting Tibetan river waters northward so as to feed the arid areas in the Chinese heartland. But whereas China continues to pursue ambitious interriver and interbasin water transfer projects of various kinds, India's river interlinking plan (discussed in chapter 5) has failed to take off, because it has fallen victim to the country's raucous politics and the strong activism of nongovernmental organizations.

Having entered an era of perennial water shortages that are likely to parallel, in per capita water availability, the scarcity in the Middle East before long, India and China face the prospect that their rapid economic modernization could stall due to inadequate water resources. Such a prospect would become a reality if their industrial, agricultural, and household demand for water continues to grow at the present frenetic pace. Even though India's usable arable land is larger than China's—161 million hectares, compared with 122 million hectares—the source of all the major Indian rivers except one is the Chinese-held Tibetan Plateau.[149] Although the Ganges River originates on the Indian side of the Himalayas, its main tributaries flow in from Tibet. China's ambitious interbasin and interriver water transfer projects on the vast Tibetan Plateau, and its upstream damming of the Brahmaputra, Indus, Sutlej, Karnali, Arun, and other rivers, thus pose a serious threat to Indian interests.

More broadly, the sharpening Asian competition over water and energy resources is a reminder of the risks the Asian economic renaissance faces. These risks will increase if resource constraints become a serious bottleneck in rapid economic growth. A slowing of economic growth rates due to resource shortages would also have an unsettling domestic effect, socially and politically. Furthermore, if food production failed to keep up with the changing diets and soaring demand for meat and dairy products, and the present grain-exporting or grain-sufficient countries become major food importers, significant financial and strategic costs would inexorably follow. Climate change could make water conflicts more likely, although the extent and impact of global warming, admittedly, would depend on several complex variables. More fundamentally, if intrastate and interstate hydropolitics in Asia were to turn ugly and foster inter-riparian tensions through reduced river flows from the upstream to downstream regions, water conflicts would become inevitable.[150]

CENTRAL ASIA'S COMPLEXITIES

The specter of water wars in Asia is being highlighted by increasing water stress, continuation in a number of countries of perverse subsidies that promote water profligacy, and human-made environmental degradation in the form of shrinking forests and swamps that foster a cycle of chronic flooding and droughts through the depletion of nature's water storage and absorption cover. Given their common dependence on rivers flowing in from the Great Himalayan massif and its adjoining ranges, the water futures of Central Asia, Indian subcontinent, the Indochina Peninsula, and the People's Republic of China, in a sense, are linked. The Himalayan snowmelt that feeds Asia's great rivers could be damagingly accelerated by global warming.

Even Afghanistan depends for a substantial share of its water supplies on the Hindu-Kush Mountain Range, the westernmost extension of the Himalayas and the source of the Helmand, Hari Rud, and Kabul rivers. Afghanistan's largest source of river waters, however, is a border river, the Amu Darya, formed by the confluence of the Vakhsh and Panj rivers flowing out of the Pamir Mountains (map 2.1). The Pamirs, along with the Hindu-Kush, Karakoram, Kunlun, and Tian Shan ranges, are located on the outer rim of the Himalayas.

In the broader Himalayan region, extending to glaciers and other river sources in adjacent ranges, "tensions between countries over the proper management and equitable allocation of water resources mean that the potential for international conflict is high."[151] This potential is heightened by the fact that each riparian state is seeking to develop water resources of a transnational basin on its own, and

MAP 2.1   The Amu Darya River Basin

unrestrictedly, without considering the water-utilization plans or water needs across its borders. Consequently, the relationships between upstream and downstream states are often characterized by mutual distrust, political tensions, and discord. Even when an understanding or accord exists, its faithful implementation can remain problematic.

For example, in Central Asia—a largely arid region with poor precipitation and scarce groundwater resources, but with the Amu Darya as the largest river—demographic pressures, unsustainable Soviet-era irrigation practices, artificially drawn borders, and environmental degradation have accentuated the link between water and security, sharpening the regional hydropolitics. To some extent, the interstate water tensions there also are rooted in the transformation of the political parameters of drainage basins; the Soviet Union's sudden disintegration in December 1991 turned what had been intrastate basins into internationally shared basins. The new international frontiers, bearing little resemblance to the natural contours and even to the ethnic composition in some areas, have compounded the interstate sharing of water resources.

This five-country region is geographically very diverse, stretching from the mighty mountain ranges in the south and southeast and the world's second-largest crater lake, Issyk-Kul in Kyrgyzstan, to the vast Kyzyl-Kum and Kara-Kum deserts in the northwest and southwest. Issyk-Kul, an endorheic lake (or a body of water that does not flow into the sea), also ranks as one of the world's deepest lakes. In the middle of this region is Uzbekistan, which, upon the Soviet Union's disintegration, became—after Liechtenstein—the world's second doubly landlocked country. Central Asia's freshwater reserves are concentrated in the glaciated mountain areas in its southeast.

Today, at the center of the water tensions are the competing demands of large-scale irrigated farming in Uzbekistan, Turkmenistan, and Kazakhstan and the plans of upstream Tajikistan and Kyrgyzstan to expand their hydropower-generating capacities. The upriver, energy-poor states can become major renewable energy exporters if they are able to build hydroelectric stations—projects that the larger, militarily stronger downriver states oppose, including by holding out threats. The interstate competition in the region is aggravated by intrastate instability and ethnic rivalries, with Kyrgyzstan the most vulnerable and seriously in danger of becoming a failing state. The region's natural resources, although rich, are unevenly distributed: The energy and mineral resources and much of the arable land are concentrated in Kazakhstan, Uzbekistan, and Turkmenistan, and some 81 percent of Central Asia's renewable surface-water resources fall within the borders of Tajikistan and Kyrgyzstan, whose mountain ranges are the sources of the region's two principal rivers—the Amu Darya and the Syr Darya. The resource and ethnic fault lines run deep in Central Asia, and thus contribute to increasingly fractious intercountry relations.

It is thus hardly a surprise that water disputes already have become rife in Central Asia, where Kyrgyzstan and Tajikistan have a near monopoly on water resources but the main users are Uzbekistan (which consumes more than half the region's water supply to grow cotton, rice, and wheat) and Kazakhstan, the region's largest state by total area. In fact, almost a third of Central Asia's 62 million people depend directly or indirectly on irrigated agriculture. Uzbekistan—the regional hub that shares borders with the other four countries plus Afghanistan—is alone home to 45 percent of the Central Asian population. By contrast, Kazakhstan, the world's ninth-biggest state, is almost three-quarters larger than Mexico in area, but its population is less than 15 percent of Mexico's.

An elaborate infrastructure of dams, reservoirs, and irrigation canals in the Amu Darya and Syr Darya basins was built during the Soviet period to turn this region into the Soviet Union's main cotton-growing belt, with devastating environmental consequences, best illustrated by the way the Aral Sea has shrunk to less than half its original size. Heavy water withdrawals for irrigation from the Amu Darya and the Syr Darya have reduced the inflows into the Aral Sea to a trickle. Despite confronting a growing water scarcity, Central Asia remains a major cotton-producing area, accounting for almost 93 percent of the total irrigated cotton area of the former Soviet Union.[152] The curse of cotton has led to the degradation of water and land resources in Uzbekistan, Turkmenistan, and Tajikistan.

Ominously, the construction of new dams has become a flashpoint issue in the post-Soviet Central Asia. Tajikistan's moves to complete unfinished Soviet-era hydropower projects, including the world's highest dam on the Vakhsh River, carry major implications for downstream Uzbekistan, which is likely to receive less water flows, especially in the summer. Whereas Uzbekistan is obsessed with the quantity of transboundary supplies it receives, Kazakhstan's main concern is the deterioration in the quality of water, because the Syr Darya serves as the primary source of drinking water for its population. Tajikistan and Kyrgyzstan, in fact, wish to turn water into white gold to build energy security at home and earn foreign exchange by exporting hydroelectricity.

Efforts by Kyrgyzstan and Tajikistan to fashion transboundary water supplies into strategic exports akin to the hydrocarbon exports of their larger neighbors—Kazakhstan, Uzbekistan, and Turkmenistan—have foundered, principally because they lack geopolitical weight. In fact, Kyrgyzstan and Tajikistan remain dependent on gas and oil imports from their downstream neighbors and thus vulnerable to any disruption or stoppage of such supplies. As Soviet republics, Kyrgyzstan and Tajikistan received gas, oil, and coal supplies at highly concessional prices as well as direct federal aid in return for serving as the headwaters of the vast irrigation networks leading to the downstream republics.

But once the Central Asian states became independent, Uzbekistan and Kazakhstan sought to export energy resources at international market prices to Kyrgyzstan and Tajikistan while getting free water from them. That, in turn, prompted the upstream states to seek changes in the Soviet-era water quotas, under which the bulk of the Amu Darya and Syr Darya waters remain reserved for the downstream users. The upriver nations also demanded that the downriver states pay for the maintenance and repair of the water facilities serving transboundary users.

Up to now, most water-related issues in Central Asia have remained unsettled. Indeed, there is little prospect of an early resolution. As one study has cautioned, "The region's water challenges do not necessarily or inevitably lead to armed conflict. Unalleviated, however, they increasingly threaten to undermine human security and to bring different communities and regions into dispute with each other."[153] With the quality and quantity of water resources coming under growing pressure in Central Asia, intercountry discord has intensified over the twin issues of equitable water use and ensuring that transboundary flows are not materially altered.

These are the very issues at the heart of interstate water competition and dissonance in Asia as a whole. Indeed, as the Asian experiences show, it is no easy task to balance the right to equitable and reasonable utilization of water resources with the concomitant obligation not to materially impede cross-border flows or cause significant harm to a co-riparian. The competing water needs of river basin states, coupled with their divergent priorities and interests, are accentuating Asian discord. By 2050, as Asia's population expands by another 1.5 billion people and the resource-related demands of development soar, water is likely to become a prized commodity to be sought out and possibly even fought over. The struggle over water in Asia already is being underscored by the rising demands of irrigated farming, the spread of water-intensive industries (from steel to paper making), and a growing middle class seeking high water-consuming comforts. Worse still, the fast-rising water consumption rate is affecting the integrity of the water resources base and the health of aquatic ecosystems. And with future climatic changes likely to raise sea levels and negatively influence temperature and mountain-snowmelt patterns, freshwater management is set to become a critical security issue in Asia—a situation that would demand innovative and cooperative approaches, not confrontation or conflict.

Asia needs preventive diplomacy geared toward averting water conflicts, as well as subregional collaborative mechanisms. More fundamentally, to help protect fluvial ecosystems and prevent more freshwater species from becoming extinct, Asia needs to harmonize development with nature. Other than Japan and perhaps South Korea, Asian states in general are doing poorly in reconciling development with environmental protection. One key test of internal and regional security in Asia would be the ability of its governments to address pressures on water resources by adopting better water management and efficiency standards and enhancing water productivity in agriculture to help narrow the supply/demand gap. In the business-as-usual model, such a water gap will grow sharply during the next four decades. Asian states thus have little choice but to institute a system of water governance that emphasizes equity along with efficiency in sharing and utilizing this finite resource. At the same time, the integrity of this resource must be safeguarded for future generations.

Three

The Tibetan Plateau

The World's Most Unique Water Repository

T he status of the Plateau of Tibet is unique: No other area in the world is a water repository of such size, serving as a lifeline for large parts of a continent. Indeed, the plateau plays a triple role: It is Asia's main freshwater repository, largest water supplier, and principal rainmaker. But Tibet is rich in more than just water; it also holds other resources of immense strategic value. It is a treasure-trove of minerals, including precious metals and the so-called rare-earth elements. It is the world's No. 1 lithium producer and has China's biggest reserves of ten different metals. It is the largest supplier of timber, wool, and cashmere to mainland China and boasts newly discovered energy resources. The Chinese name for Tibet since the Qing Dynasty of the Manchus—Xizang, or "Western Treasure Land"—underscores the great value that this restive region, strategically located in the heart of Asia, holds for China. With its galloping, often-improvident style of economic growth, China has depleted its own natural resources and now is avariciously draining resources from the Tibetan Plateau.

Stretching 2,400 kilometers from east to west, and 1,448 kilometers from north to south, this unique water bank is the world's largest plateau. It is also the world's highest plateau, with the average elevation in Tibet so high—more than 4,000 meters above sea level—that it is called "the Roof of the World." It is one of the world's most biodiverse regions, with the rarest medicinal plants; the highest-living primates on Earth; and scores of bird, mammal, amphibian, reptile, fish, and plant species not found anywhere else. As a land that includes ecological zones from the arctic to subtropical, this plateau has a range of landscapes extending from tundra to tropical jungles, besides boasting the world's steepest and longest canyon as well as its tallest peak, Mount Everest. Indeed, it is such a matchless biogeographical region that, as a Chinese study has highlighted, a "total of 26 altitudinal belts, 28 spectra of altitudinal belts, 12,000 species of vascular plant, 5,000 species of epiphytes, 210 species of mammals, and 532 species of birds have been recorded" there.[1] The high vascular-plant diversity alone brings out the plateau's extraordinarily rich overall biodiversity.

Lowlanders take days to acclimatize to its rarefied air, which contains about 40 percent less oxygen than is available at sea level. Environmental hypoxia causes the blood to thicken as the body churns out more red blood cells to offset the low oxygen level, leading to chronic altitude sickness—a condition that, in some cases, can develop into life-threatening lung, heart, or brain complications. By contrast, ethnic Tibetans, with low blood hemoglobin levels, have distinctive genetic features that allow them to breathe easily at very high altitudes, with scientists identifying two genes associated with hemoglobin that play a role in hypoxia adaptation and explain the Tibetans' ability to thrive in such a harsh environment.[2] These genetic differences set the Tibetans apart from their present-day rulers, the Han Chinese.

With its height, the Tibetan Plateau literally towers over the rest of Asia. It actually rises up to the middle of the troposphere—the lowest and most-dense layer of the atmosphere—and helps deflect wind outward in winter and inward in summer. It influences Asian climatic, weather, and monsoonal patterns, as well as the Northern Hemisphere's atmospheric general circulation—the system of winds that helps transport warm air from the equator, where solar heating is greatest, toward the higher latitudes, giving rise to different climate zones.[3] Due to Tibet's high topography, the jet stream—a torrent of fast-flowing air 8 to 11 kilometers above sea level—curves around the mighty Himalayas and the adjacent Karakoram, Kunlun, Hindu-Kush, Pamir, and Tian Shan ranges. The plateau's unique features and role, fragile ecosystems, and endangered endemic species make it more vulnerable to the effects of global warming than any other region in the world. It is thus little surprise that this plateau is seen as both a driver and amplifier of global warming.[4]

Although more than half the world's mountain regions play "an essential or supportive role" for the adjacent lowlands by serving as their "freshwater towers," Tibet is a life giver and water supplier for much of the world's biggest continent, Asia, especially its most heavily populated regions.[5] The abundance of runoff in mountain areas principally because of much greater precipitation makes these regions critical for supplying the Earth's land surface with blue water in the form of river runoff, with mountains actually serving as the main source of freshwater in arid zones.[6] However, in comparison with the European Alps—the water tower of Europe—the sources of freshwater originating on the Tibetan Plateau support several times larger population in the lowlands of Asia. Tibetan rivers indeed are the lifeblood of the world's two most populous nations—China and India—and the other countries that stretch from Afghanistan to Vietnam in a contiguous arc. They include Bangladesh, Burma, Bhutan, Cambodia, Laos, Nepal, Pakistan, and Thailand. Together, these countries make up 46.3 percent of the global population and contain four-fifths of the people in the larger Asia that extends up to the Bosphorus.[7] Fed by thousands of Himalayan glaciers and mountain springs, the great river systems of Asia flowing down from the Tibetan highlands constitute an ecological marvel.

The ten key watersheds formed by the Himalayas and the Tibetan highlands spread out river waters far and wide in Asia. More than 90 percent of their runoff flows downstream to China and to southern and southeastern Asia. In addition, as the Intergovernmental Panel on Climate Change has pointed out, the rivers originating on the Tibetan Plateau form eleven Asian megadeltas, which are home to megacities like Tianjin, Shanghai, Guangzhou, Bangkok, Calcutta, Dhaka, and Karachi.[8] These megadeltas are "critical diverse ecosystems of unique assemblages of plants and animals located in different climatic regions."[9] In China, the megadeltas make up a substantial proportion of that fast-rising country's total gross domestic product.

The Tibetan Plateau is called the "Third Pole" because it has the largest perennial ice mass on the planet after the Arctic and Antarctica. With its snowfields and glaciers feeding virtually every major river system of Asia—from the Indus (Sengye Khabab to the Tibetans) in the west to the Yellow (known in Chinese as Huang He) in the east—the plateau holds more freshwater than any place on Earth, other than the North and South poles. But whereas the water in the polar icecaps is all locked up, much of the water in Tibet is accessible. Yet today, the effects of human-made environmental changes and global warming are more visible on the Tibetan Plateau than in the cryosphere (i.e., the frozen part of the Earth's surface, including the polar icecaps). Given that the hydrological integrity and ecological well-being of the plateau's major watersheds depend on sustainable anthropogenic practices, the central challenge in Asia is to establish institutionalized cooperative relationships among all riparian states that depend on streams originating there.

DISTINCTIVE FEATURES

Distinctive features have helped turn the Tibetan Plateau into Asia's "water tower," which supplies freshwater far and wide in Asia—to a region extending from the unique Tonle Sap lake-and-river system in Cambodia and the arid plains of Afghanistan–Pakistan to China's heartland and Thailand's rice paddy fields.[10] Tibet's vast glaciers, hundreds of lakes, huge underground springs, and high altitude have endowed it with the world's greatest river systems. In addition to the major river systems that originate on the Tibetan Plateau, a number of other important streams also have their primary source there. They together water several parts of Asia and serve as the lifeblood for the largest concentrations of population in the world. Tibet's snowpack stores gargantuan quantities of water through the winter months, even as its mountain springs continue to supply rivers with dependable base flows perennially, thereby reducing the variability of supply. From the spring season, river flows from the Tibetan Plateau begin to increase appreciably with the aid of snowmelt.

The rivers flowing out of the Tibetan Plateau include the main rivers of China, Southeast Asia, and South Asia: the Yangtze (known in Tibetan as Drichu), the Yellow (Machu), the Mekong (Zachu), the Salween (Gyalmo Ngulchu), the Irrawaddy, the Arun (Phungchu), the Brahmaputra (Yarlung Tsangpo), the Karnali (Mabcha Khabab), and the Indus (Sengye Khabab). The Ganges, which has the largest sediment river discharge in the world due to its relatively short upstream area and the high elevation from which it rapidly plunges into the plains, rises on the Indian side of the plateau's Himalayan rim. But whereas the Ganges' primary source—the Gangotri Glacier—and point of origin are on the Indian side of the Himalayas, this mighty river's main tributaries flow in from the Chinese-controlled Himalayan areas, including the Karnali, the Gandak, and the Kosi (whose uppermost part is called the Arun). The Karnali, the Gandak, and the Kosi actually are Nepal's principal river systems, and each of them, coincidentally, is made of seven tributaries.

The three great river systems of the Indian subcontinent—the Ganges, the Indus, and the Brahmaputra—alone support half a billion people, who are dependent on their waters for agricultural and other economic practices as well as daily personal needs.[11] However, in terms of a single basin, the Yangtze basin supports the largest concentration of population in Asia, whereas the Ganges basin boasts the highest population density.

As table 3.1 shows, three of the world's five largest rivers by discharge originate in the Himalayas and the Tibetan highlands. The Brahmaputra is the wettest major basin in Asia and the Yellow, with less than two-fifths of the Brahmaputra's precipitation level, is the driest. The Yellow and the Yangtze basins contain very little glaciated area, but the opposite is true of the Brahmaputra and the Indus, which flow extensively through high-altitude terrain. The Indus, the Yangtze, and the Ganges support the three largest irrigation networks in the world. The difference between basin precipitation and net irrigation demand, however, is the highest in relation to the Indus, which is exceptionally dependent on flows generated by

TABLE 3.1   The World's Five Largest Rivers by Discharge

River	Average Discharge at River Mouth (cubic meters per second)
Amazon	212,000
Congo	40,000
Yangtze	22,000
Brahmaputra	20,000
Ganges	19,000

Sources: UN-Water, 2011; waterencyclopedia.com.

snow and glacier melt. The meltwater share of the total river discharge of the Indus is easily the highest of any major Asian river, making its flows particularly susceptible to global-warming-driven shifts in melt characteristics.[12]

The western rim of the larger Himalayan region is the starting place of two key Central Asian rivers whose flows also heavily rely on melting snow and ice—the Amu Darya and the Tarim. Today, five rivers originating in the Himalayas and the Tibetan highlands rank among the world's top ten endangered rivers—the Yangtze, the Indus, the Mekong, the Salween, and the Ganges.[13] In addition, the overstressed Yellow is widely seen as having been ecologically damaged by over-damming and pollution, and untreated sewerage still finds its way into the river, including its upstream portions.

Such is Tibet's centrality in Asia's hydrological cycle and weather and climatic patterns that the plateau also plays a pivotal role in the Asian summer monsoons.[14] By serving as a high-elevation heat pump, it draws into the hinterland the mon-soonal currents from the oceans stretching from the East and South China seas to the Arabian Sea. Whereas in winter the massive plateau deflects the cold jet stream to the high Himalayas in a wavelike pattern, in summer Tibet's rocky and lofty terrain heats up quickly to form a low-pressure system that helps attract the mon-soons from the east, southeast, and southwest.

Scientific studies have shown that the plateau, though a heat sink during winter, turns into a heat source from spring to fall, with the heating maximum in the summer.[15] That thermal effect helps to intensify the East Asian monsoon and bring heavy rains to the Indian subcontinent and the Indochina Peninsula, the two regions with the highest precipitation in Asia. In other words, the plateau acts as a huge elevated "heat island" in the summer to induce movement of the monsoonal currents deep into the Asian landmass, facilitating the long-distance transportation of moisture from the tropical and ocean regions. Tibet thus is not only Asia's largest freshwater repository and water supplier but also a rainmaker for southeastern, southern, and central Asia as well as China and Japan.

Another remarkable facet of the Tibetan Plateau is that it has the largest concentration of tall mountains in the world. Most of the world's mountain ranges are located in the Northern Hemisphere, but all the mountains of more than 7,000-meter height are situated in Asia, largely on the Tibetan Plateau and in the Himalayas.[16] In fact, the world's tallest peaks above 8,000 meters are all located in the Great Himalayan Range, which straddles the Tibet–India border. This range actually extends nearly 3,500 kilometers from Burma to the Hindu Kush in Afghanistan.

The height of the Great Himalayan massif helps generate in the mountainous regions heavy precipitation, which, along with the water-storing capacity of the Himalayan glaciers, gives this mountain range a hydrological role unmatched any-where else in the world. The sudden rise of the Himalayan mountains from less than 500 meters to more than 8,000 meters results "in a diversity of ecosystems that range, in only a couple of hundred kilometers, from alluvial grasslands (among the tallest in the world) and subtropical broadleaf forests along the foothills, to temperate broadleaf forests in the mid-hills, mixed conifer and conifer forests in the higher hills, and alpine meadows above the tree line."[17]

There are more than 18,000 high-altitude glaciers in the Great Himalayas, where a zone of permanent rock and ice begins at about 5,500–6,000 meters. The glaciers, spread over 42,946 square kilometers, cover 17 percent of the Himalayas.[18] The Himalayan portion in Tibet has at least three times more glacier area than the part in India. About 10,000 square kilometers of the Himalayan glacier area is in India, compared with more than 30,000 square kilometers under Chinese territorial control. In fact, other than some glaciers in Xinjiang, China's glaciers are concentrated on the Tibetan Plateau, including the areas that have been taken out of Tibet to be either merged with Sichuan, Gansu, and Yunnan or turned into the separate province of Qinghai. The Himalayas, however, extend beyond Tibet and India to Nepal, Bhutan, Pakistan-administered Kashmir, and the northern tip of Burma, and each of these regions boasts glaciers.

The Tibetan Plateau, in addition to being the highest elevated land in the world, stands out for its extensive *permanently frozen layer of earth*, or permafrost, and numerous lakes and mountain springs that feed the river systems. The high-altitude permafrost helps store subsoil water, the wellspring of wetlands, lakes, and grasslands. The water and heat exchange between the atmosphere and ground surface that occurs through the cycle of soil freezing and thawing influences the Asian climate significantly. According to one study, "The greater the moisture content in the soil, the greater is the influence of the freeze-thaw cycle on the heat exchange."[19] But the greater evaporation of water that is happening due to warming trends means less soil moisture on the whole. Tibet's permafrost regime is characterized by a strong diurnal, or daytime, pattern influenced by intense solar radiation inputs at the surface, as well as by a high gradient related to the Earth's heat—elements that make it very susceptible to thermal disturbance.[20]

More than 1,500 lakes, many located at an altitude of 4,000 to 5,000 meters and with steep banks and impressive water depths, highlight the Tibetan Plateau's amazingly rich water resources. The lakes include Mansarovar (also called Mapham Tso), Nam Tso, Yamdrok Yumtso, and the largest of all, Ngonpo Tso, which is still better known by its old Mongolian name, Kokonor, despite China renaming it Qinghai Lake. According to an assessment by the Qinghai–Tibet Plateau Study Institute of the Chinese Academy of Sciences, these lakes—spread over 45,000 square kilometers of area—hold 608 billion cubic meters of water, which constitutes 70 percent of China's total lake-water reserves.[21]

Add to the picture the extensive glaciers, and what emerges are colossal water resources. According to Chinese experts, there are about 15,000 *large* glaciers just in the Himalayan region of Tibet, with a volume of locked water estimated to total up to 12,000 cubic kilometers.[22] The Food and Agriculture Organization of the United Nations, however, estimates the number of large glaciers in the entire Himalayan region at 5,000, storing approximately 3,870 cubic kilometers of water.[23]

The glaciers serve as massive storehouses of freshwater. Although in wet or cold seasons the glaciers grow with snow, their edges slowly melt in dry and hot seasons, thereby feeding lakes, rivers, and mountain springs. But the glaciers' accelerated thawing due to climate change means increased runoff, a process that could make the glaciers gradually smaller. On the positive side, however, the rise in average temperatures owing to global warming is triggering increased precipitation in large parts of the Himalayas, and the Intergovernmental Panel on Climate Change has predicted that the mean annual precipitation on the Tibetan Plateau will increase 10 to 30 percent by 2080.[24] However, the increase in precipitation on the Tibetan Plateau, as a 2009 Chinese study discovered, is "not as pronounced as the increase in temperature."[25] The greater precipitation also is being offset by the higher temperature-linked increased evapotranspiration, or the loss of water to the air through evaporation and plant transpiration.

Still, it is not a surprise that two-thirds of China's hydropower potential is located on the Tibetan Plateau or that the present dam-building activities of China, Burma, India, Bhutan, Nepal, and Pakistan are concentrated in the extended Himalayan range. But as one scientific study has put it, "Perhaps the most critical region in which vanishing glaciers will negatively affect water supply in the next few decades will be China and parts of Asia, including India (together forming the Himalaya–Hindu Kush region), because of the region's huge population. The ice mass over this mountainous region is the third largest on Earth, after the Arctic/Greenland and Antarctic regions. The hydrological cycle of the region is complicated by the Asian monsoon, but there is little doubt that melting glaciers provide a key source of water for the region in the summer months."[26] Another study has reported that because snow and glacier meltwater is far more important in the Indus and Brahmaputra basins than in the Ganges, Yangtze, and Yellow basins, the vulnerability of the first two rivers to climate change–driven reduced flows is greater, thus posing a serious threat to food security in their downstream regions.[27] Their late-spring and summer discharges are expected to reduce "considerably" between 2046 and 2065, according to the study, "after a period of increased flows due to accelerated glacier melt."

Tibet's natural forests on the remote, steep slopes play a hydrological role by serving as land cover in its mountain watersheds, helping to control runoff peaks. They also play a crucial role in maintaining "ecological services" connected with the water and carbon cycles, including by storing carbon, generating rainfall, and conserving soils. Additionally, they aid river flows by protecting stream banks. In fact, these forests are a huge reservoir of biological diversity, serving as home to 90 percent of the land-based plant and animal species on the plateau. Concentrated in the water-rich southern and southeastern belt of the plateau, the Tibetan forests are of a varied lot: Tropical-montane and subtropical-montane coniferous forest, with evergreen spruce, fir, juniper, pine larch, cypress, birch, and sclerophyllous oak being among the main species of trees.

Yet Tibet's mountain forest ecosystems, including cloud forests, rank among the most endangered ecosystem types in the world. The felling of these forests has continued under the more than six-decade-old Chinese rule, despite growing recognition in China of their critical ecological role. In fact, after more than 4,000 people were killed in the devastating flooding in the Yangtze basin in 1998, which Chinese president Jiang Zemin blamed on forest-cover depletion in the upper reaches of the river, China banned further logging in the upstream area on the Tibetan Plateau and even launched a replanting program. Between 1957 and 1986 alone, according to the Chinese government, the forest cover in the Yangtze upper catchment declined from 22 percent of the total area to 10 percent, leading to soil erosion and sediment problem. A similar ban was clamped on the Yellow River upper basin after some Chinese studies linked the falling downstream river flows to the deforestation in the upstream catchment region.

Chinese domestic regulations, however, are sometimes promulgated to blunt criticism, rather than actually be put in force. Beijing has been unwilling or unable to put an end to reckless logging practices across the Tibetan Plateau, especially in the upper catchments and river valleys. Since the logging bans in the upper Yangtze and Yellow catchments, the size of the Chinese economy has quintupled, putting greater pressures on land, river systems, and forest resources. In fact, deadly flooding again racked the Yangtze basin in July 2010, with floodwaters with speeds of 70,000 cubic meters per second hitting the giant, newly completed Three Gorges Dam in Hubei Province.

Several of the major rivers in Tibet, including the Indus, the Brahmaputra, the Sutlej, and the Karnali, actually originate in the same area located in the southwestern corner of the Tibetan Plateau, near the border with India. The rivers start off from an area that has Mount Kailash (Gang Rimpoche in Tibetan) in the center, surrounded by Lake Mansarovar (Mapham Tso, or "always invincible"), Lake Rakshastal (La'nga Tso, or "the lake of the demon"), and some very large glaciers. Mount Kailash—whose own 6,638-meter main peak sits in the middle of other peaks to resemble a mammoth eight-petal lotus—and the large, 412-square-kilometer Mansarovar ("the lake of consciousness and enlightenment") constitute the sacred mountain-and-lake duo of four faiths: Hinduism, Buddhism, Jainism, and the indigenous religion of Tibet, Bon. Bon was firmly established in large parts of the Tibetan Plateau before the introduction of Buddhism in the seventh century CE reduced its adherents to a minority, and Bon continues to thrive in pockets of present-day Tibet.[28]

Mount Kailash, the legendary center of the world, is worshipped by believers as the abode of the father and mother of the planet, the gods Shiva and Uma—the place where Lord Buddha manifested himself in his super-bliss form, and where the first prophet of the Jain religion, Rishabha (Rishabhadeva), achieved nirvana or spiritual liberation.[29] The circumambulation of Kailash is a must for the pilgrims who manage to trek to its forbidding surroundings. The renowned ancient Indian poet, Kalidas, wrote in the fourth century CE about Kailash: "At the center of

Earth, there stands a great mountain, Lord of Snows, majestic, rooted in the sea, its summit wreathed in clouds, a measuring rod for all creations." Kailash means "crystal" in Sanksrit, whereas the mountain's Tibetan name stands for "the precious jewel in the snows." The Bon call the mountain Yung-drung Gu-tzeg, or "the nine-story swastika."

Mansarovar, the world's highest freshwater lake at 4,557 meters above sea level, and the saline lake, Rakshastal, are wedged between Kailash and Gurla Mandata, the "Mountain of Goddess." Mansarovar is believed by Hindus to be a lake created by Brahma, the first god in the Hindu trinity, and its icy, sapphire-like waters are regarded as holy.

Tibet's richest water resources indeed are located in its region along the border belt with India stretching from the southwest to the southeast. The reason for the concentration of the water resources in this belt is simple: The Great Himalayan Range blocks the advancement of the summer monsoons from the Bay of Bengal and the Arabian Sea further northward, causing heavy and widespread rainfall on the slopes facing south. The Himalayas also help deflect the precipitation system in an eastward direction. Apart from the water-rich southern and eastern belt—home to most of Tibet's numerous lakes—the rest of Tibet is semiarid. Although Tibet is characterized by extremes of altitude, relief, and climate, the Himalayan-influenced precipitation patterns explain why much of the Tibetan Plateau is dry. Each successively higher mountain range serves to decrease precipitation from south to north, culminating in the high-altitude aridity of most of the plateau.

The water-rich southern Tibetan belt, the Himalayan rim, serves as the headwaters of the two major river systems—the Indus and the Brahmaputra—as well as several other important rivers for South Asia, such as the Karnali and the Kosi, which empty into the Ganges. The 1,550-kilometer-long Sutlej (Langchen Khabab to Tibetans), which flows through India to ultimately drain into the Indus in Pakistan, also originates in this belt, from the southern slopes of Mount Kailash. The southeastern and eastern areas of the Tibetan Plateau are also water rich. The Salween, for example, has its primary source near the town of Nagchu in the Tibet Autonomous Region, and the Mekong originates in the remote Thangla Mountains of Tibet's Amdo Region, now in Qinghai Province.

In their southward course, the Salween and the Mekong run in parallel through the Tibetan Plateau into Yunnan before separating, the former entering Burma and the latter, joined by the Ngomchu River, flowing into Laos. The Yangtze (Asia's longest river) and the Yellow also originate in the eastern part of the Tibetan Plateau, with the Yellow's primary source being in what China has designated the "Yushu Tibetan Autonomous Prefecture." (Yushu, or "Jade Tree," is the Mandarin name for a place the mostly Tibetan local population knows as Kyedudo.) The Irrawaddy, Burma's major river, is fed by three Tibetan streams in Zayul County, near the border with India.[30] Similarly, one source of Manas (or Lhodrak Sharchu to Tibetans, and Norbu Lakchu to Bhutanese)—a 376-kilometer river of Bhutan and northeastern India—is in Tibet.[31]

Such is the Tibetan Plateau's southeast-to-northwest precipitation gradient that its southeastern part receives copious precipitation from India's Southeast Monsoon from the Bay of Bengal, whereas the rest of the southern Tibetan belt gets abundant precipitation from both the Southeast and Southwest Monsoons.[32] By contrast, the low precipitation rates in Tibet's center and northwest are reflected in those regions' extreme continental conditions. The evolution of lakes on the Tibetan Plateau is also tied to the natural environment, in particular the climatic conditions. There is a general decrease in the salinity of lakes from the plateau's arid northern and northwestern areas to the water-rich southern and southeastern areas.[33] The location of Tibet's ice cores and freshwater resources in a relatively small belt tells the story about where the precipitation is concentrated. It is thus no surprise that a narrow belt running along the Himalayas is the source of some of the world's greatest rivers.

Such are the extremely high precipitation levels in the entire Himalayan region that the Chinese Water Resources Ministry has pointed out that "the annual precipitation at the downriver portion of the Yarlung Tsangpo (Brahmaputra), near the Sino-Indian border, can approach 5,000 millimeters."[34] By contrast, the total annual rainfall in the water-rich hill regions along China's southeast coast averages 1,600 to 2,000 millimeters, or roughly one-third. Within Tibet itself, the annual mean precipitation decreases from nearly 2,600 millimeters in the botanically diverse southeast to between 50 and 80 millimeters in the barren and very cold northwest. That gradient, significantly, is matched by a corresponding decrease in temperature as well as in biodiversity.

In this light, it is really the Himalayan corridor of the sprawling Tibetan Plateau that stands out for its unmatched water resources, just as the Himalayan areas in India, Nepal, Bhutan, Burma, and Pakistani-administered Kashmir are known for their bountiful water reserves. Together, these areas constitute the Great Himalayan Watershed, which now is the focal point of dam-building projects by several countries. The Chinese water megaprojects have prompted India to initiate its own dam-building program along the border with Tibet. China and India are not only competing to dam rivers along their disputed frontier, with the former holding a major advantage as the dominant upper-riparian state, but are also aiding other states to tap the resources of the Great Himalayan Watershed. Chinese state-owned firms are involved in dam building in Pakistan, Nepal, and Burma, and India is financing some Bhutanese and Nepalese dam projects.

THE REALITY ABOUT TIBET

The Tibetan Plateau lies in the center of Asia and at the crossroads of major civilizations. It is not an area the size of Brunei, Bhutan, or Switzerland, but rather a large region almost two-thirds the size of the entire European continent. The plateau's size, rich natural resources, and vantage-point location underline its geopolitical importance. Furthermore, its ecological integrity is critical for the well-being of countries that are dependent on its water resources and rainmaking capacity.

Political control over the 2.5-million-square-kilometer Tibetan Plateau has armed China with tremendous leverage, besides giving it access to Tibet's vast natural resources. Three-fifths of historical Han China remains water poor. But the present-day People's Republic of China is extraordinarily water rich, thanks to its forcible absorption of the Land of Snows. Control over the "blue gold" wealth of the Tibetan Plateau makes China a potential water power in the way Saudi Arabia is an oil power.[35] In fact, through its control over Tibet, China controls the ecological viability of several major river systems that are the lifelines for the nations of southern and southeastern Asia. But as one case study has pointed out, Chinese rule already has been "a significant contributor to the decline of Tibet's natural resources" and to the "resulting environmental impairment."[36] The reckless exploitation of resources has extended to China proper and, consequently, the country as a whole is paying significant environmental and other costs.[37]

In the twenty-first century, China's attention increasingly has turned to the exploitation of water resources on the Tibetan Plateau, which offers a range of tempting sites for megaprojects to a country that has long believed in subduing nature, with little regard for the long-term ecological effects (map 3.1). The advertisements for bottled Tibetan water on billboards in Chinese cities symbolize China's new covetous focus on Tibet's waters. In fact, as water woes have intensified in its northern and central provinces owing to unsustainable consumption patterns in agriculture and industry, China has progressively turned its attention to the copious water reserves that the Tibetan Plateau holds. The Huai River basin—an intricate network of rivers, lakes, and fishing villages—has come to epitomize the overexploitation and contamination of water resources in mainland China. A once-pulsating lifeline of the densely populated Henan, Shandong, Jiangsu, and Anhui provinces, the Huai now is clogged with the toxic effluents from industries along its banks, and some of its fishing villages are troubled by exceptionally high cancer rates.

Having brought the resources of its own major rivers under severe stress in the Han heartland, besides creating a serious problem of water contamination, China now is pursuing major interbasin and interriver water transfer projects on the Tibetan Plateau. Furthermore, most new Chinese megaprojects or plans for building dams, barrages, and diversion facilities now are centered in southern and southeastern Tibet, close to the frontiers with other countries and involving international rivers. That is the portion of Tibet with high humidity, heavy precipitation rates, and abundant water resources.

The Chinese projects thus have a direct bearing on the water interests of other riparian countries After all, unless a significant portion of a river system's main

MAP 3.1   The Major Asian Rivers Originating in Tibet

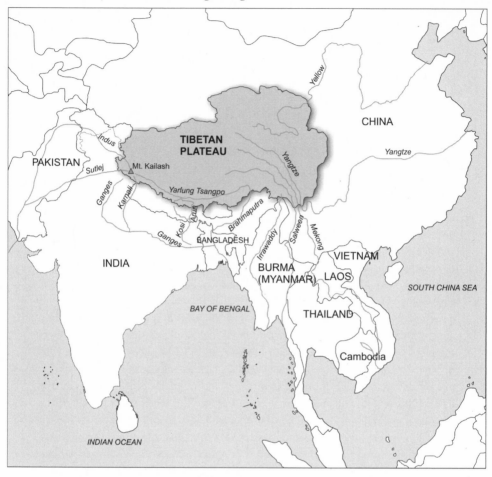

catchment area extends to a downriver state, there is a virtual straight-line relationship between water use upstream and water availability downstream. If excess
water is consumed or diverted upstream, there will be less water available for
downriver users, besides leading gradually to lower water quality and damage to
the fluvial ecosystems. Today, as it turns its attention to Tibet to meet its thirst for
water and energy, China threatens the ecological well-being of river systems that
are indispensable to other countries. The major hydroengineering projects Beijing
undertakes in Tibet will ultimately affect everyone downstream, including those
in the downriver basins in China itself.

One obvious reason for China's determination to hold onto Tibet is that the
region is very rich in the water, mineral wealth, and energy resources so desperately
needed in mainland China. At a time when China has aggressively sought to secure

supplies of energy, metals, and strategic minerals from overseas, it has viewed the recrudescence of overt separatism in resource-rich Tibet with political alarm. This explains why China continues to employ brute force to enforce its writ in Tibet. In this respect, little has changed since the Mao Zedong era.

In more recent years, as it has increasingly sought to exploit Tibet's water and mineral resources, China has poured money into infrastructure development on the plateau in a big way. Between 2000 and 2009 alone, Beijing invested some $46 billion in the so-called Tibet Autonomous Region to help build roads, railways, telecommunications, and other infrastructure in order to integrate Tibet more closely with China proper and to facilitate resource exploitation.[38] Billions of dollars of additional investments are now being poured into this region to upgrade its transportation grid, including extending the strategic railroad and expanding the expressway network to 70,000 kilometers. This infrastructure development is paving the way for the launch of hydropower and other water megaprojects on the plateau. Yet there is little discussion in China about the international nature of the plateau's water resources.

The more the Chinese government has sought to present Tibet as a "core" sovereignty issue for China, the more it has helped highlight Tibet as a key lingering problem. And the more it has sought to portray Tibet as its "internal" matter, the more Tibet has emerged as a region where Chinese activities hold international implications. The transboundary effects of Chinese megaprojects on the Tibetan Plateau have begun to complicate Chinese diplomacy with riparian neighbors. Tibet itself remains at the heart of the China/India divide. The tallest mountain peaks in the world are in the Great Himalayan Range, the scene of a thirty-two-day China–India war in 1962 and continuing military tensions to date between the two demographic titans. As a triumphal symbol of its rule over Tibet, China took the Olympic torch in 2008 through Tibet to the 8,848-meter Mount Everest, located along the Tibetan–Nepalese border. Taking the torch to the world's tallest mountain was Beijing's way of reinforcing its tall claim on Tibet.

But 2008 also served as a reminder of the troubles wrought by Tibet. First came a monk-led Tibetan uprising, which spread like wildfire across Tibet and even beyond to the traditional Tibetan areas that have been incorporated in Han provinces. The revolt was a rude jolt to what is now the world's largest, strongest, and longest-surviving autocracy, highlighting the signal failure of state-driven efforts to pacify Tibet through more than half a century of ruthless repression and laying bare China's Achilles' heel. The open backlash against the Tibetans' economic marginalization, the rising Han influx, and the state assault on Tibetan religion and ecology constituted, in its geographical spread, the largest rebellion in Tibet since 1959, when the Dalai Lama and his followers were forced to flee to India. That revolt was followed a couple of months later in 2008 by the giant Sichuan earthquake, which killed more than 87,000 people, and by smaller tremors along the Tibetan Plateau's rim. The quakes, in the view of geologists, resulted from the tectonic plate of Tibet, the world's highest elevated land, pressing down on China's southwest and midwest lowlands. The giant quake, emanating in the eastern margins of the plateau, indicated that the tectonic plate was beginning to shift.

TRUTH AND RECONCILIATION

The incontrovertible fact is that the only occasions in history when Tibet was clearly part of China was under non-Han dynasties—that is, when China itself had been conquered by outsiders: the Mongol Yuan Dynasty, from 1271 to 1368; and the latter half of the Manchu Qing Dynasty, which lasted from 1644 to 1911. What Beijing today asserts are regions "integral" to its territorial integrity are really imperial spoils of earlier foreign dynastic rule in China.[39] Yet revisionist history under Communist rule has helped indoctrinate the Chinese to think of the Yang and Qing empires as Han. When a dynasty was indeed ethnically Han, such as the Ming (founded between the Yang and Qing empires), Tibet had scant connection to the Chinese rulers.

Consider the period of Mongol rule over China and Tibet, when Genghis Khan and his successors carved out one of the largest empires in world history. Tibetan leaders cleverly befriended Genghis Khan as the Mongol leader's advancing armies were on a rampage in the early thirteenth century; by pledging political loyalty and offering religious blessings, they sought and secured Mongol patronage and protection in return. So, when the Mongols eventually conquered China and extended their sway to the whole of Tibet, the Tibetans were permitted greater autonomy than the other Mongol-conquered lands, including the Han-populated territories.

Yet, in a gross misappropriation of Genghis Khan's legacy, Communist China's official history treats the Yuan Dynasty as Chinese. In fact, the official Chinese White Paper on Tibet unabashedly dates China's purported incorporation of Tibet to the Mongol period. "In the mid-thirteenth century, Tibet was officially incorporated into the territory of China's Yuan Dynasty," the White Paper asserts.[40] The Yuan Dynasty, however, was not Han but Mongol. Such misrepresentation is redolent of the expansive view of China's history, underlined by Beijing's more recent request to the United Nations to list Kyrgyzstan's traditional poem—the Epic of Manas—as a Chinese contribution to world cultural heritage, stirring outraged charges of cultural theft.[41] Tibet's inclusion in China as part of the Mongols' Yuan Dynasty was like Burma being part of the British India Empire until 1937.

In fact, among the Mongols' conquests, Tibet was administered separately from China during the Mongol rule.[42] The Mongols imbibed Tibetan religious and cultural values and patronized Tibetan Buddhism. The Mongol–Tibetan relationship was "an expression of a racial, cultural and, above all, religious affinity between the two peoples—an affinity that neither shared with the Chinese."[43]

During the period of the ethnic-Han Ming Dynasty (1369–1644), Tibet was independent; it was ruled by the Phagmodru, Rinpung, and Tsangpa Tibetan dynasties in succession. Underscoring China's limited borders in that period, the Great Wall as it exists today was built by the Ming Dynasty mainly to denote the edge of the Han Empire's political frontiers. Today's China, however, is three times as large as it was under the last Han dynasty, the Ming, with its borders having extended far west and southwest of the Great Wall. Territorially, Han power is at its zenith, symbolized by the fact that the ancient city of Kashgar, in Chinese-ruled Xinjiang, is closer to Baghdad than to Beijing, and that Lhasa, Tibet's capital, is almost twice as far from the Chinese capital as from New Delhi.

In fact, it was the non-Han dynasty that came after the Ming rule, the Manchus' Qing, which represented the historical peak of Beijing's intervention in Tibet, especially in the late eighteenth century.[44] Still, the Chinese name for Tibet since the Qing Dynasty—Xizang (*xi* is Chinese for western, and *zang* means treasury)—implies that Tibet is a distinct land, west of China rather than part of China. It was not until the Qing Dynasty collapsed in the early twentieth century that Tibet regained its independence, a development that coincided with the 1911 uprising in the central Yangtze Valley city of Wuchang. The uprising triggered the anti–Manchu Chinese revolution, which, in turn, led to the establishment of the Republic of China by the provisional government of Sun Yat-Sen, leader of the Republican movement.

However, it was not until after the Communists came to power in China in 1949 that Tibet, for the first time in history, came under direct Han rule. In October 1950, with global attention focused on the Korean War, Mao's government swiftly captured eastern Tibet, a success that emboldened Mao to enter the Korean War days later.[45] By 1951 Communist China had annexed the entire Tibetan Plateau.

Tibet, in the shape and size it existed independently up to 1950, makes up approximately one-fourth of China's landmass today, and it has given the Han society, for the first time in history, a contiguous frontier with India, Nepal, and Bhutan. Before Tibet's annexation there was no instance in history of Han forces being deployed along the Himalayas. The disappearance of the traditionally neutral buffer between the Chinese and Indian civilizations has had a tremendous effect on the relationship between Asia's two largest powers. Within eleven years of Tibet's forcible absorption, China waged a bloody war with India, with the shadow of the 1962 Himalayan conflict still clouding the Sino-Indian relationship.

Tibet traditionally has encompassed the regions of Ü-Tsang (the central plateau), Kham, and Amdo, as map 3.2 shows. After annexing Tibet, China gerrymandered the Tibetan homeland by incorporating much of the Amdo Region (the present Dalai Lama's birthplace) into the new province of Qinghai and merging large parts of Kham into the Han provinces of Sichuan, Yunnan, and Gansu. A slice of Amdo also was transferred to Gansu and Sichuan. There now are two

MAP 3.2   Tibet Before It Was Occupied by Communist China

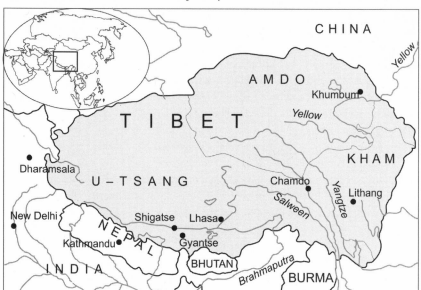

"Tibetan autonomous prefectures" and one "Tibetan autonomous county" in Sichuan Province,[46] one Tibetan autonomous prefecture and one Tibetan autonomous county in Gansu Province,[47] and one Tibetan autonomous prefecture in Yunnan Province.[48] Apart from its water-rich southern and southeastern belts, Ü-Tsang is arid, along with the north and west of Amdo.

The traditional Tibetan region is a distinct cultural and economic entity. But with large, heavily Tibetan-populated areas having been severed from Tibet, what is left as Tibet is just the 1965 creation—the Tibet Autonomous Region (TAR), the central plateau comprising Ü-Tsang and the westernmost part of Kham, or roughly half the Tibetan Plateau. When China now refers to Tibet, it means just TAR, which is the size of South Africa, one of Africa's largest countries. Yet China has changed even the demographic composition of TAR, where there were hardly any permanent Han settlers before the Chinese annexation. Eastern Kham and Amdo, by contrast, have had many Han settlers for centuries. Today, though, the Han people constitute the majority in eastern Kham and Amdo, whose political control in history has alternated between Tibetan and Han rulers.[49] The principal city in the central plateau, Lhasa, also has come under Han domination.

TAR, home to less than half of the 6.5 million Tibetans in today's China, was the last "autonomous region" created by China, the others being Inner Mongolia (1947), Xinjiang (1955), Guangxi Zhuang (1958), and Ningxia (1958). In addition, China has 30 "autonomous prefectures," 120 "autonomous counties," and 1,256 "autonomous townships." All the so-called autonomous areas are in the lands of ethnic minorities, which make up 60 percent of the territory of the People's Republic of China. The policies of forced assimilation in Tibet and Xinjiang—which, by themselves, make up nearly half of China's landmass—began after the Mao regime created a land corridor link between the two rebellious regions by gobbling up India's 38,000-square-kilometer Aksai Chin, part of the state of Jammu and Kashmir. Aksai Chin provides the only accessible Tibet–Xinjiang route through the Kunlun mountains in the western Himalayan rim. Like Tibet, most of the other ethnic homelands were ruled historically from Beijing only when China itself had been conquered by foreigners.

Today, these areas are "autonomous" only in name, with that tag designed to package a fiction to the ethnic minorities. Apart from not enforcing its one-child norm in those sparsely populated but vast regions, China grants them no meaningful autonomy. In fact, China has relegated governance of minority homelands to local Han satraps who take orders directly from the central government in Beijing to enforce Chinese control. To help Sinicize the minority lands, Beijing's multipronged strategy has involved five key components: cartographically altering ethnic-homeland boundaries, demographically flooding non-Han cultures, rewriting history to justify Chinese control, enforcing cultural homogeneity to help blur local identities, and maintaining political suppression. The Manchu assimilation into Han society and the swamping of the locals in Inner Mongolia have left only the Tibetans and the Turkic-speaking Muslim ethnic groups in Xinjiang as the holdouts. But as underscored by events in recent years, the strategy of ethnic and economic colonization of the traditional Tibetan and Uighur lands is stoking deep unrest.

The preservation of what China's leaders call "stability" and "harmony" serves as their justification to maintain state power through control of even religious institutions, as in Tibet, with President Hu Jintao's slogan of a "harmonious society" designed to undergird the theme of conformity. Although it officially comprises fifty-six nationalities, China honors artificially enforced monoculturalism. China grants genuine local autonomy just to two areas, both Han—Hong Kong and Macau. In the talks it has held with the Dalai Lama's envoys since 2002, the Chinese government has flatly refused to consider the idea of making Tibet a special administrative region like Hong Kong and Macau. It also has rebuffed the idea of restoring Tibet, under continued Chinese rule, to the shape and size it existed in 1950.

The population transfer that is transforming Tibet's ethnic composition is just one dimension of a systematic Chinese policy that threatens the survival of the distinct Tibetan culture and natural environment. More broadly, Tibet has come to symbolize some of the key Asian challenges. One challenge relates to ecology: Safeguarding the ecological interests of large parts of Asia, after all, requires protecting the delicate Tibetan ecosystems. Environmental degradation in Tibet holds serious implications for other states because the plateau is a barometer of climatic conditions in southern, southeastern, and central Asia, as well as in mainland

China. The plateau already is witnessing accelerated thawing of its glaciers, soil erosion, degradation of its vegetated riparian buffer zones, deterioration in watershed quality, and water pollution problems. Add to that picture the local effects of warming temperatures and degraded pastoral lands.

Because of its extremely high elevation, the plateau is warming faster and earlier than the surrounding lowlands. So it is little surprise that the average annual temperature in Tibet is rising at a rate much higher than the average in China and the world—a development that will have a significant impact on climatic stability in the rest of Asia, according to a Chinese official report written by the Tibet Regional Meteorological Bureau and titled "Tibet's Climate under the Global Warming Trend."[50] Extreme weather events in Tibet, as a consequence, are becoming more frequent. "Problems like receding snow lines, shrinking glaciers, drying grasslands, and desert expansion are increasingly threatening the natural ecosystem in the region," according to the director of the Tibet Regional Meteorological Bureau. "Natural disasters like droughts, landslides, snowstorms and fires are more frequent and calamitous now."[51]

Another Asian challenge relates to the changing patterns of mountain snowmelt and glacier thawing. The Tibetan and Himalayan glaciers constitute, metaphorically, a water bank account built up over thousands of years. If the present trends of accelerated glacier thawing continue, this bank account eventually would become empty. The Intergovernmental Panel on Climate Change has expressed regret for wildly exaggerating the Himalayan glacier retreat and making an unsubstantiated claim that the "likelihood" of these glaciers "disappearing by 2035 and perhaps sooner is very high."[52] But several studies, international as well as Chinese, have pointed to accelerated glacier thawing in the Himalayas and the Tibetan highlands. According to one study, the Tibetan glacier thawing in the 1990s alone resulted in a 5.5 percent increase in river runoff in northwestern China.[53] Another study, conducted by the Remote Sensing Department of the government-run China Aero Geophysical Survey, warned that the Tibetan and Himalayan glaciers could be reduced by nearly a third by 2050 and up to half by 2090, seriously depleting Tibet's water resources.[54] The *China Glacier Inventory* of the Chinese Academy of Sciences has recorded a decrease in the area and mass of the plateau's glaciers.[55]

Various scientific studies have underscored the link between the ecological health of Tibet and the water-related interests of Asian societies, including the stability of the monsoonal cycle and weather patterns. In a sense, sustainably managing Tibet's key strategic resource—freshwater—is critical to Asia's long-term economic growth and security. Indeed, the Tibetan Plateau symbolizes that a sustainable Asian order has to be built on a balance among the market, culture, and nature so that Asia can address its development, energy, and security needs. The imperative to forge such a balance is also being highlighted by the spreading desertification, grassland degradation, and water scarcity in China proper.[56] State policies are beginning to export China's water and environmental problems to the Tibetan Plateau. Even as China remains unmindful of the wider environmental impact of its water projects and mineral resources exploitation in pristine areas, such activities are beginning to have transboundary effects.

With Tibet locked behind an iron curtain, the economies and cultures of the entire Himalayan region have been isolated and weakened, whereas historically the Himalayan communities were closely integrated. Chinese policies continue to promote the economic marginalization of the Tibetan people and the Sinicization of Tibet's environment, to the detriment of the wider region's ecological well-being. A resolution of the Tibet issue through a China-initiated process of reconciliation and healing, and environmentally conscious Chinese policies, have become necessary to help protect Asia's "water tower." Otherwise, the 2 billion Asian users of waters flowing in from the Tibetan Plateau are certain to confront a serious crisis.

In this light, Tibet could well determine whether we will see an Asia where states act as "responsible stakeholders" in the international system or an Asia that becomes an arena of old-style, balance-of-power politics. The choice, in other words, is between a stable, peaceful Asia that expands its economic and cultural renaissance and an Asia racked by great-power rivalries and murky hydropolitics.

THE TANGIBLE IMPACT ON NATURAL ECOSYSTEMS

The Tibet issue has been presented more often than not in the international literature in political or cultural terms, with the Chinese government and ethnic Tibetans supposed to be the principal players. But the Tibet issue is much larger and more fundamental: It is about Asia's water and climate security and its ecological interests. It also is about access to vital resources. Fundamentally, it is about securing Asia's future.

The nature-friendly Tibetan way of life had helped preserve the plateau's pristine environment through the centuries. Conservation actually is embedded in Tibetan culture, with plants regarded as medicinal or spiritual, or both. Mountains and glaciers, for their part, are revered by the Tibetans as embodiments of deities and spirits. Tibetans "who inadvertently remove material from a *yul-lha* (divine) habitat have an opportunity to make amends," such as by replanting trees that have been felled, thus putting a cultural premium on maintaining balance with the natural ecosystems.[57]

The sacredness or taboo associated with particular species of trees or with specific mountains, valleys, rivers, caves, and lakes greatly promoted nature conservation. Tibetan Buddhism, for example, contributed to the preservation of aquatic life by frowning upon the eating of fish. But the demographic transformation of the plateau under Chinese rule, along with the environmentally unsustainable exploitation of its mineral and water resources, have disturbed the region's ecological stability and endangered the survival of many plant and animal species. Han settlers have hunted wildlife for meat and for the lucrative profits from trade in animal parts and products.

Land transformation through deforestation, the elimination of grasslands, and the introduction of Western-style agriculture, along with the impact of water mega-projects, are leading to high rates of loss of genetic variability and the extinction of species on the Tibetan Plateau. Human alterations of aquatic biological systems, for example, are causing the demise of native fish. In addition, the introduction of nonindigenous plant species by Han settlers in Tibet has created another threat in the form of "biological invasion." Such invasions by alien species can upset ecosystem processes, degrade biological diversity, and affect the health of local human populations and other species. The large-scale influx of Han settlers is by itself affecting Tibet's fragile ecosystems and, along with the role of commercial harvesters, loggers, and hunters, leading to habitat loss. The human-induced changes "not only impact local climate and environment, but also have important hydrological implications for the rivers which originate from the plateau."[58]

China's water and other engineering megaprojects on the Tibet Plateau promise to have ripple effects far into future and potentially alter regional ecosystems forever. No independent studies are available on whether China's atmospheric nuclear tests—carried out at the next-door Lop Nur site in Xinjiang between October 1964 and October 1980—caused any lasting damage to the core of Tibet's water reserves: the glaciers and the permafrost. Tibet's ice fields yield the dry-season runoff for the transnational rivers and for China's own two main rivers, the Yangtze and the Yellow. A total of twenty-three atmospheric nuclear tests were conducted by China, with the yield of the largest one in November 1976 measuring 4 megatons.[59] But suspicions that China was storing or disposing of nuclear waste on the Tibetan Plateau were confirmed by a 1995 Xinhua report about a radioactive dump in the Haibei Tibetan Autonomous Prefecture.[60]

Haibei actually was the site of China's oldest nuclear-weapons complex, the "Ninth Academy," also known as the Lake Kokonor complex. Located 16 kilometers from the Tibetan Plateau's largest lake, Kokonor (Ngonpo Tso), the complex designed China's first fission warhead and hydrogen bomb. Before it was shut down in 1987, the US Defense Intelligence Agency called it China's leading nuclear-weapons research and development complex and a "major weapons fabrication center as well."[61] Haibei prefecture and a couple of other places in Qinghai Province, carved out of Tibet's Amdo Region, have been identified as China's major nuclear deployment and storage sites.[62]

Several studies, including one by the Chinese Academy of Sciences, have documented the growing threat to Tibet's freshwater reserves from human activity, ranging from mining and manufacturing pollution to deforestation, which is promoting soil erosion, sedimentation in lakes and reservoirs, and the degradation of watershed areas. Chinese water projects and other developmental work, coupled with the demographic changes resulting from a continuing Han influx, are upsetting the fine balance between soil, water, and plant species. Reliable downriver water flows thus are in danger of being seriously upset. As Michael Zhao and Orville Schell have pointed out, "Over the next 25 years, 'the Roof of the World,' where most of Asia's great rivers find their headwaters, could well deliver an ecological crisis to Asia's billions of people. With glaciers melting away faster than anyone predicted, the people of China, South Asia and Southeast Asia are confronting the prospect of diminished water resources. For, while irregular water flows may be accelerated in the near term by the melting ice, the long-term flows would be diminished."[63]

The thawing of Tibet's permafrost represents one symbol of the impact of human activity on ecosystems. When the top layer of permafrost melts, it affects the subsoil water supply, influencing, in turn, water levels in lakes and wetlands and also contributing to shrinking grasslands. Tibet's permafrost is said to be warming faster than anywhere else on the planet, other than the poles. With the mean annual surface temperature warming, and temperatures at 20-meter depth having increased by an average of 0.2 to 0.3 degrees Celsius in the period since 1990, the permafrost on the Tibetan Plateau is set to degrade and shrink, according to a study funded by the China Natural Science Foundation and the Lanzhou Institute of Glaciology and Geocryology.[64] Another study by two Chinese experts has identified permafrost degradation as "one of the main causes responsible for a dropping groundwater table at the source areas of the Yangtze River and Yellow River," resulting, in turn, in the lowering of lake-water levels, the drying of wetlands, and the shrinking of grasslands.[65]

The mid-2006 opening of the China–Tibet railroad, while facilitating the exploitation of the plateau's natural resources, has exposed the fragile regional ecology to accelerated human alterations of the natural environment. Ranking as the highest railroad in the world, with its uppermost point more than 5 kilometers above sea level, it cuts through 550 kilometers of permafrost to link the Tibetan capital with China's national railway network. China first took its national railroad network to the northern Tibetan Plateau, completing the railway from the Qinghai city of Siling (Xining in Chinese) to Gormu (Golmud) in 1984, before extending the line southward to Lhasa. Since then, China has not only built a second Siling–Gormu railroad but is also expanding the railway from Lhasa to the Himalayan frontiers in an inverted "Y" shape—with one spur running to Shigatse (Xigaze) city near the border with Nepal, and another line to reach a remote water-rich prefecture adjoining India's Arunachal Pradesh state.[66] All the railroads in Tibet pass through ecologically sensitive zones. For example, the 253-kilometer railroad from Lhasa to Shigatse—seat of the Panchen Lama's Tashilhumpu Monastery—has been routed through natural reserves.

In areas on the Tibetan Plateau where the permafrost has been disturbed by human activity, such as the railroads, the rate of warming of the frozen soil is 0.6 degrees Celsius, or double what it is in unspoiled places, according to a United Nations Environment Program report.[67] The high-altitude frozen soil on the plateau comprises the largest continuous subarctic permafrost region on the planet, and the railroad-caused land transformation has exposed it to greater effects of climate warming. Indeed, the $6.2 billion Gormu–Lhasa Railroad, by adding warmth, threatens to slowly destabilize its own track's frozen underpinnings, although Chinese engineers, drawing on techniques used in Serbian and Alaskan projects, have drilled ammonia-filled steel tubes (called "thermosiphons") along the sides of the tracks to refrigerate vulnerable parts of the soil.[68] Tibet's permafrost is different from the frozen soils elsewhere: It is characterized by intense salinity, which, along with the plateau's relatively higher temperature, diminishes its capacity to endure thermal disturbances.

Human-made environmental change already has started affecting the Tibetans' traditional nomadic way of life. The quality of summer pastures is of prime importance for "animal husbandry on the Tibetan Plateau because during the winter when the grass is covered by snow, livestock must survive by burning fat stored during the short months when the pasture is lush. However, if this cycle of feast and famine (to which animals on the plateau have uniquely adapted) is disrupted, it affects not only the animals, but the lives of the nomads themselves, whose subsistence is entirely dependent on their herds."[69] Projects-tied land transformation and other ecological alterations, along with changing weather patterns, are shrinking the size and quality of grasslands, promoting dust storms as far south of the plateau as Lhasa and aiding the growth of desertification. This, in turn, is forcing an increasing number of traditional nomads to move to towns in search of menial jobs.

In the name of halting shrinking of grasslands, local Chinese authorities, in fact, are moving increasing numbers of nomadic herdsmen into new "resettlement towns," endangering the Tibetans' centuries-old tradition of herding yak, cattle, and sheep across the plateau's grasslands. The government-run Qinghai–Tibet Plateau Study Institute has reported that the loss of grasslands on the plateau since the beginning of the 1990s has reached an alarming rate of 0.725 percent a year, "or more than 1,500 square kilometers of grassland being reduced to bare land" annually.[70] Herd levels also have continued to fall on the plateau.

Water Contamination by Ore Tailings

Water is not the only resource on the Tibet Plateau that China is seeking to exploit. The unbridled exploitation of Tibet's mineral resources is contributing to the contamination of river waters through tailings and land erosion. There is a big store of valuable minerals on the Roof of the World. In fact, through its control of the Tibetan Plateau, China has access to 126 different minerals, including its largest reserves of copper, iron, chromites, boron, corundum, crystal, sulfur, magnesite, lithium, and mica. The plateau also has significant deposits of uranium, gold, molybdenum, zinc, and lead, as well as smaller reserves of hydrocarbons, silver, and cesium.

Furthermore, through its myriad saline lakes, Tibet has become the principal global source of lithium. As a result, China has emerged as the world's largest producer and exporter of lithium-ion batteries. Because lithium powers laptop computers, cellphones, personal electronic gadgets like iPods, and other high-end technology, there is a little bit of Tibet in the devices we commonly use. Indeed, the next-generation plug-in hybrid and all-electric automobiles are nearly all being developed with lithium technology. Tibet's 247-square-kilometer Chabyer (Zabuye) bittern-salt lake, located at an elevation of 4,421 meters on the outer Himalayan rim not far from Mount Kailash, is the single largest source of lithium for China—and the world. The Chinese railroad to Tibet—equipped to handle 150,000 tons of cargo monthly, with the freight-carrying capacity being further expanded and the railway itself being extended toward the Himalayan frontiers— has helped boost the extraction and transportation of Tibet's mineral resources, whose value in 1995 was officially estimated at 650 billion yuan, or $100 billion.[71]

Since then, China has made discoveries of vast new mineral deposits on the plateau, listing more than 3,000 proven reserves of as many as 102 types of minerals.[72] According to the findings of a seven-year, $44-million survey by China's Ministry of Land and Resources—which was unveiled soon after the opening of the railroad—Tibet, among other minerals, has more than 1 billion tons of untapped high-grade iron ore, up to 40 million tons of copper, and 40 million tons of lead and zinc. The previously unknown deposits of a number of valuable minerals, along with the introduction of the railway, have helped transform the Tibetan Plateau into one of the most important mining centers in Asia. The Chinese government has designated at least nine special mining zones across the Tibet Autonomous Region, or the rump Tibet, as it openly seeks to make this region a raw-material appendage of the national economy.

Rich gold deposits located in northern Tibet's Chokle Namgyel Mountains and in the Tibetan prefectures of Gansu and Sichuan provinces have been opened to development, including by foreign mining companies. On the plateau's eastern rim, there also have been finds of rare-earth elements, which are vital for a wide range of green energy technologies and military applications and whose global supply China dominates. Deng Xiaoping remarked in 1992 that while "the Middle East has oil, China has rare-earth minerals," implying that Beijing could leverage international supply of rare earths the way the Organization of the Petroleum Exporting Countries has sought to do with oil.

In fact, after first making local mining and refining of rare earths unprofitable in a number of overseas markets by flooding the world with cheap exports since the 1980s, China in recent years has tried to gain enhanced leverage over other major economies by limiting exports of rare earths—seventeen minerals critical in the manufacture of a vast array of products ranging from missiles and lasers to computers and energy-efficient light bulbs. It is not the Tibetan Plateau but another minority homeland, Inner Mongolia, however, that is the largest source of rare earths for China, which—while controlling more than 95 percent of the global production—employed an unannounced embargo of such exports to Japan as a coercive-diplomacy tool after the Japanese arrest of a Chinese fishing-trawler captain in September 2010 renewed tensions between the two countries over the disputed Senkaku/Diaoyu Islands. By resorting to economic warfare, even in the face of an insignificant provocation, China has involuntarily served notice on the other major economies to find ways to reduce their reliance on imports of Chinese rare earths.[73]

Moves by Western companies to cash in on the new mining opportunities on the Tibetan Plateau even before the railroad was opened prompted the exiled Tibetan leader, the Dalai Lama, to use an open letter in 2003 to say, "I appeal to all foreign mining companies and their shareholders thinking about working in Tibet to consider carefully about the ethical values when embarking on such ventures." That appeal was followed in 2004 by the "Guidelines for International Development Projects and Sustainable Development in Tibet," in which the Tibetan government in exile declared to foreign donors, lenders, and investors that Tibetans do not support any development that degrades the environment and "deprives future generations of Tibetans" of natural resources.[74] The railroad and the opening of five high-altitude airports in Tibet, however, have helped attract more interest from Western mining firms. In 2010 alone, China opened a civilian airport at a height of 4,274 meters in Ngari, in southwestern Tibet, and another one at Shigatse, Tibet's second main city.

Chinese state-owned firms, for their part, have moved aggressively to establish new mines on the plateau. Major production of copper, for example, has commenced at several places after that malleable metal was found at 329 different sites in Tibet, with the Qulong Mine alone containing proven reserves of more than 8.95 million tons.[75] Qulong is part of a rich, 400-kilometer copper belt discovered close to the Brahmaputra (Yarlung Tsangpo) Gorge, which boasts Asia's largest concentration of freshwater resources. Although the copper mines in this belt began operations only in recent years, tailings already have started polluting local water resources. In many mining operations, harsh chemicals are used to recover valuable minerals from the extracted ore. A by-product of ore separation is tailings—a mixture of water and insoluble, finely ground rock from which most of the minerals of value have been removed. Because leaching of gold, uranium, silver, and copper ores with arsenic, cyanide, or sulfuric acid is common, with the slurry then pumped into leaky artificial ponds with earthen dams, the tailings left over from such operations are toxic. Large-scale Chinese ore processing in Tibet now not only appropriates vast quantities of local water but has also opened aquatic and terrestrial ecosystems to degradation.

The Hydrological Impact of Deforestation

Continued deforestation on the Tibetan Plateau is a major ecological concern because it is upsetting the water-runoff regime and reducing natural habitats and native species. Natural forest cover in the Tibetan watersheds is indispensable to the maintenance of the hydrological integrity and ecological health of the major river systems originating there. The forests on the plateau serve key functions, ranging from controlling stream flows and regulating climate to providing a major carbon sink and sheltering biodiversity. Indeed, most forests are located on the remote, steep slopes of river valleys in the plateau's water-rich southern and eastern belts.

Such forest cover, however, is being depleted on the plateau, including in riparian buffer zones, although natural vegetation in such buffers is invaluable as a sediment trap and river-bank stabilizer. The term "riparian buffer" refers to lands adjacent to rivers where the native vegetation—from trees and shrubs to flowers and grasses—is strongly influenced by the presence of water. Riparian vegetation ensures clean, cool water, provides valuable habitat for wildlife, controls floodwaters, and filters pollutants. Removal of such vegetation degrades water quality; reduces wildlife and fish populations; causes stream-bank erosion, leading to wide, shallow and slow-flowing rivers; and diminishes the water-storage capacity of the riparian area, including groundwater recharge. Yet, as one study has pointed out, there is "a disturbing deforestation trend" in some Tibetan regions—with serious implications for freshwater reserves and stream-flow regimes and the survival of endemic species—"due to overcutting, inaccurate government reporting of forest cover, and poor land-use decisions."[76]

On the Tibetan Plateau, deforestation is a problem that extends from catchment areas to riparian plains. Traditional pastoralism, with herdsmen turning forested areas into pastures, and the felling of tress by locals for firewood and construction timber have contributed to the problem. However, it is the commercial mining of Tibetan forest resource for shipment to mainland China that has led to significant forest-cover depletion. Deforested lands in Qinghai Province have turned into desert. The extremely biodiverse tropical rainforests in the plateau's southeastern river valleys, including in eastern Kham, have also been targeted by commercial loggers.[77] In south-central Tibet, vast tracts of forests and scrubs have turned into open steppe.

The Chinese government has been slow to respond to the large-scale deforestation that is threatening Tibet's biological highways, the river valleys. Even if it has not been able to effectively enforce its directives, Beijing at least has banned logging around the primary sources of China's two main rivers, the Yangtze and the Yellow, and initiated the "Natural Forests Conservation Program" in their upper reaches on the Tibetan Plateau.[78] By contrast, feeble attempts have been made to halt logging in the upper catchments of the rivers that flow from the plateau to other countries.

Starting in the Mao era, the Tibetan Plateau was made the major source of timber supply to mainland China. A Chinese official estimate in 1995 put the size of forest reserves in Tibet at 7.2 million hectares, down from 13.6 million hectares in 1985 and 25.2 million hectares in 1959. Although no official figures are available after 1995, deforestation remains a serious problem in riparian corridors and elsewhere on the plateau, even as the Chinese government has initiated a reforestation program across the country. The film *Cutting Down Tibet*, made secretly by a Tibetan and telecast by the BBC in 1996, showed large-scale logging in southern

Tibet and trucks loaded with giant trunks up to 3 meters in diameter, indicating that the operations enjoyed the sanction of local government and military authorities. Between 1950, when China forcibly absorbed Tibet, and the early 1990s, the Tibetan Plateau was denuded of most of its natural forests, as the satellite-data maps in figure 3.1 show. What the maps reveal is that in about four decades under Chinese rule, the plateau was stripped of its largest forest resource: the boreal coniferous forests in the southeast. Land transformation through conversion of forests and grasslands to cropland, urban housing, and other uses has continued on the plateau beyond the early 1990s, according to one study that employed high-resolution satellite imagery from the Landsat Thematic Mapper between 1990 and 2000 to look at the entire territory of China.[79]

Frequent flooding in India's Arunachal Pradesh State and in Bangladesh, located farthest downstream, has been linked to deforestation in southeastern Tibet, whose premium forests traditionally boasted an outstandingly high stock density, with the majority of trees more than two centuries old. This region has the main concentration of virgin forests still intact in China. The hydrological effects of the deforestation there actually extend to the basins of other rivers like the Salween, the Mekong, and the Yangtze that flow through the southeastern Tibetan Plateau, a mountainous region with an elevation between 3,000 and 7,000 meters above sea level that comprises northern Yunnan, western Sichuan, southwest Gansu, southeast Qinghai, and the southeast Tibet Autonomous Region.

One scientific study has found that the deforestation in this region carries two major hydrological implications extending beyond the plateau. First, it induces decreased transpiration (evaporation of water from plants) but greater precipitation on the plateau, with the loss of forest cover possibly leading to increased runoff into the rivers and consequent downstream flooding. Second, it has a broader impact on the Asian climate, even as the Tibetan Plateau on the whole becomes warmer and wetter in summer, and colder in fall and winter.[80]

Rates of deforestation have lowered in the twenty-first century, with the Chinese government also undertaking a tree-plantation program. Reforestation in Tibet, however, remains small compared with the number of original trees being cut down. The planting of fast-growing poplars and willows in deforested river valleys, though a welcome step, is not an answer to the loss of primary forests, especially because the natural regeneration of forests is a slow process and the reforestation of boreal coniferous forests has been found wanting. Although vegetation restoration with indigenous tree species is difficult, the focus ought to be on recreating natural ecosystems, to the extent possible. The authorities also have done little to put into action sustainable practices for forest resource management, including enforcing rules for the timber industry. However, given the dramatic increase in wood demand in mainland China, the timber supply from Tibet, Manchuria, and other remote regions now is being augmented by major imports, especially from Russia, Malaysia, and Indonesia.

FIGURE 3.1   Deforestation on the Tibetan Plateau under Chinese Rule

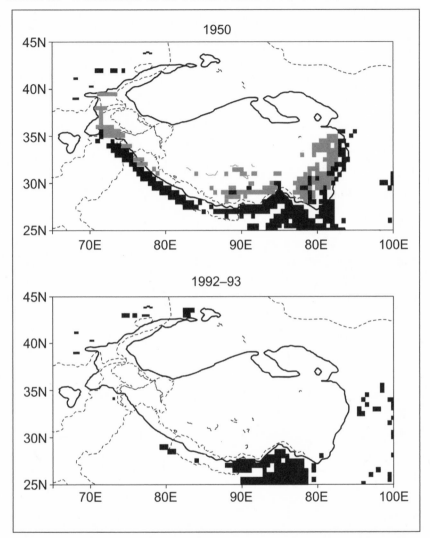

Note: Whereas the 1950 drawing is based on the International Satellite Land Surface Climatology Project Initiative II data collection, the 1992–93 sketch employs 1-kilometer Advanced Very High Resolution Radiometer data released by the US Geological Survey. In the maps, light gray denotes boreal coniferous forests, while dark gray represents warm broadleaf forests.

Source: Earth Interactions 11, no. 15 (September 2007).

The ecological conservation of Tibet—including the protection of its hydrological systems, biological resources, glacial and climatic conditions, and virgin forests—is vital to the sustenance of both human populations and the extremely fertile agricultural lands that have evolved downstream through river-water flows from the Tibetan Plateau. In fact, the Tibetan Plateau constitutes a life support system for much of the planet, with the tree line there extending to elevations up to 4,850 meters—the highest in the world. Forest ecosystems have evolved on the plateau with such an adaptive capacity that juniper forests, for example, manage to thrive even in conditions of modest precipitation with the annual mean temperature touching the freezing point. Junipers are the religious landmarks of Tibetan Buddhism, and the "largest stands of juniper trees are even pilgrimage sites," including the Reting Forest, north of Lhasa.[81]

More specifically, safeguarding Tibet's fluvial and forest ecosystems and mountain biodiversity is essential for the supply of clean water, including for aquatic life. For decades, the Chinese authorities looked at the plateau's forests merely as a source of timber, ignoring their key hydrological functions. As a result, forest ecosystems have been seriously compromised. Anthropogenic land changes in the Himalayas and the Tibetan highlands directly affect hydrological-cycle intensity and erode the stability of the Asian monsoons. A good vegetative cover in upper catchments is indispensable to soil erosion control so as to ensure the stability of river directions and flows, to moderate flooding, and to allow China and the countries located downstream to build and sustain greater hydropower-generating capacity. The linkage between vegetation, soil, and water is central to the principal hydrologic unit—the watershed, which controls the water yield for river systems. Preserved natural forests in catchment areas help guarantee clean, pure water. In a regional hydrology dominated by the monsoons and international rivers, the depletion of natural forests on the Tibetan Plateau portends long-term ecological and hydrological ill effects.

Vanishing Species

Besides its rich water and mineral resources, the Tibetan Plateau is known for its endangered and endemic species of animals, plants, and algae. The immense biodiversity of its forests "contains a great variety of genetic resources which need to be protected for the future."[82] Commercial harvesters and hunters, however, are having a major impact on the biodiversity in the plateau, where before the Chinese takeover a strict ban on hunting was in force.

The region's rich biological resources include many high-altitude species and genetically distinct populations and a range of wildlife habitats. The wide diversity of elevation and climatic conditions on the plateau has given rise to a varied and complex range of natural habitats for flora and fauna. Significantly, more than four-fifths of the Tibetan plant and animal species are concentrated in less than one-fifth of the plateau—the water-rich southern and southeastern areas along the borders with India, Nepal, Bhutan, and Burma. Through the centuries, this region has served as one of the main global centers of species formation and differentiation.[83] The approximately eighty natural reserves designated by the Chinese government on the plateau are concentrated in this region.

The plateau is the source of prized medicinal plants, including dozens of rare species, such as the Tibetan snow lotus, which grows high up in the mountains and is known in traditional Chinese medicine as *xue lian* and in Tibetan medicine as *ganglha metok* ("glacier deity"). Indeed, some 2,600 varieties of medicinal herbs used in the traditional Indian, Chinese, and Tibetan medical systems are derived from plants grown on the plateau, including rhododendron, high-mountain rhubarb, saffron, bottle brush tree, Himalayan alpine serratula, and hellebore. In the Tibetan school of medicine, the most commonly used herbs are classified under sixty different heads.[84] Some exotic flora found in the West—like saxifrage, Tibetan hellebore (*helleborus thibetanus*), and rhododendron—were originally taken from the Tibetan Plateau by European and American explorers in the nineteenth and twentieth centuries. Tibet's southeastern region actually has some two hundred species of rhododendron. One of Tibet's best-known flowers, a rhododendron known as Meconopsis—a type of Himalayan poppy—is also a medicinal plant. The pea-sized white bulbs of a Tibetan plant of the Liliaceae family, *fritillaria cirrhosa*, known in Tibet as *pema*, are used to make the *yao jiu* medicinal schnapps in China. Tibet's wild plants also are valued as potential material for genetic engineering.

Although conservation is integral to the Tibetan culture, the growing demand for Tibetan flowers, tubers, and other plant parts in China for medicine and also as table delicacies (e.g., lily bulbs) has brought a number of species to the brink of extinction, while some others already have vanished. This has reinforced the imperative to harvest plants in a sustainable manner. There is also another lurking danger: A study by Chinese experts has concluded that "because of the long-term influence from Han community's culture and way of life, traditional Tibetan medicinal culture is facing the danger of dying out, which would be a great loss not only to the Tibetan cultural wealth, but also to the great culture diversity of China."[85]

The Tibetan Plateau is home to the majority of the world's black-necked cranes (known as *trung trung kaynak* in Tibetan, and among the world's most engaging birds), and it is also the abode of some 70 percent of all bird families found in China, including raptors, white storks, Crested Serpent eagles, wild swans, parrot bills, large-billed bush warblers, Blyth's kingfishers, ruddy shelducks, shorebirds, brown-chested jungle flycatchers, redstarts, finches, grey-sided thrushes, wagtails, chickadees, bearded vultures, woodpeckers, nuthatches, brow-necked toucan, and kestrel. As a Chinese government website acknowledges, Tibet, with its unique natural environment and traditional customs emphasizing conservation, has provided "an ideal physical and social environment" for the breeding and inhabitation of rare species.[86]

Although the Chinese authorities have sought to protect seventy-two rare bird species on the central Tibetan Plateau (the so-called Tibet Autonomous Region), some varieties of birds are becoming hard to find, including the golden pheasant, which has been heavily hunted for food. In the case of the cranes that have black necks but vanilla-white stomachs, human encroachment on their nesting and wintering grounds has driven them to near extinction. A train station, for example, has been built within the Gulu wetlands, a pristine breeding ground for the black-necked cranes and also for the yellow ducks, which lead a couples-only existence to the point that if one partner dies, the other commits suicide.

Tibet's forests, mountains, and steppes also are rich in wildlife, including the statuesque *chiru* (or Tibetan antelope), white-lipped deer, Tibetan gazelle, argali sheep, kiang (or large wild ass), wild yak, red *ghoral* (or small goat-antelope), Asiatic black bear, giant panda, red panda, snow leopard, wolf, wild Bactrian camel, snow monkey, Himalayan black bear, and takin ("its face a peculiar profile reminiscent of its closest relative, the musk ox").[87] The Chinese government has sought to shield some 125 fauna species in Tibet by listing them as rare—including the snow leopard, Tibetan antelope, black-necked crane, wild yak, musk deer, and snow chicken—yet it has failed to put an end to the poaching that is threatening to wipe out endangered animals.[88] Worse still, traditional Chinese medicine uses deer antlers, musk, bones, and other parts of wild animals. And the meat of the Tibetan antelope, blue sheep, wild yak, and gazelle are much-sought gastronomic delicacies in China, Hong Kong, Taiwan, and elsewhere.

Trade in animal parts and products has continued to thrive, at times with the involvement or connivance of local government officials. For instance, chiru antelopes, native to the vast, remote Tibetan steppes and prized for their wool or *shahtoosh*, have been identified as an endangered species under the Convention on the International Trade in Endangered Species of Wild Fauna and Flora since 1979 because of still-unchecked poaching.[89] The poachers, many of them Huis or Muslim Hans, make their money by smuggling *shahtoosh* (or "king of wool" in Persian) to India and the West, where demand is high among the wealthy. Made from the fleecy underwool of the chirus' neck, the amazingly soft and warm *shahtoosh* is turned into 2-meter-long shawls that weigh just 160 grams but cost several times more than equivalent gold in weight. Two to three chirus have to be skinned to make one *shahtoosh* shawl, which is so fine and light that it actually can pass through a finger ring. The wool is often smuggled from Tibet to the Indian state of Jammu and Kashmir, where it is woven into shawls and even scarves and then exported illegally to the West.[90] The chiru population in Tibet has shrunk from several million in the early twentieth century to as low as 65,000 today.

Another endangered animal, the panda, has become so synonymous with China—which has made this cuddly-looking creature its national mascot—that not many know that it is native to the Tibetan Plateau. The plateau actually is home to both the giant panda (a large mammal with bold black-and-white markings, including black patches over the eyes) and the red panda (which is just the size of a house cat but with a long, bushy tail). The red pandas, living in the mountains of the Tibetan Plateau, Nepal, Bhutan, Indian Himalayan region, and northern Burma, are endangered because deforestation and the spread of agriculture have shrunk their natural habitat. The giant pandas, native to the high-mountain bamboo forests of the southeastern Tibetan Plateau and the adjacent region in central China, are seriously in danger of extinction, with only about a thousand left in the wild.

Yet, ever since Chairman Mao famously gifted a pair of giant pandas to US president Richard Nixon in 1972, China has made these oversized, bamboo-eating, furry mammals a part of its diplomatic outreach, giving away giant pandas as gifts to select foreign governments. As part of its "rent-a-panda" program, China also allows zoos around the world to "borrow" pandas for exhibit by paying handsome rental fees, underscoring how the "panda has become a lucrative commodity."[91] For example, Japan, which has a number of giant pandas in its zoos, is paying about $1 million a year for each pair on loan from China.

Beijing's panda diplomacy or rent-a-panda program, however, cannot obscure the panda politics between Tibet and China, which is exemplified whenever Tibetan activists, wearing panda costumes and panda hats, distribute flyers outside zoos in other countries saying that the pandas exhibited there are from Tibet.[92] The largest natural habitat for giant pandas in China, the Wolong Nature Reserve, is located in what the Chinese government has designated as the Aba Tibetan-Qiang Autonomous Prefecture of Sichuan Province, in the southeastern corner of the Tibetan Plateau.

Yet another endangered animal, the snow leopard, which lives in the Himalayan region and other mountainous parts of Tibet, is hunted for its beautiful, warm fur, and—like another Asian big cat, the tiger—for its body parts, which are used in traditional Chinese medicine. The illegal trade in pelts and body parts, along with habitat loss and a decline in available prey, has left only a few thousand snow leopards in the wild in Tibet. Similarly, with tiger organs occupying a notable place in Chinese pharmacopoeia, the Bengal tiger, an important part of Indian tradition and lore, is falling victim to illegal hunting for body parts, despite China's trade ban since 1993.[93] Weaning many Chinese off a culinary taste for wildlife poses a separate challenge by itself, underscored by the popular joke the Chinese recite about their own dining preferences: "'Eat anything that flies except airplanes; eat anything with legs except the table."

The planet's high-altitude regions are richer in biodiversity than its lowlands and, therefore, hold prime conservation value. Tibet's abundant biodiversity, of course, is tied to its unique features, including its extremes of topographical relief. The abrupt variations in relief and altitude occurring over relatively short lateral distances have helped support a complex medley of topo-climates on the Tibetan Plateau, ranging from arid and tropical climates to temperate and arctic climates. The majority of Asia's biodiversity hot spots indeed are concentrated on the Tibetan Plateau, whose already-fragile ecosystems have come under assault from anthropogenic factors, including the influx of new Han settlers, the introduction of extractive industries, the initiation of large hydroengineering works, deforestation, water pollution, soil erosion, poor management of river basins, unsustainable agricultural practices, and vanishing aquatic, wildlife, and plant species.

Broader Effects

According to the ministerial declaration at the Second World Water Forum in The Hague in 2000, the world has "one common goal: to provide water security in the twenty-first century. This means ensuring that freshwater, coastal and related ecosystems are protected and improved; that sustainable development and political stability are promoted; that every person has access to enough safe water at an affordable cost to lead a healthy and productive life; and that the vulnerable are protected from the risks of water-related hazards."[94] The call for preserving the integrity of fluvial and other ecosystems through sustainable water resources management is especially relevant for the Tibetan Plateau, where ecological changes are occurring due to the reckless exploitation of Tibet's mineral wealth and water and land resources.[95] Land-cover changes arising from deforestation, the transformation of grasslands into new cropland, and large-scale mining have contributed to habitat destruction, serious river-sedimentation problems, and watershed degradation.

In fact, the Tibetan Plateau has been warming at an accelerated rate of 0.16 degrees Celsius per decade, with its winter temperatures going up even faster—by 0.32 degrees per decade.[96] In comparison, China's overall national average temperature rise has registered 0.05 to 0.08 degrees every ten years.[97] What is even more disturbing is that the linear rates of temperature rise for the Tibetan Plateau are higher than those for other areas in the same latitudinal zone, underscoring the manner human alterations of ecosystems are adversely affecting conditions in Tibet. It also brings out that with its sensitive ecology, the plateau is more easily falling prey to human-made environmental change and global warming.

Yet another indicator of this growing susceptibility is the recorded decrease in the length of the snow-cover season at elevations between 4,000 to 6,000 meters above sea level across the Tibetan Plateau, along with the earlier snowmelt at elevations up to 5,500 meters above sea level.[98] Such changing patterns attenuate the regional albedo (or the degree to which the incoming sunlight is reflected back to space) and possibly enhance the rapidity and spatial scale of the Himalayan glacier retreat. The sun's radiation reflects off the bright white snow and escapes back out to space, which helps to cool the temperature. But when the albedo effect diminishes, more radiation from the sun gets absorbed regionally, which raises Asian temperatures. Although the decline in the total surface area of the Himalayan glaciers in Tibet and India has been well documented by satellite imagery—as available, for example, from the Advanced Spaceborne Thermal Emission and Reflection Radiometer (known as ASTER), Indian Remote Sensing (IRS) satellites,

China–Brazil Earth Resources Satellite (CBERS), and Landsat Thematic Mapper—scientific evidence indicates that the glacier retreat is occurring right across the Tibetan Plateau and at a rate unmatched elsewhere in the world.[99]

The impact of demographic transformation on the ecosystems cannot be underestimated. Of all the regions in the world that are above an elevation of 2,500 meters, the Tibetan Plateau is now the most populated region, thanks largely to China's "Go West" Han migration campaign. Demographically, what Beijing is pursuing in Tibet, according to critics, is not ethnic cleansing but ethnic drowning, with the state-sponsored "Go West" campaign tantamount to an attempt to annihilate the distinct Tibetan culture and identity.[100] Under the population-transfer policy designed to gain tight control over a restive region, vantage locations in towns were cleared of their Tibetan residents and new modern homes, shops and offices were built there for Han settlers. The Chinese part of any town in Tibet usually straddles or overlooks the Tibetans' cultural sites and dilapidated quarters. The incontrovertible fact is that the still-continuing influx of Han migrants, the surging number of tourists from mainland China, and the growing number of resource development projects on the plateau are altering Tibet irrevocably. An old saying that China's prosperity depends on the happiness of Tibet has been turned on its head, with China pursuing its economic growth and security in such a way as to seek Chinese happiness in Tibet through greater ethnic and economic colonization.

The distinctive cultural traditions that helped protect the natural environment have given way to the Communist system's conviction that taming nature is essential for China's rapid development and to transform Tibet from what officials say was a state of "backwardness." Human activities, including engineering projects, have become the principal driver in altering the Tibetan Plateau's climate and natural ecosystems and undermining its species diversity. For example, one study by four Chinese scientists using remote-sensing and climate data found that "human activities have adversely affected" the huge, lower-altitude grassland ecosystem on the northern Tibetan Plateau.[101] In fact, an extensive study carried out over several years by a group of scientists with China's state-run Qinghai–Tibet Plateau Study Institute has warned that the plateau "faces serious ecological threat" and that "its environment will continue to deteriorate because of climate change, overgrazing and increasing human activities."[102] The changes to natural ecosystems and climate in Tibet directly affect much of Asia's water resources because of the plateau's role as freshwater supplier to other societies and as rainmaker.[103]

The degradation or impairment of natural ecosystems indeed undermines the sustainability of freshwater resources. Ecosystem and landscape changes that directly or indirectly impinge on the long-term integrity and sustainability of water resources, according to the United Nations, include deforestation, the conversion of grasslands or other natural terrestrial ecosystems to farmland or grazing land, urbanization (if it leads to changes in water runoff patterns and to pollution), wetlands removal, new transportation routes cutting through protected or ecologically sensitive areas, and mining in quarries or large-scale open pits.[104] All such land-cover changes on the Tibetan Plateau have become commonplace under Chinese rule, even as the government in Beijing has begun to recognize in more recent years the importance of environmental protection and conservation. Even the rapid rise of China's mineral-water industry has been at the expense of Tibet's natural ecosystems. The industry, with its sales of bottled water skyrocketing, sources its water in Tibet by siphoning the runoff from glaciers that normally would flow for "ecosystem services" extending from the recharging of wetlands to the sustenance of biodiversity.

Excess sedimentation in streams often results from land-use changes—including the removal of riparian vegetation—and poor agricultural practices. Today, the integrity of the major watersheds on the Tibetan Plateau has come under growing pressure due to upstream soil erosion, with the Chinese introduction of large-scale agriculture and the use of chemical fertilizers and pesticides leading to both surface attrition and water pollution problems. Agricultural practices in Tibet now extend beyond terracing, whose soil conservation worth is well known. The result is that sediment loads and pollutants from eroded watersheds threaten to affect river flows and aquatic life (including fisheries), and reduce water quality overall.

How ecosystem changes on the Tibetan Plateau can exact serious environmental costs far beyond is illustrated by the manner the damming of rivers upstream and other water diversion is affecting China's own megadeltas, which are the centers of economic boom. The nutrients and minerals received by oceans from the rivers are critical to marine life. But with the nutrient supplies to many Asian megadeltas being reduced by the upstream construction of dams on rivers originating in the Tibetan Plateau, these delta regions, according to the Intergovernmental Panel on Climate Change, have become "much more vulnerable" to the effects of climate change and sea-level rise. Owing to such continued nonclimatic pressures, these Asian megadeltas are becoming "highly threatened by climate change, and responding to this threat will present important challenges."[105] Indeed, there already is sufficient evidence pointing to the "retreat of megadeltas fed by rivers originating from the Tibetan Plateau."[106] In some downstream basins, including within China, the upstream damming of rivers flowing out of the plateau has resulted in the loss of the yearly gift of highly fertile silt, which would be deposited on the plains by the natural flooding cycle. Farmers have sought to compensate for this loss through the increasing use of chemical fertilizers.

The Tibetan Plateau already has the dubious distinction of having the largest concentration of endangered river systems in the world.[107] As one observer has put it, "It was not so long ago that the Tibetan Plateau was seen as a region of little consequence, save to those few Western adventurers drawn to remote regions that the early-twentieth-century Swedish explorer Sven Hedin once called the 'white spaces' on the map. Today, these white spaces play a crucial role in Asia's ecology."[108] At stake are the integrity and sustainability of Asia's main watershed and river systems, as well as the regional precipitation, natural-water runoff, and climate regimes. Tibet's ecological crisis potentially affects the 2 billion people in Asia that rely on freshwater flows from sources located on the plateau.

WATER MEGAPROJECTS ON THE TIBETAN PLATEAU

When China annexed Tibet, little of the river waters were being consumed on the plateau itself. The "negligible utilization rates in Tibet meant that nearly all the water was transferred to the countries in downstream basins including India, Nepal, China, Bangladesh, Pakistan, Bhutan, Vietnam, Burma, Cambodia, Laos, and Thailand."[109] Now, with the river waters increasingly being diverted for electricity generation, irrigation, mining, and other economic activities on the plateau and with China significantly expanding its water infrastructure there and pursuing interriver and interbasin transfer projects, the transboundary implications of China's hold over Tibet are becoming stark. Because China cannot address the water stress in its heartland the way it meets its needs for other resources—through import deals clinched on the back of its rising economic and political clout—its planners have devised ambitious interriver and interbasin water transfer projects on the Tibetan Plateau, largely to redirect flows to the depleted Yellow River, which flows from the northeastern plateau across China into the Bohai Sea, the innermost bay of the Yellow Sea.

The growing number of Chinese megaprojects on international rivers on the plateau is contributing to making water a divisive issue in interstate relations in Asia. As one Chinese analyst has admitted, "China's water-supply crisis has taken on an international dimension, not only in respect of other countries affected by the pollution in China, but also in disputes over water resources."[110] A rapid expansion of hydropower capabilities and a further exploitation of the irrigation potential of rivers are key elements of China's fifty-year infrastructure development program launched in its western region in 1999. Water resources development on the plateau is tied also to publicly unveiled plans to take Tibetan waters to China's parched north. Even as new dams and reservoirs are being built or planned, the existing hydroengineering facilities have started affecting the hydrology of the rivers flowing out of the plateau and their sediment loads, besides promoting riparian-vegetative attrition and stream-bank erosion and disturbing or depleting aquatic life.

Since annexing Tibet, China has tried everything—from Tibet's cartographic dismemberment and rewriting Tibet's history, to altering the region's ethnic composition through large-scale Han migration and trying to systematically undermine Tibetan religious institutions. Half the traditional Tibetan region has been hived off from Tibet, leaving 60 percent of the Tibetans living outside the area that China now calls the Tibet Autonomous Region. Yet, given the Tibetan Plateau's status as Asia's freshwater repository, water supplier, and rainmaker, much more than Tibet's political future or religious autonomy hangs in the balance. With Asia's environmental security tied to the preservation of the fragile natural ecosystems of Tibet, the new megaprojects on the plateau to dam rivers or to divert river waters threaten to wreak lasting ecological damage.

The rivers originating on the Tibetan Plateau serve the largest and most densely populated region in the world. In mainland China, demands on water resources from both industry and agriculture have skyrocketed elevenfold since the Communist takeover. As water woes have aggravated in its north owing to environmentally unsustainable irrigation, water-intensive manufacturing, growing urban needs, and water contamination, China increasingly has sought to tap the bounteous water reserves on the Tibetan Plateau, with the third leg of the so-called Great South–North Water Transfer Project focused on Tibet. The Chinese hydroengineering projects on the plateau have a direct bearing on the quantity and quality of river-water flows to southern and southeastern Asian countries.

China has dammed every major river on the Tibetan Plateau—including the Mekong, the Salween, the Brahmaputra, the Yangtze, the Yellow, the Indus, the Sutlej, the Shweli and the Karnali. China has unveiled plans to dam the rivers that still remain free flowing, such as the Arun and the Subansiri (or Lorochu, which enters India's Arunachal Pradesh to drain into the Brahmaputra). A cascade of five major dams have been planned on the Arun near the Tibet–Nepal frontier, with the uppermost dam to be located at Kanggong and the lowest at Shali, almost on the international boundary. In addition to existing dams, a series of giant new dams are planned or under construction on the Mekong, the Salween, and the Brahmaputra. A large dam has already been built on the Indus near the town of Shiquanhe, in the southwestern Ngari Region bordering India, Nepal, and Xinjiang, whereas the major dam on the Karnali is located in Pulan County, home to Mount Kailash and Lake Mansarovar.

More significantly, China's water megaprojects have steadily been moving from the Han heartland to ethnically distinct lands—that is, from east to west—with dam-building works now increasingly concentrated in the minority provinces of Yunnan and the Tibet Autonomous Region along the southwestern belt with neighboring countries. The portion of Yunnan where dam-construction activity is concentrated is largely part of the Tibetan Plateau. The building of major new dams on the upper catchments of the Mekong and the Salween and on the middle reaches of the Brahmaputra attests to China's greater resource development focus on the Tibetan Plateau, especially its extraordinary water-rich southeastern region.

In fact, before the countries in the lower Mekong basin could realize the larger implications, China quietly went ahead and completed the 1,500-megawatt Manwan Dam on the Mekong in 1996 with little publicity. Manwan is located 100 kilometers south of Dali in Yunnan. More dams on the Mekong followed in quick succession: the 1,350-megawatt Dachaoshan, located in the Dachaoshan Gorge; the 750-megawatt Gongguoqiao; and the 1,750-megawatt Jinghong, near Jinghong city, about 300 kilometers north of Chiang Rai, Thailand—all completed in the first decade of the twenty-first century. These have been followed by the construction of another series of dams on the upper Mekong, including the giant 4,200-megawatt Xiaowan and 5,850-megawatt Nuozhadu. This frenetic dam building, which is uprooting tens of thousands of ethnic-minority people in Yunnan, has proceeded apace despite the fact that downstream countries have repeatedly voiced their concerns. Indeed, these concerns have been accentuated by the transboundary effects of the river damming, including the reduction of the lower Mekong's flow to a fifty-year low in 2010—a development also linked to a severe drought (map 3.3).

Nothing better illustrates China's new focus on Tibet's water resources than its plan to build the world's largest dam and hydropower station on the Brahmaputra at Metog ("Motuo" in Chinese), just before the river enters India. The dam, by impounding water on a gargantuan scale, will generate, according to the state-run HydroChina Corporation, 38 gigawatts of power, or more than twice the capacity of the Three Gorges Dam, which came with a price tag of $30 billion.[111] Hydro-China, in its own words, is in charge of "conducting the hydropower planning for the upper reaches" of the Mekong, the Salween, the Jinsha, and the Yellow and the middle reaches of the Brahmaputra—activities that focus on the Tibetan Plateau.[112] Such is the proposed scale of the Motuo Dam, as it is officially called, that the

MAP 3.3   The Mekong River Basin

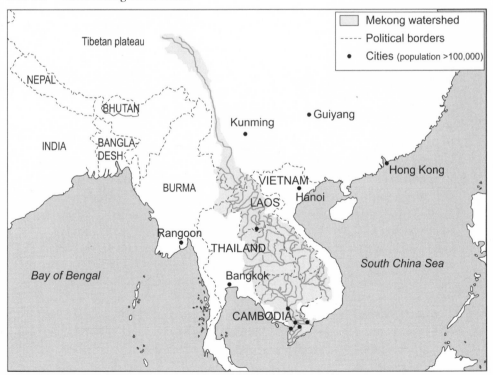

project will by itself produce the equivalent of three-quarters of the total capacity Australia had in 2010 to generate electricity from all energy sources. China is also building a series of six major dams in the upper-middle reaches of the Brahmaputra, with the construction of the first—at Zangmu—beginning in 2009. This cascade has come on top of the more than a dozen smaller dams China already has built on the Brahmaputra and its tributaries, including at Yamdrok Tso, Pangduo, Nyingtri-Payi, and Drikong.

The plan to build the colossal Motuo Dam—a project for which leaders of China's state-run hydropower industry have actively lobbied—could be linked to China's interest to reroute a sizable chunk of the Brahmaputra waters northward at the Great Bend, the point where the river makes a sharp turn to enter India. The infrastructure work around the Great Bend, which holds one of the greatest concentrations of river energy on Earth, is designed to pave the way for massive hydropower generation and possible water diversion. In fact, Motuo is not the only megadam planned at the Great Bend. The map of planned dams released by HydroChina Corporation in 2010 also cited Daduqai—almost on the disputed border with India—as the site of a giant dam, which is to produce electrical power by exploiting the river's mighty 2,000-meter fall as it hurtles down to India. Another map published in 2010 by the State Grid Corporation of China, the country's main builder and operator of power grids, showed that the Great Bend area will be connected before long to the rest of China's national grid—a pointer to the launch of energy megaprojects there to supply electricity to the booming industrial areas in the east.

China thus far has dammed rivers on the Tibetan Plateau to produce energy and to channel their waters for irrigation and mineral resource extraction. Its new projects, however, carry loftier hydroengineering objectives, including interbasin transfers. It also has steadily scaled up the sizes of its dams, with the new ones under construction or planned being huge by global standards. Water indeed has become integrally linked with China's strategic priorities and ambitions. It is pursuing massive interbasin and interriver water diversion projects, with the Tibetan Plateau at the center of the largest planned transfers. In the same way that it has voraciously sought to secure assured, long-term supplies of other natural resources by employing its newfound economic power, China is aiming to increase its water supply by launching multi-billion-dollar water diversion projects. But while it is buying the other resources through trade deals, including with pariah regimes, its water avarice is prompting it to turn its attention to the Tibetan Plateau's international rivers. This means that water issues increasingly will be a factor in its relations with its riparian neighbors, as hydropolitics casts a growing shadow on Asian interstate relations. Thus, China's water transfer projects involving international rivers actually carry the seeds of inter-riparian conflict.

No less significant is the fact that the large-scale damming of transnational rivers upstream creates greater variability in transboundary water flows, making it harder for downstream users to predict assured flows. China already has contentious relations with most co-riparian states over its upstream hydroengineering projects. This is illustrated, for example, by its megaprojects on the Mekong River, which have inflamed passions downstream in Vietnam, Cambodia, Laos, and Thailand. It appears to be in a rush to deny India substantial resources of the Brahmaputra to tap; the more river resources China exploits upstream, the less there will be for India to potentially harness. In this pursuit, China is seeking to denude sensitive areas of their natural forests. For example, the reservoir of the Motuo Dam will have to be much larger than the Three Gorges reservoir, which, with its length of more than 630 kilometers and average width of 1.3 kilometers, inundated some 1,300 archeological sites and altered the majestic beauty of the limestone cliffs of the Qutang, Wu, and Xiling gorges (the "Three Gorges"). But Motuo is the site of Tibet's greatest natural reserve and "the largest and best preserved virgin forests in China."[113]

China's hydroengineering projects also affect the hydrology of rivers, posing a threat to the fluvial ecosystems. In fact, having depleted and extensively contaminated its own major rivers and groundwater sources through unbridled withdrawals and lax antipollution controls, China, in its bid to meet its thirst for water and energy, now threatens the ecological viability of river systems linked to southern and southeastern Asia. There is plenty of evidence to indicate that the upstream dams, barrages, and other water projects on the Tibetan Plateau, besides leading to forest removal and soil and stream-bank erosion, are already contributing to greater fluctuations in transboundary flows and causing downstream flooding at times.

For example, a breach in an upstream dam in Tibet in mid-2000 not only triggered flooding in the northeastern Indian state of Arunachal Pradesh but also led to Indian and Chinese border troops being put on alert. The breach raised the level of the Brahmaputra by more than 30 meters and caused serious flood damage downstream, leaving at least 26 residents dead and 35,000 homeless in Arunachal Pradesh and stoking an Indian furor.[114] Worse still, the Chinese government provided no flood warning to India, and it suppressed publication of the news of the dam burst in its own domestic media.[115] Later, however, the Chinese government admitted the dam burst, identifying the location as Yiong, beyond Mount Namcha Barwa, and claiming that it was a 60-meter-high "natural dam" that gave way—a claim that was received skeptically by those downstream.

China, however, was at a loss to offer a plausible explanation when its water works in Tibet repeatedly triggered flash floods in 2000, 2001, and 2005 in another Indian Himalayan state, Himachal Pradesh. The flash floods in that state, located north of New Delhi, prompted one Indian newsmagazine to coin the phrase "Made-in-China floods."[116] Using satellite imagery, the Indian Space Research Organization actually identified the cause of the flash floods in 2000—which killed more than 100 people—as the Chinese release of excess water from its Sutlej basin hydro works without any forewarning to India.

It is apparent that Chinese dams and other hydroengineering structures on the international rivers on the Tibetan Plateau have a bearing on water flows into neighboring countries. But despite repeated demands by Thailand, Laos, India, and other states for greater transparency, Beijing has been loath to share information about its water projects. As a result, India has had to rely on its technical intelligence capability to detect new Chinese dam projects. The only area where China has been willing to cooperate with downstream states is in sharing flood-related hydrological data during the monsoon season. It has agreed to supply such hydrological information to the lower Mekong basin states and India. But whereas India supplies hydrological data free to downriver Pakistan and Bangladesh, China charges a fee.

After the flash floods in India's Himachal Pradesh State, China agreed in 2005 to provide New Delhi with data on any abnormal rise or fall in the upstream level of the Sutlej River, which it has quietly dammed. Furthermore, after the series of flash floods in Arunachal Pradesh State, China, in June 2008, signed a memorandum of understanding with New Delhi to share flood-season data on the Brahmaputra and two of its tributaries—the Parlung Tsangpo and the Lohit, which Beijing calls Zayu Qu. The memorandum of understanding was intended to help India improve its flood forecasting and timely warning on the plains of Assam. Since 2002, China had already been sharing hydrological information with India on the Brahmaputra but not on the two tributaries. India now needs to persuade China to extend the memorandum to cover all rivers flowing in from Tibet and also provide regular hydrological data not just related to flooding but also about below-average precipitation at the river source so that downstream users can be forewarned of a potential drought.

Given that the major watersheds formed by the Himalayas and the Tibetan highlands spread out river waters far and wide, greater cooperation is needed in an institutionalized form between China and the other riparian states. This imperative is being reinforced by the new, larger-scale Chinese hydroengineering projects on the Tibetan Plateau. After all, with China seeking to expropriate greater resources of the rivers originating on the plateau, the long-term geostrategic, economic, environmental, and even social implications of its megaprojects can no longer be ignored by the downstream countries and other players that have a stake in Asian peace and stability.

The Great South–North Water Transfer Project

With water scarcity beginning to haunt its northern plains, China has pursued with unflinching resolve the Great South–North Water Transfer Project, the biggest hydraulic project ever designed in the world. In addition to damming rivers and diverting river waters for energy, irrigation, and mineral resource extraction, China has launched interbasin and interriver transfer ventures, which now largely fall under the umbrella of the South–North Water Transfer Project. The third leg of the megaproject is centered on the Tibetan Plateau. The water-transfer plans in the third phase involve international rivers and, when fully implemented, they will arm China with considerable leverage over its riparian neighbors—a leverage it can employ to keep any downriver state on good behavior.

With the hydropower potential of the rivers on the Tibetan Plateau being among the highest in the world, thanks to the unmatched heights from which their waters rapidly descend, an energy-hungry China has sought to exploit those waters for generating electricity to meet the fast-rising demand in its east, as illustrated by its megadams on the upper reaches of the Mekong and Salween, which has prompted one analyst to say that Yunnan has been turned into the "powershed" of Guangdong.[117] But China also is seeking to divert waters from the Tibetan Plateau to its arid and semiarid areas. To garner wider backing for such plans, some official and Communist Party institutions in Beijing have encouraged the publication of supporting material. For example, an officially blessed book, enlighteningly titled *Tibet's Waters Will Save China*, has supported interbasin and interriver water transfer projects in Tibet and championed the northward rerouting of the waters of the Brahmaputra.[118] Some 10,000 copies of this book, written by a former officer of the People's Liberation Army (PLA), Li Ling, were bought by the Chinese government and its agencies for circulation to officials.

The 2005 book seemed to bear the PLA's imprimatur. Li Ling's ideas on how Tibet's waters can save China, however, are not new, including the suggestion that China go beyond the northward diversion of the waters of the Yangtze's Tibetan tributaries and actually reroute the Brahmaputra waters to the Yellow River. After all, the PLA has been enthralled by such ideas since at least the 1980s. However, the book's publication and wide distribution in military and civilian circles signaled that those ideas had become ripe for larger dissemination and that the PLA probably was ready to join hands with civil hydrologists and engineers in planning the rerouting of Tibetan river waters to China proper.

Given that such a redirection of waters would involve boring many channels and tunnels through mountain ranges, the PLA's expertise in blasting and tunneling would be vital to help accomplish such an unparalleled diversion. The challenges of building tunnels in one of the world's roughest environments are enormous. Li's own 1,239-kilometer interbasin diversion proposal called for 56 kilometers of tunneling through six mountain ranges. Such a route would cross five rivers, collecting their waters with the help of dams, before entering the Yellow River at the tri-junction of three Chinese provinces—Qinghai, Sichuan, and Gansu, each of which incorporates Tibetan regions.

The origins of the Great South–North Water Transfer Project actually date back to August 1958, when a meeting of the politburo of the Chinese Communist Party was held soon after the launch of the "Great Leap Forward"—a catastrophic charge toward forced collectivization initiated by Mao Zedong that eventually led to mass starvation and millions of deaths. The politburo meeting, under Mao's

influence, passed the so-called Directive on Hydraulic Works (Guanyu Shuili Gon-
gzuo De Zhishi), coining the phrase "south-to-north water diversion" (*nanshui beidiao*).[119] Immediately thereafter, Mao ordered work to begin on a giant reservoir at
Danjiangkou, on the Haijiang River in Hubei Province, as a first step in the
planned water diversion. The Danjiangkou Reservoir, however, could not be completed until the "Cultural Revolution"—another disastrous initiative of Mao that
started in 1966—was at its height.

In the disorder and economic disarray that engulfed China during the decade-
long Cultural Revolution, the grand water diversion plans were forgotten, with
efforts concentrated on modest dams, barrages, and irrigation canals. The south–
north transfer plans were not revived until the late 1980s, when hydroengineer-
turned-premier Li Peng lobbied for their revival. In 1991, the National People's
Congress, China's rubber-stamp legislature, included the south–north project in
the country's five-year and ten-year plans, and in the following year, it gave the
go-ahead to the resumption of work on the Three Gorges Dam. But it was only in
2002 that the implementation of the South–North Water Transfer Project (Nanshui
Beidiao Gongcheng Zongti Guihua) was approved by the State Council.[120]

The South–North Water Diversion (SNWD) Project is an overly ambitious
engineering attempt to correct the imbalance in water availability, with the south
holding four-fifths of China's water resources. China is currently home to one-fifth
of the world's population, which is projected to grow from 1.35 billion in 2010 to
1.6 billion by 2045, and it fancies interbasin and interriver water transfer projects
as a way to address the demands of its increasingly water-stressed economy. Beijing,
however, has not factored in the likely environmental damage that such mammoth
diversions would wreak, or the potential impact of climate change on the long-
term availability of the water resources it is eyeing on the Tibetan Plateau.

It should not be forgotten that the northward diversion of the waters from the
Tibetan Plateau is an idea enthusiastically backed by a succession of Chinese leaders, including Hu Jintao, a hydrologist who made his name through a brutal martial-law crackdown in Tibet in 1989. Indeed, Hu owed his swift rise to the top of
the Communist Party hierarchy to that martial-law crackdown. In using PLA
troops to brutally crush protestors at Tiananmen Square two months later, strongman Deng Xiaoping actually took a page out of Hu's Tibet playbook. The March
2008 Tibetan uprising, coinciding with Hu's reelection as president for a second
term, however, drew attention to the counterproductive nature of the Hu-backed
policies—from seeking to change the demographic realities on the ground in Tibet
through the "Go West" Han migration campaign, to draconian curbs on Tibetan
farmland and monastic life. The Tibetans' feelings of subjugation and loss have
been deepened as they have been pushed to the margins of society, with their
distinct culture being reduced to a mere showpiece to draw tourists and boost the
largely Han-benefiting local economy in Tibet. Tibetan representatives have been
given no say in China's pursuit of major water projects on the Tibetan Plateau,

even though the projects have an impact on local Tibetan communities and the natural environment.

The SNWD Project works have gradually been ramped up. The project was launched with $5.86 billion in credit from state-run Chinese banks, with the federal government pumping another $7 billion into more than seventy subsidiary projects under the megaproject.[121] By 2008, according to the director of the SNWD Project office, Zhang Jiyao, the available investment for the eastern and central routes had swelled to the equivalent of $37 billion.[122] In fact, the State Council has approved a total budget of $62 billion for the SNWD Project, but the actual cost is likely to be much higher.

Among the components of the megaproject are water diversion routes connecting the Yangtze River, the Huai River, the Yellow River, and the Hai River to help bring water to parched northern regions, such as Shandong Province and the municipalities of Tianjin and Beijing. The project is designed to create three new waterways to run along the east, center, and southwest of China. Just the first phase of SNWD entails an investment of at least $15 billion and the relocation of more than 440,000 residents, the vast majority of them living in Henan and Hubei provinces. Work on the western route is expected to start once the central route is fully complete. Parts of the eastern and central routes already have been completed, but some works have run into engineering and other roadblocks.[123] But unlike the western route, the eastern and central routes involve the diversion of waters from China's internal rivers and thus hold no international implications. The eastern and central routes, however, are designed as stepping stones to the much bigger western route (map 3.4).

The project's eastern route, designed to take 14.8 billion cubic meters of water per year from the Yangtze in Jiangsu Province right up to Tianjin in the north through a tunnel burrowed beneath the Yellow River, involves expanding the 1,600-kilometer imperial Grand Canal into the world's longest aqueduct.[124] The Grand Canal was built during the Sui Dynasty—which lasted from AD 589 to 618—to ferry rice northward from the fertile southeast; it runs from Hangzhou to Beijing. A branch line of the eastern route would link the Shandong Peninsula with the Yangtze. Work on the eastern route began within months of the 2002 State Council approval of the SNWD Project. Technologically, the 1,156-kilometer eastern route is the simplest of the three diversion projects, involving less than 9 kilometers of tunneling from the outlet of Dongping Lake to the inlet of the Weilin Canal. Parts of the eastern route actually were completed and put into operation in 2008.

The more difficult 1,421-kilometer-long central route—under construction since late 2003—is also intended to relieve pressure on the resources of the Yellow River by diverting up to 14 billion cubic meters of water per year northward from the Yangtze basin.[125] The route will pass beneath the Yellow, too, in channeling waters to the Beijing area. The nearby city of Tianjin also will draw water from a trunk line. The route's gravity-fed flow is designed to pass through tunnels in the

Map 3.4   China's Great South–North Water Transfer Project

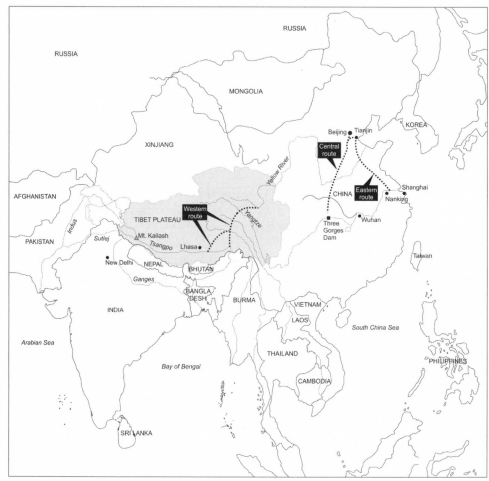

Funiu and Taihang mountains on its way to Beijing's Yuyuantan Lake. But its most complex part involves burrowing tunnels under the Yellow at Gubaizui.

The central route—racked by engineering challenges, cost overruns, pollution, and the burden of resettling large numbers of displaced rural residents—is running several years behind schedule.[126] In fact, this conduit has faced protests from local farmers that are in the process of being uprooted, as happened in 2009 when some 350,000 residents were sought to be relocated from near Hubei Province's Mao-era Danjiangkou Reservoir, which is being enlarged at a cost of $365 million to serve as the point of origin of the central route. The reservoir's height has already been raised almost 15 meters to add 11.6 billion cubic meters to its storage capacity of 17.45 billion cubic meters and to create an incline to help transport water northward.

Popular protests are unlikely to stall the conduit's completion. The Chinese state machinery has long years of experience in effectively stifling protests and evicting residents, including from Danjiangkou. After all, by the time the Danjiangkou Reservoir had filled in 1974, the area around what became Asia's largest human-made lake already stood depopulated. The forced resettlement for the SNWD Project is China's biggest since displacing a record number of local residents to build the Three Gorges Dam. Many of those displaced by the enlargement of the Danjiangkou Dam are being resettled in the adjacent but crowded province of Henan, China's most-populous region, which has nearly 100 million people. Today, declining water levels in Danjiangkou have prompted suggestions to draw water from the Three Gorges Dam—located also in Hubei Province—to help augment supplies to the central route.[127]

The Chinese authorities seem determined to complete the central route's first and largest phase by the revised deadline of 2014 and the entire eastern route by 2013. Once fully operational, the central and eastern routes together would be supplying almost 29 billion cubic meters of water to the north every year. This transfer capacity would be three times greater than America's diversion of 9.3 billion cubic meters of water from the lower Colorado River to California, Arizona, and New Mexico.[128]

The truly gargantuan part of the South–North Water Diversion Project, of course, is the third leg, known as the western route. It will be the source of the bulk of the waters to be transferred to the north under the SNWD Project. This leg centers on unparalleled plans to divert to the Han heartland the river waters cascading from the Tibetan highlands. This extremely complex engineering leg, which involves working at elevations of 4,000 to 5,000 meters above sea level or more, seeks to fuse different component projects into one program under the banner of the western route. The interbasin transfer of the waters from the Brahmaputra, with its bounteous flow, to the Yellow (known as Machu to the Tibetans and Huang He to the Chinese) forms the most ambitious part of the multidecade western route plans.

Broadly, the western route of the south–north project aims to tap into the waters of the four large rivers flowing out of the Tibetan Plateau—the Salween (Nu in Chinese), the Mekong (Lancang to the Chinese), the Brahmaputra, and the Jinsha (or "River of Golden Sands," which originates in the same county—Yushu—as the Yellow River). The Jinsha, the westernmost major tributary of the Yangtze, already is the scene of sixteen dam projects, most of them in its upper reaches in Tibet's Amdo Region (Qinghai Province). One challenging plan in the larger western route involves building a series of canals and tunnels along a 1,215-kilometer route bisecting the eastern Tibetan Plateau to connect the higher reaches of the Yangtze with the upper catchment of the Yellow. Initially under the western route, some

300 kilometers of tunnels and channels would be built to draw waters from the Jinsha, as well as from the smaller Ngyagchu (Yalong in Chinese) and Gyarong Ngulchu (Dadu He to the Chinese) rivers, located on the plateau's eastern rim. The tunnels would have to be cut through the earthquake-prone Bayankala Mountains.

Even though the western route involves digging into the Roof of the World, China's resolve to embark on this venture is not in doubt. Indeed, the dam-building spree on the Mekong, the Salween, the Brahmaputra, and other rivers on the Tibetan Plateau shows that China already is starting to tap the waters of the key southwestern rivers in a major way. The big question is when China will go from building dams on these rivers to generate electricity for its eastern regions to constructing tunnels and channels to send waters from the Tibetan Plateau northward as part of the western route. It seems likely that work on some aspects of such a water diversion will begin as soon as the central route's main phase is ready by 2014. Officially, the entire western route is supposed to be fully completed by 2050.[129]

It is doubtful, though, that the water demands of China's northern plains, which make up 64 percent of the country's cultivated land, can be met even with the transfer of hundreds of billions of cubic meters of water annually through the SNWD Project. If anything, the SNWD Project—which is being implemented directly under the supervision of the State Council—is certain to exact heavy environmental costs. Besides affecting the ecosystems of the rivers targeted for water diversion, the project is likely to spur sediment buildup, erratic flow speeds, contamination, and other problems in the new human-made waterways. Despite Premier Wen Jiabao's 2006 assurance to the National People's Congress that the government would emphasize "the prevention and treatment of pollution at the sources and along the routes of the South–North Water Diversion Project," water contamination already has emerged as a problem in the eastern route, with the director of the SNWD Project office admitting that authorities have "still a long way to go" to transform "the eastern route into a clean-water corridor."[130] Efforts to prevent pollution and treat contaminated water are adding significant costs to the water transfer.

River depletion through diversion, in fact, is inevitably going to lead to water pollution, as has already happened in the Yangtze because of the Three Gorges Dam. The Yangtze—the source of waters for the first two legs of the SNWD Project—has become so polluted that it has been identified as the single largest source of the pollution of the Pacific Ocean.[131] Millions of cubic meters of water in the new canals channeling the "blue gold" to the north are likely to be lost annually to evaporation. Instead of dealing with the unsustainable agricultural and industrial practices in the northern provinces by enforcing water productivity and efficiency standards and promoting conservation, Chinese planners are intent on manipulating the natural flows of the rivers in the south to meet the unquenchable water needs of the north. However, they need to recognize that the Tibetan Plateau and its ecosystems, including the great rivers that arise there, are part of the ecological heritage of Asia and other regions in the Northern Hemisphere.

Four

Exploiting the
Riparian Advantage

A Key Test Case

The mighty Brahmaputra River, or Yarlung Tsangpo ("the Purifier"), which China has renamed as Yaluzangbu, runs due east for almost 2,200 kilometers along Tibet's southern border with India, draining the runoff from the Himalayan slopes, before abruptly making a sharp southward turn to enter into India and Bangladesh. Among the world's major streams, this is the highest river and one of the fastest flowing. It actually ranks as the fourth-largest river in the world by discharge. It has numerous small and large tributaries. One of Brahmaputra's tributaries in Tibet also feeds into the Mekong River. In India, where two major tributaries from Tibet and smaller Indian rivers merge with it, the Brahmaputra becomes as wide as 10 kilometers before flowing into Bangladesh.

The main river is known by different names locally—from first the Siang and then the Dihang in the remote northeasternmost Indian state of Arunachal Pradesh to the Jamuna in Bangladesh, where it becomes the Padma after merging with the Ganges. Most rivers of the Indian subcontinent carry female names, but the Brahmaputra means the "putra," or son, of Brahma, the god of creation. The entire Brahmaputra basin extending downward from Tibet supports very rich biodiversity, including thousands of species of plants and angiosperms, as well as a great variety of ferns and gymnosperms, besides rare animals, birds, and fish.

The Brahmaputra originates from Mount Kailash near Lake Mansarovar, drawing waters in the warm months from the adjoining Gyema Yangzom Glacier. Before dipping into India through the Himalayan divide, the Brahmaputra flows eastward in Tibet through Shigatse city, the second-largest city in the so-called Tibet Autonomous Region, and south of Lhasa at an average altitude of more than 4,000 meters, making it the world's highest-flowing river system. All along its

141

journey through Tibet's Himalayan belt, it collects more water. Several tributaries join the Brahmaputra in Tibet itself, including the Raka Tsangpo, Dokshung Tsangpo, the Lhasa River that runs past the Tibetan capital, the Gyamda, and the Nyangchu (or "Nyangqu" in Chinese), which flows more than 300 kilometers before entering the main stream in southeastern Tibet. Just before the Brahmaputra bends around the Himalayas to cross over into India, the Po Tsangpo tributary, flowing in swiftly from the north, drains into it, increasing the ferocity of the river's flow.

In the same way that the Yellow River has been a lifeline of the Han civilization since Neolithic times, the basin of the Brahmaputra or Tsangpo running across southern Tibet has been the cradle of Tibetan civilization. Tibet's unique culture and religion developed on the banks of the Brahmaputra. Given that the river skirts Tibet's border with India, it is no accident that the Tibetan and Indian civilizations have shared historical intimacy. Until Tibet was annexed by Communist China, its roads and other links faced southward to India. Historically, the Brahmaputra basin has served as the common bond between Tibet and India.

Just before going into India, the Brahmaputra makes a U-shaped turn to form the so-called Great Bend in the Nyangtri Prefecture of the Tibet Autonomous Region. Nyangtri, ranked as the most biodiverse part of the Tibetan Plateau, is known for its breathtaking scenery, virgin forests, and wildlife. To make the U-turn, the Brahmaputra, in a series of rapids and cascades, cuts through deep gorges between two giant Himalayan peaks, Mount Namcha Barwa and Mount Gyala Peri. At 7,782 meters, Namcha Barwa is the highest peak in the eastern Himalayan range, whereas Gyala Peri is 7,294 meters high. In making the U-turn, the river not only cleaves the Himalayan range in two but also forms the steepest and longest canyon in the world. The Brahmaputra Canyon indeed is twice as deep as the Grand Canyon carved by the Colorado River in the United States.

The "Yarlung Tsangpo Great Canyon," as China officially calls it, is spread over an area of 64,300 square kilometers. The canyon is 504.6 kilometers long, 21 kilometers wide on average, and so deep that the average depth of its core section is 2,673 meters. The deepest point recorded in the canyon is at 7,057 meters,[1] with the villages of the Abor (Lhopa) and Monpa tribespeople—who inhabit the Great Canyon—located at depths of even 6,000 meters.[2] Its wall-like slopes are far more precipitous than those of the Grand Canyon in the United States, which, at 448 kilometers, is 12.5 percent shorter. The Brahmaputra Canyon also boasts the deepest points in the world, but in terms of average depth throughout, the short, 90-kilometer-long Colca Canyon in southern Peru has a median deepness of 3,200 meters.

The massive hydropower potential at the Great Bend—among the greatest in the world—arises from the fact that the Brahmaputra at that stretch plunges several thousand meters by cutting through the high mountains, with the white foaming rapids creating a natural source of immense energy. The Brahmaputra's Great Canyon indeed has the largest slope deflection of any river surface in the world—

75.35 percent—which is the ratio of the difference in the elevation of a section with its distance.[3]

Although China has sought to tap the resources of all the international rivers originating on the Tibetan Plateau, this chapter is a case study of just one river—the Brahmaputra—and the larger geopolitical, economic, and environmental implications of the Chinese hydroengineering projects and plans in its basin. There are at least four reasons why this river has been chosen as the focus of the analysis in this chapter.

First, the Brahmaputra is by far the most important river flowing from Chinese-controlled territory into any other country in terms of the sheer volume of cross-border flows. As table 4.1 indicates, the Brahmaputra's mean annual transboundary runoff volume is nearly equal to the aggregate volume of cross-border flows of all the other rivers directly flowing into India from Tibet. The figures in the table also reveal why the Brahmaputra is such a water diversion magnet for the engineers-turned-politicians who dominate China's top leadership: The average annual transboundary flows into India of just the Brahmaputra are greater than the combined cross-border flows (142,370 cubic kilometers, km³) of the two main Tibetan Plateau rivers—the Mekong and the Salween—flowing into the Southeast Asian countries. The average cross-border runoff volumes of the rivers flowing from China into Kazakhstan and Russia—the Irtysh, the Illy, and the Amur—are even smaller than the transboundary flows of the Mekong and the Salween.

Second, no less revealing is heavily populated India's acute dependency on cross-border river flows from Tibet and the consequent vulnerability to China's potential use of water as a political instrument. Although the mean transboundary runoff volume from Tibetan rivers aggregates 185,660 km³ per year in the

TABLE 4.1 The Volume of River Waters Flowing Out of the Tibetan Plateau to Countries other than China

River System	*Direct Destination*	*Mean Annual Runoff Volume Flowing Out (km³)*
Brahmaputra (Yarlung Tsangpo) and tributaries	India	165,400
Rivers from southwestern and western Tibet	India	181,620
Rivers from southern Tibet	Nepal	12,000
Salween (Gyalmo Ngulchu, or Nu)	Burma (Myanmar)	68,740
Mekong (Zachu or Lancang)	Laos and Burma	73,630
Tibetan rivers flowing out from western Yunnan	Burma	31,290

Source: Aquastat online data, Food and Agriculture Organization of the United Nations, 2011.

case of the other riparian neighbors of China combined, the figure totals 347,020 km³ per year in relation to India. Given that fact, the Chinese hydroengineering projects on the Tibetan Plateau, in general, hold greater direct implications for India than for any other country. Because India—a potential peer rival—is the main beneficiary of transboundary river flows from Tibet, China may only see an incentive to aggressively exploit or divert Tibetan river-water resources. China/India geopolitical competition indeed has emerged as a defining feature in the twenty-first century, even as the two giants seek to downplay their rivalry by trying to showcase cooperation.

Third, the greatest impact of the upstream diversion of the Brahmaputra waters by China, however, would likely be borne by the weakest, poorest, and most densely populated state in the basin, Bangladesh. The Brahmaputra is Bangladesh's most important river, and the Chinese diversion would mean environmental devastation of large parts of that country. Bangladesh's reliance on transboundary water flows is one of the highest in the world: It depends on India for 91.33 percent of its water supply, receiving some 1,105.6 km³ of river waters per year.[4] If Chinese megaprojects diminish the Brahmaputra's flows into India, Bangladesh, as the country located farthest downstream, would be the hardest hit, with the impact likely to extend from agriculture to people's livelihood.

Fourth, the scale of the Chinese strategy to exploit the resources of the Brahmaputra is unparalleled—from the plan to build a dam more than twice as large as the Three Gorges Dam at the Great Bend (the 38-gigawatt Motuo Dam[5]) to the interest to partially redirect northward the natural southward flow of the river. Indeed, China's dam-building projects on the Brahmaputra are beginning to move toward the Great Bend area, where the largest water resources are concentrated.

The Chinese interest in rerouting the Brahmaputra waters from "the Roof of the World" to the Yellow River is a proposition of Olympian scale that has injected a new unfavorable element into the troubled Sino-Indian relationship, with the Bangladesh factor adding to the complexity (map 4.1). Water is becoming a key security issue in India–China relations as a result of China's water megaprojects on the Tibetan Plateau, including interbasin and interriver transfer plans. Flash floods in India's Himachal Pradesh and Arunachal Pradesh states have served as a reminder of the costs for the lower riparian of China's opaquely pursued water projects in Tibet.

Water indeed adds an ominous new dimension to an India–China situation characterized by territorial disputes, deep-seated mistrust, border tensions, and geopolitical rivalry. In that setting, Beijing has not shied away from upping the ante against New Delhi. For example, since 2006 it has publicly raked up an issue that had remained dormant since the 1962 Sino-Indian war—Arunachal Pradesh, a region offering a cornucopia of natural resources and that China claims largely as its own on the basis of the territory's putative historical ties with Tibet. In fact, the Chinese practice of describing Arunachal, with its 1.3 million residents, as "Southern Tibet" started only in 2006.

Map 4.1   The Brahmaputra River Watershed

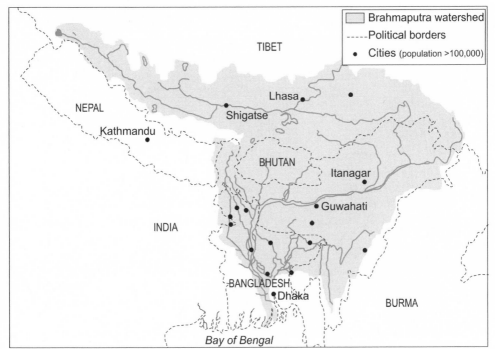

In fact, through its hydro projects in Tibet—where the fragile ecosystems already are threatened by reckless resource exploitation and global warming—China is likely to acquire the capability to use water as a source of political leverage against India. Its fast-growing exploitation of water and mineral resources on the Tibetan Plateau has helped highlight why it regards Tibet as its most treasured acquisition since the 1949 Communist "revolution." As one analyst has put it, "Current efforts on behalf of China to divert the water resources of the Brahmaputra River away from India will compound a situation that has remained tenuous since the 1962 Indo-China war."[6] Although doubts still persist over the economic, environmental, and engineering feasibility of channeling Tibetan waters northward, few can discount the possibility that the mammoth diversion of the Brahmaputra could begin as water shortages become more acute in the northern Chinese plains and China's foreign-exchange hoard continues to brim over. The 2030 Water Resources Group, a consortium of private social-sector organizations, has projected that the greatest global growth in water use by industry will come from China, the world's back factory, where changing diets already are fueling demand for significantly increased food production.[7]

THE SACRED AND THE PROFANE

The Great Bend, where the Brahmaputra River makes a hairpin-style turn around Mount Namcha Barwa, forms not just the world's longest and steepest canyon; it also is revered as a sacred place in Tibetan Buddhism. The Tibetans believe the Great Bend, one of the rainiest places in the world, personifies Tibet's protecting deity, Goddess Dorjee Pagmo (Vajravarahi in Sanskrit), with each mountain, cliff, cave, and waterway there being part of her body and the Brahmaputra representing her spine. Mount Gangri Karpo, which faces the northeast, symbolizes her head, Mount Dorjeyang her neck, Mounts Gongdu Podrang and Pemasiri her breasts, and Mount Richenpung her navel.[8]

This forbidding abode of Dorjee Pagmo—Buddha's five-chakra consort and a symbol of enlightenment—is known locally as Pemako, or the "Hidden Lotus Land," the place where real happiness supposedly lies in concealment in a monstrously steep gorge within a gorge, with the narrowly separated cliff sides casting perpetual shadows. The verdant Pemako, covering a rain-drenched area of some 30,000 square kilometers in southeastern Tibet, blends giant snow-covered, mist-shrouded peaks and cliffy slopes with deep, subtropical valleys and virgin, wildlife-rich forests that are home to rare medicinal plants.

To the Tibetans, this earthly paradise in the borderland between Tibet and India is a holy site blessed by Padmasambhava, the eighth-century sage known as Guru Rinpoche who helped establish Buddhism in Tibet. An ancient monastery in ruins at Pemakochung, the gateway to the Brahmaputra's Great Canyon, serves as one of the holiest pilgrimage places in this inhospitable area for those seeking enlightenment.

The Great Canyon, with its pure water and dense, leech-infested jungles, has "lived in legend as the site of fabled waterfalls and magic portals to other worlds,"[9] inspiring the imaginary utopian Tibetan lamasery Shangri-La in James Hilton's 1933 novel *Lost Horizon* and the subsequent movie of the same name.[10] The concept of Shangri-La actually has its origins in ancient Tibetan Buddhist texts describing *beyul*, or sacred sanctuaries, which are said to store the essence of the Buddhist Tantras and to reveal themselves only to devout pilgrims. In fact, underscoring the centrality of nature conservation in their culture, the Tibetans have three categories of sacred landscape. Two are Buddhist—*beyul* valleys and *neri* (or cult) mountains that have given rise to major Tibetan pilgrimage centers and *beyul* and mountain-deity worship[11]—and the third is pre-Buddhist: *yul* landscapes, which are symbolized by a divinity with human personality (*yul-lha*) and thus demand respect for and protection of the natural environment.[12] In fact, safeguarding *yul* landscapes from despoliation is considered essential for the well-being of the land and its people.

The greatest of all hidden lands, or *beyul* valleys, according to the Tibetan Buddhist texts, "lies at the heart of the forbidding Tsangpo Gorge, deep in the Himalayas and veiled by a colossal waterfall."[13] In the words of the present Dalai

Lama, the revered texts, discovered centuries ago, "describe valleys reminiscent of paradise that can only be reached with enormous hardship. Pilgrims who travel to these wild and distant places often recount extraordinary experiences similar to those encountered by spiritual practitioners on the Buddhist path of liberation. One of the most renowned of these hidden lands lies in the region of the Tsangpo gorges in southeastern Tibet. It is called Beyul Pemako, 'the hidden land shaped like a lotus.' Many pilgrims have journeyed there in search of the innermost sanctuary. From a Buddhist perspective, sacred environments such as Pemako are not places to escape from the world, but to enter them more deeply."[14]

Indeed, after quiet attempts by Indian voyagers in the second half of the nineteenth century to probe the secrets of the Brahmaputra and penetrate Pemako's mysterious depths on behalf of the Survey of India institution, British explorers tried unsuccessfully to reach the largest waterfalls in the Brahmaputra's Great Canyon, dubbed the "Hidden Falls." Although some Tibetans believe that the Hidden Falls are the entrance to Yangsang—Pemako's secret sanctum sanctorum—the British explorers were motivated by the prospect that those colossal falls in the depths of the canyon could hold geopolitical value akin to southern Africa's Victoria Falls, which by 1900 became a symbol of European imperial power. The Tibetan religious texts inspired several ill-fated British expeditions in search of the legendary waterfalls, the story about which had become known as "the great romance of geography."[15] The botanist Frank Kingdon-Ward managed to make his way into the labyrinth of the Great Canyon in 1925 but was unable to locate the Hidden Falls. That led Kingdon-Ward—who later was briefly arrested by authorities of the then-independent Tibet in 1935 for crossing the 1914-drawn "Red Line" and illegally entering Tibetan territory from India's Tawang Tract[16]—to deceptively declare that he had solved "the riddle of the Tsangpo Gorge" and that the falls were just a "religious myth." Wrote Kingdon-Ward after his 1924–25 foray:

> Not only is Pemako extraordinarily difficult to reach from any direction, it is still more difficult to penetrate and explore when reached. Surrounded on three sides by the gorges of the Tsangpo, the fourth is blocked by the mighty ranges of snow mountains, whose passes are open only for a few months in the year. Beyond these immediate barriers to east and west and south, are dense trackless forests, inhabited by wild, unfriendly tribes. . . . Add to this . . . a climate that varies from the subtropical to arctic, the only thing common to the whole region being perpetual rain, snakes and wild animals, giant stinging nettles and myriads of biting and blood-sucking ticks, hornets, flies and leeches, and you have some idea of what the traveler has to contend with.[17]

The 33-meter, rainbow-ringed Hidden Falls were not reached by outside explorers until 1998. After the Chinese annexation of Tibet, the natives shared little information about Pemako's mysterious depths with their occupiers. To prevent tampering with a sacred site—the last hidden Shangri-La—the locals had concealed the waterfalls from the Chinese authorities.[18] After all, in the battle to protect sacred Tibetan places from the demands of Confucian materialism, the sacred hardly stood a chance of surviving unspoiled.

It was only after an expedition by Chinese scientists in 1998, according to an official Chinese claim, that "the mystery of the canyon" was "finally unraveled."[19] A rival claim is by National Geographic Society's Expeditions Board, which has contended that the American explorers it sponsored—Ian Baker, Ken Storm Jr., and Brian Harvey—were the first to find the Hidden Falls in November 1998, ahead of the Chinese team. Baker, a Tantric scholar based in Kathmandu, detailed in his memoir the experiences that led him and his colleagues to the falls, whose search had previously been dismissed as "one of the most obsessive wild goose chases of modern times."[20] Lasting seventeen days, Baker's expedition approached the gateway to the mystical paradise from the north, following hunting and animal trails. With that discovery, the stretch of the Great Canyon unexplored by outsiders has shrunk to a few kilometers, but it includes the fabled sanctum sanctorum.

Against that background, it is apparent that Pemako is more than just the source of the legend of Shangri-La; it is integral to the beliefs and practices of Tibetan Buddhism. Today, however, China pays little heed to Pemako's sacredness. With an eye on Pemako's bountiful water resources—which include numerous glaciers that are so vast that they cover 68 percent of the land surface area of the newly created prefecture of Nyangtri (also spelled "Nyingtri" and "Nyingchi")—it has unveiled its intent to construct dams in Pemako's vicinity, including the world's largest. It already has built a highway to that area, as well as an airport there that the *People's Daily*, the Chinese Communist Party's turgid broadsheet, has boasted is "the world's most difficult airport to take off from or land."[21] Located close to the Great Canyon at Nyangtri, the main city in Nyangtri Prefecture, it is—at 2,949 meters—one of the world's highest airstrips. Now the Chinese Ministry of Railways has unveiled a plan to build a railroad from Lhasa to Nyangtri, which means "The Throne of the Sun" in Tibetan.[22]

Building such access by road, rail, and air is a prerequisite to tapping the resources in that remote prefecture, whose capital is a low-altitude former military base populated almost entirely by Han Chinese, Bayi (which means "August 1," the anniversary of the founding of the People's Liberation Army). Significantly, official Chinese maps include two counties in Nyangtri Prefecture that are part of Indian-administered Arunachal Pradesh. The new copper mines that have come up in this prefecture near the Tsangpo Gorge, with their tailings beginning to pollute the holy waters, followed geological discoveries that identified this area as home to the richest copper deposits in China. The capital, Bayi, for its part, has emerged as the principal center supplying timber and wool to the Han heartland from this resource-rich prefecture. Yet Beijing admits that the vast virgin forests of this area, along with its 6,783 square kilometers (km^2) of glaciers and permafrost, "function as the source of the climate and ecology for Tibet and even the entire country and Southeast Asia."[23]

With Chinese authorities violating Pemako's sacred inviolability, the fears that had prompted the local Tibetans to hide parts of the site have come true. To the Tibetans, the planned damming of the Brahmaputra at the Great Canyon and the ongoing mining operations in the vicinity constitute the environmental desecration of sacred landscapes. And this environmental desecration has come atop the assault on Tibetan cultural traditions under Chinese rule. The damming at the Great Canyon will flood vast tracts of virgin forests, which are home to one of the largest wildlife preserves in Asia, and uproot the jungle-dwelling Abor and Monpa tribal communities that have lived there for thousands of years. One wildlife sanctuary, Gongdu Dorsem Podrang, consecrated to a meditational deity, extends to the disputed border with India. So holy is Pemako for the Tibetans that an ancient Buddhist text discovered in the area in the seventeenth century declares, "Just taking seven steps toward Pemako with pure intention, one will certainly be reborn here. A single drop of water from this sacred place—whoever tastes it—will be freed from rebirth in the lower realms of existence."[24]

Chinese officials, however, want to utilize Pemako's holy waters not to be "freed from rebirth in the lower realms of existence" but to meet Han material needs in distant provinces, including for energy. The Great Bend is located in an area of high seismic activity close to the fault line where the Indian Plate collides against the Eurasian Plate. China's Great Water Diversion plans, as part of the western route of its south-to-north transfer project, could trigger great earthquakes in the region.

A reminder of that danger came in May 2008 when a massive earthquake struck the Tibetan Plateau's eastern rim. Dubbed the "Great China Quake," it left more than 87,000 people dead and 5 million homeless, mostly in Sichuan Province. That earthquake was very likely triggered, according to a number of experts, by China's new 156-meter-high Zipingpu hydropower dam, located 5 kilometers from the quake's epicenter and barely 500 meters from the critically stressed fault line where the giant tectonic plates collide. The correlation between fluid-driven local seismicity and stress change potentially hastened the earthquake.[25] It is believed that the tremendous weight of the several hundred million tons of water impounded in the reservoir put unnatural stress on the geological fault line. Fan Xiao, chief engineer at the Sichuan Geology and Mineral Bureau in Chengdu, said the gradual filling of the reservoir during 2004–5 very likely affected the pressure on the fault line underneath, causing the quake, which measured 7.9 on the Richter scale.[26] Another powerful earthquake in April 2010 struck the area where the Yellow River originates—Yushu Prefecture of the Tibetan Plateau—causing serious damage to a dam and killing nearly 3,000 people. The epicenter of that 7.1-magnitude quake was related to the northward thrust of the Indian Plate against the Eurasian Plate, the same root cause of the May 2008 quake.

Instead of seeking to bend nature in the environmentally sensitive Great Canyon area, China ought to be emphasizing nature conservation there, consistent with the Tibetan tradition. In addition to being sacred, the Great Bend region—with its ice falls, snow peaks, subtropical jungles, hot springs, and abrupt, imposing cliffs—is ecologically unique. Its diverse climatic zones, spread vertically as the altitude descends from more than 7,000 meters to 600 meters over a relatively short distance, have supported several thousand plant and animal species, including snow leopards, Bengal tigers, gibbons, and a horned mammal called the takin, sacred to Tibetan Buddhists. The area's nine climatic zones range from the Alp ice-snow belt to tropical seasonal forests, earning it the reputation of being a "natural arboretum," "natural zoo," and "plant gene bank." It is simply an unparalleled natural park. Although China has recognized that fact by opening the "Yarlung Tsangpo Grand Canyon National Reservation," its infrastructure projects and water-impoundment plans run counter to that initiative.

China's tampering with holy lakes and rivers in Tibet, in fact, has appalled ethnic Tibetans for long. Although lakes and rivers play a central role in the religious and cultural lives of the Tibetan people, China makes little effort to consult them about its water projects in their homeland. One classic case of defilement of a sacred watercourse is Yamdrok Tso (Yangchouyong in Chinese), the largest freshwater lake in southern Tibet, located at an elevation of 4,441 meters southwest of Lhasa. With a surface area of 638 square kilometers overlooking the mountains of Bhutan, Yamdrok Tso is one of the four major holy lakes in Tibet, along with Mansarovar, Lhamo Latso, and Nam Tso. Shaped like a giant scorpion with its claws outstretched and with the famous Samding monastery on its shores, Yamdrok Tso is revered as a "life-power lake" by the Tibetans, who for centuries have made offerings by its once-pure, turquoise waters, regarding it as the abode of the soul (*bla*) of the Tibetan nation.

Between 1989 and 1995,[27] more than 1,500 troops of the People's Armed Police and the People's Liberation Army, using explosives and drilling equipment, bore four 6-kilometer-long tunnels through the Gambala Mountains to create waterfalls from the lake into the Brahmaputra below.[28] A hydropower station, built by the riverside, began operating in 1996. Exploiting the lake as a reservoir, with its manipulated waterfalls, and employing pumped-storage technology that recycles water on a continuing basis, the station—without the need for a dam—produces 90 megawatts of electricity for supply to the increasingly Sinicized Lhasa area. The 742-meter tunneled waterfalls from the lake power the station's turbines, with stored electricity in off-peak periods being utilized to replenish the lake by pumping back water from the Brahmaputra through the use of reversible turbines. The project not only constitutes an act of defilement of a sacred lake but is also damaging Yamdrok Tso's ecosystem by slowly but continually replacing its pure, snow-fed waters with the river's sediment-laced waters.

The lake was almost a closed hydraulic system, with the inflow coming from mountain snowmelt and rainfall and a small outflow to a tiny tributary of the

Brahmaputra. Its waters were believed to have a healing power. Now the continual exchange of the Yamdrok Tso's waters with the Brahmaputra's waters has increased acidity and nitrate levels in the lake. For devout Tibetan Buddhists, eating fish is a sacrilege, in keeping with the saying "A fish is without a tongue, so killing it is indefensible." But Han Chinese have valued Yamdrok Tso as the "Fish Barn of Tibet," with a thriving fishing industry coming up in the area in the period since the fall of Tibet to China. The rise in the lake's acidity and nitrate levels, coupled with overfishing and illegal fishing practices involving, for example, the use of explosives, has resulted in a drop in the annual catch from Yamdrok Tso in recent years, according to Chinese media accounts. No studies thus far have been conducted on the hydropower project's larger environmental effects, including on the already-endangered black-necked cranes for whom the lake area is an important habitat.

No sooner had the Yamdrok Tso project been completed than the state-run Chinese hydropower industry unveiled a plan to dam another sacred lake—Megoe Tso (Mugecuo to the Chinese).[29] Perched at an altitude of 4,000 meters on the eastern rim of the Himalayas in the portion of the Tibetan Plateau that now is in Sichuan Province, this pilgrimage lake is surrounded by more than thirty smaller lakes, primeval forests, and hot springs. The nearby 7,556-meter Minyak Gangkar (White Snow of Minyak)—the highest peak in the easternmost Himalayas—and Megoe Tso constitute a sacred mountain-and-lake duo in the same way as Mount Kailash and Lake Mansarovar in the western part of the plateau. The government plan to dam Megoe Tso for energy production ran into stiff opposition from local Tibetan communities, which actually had been demanding for long that the area be declared a UNESCO World Heritage site. In 2003, they wrote a letter to Premier Wen Jiabao urging that the hydropower plan be scrapped. Chinese environmentalists also voiced concern that the project could seriously undercut the natural heritage of an area that attracts large numbers of Chinese tourists. Following a fresh environmental impact assessment ordered by the federal government, local authorities announced the project's indefinite suspension in late 2006.[30]

Other sacred places have not been so lucky. A Western researcher has described the assault on one of Tibet's most venerated natural places—the snow-covered peak named Pure Crystal Mountain in Tsari, located near the border with India, to the east of Bhutan. After the 1959 Tibetan uprising, which led to the Dalai Lama's flight to India, the monasteries and temples in Tsari were "looted and razed. All pilgrimages around the mountain were banned for over two decades. . . . Nowadays, a gravel road runs down the course of the Tsari River Valley, along part of the former pilgrimage route. It provides strategic access to a Chinese military base on the disputed Sino-Indian border just below the village of Lo Mikyimdun. Logging trucks also use it to haul timber cut from forests along the mountain's flanks. Wild animals have virtually disappeared; most have now been shot or trapped. Soldiers and hunters patrolling the upper mountain relieve themselves without concern for polluting its sacred slopes."[31]

It is the combination of the Mao-era mindset to subdue nature through engineering feats and the greater national emphasis both on renewable energy, especially hydropower, and on interbasin water transfers that explains China's relentless exploitation of water resources, including at sacred sites. Had China been a more open society with a vigorous civil society, the serious environmental problems the Three Gorges Dam has spawned—from altering the local ecosystems to attenuating the Yangtze flow—would likely have given pause to other water megaprojects. The Three Gorges Dam's growing problems have been exemplified by recurrent landsides in the area surrounding its gigantic reservoir (which sits on two major geological fault lines), by intractable water pollution, and by concerns over reservoir-induced seismicity.[32] By diminishing the river-delivered nutrient supply on which sea life depends, the Three Gorges Dam also threatens to reduce productivity in the East China Sea.[33]

But in a one-party system with Internet and media censorship that is among the most stringent in the world, such problems have done little to tamp down official enthusiasm for water megaprojects. In fact, twenty new dams are being built on the Yangtze itself, including its tributaries.[34] The ecologically distressed Yangtze already is one of the most dammed rivers in the world and the most polluted river of China. More ominously, China's attention has turned to the sacred Tsangpo Gorge, where the official plans are to replicate the Three Gorges Dam on a larger scale.

A GRAND WATER LARCENY IN THE MAKING

With the resources of the Yangtze River and its tributaries already exploited heavily, the Brahmaputra River has loomed large in China's diversion plans as it is the only major Tibetan Plateau river whose waters remain, in the Chinese eyes, largely untapped. Indeed, in terms of annual mean transboundary runoff volume flowing out of Chinese-controlled territory, the Brahmaputra, as table 4.1 has shown, easily ranks No. 1, with its water flows across the international boundary totaling more than the combined transboundary flows of China's next two largest cross-border rivers—the Mekong and the Salween—whose resources Beijing now is aggressively exploiting. This helps explain the centrality of the Brahmaputra in the Chinese damming and water-rerouting plans. The Chinese hydroengineering focus on the Great Himalayan Watershed has been highlighted by the series of dams under construction or planned on the Brahmaputra and its tributaries as well as the Arun River system, with the Brahmaputra also the subject of proposed interbasin water division.

China's geoengineering projects ranging from attempts to change weather patterns to altering river courses have in part been geared to showcase its technological prowess. Big dams and other water diversion projects have actually been flaunted as national trophies symbolizing China's engineering and economic might, with the colossal Three Gorges Dam serving as one such example. But its growing thirst for water "must lead to worries that Chinese engineers may devise new ways of geoengineering in the Himalayas to prove themselves."[35] Harnessing the Brahmaputra's resources to meet the needs in the Han heartland has been referred to as the "Tsangpo Project" by some Chinese officials and newspapers. The proposed Brahmaputra diversion to channel the river waters all the way to the northeastern megacity of Tianjin stands out for the sheer audaciousness of scale.

More broadly, China's focus on the international rivers originating on the Tibetan Plateau and in another restive minority homeland, Xinjiang, has been part of a policy strategy since the 1990s to rapidly develop river resources in the western region, including for hydropower and irrigation. To help accelerate progress toward that end, then President Jiang Zemin publicly unveiled in 1999 a larger infrastructure development program named *xibu da kaifa* (which translates as the "Great Western Opening Up" or the "Great Western Extraction"). The state-run Chinese English-language media, however, called it the "Great Western Development" program, a label that gained currency in the international literature.[36] The Go West development plan, however, has been part of Chinese strategy since the Mao Zedong years, with infrastructure being viewed as the key to enforcing effective political control over the minority homelands that make up three-fifths of China's land territory. Mao indeed had said openly: "The Han nationality has the population, the minority nationalities have the land. . . . It is thus imperative that the Han assist the minorities in raising their standard of living and socialist ideological consciousness, while the minorities provide the natural resources necessary for the industrialization and development of the motherland."[37]

The *xibu da kaifa* program thus marks only the newest phase in China's strategy to integrate and assimilate ethnic minorities and facilitate greater exploitation of their natural resources. Significantly, the program incorporates a core hydraulic component that proponents in China have called the "Great Western Route." That route is centered on the waters of the Brahmaputra, the Salween, the Mekong, and the three Yangtze tributaries located on the eastern rim of the Tibetan Plateau— the Jinsha, the Yalong, and the Dadu. The Great Western Route is also known as Shoutian—a name that represents a fusion between the first four letters in Shoumatan (the Chinese name for the Suma Tan site on the Brahmaputra where the uppermost dam for the purpose of river-waters rerouting is to be built) and the port city of Tianjin, the end point of the Yellow River, to which the waters from the other rivers are to be diverted.[38] Interestingly, *shuo tian* translates as "reverse flow" in Mandarin. So, the Great Western Route is indeed what it entails—a reverse-flow canal.

The idea of rerouting Tibetan river waters through the *shuo-tian* canal linking several streams with the Yellow was actively promoted for several years by the hydrogeologist Guo Kai, prompting then Water Resources Minister Zhang Jinong to establish in 1989 a "preparatory committee" headed by three People's Liberation Army (PLA) generals to examine the possible implementation of the proposal. By the late 1990s, the proposal had received the support of 208 deputies of the National People's Congress (China's quasi-parliament), many delegates to the Chinese People's Political Consultative Conference (a 2,252-member advisory body), and a number of PLA generals.[39] President Jiang, even before he unveiled his *xibu da kaifa* program, gave his imprimatur in principle to the *shuo-tian* proposal, prompting the dispatch by federal authorities of an 11-member scientific team in 1999 for an extensive on-the-spot survey on its technical feasibility. The survey team, covering the entire route of the proposed interriver and interbasin diversion, reported that 600 billion cubic meters of the waters on the Tibetan Plateau, according to the Chinese media, was going "waste" annually because of lack of infrastructure to impound them for beneficial use within China.[40]

More moves followed in the first decade of the twenty-first century in support of the idea to channel river waters northward from the Tibetan Plateau. The publication of Li Ling's book *Tibet's Waters Will Save China* in November 2005 and its government-sponsored distribution among policy and engineering circles signaled an official interest in launching the Greater Western Route project, with the Brahmaputra at the center of the grand interbasin design.[41] Li reportedly spent more than a decade working on his book, which details the ambitious Brahmaputra-to-Tianjin diversion plan.

Although the Chinese government has identified the Great Bend as holding the greatest untapped water reserves, Li's plan has sought to overcome the obstacles posed by the tall mountains and the world's longest, steepest canyon there by moving the main diversion point farther upstream. By rerouting the Brahmaputra at the 3,588-meter-high Shoumatan (Suma Tan) site—near the Tibetan Buddhist pilgrimage center of Tsethang, famous for its eighth-century Tantric meditation cave of Guru Rinpoche—Li's plan seeks to reduce the need to pump water uphill, thereby ensuring that the construction of the 1,239-kilometer route to the Yellow River does not openly defy the laws of physics (map 4.2). Shoumatan, located next to sacred valleys in the shadows of two cult peaks, Lhamo Latso and Lha Gyari, is several hundred kilometers to the west of the Great Bend. The Shoumatan Dam is likely to flood *yul* landscapes.

It was actually at the first international conference of the Global Infrastructure Fund, held in July 1986 in Anchorage, that the idea to reroute the Brahmaputra was openly discussed at a venue outside China. For more than a decade thereafter, it appeared that engineering and other challenges would prevent the proposal from getting beyond the drawing board. Because the plan has been very controversial from the beginning, the Chinese government has chosen not to speak about it in public. Yet long before Li Ling's book was published, a flurry of reports appearing in the Chinese state-run media indicated that the mega-idea was making a strong comeback in policy deliberations. The reports suggested that, while still wanting to divert waters from the Brahmaputra to China's northern plains, federal authorities were veering toward the idea of building a mammoth, unmatched-in-size dam at the Great Bend to generate hydropower. Several years before the state-owned HydroChina Corporation identified that site by name in 2010, media reports had

Map 4.2 The Proposal to Reroute the Brahmaputra River Not from the Great
Bend but from Shoumatan, to the West

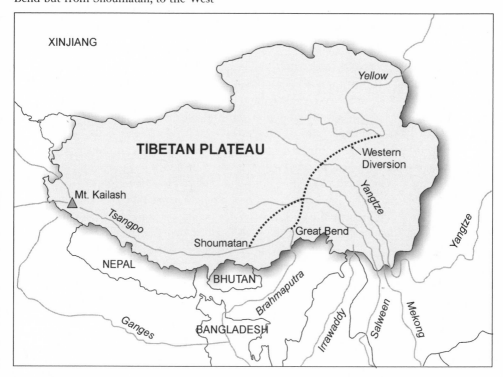

said the 38-gigawatt project would be located at Motuo, harnessing the force of a
2,982-meter precipitous drop in the river's height as it takes a sharp southerly turn.
In another pointer to those plans, the authoritative *People's Daily* reported the
launch of a feasibility study in 2003, saying the Tibet portion of the Brahmaputra
"boasts hydropower reserves of about 100,000 megawatts, or one-sixth of China's
total, ranking second only to the Yangtze River."[42]

In fact, it was only after the State Council—China's Cabinet—approved the
plan in principle in 2002 that the hydropower-planning authorities started the feasibility study to build the world's largest power station at the Great Bend. A preliminary assessment was first conducted at the site by an expert team in mid-2003
before the full-fledged feasibility study was initiated in October of that year.[43] By
2005, the government interest had broadened and the state-run China Hydropower
Engineering Consulting Group Corporation was pressed into service to assess the
Brahmaputra's hydro potential at key points on its course in Tibet and to put
forward concrete suggestions on potential resource exploitation.[44]

The following year the State Council took the next important step of authoriz-
ing detailed planning of the so-called Tsangpo Project at the Great Bend, with
Chen Chuanyu of the Academy of Engineering Physics being appointed the chief

planner. As publicly sketched by Chen, the project would "involve using nuclear explosives to blast a 15-kilometer-long tunnel through the Himalayas" to reroute the river flow partially northward.[45] Also in 2006, Liu Changming, a hydrologist at the Chinese Academy of Sciences who was advising the government on the project, said in a media interview: "Now the Western Route isn't just an abstract plan; it will go ahead."[46]

Significantly, China's resurrection of its long-dormant claim to India's Arunachal Pradesh State in 2006 coincided with Beijing's going ahead with detailed project planning of the massive damming of the Brahmaputra at points close to the disputed Tibet–Arunachal frontier. The entire Great Bend is located in the borderland with India, which controls the lower part of the bend and is pursuing its own hydropower development there. One key reason why China has refused to settle its territorial disputes with India is that it wants the latter to cede the upper, water-rich parts of Arunachal Pradesh. The edges of Arunachal and Tibet now constitute one of the world's most militarized zones, with Beijing accusing the Indian army of pursuing attrition warfare with the PLA forces stationed there and the Indian military, for its part, reporting growing cross-border Chinese incursions in that region and other parts of the Himalayan borderlands.

No less significant is the fact that the Tsangpo Project has been actively supported by the PLA, whose generals were the first to encourage federal authorities to examine the vision outlined by Guo Kai (who, ironically, was imprisoned during the Mao-era Cultural Revolution before being rehabilitated under Deng Xiaoping). The megaplan proposal not only received the support of a number of PLA generals, but the technical assessments that had been carried out until then prompted the influential General Zhao Nanqi in October 2000 to declare: "Even if we do not begin this water diversion project, the next generation will. Sooner or later it will be done."[47] In 2006 Li Ling, the author of *Tibet's Waters Will Save China* and an ex-army officer himself, was quoted as saying, "Many of the generals have lived and traveled in western China, so they know how serious the water shortage is there and how difficult life is," while the aging Gua Kai declared: "With one engineering project we could solve all of northern China's water problems."[48]

Today, the PLA remains the most enthusiastic backer of the plan, which actually comprises two projects: The construction at the Great Bend of a dam more than twice as large as the Three Gorges Dam to generate energy for China's eastern belt, and the Brahmaputra's diversion as part of the Great Western Route. The gigantic dam itself would significantly deplete transboundary river flows.

The Great Western Route, for its part, involves much more than the rerouting of 17 km³ of waters per year of the Jinsha, the Yalong, and the Dadu proposed in the more modest version of the western leg of the Great South–North Water Diversion (SNWD) Project. The Great Western Route plan actually calls for waters to be diverted from three big rivers in addition—the Brahmaputra, the Mekong, and the Salween. The diverted waters are to flow northeast through hundreds of kilometers of aqueducts, tunnels, and reservoirs, with Tibet's greatest lake, Kokonor, along with Lajia Gorge, to be used as the main storage center and conduit. Thus far, the official plans for the Mekong and the Salween have centered more on exploitation of their hydropower potential than on water diversion to China's northern plains, although the Great Western Route calls for some of their waters to be eventually diverted to the Yellow River. The upper Salween and Mekong, as the Chinese Water Resources Ministry has noted, flow between towering mountains and, although their drainage basins are small, their "great drops in height" just before they dip into Southeast Asia create "an enormous flow that offers an abundant source of power."[49]

Because of the sheer volume of its discharge, the Brahmaputra is at the heart of the Great Western Route plan, which demands the annual diversion of at least 200 billion cubic meters of that river's water. That figure is almost five times more than the 44.8 billion cubic meters of water per year planned to be diverted via the other projects combined in the eastern route, the central route, and the narrowly defined western route of the SNWD Project. The Chinese government, despite touting the Tibetan Plateau as "an inexhaustible source of water," has preferred not to talk about the Great Western Route or even the Tsangpo Project, so as not to intensify the international controversy and concerns about its megaplans. Indeed, it has remained economical with information about its present and prospective projects in Tibet. While making halfhearted attempts to stanch Bangladeshi and Indian fears about the diversion of the Brahmaputra, China has not shied away from identifying the Great Bend as holding the largest untapped reserves for potentially meeting its water and energy needs.

The identification of the Brahmaputra bend as the site for the construction of a hydropower project larger than the 2.3-kilometer-long Three Gorges Dam—which itself is almost nine times bigger than America's Hoover Dam in terms of installed hydropower-generating capacity—is significant because China has harnessed the power of the Yangtze also at a major bend. The Three Gorges Dam has been built at the uppermost of the Yangtze's famed gorges, formed by an assembly of high, steep cliffs round which the river curves. The rich biodiversity of the Three Gorges area, underscored by its large concentration of "seed plants" (plants that are reproduced by means of seeds), did not prevent China from building the mammoth dam there and flooding some natural habitats; it seems set to similarly disregard the unique ecological status of the Great Bend. Although China has built more dams than the rest of the world combined in the past five decades, the most controversial of them has been the Three Gorges Dam, whose completion constituted only one part of the much broader water strategy centered on the SNWD Project and the big western line.

The ongoing infrastructure development in the county of Metog (home to the sacred Pemako and site of the planned largest dam in the world) is a pointer to China's intent to tap the Brahmaputra's resources in a big way. Some of the infrastructure development also is designed to draw hordes of tourists to the Great Canyon (map 4.3). But much of the infrastructure activity in Metog (also spelled

MAP 4.3   The Great Bend Area in Tibet

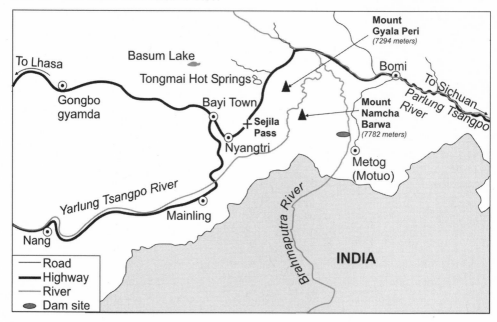

"Medog," and called Motuo in Chinese)—located in Nyangtri Prefecture—seems designed to support the ambitious hydro plans. In fact, the main reason why the Chinese government, despite its frenzied construction of dams in the Han provinces, was slow to undertake similar projects in Tibet in the past was the lack of supporting infrastructure. That shortcoming has been sought to be remedied through the construction of new highways, airports, and railroads. The advent of better infrastructure already has led to a spurt in dam building in the water-rich southeastern areas of the Tibetan Plateau, as is apparent from the parallel cascade of dams being built on the upper reaches of the Mekong and Salween in Yunnan and from the new hydropower projects on the Brahmaputra at sites located upstream to the Great Bend.

China already has built a number of dams on the Brahmaputra, as table 4.2 shows. These dams are all located upriver from the Great Bend. An official Chinese newspaper quoted a Chinese scholar as saying that, "Although some water dams are operating on the tributary of the river, they do not impact the downstream Brahmaputra River in India."[50] That is true: Their size is such that the downstream flows are unlikely to be materially affected. Some of the dams are linked to the Three Rivers Development Project involving the Brahmaputra and its two key tributaries, the Kyichu (or the Lhasa River) and the Nyangchu. Also called the "One River, Two Streams" plan, the Three Rivers Development Project has since 1991 focused on large-scale irrigation, hydropower, and economic development in

TABLE 4.2   Dams Built by China on the Brahmaputra River and Its Tributaries (Partial List)

Project Name	Location	Intended Use	Generating or Storage Capacity (MW)	Construction Status
Pangduo	Lhasa River	Irrigation and Power	120 megawatts (MW) 687 million cubic meters (m³)	Completed or under construction
Zangmu	On Brahmaputra, in Lhoka prefecture	Power	510 MW	Under construction since 2009
Yamdrok Tso	Lake Yamdrok	Power	90 MW	Completed in 1987
Manlha	On Nyang Chu, between Nagartse and Gyangtse	Irrigation and Power	20 MW 157 million m³	Completed in 2002
Chonggye	Near Chonggye township	Irrigation	11.58 million m³	Completed in 1997
Nyangtri-Payi	Nyangtri (Kongpo) Chumo Gully in Sangri County,	Power	84 MW	Completed in 1995
Wolka	Lhoka	Power	20 MW 4.5 MW	Completed in 1998
Yangjungshi Tago (Tiger Head)	Lhasa River basin	Mainly irrigation	81 million m³	Completed (year unknown)
Reservoir	Lhasa River basin	Irrigation	12 million m³	Completed (year unknown)
Suo Chang	Nye Chu, Panam County	Irrigation	18 million m³	Completed (year unknown)
Chun Sun	Nye Chu, Panam County	Irrigation	24 million m³	Completed (year unknown)
Drikong	Lhasa River	Power	30 MW	Completed or under construction

Sources: Environment and Development Desk of Central Tibetan Administration; internationalrivers.org; *China Daily.*

the Brahmaputra basin area between the Kyichu ("the river of happiness") and the Nyangchu ("the mother river" to local communities). Although the climate and soil are not suitable for large-scale agriculture, the Chinese authorities have turned grasslands into irrigated farms in this region, with the land transformation accelerating environmental degradation.[51]

In March 2009, however, the chairman of the Tibet Autonomous Regional Government, as if to intensify China's dam-building spree in Tibet and Yunnan, unveiled plans for major new hydropower stations on the Brahmaputra, besides the Salween, Mekong, and Jinsha rivers. A series of six big dams will come up in the upper-middle reaches of the Brahmaputra, to the southeast of Lhasa, with construction of the first—the run-of-the-river Zangmu hydropower project—beginning in 2009 itself. India, through its technical-intelligence capability, however, has identified twenty-four Chinese projects in progress on the Brahmaputra, a majority of them small dams. The official Chinese announcement of a cascade of dams on the Brahmaputra coincided with reports in the state-run media that China Gezhouba Group Corporation had been awarded the contract to design and complete by 2015 the Zangmu Dam, whose groundbreaking was hailed by local authorities as opening the path to major dam building in Tibet.[52] As part of the new cascade, four other large dams are officially coming up downstream from Zangmu at Jiacha, Lengda, Zhongda, and Langzhen. The sixth, at Jiexu, is upstream to Zangmu and is intended to help flush silt buildup in the lower dams with the aid of its huge reservoir. Significantly, this cascade is in the same portion of the Brahmaputra as Shoumatan, the proposed river diversion point.

Dam building is to apparently concentrate around the Great Bend in the next phase. In fact, after the completion of the Gormu-to-Lhasa railroad in 2006, some of the 230,000 engineering and support staff employed on that mission were sent to work on new infrastructure development projects in Metog and other remote counties in Nyangtri Prefecture. To help facilitate the movement of heavy machinery for tunneling and boring to the Great Bend for the start of any water megaproject, Chinese authorities, for example, unveiled an $87.5 million venture in 2007 to build an all-weather road from Metog town—which is close to the border with India and has less than 10,000 residents, although it is the main settlement in Metog county—to Bomi city, located 141 kilometers to the north at an altitude of 2,720 meters (map 4.3). That newly built road, passing through the 3,750-kilometer-high Galongla Tunnel, links up with Tibet's main highway to Sichuan Province (known as Highway No. 318), which is to serve as the route for transporting supplies of equipment and material for hydro works at the Great Bend. A Tibet–Sichuan railroad running through Bomi is also planned, in addition to the six new railway lines already in the works on the Tibetan Plateau.

China's state-owned media has not tried to conceal the linkage between infrastructure development in the region and official plans to harness the Brahmaputra's resources. For example, Xinhua, the government-run news agency, quoted a local tourism official as saying that the new highway from Metog to Bomi "will allow investors to tap the rich water resources from the Brahmaputra canyon."[53] The Motuo Dam site is barely 20 kilometers north of Metog town. Daduqia, almost on the border with India, has been identified as the site for another megadam to impound the Brahmaputra's waters. After the opening of a high-altitude airport in Nyangtri city not far from these two dam sites, building a railway to the region became the next logical step.[54] Plans thus were unveiled to extend the railroad to Nyangtri Prefecture so as to assist in the construction and upkeep of the multiple water projects intended to be initiated in this resource-rich but seismically active region. Once sufficient local infrastructure has been erected, work on the impoundment and diversion of the Brahmaputra waters is likely to begin unannounced.

The Nuclear-Explosives Idea

By 1995, China began openly toying with the idea of carrying out "peaceful nuclear explosions" (PNEs) to excavate an underground tunnel, 15 to 20 kilometers long, through the Himalayan range to the north of the Brahmaputra to help redirect massive volumes of water from the river to its northern plains.[55] In a meeting at the Chinese Academy of Engineering Physics in Beijing in December 1995, for example, engineers contended that, though it would not be possible to reroute the Brahmaputra with conventional methods, the mission definitely was attainable with nuclear explosives—a statement that, as an article in an American scientific publication then put it, was "just one of many lately in which Chinese technologists and officials have touted the potential of nuclear blasts for carrying out nonmilitary goals."[56] Given the deep gorges flanked by mighty mountains in the Great Bend, the proponents of rerouting always have contended that the diversion has to be engineered at a point before the river has embarked on its U-turn.

The Chinese government's desire to divert the Brahmaputra waters by employing nuclear explosives actually found expression in the international negotiations in Geneva in the mid-1990s on a Comprehensive Test Ban Treaty (CTBT). China confounded every other state in the negotiations by introducing a proposal to exempt PNEs from the CTBT purview. PNEs had fallen out of international favor in the period after India surprised the world in 1974 by conducting what it called a PNE.

China had not done a PNE—or at least not acknowledged carrying out one. But the United States and the Soviet Union had large PNE programs. From 1961 to 1973 the United States conducted 27 PNEs involving 35 individual detonations as part of the program called "Project Plowshare," a name derived from a line in the *Old Testament*: "And they shall beat their swords into plowshares, and their spears into pruning hooks." US nuclear scientists considered the PNE technology as best applicable to large excavation projects, including the building of harbors, dams, canals, and highway and railroad cuts through mountains.[57] The Soviets, for their part, carried out a total of 128 PNEs between 1965 and 1988, with most yields ranging between 2 and 20 kilotons, although larger detonations also were done.

The Soviets conducted PNEs for a wide range of missions, including to create caverns to store gas condensate, boost oil and gas production, bore canals and tunnels, build dams and water reservoirs, employ the underground-mining method known as "block caving," bury biologically hazardous industrial waste, and stop gas escaping from coal mines.[58]

The Indian PNE, however, became an international symbol of how to acquire nuclear-weapons capability in the garb of peaceful activity. So when Beijing, more than two decades after the Indian detonation, proposed a PNE exemption in the CTBT draft, it took everyone by surprise. Chinese negotiators argued that their country should not be compelled to foreclose the option of using nuclear explosions for peaceful purposes, especially when such detonations could bring economic benefits.[59]

The fact is that the Soviet use of PNEs in resource-related and other economic projects had impressed Chinese leaders and scientists. Indeed, "before 1960, the megaproject propensities of the Soviet experts working in Mao's China left a deep imprint on China's water engineers,"[60] who earlier had been awed by Joseph Stalin's plan—abandoned after his death—to redirect to arid Soviet Central Asia the north-flowing Irtysh, Ob, and Yenisei rivers of Western Siberia. To be sure, the post-Stalinist Soviet Union used PNEs to successfully excavate water reservoirs and canals.[61] The largest Soviet PNE experiment, code named "Project 1004," produced two lakes from a river.[62]

Even the American PNE program sought to experiment with water resources–related uses of nuclear explosives under a 1968–70 project code named "Aquarius." The project—not executed—was designed to modify underground aquifers, create subsurface storage, dam rivers, and manage water resources, while another unimplemented project sought to connect the Tennessee and Tombigee rivers via an excavated canal.[63] The United States, unlike the Soviets, did not employ PNEs on an industrial basis. Yet, in the period after the 1974 Indian detonation, the United States teamed up with the non-nuclear-weapons states Thailand and Egypt to enter into agreements with private companies to carry out feasibility studies on two water-related projects involving nuclear excavations.

One was the Kra Canal Project in Thailand, which sought to link the Gulf of Thailand with the Andaman Sea using 139 nuclear explosives ranging from 100 to 1,000 kilotons. Another proposal was to take Mediterranean Sea water some 54 to 79 kilometers into the Qattara Depression in Egypt, employing "the difference in elevation to generate hydroelectric power"—a project that called for the use of at least 181 nuclear explosives in the 150-kiloton to 500-kiloton range.[64] Neither project, however, went beyond the feasibility study. The 1976 Peaceful Nuclear Explosions Treaty between the United States and the Soviet Union, in any event, imposed a 150-kiloton ceiling on such detonations.

It was against this background that China proposed at the United Nations' Conference on Disarmament in Geneva that PNEs be exempt from the scope of the nuclear test ban treaty. After tabling a working paper on PNEs in mid-1994, it came out openly and strongly in March 1995 in favor of PNE exclusion, contending that the experience of "some countries with advanced nuclear technology has proved that peaceful nuclear explosions have extensive prospects for application which will benefit mankind as a whole."[65] China said it would be preposterous to ban nuclear explosions for peaceful purposes when nuclear detonations were not outlawed in war. In support of its position, it also cited Article 5 of the 1970 Nuclear Non-Proliferation Treaty (NPT), which seeks to extend PNE benefits to even non-nuclear-weapons states by proclaiming:

Each party to the Treaty undertakes to take appropriate measures to ensure that, in accordance with this Treaty, under appropriate international observation and through appropriate international procedures, potential benefits from any peaceful applications of nuclear explosions will be made available to non-nuclear-weapons states party to the Treaty on a nondiscriminatory basis and that the charge to such parties for the explosive devices used will be as low as possible and exclude any charge for research and development. Non-nuclear-weapons states party to the Treaty shall be able to obtain such benefits, pursuant to a special international agreement or agreements, through an appropriate international body with adequate representation of non-nuclear-weapons states. Negotiations on this subject shall commence as soon as possible after the Treaty enters into force. Non-nuclear-weapons states party to the Treaty so desiring may also obtain such benefits pursuant to bilateral agreements.

Three possible uses of PNEs were put forward as justification by China, including diverting waters from Tibetan mountains through canals to China's parched areas.[66] It proposed that the CTBT specify that "only nuclear-weapons states can conduct such peaceful nuclear explosions, either for themselves or for non-nuclear-weapons states as well." Nearly all other countries in the negotiations, however, opposed China's PNE demand, which they feared would leave a major loophole in the treaty. In fact, a final document of the April–May 1995 NPT review conference in New York, which indefinitely extended the NPT while negotiations on the CTBT were going on in Geneva, recommended that the UN body in Geneva "take . . . into account while negotiating a comprehensive nuclear test ban treaty" that "peaceful applications of nuclear explosions envisaged in Article 5 of the Treaty [NPT] have not materialized."[67]

China, however, remained defiant until mid-1996. The CTBT was eventually concluded after China on June 6, 1996, dropped its insistence on excluding PNEs, but not before it extracted a formal concession that the issue would be revisited at a treaty review conference ten years after the pact had come into force.[68] Although some states like Canada and Japan sought to block the concession, saying a specific mention of the PNE issue could provide countries with a lawful excuse to pursue PNE research and development programs until a review of the CTBT had been able to sort out that matter, the final treaty text incorporated the compromise. CTBT's Article VIII, titled "Review of the Treaty," reads:

1. Unless otherwise decided by a majority of the states parties, 10 years after the entry into force of this Treaty a conference of the states parties shall be held to review the operation and effectiveness of this Treaty, with a view to assuring itself that the objectives and purposes in the Preamble and the provisions of the Treaty are being realized. Such review shall take into account any new scientific and technological developments relevant to this Treaty. On the basis of a request by any state party, the review conference shall consider the possibility of permitting the conduct of underground nuclear explosions for peaceful purposes. If the review conference decides by consensus that such nuclear explosions may be permitted, it shall commence work without delay, with a view to recommending to states parties an appropriate amendment to this Treaty that shall preclude any military benefits of such nuclear explosions. Any such proposed amendment shall be communicated to the Director-General by any state party and shall be dealt with in accordance with the provisions of Article VII.

2. At intervals of ten years thereafter, further review conferences may be convened with the same objective, if the conference so decides as a matter of procedure in the preceding year. Such conferences may be convened after an interval of less than ten years if so decided by the conference as a matter of substance.[69]

Years later, the CTBT has yet to come into force. China has signed the treaty but not ratified it. It presumably continues with its PNE research in order to retain the option to make use of nuclear technology for massive excavation. The People's Liberation Army's expertise in using conventional boring and blasting techniques to build tunnels and channels, in any case, will be relied upon for any rerouting of the Brahmaputra waters because, to link up with the Yellow River, the diversion path will have to cross a number of streams and mountain ranges. The six-river Greater Western Route to the Yellow will necessitate extensive burrowing in a region that is prone to major earthquakes.

The plain truth is that China retains an unconcealed interest in nuclear excavations on the Tibetan Plateau to impound or divert river waters. In fact, a spate of reports in the state-run Chinese media in 2000 about the Brahmaputra's centrality in the plans to address water scarcity in China's northern plains gave rise to speculation in the Western press that China was drawing up plans to employ PNEs to create a diversion path through the Himalayas.[70] In an interview telecast in early 1998, Chen Chuanyu, who subsequently was appointed the chief planner of the Tsangpo Project, told the German state-owned television ZDF that the nuclear plan was to excavate a 15-kilometer tunnel through the Himalayas that would make the river plunge precipitously, thereby creating a gravity-driven northward diversion and generating 40,000 megawatts of hydropower.[71] That figure was later revised to 38,000 megawatts.

The Great Bend area has remained at the center of the Chinese plans to tap the Brahmaputra's resources in a major way by building tunnels through high mountains. Even if the Brahmaputra's flow were partially deflected from upstream Shoumatan, the exploitation of the unparalleled energy resources at the Great Bend—where the river is joined by swift-flowing tributaries, especially the powerful Parlung Tsangpo—would demand mammoth excavations. After all, a reservoir to help generate 38 gigawatts of electricity would be substantially larger than the Three Gorges reservoir, which is bigger than North America's Lake Superior in length. Such a reservoir would inundate vast tracts of virgin forests and rich biological resources in an ecologically sensitive region that is home to half of all species found on the Tibetan Plateau. The environmental effects would be further exacerbated if small-yield nuclear explosives were employed, even if without official acknowledgment, for tunneling.[72] A nuclear device with a very low yield is still more powerful than the largest conventional explosives.

Not "If" but "When"

Tibet's immense strategic and resource value for China is obvious. As one observer has put it, "The Chinese Communist Party has always referred to Tibet as China's 'water tower' and considers it a key to sustaining China's northwest in water, revitalizing its deserts and the Yellow River itself, as well as being crucial to its Himalayan strategy."[73] China's interbasin and interriver water transfer plans on the Tibetan Plateau are likely to proceed the way its mineral-wealth-exploitation strategy in that region has been implemented—quietly.

The Brahmaputra, which has gushed across the Himalayas with such force as to carve the world's steepest and longest canyon and to form Asia's most biodiverse basin, is all set to be tamed. On its plans to siphon the Brahmaputra flow for its energy and water needs, China has not only been frugal with information but has also sent out confusing signals. As Indian opposition leader Jaswant Singh recalled in Parliament in 2008, he, as foreign minister between 1998 and 2002, raised the issue of the Brahmaputra's diversion with his Chinese counterpart, only to be told that there were no such plans. "But having denied it vehemently for many years, China's official news agency, Xinhua, has confirmed plans for the Tsangpo diversion project. This is a very serious development," he said.[74]

In fact, Chinese officials have been publicly contradicting themselves on the feasibility of diverting Tibetan waters northward. That could imply differences over the Great Western Route among important figures or groups within the Chinese Communist Party, which is said to be now racked by "chronic factionalism."[75] Another possibility in the case of nonconforming comments is that the concerned functionaries themselves misspoke and inadvertently punctured the regime's carefully crafted public relations line. The voices of skepticism occasionally heard could also reflect genuine doubts within the party and government establishment about the technical and environmental advisability of going against the laws of nature and carrying out massive transfers of water across inhospitable terrain.

Whereas the then–Chinese water resources minister, Wang Shucheng, told a Hong Kong University meeting in October 2006 that, in his personal "academic" opinion, the idea to reroute waters from the Tibetan highlands did not seem viable (though, he hastened to add, the government had yet to make a final decision),[76] the director of the Yellow River Water Conservancy Committee, Li Guoying, said publicly around the same time that the megaproject enjoyed official sanction and was likely to begin after certain engineering and environmental issues had been resolved.[77] "When the economic and social development of the northwest reaches a certain level and the potential of water-saving measures is exhausted, this project will be launched," Li added at a news briefing.

Wang, who served as the water resources minister for nine years up to 2007, has described China's water crisis in these ominous words: "To fight for every drop of water or die, that is the challenge facing China."[78] But after leaving office, Wang cautioned that the proposal to divert 200 billion cubic meters of water per year from the Brahmaputra to the Yellow would trigger such water pressure as to damage many dams and embankments along the latter river.[79] That concern had been voiced earlier by some others, including Guo Qiaoyu, a water expert with the Nature Conservancy's Beijing office, who said the big western line would cause the Yellow to flood and damage aquatic ecosystems.[80] A 2000 report titled "A Strategic Study on Sustainable Development of China's Water Resources in the Twenty-First Century," by Qian Zhengying and Zhang Guangdou of the Chinese Academy of Engineering, underscored the risks of building a giant dam at Shoumatan to reroute the Brahmaputra, reckoning the cost of the Great Western Route at $125 billion, or five times higher than the estimate of its proponents.[81]

Wang, the most-prominent person to speak out, may have genuine doubts about the wisdom of going ahead. But just as the Chinese government commenced work on the eastern and central routes despite some domestic experts openly expressing misgivings about the entire South–North Water Diversion Project,[82] it is unlikely to be swayed by the views of Wang and other skeptics on the different planned elements of the Big Western Route. Although the Brahmaputra-related massive damming and diversion plans remain a continuing subject of debate in Chinese newspapers and think tanks, it is apparent that this dual-purpose megaproject is not only under serious consideration at the government level but is also likely to be launched.

All official indicators point in that direction, including government-conducted engineering surveys and infrastructure development in the Great Bend area and farther upstream. The construction of a cascade of dams in the upper-middle reaches of the Brahmaputra, in fact, has underlined Beijing's new focus on the Brahmaputra. The muted Indian and Bangladeshi response to the new projects can only encourage China to construct bigger dams downstream closer to the Great Bend and embark on building the largest dam ever conceived in human history—at

Motuo. Bangladesh has stayed mum, whereas India has done little more than regurgitate the Chinese government assurance that transboundary water flows will not be affected—the same assurance Beijing has proffered the lower-Mekong countries while blithely building bigger dams upstream.[83]

Such is the importance of the Tsangpo Project that, by helping to top up the Yellow River, it can, according to its promoters, alleviate water shortages in six hundred cities in northern China. But as the Yellow will not be able to accept mammoth transfer of water in one go, a gargantuan storage reservoir would need to be separately engineered for calibrated release of water to the Yellow, especially in the lean season. The same storage reservoir would also receive waters from the five other rivers included in the big western line. The most likely plan, as suggested by Guo Kai and Li Ling, is to employ Lake Kokonor and the Lajia Gorge to its south, linked together by a specially constructed canal, as the central site to store and redirect water flows on a mass scale. Kokonor, whose water level has sunk over several centuries, is to be enlarged and filled to the brim, while Lajia will be dammed. That would allow water to be channeled not only to the Yellow but also to desert lands in the northwest to help end the sand squalls that now intermittently blanket Beijing and other northern Chinese cities in the dry season.

The other mission of the Tsangpo Project—energy—is already being put into action, with bigger dams planned or under construction. Plans also have been unveiled, as detailed in chapter 3, to build the world's largest hydropower station, whose reservoir is to impound colossal waters at the river's most fragile area, ecologically and seismically. The energy-related part of the Tsangpo Project actually is moving ahead in conjunction with the damming of the upper Mekong and Salween, the other key international rivers in the Great Western Route plans.

China's ambitions to channel Tibetan waters northward actually have been whetted by two factors: the completion of the Three Gorges Dam, which, despite the project's glaring environmental pitfalls, China continues to trumpet as the greatest engineering feat since the completion of the Great Wall; and, as discussed earlier in the book, the dominance of engineers in the Chinese political hierarchy. Since the 1980s, many of China's leaders have been engineers, and they have focused on what engineers like to do—infrastructure development. President Hu Jintao, who graduated as an engineer with a major in hydropower in 1964, served as Tibet's martial-law administrator in the late 1980s. He thus fused two key elements in his persona—water and Tibet. But as others are discovering, water plus Tibet equals trouble. Premier Wen Jiabao, a geological engineer who rose to prominence after the June 4, 1989, government crackdown on prodemocracy demonstrators, also boasted an old Tibetan connection, having done geological work in the part of the Tibetan Plateau that now is in Gansu Province.

This may explain Beijing's obsession with water megaprojects and its drive to exploit the rich resources on the Tibetan Plateau. The Three Gorges Dam indeed was planned as a stepping stone to the much wider water strategy pivoted on the South–North Water Diversion Project. The environmental problems that the

Three Gorges Dam is spawning—from landslides to water pollution—have thus not dampened the enthusiasm of the Chinese officialdom for the south-to-north program, whose eastern and central routes are scheduled to be largely operational by 2014. That would allow the authorities to concentrate on the western route.

Dam building has been an integral part of state ideology in Communist China, and is still presented to the public as an indispensable tool of national development. The "iron fist of authoritarianism was used to silence" those who opposed the Three Gorges Dam, such as the female author Dai Qing, who was imprisoned for publishing a collection of essays critical of the project.[84] Just as the Chinese government has ignored criticism by foreign (and some daring domestic) experts of its past or ongoing water megaprojects, it will not allow downstream states' displeasure or condemnation to get in the way of its exploitation of the resources of the Brahmaputra, the Salween, and the Mekong.

In this light, as one Western expert on China-related environment issues has put it, it "would not be exaggeration or nationalistic paranoia for India to think that the next westward step in China's megaprojects" is likely to center on one of the world's mightiest rivers, the Brahmaputra.[85] A Beijing University professor of international studies—while deriding concerns about a potential Sino-Indian water conflict as attempts at "myth-making"—has revealed that advocates of the "new complex western route to link watersheds in Tibet and western China have stated that construction could start as early as the mid-2010s. Given that China has already started the eastern and central routes of its controversial south-to-north water diversion plan, there is indeed ground for concern that the Chinese authorities and hydroengineers may again be determined to prevail over the forces of nature."[86]

It is thus apparent that the issue is not *whether* China will expropriate a major chunk of the Brahmaputra's waters for its use but *when*. Such commandeering of the Brahmaputra's waters, however, is an idea China will not discuss in public, because the plans imply environmental devastation of India's northeastern plains and eastern Bangladesh and would be akin to an undeclared water war on India and Bangladesh. As a headline in *The Times* of London encapsulating downstream concerns read, "Millions Live in Fear That China Aims to Steal Their River."[87] For its part, the Hong Kong–based *South China Morning Post*—in an article titled "The Great River Theft," about the "sheer effrontery of diverting a river of such importance"—said that the Chinese government's plans are "to punch a great hole" in Tibet's massive natural water tank and "siphon water away from its neighbors through a buried pipe no one seems to have noticed."[88] Once the Chinese authorities complete their preparatory work, they will start building megadams on the Brahmaputra for energy and water diversion, presenting the program as a fait accompli.

Such a water strategy carries serious potential to damage the interests of co-riparian states, raise political tensions, and engender inter-riparian conflict. The covetous exploitation of the resources of international rivers with little regard for transboundary effects is not a recipe for regional stability. Yet a newly powerful China, sitting prominently at the tables of global governance, is becoming increasingly repressive in Tibet and dismissive of international calls to protect that plateau's unique culture and ecology. Success breeds confidence, and rapid success spawns arrogance. That, in a nutshell, is the China problem facing downstream Asian states. Regrettably, China's authoritarian assertiveness, underpinned by the country's rise as America's largest creditor and its belief that US economic power and political influence are on the decline, has emerged as the key obstacle to the adoption of a sustainable approach to the resources of the Tibetan Plateau and to the formation of basinwide Asian communities to help manage transnational water resources in an integrated, holistic fashion.

STARK IMPLICATIONS FOR LOWER RIPARIANS

The water megaprojects and plans on the Tibetan Plateau cannot be regarded as China's internal matter alone, given the likely transboundary effects, the threat to the health of transnational rivers, and the environmental degradation already being witnessed in Asia's "water tower." Environmental changes on the plateau will, for example, adversely affect the Asian monsoons, introducing greater variability and unpredictability in rainfall patterns. Indeed, the Chinese moves to aggressively dam international rivers have set a wrong example, as underscored by the dam building initiated by the lower-Mekong countries and the nations along the Himalayan belt. Not to be left out of the water-harnessing game, these riparian states have launched their own projects.[89] China's dams, however, are much bigger in size and purpose, and carry the most profound transboundary implications. That country's hydraulic interventions through gigantic projects actually translate into much increased geopolitical risks in water-stressed Asia.

The planned construction of the world's largest dam at the Great Bend, for example, would reduce cross-border flows into India and Bangladesh and affect fluvial and aquatic ecosystems in ways even more significant than the impact of China's upper–Mekong River basin hydropower projects on Laos, Thailand, Cambodia, and Vietnam. Yet it has been speciously claimed in China that the massive upstream damming of the Brahmaputra River, or even the partial deflection of its flow northward, will not "significantly" affect downstream-basin states but rather "help reduce flood damage" in India and Bangladesh.[90] It is even claimed that a lot of the Brahmaputra water goes "waste" through discharge into the ocean. These claims actually mirror the ones that have been made in relation to the Mekong.

Such contentions overlook the plain fact that fish and other marine life depend on the nutrients and minerals received through such emptying of a river. If the Brahmaputra's discharge were reduced to a trickle, it would ravage the delta and coastal marine areas in the Bay of Bengal that together are among the most biologically productive areas on the planet, supporting countless species. The impoundment and diversion of the river's waters in Tibet would also seriously disrupt the

Brahmaputra's annual flooding cycle, which helps spread valuable nutrients into the floodplains of northeastern India and Bangladesh and allows for the cultivation of rice paddies in natural-pond conditions, besides creating a giant nursery for fish—the main source of protein for the poor.

The rich, fertile soil in the lower Brahmaputra basin owes a lot to nature's yearly gift of silt; the Chinese megaprojects will block delivery of that gift. Much of the river's nutrient-rich sediment load, instead of being naturally transported downstream, would get trapped by the upstream projects—in the same way that the Three Gorges Dam already is disrupting heavy silt flows in the Yangtze and causing silt buildup in its reservoir itself, besides creating fluvial imbalance upstream and denying essential nutrients to agricultural land and fish downstream.

The Chinese plans to divert the Brahmaputra waters partially away from India and Bangladesh also have to be viewed against the likely impact of climate change on the snowmelt and glacial melt that significantly feeds this river, Tibet's longest and the world's fourth largest. The shrinking Himalayan glaciers along the route of the Brahmaputra in Tibet underscore the creeping impact of climate change. If the sources of river flow begin to be seriously affected, massive impoundment and diversion of the Brahmaputra's waters upstream would be an invitation to an eco- logical catastrophe in Tibet itself, besides devastating the plains of northeastern India and more than half of Bangladesh. By the middle of this century, global warming is projected to adversely affect the dry-season availability of Brahmaputra waters downstream while increasing wet-season flooding.[91]

The Brahmaputra ecological health already is beginning to be affected because of the growing number of upstream hydropower plants and irrigation reservoirs on the main river and its tributaries, with India also seeking to emulate China's example by unveiling dam-building projects in Arunachal Pradesh State. Ecologists have warned that such overexploitation of water resources would diminish the movement of nutrient-rich sediments downstream, affecting agriculture on the Assam plains of India and in Bangladesh and eroding the river-centered biodiver- .sity. In fact, owing to the high ambient salt levels in the Brahmaputra watershed, the irrigation-induced salinity resulting from the introduction of widespread farm- ing in the upper-middle basin in Tibet has already emerged as a threat to down- stream agriculture.

With the leadership in Beijing having decided that the Tibetan Plateau's waters are the answer to China's water crisis, the Brahmaputra and the Mekong are likely to join the list of the world's endangered rivers. As symbolized by the cascade of dams that China is building on these rivers, with little regard for the transboundary impact on co-riparians, its upstream hydroengineering projects on the plateau carry dire environmental risks as well as major interstate political implications. Its moves, in fact, threaten to turn international rivers like the Mekong, the Salween, and the Brahmaputra into mirror images of its main rivers, the Yellow and the Yangtze: hydrologically degraded, heavily polluted, and ecologically dying. Of all the Chi- nese hydroengineering plans on the plateau, the ones relating to the Brahmaputra are the most far-reaching.

The Impact on Bangladesh

The greatest impact of the upstream impoundment and diversion of Brahmaputra waters would clearly be borne by deltaic Bangladesh, whose future already is threatened by saltwater incursion and more-frequent extreme weather events. The Chinese diversion would mean environmental devastation of large parts of Bangladesh, which is not a small state but the world's seventh most populous nation, with more than 167 million citizens. Although tiny Monaco boasts the world's highest population density, the country with the greatest population density other than a microstate is Bangladesh.

With 1,131 inhabitants per square kilometer, Bangladesh's freshwater resources are coming under an increasing strain, although more than two-thirds of the population lives in remote villages with few basic facilities. Farming is a critical link in Bangladesh, accounting for nearly half of overall employment. But most farms are very small, with less than 1 hectare of land; indeed, a large number of them have even less than 0.2 hectares.[92]

A Chinese diversion of 200 billion cubic meters of waters from the Brahmaputra is likely to dry up several streams in northeastern India and Bangladesh, besides seriously affecting the main river's hydrology, sediment load, and water quality. In fact, some small tributaries will desiccate before reaching Bangladesh. Increased salinity in the delta area will threaten the survival of the Sunderbans (Forests of Sundari Trees), a UNESCO World Heritage site located along the Bay of Bengal in Bangladesh and India. The Brahmaputra forms a common delta in Bangladesh with the Ganges and a third river, the Meghna, which originates in the hills of eastern India.

As a fused entity, the Ganges-Brahmaputra-Meghna basin has 2.5 times the discharge of the Mississippi, North America's largest river, and is second in the world only to the Amazon in its annual discharge. The Brahmaputra contributes by far the biggest volume of water to this delta, which "contains the largest number of the world's poor in any one region."[93] Whereas China has about twenty-four thousand large dams, Bangladesh has only one important dam and three irrigation barrages at present. Upstream impoundment and diversion of the river waters would devastate Bangladesh's deltaic plains, undermining farm production, exacerbating poverty, and damaging the ecology.

The Sunderbans, which serve as a natural bulwark against the impact of hurricanes and the encroachment of saline water from the Bay of Bengal, are the world's largest contiguous mangrove forests and home to river dolphins, estuarine crocodiles, and the famous but dwindling Royal Bengal tiger population.[94] In the past three decades, the rising sea level has already swallowed up about 100 square kilometers of the 9,630-square-kilometer mangrove swamps of the Sunderbans, which are made up of hundreds of islands that are crisscrossed by narrow water channels. The Sunderbans ecosystem is pivoted on a fine balance between freshwater from the delta and saline water—a balance that threatens to get upset. Some aquatic species are found in mangrove channels with high freshwater inputs, while other species prefer more salty channels further downstream. Increasing water salinity due to several factors—including upstream irrigation, geotectonic movements, and global warming—has already led to vegetation depletion and encouraged coastal species like the finless porpoise to migrate to the Sundarbans.

About four-fifths of Bangladesh actually is made up of alluvial lowlands at the confluence of the three great rivers and their tributaries. Given the fact that Bangladesh is crisscrossed by 230 major rivers—54 of them (especially the largest ones) flowing in from India—it is hardly a surprise that watercourses cover 7 percent of the country's total land area. The annual monsoonal flooding, aided by overflowing rivers and the country's low-lying topography, often causes major damage or destruction in Bangladesh, with the Food and Agriculture Organization of the United Nations estimating that, on average, 18 percent of the country gets inundated during the four-month summer monsoon season.[95] If the flooding were to be severe, the affected area could be more than twice as large. In the 1998 floods, which were among the worst ever, 66 percent of the country was submerged. But with much of Bangladesh located within the floodplains of the three major river systems, the floodwaters play an important role in renewing the country's rich soil fertility by spreading essential nutrients.

The Brahmaputra is the most important river of Bangladesh. With the indigenous renewable water resources estimated at just 105 km^3 per year—of which the groundwater part is limited to 21.1 km^3—Bangladesh heavily depends on the inflowing rivers from India that originate either there or in Tibet.[96] Those rivers bring in 1,106 km^3 of water per year.[97] That the waters of the Brahmaputra are the lifeblood for the largest number of Bangladeshis can be seen from the fact that more than half of Bangladesh's total quantity of transboundary waters are delivered by this river alone.

The Brahmaputra's annual inflow into Bangladesh is estimated at 599 km^3 per year, while the cross-border contribution of the Ganges—the next important river for Bangladesh—is 344 km^3 per year and of the Meghna 163 km^3 annually.[98] The Brahmaputra's contribution to transboundary river inflows thus is 54 percent, while its share of Bangladesh's total renewable water resources—from endogenous and exogenous sources, and including both surface and underground waters—is 49.5 percent.[99] The Brahmaputra's drainage basin in Bangladesh is also that country's largest basin; the river drains a 270-kilometer-long region from north to south before joining the Ganges west of Dhaka, the capital.

India, according to international estimates, has a 33.4 percent dependency on waters originating from across its frontiers, largely Tibet.[100] But Bangladesh's external water dependency—91.33 percent—is one of the highest in the world.[101] Its per capita freshwater availability, 7,569 cubic meters per year, however, is almost five times higher than India's.[102] That offers small consolation in view of Bangladesh's high vulnerability to transboundary appropriation of river resources by China or India.[103] If the Chinese megaproject plan to reroute the Brahmaputra waters to the Yellow River takes off, the effects in Bangladesh would be ruinous. Even the impoundment of waters by the planned gigantic dam at the Great Bend would be most damaging for the country located farthest downstream, given the extent of Bangladesh's reliance on the Brahmaputra waters and that river's centrality in the livelihood and security of tens of millions of Bangladeshis.

Bangladesh indeed illustrates that the claims put forward by Chinese officials and engineers in support of their Brahmaputra water-harnessing plans reflect extraordinary naïveté on issues of hydrology and ecology. The Chinese have touted their plans as potentially offering dual benefits to the downstream states: flood control, and the option to purchase hydropower from China. Even if energy-hungry China had surplus hydropower to export, it has no common border with Bangladesh to sell electricity directly. To sell electricity to Bangladesh via India would not be easy in the absence of a regional energy grid and trilateral cooperative mechanisms. The flood control benefit also is unpromising. In fact, by disrupting the annual flooding cycle, which helps spread fresh deposits of rich silt to replenish the fertile but overworked soil, the Chinese plans will seriously affect rice paddy cultivation on the Assam floodplains of India while delivering a major blow to agricultural production in Bangladesh's Brahmaputra basin.

In Bangladesh, agriculture dominates the economy, politics, and society, with domestic stability tied to growth in the farm sector. Although this sector also includes fisheries, livestock, and forestry and serves as the main source of raw materials for most industries, food grain production—especially of rice, the staple crop—remains the leading economic activity in the country. Yet that is the very area that will bear the brunt of Chinese impoundment and diversion of waters. Despite impressive increases in rice and other cereal production since the time Bangladesh became independent in 1971, the country remains one of the world's leading rice importers.

Owing to several constraints—ranging from the lack of additional arable land and the ravages of extreme weather events—grain production increases have failed to keep up with the increased demand arising principally from the yearly addition of about 3 million people to the national population. Food insecurity is a major problem also "because of the lack of purchasing power and thus of access to food" among the very poor.[104] The government has identified food security as holding the key to socioeconomic stability and thus has continued, despite a rising import burden on the national treasury, to market subsidized rice in a country where rice is life. China's Brahmaputra plans add a major new challenge to Bangladesh's efforts to significantly boost rice yields in order to cope with population growth, climate change effects, and natural forces such as floods, droughts, heavy rainfall, and salinity.

The central problem Bangladesh faces is that it has too much water during the monsoon season (when 80 percent of the total annual rainfall occurs) and too little water from late fall to the beginning of summer. The upstream appropriation of the Brahmaputra waters threatens to compound that problem by reducing the transboundary flows when water is most needed—during the dry season. Diminished dry-season flows will mean less freshwater availability not only for irrigated farming and other economic and human needs but also for salinity control and ecosystem services. Increases in crop yields in Bangladesh have been achieved both by planting genetically improved varieties that respond well to chemical fertilizers and agrochemicals and by improving irrigation water management practices. But due to the volatility of river flows, the limited availability of surface waters during the dry season, and the country's flat terrain, the goal of building an extensive, reliable network of gravity irrigation has proven elusive.

As a result, rampant exploitation of groundwater for agricultural, urban, and industrial needs has become commonplace in Bangladesh, resulting in a rapidly falling water table and accelerated reduction in dry-season river and stream flows.[105] The overexploitation of groundwater resources—best symbolized by the near depletion of the aquifer system serving Dhaka, a megacity with 12.5 million people—has accentuated environmental problems, including arsenic contamination, intrusion of saline water in coastal areas, and land subsidence (a condition whereby the subsoil becomes compacted because of the excessive withdrawal of water from certain types of rocks, causing the land level to drop). The contamination of groundwater with naturally occurring inorganic arsenic has been described as "the largest mass poisoning of a population in history," bigger in scale than the fallout of the 1986 Chernobyl nuclear disaster or the 1984 Bhopal gas catastrophe.[106] Surface-water shortages in the dry season have prompted farmers to drill hundreds of thousands of tube wells, many of which—without any arsenic-contamination test—have also become a drinking-water source.

Given the pivotal importance of the Brahmaputra in the dry season, China's upstream plans spell serious trouble for Bangladesh. The Ganges, which flows in an east–southeast direction, is an overstressed river even before it enters Bangladesh. It gets so depleted within Bangladesh that increasing salinity has emerged as an important problem in its basin, prompting the government to plan the ambitious, multi-billion-dollar Ganges Barrage.[107] The barrage is to boost dry-season water supplies in the southwestern region by diverting Ganges waters to twenty-four streams. Under a 1996 treaty with Bangladesh, India is committed to maintain cross-border Ganges flows at prescribed levels round the year, with the sharing formula guaranteeing Bangladesh 35,000 cubic feet of water per second of time ("cusecs," also known as "c.f.s") in alternative three ten-day periods between March 1 and May 10, which is the driest period.[108] The pact, a major water-sharing arrangement, has not helped close the supply/demand gap or stem the salinity problem because rising downstream water use has only increased the supply shortfall in the dry season. In fact, saline-water encroachment in Bangladesh's coastal areas has accelerated in the face of declining freshwater outflows to the sea.

Against this background, a significant decrease of the Brahmaputra flows due to China's Tibet projects is bound to have a cascading effect downstream in Bangladesh, compounding a range of problems stretching from paucity of surface-water availability in the dry season to increasing salinization. Sediment retention upstream resulting from the building of multiple large dams on the Brahmaputra, including one that is planned to be bigger than the Three Gorges Dam, is certain to extend harmful environmental effects all the way down to coastal fisheries, which depend on nutrient inputs from the river discharge. According to one Western observer, "There is no doubt that China needs the water. But so do India and Bangladesh. In this context, water is a matter of life and death, which is why the decision to be made in Beijing whether to go ahead with damming the Brahmaputra makes this tiny corner of Tibet potentially the most dangerous place on Earth."[109] China, however, is unlikely to be deterred by the downstream ecological and economic costs of its water projects, whose main beneficiaries will be Han Chinese but with local Tibetan and downriver communities paying the price.

Broader Implications for India

India is dependent not on just one river system originating in Tibet but on multiple major rivers that have their primary source there. In addition to the Brahmaputra, the Indus, and the Sutlej, which flow into India from Tibet, the seven-stream Kosi—a major Nepalese river system that commands an average outflow of 47.3 km³ per year and drains into the Ganges in India—has its topmost catchment area on the Tibetan Plateau. This is also the case for two other important Nepalese inland river systems, the Karnali and the Gandak, which both empty into the Ganges in India.

India, in turn, is the source of major cross-border river flows to other countries: Bangladesh, at 1,105.6 km³ per year, is the biggest recipient of waters from India by far, followed by Pakistan, which gets 183 km³ per year, and Burma, the beneficiary of a much smaller volume of waters estimated at 20 km³ per year.[110] Yet given India's significant dependence on multiple rivers originating in Tibet, the Chinese water-harnessing projects encompassing almost all the transnational rivers directly impinge on Indian interests.

The implications of China's building of upstream dams and barrages on international rivers—without transparency or information sharing—were driven home to lower-riparian India by the surprise flash floods that ravaged parts of its Himalayan states of Himachal Pradesh and Arunachal Pradesh between 2000 and 2005. Indeed, the saga of endless and fruitless Sino-Indian border talks since 1981 has helped deflect attention from a more central issue: China's opaquely pursued hydroengineering projects in Tibet that threaten to significantly diminish transboundary river flows. Between nuclear-armed, continental-sized China and India, the water bomb is no less potent than the nuclear bomb.

China's hydropower and irrigation works and plans for megadams in Tibet, indeed, are highlighting Indian vulnerability on the water front even before India has plugged its disadvantage on the nuclear front by achieving the objective to erect what it calls "a credible but minimal deterrent." Growing national water demands, the depletion and degradation of water resources, and climate change together are altering the balance of power between the two Asian giants by increasing the importance of water, a variable that China controls to a large degree through its hand on Asia's faucet, Tibet. This riparian ascendancy is reopening old wounds and subtly bringing Tibet back to center stage in the relationship between India and China.

In fact, Tibet is central in India's water resources picture. The Indian Peninsula ranks as the largest in the world, but the rain-fed rivers there have fluctuating volumes and several of them are not even perennial. South of the Godavari basin, the only major rivers are the Krishna and the Cauvery, with average annual runoffs of just 78.1 km³ and 21.4 km³ per year, respectively.[111] Most coastal rivers in peninsular India—popularly known as the Deccan Plateau—have small catchment areas and thus are seasonal. It is the mighty rivers that flow in from the Himalayas and the Tibetan highlands that are the lifeblood for the majority of the Indian population, concentrated in the northern plains. Most of these rivers, fed by mountain springs, rainfall, and snowmelt and glacial melt, have reasonably good flows during the lean season, with their monsoonal flooding cycle spreading valuable nutrients and sediment into the floodplains. In this light, it is hardly a surprise that the Indo-Gangetic plains of northern India are the most fertile areas of the country, "contributing to 65 percent of the total food basket."[112] The Ganges-Brahmaputra-Meghna basin covers 34 percent of India's land area but contributes nearly twice as much (62 percent) to the country's water resources, highlighting the spatial imbalance in resource distribution within the country.[113]

China has declined to get into institutionalized water-sharing cooperation with any of its riparian neighbors. By contrast, India, though no paragon of virtue, virtually stands out as a role model for having entered into an international water-sharing treaty with each of the two countries that are downstream to it—Bangladesh and Pakistan. Through its control over several major rivers vital to South Asian water and food security, China enjoys strategic and riparian advantage, which it has sought to selectively exploit by undertaking a growing number of water projects.

Its riparian preeminence is underpinned by glaciological dominance. Glaciers are key contributors to river waters when the demand for water is the greatest—in the hot season. Of the nearly 43,000 square kilometers of glacier area in the Himalayas, China controls more than three-fourths.[114] From channeling the glacier runoff to its newly built reservoirs and to its bottled-water industry and unveiling large dam projects, China is seeking to reap the full advantage of its hold over Tibet. Its hydropower, irrigation, and other projects on India-linked international watercourses serve as a glaring reminder that Tibet is at the heart of the India/China divide.

These projects also raise a larger question: Is China entitled to be the sole arbiter of the future of river systems that are the lifeline of downstream countries? To a large extent, India's plight, however, is of its own making. With China seeking to exploit—to India's detriment—its riparian dominance, New Delhi's self-injurious acknowledgment of Tibet as part of China has become more apparent. India has seriously compounded its problems by accepting Tibet as an integral part of China. If Tibet's annexation was the single most adverse event to affect Indian security in the twentieth century, India's formal recognition of Chinese sovereignty over Tibet constitutes the single biggest security blunder with lasting consequences for Indian territorial and river-water interests.

Take land first. By accepting Tibet as part of the People's Republic of China, India has ended up encouraging Beijing to assert Tibet's claims on Indian-administered territories, such as the resource-rich northeastern state of Arunachal Pradesh, which includes the Tawang Valley—the gateway to the Dalai Lama's 1959 escape from his homeland. A perceptible hardening of China's stance toward India in recent years is at the hub of the bilateral tensions, reflected in renewed Chinese muscle flexing along the 4,057-kilometer disputed Himalayan frontier. According to the US Defense Department, China has deployed solid-fueled, road-mobile CSS-5 nuclear missiles against India in place of the aging liquid-fueled CSS-3s; it also may be "developing contingency plans to move airborne troops" into the Himalayan border region.[115] By building new railroads, airports, and highways in Tibet, China now is in a position to rapidly move additional forces to the border to potentially strike at India at a time of its choosing. India, in response, has beefed up its force levels and announced plans to upgrade its logistics along the Himalayas.

Since ancient times, the Himalayas have universally been regarded as the northern frontier of India. But having annexed Tibet and then seized some Indian territories through conquest, China has laid claim to areas far south of the Himalayan watershed, as underscored by its claim to much of Arunachal Pradesh—which means "The Land of the Rising Sun" but which Beijing has been calling "Southern Tibet" since 2006. That Tibet remains at the core of the India/China divide is being underlined by China itself, because its claim to additional Indian territories is based on alleged Tibetan ecclesial or tutelary links to them, not on any professed Han connection. This attempt at incremental annexation draws quiet encouragement from India's imprudent acceptance of Tibet as part of the People's Republic of China. At the center of the Chinese strategy is an overt refusal to accept the territorial status quo vis-à-vis India. As a result, the wounds of the 1962 war have been kept open by China's aggressive claims to further Indian territories. Even as China has emerged as India's largest trading partner, the Sino-Indian strategic dissonance and border disputes have become more pronounced.

Although India has come to virtually accept the Chinese occupation of Aksai Chin—a Switzerland-size plateau that was part of the state of Jammu and Kashmir before it was captured by the People's Liberation Army—an emboldened China, in the name of upholding Tibetan interests and sentiments, presents itself as Tibet's supposed guarantor vis-à-vis India, laying claim to large chunks of Indian territory on the basis of their putative historical links with Lhasa. The larger, Austria-size

Arunachal Pradesh, bordering Burma, is located at the other end of the Himalayas as compared with Aksai Chin.

With its rich water resources, Arunachal Pradesh has untapped hydropower reserves of at least 57,000 megawatts,[116] which the Indian federal government is seeking to partially develop to help the state earn annual revenues of up to $850 million through the sale of electricity to other parts of northeast India.[117] Arunachal Pradesh's virgin forests, freshwater reserves, and unexploited mineral resources—ranging from coal and dolomite to hydrocarbons and graphite—highlight its impressive natural wealth. With its varied flora and fauna, including fifty-seven medicinal and aromatic plants in high demand, Arunachal actually is one of the global "hot spots" of biodiversity, along with the rest of the Eastern Himalayan region. In fact, unlike the biodiversity loss and environmental degradation in Tibet, Arunachal largely retains its pristine form.

As India gets sucked into a pre-1962-style trap, history is repeating itself. The issue then was Aksai Chin; the issue now is Arunachal. By asserting that Arunachal is part of Tibet and thus of China, Beijing wants other countries as well as multilateral institutions to treat that region as "disputed." Still, India is shy to publicly shine a spotlight on Tibet as the lingering central issue so as to help redirect attention to the source of China's claim. China, after all, has significantly raised the stakes by identifying Tibet as a "core issue" to its sovereignty, just like Taiwan, especially since the resistance to its rule in Tibet emerged as an open rebellion in the spring of 2008. Tibet now holds as much importance in Chinese policy as Taiwan. In ratcheting up the Arunachal issue with India, China seems to be drawing another analogy: Arunachal is the new Taiwan that must be "reunified" with the Chinese state. The Dalai Lama has publicly said that Arunachal Pradesh was never part of Tibet, using that detail to explain why Arunachal was not included in Tibet in a 1914 agreement that demarcated the borders between the then-independent Tibet and British-ruled India.

Beijing does not recognize that agreement because China's acceptance of the 1914 border would be an admission that Tibet was once independent, which would seriously undercut the legitimacy of its control over the restive region. But the very fact that the Republic of China—the predecessor to the People's Republic of China—took part in the tripartite conference in Simla, India, with the Tibetan and British Indian governments was a testament to Tibet's then-independent status. In fact, by accepting the credentials and full participation of the Tibetan plenipotentiary at Simla, Beijing acknowledged Tibet's power to enter into international obligations. According to Sir Charles Bell, a British officer who played a key role in the Simla Conference, China agreed both to "the transfer of negotiations from Peking to India" and to "the presence of the Tibetan plenipotentiary on an equal footing" with the British and Chinese representatives.[118]

The Simla Conference yielded four agreements—the Tripartite Convention between Great Britain, China, and Tibet; the Anglo-Tibetan Trade Regulations Agreement; the Tibet-India border accord; and the Anglo-Tibetan Declaration, which turned the Tripartite Convention into a bilateral treaty after the Republican government in Beijing, on second thought, balked at approving it. The Chinese plenipotentiary actually initialed the map at Simla delineating the India–Tibet border, or what became popularly known as the McMahon Line; thereafter, no dispute was raised by Beijing at the conference or in the subsequent years about the legitimacy of that boundary.

The Republic of China had objected to the delineation of the borders between so-called Inner Tibet and Outer Tibet, but not to the McMahon Line, which marked the Indo-Tibetan frontiers in the east. Those frontiers stretched from Bhutan to the Isurazi Pass in Burma, which was part of the British Indian empire at that time. A united Burma had been brought into British-ruled India in 1886 and remained part of it until being made a separate colony in 1937. As per the McMahon Line, the boundary runs along the crest-line of the eastern Himalayas into Burma.

The sole dispute at Simla that blocked the Republic of China from granting consent to the Tripartite Convention centered on defining the boundaries between Inner and Outer Tibet.[119] That was confirmed even by Communist China's official White Paper on Tibet. The White Paper makes no mention of any disagreement at Simla on delimiting the Tibet–India border, but admits the real dispute there was over the Tibetan representative's claim that the "Tibetan territory includes Qinghai, Litang, Batang and Dajianlu"—demands that "were rejected by the representative of the Chinese government."[120] Yet publicly, Beijing has continued to rail against what it calls a colonial line, even though it has recognized several other British colonial-era agreements.

Tellingly, the People's Republic of China has accepted the McMahon Line portion with Burma but not the section with India (map 4.4). When at Indian independence in 1947, the British diplomatic mission in Lhasa became the Indian mission, the precommunist Republic of China itself maintained such a mission there, underscoring the independent status Tibet enjoyed until Communist China annexed it. Having seized Tibet in violation of international law, China's nonrecognition of the McMahon Line with India became essential to legitimize its claims to areas south of that line, such as Arunachal Pradesh. In fact, with the Dalai Lama having publicly repudiated the Chinese claim that Arunachal Pradesh, or even just the Tawang Valley, was part of Tibet, a discomfited Beijing has sought to impress upon his representatives in the dialogue process since 2002 that for any larger political deal to emerge, the Tibetan government in exile must support China's position that Arunachal had been part of traditional Tibet. The plain fact is that with China's own claim to Tibet being historically dubious, its claims to Indian territories seem doubly suspect.

China originally fashioned its claim to resource-rich Arunachal Pradesh—a territory almost three times larger than Taiwan—as a bargaining chip to compel India to recognize its occupation of the Aksai Chin Plateau. For this reason, China withdrew from the Arunachal areas it had invaded in the 1962 war but retained its

MAP 4.4   China–India Territorial Disputes

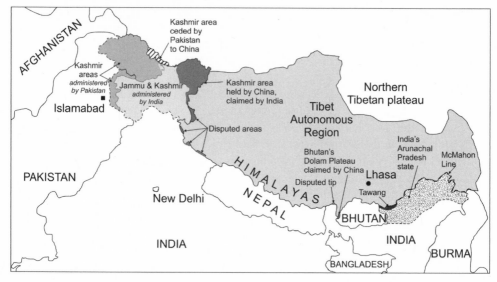

territorial gains in Aksai Chin, which provides the only passageway between its rebellious regions—Tibet and Xinjiang. Chinese leader Deng Xiaoping even broached the exploratory idea of a package settlement: New Delhi would accept Chinese control over Aksai Chin, and Beijing would drop its claim to Arunachal, subject to "minor readjustments" in the line of control. In his meeting with the visiting Indian foreign minister in February 1979, Deng said the package settlement would consist of India ceding its claims in the west and China ceding its claims in the east, taking the actual position on the ground as the starting point for a negotiated resolution. In elaboration, he stressed that this proposal was on balance to the advantage of India as the disputed territory in the east was vast in area, well inhabited, and rich in resources, whereas the area in the west was smaller and desolate.[121]

In the years since, however, as water stress has grown in China and water diversions have become popular in official policy, Beijing has begun eyeing Arunachal Pradesh's plentiful water resources. This has led to its plan to build near the Arunachal border the largest dam ever conceived in world history. China's resource-driven resurrection of its claim to Arunachal parallels the way it became covetous of the Japanese-controlled Senkaku Islands—which it calls Diaoyu Islands—only after the issue of developing petroleum resources on the continental shelf of the East China Sea came up in the 1970s. China had expressed no objection to the Senkaku Islands (controlled by Japan since the 1890s) coming under the administration of the United States under Article III of the 1951 San Francisco Peace Treaty. Nor did it object when, under the 1969 Okinawa Reversion Treaty, the United States agreed to return Okinawa and its "southwestern islands," including the Senkaku chain, to Japan. In fact, a world atlas published in China in 1960 showed the Senkaku Islands as part of Japan's Okinawa Prefecture. After staking a claim to the Senkaku Islands in the second half of the 1970s, China went one step further in 1992 by listing the Senkaku/Diaoyu Islands in its "law for territorial waters" and declaring its intent to use force to expel foreign ships entering any part of its territorial waters as defined in the promulgation.

Now that Aksai Chin is no longer a real issue bilaterally with India, Beijing has successfully put the "dispute" over Arunachal Pradesh at the center of its relationship with New Delhi, openly coveting that state as a cultural extension to Tibet. And to leave an international question mark hanging over the legitimacy of India's control of Arunachal, Beijing has sought to compel multilateral lending institutions and major countries to chart a course of neutrality on this "dispute." At the same time, to help aid the strategy of Pakistan, which China has continuously courted as a key proxy in its geopolitical competition with India, Beijing has found innovative ways in recent years to question India's sovereignty over the Indian-administered part of Jammu and Kashmir State—from refusing to allow the top Indian army general in Jammu and Kashmir to visit Beijing for a regular military-to-military meeting in 2010 to issuing visas on a separate sheet to residents of that state so as to set it apart from the rest of India. In addition, it has purged its frontier with Indian Kashmir from the total length of the border it claims to share with India. All these provocations have occurred as India has continued to gratuitously declare that Tibet is part of China.

In fact, just as India had retreated to a defensive position in the border negotiations with Beijing in the early 1960s after having undermined its leverage through a formal acceptance of the "Tibet Region of China," New Delhi similarly has been left in the unenviable position today of having to fend off Chinese territorial demands. Whatever leverage India still had on the Tibet issue was surrendered in 2003, when it shifted its position from Tibet being an "autonomous" region within China to it being "part of the territory of the People's Republic of China." There is thus little surprise that the spotlight now is on China's Tibet-linked claim to Arunachal Pradesh rather than on Tibet's status itself. That is why Beijing has invested so much political capital over the years in getting India to gradually accept Tibet as part of China. Its success on that score has helped narrow the dispute to what it claims.

This neatly meshes with China's long-standing negotiating stance: What it occupies is Chinese territory, and what it claims must be on the table to be settled on the basis of give-and-take—or as it puts it in reasonable-sounding terms, on the basis of "mutual accommodation and mutual understanding." So, while publicly laying claim to the whole of Arunachal Pradesh, China in private is asking India to cede at least that state's strategic Tawang Valley[122]—a critical corridor between Lhasa and Assam of immense importance because it can militarily open the way to throttle India's hold on its northeastern region. In fact, to place itself in a position to potentially chop off the northeast from the rest of India, China has laid claim to tiny Bhutan's Dolam Plateau, which directly overlooks the 21- to 40-kilometer-wide chicken neck that connects India with its northeast. China also has staked a claim to an area in Bhutan's north, but that claim appears designed as a bargaining chip to force Bhutan to make territorial concessions in the Dolam Plateau.

Now let us consider river waters. India is set to pay a heavy price on that front in the years ahead for its blunder on Tibet, the point of origin of most Himalayan rivers of India other than the main Ganges River. Only one small stream with an average annual outflow of just 0.117 km^3 per year, the Ruxu Tsangpo,[123] enters Tibet from the Indian Himalayan region. India thus is critically dependent on cross-border water inflows from Tibet. If Tibet is at the heart of the Chinese/Indian divide, water is at the center of the India–Tibet connection. But until the advent of the twenty-first century, no Indian leader had even mentioned the "w" world in public in relation to Tibet or China. It was only after flash floods devastated some downstream areas in the Sutlej and Brahmaputra basins that India gingerly raised the matter with China about its upstream hydroengineering works on those rivers and sought flood-related hydrological data on a regular basis. The first Indian leader who bilaterally raised the issue of water as a component of the India–China equation was Prime Minister Manmohan Singh during a 2009 Beijing visit.

When, in the 1954 Panchsheel (Five Principles) Treaty with Beijing, Indian prime minister Jawaharlal Nehru implicitly accepted China's annexation of Tibet without securing or even seeking Beijing's recognition of the then-existing Indo-Tibetan border, he did not even think that his action would have an impact on India's water interests in the future.[124] Under this eight-year pact governing India's relationship with the "Tibet Region of China," India forfeited all the British-inherited extraterritorial rights and privileges in Tibet. The accord recorded India's agreement to fully withdraw within six months its "military escorts now stationed at Yatung and Gyantse" in the "Tibet Region of China" and "to hand over to the Government of China at a reasonable price the postal, telegraph and public telephone services together with their equipment operated by the Government of India in Tibet Region of China."[125]

China's water-related focus on the Tibet Plateau dates back to the immediate aftermath of Tibet's forcible absorption. Mao Zedong, who knew that political control over the Tibetan massif was the key to dominating the Himalayas and major watersheds, famously observed in 1952 that, "The south has a lot of water, the north little. . . . If possible, it is okay to lend a little water." Even as Mao initiated a major program to build dams—a program that eventually resulted in the building of between 22,000 and 24,000 large dams in Han China and the Tibetan Plateau in the first five decades after the establishment the People's Republic of China[126]—Nehru signed away Tibet's long-held independence in a treaty with the occupying power without factoring in how his action could affect his country's water and other interests. Water as a potential bilateral issue was remote from his mind at a time when water shortages were not known in most parts of

India, and water availability had been taken for granted. That was the same reason why Nehru in 1960 charitably gave away 80.52 percent of the Indus system waters to Pakistan through a treaty of indefinite duration. India entered into Indus water-sharing negotiations with Pakistan in the 1950s under American and British persuasion to settle an issue left over by the 1947 partition of the subcontinent.

By contrast, there had never been a water-related issue between India and Tibet in history. So no one in the didactically quixotic government in New Delhi at that time thought that China's occupation of Tibet would change that record. Indeed, the romanticism that came to govern India's China policy up to the 1962 war was set in motion by Nehru himself when he recorded the following note in a policy advisory in July 1949 just before the Communist victory in China: "Whatever may be the ultimate fate of Tibet in relation to China, I think there is practically no chance of any military danger to India arising from any change in Tibet. Geographically, this is very difficult and practically it would be a foolish adventure. If India is to be influenced or an attempt made to bring pressure on her, Tibet is not the route for it. I do not think there is any necessity for our Defense Ministry, or any part of it, to consider possible military repercussions on the India–Tibetan frontier. The event is remote and may not arise at all."[127]

What Nehru believed would be a "foolish adventure" was successfully executed, bringing Han Chinese military forces to India's Himalayan frontiers for the first time in history. Yet even in 1954, Nehru was still unable to visualize the threat to India's territorial and water interests from the disappearance of Tibet as a buffer, even though the Tibet Plateau is more than three-quarters the size of India. The very essence of a dynamic and effective foreign policy is the ability to think ahead. While important countries in the 1950s were pursuing strategies of "balance of power," "balance of threat," or "balance of interest," the Nehruvian foreign policy was organized around developing-world solidarity, including India–China friendship, without being anchored in a distinct strategic doctrine. With idealism compensating for the absence of goal-oriented statecraft, the propensity to act in haste and repent at leisure ran deep in Indian policy. When China invaded India in 1962, Nehru admitted to the nation that

> a powerful and unscrupulous opponent, not caring for peace or peaceful methods, has continuously threatened us and even carried the threats into action. . . . Perhaps there are not many instances in history where one country has gone out of her way to be friendly and cooperative with the government and people of another country and to plead their cause in the councils of the world, and then *that country returns evil for good* and even goes to the extent of committing aggression and invades our sacred land. No self-respecting country, and certainly not India with her love of freedom, can submit to this, whatever the consequences may be. (emphasis added)[128]

To be sure, water as a potentially aggravating bilateral factor was not even in Prime Minister Atal Bihari Vajpayee's calculations decades later when he surrendered the remaining Indian leverage on Tibet in 2003 in Beijing, officially completing the process of India's sacrifice of its traditional buffer. A declaration signed by

Vajpayee and Chinese premier Wen Jiabao recorded the following unilateral Indian concession: "The Indian side recognizes that the Tibet Autonomous Region is part of the territory of the People's Republic of China and reiterates that it does not allow Tibetans to engage in anti-China political activities in India. The Chinese side expresses its appreciation for the Indian position and reiterates that it is firmly opposed to any attempt and action aimed at splitting China and bringing about 'the independence of Tibet.'"[129]

Let alone water, even the territorial implications escaped the attention of the aging and ailing Vajpayee when he formally recognized the Tibet Autonomous Region (TAR) as "part of the territory of the People's Republic of China." The declaration incorporated the worst possible phrasing for Indian interests. After all, TAR, as shown by China in its official maps, incorporates some Indian Himalayan territories, including the entire state of Arunachal Pradesh. Yet, unthinkingly, Prime Minister Vajpayee signed a declaration in Beijing recognizing TAR as part of China. Also, by narrowing Tibet to just TAR, Vajpayee gave India's imprimatur to Tibet's cartographic dismemberment. China has hived off extensive parts of traditional Tibet to shrink Tibet in size, divide the Tibetan population, and Sinicize the entire Tibetan Plateau. With its sense of history and its eye on Arunachal Pradesh's water resources, China is sure to confront India with the 2003 document in the future to argue that the Indian case on Arunachal is weak in terms of bilateral agreements. Indeed, it is no accident that China's resurrection of its claim to Arunachal has drawn encouragement from and followed India's 2003 forfeiture of its remaining leverage on Tibet.

The truth is that India is still in transition from the traditions of Nehruvian foreign policy to a post-Nehruvian approach to world affairs. It has imbibed greater geopolitical realism by abandoning moralizing diplomacy and doctrinaire non-alignment. But it has not yet fully embraced realpolitik. Nor is it an assertive pursuer of self-interest, in the way China, with its aspiration to great-power status, has been. Indeed, India—home to more than one-sixth of the human race—continues to punch far below its weight. Internationally, it is a rule taker, not a rule maker. Yet India's growing geopolitical importance, high rate of economic growth, and abundant market opportunities have helped increase its international profile. As a "swing" geopolitical actor, with the world's most assimilative civilization (which has managed to accommodate an extraordinary degree of diversity within its borders), India can truly play the role of a bridge between the East and the West, including serving as a link between the competing demands of the developed and developing worlds.

China's Legal Upper Hand

Although China's aggressive water-development strategy is driven by its fast-rising water and energy needs, it is the legal upper hand that encourages it to pursue projects designed to manipulate international river flows. By having consistently refused to get into binding sharing arrangements with its riparian neighbors, China remains legally unencumbered to appropriate river waters and increase downstream dependency. In fact, the lower-riparian states have little leverage to stop China from acquiring the capability to potentially employ water as an "asymmetric" political tool against any of its neighbors. Despite the great number of basins in the world that are shared between nations and the recurrent incidence of interstate water disputes, there is no universal water treaty or convention currently in force.

China is also on strong legal foundation vis-à-vis India, which has formally accepted full Chinese sovereignty over TAR, the headwaters of many rivers. Had India acknowledged only Chinese suzerainty—or restricted sovereignty—over that region, it could have cogently and compellingly pushed for international recognition of Tibet's waters as a common resource of all, with an attendant obligation on China to protect Tibet's natural ecosystems and refrain from causing harm to downstream communities. It is apparent that India's past mistakes are going to haunt it on the water issue with China. By conceding full Chinese sovereignty over Tibet, India has accepted China, in a de jure sense, as the uppermost riparian state in relation to the transnational basins that stretch from the Tibetan Plateau to the Indian subcontinent.

An upper-riparian state, according to the basic principles of customary international law, has the first right to exploit basin resources. International law rests primarily on treaties and customary (or unwritten) law, with the subsidiary sources of law being decisions of international courts and arbitral tribunals as well as the "teachings of the most highly qualified publicists of various nations."[130] Because no written international water law has been in force up to now, the principles of customary water law remain dominant.[131] The 1997 United Nations Convention on the Non-Navigational Uses of International Watercourses "codifies," or writes down, many of the principles of customary water law.[132] The entry into force of this "codification" convention still seems distant because of meager number of ratifications. But the principles and guidelines that the convention incorporates are increasingly being invoked in international forums because they reflect customary international law. Still, until the convention comes into force, it can at best only serve as a nonbinding guide.

In that light, on what legal grounds can India object to the upper riparian's construction of hydroengineering structures on the international rivers flowing to the subcontinent, even if such projects lead to diminished transboundary flows? Even politically, India cannot compare its position on Tibet with that of other powers. When the United States and Britain accepted Chinese sovereignty over Tibet—the United States has done that since the Richard Nixon administration, and Britain only since 2008, when it unveiled a historic reversal of position[133]—they had nothing to lose on the territorial or water fronts. For them, Tibet is a moral issue, not a strategic issue. That is why these powers could strike a separate deal with Beijing to recognize Chinese direct rule over Tibet, although they still support

Tibetan autonomy, especially in culture and religion.[134] But for India, Tibet is critical to its water security and larger national security. Chinese actions in Tibet directly affect Indian interests—from projects-related ecological degradation (which promotes climatic and monsoonal variability in India) to political repression (which brings more Tibetan escapees to India).

Now that India has unequivocally recognized Chinese sovereignty over Tibet, the river-waters issue—legally and politically—is no longer between Tibet and India but between China and India. Having accepted that several major rivers flowing into India originate in Chinese territory, India cannot convincingly object to China's exercise of its rights over the shared waters as the upper-riparian state. Water rights in customary international law are analogous to property rights, and they can be exercised, mortgaged, or transferred independently of the land on which the water originates or on which it is used.[135]

Although efforts to establish a *law of reason* for all water resources have sought to tie modern water regulations to ecosystem values, rather than merely with human demand, a couple of key doctrines of customary international law support China's prior entitlement vis-à-vis India and its other neighbors on the river-waters issue. One is the *doctrine of prior appropriation*, under which a priority right falls on the first user of river waters. It favors the upper-riparian state or the first appropriator of water (called the "senior appropriator"). A priority right, however, can fall on the first user of river waters, even if it is located downstream. The right of the "senior appropriator" to meet its water requirements takes precedence over the entitlement of a "junior appropriator" to draw water from a river. The central legal element in prior appropriation is the diversion of water from a watercourse for "beneficial" applications, including irrigation, industrial or mining purposes, electricity generation, and municipal supply. The definition of the beneficial use of water has since the 1990s expanded to environmental-protection uses.

As the uppermost-riparian state, China has the right to expropriate a rational share of the waters of any Tibet-originating international river. But through its hydro works, China also is seeking to set itself as the prime user of Tibetan waters whose water rights are protected under the doctrine of prior appropriation vis-à-vis any downstream state. India's own tardy moves in recent years to initiate water-harnessing projects in Arunachal Pradesh have been driven by its apparent intent to assert a priority right as the first user of river waters.

Then there is the *law of riparian rights*, which confers proprietary water rights on the owner of land contiguous to a river. After all, the term "riparian" comes from the Latin *ripa*, meaning "the bank of a stream," with the riparian landowner in customary law being the one whose continuous ownership title extends beyond the riverbanks. India has accepted that China, by law, is the rightful owner of the transboundary basins in Tibet. China thus cannot be challenged over its assertion of sovereign "riparian rights" on those shared water resources. The law of riparian rights indeed empowers upper-riparian China to a reasonable water share, but without reasonableness being defined.

China thus is within its riparian rights to dam or divert the waters of any international river for its own use, even if the consumers of water or beneficiaries of energy generated from water are not the people in Tibet but the residents in the Chinese heartland. In fact, under the *doctrine of prior appropriation*—which in the American West evolved as a means of establishing the right to use scarce waters from rivers and streams, and now is popularly known as the "Colorado Doctrine" of water law, after the US Supreme Court case *Wyoming v. Colorado*—an appropriator may remove the water from its source and put it to beneficial use at another location, in contrast to the geographical limitation that the *law of riparian rights* incorporates.

The large infrastructure of dams, barrages, irrigation canals, and other diversion channels that China is building on the Tibetan Plateau aims to give effect to the customary dictum "First in time, first in right." The first user or appropriator of water acquires the right (called a "priority") to its future use, as against later users or appropriators. Also, in keeping with the maxim "Use it or lose it," water rights can be lost due to nonuse.

China actually has staked a maximalist position vis-à-vis all its riparian neighbors by tacitly asserting *absolute territorial sovereignty*, or the right to do whatever it chooses with the rivers originating in Chinese-controlled territory, irrespective of the effects on the other nations or on ecosystems. Its frenetic and unilateral construction of dams on international rivers unmistakably signals that intent. By contrast, India, as the upper-riparian state in relation to Pakistan, accepted the *theory of restricted sovereignty* over transboundary rivers in signing the Indus Waters Treaty, going to the extent of agreeing to set aside four-fifths of the Indus River Basin waters for downstream Pakistan. In actual fact, India set a new precedent in international relations by effectively *ceding sovereignty over waters* of the largest three rivers of the Indus system, two of which originate within its territory and the third one of which arises in Tibet but collects its largest share of waters in India. In accepting the "block" reservation of those three rivers for Pakistan, India agreed not to make use of their waters in a way that could "materially change, on account of such use, the flow in any channel to the prejudice of the uses on that channel" by Pakistan under the provisions of the treaty.[136]

China's claim to absolute sovereignty over transboundary basins and their resources is probably intended to strengthen its bargaining leverage. It is apparent that until China completes the water infrastructure to enforce its perceived rights— even if such a water complex ends up significantly altering transboundary flows—it is unlikely to contemplate entering into any water-sharing negotiations with India or another riparian neighbor. Indeed, until then, Beijing is likely to maintain strategic silence on its water diversion activities to keep any co-riparian state guessing. Any talks to be held subsequent to China's completion of its megaprojects would thus be over the remaining waters not already appropriated.

Such an approach clearly draws comfort from the unfortunate fact that there still is no international treaty in force regulating the use of transnational water resources. There are only several basic international water law rules, but these are in the form of customary principles that have not been fully fleshed out or universally accepted. China indeed has been the lead opponent of the UN Convention on the Law of the Non-Navigational Uses of International Watercourses; it even tried to block its passage through the UN General Assembly but could get only Turkey and internally torn Burundi on its side in a vote that went 103 to 3 in favor of approval, with 27 abstentions. Turkey enjoys a riparian ascendancy in the Middle East almost similar to China's in Asia.

The so-called Helsinki Rules on the Uses of the Waters of International Rivers were the first to outline the principle of "equitable utilization" of shared inter-country watercourses and the obligation not to cause "substantial injury" to co-riparian states.[137] But in seeking to frame reasonable and equitable utilization as the cardinal rule of international water law, the 1966 Helsinki Rules have identified existing utilization of waters as one of the eleven factors that should determine what is reasonable and equitable.[138] The Helsinki Rules thus accord respect to prior appropriation—a path on which China is firmly set. The Helsinki Rules have been embraced by a number of international organizations and states. For example, meeting in New Delhi in 1973, the Standing Sub-Committee on International Rivers of the Asian–African Legal Consultative Committee adopted the principle of reasonable and equitable share, largely embracing the factors identified by the Helsinki Rules to determine equitable utilization.[139] Although they lack a legally binding effect, the Helsinki Rules have long been treated as reflecting the principles of customary international water law.

The Helsinki Rules actually helped shape the provisions of the UN Convention. The imprint of the Helsinki Rules on the UN Convention is so distinct that this convention also endorses the principle of prior appropriation, identifying "existing and potential uses of the watercourse" as one of seven factors relevant to equitable and reasonable use of shared interstate resources.[140] The convention, however, notes that "in determining what is a reasonable and equitable use, all relevant factors are to be considered together and a conclusion reached on the basis of the whole."

Yet the International Law Commission, which helped draft the UN Convention, has suggested that under this convention's mandate, "a watercourse state should first attempt to determine its legal entitlement to the beneficial uses" of a transboundary river flowing through its territory, before it considers other factors relevant to ensuring that the correlative rights of other riparian states are respected.[141] That reading jibes with what China claims to be doing. Indeed, China can only draw encouragement from the international precedent that India set by conceding four-fifths of the waters of the Indus Basin to downstream Pakistan on the principle of prior appropriation. As the upper-riparian and most powerful state in relation to its neighbors, China is in a position to enforce this principle by simply presenting a fait accompli.

Admittedly, the development of comprehensive, widely accepted international water laws on transboundary watercourses, backed by a neutral enforcement mechanism, remains elusive. Even customary international water law is still undeveloped institutionally to be able to help manage transboundary water disputes or conflicts. But to the extent principles of customary international law exist and are broadly recognized, China feels emboldened by them to stay on the present course of unilaterally appropriating an increasing share of the waters of international rivers. But even if there had been no customary principles serving as international standards in the most general sense, China—well accustomed to assertive advancement of its interests, including through unilateralist actions on the ground—would likely have done exactly what it has embarked upon.

The High-Stakes Himalayan Competition

Just like the now-famous motto "To get rich is glorious," the title of Li Ling's book, *Tibet's Waters Will Save China*,[142] reflects policy thinking in China. Control over Tibet's water resources gives China "enormous strategic latitude with its neighbors; when one of those countries is a rival, such as India, it becomes an effective bargaining tool and potential weapon."[143] Add to the picture the fact that China's Soviet-style political system normally does not back away from plans the top leadership has approved.

Unless there is internal political upheaval, it seems almost inevitable that China, given its own water shortages in the northern plains and its ongoing interriver and interbasin diversion projects, would—in due course—siphon off a sizable share (calling it a "reasonable" share) of the waters of the Tibetan rivers flowing southward. That the large-scale appropriation will have a serious economic, social, and environmental impact on the downstream basins, besides wreaking havoc on the natural ecosystems, is unlikely to give pause to the Chinese water diversion plans. "When faced with any question as to China's interests, especially in regard to territory and resources, the façade of good neighborliness quickly drops," as one scholar has pointed out, while warning that the "ongoing territorial disagreement between China and India could be but the prelude to a far more serious dispute should China proceed with plans to divert the water resources she controls in Tibet in ways that would benefit China at India's expense."[144]

A government structure capable of taking decisive action has armed China with unusual power to mobilize resources and rapidly execute new projects. China has the necessary capital, hydroengineering capabilities, and political determination to undertake water diversion megaprojects in the Himalayas, and it is unlikely to be swayed by international or Indian opinion. Whereas India has been slow to tap hydropower reserves in the Himalayan region, China has aggressively sought to bring the doctrine of prior appropriation into play by asserting its prior use through an increasing number of projects on transnational rivers in Tibet. It also has sought to impede India's water development projects in Arunachal Pradesh through moves to block multilateral credit lending to such plans.

China's efforts in 2009 to stymie a $2.9 billion Asian Development Bank credit plan for India because it included a $60 million flood management project in Arunachal were doubly paradoxical. For one, Beijing lays claim to India's largest state by area in the northeast as if the views of the 1.3 million residents of Arunachal Pradesh do not matter. For another, the watershed management project in Arunachal had been necessitated by deforestation, land and riverbank erosion, and other anthropogenic changes on the Chinese side of the Brahmaputra basin, leading to recurrent flooding downstream. As the Indian foreign minister put it, "China's objection on political grounds is a clear violation of the Asian Development Bank's charter which prohibits the Bank from evaluating any proposal on grounds other than economic."[145] China, even as it seeks to block multilateral funding of any project in "disputed" Arunachal, is merrily building dams—in the face of Indian objections—in a region that is internationally recognized as a disputed zone: Kashmir. Several Chinese projects have been initiated in the Pakistani part of Kashmir, one-fifth of which is under China's control. The Brahmaputra basin, according to the Asian Development Bank, has become "one of the most flood-prone parts of the world,"[146] thanks to the ecological and fluvial-system damage upstream.

India's flood management and hydropower production plans in Arunachal— most of whose rivers flow in a north–south axis and ultimately empty into the Brahmaputra—have made slow progress due to environmental concerns and local resistance. But with the Indian government committed to their implementation, the projects have come to symbolize the geopolitical competition with China over utilization of Himalayan resources. Indeed, the Indian environment minister publicly said in Beijing that "the answer" to Chinese water diversion plans is for India "to be much more aggressive in implementing its own hydro projects . . . so that our negotiating position vis-à-vis China improves."[147] But as India is downriver, it is taking important risks by pushing ahead with projects vulnerable to large-scale Chinese water impoundment and diversion.

Both countries face a growing water deficit. But whereas China is a water-stressed country, the situation in India is worse. India's per capita availability of freshwater is one of the lowest in Asia, with large parts of the country headed for a serious water crisis—a specter that is being reinforced by unsustainable rates of groundwater extraction.[148] On resources such as oil, gas, and minerals, a cash-rich China has demonstrated its nimbleness to outmaneuver rivals by using state-owned corporate behemoths to sign up international contracts. But because it cannot secure water through international deals, China has turned its attention to the exploitation of Tibet's "blue gold" wealth. Its water diversion projects and plans in Tibet are set to exacerbate India's water challenges. China's utilization of the Brahmaputra's average annual upstream runoff, through existing dams and reservoirs, is modest for now. But as its utilization of the total volume of the basin waters rises substantially through new large dams and other projects, the enhanced exploitation is likely to upset the Brahmaputra's hydrological integrity and have a damaging impact in northeastern India and Bangladesh. And if the projects to divert the Brahmaputra waters to the Yellow River and build a dam at the Great Bend larger than the one at the Three Gorges take off, the downstream effects would be ruinous.

India thus must prepare for its interests to come under growing pressure from China's water megaprojects. When China has refused to cease building more dams on the Mekong River, even though such construction has been without prior consultations with co-riparian states or an objective assessment of the transboundary effects, it is not going to be more considerate of India's interests in impounding or diverting the waters of any southward-flowing river. Multiple big dams on major Tibetan rivers, especially the Brahmaputra, are indeed likely to increase the risks of downstream flash floods in India triggered by sudden large releases from Chinese rain-swollen reservoirs or by a powerful earthquake wrecking a dam. The southeastern portion of the Brahmaputra basin in Tibet has one of the highest annual precipitation levels in the world, with much of the rainfall concentrated in the monsoon season. While holding back water for power generation and irrigation during the dry season, local Chinese authorities could be compelled to release water from their reservoirs during the monsoon season, wreaking havoc downstream.

Although the southeastern region of the Tibetan Plateau is prone to strong earthquakes, China has ramped up construction of more dams and reservoirs in Tibet and Yunnan. Yet, according to the Chinese state media, "improper construction procedures, [use of] disqualified workers, embezzlement of construction funds and mismanagement" have resulted in a situation where several large dams in Gansu, on the rim of the Tibetan Plateau, "are near collapse just one or two years after their construction."[149] A total of fifty-nine dams were breached in China between 1999 and 2008 alone.[150]

The diversion of the Brahmaputra waters is central to the Great Western Route of the ongoing Great South–North Water Diversion Project—a route that will bisect the Tibetan Plateau to link up the Brahmaputra and Yellow basins through a network of mountain tunnels and multiple dams in this quake-prone region. The intended diversion of at least 200 billion cubic meters of Brahmaputra waters per year is, as discussed above, nearly five times greater in volume than the combined waters to be rerouted to China's north through all other plans in the SNWD Project. The Brahmaputra waters thus hold the key to the Chinese plans to revitalize the Yellow and halt the spreading desertification in the northwest and north. Without the Brahmaputra being rerouted, the SNWD Project will make only a marginal impact in improving water availability on China's northern plains.

But for India, the Brahmaputra constitutes a critical basin, representing almost 30 percent of the country's water resources potential and 41 percent of its total hydropower reserves.[151] In fact, 58 percent of the total Brahmaputra drainage basin area of 651,334 km^2 falls in India, covering much of the country's northeast, plus the state of Sikkim and the northern slice of West Bengal State. Only 20 percent of the basin area is under Chinese control. India thus has a greater right to the river's resources. But China is unlikely to buy that argument over a river that flows through some of the most heavily militarized areas in southern Asia, with Beijing continuing to show much of the 83,743-square-kilometer Arunachal Pradesh in its maps as its own territory. In fact, China's resurrection of its long-dormant claim to

Arunachal Pradesh can be seen as part of a diplomatic strategy tied to its upstream water diversion plans. By laying claim to such sizable real estate located directly downstream, China seeks to nullify Indian complaints about the effects of upstream activities on Arunachal, which is on the frontlines of China's planned grand water larceny.

If upstream water infrastructure helps create a situation where India is at the mercy of China with regard to cross-border river flows, such dependency can only aid the Chinese strategic aim to keep New Delhi on good behavior so that it does not directly challenge Beijing and steers clear of a military alliance with Washington. The capability China is seeking to develop "to turn the 'taps' on or off," as an article in a Hong Kong newspaper put it, holds stark implications for others: "Control over Tibet's largest river [the Brahmaputra] is as great a political tool as any military force—like laying siege to an enemy fortress from the safety of your own home."[152] The article also said that India's "meek" response to Chinese hydro plans "has been likened by one Tibetan publication to the Indian fable regarding a rural simpleton who chopped off a tree branch he was sitting on," adding that "if India is not prepared to stand up to the mainland [China], then Bangladesh is up the proverbial creek without a paddle." Still, despite the supposed meekness, India has faced growing Chinese criticism in recent years, with the *People's Daily*, for example, berating New Delhi for its "recklessness and arrogance"[153] and the Chinese Foreign Ministry labeling the Indian prime minister's 2009 Arunachal Pradesh tour a "disturbance" that should not be repeated.[154]

It is more Tibet than Arunachal Pradesh, however, that raises controversial political questions on interstate water resources. China's construction of new roads and an airfield in the vicinity of the Brahmaputra's Great Bend and its plan to bring the railway to that area are pointers to what is in store for India on the water front. Such supporting infrastructure is critical for any giant engineering project, especially building the largest dam ever designed. The Chinese intentions to also redirect the Brahmaputra flows have been manifest for long. In fact, having successfully inserted a provision in the Comprehensive Test Ban Treaty's Article VIII that the peaceful nuclear explosions issue be examined anew at the treaty's review conference, China presumably is continuing with its PNE research in order to retain the option to do nuclear excavations in the Himalayas to take the Brahmaputra waters to the parched Yellow River. However, it may simply settle for the use of conventional excavation technology—a safer bet. Once the authorities have completed their various technical assessments and the Brahmaputra diversion receives the political go-ahead, the effort will be to carry out the project quietly, to the extent possible, and present it as an unalterable reality. A similar strategy was employed in the 1950s when China made furtive encroachments on Indian border areas to help incrementally create new realities on the ground.

Before the arrival of the Chinese military on the Tibetan massif, there was little utilization of water resources upstream in Tibet and the rivers flowed across the borders unimpeded. The Tibetans practiced small-scale traditional irrigation for centuries to grow their staple food, barley, which is roasted and ground into flour (*tsampa*). But their water consumption was negligible. Today, the story is fundamentally different as Tibet's new ruler, China, after building a series of dams, seeks to commandeer a growing share of the international river waters, unmindful of the downstream impact. That serves as a powerful reminder of how its annexation of Tibet is increasingly affecting the interests of downstream communities. For its part, India, by sacrificing its British-inherited extraterritorial rights in Tibet and legitimizing China's Tibet grab, ended up betraying its own interests.

China can be faulted for its lack of transparency on the hydroengineering projects in Tibet that carry significant implications for cross-border flows. But as the legitimate owner of Tibet's resources, by India's own reckoning, China has the right to harness river waters for its beneficial use. India, of course, can appeal to China not to ignore its interests by citing the principle of equitable distribution, which regards a river as an indivisible unit that should be developed for the benefit of the maximum number of people, regardless of territorial boundaries. But that can only be a plea because China does not have, and is unwilling to enter into, a treaty with India on shared rivers, unlike India's own water treaties with Bangladesh and Pakistan or the omnibus pact of 1909 between the United States and Canada that covers all their boundary water resources.

India also can cite the theory of limited territorial integrity, which asserts that every riparian state has a right to use the waters of an international river but is under a corresponding duty to ensure that such use does not cause substantial injury to any co-riparian. However, this theory, which is based on the equality of all riparian states and serves as the basis for some international customary rules, rests on two principles that have not been clearly defined or reconciled—the right to use the waters of a shared watercourse, and a parallel obligation not to cause appreciable harm to another riparian.[155] One unresolved issue is whether the right to utilize the resources or the duty not to cause appreciable harm is primary.

China, in any case, is sure to deny causing any harm to India through its upstream projects. Indeed, in an echo of the Chinese Foreign Ministry's earlier statement that as "a responsible upstream country," China had "fully considered the concerns of downstream countries" before launching its giant dam projects on the upper Mekong, Premier Wen Jiabao sought to assure India during a visit at the end of 2010 that "China takes seriously India's concern about the transborder rivers, and we are ready to further improve the joint working mechanism. We will do whatever we can and do it even better. I would like to assure our Indian friends that all the upstream development activities by China will be based on scientific planning and study and will never harm downstream interests."[156] Still, by reactivating its claim to Arunachal Pradesh, China has created strategic leeway to potentially argue that the downstream effects of its waterworks in that region are its own internal matter. Put simply, China has leveraged its position vis-à-vis India on water and other issues by resurrecting its claim to Arunachal.

When China builds a dam larger than Three Gorges at the Great Bend or starts partially rerouting the Brahmaputra, it will justify its plan in the same way that it has defended its building a cascade of dams on the upper Mekong—that reshaping the river's flow holds minimal impact downstream and indeed may be beneficial both in easing the annual cycle of flooding in India and Bangladesh and in making the Brahmaputra more navigable for promoting subregional trade. Some in India actually will buy and regurgitate this spiel, just as some Indians still repeat China's old accusation that it was India's forward-deployment policy, not the Chinese annexation of Tibet and the consequent nibbling at Indian territory, that caused the war in 1962. Yet the message that would go out clearly to the world is that China has once again acted unilaterally and stealthily.

The real problem India faces, however, is that it has ended up constraining its own options vis-à-vis China. As on the territorial issue, so too on the water issue, India sought no quid pro quo from China before a succession of Indian governments began shouting from New Delhi's Raisina Hill—seat of Indian officialdom—that Tibet is part of China. Prime minister after prime minister could not refrain from recording in joint Sino-Indian communiqués India's commitment to a "one China" policy, even as China not only declined to reciprocally make a one-India pledge but also overtly mocked India's territorial integrity.

Worse yet, little thought was given that by progressively bringing India's Tibet stance into complete alignment with China's demand, it would boost Chinese leverage, not result in any lasting gratitude from Beijing. Had New Delhi maintained a consistent stance over time that Tibet was a disputed territory (in the same way that Beijing treats the Jammu and Kashmir region as disputed, but not the one-fifth of it that China occupies), it would have enjoyed a stronger case against China's hydroengineering moves to diminish the flows of India-bound rivers. But now India's only option is to raise such matters bilaterally with the very country that has a record of flouting international norms and even bilateral commitments. For example, three of the five principles in the 1954 Panchsheel Treaty—"mutual respect for each other's territorial integrity and sovereignty," "mutual nonaggression," and "peaceful coexistence"—went up in smoke when China invaded India in 1962.

In fact, if China had been in India's place, it is unthinkable that it would have entered into Indus water-sharing negotiations with Pakistan in the 1950s, let alone sign away 80.52 percent of the water share. Instead of treating the water issue as a leftover issue from India/Pakistan Partition that needed to be resolved, China, in that role-change situation, would have lambasted the "colonialists" for arbitrarily rejigging international borders without any regard to the natural geographical and hydrological unit, and would have called upon them to pay for their sins. By contrast, India did not exercise its water leverage vis-à-vis Pakistan even to get the latter to withdraw from the more than one-third of Jammu and Kashmir it occupied by waging aggression in the years 1947–48. It continued to release the bulk of the Indus system waters to Pakistan on an interim basis for thirteen years—

maintaining the pre-Partition distribution patterns—until the terms of the Indus treaty could be finalized and brought into force. Generosity or charity, however, is not a principle of international relations. India's unprecedented bigheartedness toward Pakistan in the Indus treaty is not a model that China can even countenance. The Chinese strategy since the Mao era has been founded on a single-minded focus on building comprehensive national power as the key to China's emergence as a great power. That has entailed a ruthless pursuit of self-interest, including the assertion of its power and prerogative as the upper riparian.

So, when Prime Minister Singh raised the water issue with the Chinese leadership in 2009, as he admitted publicly, what did he expect from Beijing? The Chinese response, in essence, was to give a cold shoulder to India's stated concerns. China remains unwilling to go beyond informal oral assurances. As one analyst has cautioned about the Brahmaputra diversion plans, "the deliberate cold-blooded intent to steal water to support uncontrolled and unsustainable development in northwestern China . . . is reckless in the extreme and poses the real possibility of China being held responsible for plunging Asia into the unthinkable—the first major international water war."[157] It is doubtful, however, that India has the political will or capacity to retaliate to large-scale Chinese water impoundment or diversion that significantly affects downstream Indian users. "What can be stated with relative confidence is that it won't be the United Nations or any other such international organization, treaty or agreement that will forestall or avert crises resulting from the competition for water resources," according to another scholar. "China has shown no inclination to binding herself to any international agreement regarding water resources. China, despite becoming part of the so-called 'world community' and her talk of 'shared visions' with India, Russia and other neighbors, has not repudiated or even compromised on the old territorial claims that have persisted since Mao and before, and on this basis there seems little optimism for expecting an altruistic or 'neighborly' aptitude from China towards its neighbors if survival depends upon exploiting and diverting water resources at the expense of her neighbors."[158]

The Chinese erection of an extensive water infrastructure in Tibet has a bearing not just on the transboundary Brahmaputra flows but also on the other rivers that are directly or indirectly tied to India's treaty obligations with Bangladesh and Pakistan. Additional Chinese damming of, and water diversion from, the Sutlej would diminish that river's cross-border rate of flow, affecting India's ability to tap its entitlement of waters in the Indus system under the treaty with Pakistan. The Sutlej is the longest of the three eastern rivers of the Indus system reserved for India's use under the treaty. Another example relates to the Indo-Nepalese river of Kosi, which receives a contribution of some 12 km^3 per year from its Tibet-based upper catchment area and ultimately drains into the Ganges. China has unveiled a cascade of dams to be built near the border with Nepal on the Arun, part of the Kosi river system. Such significant water capture from the Arun and other Ganges tributaries would affect average annual flows in the lower eastern stretch of the overstressed Ganges, potentially making Indo-Bangladesh sharing of waters at the Farakka Barrage problematic.

As China blithely seeks to reap the fruits of its riparian ascendancy, India's recognition of Chinese sovereignty over Tibet hangs as an albatross round its neck. Just as India has retreated to an increasingly defensive position territorially, with the spotlight now on China's Tibet-linked claims to Arunachal Pradesh than on Tibet's status itself, New Delhi's self-fashioned policy straitjacket on Tibet leaves it little room to do anything about Beijing's reckless exploitation of its riparian dominance while rebuffing the idea of a cooperative interstate water regime. Accepting Tibet and the developments there as China's "internal" affairs, rather than evolving a balanced and nuanced China policy that puts the premium on leveraged diplomacy, has proven a leviathan misstep for India—one that will continue to exact increasing costs.

With Tibet becoming a theater for China to flex its military and hydro muscles, India thus must blame itself, not China, for its growing concerns over the Himalayan waters issue, which holds direct implications for its looming national water crisis. China, as is its wont, is asserting its riparian power over the Tibetan Plateau's resources, bolstered by its rising national strength. But it is doing so quietly, because talking about its rights or publicizing its water diversions would only highlight the emerging riparian conflicts with India and Southeast Asia. Chinese diplomacy aims to minimize the range of issues between China and its neighbors. Placing water—a sensitive and emotive issue—in the domain of public diplomacy just does not serve the Chinese interest, given that Beijing treats Tibetan waters as its own strategic asset. Yet China does not disguise its objective: To steal a significant portion of Asia's water supplies by quietly diverting them for its own use.

Indeed, China today seems to recognize no technological, political, and ecological limits to its exploitation and diversion of water resources. As underscored by its latest dam-building boom and in keeping with its larger resource-grab strategy, China is determined to do what it can get away with. It seems "willing to risk open conflict in order to hoard as much water as it can" before India and its other riparian neighbors can get their act together to "challenge the continent's biggest water hog."[159] To the extent that it can, China will try to present its actions as a fait accompli. The choice for Indian policymakers, therefore, is to stay limp-wristed or to rectify past mistakes before it becomes too late. Diplomacy, after all, encompasses the art of setting right a course and repairing any damage.

Tibet ceased to be a Sino-Indian political buffer when China annexed it. For Tibet now to become a political bridge between the two Asian giants that have important roles to play in shaping the new international order, water must be a source of cooperation, not conflict. Although the United States remains concerned about the China–India border situation, it will, according to a high-ranking State Department official, "likely be involved in a different issue on the Himalayan border—which is the dire shortage of water in both nations, and the role Tibetan waters can play in addressing it."[160] In fact, in March 2010 the State Department upgraded water as "a central US foreign policy concern," noting that as rising populations face diminishing water resources, "the probability of conflict will increase."[161] But America's manipulation of the Colorado River's flows to Mexico, in terms of both quantity and quality, has only set a wrong example that China is seeking to emulate on a much larger scale.[162] The once-mighty Colorado River's waters are siphoned by seven American states before the river dribbles into Mexico. Still, the United States, as a major partner of India and China, can play a key role in helping to contain Sino-Indian friction, including by cautioning Beijing against crossing well-defined red lines or going against the self-touted gospel of its "peaceful rise."

The plain fact is that nowhere in the world are the stakes higher on shared water resources than in the Himalayas and the Tibetan highlands, where the interests of the most-populous basins converge. If water is not to accentuate Sino-Indian strategic dissonance or instigate confrontation, the protection of these basins' shared resources must become part of bilateral and multilateral cooperation. For this to happen, there must be a fundamental shift in Chinese thinking and policy. Otherwise, the China/India water conflict, however one-sided it may be in its eventual outcome, will dwarf the fight over water in other parts of the world, including the Middle East.

Five

Managing Intrastate Water Conflicts

Intrastate water-sharing disputes already are rife in large parts of Asia—from Southeast Asia and the Indian subcontinent to Central Asia and China. According to the United Nations, growing competition over water resources has "led to an increase in conflicts over water" in the region, with conflicts within nations "dominating the picture, particularly since 1990."[1] As in the intercountry context, an intrastate water discord can arise as an extension of another dispute or conflict, including over a new boundary demarcation or projects designed to offer structural solutions in the form of dams, reservoirs, irrigation canals, and levees.[2] Because supply-side approaches centering on storage and diversion are often intended to address spatial imbalances in resource distribution, disputes can arise between provinces or regions over perceived excessive or inadequate water channeling. At times, more than one source of water-related conflict may be present in a situation. Water scarcity or the threat of a water crisis, however, is usually the key driver for a dispute to escalate to violent conflict.

Asia illustrates how rapid rates of population growth, development, and urbanization, together with shifts in production and consumption patterns, can place unprecedented demands on water resources, bringing them under growing pressure and fostering domestic discord. As the global center of the overuse and misuse of water resources—in keeping with its larger mismanagement of natural resources—a fast-developing Asia now must cope with inadequate water availability for many citizens, growing water pollution, and dwindling wetlands (which are an important source of groundwater recharge and waste treatment and detoxification services). The impact of overappropriation of stream flows on fluvial ecosystems is threatening the livelihoods of the people who depend on rivers, besides triggering interprovincial disputes and putting aquatic ecosystems at risk. Add to the picture the overexploitation of groundwater due to insufficient surface-water availability. With water quality having a bearing on public health, diseases caused by water contamination continue to claim many Asian lives every year, especially of the very young.

Asia clearly is headed toward a serious water crisis, underscored by the high extraction rates, soaring demand, scarce availability, falling quality, heavy dependence of many states on cross-border supplies, and threats to the sustainability of resources. To add to its woes, global warming and human-made environmental change are fostering a recurrent cycle of too much water from extreme weather events like river floods and typhonic storms from the oceans, and yet too little freshwater to meet national needs. As a newspaper headline put it following Pakistan's devastating flooding in mid-2010, "Drowning Today, Parched Tomorrow."[3]

Although the spotlight has been on interstate water issues in Asia, the intrastate water tensions and wrangles are no less serious. Asia, in fact, is discovering the hard way that hydrological, ecological, developmental, and social processes are closely woven together, and that poor management of freshwater resources can seriously constrain national, community, and individual choices. Except for a few countries—principally Bhutan, Burma, Kyrgyzstan, Laos, and Malaysia—Asian states already face water shortages, which are intensifying domestic political and environmental challenges.

Generally, the more populous a subregion, a nation, or an area within a country, the greater are its water challenges, with water stress often being accompanied by a fall in water quality. But when water quality is maintained, the paucity of water can be better managed. For example, Japan and South Korea have low per capita availability of freshwater compared with the global average of 6,466 cubic meters (m^3); yet their overall good water quality better positions them to meet their national needs. Groundwater depletion serves as another warning sign of the looming water crisis in the most populous parts of Asia.

A very different water-related problem confronts low-lying states like Bangladesh and the Maldives. Their very future is at stake due to creeping saltwater incursion and frequent flooding. Bangladesh, for example, has too much water, yet not enough to meet its needs. Born in blood in 1971—a war of secession that left 3 million people dead and ten times more women raped than during the subsequent 1992–95 Bosnian war—Bangladesh today faces the specter of a watery grave.[4]

Water withdrawal expressed as a percentage of the total renewable water resources (TRWR), according to the Food and Agriculture Organization of the United Nations, is a good indicator of the pressure on water resources in any country. TRWR—a measure of the maximum theoretical amount of water available to a nation—includes both external inflows and indigenous resources, which are calculated by summing surface water flow and groundwater recharge and subtracting their common part. Pressure on national water resources is said to be high when the TRWR value is above 25 percent, which is the case for India (34 percent) and South Korea (26 percent).[5] The value for China (18.57 percent) may be relatively decent, but the country remains chronically unable to meet its water needs.

In contrast, Japan, with a TRWR value of 21.26, is doing a better job than China in managing its water resources.

The good news is that the proportion of people in the Asia-Pacific region with improved access to drinking water sources increased from 74 percent in 1990 to 88 percent in 2006, even as an opposite trend of decreased access emerged in some areas, especially the Pacific Islands and war-torn Afghanistan.[6] But the bad news is that such significant improvements are likely to become more difficult to achieve as water becomes an increasingly scarce commodity in the region, exacerbating intrastate challenges. High water demand in the region from all "sectors is outstripping the natural replenishment of resources and compromising future water availability."[7]

Water shortages already are impeding the rapid expansion of industrial activities in Asia, with one state-run institute in China contending that water scarcity is causing billions of dollars worth of annual losses in industrial output in that country.[8] Because China has become the world's factory, producing cheap manufactured goods for other countries, its industrial water withdrawal is one of the highest in Asia. But with the level of industrial development advancing in several other parts of Asia, the demand for water to support manufacturing and other industrial activities is beginning to rise dramatically. The United Nations projects that industrial water withdrawals in the world will double between 2000 and 2025, with much of the increase likely to occur in the Asia-Pacific region, "given its rapidly rising status as a global industrial production center and the fast growth in subsectors with high water consumption, such as the production of transportation equipment, beverages and textiles."[9] The fastest rise, interestingly, is projected for India, whose economy now is led by the services sector but where industrial water use is expected to almost quadruple by 2050 as manufacturing rapidly expands.

The intrastate water tensions and challenges, however, are conspicuously linked with the farming sector, the dominant water user and major employer in Asia. Agriculture's share of total water withdrawals in Asia remains well above the global average. Although agricultural production in Asia since 1990 has risen faster than the world average, this continent still needs to continue to increase its food output at a faster rate to feed its burgeoning populations and meet the demands of a growing middle class that is eating better and more. Yet, at the same time, Asia must also find ways to reduce its high water withdrawals for agriculture. Such withdrawals now total between 81 and 84 percent of the annual renewable resources—compared with the global average of 71 percent—largely because of inefficient irrigation practices, which, besides accentuating water shortages, are contributing to the deterioration of water quality through soil erosion and salinization.[10] The Indian subcontinent, with 91 percent, tops the water-withdrawal-for-farming list in Asia, followed by the China–Mongolia–North Korea region, where the mean figure is 77 percent.[11] Four-fifths of the total irrigated cropland in Asia is in these two belts.

As Asia's water resources become more vulnerable to environmental changes, global warming, and human-made alterations of natural ecosystems, the availability of water will decline and the internal challenges in many countries will be exacerbated. In the coming decades, the Tibetan Plateau—where most of Asia's great rivers have their headwaters—is likely to accentuate the Asian water crisis as its ecological and hydrological stability gets disturbed by human-made and climatic changes. Even as China embarks on new water megaprojects on the plateau, this region already is experiencing—as discussed in chapter 3—the early effects of global warming and the anthropogenic transformation of ecosystems, with glaciers retreating, permafrost thawing, grasslands eroding, and desertification spreading. An increase in near-surface air temperature is expected to unfavorably alter the hydrological cycle in snowmelt-dominated regions in the world by spurring seasonal shifts in stream flows, which, in turn, would heighten regional water shortages.[12] This is especially true of Asia, given the reliance of many Asians on rivers whose flows heavily draw on snow and glacier melt.

Against this background, it is hardly a surprise that the upstream damming of rivers is a source of growing friction in Asia not just between countries but also within nations. In fact, the lopsided availability of water within some Asian nations (abundant in some areas but deficient in others) has given rise to megaprojects or grand diversion plans. Yet the building of large dams and other diversion structures has run into stiff grassroots opposition in a number of Asian nations because of displacement and submergence issues. If adequately sized and designed, dams can aid economic and social development by regulating water supply, controlling floods, and facilitating irrigation, besides generating hydroelectricity and helping to bring drinking water to cities, when designed for such purposes.

But upstream dams on rivers shared by two or more provinces in an era of growing water stress often carry broader political and social implications, especially because they can affect water quality and quantity downstream. Dams can also alter fluvial ecosystems, damage biodiversity, and promote coastal erosion and saltwater intrusion. Despite the attraction of supply-side approaches, the building of new dams may no longer be a viable option to boost water supply in many parts of Asia, other than in underdeveloped countries such as Nepal, Burma, and Laos that have not adequately exploited their water resources or in autocracies that can effectively stifle protests. Most of the best dam sites in Asia already have been taken.

Yet the numerous new projects show that the damming of rivers is still an important priority for national and provincial decision-makers in Asia. The vast majority of dams in the world have been built since the 1950s. The construction of large dams, by and large, has petered out in the West but continues in full swing in Asia, where a host of countries extending from Japan to Turkey are involved in major dam-building activities. Indeed, more than half of all dams under construction in the world in 2011 were in Asia.[13]

Such a focus on dam building has only intensified intrastate water disputes, with implications for internal security and stability. A new dam, as Australia has realized, often tends to commandeer "resources from an existing use (e.g., agricultural or other forms of rural livelihood support) or from freshwater ecosystem and water-cycle support."[14] Dams also have a "multitude of socioeconomic impacts, often including the displacement of local inhabitants," besides changing river hydrology, sediment load, riparian vegetation, patterns of stream bank erosion, migration of fish, and water temperature.[15] In Asia, degraded watersheds constitute one of the most serious challenges for sustainable development. However, the continued dam building in a number of Asian nations is creating new intrastate tensions and challenges.

INTRASTATE COMPETITION

Water conflict within nations, especially those that are multiethnic and culturally diverse, often assumes ethnic or sectarian dimensions, thereby accentuating internal security challenges. Intrastate water disputes, however, rarely get the kind of international attention that interstate discords do, even though, as the ongoing internal wars in Yemen and Afghanistan illustrate, recurrent drought and water scarcity can poison interethnic or intersectarian relations and trigger bloodletting. The violent conflict in Darfur, in Sudan's far west, was rooted in disputes over water and grazing rights between sedentary farmers and semi-nomadic herders. With rainfall declining between 16 and 30 percent since the 1960s, deserts in Sudan have advanced by about 100 kilometers, exacerbating water scarcity.[16]

As exemplified by the disputes, for example, within the United States, Spain, and Australia, intrastate water conflict is not restricted to the developing world. In the United States, most water conflicts historically have been located in the arid West, but the rise of water discord in the East has been illustrated by the US Supreme Court's early 2010 decisions in two cases—the fierce dispute between South Carolina and North Carolina over the Catawba River, and the one between the state of Mississippi and the city of Memphis over the latter's overexploitation of the shared Memphis Sand Aquifer. Still, violent struggles over water are occurring mostly in developing countries, with resource scarcity often promoting environmental degradation and perpetuating poverty.

In Asia, serious or festering intrastate water rows are widespread, even if they do not receive much coverage in the local or international media. Endemic local conflicts over water in some drought-battered areas have even led villagers to engage security guards to protect their sources of freshwater, such as wells or water trucks. Despite many examples of water-related tensions and conflict, "the issue of water disputes within a nation's borders has rarely been assessed methodically. One barrier to such analyses is the intricate nature of the problem: Intuitively, it stands to reason that, as scale decreases from the international to the internal, the dynamics become more subtle and complex."[17] With so many internal water disputes raging in Asia and other parts of the developing world, scholars and international organizations tend to pay little attention to them. Indeed, in the absence of the geopolitical ingredient common in intercountry disputes, intrastate water discords usually attract little international interest.

Water Discord along Ethnic Fault Lines

Asia shows that when intrastate water disputes are between two provinces, they have a tendency to get ugly, unless the federal government initiates sincere efforts early on to settle the conflict. If the feuding provinces or areas are ethnically distinct, their water dispute also rages along ethnic lines. This pattern has been most visible on the Indian subcontinent—where water disputes between princely states and principalities were common even during British colonial rule—and also in post-Soviet Central Asia, much of whose freshwater comes from the Pamir and Tian Shan snowmelt and glacier melt that feed the region's two main rivers, the Amu Darya and the Syr Darya. These two overexploited rivers flow west and north to the Aral Sea to release just a dribble.

The intersection between ethnic identity and water insecurity in Central Asia has fostered deep-seated ill will among communities and even spawned violent conflict. Indeed, one of the underlying causes of the mid-2010 bloody riots in the Fergana Valley—a minefield of religious fundamentalism and ethnic animosities— was the local ethnic-Kyrgyz fear that Uzbekistan wanted to absorb that water-rich region of Kyrgyzstan. Kyrgyzstan controls almost two-thirds of that southern valley straddling Uzbekistan and Tajikistan. The Kyrgyz accused the Uzbeks in Kyrgyzstan of seeking to expand their control over local land and water resources—the very issue that had sparked major bloodletting in the Fergana Valley in 1990, forcing Soviet leader Mikhail Gorbachev to send in troops to quell the violence.

In the 2010 riots, several hundred ethnic Uzbeks were killed in four days of attacks by marauding bands of Kyrgyz men, who were often backed by uniformed soldiers on armored personnel carriers. The attackers, armed with bats and iron bars, said they were seeking to suppress an alleged plot by Uzbekistan to seize control of the entire Fergana Valley, Central Asia's most fertile and most densely populated area, which is drained by the Naryn Darya and Kara Darya rivers, which merge to form the Syr Daya (map 5.1).[18] Ethnic Uzbeks make up about 15 percent of Kyrgyzstan's population but rival the ethnic Kyrgyz in numbers in the Fergana Valley part of Kyrgyzstan.

Uzbekistan has been embroiled in a bitter water feud with upstream Kyrgyzstan and Tajikistan, with the regional competition for water resources loaded with both transboundary and intracountry ethnic dimensions. There also have been Kyrgyz/ Tajik water disputes in the Fergana Valley, the seat of several major dams and reservoirs that collect snowmelt and glacier melt for release in the long dry season. In a region where national frontiers do not match ethnic boundaries and some territories remain in dispute between Uzbekistan, Kyrgyzstan, and Tajikistan, the Syr Darya basin illustrates how intercountry water tensions can actually fuel intrastate ethnic hostilities. More broadly, the rise of water and ethnic feuds in Central

MAP 5.1   The Syr Darya River Basin

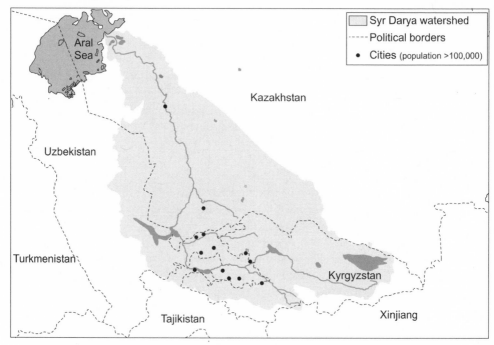

Asia is linked to the disappearance of the federally run and highly centralized regional management system the Soviets set up to integrate water, energy, and agriculture.

Intrastate Conflicts over Dams, Aquifers, and Irrigation

In several Asian countries, intrastate water conflicts have flared over the construction of large dams and the ensuing need to relocate many residents. As the world's largest democracy, with a strong and open civil society, India has been the scene of more such disputes than any other Asian nation. Organized protests by nongovernmental organizations (NGOs) over the displacement of local people by large multipurpose water projects have slowed down or stalled such works not only in India but also in other countries as disparate as Japan and Nepal. China, of course, stands out as an exception to the power of NGOs because civil society is weak there. When China built the Three Gorges Dam, it created a 630-square-kilometer reservoir that necessitated the displacement of a staggering 1.4 million people officially, all of which was accomplished in about a decade without much of a fuss, with the forced eviction of another 300,000 residents initiated in 2010 to fix environmental problems created by that project.[19] By contrast, India's much smaller Narmada Dam, aimed at bringing irrigation, drinking water, and electricity to millions of people in four central Indian states, has seen environmental groups, human rights activists, and advocates for the displaced battle the federal and state governments for decades now, with the project yet to be fully completed.

Intrastate water wrangles also have arisen in Asia from the overpumping of water from aquifers shared between provinces and communities. By depleting groundwater resources, overexploitation opens an underground source to pollution. Indeed, the reckless extraction of groundwater resources is leading to the deterioration of water quality and to a rapid lowering of water tables across much of mainland China, the Indian subcontinent, Afghanistan, Iran, Iraq, Jordan, the Arabian Peninsula, Indonesia, and the Philippines, promoting the consequent exploitation of deeper, very-slow-to-recharge aquifers. Such practices jeopardize the interests of other communities not engaged in overexploitation. As a United Nations report warned, excess extraction of groundwater for irrigation and other purposes dries up villagers' shallow drinking-water wells and exacerbates shortages in groundwater-dependent Asian cities, ranging from Jakarta to Dhaka; the Pakistani city of Quetta, for example, is in danger of running out of water as early as 2018, given the rate at which its water table is plummeting.[20]

Asia's experiences during the past quarter century actually demonstrate that intrastate water conflicts, in reality, tend to be more damaging and violent than international water disputes. Consider Sri Lanka, where the now-crushed Liberation Tigers of Tamil Eelam, which waged a guerrilla war and ran a de facto state in the north and east for years, accused the Sinhalese-dominated government of deliberately not supplying water to the Tamil minority areas. A dispute over the July 2006 closure of the Maavilaru Dam's sluice gates escalated into bloody clashes between the rebels and government forces, leaving at least 425 people dead in a ten-day period.[21] Another example was the punitive action of the Sri Lankan government in trimming the size of a World Bank–funded irrigation project—designed to draw waters from the island state's largest river—so that Tamil areas did not benefit from the project. In yet another example from Sri Lanka, intersectarian tensions and clashes between the Sinhalese majority and Muslims contributed to environmental degradation in the small but environmentally fragile Pinga Oya watershed. During the protracted confrontation between the Muslims, located downstream, and the upstream Sinhalese, illegal buildings were built on both banks of the river, polluting its waters.

Water disputes have triggered armed clashes between government forces and local tribespeople in Pakistan's Baluchistan Province—racked by a long-festering tribal insurrection—and in Afghanistan's Hazarajat Region, home to the Hazara minority. The Persian-speaking, predominantly Shiite Hazaras in central Afghanistan live by subsistence agriculture, a practice made difficult by a harsh climate, short growing season, and acute water scarcity.[22] Baluchistan, the seat of a strong Baluch national movement,[23] makes up a third of Pakistan's territory. Strategically located where the regions of South Asia, Central Asia, and the Middle East converge, Baluchistan is rich in hydrocarbons, copper, gold, onyx, sulfur, zinc, and coal. The eastern part of Baluchistan falls in the Indus River basin, while the Mashkel and Marjen rivers are the principal source of water in the western section. These rivers drain into the Hamun-i-Mashkel Lake on the border with Iran.

Baluch nationalists have long accused the Pakistani government of overexploiting the natural gas reserves and mineral wealth in Baluchistan while depriving local people of water and energy.[24] The degradation of fluvial and coastal ecosystems also has agitated the Baluch tribespeople, who blame settlers from outside, largely from Punjab Province, for depleting and polluting the waters of the Hob, Porali, Hingol, and Dasht rivers in the arid coastal zone of Makran, along the Arabian Sea. Since the late 1990s, state-run Chinese companies have ploughed billions of dollars into projects in Baluchistan, including a deepwater port at Gwadar, copper and zinc mines, an oil refinery, and a highway, airport, and railroad.[25] China's construction of the Gwadar port and new Pakistani naval bases at Gwadar, Pasni, and Ormara has brought more settlers to the Makran coast, fanning Baluch resentment. Thrust together by their shared rivalry with India, China and Pakistan are old military and political allies, and Chinese warships in the future could use Gwadar, Pasni, or Ormara as a base. Some of the Chinese projects in Baluchistan, however, have come under guerrilla attacks.

Even when not accompanied by violence, intrastate water disputes in Asia have often proven politically intractable, provoking popular passions, unruly demonstrations, and crippling strikes. In addition to the social, economic, and political costs, a number of Asian countries are paying ecological costs by overdrawing resources beyond the renewable capacity of the forces of nature. Unsustainable water consumption patterns actually spur a vicious cycle of heightened resource scarcity, environmental degradation, and social and political conflicts within societies. Water disputes rooted in ethnic, sectarian, or political divides are endemic in many countries—from Uzbekistan and Kazakhstan to Iran and Saudi Arabia. But such intrastate water conflicts are particularly worrisome in China, Pakistan, and India, while a national water project has divided South Korea.

The chapter, from this point onward, examines these four densely populated countries as illustrative cases of the costs of internal water-related wrangles. Even though South Korea, China, Pakistan, and India are clearly different from each other, their internal water disputes spotlight the same lesson: the limits of a purely supply-side approach in addressing water challenges and discord.

India's Intensifying Water Wrangles

Conflict management between warring states has become a central feature of the water distress in India. The federal government and the country's Supreme Court repeatedly have had to intervene in unending water wrangles between states— between the states of Tamil Nadu and Karnataka, Tamil Nadu and Kerala, Punjab and Haryana, Punjab and Rajasthan, and Uttar Pradesh and Delhi, to cite some ongoing disputes. Settlement of the dispute between Maharashtra, Karnataka, and Andhra Pradesh states over the sharing of the waters of River Krishna was the subject of two separate tribunals that delivered their decisions in 1973 and 2010, yet this wrangle is far from over. The country's democratic system has served as an open forum to ventilate and agitate water-related and other grievances.[26] "Water has emerged as a critical and contentious issue across the country," the Indian prime minister admitted in a 2004 address to the nation. "Even access to safe drinking water remains a problem in many parts of our country. Water-management policies have to be so formulated as to address the needs of farmers and weaker sections, especially women, as well as those of city-dwellers."[27]

Intracountry allocation of scarce water resources has emerged as "the principal cause of water conflicts."[28] In fact, water disputes between Indian states have begun to roil domestic politics to such an extent that when a new coalition came to power in national elections in 2004, it had a separate section titled "Water Resources" in its so-called Common Minimum Program of governance. The United Progressive Alliance government "will take all steps to ensure that long-pending inter-state disputes on rivers and water-sharing, like the Cauvery Waters dispute, are settled amicably at the earliest, keeping in mind the interests of all parties to the dispute," the governance program declared, adding: "Providing drinking water to all sections in urban and rural areas and augmenting availability of drinking water sources is an issue of topmost priority. Harvesting rainwater, de-silting existing ponds, and other innovative mechanisms will be adopted."[29]

But despite the fact that this government—reelected in 2009—has made water a priority in policy, water stress in India has accentuated and interprovincial disputes have escalated. For example, Punjab State's refusal to release more river waters for downstream users resulted in violent protests in 2005 by farmers at the tail end of the irrigation system in Rajasthan State, leading to at least five deaths.[30] Disputes also have flared within Indian states over water allocations to different sectors. In late 2007, for instance, police used force to scatter some 30,000 farmers who laid siege to the Hirakud reservoir in southeastern Orissa State to protest the diversion of irrigation water to local industries.[31]

The recrudescence of the dispute over the sharing of the waters of India's southern Cauvery River has generated serious tensions, mass protests, lawsuits, and political rancor between the states of Tamil Nadu and Karnataka, with each of the two demanding a larger share of the waters to meet its irrigation and agricultural needs. The Cauvery dispute also involves another state, Kerala, and the federally administered territory of Pondicherry. India's federal government, on a specific direction from the country's Supreme Court, set up the Cauvery Water Disputes Tribunal in 1990 to adjudicate the bitter conflict over the sharing of the river waters. It took the tribunal seventeen long years to reach a final decision, only to provoke fresh litigation in the Supreme Court.[32]

Under India's 1956 Inter-State River Water Disputes Act, the final decision of a tribunal is equivalent to a judicial ruling and thus open to review by the tribunal itself but not by any other court of law. Yet having first directed the government to appoint the Cauvery Tribunal, the Supreme Court later agreed to hear a legal challenge to the tribunal's final order, making it, as one analyst put it, "very difficult, if not impossible, for the tribunal to function in accordance with the Inter-State Water Disputes Act."[33]

The Cauvery River originates at an elevation of about 1,340 meters in the Coorg Mountains of Karnataka State, where it is joined by six local tributaries and a seventh stream flowing in from Kerala State. In downstream Tamil Nadu State, three other tributaries join the Cauvery, making it a river drawing waters from three states. But whereas its upper-catchment areas in Karnataka and Kerala states draw water from the dependable southwest summer monsoon, its lower catchment in the plains of Tamil Nadu State is serviced by the capricious northeast monsoon in the period from October to December.

Irrigation in the Cauvery basin is centuries old, with the oldest irrigation canal—the Grand Anicut—dating back nearly two thousand years. The intrastate water dispute, however, goes back to the mid-1970s, when four new dams built upstream by the state of Karnataka reduced cross-border flows into Tamil Nadu.[34] Equitable water sharing between the two states has been complicated by historical and hydrological factors: Tamil Nadu, with 54 percent of the basin area, has invoked "historic rights" to assert priority of use and block greater upstream utilization, whereas Karnataka, as the contributor of more than half the basin waters, has demanded a share larger than the 36.5 percent awarded by the tribunal in 2007.

India's Supreme Court also has been trying to resolve water disputes among Punjab, Haryana, and Rajasthan states, with upstream Punjab seeking to control the flow of river waters to the other states and the nonriparian Rajasthan at the mercy of Punjab and Haryana for receiving its agreed-on share of the waters. A number of other water feuds involving dams, environmental or public health issues, or the project-related displacement of local residents have reached the Supreme Court.

Although the right to water is not enshrined as a fundamental right in the Indian Constitution, courts have interpreted Article 21 of the Constitution on the right to life as encompassing the right to water. Yet the right to water, in practice, exists only as an idea, even as interprovincial water feuds continue to rage despite interventions by courts.[35] Indeed, such is the intensity of the water disputes in India that elected officials in the state of Uttar Pradesh dragged their feet over releasing water for the federal capital, New Delhi, from the Tehri Dam in the foothills of the Himalayas. The building of the Tehri Dam, located in Uttarakhand State, itself generated a lot of public controversy as the issue became emotionally surcharged, preventing a rational debate.[36]

The record of the country's highest court on water settlement issues has been anything but glorious. The Supreme Court has struggled for years to resolve water disputes between various states, only to find the parties returning to litigate again on new grounds. Despite such an unflattering record, the Court has demonstrated a proclivity to deepen its involvement in water wrangles. For example, the Court, after hearing the matter on and off for a decade, ordered the establishment of a high-level committee in 2010 to examine safety and other issues related to a dispute between the states of Kerala and Tamil Nadu over Mullaperiyar, an old dam constructed at the end of the nineteenth century.

The dam is located in Kerala but supplies much of its water to Tamil Nadu, which actually operates the dam. Tamil Nadu had sought to implement a 2006 Supreme Court decision permitting an increase in Mullaperiyar's water-storage level from 41.5 to 43.3 meters. But Kerala, citing safety concerns and the consequent need to dismantle the dam, passed state legislation effectively overriding the court decision by classifying Mullaperiyar as an "endangered dam." Instead of taking Kerala to task for flouting its decision, the Supreme Court appointed a committee to examine the safety aspect—an issue the Court should have looked at before it earlier permitted an increase in the storage level, given that the dam's safety had been a public matter since 1979.[37] Even the Office of the Comptroller and Auditor General of India—an autonomous authority—has intervened in water issues, presenting a report in 2010, for example, that, on environmental grounds, criticized the decision of the northern state of Uttarakhand to permit private-sector development of river resources for hydropower.

The blunt truth is that judicial and other interventions in Indian water disputes have not been able to put an end to wrangles. In fact, interventions by courts, while helping to calm public passions, have only succeeded in keeping water disputes lingering. Kerala is not the only state that has balked at implementing court orders. For example, in the Cauvery and Indus water disputes, the states of Karnataka and Punjab have on occasion flouted judicial orders, with the courts unable to bring them to heel. Litigation has spawned more litigation. Taking disputes to courts also has proven costly in terms of time. Indeed, some disputes repeatedly have been taken to the courts on purpose by one party or the other to ensure that they are never resolved. The lesson to be learned from India's experiences is that water disputes are not legal but political matters, and thus must be resolved politically or through arbitration by institutional mechanisms in which all parties are represented and have full faith in their objectivity and efficacy.

Another lesson to emerge is that government plans for mammoth water projects do not jibe with the grassroots empowerment and the rise of influential civil society groups in a country that prides itself as the only real democracy in the vast contiguous arc from Jordan to Singapore. NGOs funded by international donors and domestic sources are ever ready to take up the cause of local residents facing potential dislodgment from homes located in project areas. The power of these organizations to organize grassroots protests has been demonstrated in several dam projects and the case involving the reckless extraction of groundwater and soil and water contamination by the Coca-Cola Company in the state of Kerala.[38]

With the demands of industrialization putting increasing pressure on local water resources, NGOs and citizens groups also have led grassroots movements against the setting up of water-intensive manufacturing facilities, delaying the plans of giant corporations like the Luxembourg-based ArcelorMittal and Posco of South Korea, for example, to build large multi-billion-dollar steel plants in India's iron ore belt. The 160 million tons of annual steel capacity planned in India to help cut dependence on imports would, according to the average consumption of US steel mills, utilize 640 billion gallons of water, making water rights a contentious issue between local communities and companies.[39] NGOs in India, in fact, have helped spawn some of the most interesting social movements found anywhere in the world. With anti-dam woman leaders like Medha Patkar and Arundhati Roy spearheading popular protests, these organizations wield considerable clout.[40]

Add to the picture India's labyrinthine political and bureaucratic processes, which are slow moving and bendable to public pressures—however contrived—as was exemplified by the 2010 federal-government decisions to abandon three dam-building projects on the Bhagirathi, one of the tributaries of the Ganges, including one project midway that resulted in the loss of several hundred million dollars of taxpayer money.[41] Such was the "competitive populism" that forced the government's hand on those projects, as one newspaper put it, that federal authorities actually went one step ahead to unveil India's first dam-free zone, through which this river will flow freely for 135 kilometers in the foothills of the Himalayas.[42]

Although democracy remains India's greatest asset, it comes with a glaring weakness: a badly splintered polity. Since the late 1980s, coalition federal governments comprising multiple parties have become the national rule. Worse still, Indian democracy tends to function by the rule of parochial politics—in fact, by the lowest common denominator. Much of the bickering in India usually is over partisan politics, not over policy choices. Shying away from hard decisions indeed has become a political norm in a country increasingly battered by the pervasive misuse of public office for private gain. Few politicians are prosecuted and convicted for corruption, nepotism, and cronyism. In a rare case, the Supreme Court in 2011 convicted and sentenced to one year's hard labor a former Kerala State minister who had been involved in a 1982 bribery scandal involving the Idamalayar Dam.

Against this background, it seems extraordinary that the Indian government conceived of an overly ambitious, \$120 billion National River Linking Program to help connect thirty-seven Himalayan and peninsular rivers in a pan-Indian water grid. This is a plan of the dream world, not the India its citizens have known: A colossal water grid to handle 178 billion m^3 of interbasin water transfers a year through the construction of 12,500 kilometers of new canals, generating 34 gigawatts of hydropower, creating 35 million hectares of additional irrigated land, and opening extended navigation networks.[43] This is the kind of program that only a large, ruthless autocracy like China can launch and implement. So it is of little surprise that India's river-interlinking program has remained for years at the planning phase—a stage where it promises to stay for the indefinite future.

The powerful ruling-party politician, Rahul Gandhi, has publicly rejected the program as a "disastrous idea," saying, "It is an idea that will be extremely dangerous to the environment of the country." He went on to add that it "is not a good idea to play with nature on a massive scale."[44] Taking his cue from the remarks of the ruling party's heir apparent, the Indian environment minister also went public to debunk the proposed program as imbued with the potential to unleash "a human, economic, and ecological disaster" (map 5.2). Yet, while seeking to discredit the water-grid program, Rahul Gandhi, driven by local partisan politics, has lent support to one component of it—the linking of two small rivers, the Ken and the Betwa, to provide irrigation facilities in fourteen backward districts in the Bundelkhand Region of Uttar Pradesh and Madhya Pradesh states. Construction of the 231-kilometer canal to link the Ken and the Betwa, however, has stalled in the face of environmental concerns, including the likely submergence of a portion of the Panna tiger reserve in Madhya Pradesh.

To be sure, it was India's Supreme Court—in an overt display of judicial activism—that prodded the federal government in 2002 to embark on such a water-grid program. It also is true that partisan politics has been at play—something endemic in India—with the succeeding government loath to endorse its predecessor's river-interlinking program. The succeeding government indeed told the national Parliament in late 2009 that the proposed program, centered on the separate linking of the Himalayan and peninsular rivers, "involves massive expenditure" and "such kind of money is not available to us."[45] Yet it has not tried to put forward a cost-effective alternative to a program that the National Water Development Agency and the National Commission for Integrated Water Resource Development say is essential to double India's food production to more than 450 million tons of grains per year to help meet the demands of increasing prosperity and a growing population, projected to stabilize at between 1.35 billion and 1.58 billion by 2050.[46]

Given the regular flooding in the Ganga-Brahmaputra-Meghna basin during the monsoon season and the recurring drought in western India and the peninsular basins, the National Water Development Agency has argued that "one of the most effective ways to expand the irrigation potential for increasing the food grain production, to mitigate floods and droughts, and to reduce regional imbalance in the availability of waters is the Inter-Basin Water Transfer (IBWT) from the surplus rivers to the deficit areas."[47] To produce 450 million tons of cereals annually even with improved farming techniques and new plant varieties, India will have to substantially expand irrigated farming. Otherwise, a growing reliance on food imports seems inevitable. Whether the spread of irrigation for water-intensive cereal cultivation would be a prudent use of water resources, however, is a moot question. As part of the imperative to incentivize water productivity and efficiency in agriculture, India needs to rely more on "virtual water" through both domestic

MAP 5.2   India's Dream Plans: The National River Linking Program, with the Plan for Interlinking Himalayan Rivers in the Upper Half and the Peninsular Component in the Bottom Half

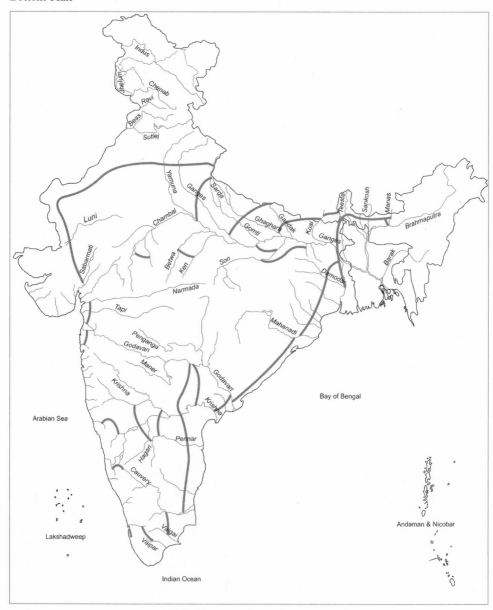

Source: National Commission on Integrated Water Resources Development, 1999.

trade and international trade. The country's agriculturally underdeveloped but water-surplus eastern region has considerable potential to grow a lot more food.

It is true that interbasin water transfers have been in successful operation in several parts of the world.[48] China's Great South–North Water Diversion Project, in fact, stands out as the largest interbasin water transfer initiative in world history. But India is not China, where the lack of democracy is an advantage in ramming through changes. India has shown over and over again that it has no ability to make long-term strategic plans and then execute them clinically. The focus of those in power in India is largely on domestic firefighting, including dousing the flames of public outrage over the newest political corruption scandal, and on electoral considerations, given the frequency of state-level elections in the country. When India has struggled for decades to complete the multipurpose Narmada River project, how could it realistically imagine implementing the grand National River Linking Program?

The river-linking plans indeed carry implications for downstream Bangladesh, which has been concerned that—as in the case of the Indian construction of the Farakka Barrage between 1962 and 1974—it could end up as the loser. The interlinking of the Ganges and the Brahmaputra rivers in India would likely upset the natural balance of water flows and sediment supply to Bangladesh, especially from the Brahmaputra.[49]

The plain fact is that organized protests by NGOs, by driving up costs or stalling plans, have acted as a damper to hydropower and other water projects in India, discouraging public and private investments. As a result, the attraction of hydroelectricity has faded, although the country's sprawling Himalayan region holds immense hydropower reserves. The share of hydropower in India's total electricity supply actually fell from 50 percent in 1962–63 to about 23 percent in 2009–10. Despite federal government efforts in the twenty-first century to reinvigorate a shrinking hydropower sector, grassroots protests, environmental concerns, protracted litigation over land acquisition, and advance premiums on projects sought by state governments have shelved many dam-building plans across the Himalayan belt but especially in the states of Uttarakhand and Sikkim.

The plan to harness the 1,300-kilometer-long Narmada River in west-central India for irrigation and hydropower actually dates back to the period just after Indian independence. Feasibility studies were ordered in 1948 on four projects on the river, which flows through the states of Madhya Pradesh, Maharashtra, and the often drought-afflicted Gujarat. In 1961, with much fanfare, Prime Minister Jawaharlal Nehru laid the cornerstone of a 50-meter-high dam at Gora in Gujarat State. The dam project, however, quickly ran into a water-sharing dispute between Gujarat and upstream Madhya Pradesh State. To resolve this dispute, a federal government–appointed panel in 1965 recommended that the dam's height be raised to 152.4 meters. Madhya Pradesh's rejection of the panel report compelled the federal government to invoke the Inter-State River Water Disputes Act and appoint an arbitral tribunal, which took ten years to pronounce its final order in

1979. The final decision of the tribunal, headed by a Supreme Court justice, ran the gamut, from land acquisition and rehabilitation of displaced people to apportionment of river waters between the two states and the design of the main Narmada Dam, formally known as the Sardar Sarovar Dam.[50]

Yet even that elaborate decision did not end the travails of a project intended to irrigate an area of about 1.8 million hectares, deliver drinking water to 8,000 villages, and generate 1,450 megawatts of hydroelectricity. Numerous official and independent committees went into the project design and other technical issues. Aided by international environmental campaigners, a new grassroots activist organization, the Narmada Bachao Andolan (Save Narmada Campaign), organized protests to stall work, which forced the World Bank to withdraw from the project in 1993.[51] As an Asian Development Study has pointed out, "During the 1980s and 1990s, large water-development projects all over the world, and especially in Asia, came under considerable criticism from social and environmental activists and the nongovernment organization movement. This movement probably reached its peak with controversies associated with the construction of some large dams—the Sardar Sarovar and the Tehri dams in India, and Arun II Dam in Nepal—and the Nagara Barrage (to prevent saltwater intrusion) in Japan."[52] Such organized protests, of course, could be mounted only in democracies.

The anti-Narmada project activists took the matter to India's Supreme Court in 1994. It took the Court more than six years to deliver its final judgment on the project, a period during which it first restricted in 1995 the construction of the dam to a height of 80.3 meters, before allowing it in 1999 to rise to 85 meters, with a 3-meter hump. Subsequently, between 2000 and 2006, further increments in height were cleared to permit the dam to be constructed up to 121.9 meters. The key point is that decades after it was initiated to help lift millions from poverty and make drought-stricken areas "drought-proof," the project—marred by repeated interventions by courts—is still not fully complete, and a lower-court injunction against canal construction was challenged in the Supreme Court in 2010. By contrast, China, with its authoritarian ability to steamroll any local resistance, completed building the Three Gorges Dam ahead of schedule to generate 18,300 megawatts of power—more than 12½ times the capacity of the Narmada project.

The legal, logistical, bureaucratic, political, and NGO-activist hurdles the Narmada project has faced reflect the true reality in implementing any large developmental project in a country as politically diverse and disorganized as India, whose red tape and susceptibility to pressures are legendary. As one American newspaper put it, "India's political culture, if prized for its commitment to democracy, often seems unable to transcend its own dysfunction."[53] Just as India has no articulated national security strategy, defined defense policy, or declared counterterrorism doctrine, it also has no national water-security strategy, even though its then–prime minister acknowledged in 2002 that the grave water situation leaves the country with "no alternative but to think radically and come up with innovative and bold responses to the enormous challenge that our nation and our citizens are facing."[54]

A succeeding prime minister in 2010 agreed to launch a program to create a public water-resources data bank to help promote conservation and better management.

Yet ad hoc, personality-driven actions have continued to trump institutionalized, holistic policymaking. Worse still, the country's hydra-headed management style, characterized by a multiplicity of governmental agencies but the absence of any linear command structure, has only promoted delays, dithering, and a lack of accountability. With that kind of a record and lackadaisical approach, India is set to face sharpening domestic water disputes in the coming years.

Pakistan's Exploding Population, Rising Extremism, and Water Crisis

In Pakistan, the internal water disputes are very serious because they have helped foment ethnic and regional discontent and thus have a bearing on the country's unity and territorial integrity. Having been carved out of British-ruled India as a homeland for the subcontinent's Muslims, Pakistan (or "Land of the Pure") became the world's first modern nation-state founded solely on Islam, going on to name its newly built capital city "Islamabad" (Abode of Islam).[55] Yet, since its bloody birth, Pakistan—despite Islam's continued centrality in national life—has been particularly susceptible to separatist tendencies. As Hilary Synnott has pointed out, "In contrast to India, whose national narrative includes an ancient and proud history and whose overriding priority in the first half of the twentieth century was to gain independence from the British Raj, Pakistan had no preexisting national identity. Its priority was separation from Hindu-dominated India. Its disparate components, including different ethnic groups (Punjabis, Sindhis, Pashtuns, and Baluchis, each with separate languages) and religious communities (including Shia and Sunni Muslims, the latter of which can be further divided into Deobandis, Barelvis, and Sufis), had little reason to cooperate toward any goal of state- or nation-building."[56]

Throughout its short history, Pakistan has had to rely on Islam, its army, and its Kashmir conflict with India to prevent its disintegration into separate nations along ethnolinguistic lines—a threat underscored by developments extending from the separatist Pashtunistan movement in the 1950s to the ongoing Baluch insurgency. Roiling the ethnic divide today is Pakistan's grave water crisis, with river waters being largely expropriated by the dominant Punjab Province and the water table falling across the country.[57]

The water crisis is largely due to four factors: Pakistan's explosive population growth (it is now the world's sixth-largest country and second-most-populous Islamic state); the mismanagement and malfeasance involving water resources; the introduction of widespread irrigated farming in a largely semiarid country; and the long-standing focus on cultivating water-intensive crops, such as wheat, rice, sugarcane, cotton, corn, and oilseeds, especially for export. According to figures of the Pakistani government and the Food and Agriculture Organization of the United Nations, a staggering 94 percent of the total water withdrawal in Pakistan is for irrigation and other agricultural needs, with municipal and industrial withdrawals of water making up barely 6 percent.[58]

Add to the picture another unusual statistic: About 80 percent of the country's cultivated area is irrigated, largely with the waters of the Indus system rivers flowing in from India. Irrigated agriculture is much more expensive and labor-intensive than rain-fed agriculture, but on the prodigal scale it is practiced in Pakistan, it serves as the principal cause of river depletion. Unlike the services-led Indian economic growth, agriculture is the single largest sector of Pakistan's economy and contributes more than 60 percent of all foreign-exchange earnings.[59]

The massive but aging national hydraulic infrastructure that supports "the world's largest contiguous irrigation network," as Pakistan calls it, is not easy to maintain in an era of declining public investments in basic maintenance, looming resource scarcity, and growing demands by those who have been left out from its benefits. According to a World Bank report, Pakistan needs to construct major new storage capacity in the Indus basin and provide drinking water and sanitation services to those without such access, while stemming rising environment costs by treating municipal and industrial wastewater and making major investments to rebuild "many elements of the vast hydraulic system now reaching the end of their design lives."[60] Under its latest multi-billion-dollar economic aid program for Pakistan, the United States has stepped in to shore up that country's national storage capacity, irrigation, safe drinking water, and electrical power production. But if Pakistan is to sustainably manage its water resources, it cannot rely on just international assistance. As a former Pakistani finance minister has suggested, "Foreign donors must insist that Pakistan reform its economy in order to escape the moral hazard implied by continued dependence on aid flows."[61]

In fact, the devastating 2010 monsoonal flooding, which struck more than one-fifth of Pakistan's territory, was a reminder of the costs of neglecting flood-hazard mitigation in a country where flooding and drainage problems are getting worse because of anthropogenic land-cover and fluvial-system changes. Despite recurrent flooding in the Indus basin since its creation, Pakistan has remained focused on irrigation and hydropower development, paying limited attention to the flood-related challenges.[62] Yet the "precarious state" of some of its major structures, such as the colonial-era Sukkur Barrage in Sind Province and the 1958 Taunsa Barrage in upstream Punjab, "puts the well-being of tens of millions of people at risk," with the 2010 flooding serving as another warning.[63] The dilapidated state of the water supply infrastructure, including irrigation canals and pipes, also leads to large water losses. Yet the destruction from the 2010 super floods set back general infrastructure by years.

Pakistan's real problem, however, is not too much water but too little water, especially safe water. Deteriorating water quality has emerged as a principal challenge. Unsustainable irrigation practices, especially in Punjab Province, have been blamed for the degradation of both land and water resources, including the ingress of saline water into overexploited aquifers and the adverse ecological changes in the

Indus delta. Intensive irrigation, coupled with poor drainage, has led to increasing problems of waterlogging and soil salinity, with "serious environmental and poverty impacts," according to a study for the World Commission on Dams.[64] Overuse of water in many irrigated areas has been held to be the main cause of waterlogging and soil salinity.

The World Bank has pointed out that more than a third of Pakistan's irrigated land is affected by waterlogging and soil salinity, leading to a perceptible decline in crop yields, with the drop in yields the greatest in the areas farthest downstream in the Indus basin. Farmers have sought to minimize the effects of salinity by using groundwater for irrigation when crops begin to show signs of salt-induced water stress. The heavy extraction of groundwater has, to some extent, reduced the waterlogging problem but done little, as another study has shown, to tackle sodicity, or the toxic effect on soil of the excess presence of sodium in irrigation water.[65]

Sodic soils and water pollution have kept Pakistani crop yields—both per hectare and per m³ of water used—low by international standards.[66] The government's own *Pakistan Water Sector Strategy* report has acknowledged the gravity of the problem: "Waterlogging and salinity, as well as water shortages (especially in tail end areas), contribute substantially to the low yields."[67] The gap between Pakistani crop yields and the yields in other countries is especially wide in wheat, Pakistan's staple food, as table 5.1 illustrates. In fact, despite the similarity in agricultural conditions in Pakistan's Punjab Province and India's Punjab State, the wheat yield per hectare in the former is less than half of the latter and 3.3 times lower than in France.

Pakistan admits that "Waterlogging and salinity pose a major threat to the sustainability of irrigated agriculture. About 30 percent of irrigated lands are affected, mostly in the Punjab and Sind. Overuse of water contributes directly to waterlogging and salinity. . . . The impact of salinity on agricultural productivity is severe, resulting in an estimated 25 percent reduction in output of major crops

TABLE 5.1 Pakistan's Crop-Yield Gap in Wheat Production, Relative to Other Countries

Country	Yield (tons per hectare)
France	7.60
Egypt	5.99
Saudi Arabia	5.36
India—Punjab State	4.80
Pakistan—Punjab Province	2.32
Pakistan—national average	2.24

Sources: Pakistan Ministry of Water and Power, *Pakistan Water Sector Strategy*, Detailed Strategy Formulation, vol. 4 (Islamabad: Ministry of Water and Power, 2002), relying on FAO Yearbook for data on other countries.

in Sind Province, where the problem is much more severe than elsewhere."[68] Yet, seeking to compound its water problems, Pakistan initiated controversial plans in 2009 to sell or lease hundreds of thousands of hectares of farmland to Arab and other foreign investors looking to secure food supplies to their countries.[69]

Although international attention has focused on the security of Pakistan's nuclear arsenal, including the challenge posed by the insider jihadist threat, a potentially more potent bomb is ticking in that country: the population bomb. With blazing population growth, Pakistan is on the verge of a crippling demographic crisis, as it unstoppably hurtles to become the fourth-most-populous country in the world. It has the dubious distinction of maintaining one of the world's highest population growth rates. The population explosion already is exacting serious social, economic, and political costs, with the ramifications extending to the water sector. Per capita freshwater availability in Pakistan, once higher than in India, has declined markedly due to high population growth. Indeed, it has fallen dramatically in the past two decades alone.

According to estimates by the Food and Agriculture Organization of the United Nations, Pakistan's per capita availability of renewable water resources now is 1,273 m^3 per year—slightly lower than India's (1,591 m^3) but only a fraction of America's (9,847 m^3).[70] But as Pakistan's population swells further, the present situation of water stress there seems set to slide into outright water scarcity by 2035.[71] With Pakistan unable to provide jobs, education, and health care to its existing population, the surging population threatens to overwhelm its fragile, foreign-aid-dependent economy, triggering high unemployment, pollution, disease, unrest, and greater extremism. The specter of Pakistan becoming the first failed nuclear-armed state— the world's Terroristan rolled into an Anarchistan—looms large at a time when it already is a global terrorist-training hub.

When it was established in 1947, Pakistan (excluding what later became Bangladesh) had the same population as Iran, roughly 15.5 million, according to United Nations estimates. But between 1947 and 2011, Pakistan's population swelled almost twelvefold. Now Pakistan has more than 180 million people to Iran's 75 million, and, according to the UN's midrange demographic projections, is likely to have 335 million citizens by 2050.[72] While Pakistan's population has ballooned, the quantity of water in the single river system on which the country is dependent, like Egypt, has remained the same. With per capita availability of freshwater sinking 5.44 times over a period of about six decades,[73] Pakistan has gone from being a water-surplus country to a water-distressed nation. In fact, because Pakistan's per capita water availability is declining yearly at the pace that its population grows, it is slipping behind countries of which it was comfortably ahead not long ago.

Had East Pakistan not seceded in 1971 to become Bangladesh, a united Pakistan long ago would have overtaken Indonesia as the world's most populous Islamic state. But even after losing its east wing (which now has 164 million people), Pakistan is set to overtake Indonesia's population, presently estimated at 230 million.[74]

Pakistan, already the world's sixth-most-populous nation, would surpass the population of Brazil by 2015 and Indonesia before 2030, a feat that would place it fourth in the world population rankings behind China, India, and the United States.[75] In 2030, Pakistan—the top country of origin for Muslim immigrants to the United States—is projected to have 256.1 million people, compared with 238.8 million in Indonesia and 89.6 million in Iran, while Afghanistan would have nearly doubled its population to 50.5 million.[76] The Afghanistan-Pakistan ("Afpak") belt is already the main sanctuary of transnational terrorists.

In Pakistan, average fertility rates have declined appreciably from the peak of 6.8 children per woman between 1960 and the mid-1980s, owing to the progressively higher ages at marriage, especially in urban areas, and the advent of abortion clinics in cities.[77] But with the pace of decline slowing in recent years, fertility rates remain comparatively high.[78] The country's population is increasing by 4 million annually, and increasing numbers of Pakistanis are moving from the countryside to overcrowded cities. With its present total fertility rate of 3.96 babies per woman (or more than twice Iran's rate of 1.81)—India's is 2.68 and America's is 2.12, with the global average being 2.54—Pakistan faces related problems: "Less than a third of Pakistan is literate—many Pakistanis still live as serfs for feudal landlords."[79] Add to this picture the growth of extremism that has made Pakistan a global crucible of international extremism and terrorism. The flight of professionals from Pakistan has exacerbated the country's woes. The United Nations projects that in the period 2005–50, Pakistan would have the world's fifth-largest level of net migration, with 167,000 Pakistanis on average emigrating every year.[80] That suggests that Pakistan is doomed to struggle endlessly with poverty, instability, extremism, and militarism.

An increasingly radicalized Pakistan, with an exploding population and multitudes of angry unemployed young men, will pose a growing threat to regional and international security. The median age in Pakistan was just 21.3 years in 2011. Although the Federally Administered Tribal Areas and the North-West Frontier Province are the most lawless parts of the country, the most radicalized region is Pakistan's heartland—Punjab Province, home to more than 55 percent of the country's population. Half of Pakistan's urban population today is concentrated in the six largest cities, some of which have turned into hotbeds of extremism. With the urban population increasing at a rate of 3.7 percent a year, the majority of the Pakistani population (52 percent) is projected to be concentrated in cities by 2025.[81]

Osama bin Laden's killing and the capture of a number of other al-Qaeda and Taliban leaders from urban centers in the heartland of Pakistan in the decade after the September 11, 2001, terrorist attacks in the United States have shown that leading militants operate not from mountain caves but from Pakistani cities, which have turned into citadels of jihadist organizations, including state-reared terror groups like the Lashkar-e-Taiba, which means "the Army of the Pure." Such Islamist groups, which run charities and madrassas while offering training for jihad, have become part of mainstream society in Pakistan. As US Senate Foreign

Relations Committee chairman John Kerry has put it bluntly about Pakistan, a "single country has become ground zero for the terrorist threat we face."[82]

There is a pernicious link between Pakistan's rapid population growth and the spread of the jihad culture there—a link reinforced by the astonishing illiteracy levels (more than half of all adults cannot sign their own name), high unemployment rates, growing income disparities, and the Islamization of the public education system, a process introduced by military dictator Zia ul-Haq in the late 1970s.[83] These different elements threaten to blend into a lethal cocktail of disorder. Not only has secular education withered away with the Islamized curriculum taking deep roots, but the public schools, along with the mushrooming madrassas, have also inculcated an Islamist and anti-Western mindset, with the most active jihadists coming from the lower middle class. Still, the most powerful forces in the country, including the army and the mullahs, have stymied efforts to reform the public school curriculum, even though it "glorifies violence in the name of Islam and ignores basic history, science and math" and instills the belief that "non-Muslim nations are out to destroy Pakistan and that the army is the only protection Pakistanis have from certain annihilation."[84] So it is of little surprise that in a 2010 survey conducted by the Washington-based Pew Research Center, roughly six in ten Pakistanis described the United States—their country's biggest economic and military aid donor—as an enemy.[85]

The linkages between burgeoning population, water scarcity, rising unemployment, widespread illiteracy, Islamization, and spreading extremism are also conspicuous in another Asian case, Yemen, now the seat of al-Qaeda in the Arabian Peninsula, a transnational terrorist organization formed by the merger in early 2009 of two al-Qaeda offshoots operating in the Saudi Arabia–Yemen belt. The bustling Yemeni city of Sanaa, with more than 2 million residents, is in danger of becoming the world's first capital to run out of water, even as its population continues to grow exponentially. The intrastate competition for water in Yemen is really fierce, despite the country having built 347 dams to store rainwater. While government forces battle a Shiite insurrection in the north, secessionists in the south, and al-Qaeda militants in the ungoverned countryside, violent protests over water are becoming common.[86] In the absence of running water in most homes in Yemen, water is delivered by truck to households that can afford it. But because water is more precious than even gasoline in parts of that violence-scarred, riverless nation, the water trucks are often driven by Kalashnikov-wielding tribesmen.[87] Yet, as in Pakistan, Yemeni irrigated farming consumes 90 percent or more of all water withdrawals in the country, with the extraction of subterranean water resources exceeding the annual groundwater recharge.[88]

The growing Pakistani youth bulge—with more than a million people a year pouring into the saturated job market—has actually spawned "a new generation that has made militant networks in Pakistan more sophisticated and deadly."[89] For its part, the public education system, instead of producing employable youths, has fostered anger and alienation, compounded by rampant unemployment and under-employment.[90] Controlling the unbridled growth of population and extremism demands education reforms.

For its own domestic stability and future unity, Pakistan must overhaul a violence-glorifying public education system that infuses a jihadist outlook and compounds its developmental and environmental challenges.[91] It can draw on the experience of next-door Iran, which, despite a clerical regime, has pursued a forward-looking approach both to family planning (propagated even in mosques by imams) and to public education. In fact, to get a marriage license in Iran, it is compulsory to attend a prenuptial birth-control class. As a result, Iranian women use birth control at exactly the same rate as American women—73 percent—and have among the fewest children of any women in the Islamic world.[92]

Without defusing its population bomb, Pakistan will find it hard to deal with its water crisis. After all, there is a direct link between population futures and water futures of nations. As the Pakistani government itself has acknowledged, "Population growth is the single most important driving force affecting the water sector," with the demands on irrigated farm production and nonagricultural water services increasingly rapidly.[93] The keys to arresting Pakistan's growing water crisis lie in its own hands. The exploding population, in actual fact, is a ticking time bomb that threatens to rip asunder what already is looking like an unmanageable and ungovernable nation.

Interprovincial water disputes, significantly, have continued to fester despite Pakistan's own domestic Indus basin agreement, which is overseen by the Indus River Systems Authority, made up of five members—one from each of the country's four provinces, plus a national member. Pakistan's 1991 Indus Water Apportionment Accord was designed to equitably apportion the Indus waters among the provinces, but its implementation has run into mounting difficulties and unresolved issues, with the World Bank suggesting its replacement with a more credible arrangement acceptable to all stakeholders.[94] The Pakistani authorities have themselves admitted that despite the domestic accord, "there are frequent disputes over water allocation," which have "led to a culture of mistrust and interprovincial rivalry."[95] The accord called for stepping up the canal diversion of Indus waters to 114.35 million acre feet (141 billion m^3), despite the already very high water withdrawals for irrigation.

The interprovincial disputes actually extend beyond water diversion and distribution to the degradation of underground and surface water resources, deterioration of deltaic ecosystems, and other environmental costs. Water and soil salinity will remain a serious problem until the excessive irrigation practices give way to more sustainable practices. In fact, parts of the restive province of Sind—home to the delta of the mighty Indus River—are now becoming arid because of the expropriation of water resources by upriver Punjab Province. The attenuation of river flows to Sind and other downstream areas also has seriously impeded the natural movement of silt, adversely affecting the deltaic belt in particular.

Such water usurpation is stoking Sindhi, Pashtun, and Baluch nationalism. The backlash in downriver provinces against the construction of dams and reservoirs in Punjab, for instance, helped suspend one plan championed by then–military dictator Pervez Musharraf. General Musharraf's campaign to launch the Kalabagh Dam ran into stiff opposition from three of the four provinces, which believed the project would allow Punjab to siphon off more of the Indus waters. Whereas Sind was worried about greater desertification and saltwater intrusion in the Indus estuary, the upper-riparian North-West Frontier Province was concerned the project could promote waterlogging and salinity in the upstream valleys. The dispute became a flashpoint for leaders in Sind to ask the federal government to choose between Kalabagh and federation, implying that Sind could seek to walk out of the Pakistani federation by reviving a movement for independence. After Musharraf was forced out of office in 2008, the successor civilian government shelved the plan to construct the dam at Kalabagh, located some 160 kilometers southwest of the capital, Islamabad, in Punjab. The 2010 flooding, however, revived official interest in the dam project.

The province of Punjab not only is economically and politically dominant in Pakistan, but also has been the main beneficiary of the 1960 Indus Waters Treaty with India. By commandeering water resources, Punjab's landowning class has prospered at the expense of others. "Equity in water allocation and access to irrigation is a major concern in Pakistan," as the *Pakistan Water Sector Strategy* report admitted, with farmers at the rearmost part of the irrigation systems "not receiving their allotted share of water because those at the head end tend to take more than their share. . . . [The] tail end farmers are usually the poorer ones, partly because of inequitable water distribution."[96]

Yet, despite being the principal beneficiary of the waters treaty with India, Punjab is Pakistan's anti-India bastion, just as anti-US sentiment burns brightly there, notwithstanding the major American aid inflow. The Indus Waters Treaty was designed to deal with the new intercountry political boundaries created in 1947 on the subcontinent. But with Punjab increasingly diverting the Indus waters for its use through new dams, including in Pakistani-administered Kashmir territories, intracountry water issues in Pakistan have remained an open national sore.

Pakistan's future as a united, cohesive state hinges on a more harmonious relationship between Punjab and other provinces, including an end to such practices as the diversion of waters and revenues away from Sind and Baluchistan and the demographic invasion by majority Punjabis of ethnically distinct areas, particularly the northernmost Gilgit-Baltistan Region in Pakistan-held Kashmir as well as Sind and Baluchistan. To deflect attention from some of these continuing practices, the Punjabi elites that rule Pakistan have sought to scapegoat India for their appropriation and gross mismanagement of water resources.

Hard-line forces in the country continue to link water with Kashmir while accusing India of diverting the waters of the western rivers of the Indus system reserved for Pakistan. But India's modest-size, run-of-the-river hydropower stations on the western rivers have no capacity to materially alter cross-border flows. The initial filling of any weir (or low dam) is restricted by treaty to the midmonsoon period, when rivers are in spate. The treaty's severe limits on "pondage" (or the limited amount of water held back to generate steady hydropower) also ensure that India has no control on the timing or quantum of transboundary flows. Although the treaty permits the building of small storage capacity upstream of up to 3.6 million acre feet (4.4 billion m³), India has no storage infrastructure on the western rivers.[97] The restricted "pondage" and other treaty conditions preclude the fashioning of a tool to diminish downstream flows or flood cross-border areas. Most Indian projects, in any case, are located more than 100 kilometers from the de facto international border in Kashmir, and any sudden release of water will first inundate populated Indian areas before causing any transboundary damage.

Yet jihadist groups like the Lashkar-e-Taiba, a largely Punjabi terrorist group reared by the Inter-Services Intelligence agency to wage a proxy war against India, have taken the lead to blame India for Pakistan's water woes. Such vile propaganda, coupled with the more recent moves of the Pakistani establishment to reopen water as a bilateral issue with India, seems designed to serve a dual purpose: To blunt the mounting complaints of the other Pakistani provinces over Punjab's commandeering of the bulk of the Indus waters, and to help unify the country by whipping up public passions against enemy India.

Still, in a rare public admission, a top Pakistani official said that Pakistan cannot "pass the buck" to India for its own "mismanagement" of water resources. "Is India stealing that water from you? No, it is not. Please do not fool yourselves and do not misguide the nation. We are mismanaging that water," Foreign Minister Shah Mahmood Qureshi told a national news conference in April 2010.[98] Despite this confession, the Pakistani government has continued to spotlight water as a contentious bilateral matter. One possible reason for its raking up the water issue in recent years is that it helps Pakistan to redirect attention away from India's focus on cross-border terrorism emanating from Pakistani territory as the core concern.

The expropriation of Indus waters by Pakistan's Punjab Province, however, raises a difficult issue for India, given that the spreading desertification in southern Sind carries significant ecological implications for India's border regions, including the Rann of Kutch, a marshland rich in biodiversity and wildlife.[99] The larger ramifications have been underscored by the rapidly degrading delta in Sind, with rivers beginning to look like canals and once-fertile fields turning into parched lands.[100] The rapid erosion of mangrove and other land cover, depleted fisheries, shrinking agriculture and vegetation, saltwater intrusion into coastal areas, groundwater contamination, and other effects in a region adjacent to India represent human-made environmental change whose long-term effects cannot stay confined to the Pakistani side of the international border. Paradoxically, India—through the multilateral Indus Basin Development Fund (IBDF), set up under the Indus Waters Treaty—partially funded the hydro infrastructure with which Pakistan's

Punjab Province began commandeering the Indus waters, to the detriment of Sind and Baluchistan. India contributed 19.4 percent of the IBDF's $895 million funds, which supported Pakistan's construction of the Tarbela and Mangla dams (among the world's biggest at that time) as well as an extensive irrigation canal network in Punjab.

Pakistan has had greater storage and hydropower-generating capacity in the Indus basin than any of the other basin states—Afghanistan, China, and India. But because Pakistan is the sole basin state totally reliant on a single river and its tributaries, it has one of the smallest water-storage capacities in Asia to serve as a buffer against drought: 150 m³ per capita, compared with India's 200 m³ and China's impressive 2,200 m³, according to the International Commission on Large Dams database. Before Pakistan embarked on new water megaprojects in recent years, its long-standing pride—the 143-meter-high Tarbela Dam—alone accounted for 54 percent of the country's total hydropower-production capacity, besides generating some 12 billion m³ of water a year for irrigation. The structure, however, has faced recurrent technical problems, prompting Patrick McCully of the US-based International Rivers Network to call Tarbela—the world's largest rockfill dam when it was completed—"perhaps the world's most problem-stricken major dam."[101] In fact, when its reservoir was first filled, a major tunnel collapsed, which required emergency works to forestall a dam break. Built between 1968 and 1976, Tarbela, together with associated barrages and diversion works, laid the foundation for Pakistan's agricultural boom and its emergence as an important food exporter. Tarbela, Mangla (which came up earlier), and the canal network, however, have had an adverse impact on the ecology and economy of the Indus delta, contributing to saltwater intrusion into the estuary and wiping out many fish species.

Pakistan, needing to build more storage for release of water in the dry season, has drawn up ambitious plans for thirty-three dams and increasingly turned to China for assistance in construction. China's growing role in the northernmost Gilgit and Baltistan areas, including the construction of dams there, has added another layer of complexity to a strategic region where the Pakistan Army and Sunni jihadist groups have sought to suppress a long-simmering rebellion against Pakistani rule by the local Shiite Muslims. The Chinese-built Karakoram Highway that has helped reinforce the Sino-Pakistan strategic nexus since opening in 1978 passes through the Gilgit-Baltistan Region—a slice of which Pakistan actually ceded to China in a 1963 agreement.[102] The Gilgit-Baltistan Region is part of Pakistan-controlled Kashmir, where there has been popular resistance to dams because they are seen to benefit only Pakistani Punjab while submerging areas upstream and dislocating local residents. The US-based group Human Rights Watch highlighted the case of Muhammad Saeed Asad, a social welfare officer in the Pakistani Kashmir government, who was suspended in 2002 for writing a book on the Mangla Dam that questioned downriver Punjab's right to commandeer Kashmiri water resources. Three books by Saeed Asad have been banned by Islamabad.[103]

Popular protests against the new 4,500-megawatt Bhasha Dam project, located 315 kilometers upstream of the Tarbela Dam, have flared in Gilgit, even as plans for more Pakistani megadams have been finalized with China, including a 7,000-megawatt project at Bunji, also in Gilgit-Baltistan. In fact, under a 2009 Sino-Pakistani agreement that followed Pakistan president Asif Ali Zardari's visit to Beijing, the state-owned China Yangtze River Three Gorges Project Development Corporation agreed to work with Pakistan's Water and Power Development Authority to set up new hydropower plants in the Pakistani part of disputed Kashmir, more than half of which is controlled by Pakistan and China.

The cornerstone of the 272-meter-high Bhasha Dam (also known as Diamer-Bhasha), which will displace tens of thousands of local residents, was laid by General Musharraf before his ouster from power. Musharraf had unveiled ambitious plans to build new dams with a storage capacity of more than 21 million acre feet (25.9 billion m³) at Kalabagh, Akhori, Kuram Tangi, and Munda, besides Bhasha. The multi-billion-dollar Bhasha Dam alone will store 15 percent of the annual discharge of the main Indus stream—an impoundment likely to compound the ecological impact on the delta in Sind.[104] Bhasha, moreover, is located in a highly unstable seismic zone, as was highlighted by the 7.6-magnitude earthquake that killed 79,000 people in Pakistani Kashmir in 2005.

If the degradation in the deltaic ecosystems is to be stemmed, upstream water use for irrigation must decline to permit better flows into the Indus delta. But new projects to meet the national need for storage and hydroelectricity threaten to accelerate the environmental change in the delta. The delta, a biologically rich area that serves as a major abode of freshwater fauna, is already experiencing biodiversity loss and rapid depletion of its mangroves due to reduced river inflows.[105] This factor is threatening to make extinct the endangered Indus River dolphin, one of the world's rarest mammals, of which there is a population of no more than 1,100. The Indus River dolphins, sometimes called "bhulans," are now largely concentrated in a small area near Sind Province's Sukkur town—the site of a giant barrage completed in 1932 before Pakistan's creation that helped introduce large-scale irrigated agriculture in the region. As a Pakistani observer has bemoaned, the "political economy of water-resources development and management in Pakistan has shifted benefits from the Indus delta to upstream users," with deltaic communities being rendered poor by willful "policy decisions."[106] Worse, according to the analyst, the "development-policy processes that caused the death of the Indus delta are still continuing."

If India wishes to stop the dominant Pakistani province from drying up downriver Sind and Baluchistan through usurper policies, it will have to look at innovative means. Such an upstream appropriation of waters, even though intracountry, does violate the spirit of the Indus Treaty, founded on the concept of open flow of river waters. Given the cross-border implications of irreversible damage to the natural ecosystems, India needs to explore prudent and feasible options. One possible option, dependent on Pakistani agreement to amend the treaty, would be for

India—instead of continuing to release all the waters to Pakistani Punjab directly or through Pakistan-held Kashmir—to build southward canals to offer substantial waters at the Rajasthan–Sind border for the benefit of the Sindhis and to save the deltaic ecosystems. Essentially, this would mean constructing a southward spur from the 649-kilometer Rajasthan Canal, also known as the Indira Gandhi Canal, which originates close to the confluence of the Beas and Sutlej rivers and terminates near the Rajasthan city of Jaisalmer.

The water delivered at the Sind–Rajasthan border will be from the Indus system's eastern rivers, which are reserved exclusively for India's use. But to compensate users in its water-stressed northern states for the water diversion to Sind, the Indian government would have to make equivalent water withdrawals from the western rivers—which are set aside for Pakistan's use but, in practice, have been meant for use mainly by Pakistani Punjab. Such Indian withdrawals could be made by reopening old canals and building new ones between the western and eastern rivers. The proposal, in essence, would seek to force Pakistan's hand to renegotiate the terms of the treaty. But its likely high diplomatic costs make the proposal politically unattractive.

The key point is that the intracountry water disputes and challenges in Pakistan are set to worsen in the coming decades. Pakistan was created as an Islamic state with a population that shared little culturally, ethnically, or linguistically. The country's rulers from the beginning have, in the absence of a national identity, used religion and the Kashmir dispute with India as the glue to hold Pakistan together. But Pakistan's rising internal challenges—from water-allocation disputes to civil–military relations—are increasingly making the use of religion as a political ideology less effective for managing state affairs. As Pakistan moves from water stress to water scarcity, there will be ominous implications for its internal security. Instead of ending its poor water management and fixing its massive irrigation inefficiencies (which have created, in the words of a Pakistani scholar, "one of the lowest productivities in the world per unit of water"[107]), a water-scarce Pakistan is likely to blame India for its woes.

Yet such finger-pointing is unlikely to stem Pakistan's growing intrastate water disputes or deflect calls for a shift from the long-standing state emphasis on dams and other engineering solutions to more resource-efficient, socially equitable, and sustainable practices that put the premium on conservation, irrigation efficiency, and water recycling.[108] In fact, with the business-as-usual model exacting increasing costs, the present pattern of more than nine-tenths of all water withdrawals being channeled for agriculture cannot continue for too long. If the Pakistani economy is to grow rapidly in support of a burgeoning population, the nonagricultural share of water consumption needs to soar from the present paltry 6 percent. But given its overexploitation of water resources, Pakistan has no capacity to inject more water into its national water grid.

If anything, it needs to get ready to make do with less water. After all, the vulnerability of the Indus system to climate-change-driven reduced flows is the greatest among the major rivers in Asia.[109] The larger three rivers reserved for Pakistan actually are more dependent than India's smaller Indus rivers on flows generated by snowmelt and glacier melt. Therefore, the flows of the rivers set aside for Pakistan are particularly susceptible to global-warming-driven shifts in melt characteristics.

Although climate-change science is still in its infancy, the projections are that accelerated glacier thaw in the western Himalayas will exacerbate problems of flooding and draining in Pakistan, especially in its lower Indus basin, in the near to medium terms before delivering a 30 to 40 percent decrease in river flows by the end of the century.[110] As one author has asked, "Consider what will happen in water-distressed, nuclear-armed, terrorist-besieged, overpopulated, heavily irrigation dependent and already politically unstable Pakistan when its single water lifeline, the Indus River, loses a third of its flow from the disappearance from its glacial water source."[111] Pakistan already ranks as one of the world's most-vulnerable and dysfunctional nations: It has remained in the top ten failed states in the Failed States Index since that annually revised list was first unveiled in 2005.[112]

Pakistan must deal with its water crisis before it becomes too late. It grows all its cotton, rice, sugarcane, fruits, and vegetables and 95 percent of its wheat under irrigated conditions.[113] These are the very agricultural items it exports in bulk. It is now the world's third-biggest rice exporter and fourth-largest cotton producer, with its fruit and vegetable exports surging rapidly. In other words, water-deficient Pakistan is a major exporter of "virtual water" in the form of cereals, cotton, oilseeds, sugar, fruits, and vegetables. As Pakistan's capacity to increasingly grow water-intensive crops for export with irrigation subsidies falters in the face of water shortages, a fundamental restructuring of the Pakistani economy will become unavoidable. Agriculture, which makes up more than 22 percent of Pakistan's gross domestic product (GDP), is not only the country's main foreign-exchange earner, but also the principal moneymaker for the country's feudal elites, who dominate the national and provincial politics.

Yet, in a country where the poor subsidize the wealthy landed and commercial class, agriculture remains untaxed, even as Pakistan's dependence on foreign donors rises. To upgrade its water infrastructure and promote integrated water resources management, Pakistan needs to generate sufficient domestic resources by reforming its economy, including its dysfunctional tax system, which collects very little money. Barely 1.7 percent of its citizens pay any income tax, for example. Even the prime minister and twenty-five of his ministers, according to their own sworn affidavits in 2010, did not pay income taxes at all.[114] "A small elite comprised of the military, landowners, and the rising urban upper and middle classes is loath to give up any of its wealth (some of which is illegally accumulated)," according to a report. "Their certain knowledge that 'the West will never let Pakistan fail' also gives the elites tremendous confidence in the status quo."[115] Pakistan indeed has one of the lowest effective tax rates in the world, equal to less than 9 percent of the value of its economy. By contrast, the tax-to-GDP ratio in the United States is about 28 percent.

China's Forced Relocation of More Than 23 Million People

China stands out not only for its intracountry water disputes but also for the large-scale forcible relocation of residents to build the thousands of dams, reservoirs, and barrages that it now boasts. After all, China is the global leader in dam construction, with at least half of all large dams in the world, even as it is building more, although almost all the best sites in the country, other than in Tibet, have already been taken.[116] Its megadams and interbasin water transfers have become proud symbols of its engineering and economic prowess.

The forced eviction of residents from and around sites chosen for water projects has been pervasive since the Mao Zedong era. In a stunning admission, Prime Minister Wen Jiabao disclosed to the National People's Congress in a 2007 report that the People's Republic of China had relocated a total of 22.9 million people to make room for large hydro projects.[117] This number is bigger than the entire population of Australia, Syria, Romania, or Chile. Still, hundreds of thousands of more residents, mostly poor villagers, have been forcibly uprooted in recent years.

Yet another surprising fact is that despite an authoritarian system, China has failed to stamp out intrastate water conflicts. If anything, such conflicts have grown since the 1990s, in keeping with the general upsurge of social ferment in Chinese society, "including a proliferation of what the authorities coyly refer to as 'mass incidents,' tens of thousands of events that in most countries would simply be called protests. There can be any number of reasons for people to be up in arms: Disputes over land rights, anger over environmental degradation, corruption and favoritism in local politics, a generalized lack of transparency and the arbitrary way that so many decisions are made here," as an account from Beijing put it.[118] Official figures actually show that such mass incidents have been growing at about the same rate as China's GDP, underscoring the threat from heightened unrest.

The very hydro structures that the authorities love to show off as engineering marvels that epitomize China's rapid rise have become a lightning rod for grassroots discontent and anger over mass displacement and persistent environmental problems. The commandeering of water resources by megacities and large corporations has further fueled unrest. A UN document says that in China, "the number of disputes related to water reached over 120,000 during the 1990s, according to official sources."[119] In the twenty-first century, with water resources coming under greater pressure and contamination becoming a serious problem, passions have run high between provinces, communities, and villages over access to safe water, triggering rampant disputes.

Since Premier Wen's admission, forced evictions have continued on a significant scale—including from near the Three Gorges Dam site and to make way for the Great South–North Water Diversion Project—triggering violent protests at times.

In a country where the government's bulldozing of historic neighborhoods and relocation of large numbers of people by fiat have become commonplace in the name of "public interest," hundreds of thousands of additional residents have been ordered in recent years to move out from sites for new water megaprojects, with any resistance being quickly crushed.

Demolition squads usually cut off water and electricity to the homes of those who refuse to leave, before calling in the police to evict them and clear the path for the bulldozing of the houses. Forcible evictions, of course, have also been carried out for other developmental projects. For example, hundreds of thousands of Beijing residents were forced to move out and their houses destroyed for the construction of the 2008 Olympics venues. Similarly, Shanghai's 2010 World Expo and the city's building of a Disneyland theme park led to the uprooting of several thousand local families. Water projects, however, stand out for displacing by far the largest number of residents since the Chinese Communists came to power.

Furthermore, with most of the country's water resources concentrated in the south and southwest, peasant protests over water shortages and pollution are becoming more frequent in the densely populated northern plains, which stretch from Beijing down to Jiangsu Province in the Yangtze River basin. Water-related protests also have flared beyond the northern plains. For example, in the eastern coastal province of Zhejiang, located to the south of Jiangsu, violent protests by thousands of peasants broke out in April 2005 over continued government concessions to a factory that had been polluting the local land and water resources and causing widespread sickness and poor crop yields.[120] According to China's Ministry of Environmental Protection, there were about 51,000 pollution-related protests in the country in 2006 alone, "many of which involved water pollution."[121] In a country where explosive economic growth has opened a yawning gap between rich and poor, as in India, water scarcity and contamination add to the problems faced by the disadvantaged.

With China having moved from being a totalitarian state to an authoritarian state, its citizens are less willing to suffer silently. Residents, in fact, are becoming more aware of their rights to property and thus are fighting back against attempts to forcibly demolish their houses to make way for projects. After all, with the erosion of the *hukou* system that tied citizens to their place of birth, the Chinese now can relocate within the country, enjoy property rights, travel overseas, make use of the latest communications technologies, and do other things that were unthinkable a generation ago. It is, therefore, little surprise that clashes between demolition teams and homeowners are becoming more common, with a few people even taking extreme steps, such as self-immolation, to highlight forced eviction. The forcible mass displacement of people—along with the state's continuing repressive impulse, as mirrored in a tightly controlled media and a pervasive security apparatus—shows that some things have not changed since the Mao era. But other things indeed have changed for the worse, such as the whipping up of ultra-nationalism and turning it into the legitimating credo of Communist rule, now the world's oldest-surviving autocratic system. Nationalism also serves as a tool to ram through megaprojects, whatever the human and environmental costs.

Water megaprojects, coupled with water shortages and pollution, have significantly contributed to the rising incidence of violent rural protests in China. Protests in the countryside, according to Chinese officials and analysts, have been increasing by more than 10 percent a year.[122] Mass incidents—the Chinese state's euphemism for rural strikes, protests, roadblocks, and other forms of large demonstrations—officially jumped from 74,000 in 2004 to 120,000 in 2008, despite the public emphasis of President Hu Jintao on *bu zheteng*, or stability, and on a "harmonious society." By comparison, officially there had been only 8,709 "mass incidents" in 1993. As for serious internal flare-ups, Shanghai's Jiatong University, in a 2011 annual report on crisis management, recorded seventy-two "major incidents" of social unrest in 2010, compared with sixty in 2009—a 20 percent increase.

Such are the rising costs of what the government calls *weiwen*, or stability maintenance, that the annual internal security budget now rivals national defense spending. In fact, according to the *Global Times*, a leading party-run newspaper, the government in 2009 "earmarked 514 billion yuan [$78.2 billion] to maintain stability, much more than the 480 billion yuan [$73 billion]" officially budgeted for national defense.[123] The fixation on *weiwen* has spawned a well-oiled security apparatus that extends from state-of-the-art surveillance and extralegal detention centers to an army of paid informants and neighborhood "safety patrols" on the lookout for troublemakers. Yet major protests by workers, peasants, and others continue to challenge the system. Housing demolition and forced relocation, the government's expropriation of rural land, pollution, and labor disputes have been identified as the leading causes of such mass protests, which are becoming more intense or violent.[124] The government's own annual report to the quasi-legislature, the National People's Congress, in 2011 identified the demolition of people's homes by state-backed developers and seizures of their land as among the key shortcomings of development. Yet given that China's latest five-year economic plan incorporates a renewed dam-building program, the path has been opened to more seizures of land, flattenings of homes, and forced relocations. The vast majority of the protests "occur in the countryside among desperate and angry peasants, and are quickly suppressed and censored. If any news emerges, it is usually only days or weeks later."[125]

The rising unrest prompted an insider in the Chinese system, Yu Jianrong, director of social issues research at the Chinese Academy of Social Sciences' Institute of Rural Affairs, to warn in late 2009 that the Communist Party's obsession with preserving its monopoly on power through "state violence" and "ideology," rather than justice, risked taking the country to the brink of "revolutionary turmoil." Yu went on to say, "More and more evidence shows that the situation is getting more and more tense, [and] more and more serious."[126] And in a 2011 article, Yu said that the government's coercion-centered *weiwen* strategy "is tantamount to drinking poison to quench one's thirst."[127]

Because of China's opaque, repressive political system, there is little room for any intrastate water dispute to come under a sustained public spotlight. Still, as pointed out by the UN, internal water disputes have become rife in China, without attracting the glare of publicity. The Three Gorges Dam occupies the pride of place in China's vast water infrastructure, but its large-scale displacement of local residents and its continuing engineering and environmental challenges have made it the subject of Chinese media attention like no other megaproject. In the largest eviction of residents for a single water project in modern world history, the Chinese government quelled grassroots resistance and forced 1.4 million people to leave their homes near the Three Gorges Dam, the world's largest global hydropower producer, which is becoming—to Beijing's acute embarrassment—one of the country's biggest environmental nightmares. The 1.4 million evictees were mostly removed in a ten-year period and resettled in other parts of Chongqing or in nearby Hubei Province.

When this project was under way on the Yangtze River between 1992 and 2008, about 16 million tons of concrete were poured to create a gargantuan reservoir that stretches back almost the length of Britain, stores 39.3 cubic kilometers of water, and drives twenty-six huge turbines. But the impoundment of such a massive volume of water, the Chinese authorities now admit, has triggered landslides in the surrounding areas, while the slowing of the Yangtze's flows has made it difficult to flush pollution from the river system. To deal with the land erosion and hydrological instability, authorities in 2010 initiated a drive to evict 300,000 additional residents, spurring greater local unrest.[128] In other words, the number of residents displaced by the Three Gorges Dam project aggregates to at least 1.7 million by official count.

China's second-largest relocation program centers on the ongoing Great South–North Water Diversion Project, launched in 2002. The total number of people likely to be displaced by this Olympian-scale project has not been disclosed by the authorities. But the relocation of about 440,000 residents, living largely in Henan and Hubei provinces, began in 2010 to facilitate work on the eastern and central legs of this three-part project, with a report in an official newspaper of the Communist Party calling the transfer of residents "a big headache for local governments."[129] Most of these evictions are linked with the central route, whose first phase, along with the entire eastern route, is scheduled to be completed by 2014.

An unspecified number of additional villagers are to be uprooted when the second phase of the central route and the big western line are launched. Zhang Jiyao, the official in charge of the gigantic project, has warned that the "intensity" and challenge of the mass relocation of residents to make way for the South–North Water Diversion Project's central route "will surpass that of the Three Gorges Dam project" because the entire process of eviction and resettlement must be completed within a much shorter time frame.[130] The relocation drive has already stirred a rising tide of complaints and triggered local unrest, which occasionally has spilled into violence.

In fact, the broader grassroots resistance to forced evictions, including violent clashes, prompted China's State Council—the equivalent of the Cabinet—to issue an edict in May 2010 ordering payment of "reasonable" compensation to displaced people and directing local authorities to refrain from "oppressive" actions. The edict, however, contained little that was new and was widely viewed as a public relations exercise to tamp down on popular anger. After all, just four years earlier, the Chinese government had promulgated what it called the "Rules of Land Compensation and People Resettlement in Medium and Large Hydraulic and Hydroelectricity Projects." According to these rules, evictees must be provided with a level of livelihood at least similar to what they had before displacement, with job creation and finding new cultivable land to be part of the resettlement plans. The rules cast the burden of responsibility on local governments.[131]

Yet forced evictions have continued as before, without many of the displaced getting what the government rules promise. Evictees have complained of having been moved to poorer lands with dim job prospects. Similarly, the State Council's edict has done little to curb the official zeal to callously remove residents in the name of the public interest.

If the eviction of 440,000 residents in Henan and Hubei in connection with the South–North Water Diversion Project and the ouster of an additional 300,000 from near the Three Gorges Dam were added to Premier Wen's 2007 figure, the number of people displaced by water projects in China would total 23.64 million—more than Taiwan's total population. This figure does not include the indeterminate number of minority-group members displaced by new dam projects in Yunnan and Tibet since 2007. It is the ability to use untrammeled state power that has allowed China to pursue grand hydroengineering projects at immense social and environmental cost. By contrast, India has to pay a "democracy tax" that not only weighs down decision making, but also complicates pursuit of development projects, as illustrated by the decades-long litigation waged by environmental and grassroots activists to stall the Narmada Dam, whose construction has stretched on interminably. Similarly in Japan—despite a dam-building tradition dating back many centuries and the construction of modern, multipurpose dams taking off with ardor from the 1950s—plans for new dams have run into obstacles ranging from grassroots resistance and environmental concerns to resettlement costs and a paucity of good sites.

In a country the size of China, given the wide disparity in the intracountry distribution of water resources and the growing water shortages and contamination in the economic-boom areas, it is proving increasingly difficult for the authorities to effectively muffle internal water wrangles, as has been exemplified by the disputes over the resources of the Juma and Daling rivers in the arid north. The federal government has often had to intervene to put an end to disputes. For instance, a nasty dispute between the prosperous coastal province of Shandong and the poor inland province of Ningxia over the Yellow River waters was settled in 2002 through a Beijing diktat in Shandong's favor, resulting in economic losses in

Ningxia as well as in Inner Mongolia. In Xinjiang, a paucity of freshwater has become a source of conflict along ethnic lines between the native Uighur communities and the large number of Han immigrants, who have introduced extensive irrigated farming in the province. The state-run Chinese media, though, carries reports on water disputes between provinces and communities in the Han heartland, but not on the Uighur/Han water conflict in Xinjiang or the displacement of ethnic Tibetans or other minority-group members due to water projects in Tibet and Yunnan.

To help tackle interprovincial and intercommunity disputes, China has tried since the 1980s to end the Maoist culture of treating water as a free commodity. After Deng Xiaoping dismantled agricultural communes in the late 1970s and allowed farmers to sell a portion of their output at open-market prices—steps that helped dramatically boost agricultural production—water still remained free. That culture promoted high resource inefficiency and a phenomenal growth in water demand in the 1980s and beyond. A replacement system under which farmers pay fixed, acreage-based irrigation charges, however, has not discouraged water from being used profligately.

In 1988, China enacted the so-called Water Law, which mandated that in the river basins under stress, a system be introduced apportioning a share of the mean annual runoff volume to each of the different riparian administrative districts (usually provinces). This law, never really enforced, was replaced by a 2002 regulation aimed at promoting integrated water resources management and emphasizing five areas: water allocation, water rights and water-withdrawal permits, river basin management, water efficiency and conservation, and anticontamination measures. The new runoff allocation plan, however, has been implemented only in the overstressed Yellow River basin.[132] In an attempt to help ease interprovincial issues, the authorities also launched a pilot project under which industrial users in some northern provinces were asked to pay farmers in upstream-river regions to acquire water rights, whereby the farmers were encouraged to raise income by selling a portion of their water rights and investing in more water-efficient crops and irrigation technologies.[133] China, however, lacks a functioning system of water rights encompassing both groundwater and surface water. Administrative decisions, often arbitrary, "substitute for a water-rights system, and the data, accurate measurement and data integrity required for a water-rights system to operate do not generally exist."[134]

As a result, about two-thirds of all water supplies in China continue to flow to farmers at next to no cost for them. To prevent the wasteful use of water, the fixed, acreage-based irrigation charges must give way to volumetric water charges, so that users pay according to the amount of water used. The federal and provincial governments also need to do more to tackle water contamination, which, by reducing availability, has become the dominant source of water conflicts in the country.[135] Although many small high-pollution factories along China's waterways have been forced to shut down and the amended Law for Water Pollution Control has strengthened legal liabilities for causing pollution, water contamination remains a serious problem. Groundwater depletion, for its part, is drying up lakes and wetlands and increasing the salinity of subterranean water. The additional waters to be brought across basins by the South–North Water Diversion Project can, at best, ease some of the acute problems in the north without ending the increasing number of disputes between villages, counties, and provinces over water quality and quantity.

South Korea's Divisive Four-Rivers Project

As a country of just 49 million people, packing 481 inhabitants per square kilometer in one of the world's highest population densities, South Korea has risen from the rubble of the Korean War into one of the world's industrial, shipbuilding, and electronics giants, which joined the ranks of the Organization for Economic Cooperation and Development in 1996.[136] Today, South Korea punches far above its weight. Yet South Korea illustrates how a national river-waters project, when pursued without also building a broad political consensus, can ignite strong popular passions and divide a country. The so-called Four Major Rivers Restoration Project, launched in early 2009, has proven one of the most divisive issues in South Korea.

One reason for the national controversy is that the Four Major Rivers Restoration Project is seen by opponents as a mere name change for the earlier idea to link the country's major rivers and create a Pan-Korea Grand Waterway. President Lee Myung-bak came to office in February 2008 vowing to build the Grand Korean Waterway. After all, transforming South Korea's rivers into a giant canal system—an idea that a government agency, the Korea Water Resources Corporation, had debunked in 1998 as technically and economically unfeasible—was Lee's main campaign issue. But after just three months in power, sensing the popular unease over his river-interlinking plan and a lack of public support for his vision, he began revising his election pledge.

The neoconservative leader announced in the central city of Daegu that his government would proceed step by step, first servicing the country's four major rivers—the Han, the Nag Dong, the Kuem, and the Young San—before considering drilling a 20-kilometer tunnel under Mount Wolak to connect the Han and the Nag Dong, the largest two rivers that supply drinking water for two-thirds of the country's population. "Since the public is uneasy about connecting the waterways, we are delaying that phase until later," the president said in May 2008. Days later, Lee formally declared at a news conference that he was canceling his grand waterway plan. He subsequently unveiled the Four Major Rivers Restoration Project in place of the Grand Korean Waterway. But to critics, this move amounted merely to a tactical retreat, not an abandonment of the grand canal plan, because they view the four-rivers project as designed to lay the foundation for interlinking the rivers.

Another reason for the national divisiveness is that the four-rivers project, even without any future move to link up the major rivers, involves the construction of more dams and barrages in a country already teeming with such human-made structures. In 2011 South Korea had about 800 large dams and more than 18,000 small irrigation reservoirs, with artificial lakes making up almost 95 percent of all the lakes in the nation.[137] The South Korean focus on regulating the course of rivers since the 1960s has been redolent of the dam-building zeal of Chinese decision makers. The widespread regulation has contributed to the deterioration of natural watercourses in a country that puts a premium on water quality.

The limited water resources and low per capita availability of freshwater in South Korea—now estimated at 1,447 m³ per year—have served as a major motivator for launching various water projects over the years, including for irrigation, flood control, community water supply, and hydropower generation.[138] The annual rainfall, though uniformly distributed across much of the nation, is concentrated mostly during the four-month summer, when typhoons sometimes wreak serious damage to crops, as do droughts before the onset of the monsoon season. In 2010, for example, an unusually long stretch of heavy rain, coupled with hot, humid weather, sharply decreased harvests of napa cabbage and other produce by early fall, resulting in a record surge in prices, especially of kimchi, South Korea's staple condiment.

About 7 percent of South Korea's total renewable water resources of 69.7 cubic kilometers per year flows in by river from across the demilitarized zone, which cuts the Korean Peninsula roughly in half and is the world's most heavily fortified frontier.[139] The percentage of the total population engaged in agriculture has shrunk from 68 in 1965 to less than 15 owing to South Korea's rapid industrialization, yet the farm sector still makes up more than half of the aggregate water withdrawals in the country. Agriculture's share of water use, however, has been on the decline in a largely rugged country where much of the arable area is reclaimed land and is thus intensively cultivated.

The Four Major Rivers Restoration Project carries a high price tag, in spite of being a trimmed-down program. The program is aimed at upgrading and repairing the Han, the Nag Dong, the Kuem, and the Young San, and it will cost taxpayers almost $20 billion, according to an official estimate. The country's fifth major river, the Seom Jin—located in the south, like the smaller Young San—has, on second thought, also been included in the project, which is widely seen to have sprung from Lee Myung-bak's desire to leave a mark through a massive "New Deal" spending initiative in the style of Franklin D. Roosevelt. Lee had initially favored building a cross-country waterway linking the Han (which flows through Seoul to empty into the Yellow Sea at Incheon, the country's No. 2 harbor) with the Nag Dong, which flows into the Korea Strait at Busan, the largest port.

The Seoul–Busan waterway, with an extensive system of locks, docks, and wharfs, was intended to be just the beginning in a planned web of river-linking canals in South Korea—and later possibly in North Korea, after the reunification of the Koreas. Before he settled for a scaled-back project centered on the four rivers, Lee had pledged to complete the 540-kilometer Seoul–Busan waterway within his initial five-year term so as to create a new transportation route to ease highway and railroad congestion. But just like his original plan to create a seamless national waterway, the four-rivers project will widen, deepen, and straighten the rivers, altering their natural course and flow (map 5.3).

In South Korea's raucous politics, the four-rivers project has proven as controversial as the abortive move of Lee's immediate predecessor, Roh Moo-hyun, to

MAP 5.3 South Korea's Four Major Rivers, Which Are Being Widened and Deepened

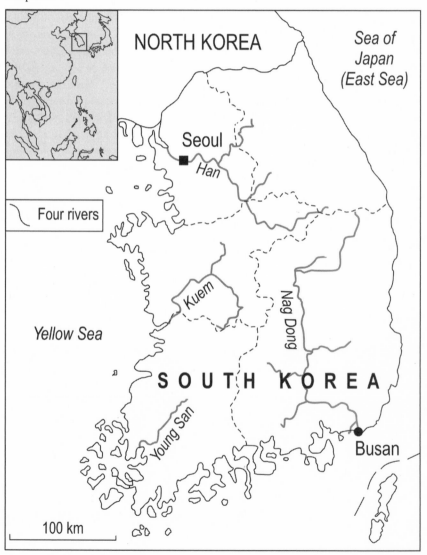

shift the national capital from Seoul to Yongi-Kongju, in the center of the country. Lee, nicknamed "the Bulldozer" from his time as a construction industry executive, also split South Korean society on another issue after becoming president: He reversed his country's decade-long "sunshine policy" toward North Korea, choosing to cut off bilateral aid and squeeze the Stalinist regime in Pyongyang, thereby prompting North Korea to scale back inter-Korean contact, carry out provocative actions including missile tests, and ratchet up bellicose rhetoric. Relations between the two Koreas actually sunk to a new low in 2010 following the death of forty-six South Korean sailors in the sinking of a warship—which was blamed on a North Korean torpedo attack—and the North's shelling of the South's Yeonpyeong island. The incidents, and threats of retaliation, spurred fears of a broader conflict.

Earlier, as the mayor of Seoul, Lee Myung-bak had pushed through another water-related project in the face of popular opposition, tearing down a busy overpass to help beautify the Cheonggyecheon stream and create a modern downtown public recreation area. But while the Cheonggyecheon project turned a rotting 5.8-kilometer stream into a concrete channel, the four-rivers project aims to reengineer more than 900 kilometers of natural waterways.

To its proponents, the four-rivers project would help alleviate water shortages, clean up and upgrade the rivers, control floods, create "eco-friendly cultural spaces" for tourists, revitalize local economies, and generate tens of thousands of jobs. The government says the project will yield 50 million m^3 of additional drinking water per year. But to its detractors, the project is a likely boondoggle that would benefit only the powerful construction industry while further degrading natural water channels and potentially proving disastrous for the environment. Lawsuits filed by civil society groups challenging different components of the program in a bid to stall work have been dismissed by provincial courts.[140]

The project, proceeding rapidly, involves the construction of twenty new large dams on the major rivers and their tributaries, the rebuilding or raising of the height of eighty-seven existing dams, the shoring up of more than 580 kilometers of riverbanks with concrete, and the dredging of 690 kilometers of river stretches. With the project requiring work at fifty-four sites to be done by local authorities, there were political skirmishes between the federal government and a couple of provincial governors skeptical of the program's touted benefits. There remains an undercurrent of religious resentment, with Buddhist groups having accused President Lee, a Christian church elder, of ignoring the threat to riverside Buddhist relics in the hills. A Zen master burned himself to death on a stream bank in 2010 in support of the demand that the project be scrapped. But most significantly, the project has pitted environmentalists, many intellectuals, and a number of grassroots activist groups against the government. An official public relations blitzkrieg failed to allay widely held misgivings about the project.

The lesson the South Korean experience presents is that in any democracy, a massive project—especially one that claims to offer national benefits—must be pursued not in a politically partisan way but through consensus building and co-option.

By upgrading, straightening, channelizing, and further damming the country's major rivers, the project is likely to deliver benefits, but these gains may come with long-term costs in terms of an adverse impact on the fluvial ecosystems. The massive investment in the project could have been more profitably channeled into developing new clean water technologies that are energy- and cost-efficient, tapping nonconventional water sources (including rainwater capture, the reuse of water, and desalination), and building greater water efficiency.

Incentivizing Water Productivity

Asia shows that intrastate water disputes are complex, with ethnic, cultural, sectarian, and environmental elements often woven in a web of entrenched social and economic grievances. Managing such disputes wisely is an important test of good governance in any nation because once they escalate to open conflict, they directly impinge on internal security and social harmony. In fact, when governance is deficient, water disputes tend to get linked with deeper socioeconomic discontent, fueling a cycle of unending unrest and sporadic violence. This, in turn, can undercut the confidence of citizens in the fairness and impartiality of public administration, erode the rule of law, and raise new threats.

With water pollution and shortages becoming more widespread, governments in Asia need to invest greater political capital to regulate water competition between provinces or communities. It has been suggested by some that one way to tamp down intracountry competition is to create an open national market where water can be priced and traded. The privatization of water supplies has been an emotive subject in Asia, and there are few takers for market-driven pricing and trading as practiced in Australia, which has taken the lead internationally in developing a free market in water. In most Asian countries, there is strong opposition to commercializing a common good like water, on the grounds that it would disadvantage poor communities and go against equity-based development.

To stop profligate use, water, however, must come with a reasonable price, even if it is not market based. The social impact of pricing can be cushioned by keeping water subsidies specifically for the poor. Rational pricing has long been held as a key element in water management and conservation.

Actually, at the heart of the Asian challenge is the need to raise water efficiency and productivity. To ease intrastate water shortages and disputes, Asian countries have little choice but to increase water productivity, especially in agriculture and industry. The frenetic pace of industrial growth in China, for example, has reduced the share of water supply for irrigation. Yet China, like the other Asian economies, needs to grow more food while concurrently seeking water savings in the irrigation sector, including by cutting conveyance losses and increasing application efficiency.

In cases where water quality and productivity both appreciably increase, conditions of water stress perceptibly lessen. South Korea's per capita water availability is close to Pakistan's, but it has done a much better job in building water quality and productivity. As a result, South Korea, while prone to the ravages of drought, does not face the serious crisis situation haunting Pakistan. The fact is that there is much scope to increase water quality and productivity in many Asian countries, including those with efficiency and quality standards that are already better, such as South Korea, Japan, and Singapore.

Too often, Asian countries have focused on supply-side approaches—which center on water impoundment, diversion, and storage facilities—and neglected demand-side options. When water resources are under pressure or stretched to the limit, as is the case in a large number of Asian states, structural responses in the form of new reservoirs, dams, and barrages can hardly offer a solution by themselves. Yet Asia needs to respond to the shifting patterns of snowmelt and glacial melt and rainfall by building greater water storage capacity so as to augment water supplies in the dry months.

The smart way is to integrate supply-side approaches with demand management, while placing as much stress on water quality as on water quantity. Even on the supply side, the adoption of nontraditional measures has become necessary, including rainwater harvesting, water recycling, and cleaning up polluted waterways. On the demand side, cutting irrigation losses has become paramount, along with greater water efficiency in industry and household water-saving measures.

To help ease internal water tensions and conflicts, the biggest water savings have to come from the main consumer of water. Agriculture contributes a small percentage of the total GDP in most Asian nations, but consumes more than four-fifths of all Asian water supplies. Agriculture's share of the GDP is 15.2 percent in China, 16.7 percent in India, 16 percent in Indonesia, 17.9 percent in Thailand, and 2.7 percent in South Korea.[141] In this light, the way to alleviate water stress or scarcity is to gradually reduce water allocations for agriculture so as to help increase availability for other needs.

Reduced water allocations for irrigation need not reduce agricultural production if altered irrigation methods are employed, more water-efficient crops are grown, recycled water is utilized, and innovations are introduced in chemicals, cultivation, harvesting, and "fertigation" (the technique of supplying dissolved fertilizer to crops through an irrigation system).[142] New plant varieties will help boost yields and crop quality. According to a World Bank report on Pakistan, reduced water supplies for irrigation can actually diminish waterlogging and salinity problems.[143] Agricultural productivity measures help improve the efficiency of water use in irrigation as well as boost crop yields on both rain-fed and irrigated lands.

As they climb up the economic ladder, Asian countries, in any case, will have to make do with smaller numbers of people in farming, as has happened in the developed world. Cropland limitations also will come into play increasingly. As cities and towns expand and new development projects are implemented, the amount of quality land available for farming will decline—a trend already visible in Asia at least since the 1990s. Given the projected sharp increase in food demand in Asia in the coming decades, difficult choices face Asian governments. To grow more food with less land, less water, and fewer farmers, Asia will need to focus on developing new techniques through application-oriented agricultural research and development. It also means that a continued supply of large volumes of under-priced water for profligate use in low-value-added agriculture will begin to exact significant costs and thus become unsustainable in the medium term.

While relying on science-based technologies to help enhance the quantity and quality of farm production, the leitmotif of development strategies in Asia needs to be the optimal use of scarce water resources. To promote water efficiency in agriculture, the current practices of free or heavily underpriced water supply in a number of countries will need to give way to more reasonable pricing and perhaps even to government rationing measures. Also, to promote the use of water recycled from treated sewage, sewerage treatment plants, along with a pipeline grid to take the cleaned water to the farms, will need to be constructed. The more wastewater Asia recycles for agriculture, the more potable water it will have for other uses. It is by adopting a mix of different measures—including greater water efficiency, water reuse, improved irrigation systems, and new farm varieties and techniques—that water-stressed Israel raised its agricultural output sevenfold between 1975 and 2000 with just a fractional increase in the use of water. It is a model that other nations must emulate to relieve their water stress.

The drip-feed irrigation system, which directs the water flow straight to the root zone of plants, can help slash agricultural water consumption by 50 to 70 percent compared with gravity irrigation, and by 10 to 20 percent in comparison to sprinkler irrigation. New computerized drip irrigation techniques provide even greater water-saving benefits through an ultralow application rate, also called "minute irrigation," that optimizes the air–water relationship in the plants' root zones. Computerized fertigation, similarly, yields important benefits. Another benefit of modern micro-irrigation systems is that they help prevent soil salinization. Traditional irrigation practices have contributed to the steady accumulation of soluble salts of sodium, magnesium, and calcium in soil to the extent that soil fertility has been compromised in some areas.

It is true that farmers will start investing in more water-efficient crops and technologies and accept recycled wastewater only when they are made to realize the true value of water and other inputs like fertilizers and seeds. Water remains free for farmers in most parts of India, while Chinese farmers—after getting free water until 1985—now pay water tariffs that are modest compared with those in countries with four times more water availability per capita. Farmers are a powerful constituency in most parts of the world, whatever the political system in a state. But their clout in Asia probably is greater than elsewhere. It is politically unacceptable for many Asian governments to make farmers pay market rates for water, electricity, seeds, and fertilizers. Yet a shift from free water or heavily subsidized tariffs to a carefully calibrated rate system has become imperative, with small, marginal farmers possibly being compensated through other types of state support.

More broadly, it makes little sense for some countries in Asia—in the name of food security—to grow in arid or semiarid areas high-water-consuming field crops, such as grains, cotton, sugar, and oilseeds. Such commodities should be imported from countries where they can be grown more efficiently, without local water resources coming under strain. Consider China: More than 50 percent of its wheat and two-fifths of its cotton are grown in the three semiarid northern provinces of Henan, Hebei, and Shandong. To sustain the intensive irrigated farming in its north, China now is transferring waters across rivers and basins—principally from the Yangtze basin to the parched Yellow basin—besides damming international rivers flowing south from the Tibetan Plateau and the rivers that head to Kazakhstan and Russia. But such practices are environmentally unsustainable and geopolitically risky and raise intrastate challenges within China over the large-scale displacement of local residents. The longer such practices remain in place, the greater will be the danger of environmental degradation and inter-riparian tensions.

There is no alternative to wise water governance. In semiarid areas, switching from irrigated wheat farming to vegetable and fruit production, for example, will be a more efficient use of local water resources while also bringing better financial returns for the farmers. By gradually slashing the domestic production of water-intensive commodity crops to rely on greater imports, water-distressed Asian countries, in effect, would be importing "virtual water," thereby mitigating their own water stress and diverting their precious water resources to alternative, high-productivity uses. Virtual-water trade may not be a means to achieving water security, yet it can improve water-use efficiency and alleviate pressures on the local environment.

Still, given the power of concepts such as "food sovereignty" and "food security," a greater reliance on imports is a politically sensitive matter in most parts of Asia. In general, many countries, especially the more ambitious ones, do not wish to lose their ability to substantially feed their own populations, or else they will be at the mercy of both global commodity markets and other governments. So any country will proceed slowly, with a great deal of circumspection, toward relying more on the international markets for water-intensive food products, even though virtual-water imports conceptually make sense for any water-stressed economy.

In an increasingly interdependent and globalized world, water-intensive commodities ought to be produced by water-rich countries for export to water-stressed economies, which, in turn, can export items whose production is less water intensive. By exporting commodities with low virtual-water content and importing those with high virtual water, water-distressed nations can help ease their water scarcity. Egypt's wheat imports, for example, save it 3.6 giga m^3 of water resources per year.[144] Conversely, water-stressed Thailand, the leading rice-exporting nation, ranks as the world's fourth-largest net exporter of virtual water, with its annual rice exports alone carrying 28 giga m^3 of embedded national water.[145]

Intracountry conflicts over the sharing of waters, in a fundamental sense, are similar to intercountry disputes, but without the geopolitical driver. The overexploitation of surface waters by one province or community, after all, imperils the interests of a downstream province or community in much the same way as an upper-riparian country's water diversion affects a downriver nation. Several principles of customary international water law thus can be applied in an intrastate context to settle disputes between water users. They include the law of riparian rights, which ties water rights to land, and the doctrine of prior appropriation, under which a priority right falls on the first or existing user of river waters. The equality of all riparians is the foundation of the theory of limited territorial integrity, which links the right to use river waters to a corresponding obligation not to cause substantial injury to another riparian. In other words, every province or county is free to use shared water resources, provided such use does not prejudice the rights or uses by other provinces and counties. There is also the principle of equitable distribution, which treats a river as an indivisible unit whose resources should be developed for the maximum number of people, regardless of territorial boundaries.

Courts in Asia that have sought to invoke such principles in the intracountry context, including India's Supreme Court, have struggled, however, to give practical meaning to them and to balance one riparian province's rights against another. For example, it has proven very challenging to determine in a practical sense what constitutes an "equitable" apportionment of waters between two or more riparian provinces—and this difficulty is compounded by shifting patterns of economic growth and water needs. Legal principles, in any event, can only be of limited help because intrastate conflicts, like intercountry disputes, are largely political in nature, with popular passions at play, even when they are driven by deep-rooted socioeconomic factors.

If internal water disputes cannot be resolved, they must be managed in such a way that social harmony, environmental sustainability, and national unity are not upset. One of the primary duties of any government is to provide basic services to its citizens, including water supply—a duty not adequately discharged by many governments in Asia. Local development projects that help bring safe drinking water to villages and towns while cutting water wastage by farms and industries double as valuable conflict prevention tools. To help sustainably manage and utilize water resources, a long-term holistic approach is indispensable. Such an integrated approach demands participatory management involving users, planners, and policymakers at all levels. Decisions made at different levels, with full public consultation and the involvement of stakeholders in the planning and implementation of water projects, not only help to avert conflict but also inculcate norms of water conservation and efficiency.

Six

Mitigating Intercountry Water Disputes or Discord

A freshwater-scarcity crisis is emerging as a defining pivot of Asian politics and security, with the set of likely consequences extending to internal and external security, economic growth, social progress, environmental sustainability, food security, public health, poverty alleviation, migration flows, and inter-riparian relations. National dependency on waters from transnational rivers or aquifers is widespread in Asia. That fact, coupled with the fast-growing water consumption and demand in Asia owing to economic and population growth, rapid urbanization, and changing lifestyles, is making interstate water competition a major security issue, increasing the likelihood of geopolitical tensions and instabilities. Add to the picture two other elements: The unmatched riparian ascendancy of China in Asia through its control of the headwaters of major rivers, and the likely impact of global warming on basin resources.

Reining in the sharpening hydropolitics tests Asia's capacity to deal with challenges and demands innovative and collaborative approaches to supply constraints and to climate change adaptation and mitigation. More than half the world's potable water supply comes from rivers, whose discharge is sensitive to long-term changes in precipitation and temperature, particularly in the snowmelt-dominated sources of origin. With Asia on the frontline of climate change, such shifts in temperature and mountain snowmelt are likely to seriously affect the hydrological stability of the majority of its river systems and other freshwater sources. The volume and timing of river flows could change significantly.

According to the grim projections of the Intergovernmental Panel on Climate Change, crop yields in Asia will decline between 2.5 and 10 percent by the 2020s and more than 1 billion people will face increased water stress in Central Asia, South Asia, East Asia, and Southeast Asia by the 2050s.[1] Furthermore, changes in the runoff volumes of river basins due to the retreat of glaciers and permafrost in

Asia could significantly effect the power output of hydropower-dependent countries, such as Tajikistan, while decreases in annual net usable water resources are
expected to haunt several areas, stretching from the Tigris-Euphrates River basin
and Lebanon to Central Asia and northern China.[2] A sharp drop in dry-season
river flows but increases in wet-season flows would create an annual cycle of scarcity and flooding. In the Great Himalayan Watershed, the cascading effects are
likely to extend to fundamental shifts in ecosystems, including fluvial and forest
systems, and lead to the extinction of a number of endemic species and other biodiversity loss.[3]

The potential for interstate water wars in Asia is underlined by the existence of
as many as fifty-seven transnational river basins there. In fact, a number of Asian
countries are significantly dependent on the inflow of river and aquifer waters
from across their national borders. Azerbaijan, Bahrain, Bangladesh, Cambodia,
India, Kazakhstan, Kuwait, Laos, Pakistan, Syria, Thailand, Turkmenistan,
Uzbekistan, and Vietnam receive 30 to 100 percent of their waters from outside
the country. Kuwait, Turkmenistan, and Bahrain have the highest water resources
dependency ratio.

Kuwait, with no perennial stream or lake but with two modest underground
fields reserved as a strategic freshwater reservoir for drinking-water purposes only,
gets barely 20 million cubic meters (m^3) of groundwater inflow from Saudi Arabia
annually and therefore relies on high-cost unconventional sources, including desalinated water and treated wastewater. Yet Kuwait's per capita water consumption is
relatively high, and more than half of all water withdrawals are for irrigated farming and gardening in that intensely arid country.[4] Turkmenistan is another interesting case: Its own internal renewable water resources amount to barely 270 m^3 per
inhabitant annually. But that figure rises sharply to 4,901 m^3 per year with transboundary inflows, brought mainly by the 1,375-kilometer, Soviet-era Kara-Kum
Canal, billed as the world's longest irrigation canal.[5]

As table 6.1 shows, the most populous states of southern and southeastern Asia
are considerably dependent on transboundary flows, with Bangladesh's dependency
ratio being 91.3 percent, Pakistan's 75.6 percent, and Vietnam's 58.9 percent. India,
although the main water supplier to Pakistan and Bangladesh, has a 33.4 percent
dependency on waters originating from across its northern frontiers, principally
Tibet. A United Nations report on the Asia-Pacific region has pointed out that in
situations where there is "water stress, coupled with high dependence on water
originating outside the country, water-security issues are becoming more important
and may prove to be a source of tension."[6]

At the other end of the Asian spectrum is China, with its upstream control of
major transnational basin resources. China receives minor water flows from Mongolia, Kyrgyzstan, Kazakhstan, India, and Vietnam, with the Food and Agriculture Organization of the United Nations defining its dependency ratio at a mere
0.9 percent—one of the lowest in the world. With its territorial size at a historical
zenith, China today likes to pride itself as a major "exporter" of water to many

TABLE 6.1   Countries in Continental Asia with a High Water-Resources Dependency Ratio

Country	Internal Renewable Water Resources (km³/year)	Actual Renewable Water Resources (km³/year)	Dependency Ratio (%)[a]	Main Source of Incoming Water
Kuwait	0	0.02	100.0	Groundwater (mostly brackish) from Saudi Arabia
Turkmenistan	1.36	24.72	97.1	Amu Darya, Murghab, and Tedzhen rivers
Bahrain	0.004	0.116	96.6	Groundwater from Saudi Arabia
Bangladesh	105.0	1,211	91.3	Brahmaputra, Ganges, and rivers from India's northeast
Uzbekistan	16.34	50.41	77.4	Syr Darya and Amu Darya rivers
Azerbaijan	8.115	34.68	76.6	Araks, Agstay, and Samur rivers
Pakistan	55.0	225.3	75.6	Indus River
Cambodia	120.6	476.1	74.7	Mekong River
Syria	7.132	16.8	72.4	Euphrates and Tigris rivers
Vietnam	366.5	891.2	58.9	Mekong, Red, Ca, Ma, and Dong Nai rivers
Thailand	224.5	424.4	47.1	Mekong and Thanlwin (Salween) rivers
Laos	190.4	333.5	42.9	Mekong River
India	1,260	1,880	33.4	Brahmaputra, Sutlej, Indus, and other rivers
Kazakhstan	75.42	109.6	31.2	Syr Darya, Irtysh, Illy, and Chu rivers

[a] The dependency ratio is equal to the part of the renewable water resources which originates outside the country.
Source: Food and Agriculture Organization of the United Nations, Aquastat online data, 2011.

neighbors—from Russia and Mongolia in the north and Kazakhstan and Kyrgyzstan in the west, to Burma and Laos in the southeast, and India and Nepal in the southwest.

China actually is placed uniquely. It is the source of water flows, among others, to India (estimated to total 347.02 cubic kilometers, km^3, per year), Burma (100.03 km^3 per year), Laos (73.63 km^3 per year, a figure that includes some supply to Burma), Vietnam (44.1 km^3 per year), Kazakhstan (22.47 km^3 per year), Nepal (12 km^3 per year), and Kyrgyzstan (0.558 km^3 per year).[7] A small quantity of water also flows to Mongolia from China through three streams—Herlen, Wursun, and Kara Ertix. Then there is the Amur, which, along with its upstream tributaries, the Argun (Ergun He) and the Ussuri (Wusuli), is a border river almost from its origin and divides Manchuria into Russian- and Chinese-held parts until it flows into Russia, giving China the right to call itself an important "exporter" of water to Russia too. Through the Amur and, to a minor degree, the Suifen River, China supplies Russia 119.05 km^3 of water per year.

China's internal renewable water resources total 2,813 km^3 per year, or 54.5 percent higher than India's, although the former's population is less than 12 percent larger than the latter's.[8] So it is of little surprise that its per capita water availability is much higher than India's. But as a Chinese official has pointed out, China has one-fifth of the global population with less than 7 percent of the freshwater and 9 percent of the arable land in the world,[9] although China's total water resources may rank as the world's fifth largest. The reality is that much of China's water resources are concentrated on the Tibetan Plateau and its adjoining areas—far from the boomtowns on the east coast. That has created water shortages where many Chinese live, especially in the northern plains. There is, in fact, a major regional disparity in water availability even within Han China: Northern China has barely one-fifth of the per capita water resources of parts of southern China.[10]

The region along the Huai, Yellow, and Hai-Luan river basins in northern China has 35 percent of the country's population but only 7 percent of the country's water resources. Yet, with the introduction of Western-style agriculture under Communist rule, this semiarid region now accounts for 67 percent of China's wheat production, 44 percent of its corn, and 72 percent of its millet. "Many rivers in the three-basin area are dry for five to eight months of the year," according to a World Bank report.[11] China's northern plains receive rain mostly in the summer during the monsoon season, with the rainfall often being sufficient, except in the hyperarid areas, to sustain cultivation of summer crops like corn and cotton. Winter crops, however, are almost entirely dependent on irrigation. Yet, with the annual variations in precipitation being higher in the north and northeast than in China's south and southeast, supplemental irrigation for crops in the north is required very often even in the summer months.[12]

Despite its impressive overall water resources, China before long is likely to reach the figure that the Food and Agriculture Organization views as an indicator of water scarcity: less than 2,000 m^3 of water per inhabitant per year.[13] The water situation, of course, is more acute in India, whose own water resources are just 1,334 m³ per inhabitant per year but are supplemented with one-third of the total water supply coming in from across its borders, mainly from Tibet. South Korea, at 1,447 m³ per inhabitant per year, confronts water shortages greater than India's, whereas the Maldives—surrounded by oceans but with just 98.4 m³ per inhabitant per year of freshwater availability—is already in the throes of a serious scarcity crisis, which is getting further exacerbated by a fast-growing population and changing lifestyles.[14]

More broadly, given the wide extent of shared transnational basin resources in Asia and the festering territorial and resource disputes, there is considerable potential for aggravated competition and conflict on the continent. There are, of course, a small number of Asian countries, especially island states, that do not share water resources with another nation. But internationally shared basins cover wide stretches of Asia. Withdrawals in an upstream country through new dams, reservoirs, irrigation systems, and other hydro facilities materially affect the volume of water available to a downstream nation. Changing patterns of water withdrawals indeed are making it more difficult to draw an accurate distinction between natural and actual river flows. Map 6.1 details the complex matrix of transboundary water flows in South and Southeast Asia, for example.

Yet, despite such dependency on cross-border flows, intercountry water resources increasingly are being seen from the national security prism by policymakers in Asia. Indeed, with water becoming a prized resource, a number of Asian nations already are jockeying to control upstream basin resources, prompting lower-riparian states to demand a say in the building of large water projects on international rivers. Competition over water resources is becoming a source of political tensions, heightening the risks of inter-riparian conflicts in the years ahead. Those risks are most apparent when, as this chapter does, the water disputes of China, Israel, and India with their multiple neighbors are examined. The analysis reveals that water has emerged as a key issue capable of shaping the direction of tomorrow's Asia—an Asia on the path of building mutual security and prosperity through harmonious, ruled-based cooperation, or an Asia driven by fierce resource competition and self-injurious power politics. Probably no country is likely to influence that direction more than China because of its unique status.

The Link between Territorial and Resource Issues

An important element in Asia's geopolitical landscape is the transnational nature of water resources in disputed or occupied territories, or in regions hit by separatist unrest, such as Tibet, Kashmir, Xinjiang, Kyrgyzstan's southern Fergana Valley, Israeli-held Palestinian areas, and Turkey's Kurdish-dominated southeastern region. Take the case of Xinjiang, which China annexed in 1949, preempting a push for independence by the Uighurs, the region's native Turkic Muslim people.

MAP 6.1   Transboundary Water Flows in Southern and Southeastern Asia (km³ per year)

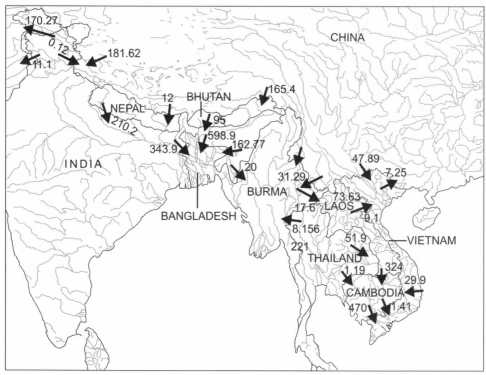

Source: FAO, Aquastat online database.

Xinjiang—an expansive land of towering, snow-capped peaks and arid deserts—is the gateway between Central Asia and Han China. It straddles the Silk Road, and was the historical route for traders like Marco Polo and for Mongol, Turk, and other invaders. For centuries, Chinese rulers had sought to control Xinjiang, but it was only in 1760 when China itself was ruled by ethnic Manchus—the Qing Dynasty—that this large western region came under the full political jurisdiction of authorities in Beijing.[15] It was the Manchus who gave the territory—which had been known as Yarkan, Qarluq, or Uighuristan for some thousand years—the name Sinkiang (Xinjiang in Chinese), or New Frontier, a place at the margins of their vast empire. But the region began to slip out of Manchu control even before the Qing Dynasty unraveled in the early twentieth century. After having been a major geopolitical battleground between Tsarist Russia and Manchu-ruled China in the nineteenth century, Xinjiang came under Soviet sway in the 1930s. In 1944, while World War II was raging, Muslim groups aided by the Soviet dictator Joseph Stalin established the East Turkestan Republic in Xinjiang.

Today, this strategic, hydrocarbon-rich minority homeland alone makes up one-sixth of the land of the People's Republic of China. The expansion of Han Chinese rule to this region—as to Manchuria and Inner Mongolia—has been largely fortified through state-sponsored migration. Millions of Han Chinese have moved to Xinjiang during the past six decades, and they have turned the region into a major flashpoint between Han settlers and Uighur and other ethnic minority communities. The bloody recrudescence of Uighur separatist unrest in 2009 highlighted a continuing challenge to Chinese rule over a region whose cultural and religious capital is Kashgar, a city of 3.5 million that is closer to Baghdad than to Beijing.

Xinjiang has decent water resources in its rivers, aquifers, lakes, and glaciers. The Illy and Irtysh rivers flow from northern Xinjiang into Kazakhstan, where the Illy empties into Lake Balkhash. Southern Xinjiang, for its part, is home to China's longest inland river, the Tarim, two of whose tributaries originate in the adjacent Chinese-held part of the disputed state of Jammu and Kashmir. But Xinjiang's profound demographic and land transformation through the large influx of Han settlers and the spread of irrigated farming to arid areas has been having an adverse impact on the quality and distribution of its water resources. Large areas of the Xinjiang Desert, as well as a number of pasturelands and wetlands, have been turned into cropland by the Han settlers under incentives-based state plans.[16] As a study by Chinese scholars has revealed, water flows in the Tarim have significantly decreased in the past three decades because of "population growth and cultivated land expansion in the upper and middle reaches of the river," resulting in water pollution and scarcity, soil salinity, loss of vegetation, desertification, and sandstorms.[17]

One tributary of the Tarim flows in from the Kashmir region seized by China from India (the Aksai Chin Plateau, which is almost the size of Switzerland) and another from the slice ceded to China by Pakistan from the Kashmir territory it holds (map 6.2). The Aksai Chin, which was an integral part of the princely state of Jammu and Kashmir before Xinjiang became a province of China in 1881 under the Qing Dynasty, provides the only accessible Tibet–Xinjiang route through the Karakoram passes of the Kunlun Mountains.

India refuses to recognize China's control over Aksai Chin. Beijing, for its part, declines to have any discussion with New Delhi on the trans-Karakoram tract (comprising mainly the Shaksgam Valley) that Pakistan ceded to China under the 1963 Sino-Pakistani Frontier Agreement.[18] India also does not recognize that territorial ceding by Pakistan to China. That transfer of territory, in fact, was a unique case in modern history of one nation gifting another with a sizable tract of land of which it had gained control earlier in a war with a third country (India).

Kashmir, where the borders of India, Xinjiang, Tibet, Pakistan, and Afghanistan converge, is just one example of how territorial disputes in Asia are often linked to resource issues, especially hydrocarbons and water. Just like the disputed islands in the South and East China seas, Kashmir is as much a resource issue as a territorial issue. In the Great Himalayan Range, watershed boundaries do not

MAP 6.2   Rivers of Southern Xinjiang and Its Neighborhood

always correspond to political frontiers. Kashmir serves as a critical waterway for Pakistan, whose external dependency ratio is high. A good deal of the waters of the Indus River system that flow from India to the Pakistani plains passes through Kashmir—both Indian-controlled Kashmir and the Pakistani-held Kashmir. Actually, a couple of rivers reenter India before returning to Pakistani territory. China holds about 20 percent of the original princely state of Jammu and Kashmir, Pakistan 35 percent, and India the remaining 45 percent. So it is of little surprise that Kashmir ranks as one of the world's largest and most militarized zones of contention.

In the water-rich, northernmost Gilgit-Baltistan Region of Pakistan-held Kashmir, Chinese state-run companies—bolstered by the entry of construction, engineering, and communication units of the People's Liberation Army into the restive area to work on various strategic projects—are building giant dams. The presence of Chinese troops in the Pakistani part of Kashmir, even if in the form of construction battalions, means that there are Chinese troops on both flanks (east and west) of Indian Kashmir. The broader Sino-Pakistan strategic nexus, extending beyond the increasing Chinese footprint in Pakistani Kashmir, presents India with a potential two-front theater in the event of a war with either country.[19]

Take yet another case: The patterns of transboundary water flows between Israel and its neighbors, especially Jordan, Syria, and the Palestinian territories, constitute a complex case involving both Israeli military conquest of water-rich lands and a subsequent water arrangement built into an Israeli–Jordanian peace treaty. For decades, water has been a cardinal concern in the subregion—an issue intrinsically tied to peace and security—largely because of a perennial struggle for that resource arising from a very low per capita availability of freshwater. The statistics highlight the prevalent water-scarcity conditions: Jordan's per capita freshwater availability averages just 152.7 m³ per year; Palestinians', 201.8 m³ per year; Israel's, 252.4 m³ per year; and Syria's, 791.4 m³ per year.[20] These figures, far below the international water poverty line, signify acute water distress.

Changes in political frontiers wrought by war have fundamentally altered the dependency ratios of various regional actors with regard to cross-border water flows. Israel proper relies on significant transboundary flows, but a large part of this water supply is derived from the territories it captured during the decisive Six-Day War in 1967—from Syria, it took the Golan Heights (the headwaters of the Jordan River); and from Jordan, it took the West Bank (the source of considerable groundwater resources). In that war, it also captured the tiny Gaza Strip, East Jerusalem, and the Sinai Peninsula (which it later returned to Egypt as part of a peace settlement signed in 1979).

Israel in 1981 formally annexed the strategic Golan Heights, which controls its major water sources, including those that feed its main freshwater lake, Tiberias (also known as Lake Kinneret, or the Sea of Galilee). The West Bank, by contrast, has modest surface water but substantial groundwater in the form of a multiaquifer system, with the groundwater outflow to Israel estimated at a sizable 325 million m³ a year and surface-water outflow at 20 million m³ annually.[21] Israel, in turn, is the source of 25 million m³ a year of water outflow to the Gaza Strip, where the overexploitation of the local resources of the Coastal Aquifer basin already has resulted in seawater intrusion in some areas.

Significantly, groundwater is a larger source of supply than surface water in this subregion. In the Israeli and Palestinian lands, there are several aquifers, but two main aquifer basins: The Mountain Aquifer, made up of three major subaquifers, is a limestone aquifer, whereas the Coastal Aquifer, running 120 kilometers along the Mediterranean coastline, is a sandstone system. Jordan, with one of the world's lowest per capita water availability figures, has been overexploiting its groundwater resources to the extent that water quality has distinctly eroded and the country has started to tap deep, virtually nonrenewable aquifers where water has accumulated over the course of many thousands of years. The most prominent such "fossil" aquifer is al-Disi, much of whose water collection lies underneath the Saudi Arabian sands but with a portion of its base extending under southern Jordan. By getting into a "quiet pumping race" with its fellow Arab neighbor, Jordan has raised concerns about a groundwater conflict with a riverless but more powerful

Saudi Arabia, whose per capita water availability is at least 60 percent lower than Jordan's.[22]

One of the developments leading to the 1967 Six-Day War, in fact, was Israel's completion of its so-called National Water Carrier, a major water-transfer network linking most of its water projects and taking surface water from the northern Lake Tiberias—now the source of one-third of its freshwater supply—to the deep south, including groundwater admixed en route. The carrier—Israel's lifeline ever since—has helped promote rapid economic progress, including a boom in agriculture that has made Israel an important exporter of farm produce.[23]

However, the 1964 completion of the carrier, which draws off Jordan River waters, set in motion a cycle of tit-for-tat actions between Israel and its Arab neighbors that culminated in the war that reshaped the region's water map. For example, a rival Arab plan to divert the river's resources from its headwaters to Syria and Jordan triggered several Israeli military strikes on the project's construction sites in Syria in the two-and-a-half years leading up to the full-fledged war. Israel's decision in the 1950s to build the National Water Carrier actually was prompted by Jordan's plan to divert part of the Yarmouk River via the East Ghor Canal to irrigate the Jordan Valley's East Ghor area. The Yarmouk, a Jordan River tributary, has the second-largest annual discharge of any river in the subregion, but much of its water now is siphoned off by Israel, Jordan, and Syria before it reaches the Jordan River. In 1969, Israel militarily attacked the East Ghor Canal (subsequently renamed the King Abdullah Canal) after accusing Jordan of stealing excess amounts of water (map 6.3). And in 1978 Israel temporarily seized the Wassani Springs, which feed the Jordan River, by invading Lebanon; a repeat invasion in 1982 lasting much longer brought Lebanon's southern waters under Israeli control.

National appropriations from the Jordan River basin now do not bear much resemblance to the sharing quotas of the nonratified US-initiated Johnston Plan, which had in 1955 recommended that 56 percent of the surface waters go to Jordan (including 17 percent specifically set aside for the West Bank), 31 percent to Israel, 10 percent to Syria, and 3 percent to Lebanon.[24] With the inflow of diaspora Jews swelling its population and water needs, Israel today has the single largest share of basin waters. The Palestinians in the West Bank are no longer permitted to take water from the Jordan River system, after Israel in the post-1967 period destroyed or seized the Palestinian irrigation pumps that drew on those waters and then turned the river stretch in the West Bank into an off-limits zone—one of the factors that has contributed to the Palestinians' overweening sense of victimization. As a result, the West Bank Palestinians source water from wells or springs.

In more-recent times, however, the subregional water situation has become less volatile, partly because the 1994 Israeli–Jordanian peace treaty incorporated a water arrangement in its Annex II, titled "Water and Related Matters."[25] The arrangement allows Jordan to store wintertime water in Tiberias, the Israeli lake, for its summer use, and permits Israel in return to lease some Jordanian land and wells. The accord also allowed Jordan to build one dam each on the Yarmouk and Jordan

MAP 6.3   Water Resources in Israel and Its Neighborhood

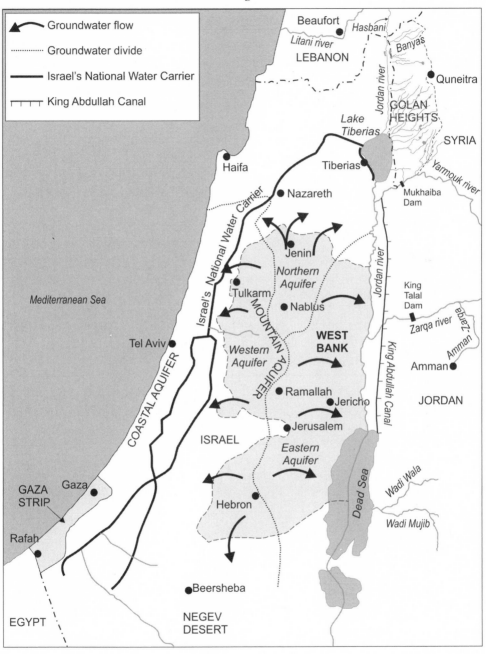

rivers, and it committed Israel to supplying Jordan with a fixed quantity of desalinated water from its saline springs.

The 1995 Israeli–Palestinian Interim Agreement on the West Bank and the Gaza Strip—popularly known as "Oslo II"—deferred the contentious issue of water rights for settlement in the future as part of the "final status" negotiations on tough issues such as Jerusalem, Israeli settlements, refugees, security arrangements, and borders.[26] Yet Israel agreed that the Palestinians, on an interim basis, should have access to 70 to 80 million m³ of water supply per year. In addition, a Joint Water Committee was set up to manage the West Bank water resources and to investigate Palestinian water withdrawals in breach of the Israeli-imposed quotas on the number of irrigation wells in operation and the amount of water pumped from them. Even as illicit water withdrawals still continue, Israel in the post-1995 period has allowed more wells to be drilled on the West Bank, thereby boosting the Palestinians' per capita water availability.

More fundamentally, Israel has consolidated its regional power, with the outcome of past wars precluding any real challenger. Its peace agreements with Jordan and Egypt have helped reinforce the message to others in the region that it is too powerful to be taken on militarily, thus leaving only political options for interstate dispute settlement.

Still, the harsh reality is that competition over subregional water resources has become more intense in the face of growing populations and soaring economic and municipal needs, with the overpumping of groundwater leading to salinization and other problems, especially in Gaza, Jordan, and, to a lesser extent, the West Bank. The failure to develop multilateral water-sharing cooperation to sustainably manage regional resources has encouraged unilateral upstream projects, including by Syria on the Yarmouk and Israel in the Golan Heights, raising risks of a reemergence of interstate conflict over water.[27] The bilateral water arrangement between Israel and Jordan, the interim accord between Israel and the Palestinian Authority, and the revised 1987 Syrian–Jordanian agreement on the Yarmouk waters are no substitute for institutionalized cooperation among all riparian states. The bilateral arrangements, in any event, have repeatedly been violated, spurring charges and countercharges.

CHINA'S CENTRALITY

China, significantly, is involved in water disputes with most of its riparian neighbors. It does not have a single water-sharing treaty or agreement with any co-riparian, despite its unique status as the world's supplier of river waters to the largest number of countries. Yet, just as it is proud of becoming the world's No. 1 exporter, biggest foreign-exchange holder, leading steel producer, and largest market for passenger vehicles, China also prides itself on its unsurpassed engineering record on water diversions, flaunting its megadams as engineering trophies. It has more dams in operation than the rest of the world combined; it boasts the largest dam on the planet and plans to construct even a bigger one; it is pursuing the most ambitious interbasin and interriver water transfer plans ever conceived by any nation; and it remains the world's No. 1 dam builder, at home and abroad. Prowess in water diversions has become an extension of its military and economic power.

Although shying away from entering into formal arrangements with its neighbors over the waters of common rivers, China has aggressively sought and signed lucrative contracts with countries both near and far to build dams and hydropower stations on their rivers. There are more than a hundred major ongoing dam-building projects involving Chinese state-run companies, the Chinese Export-Import Bank, and other Chinese financial institutions in several dozen countries across the developing world. Having emerged as the world's leading dam exporter, China also is building dams in co-riparian states like Cambodia, Burma, Kazakhstan, Laos, Mongolia, and Nepal, with the projects in Laos and Burma actually designed to supply hydropower to the Chinese home market.

At the same time, China is embroiled in water wrangles with at least nine of its neighbors. Its negative response to the idea of entering into water-sharing treaties with its riparian neighbors implies a refusal to compromise. That China is the central player in the Asian water scene also has been underlined by its own hectic dam-building activities, which are often at the root of its disputes with co-riparian states. Such activities have actually picked up tempo, although it already has at least half of all dams in the world higher than 15 meters.[28] On the Yangtze River alone, thirty-eight new Chinese dams were under construction in 2011. Worse still, China has stepped up its building of new dams on international rivers flowing from its territory to the Indochina Peninsula, the Indian subcontinent, Kazakhstan, and Russia. It has sought, on a large scale, to impound or divert waters of some of the transnational rivers.

In addition to its conflict with the four lower Mekong River basin states over its building of a cascade of upstream dams and its refusal to join the Mekong River Commission, China is involved in water disputes with Russia, India, Burma, Kazakhstan, and North Korea. The water controversy with North Korea, a client state, centers on Chonji, the crater lake on Mount Paektu, where the 33-kilometer boundary between the two countries has not been settled. Certain islands in the Yalu and the Tumen—both border rivers—are also in dispute with North Korea.

The Yalu and the Tumen (the larger of the two in total volume of water) both originate in the mountain ranges of North Korea before forming the border with China. But because they are international rivers, half their total average discharge of 20.3 km[3] per year is regarded as part of China's water resources.[29] Despite Beijing's present interest in keeping the Korean Peninsula divided, the Chinese Foreign Ministry has sought to hedge China's options vis-à-vis a potentially unified Korea by posting on its website in 2004 a revised historical claim that the ancient kingdom of Koguryo, founded in the Tongge River basin of northern Korea, was

Chinese and not Korean, as it had been considered by the Koreans and outside historians. In making this claim about a kingdom that spanned the current China–North Korea border in the period before and after Christ, Beijing seemed to signal that the present China–North Korea border may not be final for it, raising the specter of future tensions over the demarcation of frontiers.[30]

With Kazakhstan, despite establishing a Joint Committee on Transboundary Rivers as part of a 2002 accord, China still needs to resolve a raging dispute over its upstream diversion of the waters of the Irtysh and Illy rivers. China's damming of the Shweli River on its side of the border and its plans to construct thirteen new dams on the major Salween River have roiled energy-starved Burma, which sees the upstream projects as a threat to the integrity of some of its own smaller hydropower plants built in recent years or still under construction; several of these projects were funded by the Chinese Export-Import Bank and subcontracted to Chinese state-run firms such as China Southern Power Grid and Yunnan Joint Power Development Company. In its relations with India, China confronts the aggravating issue of water, given the massive hydroengineering projects that it now is undertaking in Tibet.

Intensifying Water Disputes on the Amur, Illy, and Irtysh Rivers

China's increasing exploitation of the resources of the Irtysh and Illy rivers has turned water into a major bone of contention with downstream Kazakhstan. Even in Russia, China has become a source of water-related concerns. The China–Russia lingering water disputes center on the transboundary Amur River (known as Heilong Jiang in Chinese) but extend to Chinese projects on the Irtysh, the main tributary of the Ob River, which traverses the Omsk Region in southwestern Siberia.

The Amur—with a 2 million-square-kilometer basin almost equally divided between Russia and China—actually rises in Mongolia. Formed by the merger of the Argun and Shilka rivers, the Amur, by some measures, is the world's sixth-longest river—longer than the Mekong or the Congo. China, in second half of the long reign of strongman Mao Zedong, saw the Soviet Union as a great adversary, and the Amur basin was the scene of bloody border clashes in March 1969 following a Chinese-initiated military ambush. According to a Pentagon report, the 1969 border conflict—which Beijing described as a "self-defense counterattack"—was an example, as in 1950 (intervention in the Korean War), 1962 (the invasion of India), and 1979 (the attack on Vietnam), of how "China's leaders have claimed military preemption as a strategically defensive act."[31]

Now China calls the Russian Federation a "strategic partner." But the two-decade-old honeymoon between China and Russia, despite a settlement of their border disagreements, may be ending, "with both countries reverting to their traditional suspicion and competition."[32] Although the two powers have demarcated the once-disputed islands at the Amur and Ussuri confluence and in the Argun River in accordance with a 2004 agreement, thereby ending disputes dating back some centuries, the waters of the Amur basin remain in contention.[33] China has been eyeing the Amur resources as a means to ease its grave water crisis in the north (map 6.4).

Chinese investments have spurred an economic boom on both sides of the Sino-Russian border region along the Amur. But on the Chinese side of the basin, rapid

MAP 6.4   The Amur River

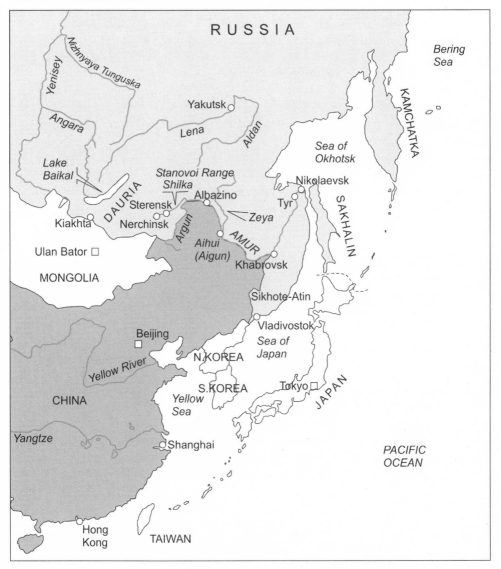

demographic and economic expansion, along with new agricultural development, have created local water shortages. The transboundary implications of the increasing Chinese water withdrawals from the river are manifest in the diminishing flows in the Amur basin, home to most of the world's Oriental white storks and Amur leopards, which are listed as critically endangered. Environmentalists are concerned that the Amur waters are being channeled for farming at the expense of wildlife habitats. China is not only further expanding agriculture in this basin, especially the cultivation of water-intensive grains, but is also toying with the idea of taking Amur waters southward to its parched-northern areas. In fact, rival Chinese and Russian plans have emerged to dam the Amur tributaries.

The fast-rising Chinese water withdrawals are by themselves making water an issue in the uneasy Sino-Russian relationship, underscoring the need for a formal water-sharing arrangement between the two giants. In addition, Chinese immigration to the Russian basin region is stoking visceral historical Russian fears of a Han demographic invasion of the Russian Far East, besides highlighting a potential threat to Russia's natural resources. Russia's thinly populated Far East, a region twice the size of Europe, is rich in natural gas, oil, iron, coal, timber, diamonds, and gold.

Despite the decades-old legacy of bilateral distrust along the Amur, resource-starved China has been signing up deals to buy Siberian metals, coal, oil, and timber. For China, such overland supplies of Russian resources are a much-desired diversification away from seaborne shipments, which it fears could be interdicted by the US Navy at the Malacca Straits chokepoint in a military conflict. The new trans-Siberian pipeline is carrying 300,000 barrels of oil a day to China, with a second pipeline to supply gas. Chinese companies also have leased more than 350,000 hectares of farmland in Russia's Amur basin left fallow by the declining population of ethnic Russians; they are employing Chinese migrants to grow soybeans and other crops for export to China.[34] For Russia, the benefits of such investment and trade have, at least for now, outweighed lurking concerns that it could spur a greater inflow of Han Chinese into Siberia's vast, unoccupied lands. Yet these lands seem set to come under increasing Chinese economic domination while technically remaining under Russian rule.

In the Irtysh and Illy basins, Chinese water diversions have increasingly become the subject of concern for Russia and Kazakhstan. China has pursued a series of canals, dams, and hydropower stations on the Irtysh and Illy rivers as part of its western development program. For example, it completed work in 2001 on a canal diverting waters from the Black Irtysh River for irrigation, despite transboundary concerns that such a diversion would affect ecosystems in Kazakhstan and Russia. Since then, it has embarked on several additional engineering projects as part of an ambitious resource development program that, as pointed out by a study, violates customary international law and threatens "both water levels in the Irtysh-Ob basin and the millions of people and dozens of ecosystems that line the Irtysh's 5,000-plus kilometer length."[35]

The canal, which links the Black Irtysh with the Karamai River in Chinese territory, came up quietly, even as Beijing was ritually denying in officials talks with Kazakhstan and Russia that it had any plans to dam or divert waters from the Irtysh basin.[36] The diversion of waters has diminished Irtysh flows and affected crop production in northeastern Kazakhstan and Russia's wheat-growing Omsk region. The Black Irtysh, after originating in the Mongolia–China borderland, flows for almost 700 kilometers through Chinese territory before crossing into Kazakhstan and emptying into the large Lake Zaisan. From the other side of Lake Zaisan, the river becomes the Irtysh proper; it "forms Kazakhstan's industrial heartland, crosses into Russia, joins the Ob River, and finally empties into the Arctic Ocean. The Irtysh flows from the most populous state in the world, through one of the least densely populated, into the largest state" in the world in land size; it ranks as the only river to flow through three of the planet's ten biggest countries (map 6.5).[37]

Ever since China launched its western development strategy, it has sought to dam the multiple rivers that flow from Xinjiang to Kazakhstan. By working to boost local water availability through such diversion, it has aimed both to meet the irrigation needs of Han farmers in Xinjiang and to raise local living standards

MAP 6.5   The Irtysh River Basin

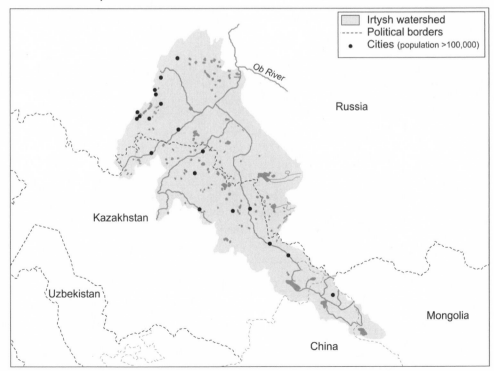

through economic development so as to help weaken the Uighur separatist movement.[38] The 2009 Uighur uprising, in spite of such government efforts, thus came as a rude shock to the Chinese leadership. The pursuit of projects on transboundary rivers with little transparency has also begun to sour Beijing's friendship with Kazakhstan, which has protested Chinese damming activities on the Irtysh and the Illy.

China has started harnessing the Illy for hydropower generation and irrigation. But the Chinese construction of dams and reservoirs is affecting transboundary flows and water quality, with upstream mining and manufacturing in Xinjiang aggravating water pollution. The water level is falling in Kazakhstan's Lake Balkhash, into which the Illy empties. With the Aral Sea shrinking to less than half its original size, Balkhash is now the largest lake in Central Asia. But Kazakh officials are warning that the Chinese diversion of Illy's waters could turn Balkhash into another Aral.

Indeed, Russian and Kazakh officials have joined hands to accuse Beijing of endlessly dragging out the separate bilateral talks with them over the resources of transboundary rivers so that China can quietly complete work on more water projects in the Irtysh-Illy basins. The Russians, for their part, have loudly complained that although an international dispute has arisen over the Chinese diversion of the Irtysh waters, Beijing remains unwilling to discuss the extensive hydro infrastructure it continues to build.[39]

China, in addition, has sought to divert the waters of an Amur tributary, the Songhua (also known as the Sungari), besides planning to tap the waters of the Yalu River, the border river with North Korea.[40] The Songhua has faced repeated contamination problems in China: Carcinogenic chemicals, including benzene, spilled into the Songhua in 2005, forcing the northeastern city of Harbin to sever water supplies to 3.8 million people for five days; and then in mid-2010, some 3,000 containers of toxic chemicals were washed into the river by floods, leading to a one-day suspension of water supply to the larger city of Jilin.

The Salween: A Reprieve for the "Angry River" Does Not Last Long

In Southeast Asia, regional concerns have focused on China's megaprojects on the upper reaches of the two big rivers, the Mekong and the Salween. While building a cascade of giant dams on the upper Mekong, China unveiled plans to construct another series of megadams upstream on the Salween, known as Gyalmo Ngulchu in Tibetan, Thanlwin in Burmese, and Nu Jiang ("the Angry River") in Chinese. It has already dammed the Shweli—a tributary of the Irrawaddy River—on its side of the border with Burma. China has completed half the eighty-eight new water projects it undertook, many of them small or medium-sized hydropower plants, on the Salween and its tributaries in Yunnan Province's Nujiang Lisu Autonomous Prefecture.[41]

What has added to the concerns over such frenetic dam building is that the Salween, the Mekong, and the Jinsha (a Yangtze tributary) run roughly parallel, north to south, through a stunning canyon region designated as the Three Parallel Rivers World Heritage Area, located on the southeastern rim of the Tibetan Plateau in Yunnan Province. The area's special topographical features—ranging from deep gorges and glaciated peaks to karst (a limestone landscape characterized by caves, fissures, and underground streams)—indicate its location at the point where the Indian Plate collided with the Eurasian Plate, a geological event millions of years ago that is believed to have resulted in the uplifting of the Himalayan Range and the Plateau of Tibet. One glacier, renamed "Mingyongqia" by China, drops spectacularly but precipitously from 6,740 meters to 2,700 meters, making it the lowest-altitude glacier in its latitude category in the Northern Hemisphere.

The convergence of temperate and tropical zones in the Three Parallel Rivers area, along with a landscape diversity characterized by a steep gradient of nearly 6,000 meters vertical, parallels the biogeographical richness of another region on the Tibetan Plateau—the Brahmaputra River's Great Bend. The Three Parallel Rivers area—inhabited by sixteen different ethnic groups and rated as one of the world's most biologically diverse temperate regions that is home to more than five thousand plant species and nearly half of China's animal species, including endangered ones like snow leopards and snub-nosed monkeys—was added to the World Heritage List by UNESCO in 2003.

But no sooner had that decision been made than China announced plans to build thirteen giant dams on the Salween in Yunnan, nine of them in its National Nature Reserves, adjacent to the world heritage area. That led the UNESCO World Heritage Committee in 2004 to express "its gravest concerns on the impacts that the proposed construction of dams could have on the outstanding universal value of this World Heritage" site and to urge China "to seek alternatives to hydropower" and let the Salween "continue to flow naturally through and beside the World Heritage area."[42] The committee, through another decision in the subsequent year, warned that damming activity within the World Heritage area "would provide a case for inclusion of the property [area] in the List of World Heritage in Danger."[43] The warning, through further resolutions in 2006 and 2007, was extended to cover "all illegal mining activities within" the heritage area, with a call for an end to such practices, which the committee said "threaten the integrity and values" of the site.[44]

China has dammed the Salween in Tibet—where it originates on the outer Himalayan rim—as exemplified by the 34-meter-high dam at Chalong in Nagchu Prefecture. But its Yunnan plans to build multiple giant dams on the river—which flows through deep gorges—not only triggered international outrage but also galvanized its own fledging environment movement into action to demand a halt to such dam building in a pristine area of global importance for biodiversity. After some Chinese scientists also raised concerns over the planned dams and members of the ethnic minorities that dominate the Yunnan–Burma border region mounted public opposition to the construction plans, Premier Wen Jiabao suspended work on the cascade and ordered a full environmental assessment to help reach "a scientific decision."

The environmental impact assessment that followed was never released to the public because hydro works on international rivers are covered by China's state secrecy law. Meanwhile, Yunnan officials, backed by China's powerful state-run hydropower companies, pressed for building the planned dams on the Salween, and a scaled-back version of the cascade was initially prepared, starting with the construction of four megadams.[45] But with the federal and provincial authorities and state electricity enterprises ramping up their hydropower ambitions, pressure built to completely overturn the 2004 suspension. In its five-year plan for 2011–15, the State Development and Reform Commission listed all the planned dams on the Salween as priority strategic projects (map 6.6). And a senior official of China's National Energy Administration publicly declared in early 2011 that dam building on the Salween was "a must" and that resumption of work thus was "certain."[46]

Few were surprised that China's dam builders had their way. After all, dam projects on the Jinsha River that had been stalled by pressure from grassroots and environmental groups were allowed, one by one, to restart, without any real effort

Map 6.6   The 271,914-km² Salween River Basin

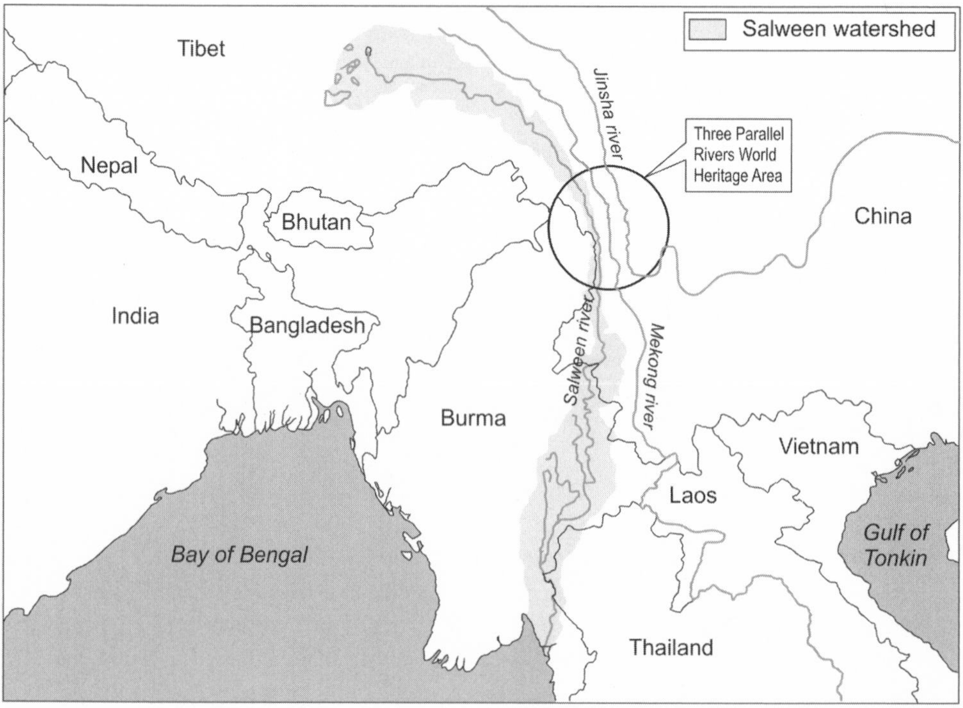

by the authorities to address the environmental concerns that these groups had raised. The authorities, by temporarily suspending a controversial plan, buy time to cool public passions, before they resurrect the project on the basis of an environmental impact assessment. And sometimes work has quietly resumed on a project even before the formal assessment has been completed.

The string of planned dams on the Salween would help generate 21,300 megawatts of hydropower—or about one-sixth more than the total installed capacity of the Three Gorges Dam. But if even more megadams were built, the Salween, according to Chinese officials, could yield up to 42,000 megawatts of electricity. The dam building is set to displace tens of thousands of ethnic-minority people who have lived in the canyon for centuries. Chinese hydropower companies, meanwhile, have embarked on multi-billion-dollar projects to harness the Salween downstream in Burma for generating electricity largely for export to China. The five-dam downriver cascade is best exemplified by the construction of the mammoth, 7,110-megawatt Tasang Dam on Burma's eastern Shan Plateau by a Chinese-led consortium of firms, which displaced Thailand's MDX Group as the main contractor. Not only is the dam situated in an area torn by internal conflict, but also tens of thousands of ethnic Shan and other minority people have been evicted from their land to make way for the project, whose reservoir extends right up to the Chinese border.

The impoundment of large volumes of river water by giant dams in Yunnan and eastern Burma threatens to seriously diminish flows to the lower Salween Valley, a major rice-growing region. The Salween, which originates in the 6,000-meter-high Dangla (Tanggula) Mountains of the so-called Tibet Autonomous Region, is the largest river by discharge to flow into Burma from the Tibetan Plateau, and this impoundment is expected to affect the cultivation of crops in its delta region and potentially open the path for seawater to infiltrate inland.

For Thailand, the Salween is a border river with Burma. In 1989 Thailand and Burma agreed to establish a joint working group to help promote and coordinate the joint development of hydropower projects within the Salween basin.[47] But as also with the case of other transnational river basins, China has not been willing to join hands with Burma and Thailand in the integrated management of Salween's resources. Its focus has been on winning dam-building contracts in Burma that offer both large profits and the sale of hydropower to the Chinese market. The Salween forms Burma's border with Thailand for 110 kilometers before emptying into the Andaman Sea. The basin of the other major river in Burma, the Irrawaddy, whose headwaters flow in from the Tibetan Plateau, extends to India's border state of Manipur, including its capital, Imphal.

The Mekong Basin: China Plays Spoiler

Of all the river basins in Asia, the Mekong has attracted the greatest international attention in recent years, largely because of upstream dam building on a massive scale. This basin holds the seeds of possible inter-riparian conflict. The Mekong, whose watershed is shared by six countries, is Za Chu ("Water of Stone") to the Tibetans, Lancang Jiang ("Turbulent River") to the Chinese, Mae Nam Khong ("Mother of Rivers") to the Thais, and Cuu Long ("Nine-Tailed Dragon," because of its nine branches that form the delta) to the Vietnamese. The 4,880-kilometer river—the world's twelfth-longest but with the eighth-biggest annual discharge—flows from the Plateau of Tibet into Laos, Thailand, Cambodia, and Vietnam, besides forming part of Burma's borders with China and Laos and Thailand's frontier with Laos. Before emptying into the South China Sea, the Mekong drains 805,604 square kilometers of land, roughly the size of the Danube River basin in Central and Eastern Europe. Nearly half the Mekong basin, however, falls in just two countries, Laos and Thailand.

The Mekong's annual flow varies widely from season to season: It averages 475 km³ in the monsoon season, but it drops precipitously to less than 17 percent of that in the dry months. Today, the Mekong is coming under growing pressure owing to multiple factors, including the rapid economic development in the basin countries, the region's thirst for electricity and water, the increasing use of the river as a cargo thoroughfare, and upstream-damming activities. The Mekong serves as a trade route between China and the downstream states; trade by riverboat between China and Thailand alone has increased by more than 50 percent since Chinese engineers dynamited a series of rapids and rocks at the beginning of the twenty-first century to make the river more navigable.[48]

The key discord in the basin centers on the exploitation of the Mekong's resources, with a clear divide emerging between the lower-basin states and an increasingly powerful and self-confident China. This equation "results in an extreme asymmetry of power relations."[49] The downstream states, despite similar concerns over upstream Chinese activities, however, have divergent basin priorities. Laos, as the single largest contributor to the Mekong's flow, is eager to harness the river's hydropower potential so as to earn hydro dollars by generating and exporting electricity, principally to China but also to Thailand and Vietnam. Vietnam is primarily interested in protecting its agricultural interests in the Mekong Delta, where 17 million Vietnamese live and nearly half the country's rice is grown. Vietnam is the world's fifth-largest, and Southeast Asia's biggest, producer of rice, although Thailand exports more rice.

Cambodia, in contrast, seeks to put the focus on conservation to help protect the Mekong's unique hydrology, pivoted on a cycle of seasonal flooding and drought. Cambodia's ecologically delicate Tonle Sap lake-and-river system is a huge breeding ground for fish. Thailand, for its part, wants to exploit the Mekong for multipurpose benefits, including energy, irrigation, and fisheries. Burma is indifferent because for it the Mekong is largely a border river. Politically, too, the basin states are dissimilar in terms of their systems, as illustrated by the military dictatorship now wearing a civilian garb in Burma, the authoritarian democracy in Cambodia, the authoritarian capitalism in China, the unstable democracy revering the world's longest-serving monarch in Thailand, and the Communist-led systems of Laos and Vietnam.

A larger issue of concern is the impact of human alterations of the fluvial ecosystem on the natural flow regime. After Latin America's Amazon River, the Mekong is said to be the world's most biodiverse inland waterway, with an estimated 1,245 species found in its waters. The Mekong, besides its rich biodiversity, is an economic lifeline for some 60 million residents downstream, many of them subsistence farmers and fishermen. Yet the overexploitation of the Mekong's resources and frenetic efforts to tap its hydropower reserves are threatening the river system's natural hydrology and ecology. Widespread logging in its catchment areas and the consequent riverbank erosion—along with the intensive application of chemical fertilizers and pesticides in the floodplains, wastewater inflows, and the use of explosives and other nontraditional fishing methods—are degrading its ecosystem.

Even as new damming activities and expansion of irrigation are under way, land-use changes thus far, including the loss of nearly 70 percent of the original forest cover in the basin, have helped highlight the negative impact on water and land quality and also on stream flows, in addition to the disappearance of habitats for a number of species. All this has helped underscore the need for integrated basin management so as to address the depletion of water resources, land erosion, environmental degradation, threats to biodiversity, and tensions among multiple and competing state users. Integrated management demands the active involvement of all stakeholders, especially the six national governments, to create a true Mekong basin community.

The hydropolitics in the Mekong basin, however, promises to get murkier as China, ignoring the concerns of downstream states, completes more upstream dams on the Mekong, even as the river's flow in 2010 fell to its lowest level in fifty years in the face of a serious drought stretching from Yunnan to parts of the Indochina Peninsula. In a region where China consciously has sought to project an image of benevolence and brotherhood, the drought in 2009–10 created a serious public-relations problem for Beijing, forcing it to counter popular perceptions in the lower basin that its new upstream dams had contributed to the drought by siphoning off the river waters.[50] Yet, while denying its dams were stealing waters, China's response to the drought was to ramp up construction of more dams and reservoirs.[51]

The river's altitude, as figure 6.1 shows, falls precipitously as it flows from the Tibetan Plateau to Yunnan Province, and then from Yunnan into the area where the borders of Burma, Thailand, and Laos converge. Through a cascade of twelve planned dams, China has sought to tap the river's hydropower reserves as it gushes from the high gorges on its route from the Tibetan Plateau to lower Yunnan. Transparency has become an important interstate issue in the basin, for the governments in Southeast Asia want Beijing to provide detailed technical information on its existing and upcoming dams. The usually cagey Thai government, for example, has publicly called for "more information, more cooperation, and more coordination" from China.

FIGURE 6.1   The Mekong River's Precipitous Drop in Altitude

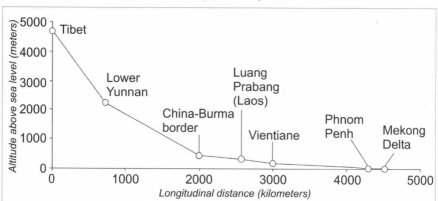

To be sure, the Mekong's rich basin resources and large waterfalls have made large-scale hydropower exploitation attractive. Emulating the example set by China, two other basin countries, Laos and Cambodia, have set out to build a series of dams either on the Mekong or its tributaries. Laos, whose catchment region generates 35 percent of the Mekong's annual flows, has drawn an ambitious program to power its development through hydropower exports by becoming "the battery of Asia." As part of its plan to employ natural resources to expand its economy, Laos wants 20 percent of its GDP to come from hydropower and mineral exports by 2020, up from about 4 percent in 2010. Paradoxically, a majority of the planned Laotian and Cambodian dams involve Chinese financial, design, or engineering assistance. In Cambodia, for example, Chinese state-owned companies are building eight medium-sized hydropower dams, including a 246-megawatt project on the Tatay River.

To make matters more complicated, Thailand is toying with the idea of taking water from the Mekong to its arid areas, besides planning its own hydropower works and agreeing to buy electricity from Chinese and Laotian upstream projects. More than eighty water projects of various types on the Mekong and its tributaries were in various stages of preparation or construction in 2011 in both the upper and lower parts of the basin. If all the planned Laotian, Cambodian, and Thai dams go ahead, they will generate 13,500 megawatts of electricity but have an adverse impact on the fluvial ecosystem. In fact, some of the Laotian and Cambodian dams being built—like the giant 1,260-megawatt Sayabouly in Laos—hold transboundary implications, besides potentially endangering freshwater species such as the Mekong giant catfish, which is the size of a car, and the Mekong stingray, which can weigh more than a tiger.

Yet it is China's cascade of upstream megadams that promises to wreak the greatest ecological damage, besides affecting cross-border flows and causing greater disquiet in downstream Thailand, Laos, Cambodia, and Vietnam. China's first two dams on the Mekong—the 1,500-megawatt Manwan, completed in 1996, and the 1,350-megawatt Dachaoshan, built 131 kilometers downstream of the Manwan and commissioned in 2003—"noticeably reduced the annual downstream flow of vital flood-borne silt and aggravated the effects of a prolonged drought."[52] Then the 750-megawatt Gongguoqiao Dam and the 1,750-megawatt Jinghong Dam came up in rapid succession.

The fifth Chinese dam—the 4,200-megawatt Xiaowan, which rises 292 meters and is located on one of the uppermost Mekong points—has a 15-billion-m^3 reservoir extending some 170 square kilometers. So large is the Xiaowan Dam that it alone is capable of producing more electricity than the 2010 installed hydropower-generating capacity of all of the lower Mekong countries together. In fact, its reservoir can store more water than in "all the [existing] Southeast Asian reservoirs combined."[53] Xiaowan is higher than Paris's famed Eiffel Tower, which without its television antenna is 276 meters.

But dwarfing Xiaowan, if not in height but volume, is another Chinese dam coming up on the Mekong—the 254-meter-high Nuozhadu, whose reservoir will hold nearly 22 billion m^3 of water in its 190-square-kilometer reservoir. The 5,850-megawatt Nuozhadu, like Xiaowan, has been designed as a mammoth reservoir system to store water in the wet season and release some of it downstream in the dry season to offset the Mekong's seasonal variability. With the first two dams—Manwan and Dachaoshan—silting up faster than anticipated, the powerful Nuozhadu and Xiaowan are also going to be used to help flush the silt buildup. But if Nuozhadu and Xiaowan themselves confront a rapid silt buildup, the dredging operations would be complex and expensive. Such a scenario is plausible, given the accelerated soil erosion and other environmental changes upstream as well as the projected global-warming-induced changes in temperature and precipitation levels.

The blunt fact is that the massive Xiaowan and Nuozhadu imperil the very hydrological stability of the Mekong on which the livelihoods of so many poor depend. China's upstream hydropower works, coupled with downstream water projects in Laos, Thailand, Cambodia, and Vietnam, also hold the threat that the Mekong could become like the ecologically degraded Yellow River, a symbol of the disaster wrought by human-made plans.[54] As Nuozhadu and more dams come on line, undesirable fluctuations in downstream water levels and sediment flows are likely to become pronounced, along with a noticeable effect on migratory fisheries. Beijing, however, continues to plough a lonely furrow on the Mekong, in defiance of the growing demands of the downstream states for institutionalized basinwide cooperation.

With the river flowing through the Tibetan Plateau and lower Yunnan for more than two-fifths of its total length, the Mekong no doubt is an important waterway for China, principally for its Yunnan Province, where the exploitation of the river's resources is concentrated. Actually, the Mekong's first 1,000-kilometer stretch is in central Tibet and Amdo, the present Dalai Lama's birthplace, which China has separated from Tibet and largely made the province of Qinghai. But as in the case of the projects on the other international rivers originating on the Tibetan Plateau, the Chinese authorities have involved no Tibetan representatives in their Mekong development plans yet given downstream Yunnan a major say. Yunnan officials have championed an aggressive strategy of building dams on the Mekong and the Salween.

With the remaining three-fifths of the Mekong basin situated in Southeast Asia—where paddy rice is the main crop grown on the river's floodplains— Chinese dams have helped inflame popular passions in Vietnam, Laos, Cambodia, and Thailand. The first six of the Chinese dams on the Mekong alone have been designed with a combined rated generating capacity of 15,400 megawatts, as compared with the 18,300 megawatts of the Three Gorges Dam, the world's largest single hydropower producer. Yet despite the significant implications that these dams hold for transboundary water and silt flows, the lower-riparian states learned of the upstream projects only after China began building the first two dams in the early 1990s. Today, important environmental effects already are "evident in terms of changes in flow patterns and sediment transport, and it is likely that the construction of further dams will exacerbate these fundamental ecological problems."[55] The effects of the Chinese dams on fishing and farming in the downstream states also are beginning to be felt (map 6.7).

By seeking to reengineer the Mekong's hydrologic regime, China's dams endanger the region's seasonal and permanent wetlands (which make up 8.7 percent of the basin) and the unique Tonle Sap lake-and-river system—a huge nursery for the Mekong's fisheries and a moderator of the severity and duration of flooding in Vietnam's rice basket, the Mekong Delta, which is already under pressure from the overexploitation of basin resources and saltwater incursion. The Tonle Sap's buffering role has been described thus by analyst Richard Cronin: "As the wet-season flood builds, the river reverses direction and the lake expands several-fold, becoming a flood buffer and giant seasonal nursery for migratory fish and other aquatic life. For about three months after the floods subside, the lake empties back into the Mekong, bringing with it the world's richest concentration of freshwater migratory fish both in numbers and species, and providing part of the Mekong Delta enough water to produce a third rice harvest."[56]

Indeed, across much of the lower Mekong, it is the rise and fall of river waters that ensures a year-round food supply: High waters in the rainy season create new fish-spawning grounds, while the retreat of waters in the dry season permits the cultivation of crops on the floodplains newly fertilized by river silt. The lower Mekong supports the planet's richest inland fisheries. The upstream damming of the Mekong by China and Laos in particular threatens to not only disrupt fish-migration routes and the natural flood cycle important to agriculture and ecosystems, but also disturb so-called recession agriculture—the practice whereby crops are planted in floodplains watered by receding floodwaters.

In this light, China has emerged as a special regional challenge: It has not only spurned invitations to join institutions like the Mekong River Commission (which

MAP 6.7   Dams Built, under Construction, or Planned on the Mekong River

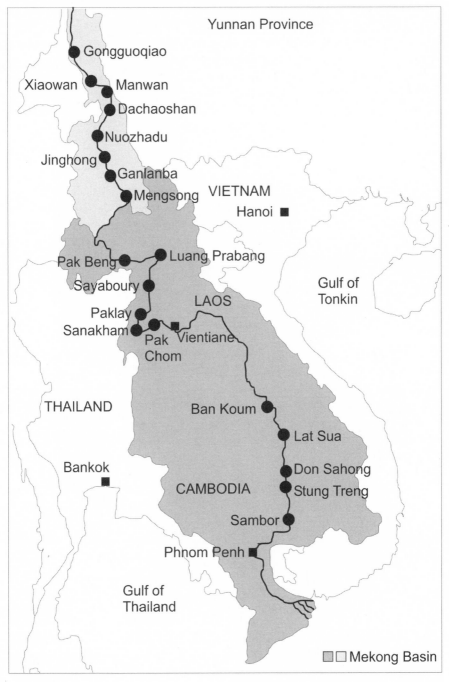

Yunnan Province

Gongguoqiao

Xiaowan   Manwan

Dachaoshan

Nuozhadu

Jinghong

Ganlanba

Mengsong

VIETNAM

Hanoi ■

Pak Beng   Luang Prabang

Gulf of
Tonkin

Sayaboury

LAOS

Paklay

Sanakham

Pak   Vientiane
Chom

THAILAND

Ban Koum

Lat Sua

Bankok

Don Sahong

CAMBODIA

Stung Treng

Sambor

Phnom Penh

Gulf of
Thailand

☐☐ Mekong Basin

was set up by Laos, Cambodia, Thailand, and Vietnam in 1995, with support from multinational aid donors[57]), but it has also continued to drag its feet on the issue of transparency relating to its hydroengineering works on the upper Mekong. As a result, building a regional basin community involving all the riparian states has proven an elusive goal. China and Burma participate in the Mekong River Commission's annual meeting as "dialogue partners" while steering clear of membership. Burma's nonmembership, however, makes little difference because the Mekong is largely a border river for that country, with the drainage basin covering just 4.2 percent of Burmese territory.

But without the membership of the dominant-riparian state, China, the intergovernmental Mekong River Commission cannot serve as an effective mechanism for cooperative water resources management. China's nonmembership thus undercuts the commission's larger mission and programs. For example, the four member-states of the commission decided in 2006 to try and maintain wet and dry season flows—within mutually agreed high and low ranges—to the 100-kilometer-long Tonle Sap River connecting the Mekong at Phnom Penh with Cambodia's endangered Great Lake, which is also known as Tonle Sap, underscoring the symbiotic relationship between the lake and its link river. But the country that can ensure such adequate flows in the dry season through its mammoth upstream reservoirs remains outside the agreement.

China has been willing to participate in infrastructural projects in the lower basin, yet it has been loath to take co-riparian states into confidence on its own upstream developmental plans. This reluctance actually is at odds with China's actions to advance regional economic integration with Southeast Asia. In fact, the world's largest free trade area by population, covering the 1.9 billion people in China and the ten-nation Association of Southeast Asian Nations, came broadly into effect at the beginning of 2010. Yet on the resources of common rivers, China wants no regional collaboration.

Where its commercial interests can be advanced, China has zealously pushed for integration in the Greater Mekong Subregion in the areas of trade, investment, communication, transportation, and energy. It has even sought to press forward its river-navigation interest, signing contracts and blasting rapids, shoals, and reefs in the lower basin to allow ships of greater tonnage to ply the Mekong. But where it can employ its riparian advantage to unilaterally exploit basin resources, China is opposed to integration, even if such resource exploitation damages the long-term interests of its trade partners. This demonstrates a selective approach anchored in China's assertive pursuit of its own interests. It is thus hardly a surprise that "indignation with China for its lack of transparency on upstream dam developments is on the rise," as it takes "what many see as a covetous and less than neighborly approach."[58] China's apparent strategy, according to another observer, is to incorporate "the natural resources of the Mekong basin into its manufacturing supply chain to expand its political and economic influence."[59] This may explain why Beijing has been reluctant to share with co-riparian states either design information about its dams, including precisely how much water is being diverted to reservoirs, or its own environmental and hydrological assessments of the projects' likely effects.

Indeed, a key reason why China has rebuffed the 1995 regional treaty seeking to create a basin community through the Mekong River Commission is that its provisions demand, among other things, prior notification, transparency, and co-riparian consultations in relation to projects with significant transboundary effects. Although separate procedures were approved between 2001 and 2006 for interstate information sharing, prior consultations and notification, water-utilization monitoring, and safeguarding of flows, the main 1995 treaty called for reasonable and equitable utilization of the Mekong's resources, maintenance of acceptable minimal "natural" flows, and a commitment "to avoid, minimize and mitigate harmful effects that might occur to the environment, especially the water quantity and quality, the aquatic (ecosystem) conditions, and ecological balance of the river system, from the development and use of the Mekong River basin water resources or discharge of wastes and return flows."[60] Contrast such obligations with the official opacity that China still maintains, to the extent that dam sites on the upper Mekong have been kept off limits to the foreign media—the police, for example, briefly detained an American journalist who tried to visit the Xiaowan Dam in 2010.[61] Yet, just as it has agreed to share limited hydrological data with India on the Brahmaputra and Sutlej rivers to help deal with flooding, China is committed through a 2002 accord to supply data on the upper Mekong water levels to downstream states during the flood season, although from only two monitoring stations.

Against this background, the Mekong has turned into a river of discord.[62] But with Southeast Asian governments seeking to muffle their concerns in deference to China's rising power and influence, it has been left to nongovernmental organizations to take the lead, even if it sometimes results in their jumping to a conclusion. For example, when the Mekong overran its banks and cut a swath of destruction through northern Thailand and Laos in August 2008, some nongovernmental organizations in the region were quick to lay the blame for the flooding on China's Yunnan dam cascade. In some areas, the flooding was said to be the worst in a century, with downstream users suspecting the cause to be China's sudden water releases from its upstream reservoirs during heavy rainfall.[63] The Mekong River Commission, however, held that the discharge from the rain-swollen Chinese dams "could not have been a significant factor in this natural flood event."[64] The 2009–10 drought was similarly blamed by many environmental activists and others in the region on the Chinese dams, although the commission found no scientific evidence to support that view. Because unusual fluctuations in the Mekong's flow now occur recurrently, such finger-pointing is likely to become more common.

Concerns of the lower-riparian states remain centered on the impact of upstream projects on cross-border flows and on agriculture and fisheries. China's unilateralist approach on exploiting the Mekong's resources, after all, has only encouraged other basin states to follow suit, as illustrated by the Laotian, Cambodian, and Thai dam-building plans and the Thai interest in additional water diversion. Downstream users are concerned that too much water could be released by the dams in the wet season, contributing to downriver flooding, but too little in the dry season, when the water is most needed. There also is concern about the effects on migrating fish. Of the hundreds of fish species in the Mekong, 87 percent have been identified by experts as migratory. The fishing industry in the lower basin, according to the Mekong River Commission, is a $2 billion annual business. More important, fish are the main source of protein for the poor, with the Mekong supplying 80 percent of the protein needs of people who live in its basin.[65] Also, with upstream dams beginning to slow the downstream flow of mineral-rich silt, there is concern about how this could affect farm productivity, especially in the Mekong Delta, Vietnam's food basket.

No regional attempt has been made to look at the Chinese, Laotian, Cambodian, Thai, and other projects as a whole to assess their long-term viability and likely effects. Their impact could extend from long-lasting damage to fish habitats and wetlands to the forced relocation of local residents. "Without good and careful management of the Mekong River as well as its natural resources, this great river will not survive," Thai prime minister Abhisit Vejjajiva warned in 2010. The country in danger of losing out the most is the one located farthest downstream, Vietnam, which has no hydropower potential to exploit in its portion of the river but whose Mekong Delta will bear the brunt of the impact of upstream hydro projects and the rise of the sea level due to global warming. A report of the Intergovernmental Panel on Climate Change has identified the Mekong Delta, along with the Ganges-Brahmaputra Delta in Bangladesh and the Nile Delta in Egypt, as the world's three "hot spots" for potential large-scale exodus of residents because of the areas' extreme vulnerability to climate change.[66] According to the same report, global warming is likely to directly affect the Mekong's hydrology and water quality, while indirect effects resulting from changing vegetation patterns could alter the food chain and increase soil erosion in the basin.[67]

A significantly decreased Mekong discharge will aggravate the problem of seawater intrusion into the delta. The expected impact of the upstream projects, however, is likely to extend beyond the delta region to other areas spread across the lower basin, affecting the interests of those who depend on the river and its tributaries for their sustenance. Significantly, most of the densely populated parts of the Mekong basin are located in the lower-riparian states, where the dams could upend the lives of millions of people who live off the fishing and farming economies. For these states that have the greatest stake in the long-term health of the river system, China's refusal to join the Mekong River Commission and help institute a region-wide basin community serves as a jarring reminder of how China has turned its back on the very principle it advocates globally—multilateralism.

Planting Seeds of Inter-Riparian Conflict

China has been the world leader in contributing to river fragmentation, or the interruption of natural flow by dams, interbasin transfers, or other diversions. Turning rivers into chains of human-made reservoirs has resulted in significant changes in the functions of fluvial ecosystems, the loss of riparian vegetation, and the disappearance of some waterfalls, rapids, and wetlands. To be sure, dams and other hydro facilities yield important economic and social benefits—from electricity for powering the economy to the expansion of irrigation and drinking-water supply. But they also can have a profound impact on freshwater ecosystems, affecting natural flood cycles, aquatic life, and the downstream movement of species-vital sediments and nutrients to deltas, estuaries, flooded forests, wetlands, and inland seas.[68]

Not content with having built more than half of all existing dams in the world, China has embarked on plans to erect dams even in areas of immense importance for biodiversity, such as the spectacular Salween River Canyon in Yunnan Province. One way it has chosen to clear the path for setting up dams in protected areas is to unabashedly redraw the boundaries of its natural reserves, as it did in 2011 in the case of a major fish reserve on the Jinsha River that serves as one of China's last sanctuaries for freshwater biodiversity. Another way is to simply claim, however implausibly, that dam building is "crucial to improving local people's lives and protecting the environment" in areas that constitute natural heritage zones, such as the Yunnan canyon.[69]

By proceeding to build a series of dams, canals, and other hydro projects on each important transnational river—and that, too, without transparency or information sharing—China is stirring up riparian tensions and threatening the hydrological cycle and integrity of river systems critical to its co-riparian states. Having learned little from the way its megaprojects of the past—including the Soviet-built, Mao-era Sanmenxia Dam on the Yellow River and the more-recent Three Gorges Dam on the Yangtze—have caused serious environmental problems, China has been blithely damming international rivers on the Tibetan Plateau, Xinjiang, and its northeast to produce hydropower and to channel their waters for irrigation and other purposes. Although the Mao era initiated the process of river fragmentation, post-Mao policies have made fluvial degradation worse through a single-minded focus on economic and water resources development and energy production, whatever the costs to the environment or downstream communities.[70]

Today China is pursuing the biggest interbasin and interriver water transfer projects ever undertaken in world history. One project, scheduled to be largely complete by 2014, involves water transfers from the Yangtze River basin to the Yellow River basin. Another more ambitious proposal aims to reroute waters to the Yellow from three international rivers on the Tibetan Plateau, especially the Brahmaputra. With China's megaprojects moving to the Tibetan Plateau, including its southeastern rim, such works threaten to export China's water crisis to the

"Roof of the World" by damaging its delicate freshwater ecosystems. The projects also carry the seeds of inter-riparian conflict in Asia. China's riparian neighbors have increasingly viewed with disquiet its construction of water impoundment and diversion works on most of the international rivers flowing out of Chinese-controlled territory. In the future, discord over such projects could easily turn into conflict that spills across international borders. Indeed, such is the possibility of water disputes between China and its neighbors flaring openly that the US National Intelligence Council—the senior analytical body within the Office of the Director of National Intelligence—has flagged the issue as "a serious enough concern" to warrant close monitoring of China's water situation.[71]

It is the growing water stress on China's northern plains that, to some extent, is promoting Beijing's assertiveness on international river resources. This stress has helped foster growing water competition in the north between agriculture, industry, and rapidly expanding urban areas. The single most significant water transfer project already in operation is the Three Gorges Dam project, which, in addition to being the world's largest hydropower producer, has been designed to transfer 70 km^3 of water per year to north China. The much greater volumes of water to be sent north by the eastern and central routes of the Great South–North Water Transfer Project will still not satisfy northern China's water demands. But as water woes have been aggravated in its north by unsustainable intensive farming, the rapid expansion of cities and industries, and a falling groundwater table, China has increasingly turned its attention to tapping the resources of transboundary rivers.

China's voracious appetite for energy is another major dam-building driver. With Beijing ramping up its hydropower ambitions and unveiling plans to install an additional 140,000 megawatts of hydroelectricity-generating capacity just between 2011 and 2015, an accelerated dam-building program has followed. The major dam-building effort is now increasingly concentrated on the Tibetan Plateau, including the Tibet Autonomous Region, Qinghai Province, and the areas incorporated in Yunnan, Sichuan, and Gansu provinces. The latest wave of dam building has coincided with an increasing government focus on exploiting this vast region's exceptionally rich mineral resources, and the newly generated electricity is coming in handy to set up local extractive and other industries that are high energy consumers.

Significantly, China is using international concerns about its emergence as the world's largest emitter of greenhouse gases to justify its aggressive dam-building activities on international rivers. Even as its carbon emissions continue to grow at the fastest rate in the world, it has set an ambitious goal of producing 15 percent of its energy from non-fossil-fuel sources by 2020 to help significantly reduce its "carbon intensity"—that is, the amount of carbon dioxide emitted per unit of economic output. This goal, China says, can be met only through a major expansion of its hydropower capacity, although it is already the world's largest producer of hydroelectricity. In truth, it embarked on a program of building megadams long before the world came to recognize that climate change is an important issue. So today, climate change serves as a convenient rationale for doing more of what it has done for decades.

The overdamming of rivers in the Han heartland, in fact, significantly contributed to China's water and environmental crisis. Over the years, China ignored the unfolding crisis, including warning signs of river depletion and the impact of growing water contamination on public health.[72] For example, such has been the overuse of the resources of the 5,464-kilometer-long Yellow River—which has served as the cradle of Chinese civilization—that the river in recent years has run dry before reaching its estuary on the east coast. There are at least eighty-six large dams, some of recent origin, on the Yellow, which suffers from serious riverbank erosion and other problems, and about 1.6 billion tons of mud and sand get washed into the stream every year on average.[73] What the Chinese traditionally have called the Mother River is drying up, prompting Beijing to even pursue a dubious cloud-seeding program involving the use of silver iodide crystals above the Yellow's source area.[74]

Just when the Chinese government has finally started making efforts to control the poisonous toxins from its industries that are biologically killing its internal rivers, it has turned its attention to exploiting the resources of international rivers. The transnational rivers flowing out of Chinese territory risk the same reckless exploitation and pollution of their waters that degraded China's internal watercourses. The chemical contamination of the Yellow River, for example, begins almost from its source, in the Tibetan Plateau's Amdo region, which boasts China's largest potash fertilizer plant, biggest asbestos production base, and second-largest lead and zinc mine. Now, tailings from the rapidly growing mining operations on the plateau threaten to pollute cross-border rivers with sulfuric acid, cyanide, and heavy metals. The continued unsustainable resource stripping of Tibet—and the attendant contamination of waterways—are issues that China cannot afford to ignore indefinitely, especially because they hold both internal and external ramifications.

Bordered by the expanding Ordos and Gobi deserts, China acknowledges that its water and energy shortages are becoming acute. But in seeking to address these shortages, its gargantuan hydro projects threaten to damage the environment and exacerbate the freshwater crisis both inside and outside China. By seeking to commandeer the waters of international rivers, some of its plans also threaten to engender inter-riparian conflict. China is not the only country building hydropower and other projects on international rivers. Several other countries located downstream from China are doing the same, even though their dams carry potentially adverse transboundary effects for the countries located further downriver. But it is thirsty China that is leading the charge in a potentially destabilizing manner. So it is of little surprise that the US National Intelligence Council has predicted that an ever-more-assertive China is "poised to have more impact on the world over the next 20 years than any other country."[75] China already is beginning to cast a lengthening shadow over Asia.

The Amur, Irtysh, Illy, Songhua, Yalu, Salween, Mekong, and Brahmaputra, among other international rivers, illustrate that China's water impoundment and diversion projects are often at the root of its increasingly tense water relations with co-riparian states. In fact, the size and scale of China's hydro works have steadily increased, with the emphasis now on megaprojects. As a consequence, China's national plans involving transnational rivers have helped turn water into a bilateral issue with almost all riparian neighbors.

The nation with the most dams under construction in the world after China is a state on Asia's western rim, Turkey, and it is easy to draw a parallel between these two countries. Like China, Turkey enjoys supreme riparian dominance in its region. It is thus no surprise that Turkey has megadams and large hydropower plants in operation or under construction on the Tigris and Euphrates rivers as part of its Güneydoğu Anadolu Projesi (GAP; Southeastern Anatolia Development Project). Under the $32 billion GAP, Turkey is set to roll out a total of twenty-two dams and nineteen hydropower plants and bring 1.8 million hectares of additional land under irrigation across nine provinces.

The GAP, one of the largest regional projects in the world, seeks to tap 28.5 percent of Turkey's total water potential. Like China's river-water diversion projects, the GAP also aims—to the consternation of lower-riparian Syria and Iraq—to divert the waters of international rivers for irrigation and industry and for hydropower generation through gigantic tunnels, canals, and reservoirs. The 1,200-megawatt Ilisu hydroelectric dam on the Tigris, for example, threatens to drastically reduce summer river flows to the northern Iraqi city of Mosul, besides uprooting thousands of Kurds and inundating several ancient caves and other historical sites in an upstream area of Turkey that traditionally has been a battleground between the military and Kurdish insurgents.

But whereas China is seeking to divert Tibetan waters across cultural zones to Han areas, Turkey's program to expand irrigation and electric power production largely aims to address the long-standing local grievances in the predominantly Kurdish southeast of the country, where popular resentment over poverty and poor infrastructure has long aided the separatist cause. Turkey's water megaprojects, however, have spurred intercountry concerns and tensions in the Middle East in ways similar to China's dam-building activities.[76] In continental Asia, which includes most of Turkey, water has emerged as a crucial element in the national security calculus of regional actors already troubled by water stress or scarcity. China's plans to divert waters from transboundary rivers affect the interests of a much larger number of countries and downstream residents than Turkey's projects. China indeed has been so aggressive in dam building that it has dammed all its important rivers, building a dam even in the remote, inhospitable southwestern corner of Tibet on the main Indus stream.

Even if China has no intention to use water as a political weapon, the fact is that it is acquiring significant water leverage over its co-riparian states. As one

Southeast Asian scholar has put it, the "most critical political ramification" of China's massive damming of the Mekong, for example, is that Beijing will be "able to control the quantity of water released to downstream countries."[77] A large upstream deflection of Mekong flows would not only have a damaging impact on the ecology and local livelihoods in downstream areas but is also likely to leave the lower-riparian states at China's mercy for adequate water releases during the dry season and for protection from flooding during the monsoon. The extensive construction of upstream dams, reservoirs, and barrages, furthermore, is likely to hold back nutrient-rich sediments vital for agricultural productivity and biodiversity downstream. China has similarly embarked on building a string of large dams and hydropower stations on the upper reaches of the Salween, Brahmaputra, Irtysh, and some other transboundary rivers.

Despite its emergence as a leading world player, China remains an insecure power governed by an insecure regime that is loath to make any course correction to the programs it has launched, including the South–North Water Transfer Project, even when its own experts warn of incalculable environmental costs. The large-scale impoundment and diversion of transnational river waters, in fact, has become another means for China to assert its rights as a resurgent imperial power in Asia. Through its unilateral approach to damming international rivers, China is beginning to reap increasing leverage, which it will be able to translate into greater power to rein in neighboring states and extend its economic and political influence. Lower-Mekong countries like Cambodia, Laos, and Thailand already avoid giving vent to their concerns about the upper-basin dams or criticizing Beijing openly on any other issue. Yet with large riparian neighbors like Russia and India, the Chinese approach risks instigating overt water conflicts.

Stemming Subcontinental Conflict

Water is a potential point of friction and hostilities on the Indian subcontinent, which is home to more than 21 percent of the world's population yet must make do with barely 8.3 percent of global water resources.[78] India, the geographical center of this subregion, is located upstream from Pakistan and Bangladesh but is downstream from Nepal and Bhutan, although its major rivers other than the Ganges tumble down from the Tibetan highlands.

The subcontinent receives about 80 percent of its total annual precipitation during the summer monsoon period from June to September.[79] The Northeast Monsoon from November to March brings rain to the southeastern belt of peninsular India and parts of Sri Lanka and the Maldives. Interstate water wrangles are common in this region, where all the countries other than the island states share land borders with India but not with each other. India thus is the focal point for subcontinental hydropolitics.

The rivers of the Indus system, for example, flow to Pakistan from the Indian-administered portion of the divided, former princely state of Jammu and Kashmir and from India's Punjab State. The small Himalayan state of Himachal Pradesh is the source of three of the six rivers in the Indus system. Hard-line forces in Pakistan—the Islamists and the military—have sought to keep the Kashmir issue alive by linking Islamabad's intent to change the territorial status quo to the control of rivers that are the lifeblood of Pakistan. Assef Ahmad Ali, an adviser to the Pakistani prime minister, went so far as to warn in 2010 that the bilateral disputes could lead to a Pakistan–India water war.[80] The book *Climate Wars* by the journalist Gwynne Dyer has outlined a scenario where Pakistan trades nuclear-tipped missiles with India over water rights.[81] But whereas India and Pakistan have an institutional mechanism for consultations and cooperation on water sharing, including a treaty that provides for division of rivers and international arbitration, China and India have no bilateral arrangement.

Water Treaties on the Subcontinent

One of the positive aspects of the interstate water struggle on the Indian subcontinent, in fact, is the existence of treaty relationships between Pakistan and India, between Bangladesh and India, and between Nepal and India on water sharing. Also, unlike China's refusal to allow officials from a lower-riparian state to inspect any of its upstream water projects, let alone to accept third-party adjudication over any issue of concern, India grants on-site access to the two states downstream to it, Pakistan and Bangladesh.

The subcontinent, moreover, serves as proof that legally binding interstate basin arrangements can be successfully concluded between adversarial states. The Pakistan–India legal arrangements have endured more than a half century of political tensions and conflicts. The complex Indus Waters Treaty, negotiated with World Bank backing, has survived wars and other major bilateral crises, and the Permanent Indus Commission has met even when the relationship between the two neighbors has been seriously strained.

Yet such is the sharpening struggle for water that no interstate relationship on the South Asian landmass other than between Bhutan and India is free of water wrangles. As an indispensable resource in short supply in many areas, water tends to raise emotive and politically charged issues on the subcontinent. Raspy hydropolitics, in fact, played no small role in souring the Indo-Bangladesh relationship just years after Bangladesh gained its independence with Indian military assistance. More fundamentally, water often serves as an ad hominem issue to deflect attention from the gross mismanagement of domestic resources by laying the blame at someone else's door. This helps magnify the risk of interstate water conflict.

The 1996 Ganges Water Treaty between India and Bangladesh is not as well known as the 1960 Indo-Pakistan Indus Treaty. But it is no less significant. Unlike the Indus Treaty, the Indo-Bangladesh pact emerged without the involvement of a third party. Even though it was the product of a quarter century of efforts, the treaty has fundamentally changed the water relationship between Bangladesh and India by easing Bangladeshi concerns. It also is a genuine water-sharing pact, unlike the Indus Treaty, which simply parceled out rivers for use by each of its two parties.

Because of the large interseasonal variations in river flows and Bangladesh's location at the farthest end of river systems, this densely populated country faces acute water shortages in the dry period from January to May. In fact, the river flows in Bangladesh in the driest month of the year represent only 18 percent of the annual average.[82] Upstream withdrawals in India significantly affect the volume of water available in the Bangladesh portion of the Ganges basin. This fact—coupled with the diversion of water by India's Farakka Barrage to a Ganges tributary, the Bhagirathi-Hooghly, to help flush silt and keep the Calcutta Harbor operational during the dry season—led to years of bilateral acrimony and disputes before a treaty was finally signed on procedures for managing the Ganges' transboundary flow.[83]

The treaty, based on the international principles of "equity, fairness and no harm to either party," guarantees Bangladesh a minimum share of Ganges waters around the year, but especially in the critical dry season.[84] The sharing formula emerged only after India climbed down from a long-standing position that it needed a minimum of 40,000 cubic feet of water per second of time ("cusecs," or "c.f.s") to flush silt from the Calcutta port. It settled for each side getting 35,000 cusecs (991 m³ per second) of water in alternative ten-day periods during the driest period from March to May. The treaty's complex water-sharing arrangement is pivoted on joint oversight of flows to help build mutual trust. And the use of the term "Bangladesh's share" in its annexure underscores an entitlement, not just a release by India. Indeed, India's recognition of Bangladesh's equality of right "led almost to an equal division" of the waters (map 6.8).[85]

The treaty covering one of the world's most populated basins was criticized in both countries for being too favorable to the other side.[86] Yet it has helped bury the hatchet over India's construction of the Farakka Barrage. The treaty, to remain in force for thirty years but "renewable on the basis of mutual consent," actually incorporates important dispute settlement provisions.[87] If the Joint Committee set up under the treaty for implementing the arrangements were unable to resolve a disagreement or dispute over the Ganges waters, the matter would be referred for settlement to the Joint Rivers Commission, which was established almost a quarter century earlier in 1972, just a year after East Pakistan broke away from Pakistan to become the independent nation Bangladesh. If the matter still remained unresolved, the two governments "shall meet urgently at the appropriate level to resolve it by mutual discussion."[88]

Largely because the treaty emerged without any international assistance, its conflict resolution provisions do not include international arbitration and adjudication.

MAP 6.8   The Ganges River Basin

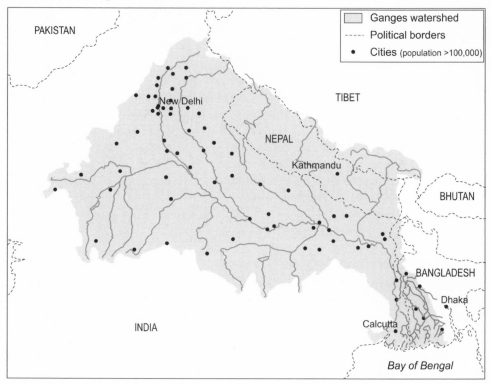

Instead, the pact reposes trust in bilateral mechanisms. No serious dispute thus far has arisen over its implementation.

New disagreements, however, have flared over other transboundary basins and projects, including India's revival of a long-dormant multipurpose plan, Tipaimukh, in the remote Manipur State bordering Burma. Located 210 kilometers upstream from the Bangladesh border on the Barak River, the Tipaimukh project—which was held up for years by local concerns on the Indian side over submergence of land and displacement of residents—is designed to control annual flooding in the region stretching up to Bangladesh's Sylhet District, improve river navigation, and generate 1,500 megawatts of hydropower. The disagreements have highlighted the need for stronger institutional bonds and better data exchanges between the two countries, including perhaps turning the Joint Rivers Commission into a Joint Waters Commission with an expanded mandate covering water quality and the integrated management of watersheds and coastal ecosystems.[89]

The Ganges Treaty, however, has made a big difference: It has not only improved bilateral relations on water issues but has also helped generate the momentum for similar water-sharing agreements covering some other transboundary basins. As a result, the path has been opened to a Ganges-style sharing pact on the Teesta River, which originates in the Himalayan Indian state of Sikkim and meets the Brahmaputra in Bangladesh. Bangladesh and India actually concluded ad hoc sharing arrangements over the Teesta in 1983. But those arrangements were not renewed and expired in 1987.

Today the two countries have joined hands to dredge their border river, the Ichhamati, and protect the fluvial ecosystems in their common basins. They have tasked their Joint Rivers Commission to resolve issues relating to the smaller transboundary rivers, such as the Feni, Manu, Muhuri, Khowai, Gumti, Dharla, and Dudhkumar. Yet with China building giant dams both on the Brahmaputra—a river central to Bangladesh because it brings 74 percent more water to the country in a year than the Ganges—and on a Ganges tributary, the Arun (the largest trans-Himalayan river passing through Nepal that contributes significantly to downstream Ganges flows), Bangladesh faces a more thirsty future.[90]

Nepal and Bhutan as Subregional Energy Hub?

The two Himalayan states of Nepal and Bhutan—sandwiched between Chinese-ruled Tibet and India—sit on vast hydropower reserves, which, if tapped with adequate environmental safeguards, could make them the hub of a long-term regional energy strategy promoting development and stability across much of the Indian subcontinent. By harnessing the natural bounty of the Himalayas to produce renewable electricity largely for export to a fast-growing India—where power shortages shrink the country's gross domestic product by an entire percentage point every year—Nepal and Bhutan would effectively turn "water into white gold," generating the hydro dollars to fuel their own development and prosperity.[91]

Environmentally sound hydropower is attractive because, although installing the capacity is cost-intensive and entails fixed maintenance costs, the station has a life span almost double that of a nuclear-power reactor and generates electricity with no fuel cost. To be up to standard, hydropower production must have a minimal impact on local ecology and not materially alter transboundary stream flows. Only sustainable hydropower projects with environmental protection built into their design must find favor with national planners, because rivers are not only sources of water and energy but also serve key ecological functions. Indeed, without the protection of watersheds and waterways, there can be no provision of water of adequate quantity and quality. The importance of following the laws of nature, rather than seeking to recklessly tame nature for economic development, has been underlined by China's hydroengineering projects, which are threatening to do to the international river systems what already has happened to the heavily dammed Yellow and Yangtze, both of which have been ecologically damaged. As opposed to China's megaprojects, smaller-scale, ecologically friendly projects in the Himalayas—if properly planned and designed, and backed by thorough and impartial environmental impact assessments—can yield major benefits without carrying environmental and social costs.

India, as the subcontinent's largest energy consumer, has sought to incentivize a subregional energy grid. Yet in a reflection of the difficulty to address all concerns, many of its own Himalayan hydropower projects have been delayed, suspended, or shelved, largely due to grassroots opposition. That has not deterred India from continuing its long-standing pursuit of freshwater diplomacy in the subregion, despite the modest returns it has yielded. In addition to doling out the bulk of the Indus waters to Pakistan by treaty and in guaranteeing Bangladesh fixed dry-season flows, India has over the years extended substantial assistance to two of its smallest neighbors, Nepal and Bhutan, in expanding their irrigation and hydropower capacities. As one Indian official put it, "All the arrangements entered into by India were considered not merely in the context of mutual and equitable benefit, but in a wider framework and with the hope that they would promote friendly ties. Accordingly, there has been more 'give' than 'take' on the part of India in these cooperative bilateral arrangements."[92] Although water cooperation has actively been used as a tool of Indian diplomacy with upstream Nepal and Bhutan, the results have varied.

In the Ganges basin, the politically unstable country of Nepal—a strategic buffer between Tibet and India—holds up to 83,000 megawatts of potential hydropower reserves.[93] Yet it produces a trifling 714 megawatts of electricity for its 30 million citizens from all sources of energy, with the result that power outages for several hours a day around the year are common even in its capital, Kathmandu.[94] A country that can be a major exporter of electricity actually imports power from India. The otherwise resource-poor Nepal has rich water reserves and controls the headwaters of, or serves as the corridor for, some rivers that flow into India's Gangetic plains. In fact, virtually all of Nepal's rivers empty into the Ganges basin. The Food and Agriculture Organization actually describes Nepal, with a per capita availability of 7,296 m³ per year, as "one of the Asian countries with the highest level of water resources per inhabitant."[95]

Five important river basins run through Nepal: The Mahakali River basin in the west, which is shared with India, with Indian tributaries contributing a flow of 15 km³ and Nepalese streams 3.4 km³ a year to the river system; the Karnali River basin, with an average outflow estimated at 43.9 km³ a year; the Gandak River basin, whose outflow is estimated at 50.7 km³ a year; the eastern Kosi River basin, which receives a contribution of 12 km³ a year from its Tibet-based upper catchment region to its net outflow of 47.2 km³ per year; and the southern river basins, which produce approximately 65 km³ a year of water flowing into India.[96] The Kosi is a seven-river system drawing waters from the Arun, Sun Kosi, Indravati, Bhola Kosi, Dudh Kosi, Barun, and Tamur rivers. Nepal has several water-sharing accords with India but none with China, which has dammed the Karnali River just before it enters Nepal and has launched work on a cascade of five dams on the upper reaches of the Arun.

Water can be to strategically located Nepal what oil is to some Arab sheikhdoms. The problem is that Nepal has been racked by severe political flux since the early 1990s. Such has been the rapidity of change in Nepal that in less than five years in the twenty-first century, Nepal ousted a feudal monarchy, converted itself from a Hindu kingdom into a secular state, established a new Constituent Assembly, and declared itself a democratic republic—but without ending the fragility of its political situation or domestic turmoil. Whereas the 1990s were a period of political evolution in Nepal, the first decade of this century heralded political revolution. And while the 1990s were characterized by instability, the next decade witnessed continuing political upheaval, with no end in sight. Nepal is clearly in danger of becoming a failed state, a development that will have major trans-Himalayan implications.

The sorry state of affairs in Nepal has seriously hampered its hydropower and irrigation expansion, even though such advance is essential to bring much-needed development and revenues to this landlocked, impoverished country and to help tame the transboundary rivers that often overrun their banks in Nepalese and Indian areas during the monsoons. Bangladesh has actively sought the construction of hydro works in Nepal to augment the Ganges' lean-season flows at Farakka, the critical downriver point where the waters are shared between India and Bangladesh. In fact, the integrated development of the Ganges basin demands a trilateral institutional structure involving multifaceted cooperation between Nepal, India, and Bangladesh, with cooperation extending to energy, transit, and port rights. Although India could make Bangladesh a fellow beneficiary of Himalayan hydropower from Nepal and Bhutan by rerouting some power through its national power grid to northwestern Bangladeshi areas, the fact is that Bangladesh has sufficient natural gas reserves to meet its present electricity needs and also export surplus power to India. Yet Bangladesh has been slow to develop its proven gas reserves.

Underscoring the difficulty in setting up a subcontinental energy network, domestic political pressures and regional geopolitics have both prevented economically sensible ideas from being taken up for implementation. In the case of Nepal, the problems that have held up or slowed hydropower development—apart from recurrent political turbulence—range from Maoist and other opposition to hydropower exports to India, portrayed as a regional hegemon, to environmental and social concerns about the impact of large projects. India, for its part, has not been sensitive to the concerns of small Nepal, where the failure of the Kosi and Gandak river treaties of the 1950s to live up to their promise has left a bad legacy weighing down bilateral cooperation and eroding trust. Consequently, several multipurpose Indo-Nepalese initiatives to tap the resources of rivers like the Karnali and the Sapt-Kosi have not been realized.

One Indo-Nepalese dispute has been over the Mahakali River, which defines Nepal's border with India in the west and is known as the Sarda River in India. Political passions were kindled in Nepal over India's 1998 construction of the Tanakpur Barrage on the Mahakali under the terms of an agreement signed earlier in 1991. In 1996, Nepal and India indeed signed a formal treaty concerning the integrated development of the Mahakali River basin, including building the Tanakpur and Sarada barrages and the Pancheshwar multipurpose project—a treaty hailed by the United Nations Environment Program as providing "India and Nepal with an opportunity for meaningful cooperation to benefit the millions of people in the two countries whose livelihood depends on the waters of the Mahakali River."[97] The treaty, which entitles both countries to utilize the waters of the river on the condition that Nepal's requirements "shall be given prime consideration," spawned the Mahakali River Commission, founded on the principles of equity, mutual benefit, no harm to either side, and dispute resolution through arbitration.[98] A Joint Group of Experts is overseeing the technical aspects of the ambitious Pancheshwar Project, designed to produce 5,600 megawatts of hydropower and irrigate 130,000 hectares of farmland in Nepal and 220,000 hectares in India.

Despite several outstanding issues, Nepal and India have made some progress in institutionalizing expanded bilateral water cooperation. To promote high-level coordination in implementing various agreements and understandings, a Nepal–India Joint Committee on Water Resources, headed by each country's water resources secretary, has been set up as the umbrella mechanism covering all water-related committees and groups. But past setbacks resulting from overambitious goals and ambiguously worded clauses in treaties continue to haunt Indo-Nepalese cooperation. Instead of treating hydropower separately from other transboundary issues, Nepal and India—seeking a holistic approach to sustainable development—actually concluded agreements that bundled together projects related to irrigation, hydropower, navigation, fishing, and forestation. The treaties on the Kosi (1954) and the Gandak (1959) were renegotiated or amended in 1966 and 1964, respectively, but their implementation remained problematic. Even the implementation of the more recent Mahakali treaty has been impeded by different interpretations of its terms. Yet Indian-aided projects during the past half century have helped bring 300,000 hectares of farmland in Nepal under irrigation, besides establishing modest hydropower-generating capacity there.

Nepal needs India, with which it shares multiple river basins, to harness the waters of common rivers for shared benefit. Still, instead of generating hydro dollars to fight its endemic poverty and help undercut the grassroots power of the Maoists, who in 2006 ended a guerrilla war and formed a political party, Nepal remains an energy importer from India. Indeed, as a water-rich country racked by underdevelopment, poverty, poor governance, and lawlessness, Nepal exemplifies what some development economists call "a resource curse." But whereas countries afflicted by the resource curse normally find it difficult to break out of slow rates of economic growth and high levels of income inequality, despite relying on major exports of natural resources, Nepal's curse has come without exploiting its resource reserves, let alone making exports.

The one country in South Asia that has used water to power its success story is Bhutan, known for its virgin forests, freshwater streams, and snow-capped mountains. This tiny, 47,000-square-kilometer Himalayan kingdom serves as an example of how a cooperative, forward-looking approach on water issues can yield rich economic dividends. Although Nepal has persisted with its political foot-dragging on joint projects with India on common rivers, Bhutan—one of the world's newest democracies—has the distinction of achieving the highest per capita income in South Asia by exploiting its hydropower reserves through environmentally sound projects, mostly small in scale and based on the run-of-the-river technology employing a stream's natural flow and elevation drop to produce electricity without the aid of a large reservoir and dam.

Bhutan has been earning substantial foreign exchange revenues by exporting electricity to India—the country that actually subsidized the environmentally friendly hydropower development by providing 60 percent of the investment in each project as a grant and the remaining amount as a loan. Bhutan, known as the "Land of the Thunder Dragon," has been guided by a vision to achieve what it calls "gross national happiness"—a measure of the state's success to preserve its environment and culture and pursue sustainable development.[99]

Bhutan is exceptionally endowed with freshwater resources, with the Food and Agriculture Organization estimating its per capita availability of renewable water resources at 113,537 m^3 per year—one of the highest in the world that puts it in the same category as Canada, Iceland, Gabon, and Suriname.[100] Bhutan's rivers, other than one small river that leads into Tibet, drain into the Brahmaputra basin in India, with the Bhutanese watercourses generally located in a north–south axis. Bhutan's dependency ratio on cross-border water flows, like Kyrgyzstan's, is virtually zero because all its rivers originate within its borders, except one—the Torsa River, which enters from India but whose inflow is negligible. The rivers originating in Bhutan, however, have caused recurrent floods in downstream areas in India, leading to land erosion in the Himalayan foothills and adjoining plains. To combat floods, the two countries set up a Joint Group of Experts in 2004. In addition, an Indian-funded network of thirty-five hydrometeorological stations has been built in Bhutan to provide flood warnings.

While seeking "the middle path" that blends preservation of its cultural and natural heritage with economic modernization, Bhutan has sought to boost its national income by exploiting its main resource. Its hydropower reserves are estimated at about 20,000 megawatts, half of which it plans to develop by 2020.[101] In 2003 King Jigme Singye Wangchuck, who later abdicated in favor of his Oxford-educated son, publicly explained his policy to integrate the Bhutanese economy with India through hydropower development by saying: "Water is to us what oil is to the Arabs."[102]

The doors to major Indo-Bhutanese hydropower cooperation actually were opened earlier by the 336-megawatt Chukha Project, funded and built by India on a turnkey basis in 1988. Chukha became the symbol of successful cooperation, providing electricity to India to develop remote areas in its northeast and yielding handsome returns for Bhutan. This $200-million project paved the way for other Indian-financed, run-of-the-river projects, including Kurichu, Basochu, and Tala (which, at 1,020 megawatts, was the biggest). Then came a slighter larger project to generate 1,095 megawatts of power from the waters of River Puna Tsang Chu, a run-of-the-river project again, to be followed by a 600-megawatt project on the Amo Chu River.

The exporting of hydropower has become the largest source of revenue for Bhutan, which also enjoys a comfortable trade surplus with India. Prospects for a subcontinental energy network, however, look as bleak as ever.

Water, the Latest Pakistan–India Battle Line

A wholly different set of issues has emerged as a challenge in the Indus River basin. In contrast to China's refusal to negotiate a water-sharing pact with any neighbor or join an interstate river commission, India is locked since 1960 in a treaty relationship with Pakistan—a treaty of indefinite duration incorporating exceptionally munificent concessions by the upper riparian. Despite its much-larger population and economy and thus far greater water needs, India's share of the total Indus system waters is barely one-fifth under the treaty, with Pakistan getting the rest. In the treaty, India also accepted severe limitations on its freedom of action vis-à-vis the so-called western rivers set aside for Pakistan—the Chenab, the Jhelum, and the main Indus stream. The first two rivers come from the Indian Himalayas, whereas the third originates in Tibet but collects its largest portion of waters in India. Today, while there are significant water shortages in Pakistan, the lopsided sharing formula has led to a 52 percent deficit between water supply and demand in India's Indus basin.[103]

The treaty, despite setting new international legal standards on interstate water relations, failed to turn water into a source of cooperation. Although the treaty is tilted in its favor, it is downstream Pakistan that has sought to keep water as a bone of contention in an already-fraught relationship with India. In reality, the Pakistan–India water wrangling is just regional politics by another name.

When relations between two neighbors are strained and tense, even an issue settled by treaty can continue to rear its ugly head. So it is of little surprise that new water disputes between Pakistan and India have continued to flare, even as old ones have been resolved or allowed to simmer on the back burner. The important difference is that water claims now take precedence over land claims. Decades after the Indus Treaty was signed and ratified, water has returned with a vengeance to bedevil India–Pakistan relations. The real issues related to water, however, are tied to the very direction of the bilateral relationship. That direction, in turn, is linked with the problem of terrorism, which has repeatedly threatened to trigger another full-fledged military conflict on the subcontinent.

Furthermore, the Indus Treaty's partitioning of rivers has proven an insurmountable barrier to the adoption of integrated basin management regionally. The need for integrated management is being underscored both by the water stress arising from population and development pressures in both countries and by climate change, which threatens to diminish basin resources. With accelerated glacier thaw and snowmelt pointing to the early effects of climate change, the sustainable optimization of the Indus water resources is becoming necessary as a hedge against increased water scarcity and hydrological uncertainties in the years ahead. However, because the treaty pivots on the partitioning of rivers and the terms to govern such an imperial-style division to complete the 1947 territorial Partition of the subcontinent, the pact leaves little room for undertaking joint projects or promoting genuine basin cooperation between its two parties.[104]

The treaty does provide both for modification of its terms and for its replacement "by a duly ratified treaty concluded for that purpose between the two governments."[105] The only time, however, either side has come close to seeking the modification, replacement, or suspension of the treaty was in the aftermath of the December 2001 terrorist attack on the Indian Parliament by five Pakistani gunmen. India responded to the daring terrorist attack—aimed at eliminating the country's elected leadership—by freezing relations with Pakistan and mobilizing its forces at land and sea for possible war. In that tense situation, which lasted until the early fall of 2002, India stopped supplying flood-related data to Pakistan and delayed holding a meeting of the Permanent Indus Commission.[106] The commission, however, has met more than a hundred times since it was established under the terms of the treaty, although it does little more than run regular consultative meetings between its two commissioners, each of whom acts on behalf of his country.

If an inherently unequal water treaty is to remain the framework for enduring cooperation in the future, the direction of the Pakistan–India relationship needs to change toward closer political cooperation and regional integration in the areas of trade, investment, communication, transportation, and energy. Such a change cannot occur unless Pakistan is able to set right its abnormally skewed civil–military relations. The military remains the country's most powerful institution, and it is loath to cede powers that it has long accumulated or to give up employing terrorism as an instrument of policy. The scourge of Pakistani terrorism emanates not so much from the Islamist mullahs as from generals who reared the forces of jihad and fathered the Taliban and al-Qaeda–linked groups such as the Lashkar-e-Taiba, a mission-oriented organization that "has emerged as potentially the most dangerous terrorist outfit on the planet."[107] Yet by passing the blame for their disastrous jihad policy to their mullah puppets, the generals have made many outsiders believe that the key is to contain the religious fringe, not the puppeteers. As one British analyst has put it, "Progressively stronger after each of its coups, the army inflates its role as 'guardian of the nation' to enrich itself and to overstate the threat from

India."[108] Given the military's vested interest in perpetuating hostilities with India, Pakistan has never been at peace with India.

The last Indo-Pakistan military conflict may have been in 1999, but even in peacetime the Pakistani military and its Inter-Services Intelligence (ISI) agency have continued to send armed terrorists into India. The military, in alliance with Islamists, has at the same time used the water issue to win popular support at home for its revanchist approach on Kashmir. Although Pakistan's objective in the formal wars was to capture the Indian-controlled part of Kashmir, the aim of its hardline forces now is broader: to unravel the Indian Republic. Ever since Pakistani dictator General Zia ul-Haq fashioned the instrument of proxy war against India in the 1980s by taking a page out of the covert war sponsored by the US Central Intelligence Agency against the Soviet military intervention in Afghanistan, the Pakistani military has been at regular war with the Indian state, orchestrating terror attacks. In fact, Pakistan has used the same term for the marauders and other gunmen it dispatched across the border to initiate wars in 1947–48, 1965, and 1999 and to carry out terror attacks since the 1980s—"freedom fighters." It is India whose label for them has changed over the decades, from raiders to infiltrators to now terrorists.

Pakistan cannot continue to bleed India by waging what responsible Pakistanis have called "a war of a thousand cuts" and yet expect India to lastingly maintain its bigheartedness on the Indus water allocations. Between Pakistan and India, as the United States has acknowledged, the "principal problem is that of terrorism."[109] Acts of terror scripted by the Pakistani army and ISI in India just in the twenty-first century—from the attacks on the Indian Parliament and Red Fort to the killing of hapless civilians in Mumbai, New Delhi, and other cities—remain a bleeding shame, scarring the bilateral relationship. Even as its military establishment continues to export terror to India, Pakistan expects eternal Indian munificence on water. But the same question must haunt Pakistan's real decision makers as it did Lady Macbeth in William Shakespeare's *Macbeth*: "Will all great Neptune's ocean wash this blood clean from my hand?" India has not sought to draw a link between water and terror. But it is apparent that a Pakistan with blood of innocent Indians on its hands cannot reasonably ask India for indefinite liberality on water supplies.

A new problem also has arisen in relation to the working of the Indus Treaty, contributing in recent years to what Pakistan labels disagreements or disputes so that it can seek international intercession by invoking the pact's conflict settlement provisions. Pakistan wants no Indian works on the western rivers, although the treaty permits India—within clearly specified constraints—to tap some of their water resources for local irrigation, hydropower generation, household, and non-consumptive uses.[110] Pakistan's efforts to deny India the treaty-sanctioned limited uses of the western rivers by raising objections virtually to every Indian project and thereby seeking to stall its construction do not augur well for the existing water arrangements' future. Pakistan's spat with India over the Baglihar run-of-the-river hydropower project, for example, ended up raising the project's costs, even though the World Bank–appointed neutral expert ultimately ruled in India's favor.[111]

Such efforts to reinterpret the treaty's terms more narrowly can only encourage India to seek a renegotiation of the pact or a new treaty in which the present "block" approach of reserving the largest three rivers for Pakistan gives way to a more evenhanded Indo-Pakistan water sharing. There is also another risk that rarely figures in the public discourse on the subcontinent: Just because the treaty is of indefinite period is no guarantee of its durability. Under Article 62 of the Vienna Convention on the Law of Treaties, a party can terminate its obligations or formally withdraw from a treaty—including one of unlimited duration—by invoking a "fundamental change of circumstances" as having both significantly altered the balance of obligations and undermined the essential basis of its original consent to the international agreement. In taking such an extreme step, the party concerned may also suspend, without further ado, the operation of the treaty.[112]

The risks that the present water arrangements may be destabilized have actually been highlighted by strident public calls in Pakistan to renegotiate the Indus Treaty, as if its current charitable terms for Islamabad can be replicated in a new pact, especially an 80 percent share of the river waters. Such calls, along with an official jeremiad against Indian policy, only egg on India to seize a welcome opportunity to try and level the playing field through a new, more equitable treaty. A process of renegotiation, however, is likely to open the path to unraveling the treaty without any hope of securing a replacement pact.

The present treaty has long been unpopular in the Indian state of Jammu and Kashmir, where it is widely viewed as denying the local economy both the water resources needed for rapid agricultural and industrial growth as well as the revenues that would accrue from such development. The three western rivers parceled out to Pakistan are the main streams of India's Jammu and Kashmir, which the treaty effectively restrains from fully exploiting the only natural resource it has— water. So it is of little surprise that the Jammu and Kashmir State legislature went to the extent of passing a bipartisan resolution in 2002 calling for a review and annulment of the Indus Treaty.[113]

Pakistan's efforts to deny the limited benefits the treaty grants India's Jammu and Kashmir by objecting and seeking to stall projects on the key rivers flowing through that northernmost state actually mesh with the Pakistani military's strategy to foment continuing discontent and violence there. In fact, Jammu and Kashmir, despite suffering from frequent electricity outages, has been able to tap barely 15 percent of its hydropower reserves and to irrigate only a small portion of its arable land, compared to the expansive irrigation covering virtually the whole of Pakistan's Punjab Province.[114] The treaty-imposed resource fetters have contributed to the underdevelopment and unrest in that Indian state. India's Punjab State—from where the surplus waters of the eastern rivers reserved for India flow into Pakistan—has been no less opposed to the Indus treaty than Jammu and Kashmir (map 6.9).

MAP 6.9   Rivers Flowing from India to Pakistan

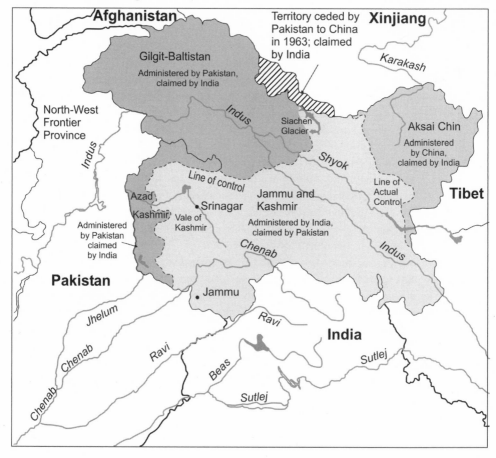

The weight behind the treaty has been put by successive federal governments in India from the time of Prime Minister Jawaharlal Nehru, with foreign policy interests trumping local concerns and demands. In fact, despite the tremendous leverage it has always held vis-à-vis Pakistan as the upper riparian on the Indus system, including a potential capacity to channel waters from the western rivers to the eastern rivers through some abandoned, colonial-era canals, India has never tried to fashion water into a political instrument. Pakistan was exceptionally vulnerable in the period up to the 1960s to India's ability to punitively cut off or withhold water supplies, given that the Partition left the headwaters of the main irrigation canals feeding the newborn country in India. Such was India's leverage then that David Lilienthal, the ex-chairman of the Tennessee Valley Authority in the United States who helped broker the start of Indus-treaty negotiations, wrote:

"No army, with bombs and shellfire, could devastate a land so thoroughly as Pakistan could be devastated by the simple expedient of India's permanently shutting off the sources of water that keep the fields and people of Pakistan alive."[115] Yet India did not use that leverage even when Pakistan waged war and occupied more than one-third of the state of Jammu and Kashmir in the years 1947–48.

Today, in the face of growing water shortages and uncertainties about how climate change will affect future availability, Pakistan has legitimate concerns about the latent control a bigger, stronger India holds over this critical resource supply. After all, unlike in India's case, a single river system serves as Pakistan's lifeline. In recent years, however, false and wild propaganda in Pakistan has accused India of all sorts of alleged transgressions—from building scores of secret dams on the western rivers, according to former ISI chief Lieutenant General Hameed Gul and militant leader Hafiz Mohammad Saeed, to quietly stealing waters from those rivers through secret tunnels.[116] As one American newspaper reported, "Anti-India nationalists and militant networks in Pakistan, already dangerously potent, have seized on the issue as a new source of rage to perpetuate 60 years of antagonism."[117]

When monsoonal floods devastated large parts of Pakistan in the summer of 2010, a rash of Pakistani media reports accused the United States of modifying weather patterns and India of manipulating river flows, prompting US State Department spokesperson P. J. Crowley to ask: "So, it was the United States and India that conspired to have the monsoons come to Pakistan? I don't find that credible." Flogging fabrications has proven so useful in shaping perceptions in a country with a penchant for conspiracies that the line between fact and fiction has blurred in the public debate in Pakistan.

To Pakistan's chagrin, the blurring of lines came out loud and clear in the Baglihar dispute when the Swiss neutral expert, appointed as the adjudicator by the World Bank with both sides' consent, demolished most Pakistani claims on the 450-megawatt project, which had been presented to the Pakistani public as asymmetrically arming India with the capability to unleash transboundary flooding, even though its weir, or low dam, is located nearly 120 kilometers upstream from the Pakistani border and any such Indian action would wreak havoc largely on the Indian side.[118] The neutral expert's final report in February 2007 gave the go-ahead to India to complete the project with marginal design changes.

The Baglihar setback, however, did not deter Pakistan from filing a case with the International Court of Arbitration in 2010 to halt India's construction of the smaller, 330-megawatt Kishenganga hydropower plant, which had been on the drawing board for decades. It sought arbitration after having initiated work on its own three-times-larger hydropower plant at a nearby border site on the same stream, putting the Chinese-aided, $2.16 billion project on a fast track to apparently gain priority right on river-water use under the doctrine of prior appropriation.

India, seeking to allay popular resentment in the state of Jammu and Kashmir over major power shortages that hamper development, has tardily embarked on a number of other hydropower projects of modest size there—all run-of-the-river plants permitted under the Indus Treaty. Such plants, in contrast to storage-type plants that depend on the impounding of large amounts of water, generate power by harnessing the forces of water flow and gravity at the point where a river has a natural drop. To produce electricity, the water is allowed to flow through low head turbines housed in a weir, with the outflow virtually the same as inflow and the water returning directly to the river without any change in the flow or water levels. As a sort of holding pond, the small dam helps moderate fluctuations in water flow. It is because such environmentally considerate plants cannot materially alter cross-border flows that the Indus Treaty permits India to build them on the western rivers.

In fact, through an elaborate series of curbs on India spelled out in its detailed annexes, the treaty precludes any Indian control over the timing or quantum of transboundary flows, including by strictly restricting the initial filling of the weir of a new run-of-the-river plant to the midmonsoon season when there is a surfeit of river waters.[119] Although the treaty permits the building of only very small permanent storage capacity of up to 4.4 billion m^3 by the upper riparian on the western rivers, India has not utilized even that limited right, building no storage—a fact hard-line forces in Pakistan usually forget.[120] Yet popular myths in Pakistan sometimes get picked up internationally; one author, for example, claimed in the *New York Times* that "untimely dam-filling by India during planting season could destroy Pakistan's harvest."[121] A 2011 majority staff report prepared for the US Senate Foreign Relations Committee also fell prey to propaganda by claiming that while no single Indian dam "will affect Pakistan's access to water, the cumulative effect of these projects could give India the ability to store enough water to limit the supply to Pakistan at crucial moments in the growing season."[122] More worrisome is the manner in which erroneous beliefs, false propaganda, and apprehensions are reinforcing the trust deficit between Pakistan and India, which is leading to what one journal has described as saber rattling over water security.[123] The distrust and antagonism is chipping away the foundation of the treaty.

If the present water-sharing arrangements were to be scrapped, suspended, or renegotiated, Pakistan has much to lose. After all, as Fred Pearce has noted, the Indus system rivers from India irrigate "an area of Pakistani desert larger than England—the largest irrigated area on the planet. Those works have increased Pakistan's economic dependence on the Indus."[124] According to the Pakistani government, the Indus basin irrigates 80 percent of the country's 21.5 million hectares of farmland through an extensive network of dams, barrages, and canals. In this light, cooperation, not confrontation, should be the leitmotif of Pakistan's relations with India. In fact, Pakistan and India need to go beyond the present Indus arrangements by undertaking bold initiatives to help optimize basin resources, exchange trusted stream-flow data, and explore climate change adaptation and mitigation measures related to water.

The India–Pakistan aim should be the satisfactory and sustainable utilization of the waters of the Indus system—in a spirit of accommodation, goodwill, and friendship—by embracing the best technological and environmental practices. The treaty, unfortunately, is more a hindrance than a help to forward thinking. Through its terms designed to underpin the "block" partitioning of rivers, the pact treats the two parties as antagonists, not partners. The treaty's entire emphasis is on defining the terms and conditions of the division of rivers, not on encouraging its parties to jointly and holistically manage basin resources. That is further underlined by its perfunctory Article VII: Although ostentatiously titled, "Future Cooperation," the article is pretty hollow.

The treaty's structure is not the only obstacle, however. Bold new moves cannot be compatible with competing visions, clashing worldviews, and conflicting goals of the two co-riparian states, especially if they imply that Pakistan and India may be locked in mortal combat. The nub of the problem is that the Pakistani military establishment sees a Balkanized India as offering Pakistan the only escape from its mounting domestic woes, including rising extremism and an unsustainably high level of military spending. But because the generals cannot militarily dismember India, they have sought to bleed it by employing the instrument of terrorism. This strategy pits an irredentist and scofflaw Pakistan against a status quo and reactive India. For Pakistan, though, the chickens have come home to roost: Some of the very extremists its army and ISI have reared now pose a mortal threat to the country itself. Yet the Pakistani military and spy agency still value terror groups as proxy forces vis-à-vis India and Afghanistan.

Real basin cooperation on sustainably optimizing water resources is thus more likely to emerge if democracy takes firm roots in Pakistan and civilian oversight is instituted over the army and the ISI. Pakistan's descent into a jihadist dungeon, tellingly, occurred not under civilian rule but under military rule: While one military dictator, Zia ul-Haq, let loose the jihadists he reared, another ruler, General Pervez Musharraf, pushed Pakistan to the very edge of the precipice. Before Musharraf's nearly nine-year rule, few in the world looked at Pakistan as a failing state. How can Pakistan become a "normal" state if its military and intelligence remain outside civilian oversight, with the decisive power still with the generals? If such an aberrant setting persists, the jihadist-infiltrated army and the ISI will continue to do what they have done for long—nurture militant groups—to the detriment of regional and international security. Existing weapons of mass destruction in a country teeming with jihadists are a matter of deep global concern; an expanding Pakistani nuclear arsenal makes the scenario nightmarish. Winning the fight against international terrorism demands a stable, moderate, deradicalized Pakistan. That, in turn, calls for sustained international political investment in building and strengthening civilian institutions there. Civil empowerment is essential to break the military's control on policy and thought processes and tame the rogue ISI agency.

A true democratization of Pakistan, whereby all institutions would become accountable to an elected government, would help create political symmetry with India and allow a strong civil society on either side of the subcontinental divide to act as a catalyst for closer bilateral cooperation. Innovative water-related mechanisms to promote the integrated, basinwide management of resources would then become more likely. In this context, it cannot be overlooked that the stronger India–Bangladesh cooperation since 2009, especially on transboundary river waters, electricity exports, and transit and port rights, has followed progress in restoring Bangladesh's secular, democratic character.

Given this background, India needs to realistically and creatively manage its Pakistan problem because it is unlikely to go away until the military's role in Pakistani affairs is rebalanced. An Indian response must deal with the institution that is at the root of the problem, without affecting the interests of the larger Pakistani public. Institutionalized basinwide cooperation is becoming necessary to deal with the human-induced degradation of water resources and the early effects of global warming on the Indus system, which is very susceptible to shifts in melt characteristics driven by climate change because the meltwater share of its total discharge is the highest of any major Asian river. Pakistan's extensive irrigation system is regulated by huge storage dams on rivers fed mainly by transboundary Himalayan meltwater. One study, while warning that "change in upstream water supply to these dams will have a profound effect on millions of people downstream," has predicted a consistent and considerable reduction in summer and late-spring river discharges by midcentury, although its results showed a substantial variation in such potential shifts.[125]

In a step-by-step approach, India and Pakistan can seek to develop integrated Indus basin management first at the subbasin, or watershed, level. One way would be to start with the most vulnerable rivers whose flows are highly dependent on the melting of ice and snow—the Chenab and the Jhelum, which also have the largest discharges in terms of per unit of catchment area.[126] Better data sharing is necessary to initiate such closer cooperation and allay suspicions or misgivings.

To help strengthen institutional mechanisms, the two-member Permanent Indus Commission ought to be reformed and expanded to include some of the productive features of the Canada-US International Joint Commission (IJC). The IJC has established twenty specialized boards and appointed a number of task forces over the years—comprising some of the leading experts on both sides of the border—to help it carry out its wide responsibilities. The IJC, with three commissioners from each country, operates as a truly international body, despite its two separate sections, in Ottawa and Washington. Decisions demand only a majority vote, but the commissioners rarely vote along national lines.[127] In fact most decisions have been unanimous. By contrast each of the two Indus commissioners constituting the full commission membership acts as his country's representative, even though all decisions require unanimity.

In helping draft the Indus Treaty, the World Bank had carefully studied the US–Canadian arrangement on transboundary water resources. But few provisions were replicated in the Indus Treaty because the North American arrangement centers not on the partition principle but on the joint, integrated management of the entire range of transboundary water resources. So, whereas the Canadian–US commission has wide jurisdiction and even quasi-judicial powers, the Indus commission's mission and functions were narrowly defined on purpose, and were mainly restricted to the negotiation of arrangements for the technical implementation of the terms of the Indus Treaty itself.[128]

To be sure, the drafters of the Indus Treaty did seek to arm the Indus commission with the investigatory authority that the Canadian–US commission has to conduct joint studies and reports. The Indus commission can "study and report to the two governments on any problem relating to the development of the waters of the rivers which may be jointly referred to the commission by the two governments."[129] But that provision remains unexplored because no such joint reference has ever been made. The Indus commission now merely serves as the main bilateral channel for water-related data exchanges and communication.

The US–Canadian commission no doubt is far from perfect; it lacks sufficient supranational powers, for example, to implement the ecosystem approach mandated by a 1987 bilateral protocol, which amended and expanded a 1978 agreement between the two neighbors.[130] The ecosystem approach recognizes that every part of the ecosystem—the air and land, the lakes, rivers, plant life, wildlife, and humans—depends on the other parts for its own health. For more than a century, the commission, however, has successfully managed the world's largest water resources governed by a bilateral mechanism, with the Great Lakes–Saint Lawrence system alone containing some one-fifth of the global surface freshwater. The commission has reportedly helped reconcile or forestall more than 130 disputes.[131]

Also consider another example: the Mexico-US International Boundary and Water Commission (IBWC). The 1944 bilateral water treaty that established the IBWC settled the overall apportionment of river waters between Mexico and the United States, leaving the commission to focus on other priority areas—the administration of irrigation and hydropower functions, flood-control and channel-control activities, seasonal water adjustments, and future river-development plans.[132] The Indus commission, by contrast, has remained stuck with the technical issues arising out of the division of river waters under the 1960 treaty. The IBWC, of course, is not in the same league as the US–Canadian commission, which has evolved into a true water council.[133]

One positive feature of the Indus commission, however, is the transparency its mandate encourages. In addition to the general tour of the Indus rivers the commission undertakes once every five years to learn more about various developments and national projects, each commissioner has the right to ask for "a tour of inspection of such works and sites on the rivers as may be considered necessary by him for ascertaining the facts connected with those works or sites." And the relevant government is obligated to "promptly" accede to such a request for inspection, allowing the commissioner to make the tour with two of his chosen advisers or assistants.[134] The treaty also obligates India to supply Pakistan six months in advance the design specifications of any works to be undertaken on the western rivers.

The transparency that the Indus Treaty promotes could serve as the underpinnings for joint cooperation through initiatives intended to surmount the dividing wall that the same pact has helped erect on the common rivers. However, building integrated water-resources cooperation on the basis of a treaty that essentially puts up dividers is no easy task. The treaty's Article VII, despite its title, "Future Cooperation," lists only modest steps, such as the two parties possibly setting up new hydrological and meteorological observation stations, carrying out drainage works, or cooperating on unspecified engineering works. The article does record initially that "the two parties recognize that they have a common interest in the optimum development of the rivers, and to that end, they declare their intention to cooperate, by mutual agreement, to the fullest possible extent."[135]

But after that introductory declaration, Article VII identifies no joint project for future cooperation and actually uses the terms "each party" or "either party" repeatedly, without once referring to "both parties." Article VII(2) indeed undercuts the token reference in the previous subclause to "a common interest in the optimum development of the rivers" by returning to the treaty's central treatment of the parties as rivals, not partners, whose competition must be moderated in every respect. It thus stipulates that if "either party plans to construct any engineering work which could cause interference with the waters of any of the rivers and which, in its opinion, would affect the other party materially, it shall notify the other party of its plans and shall supply such data relating to the work as may be available and as would enable the other party to inform itself of the nature, magnitude, and effect of the work." That otherwise prudent proviso, repeating the no-material-damage-to-the-other-party stipulation found earlier in the treaty, sits ill in a section supposedly on future cooperation.

So there is nothing in the Indus Treaty that promotes specific future cooperation or joint projects in a basin where one of the world's earliest and largest irrigation systems was developed about 4,600 years ago. If anything, joint projects are hindered by the stringent, India-specific restrictions in relation to the western rivers on the building of storages, and the limitations on pondage (the water held back in a weir to regulate the natural flow) and other uses, as a natural corollary to the treaty's partitioning of the rivers. The treaty, in effect, has left it to the two countries to devise future cooperation in pursuit of what they may come to perceive as their "common interest."

In this light, if the existing water-sharing arrangements are to rise above the treaty-built dividing wall so as to initiate joint efforts at integrated basin management, Pakistan and India will need to make a new beginning in their relationship. Realistically, this can only happen through revamped bilateral ties and better geopolitics in the region. Such developments hold the key to improving the management of India–Pakistan water issues.

Seven

Asia's Challenge

Forestalling Bloodletting over Water

At a time when Asia is in political transition, with the specter of power disequilibrium looming large, it has become imperative for Asian nations to invest in institutionalized cooperation on transnational basin resources to help underpin strategic stability and ensure that the struggle for water does not become a tipping point for war—a danger underlined by the fact that the current supplies, which already are insufficient for present needs, will not be able to meet future requirements. The water challenges in Asia surpass those in Africa, Australia, South America, and the Caribbean Islands combined. To boost current supplies, a new strategic approach is needed that centers on water conservation and recycling, efficiency and productivity gains, and, more broadly, integrated resource management that involves all basin states. Only collaborative paths that embrace all stakeholders and break free from the business-as-usual approach can help unlock solutions.

The new battle lines being drawn in Asia over transboundary water resources highlight the risks of greater interstate water conflict. At the same time, water distress is accentuating internal security challenges and, in some weak or dysfunctional states, even inciting ethnic bloodletting or fueling separatist insurgencies. Long-standing interstate tensions and internal instabilities, coupled with soaring water demand in an era of environmental degradation, have made a number of the fifty-seven transnational basins in Asia potential flashpoints for serious water conflicts. Interstate water institutions help moderate the risk of disputes flaring into overt confrontation or armed conflict, yet the vast majority of the internationally shared basins in Asia lack legally binding arrangements for water sharing and institutionalized cooperation.

Even so, a fast-rising Asia has become the defining fulcrum of global geopolitical change. The Asian juggernaut, after all, is a key instigator of the ongoing global shifts in power, which are tectonic in nature and will profoundly affect international relations. Yet Asia will also bear the greatest burden of such shifts. Asian policies and challenges now help shape the international security and economic environments. With the speed and scale of its economic rise having no parallel in world history, a resurgent Asia holds the key to the future global order.

Asia's growing importance in world affairs is being underlined by three developments. The first is the eastward movement of power and influence, once concentrated in the West. The second is the waning relevance of the international institutions that the United States helped establish after its World War II triumph and the ensuing need for far-reaching institutional reforms or even new institutions and rules. And the third is Asia's own rise as the world's main creditor and economic locomotive. Nonetheless, major power shifts within Asia itself—coupled with unresolved interstate issues out there and the territorial and resource-related assertiveness of some players—are challenging the continent's own peace and stability.

Despite its remarkable reemergence on the world stage after a relatively short period of decline in the broad span of history, Asia faces major challenges in a period of greater globalization. It must cope with fierce competition over scarce resources, especially water and energy; entrenched territorial and maritime disputes; harmful historical legacies that weigh down all important interstate relationships; the growing military capabilities of important Asian actors; increasingly fervent nationalism; and the rise of social and political extremism. Diverse transborder trends—from terrorism and insurgencies to illicit refugee flows and human trafficking—add to its challenges. Some of the challenges Asia confronts actually are unique because they center on issues that are new—from dwindling natural resources to accelerated global warming. Water is at the core of such unconventional challenges.

Asia, to be sure, is becoming more interdependent through trade and investment, money and finance, and technology and tourism. Since the 1997–98 currency crisis, Asian cooperation has grown on monetary policy and financial system stability, and free trade agreements have proliferated. But even as Asia is becoming more interdependent economically, it is also becoming more politically divided, with its principal powers at loggerheads over how to build a cooperative Asian community and institutionalize security arrangements. The rise of new Asian powers, for its part, has changed the structure of regional geopolitics.

The qualitative reordering of power under way in Asia, in fact, is beginning to challenge strategic stability and disturb power equations there. Conflict is not built into the rise of any new power. The United States, for example, rose as a great power without triggering conflict with the then-leading powers. Nor is conflict inherent in a rising nation's attempt to alter the international order so as to gain a greater say in various matters. A rising power usually is a revisionist power, even if a discreet one. The risks of conflict, however, grow when a new regional hegemon accepts norms and rules selectively and secures unfair advantage in trade, resource, security, currency, intellectual property, investment, and other issues—gains that it seeks to assertively protect or enlarge. Today, the scramble for power in Asia has unleashed potentially destabilizing forces. The resurfacing of territorial and maritime disputes is one warning sign; the increasingly fierce water and energy competition is another. Even as Asia has become the pivot of global geopolitical change, Asian power dynamics and security and resource dilemmas now play into international strategic challenges.

When Asia is compared with Europe, the political dissimilarities are striking. At least five distinctions stand out. First, whereas Europe has achieved equilibrium between its main powers, Asia is far from evolving any sort of equilibrium among its important players. The present situation in Asia, in fact, is characterized by an emerging power imbalance. Second, in Europe, the largest state and economy—Germany—does not aspire to dominance over the continent. Rather, with respect to the other European powers, Germany has learned (and accepted) to be one among equals. In Asia, the situation is the reverse. China does not hide its ambition to gain Asian preeminence. Indeed, there can be no denying that the leading Asian powers and the United States have different playbooks: Important Asian players like Japan, India, Indonesia, South Korea, and Vietnam desire a multipolar Asia and multipolar world; the United States wants a multipolar Asia, while it aims to stay the world's sole superpower in spite of the erosion in its relative economic power; and an increasingly powerful China seeks a multipolar world but a unipolar Asia. China, however, is unwittingly reinforcing America's role as the implicit guarantor of Asian security, as the overly assertive policies and actions of their next-door rising power make Asian states look to a distant protector.

Third, with the exception of Japan, South Korea, and Singapore, the other Asian economies are at earlier stages of development, as reflected in their relative per capita income levels. That is why most of them are still classified as developing or emerging economies. Fourth, most Asian nations are distinguished by wide and growing income disparities and social inequalities, along with environmental degradation. And fifth, though the community in Europe was built among democracies, the political systems in Asia are so varied—and some are even so opaque—that building intercountry trust and institutionalized political cooperation remains a daunting task. Only a small number of Asian states are really democratic. Indeed, Asia serves as a striking testament that the global spread of democracy is encountering increasingly strong headwinds, despite the popular uprisings that engulfed much of the Arab world in 2011.

The Western strategy to use market forces to open up tightly centralized political systems is not working, as illustrated by the number of one-party states in Asia. The challenge to the international spread of democratic values actually is coming from a fusion of autocratic politics and crony, state-steered capitalism that bears a distinct Asian imprint. This "model"—authoritarian capitalism—is, to varying degrees, entrenched in Asian countries as different as Malaysia, Kazakhstan, Singapore, and China. And of course China in particular, through its remarkable economic success story and fast-accumulating military power—it is in fact now the world's largest and oldest autocracy—has come to symbolize the case that authoritarianism is a more rapid and smoother way to achieve prosperity and domestic order than the tumult of electoral politics. Freedom advocates in existing autocracies may be inspired by the cases of successful democratic transition in some parts of the world. But the regimes in the world that employ brute power and tight censorship draw encouragement from the single-party Asian model. Asia thus serves as an unequivocal reminder that in countries where authoritarianism has acquired deep roots, a marketplace of goods and services can stymie the development of a political marketplace of open ideas.

This raises the question of whether, far from being liberal or rules-based, the new international order will be influenced by authoritarian powers and be centered on the classical balance-of-power strategies of its major players. And this, in turn, begs another question: Is Asia going to crimp its ability to shape the new global order by remaining an arena of old-style geopolitics? Or will the prospects of shared prosperity and stability propel Asian states to pursue growing institutionalized cooperation on the basis of shared interests? In past history, the competition for a balance of power centered on Europe. Even the Cold War was not really an East/West rivalry but a competition between two blocs over Europe. For the first time, with the world at a defining moment in its history, developing a stable and durable balance of power in Asia has become critical to international peace and security. The global power equilibrium, in fact, will be greatly influenced by developments in Asia, whose significance in international relations, in some respects, is beginning to rival that of Europe in the eighteenth and nineteenth centuries.

Yet the geopolitical risks of greater tensions, brinkmanship, and strained relationships are increasing in Asia. Present trends suggest that Asia's power dynamics are likely to remain fluid, as new or shifting alliances, strengthened military capabilities, and sharpening resource competition continue to challenge strategic stability. This has only reinforced the need to find new ways to stabilize important interstate relationships and promote cooperative Asian approaches to help tackle festering security, resource, territorial, and history issues. If Asian nations choose collaborative approaches, Asia certainly will be able to preserve peace, stability, and continued rapid economic growth, besides helping to reform global institutions in such a way that it gains a much greater say in international political, financial, and security matters.

ASIA'S TEST ON THE FRESHWATER FRONT

Against this background, water has emerged as a test case of Asia's ability to build cooperation, not competition, over a critical resource. The mounting water stress indeed is a key security challenge for Asia, where the combination of the world's fastest economic growth and the largest concentration of population is fueling spiraling demand for water and energy. Asia's economic renaissance has only whetted intercountry rivalries on matters ranging from resource acquisition to geopolitical influence. Environmentally unsustainable national developmental policies, coupled with the pursuit of narrow geopolitical objectives, have intensified interstate competition over shared basin resources. Such policies and practices represent a danger to regional and environmental security and to long-term hydrological stability. The exacerbation of resource competition due to economic and social pressures at home, interstate territorial and maritime disputes, and sharpening geopolitics threatens to engender conflict and stall Asia's continued rapid growth.

Given that the competition for water resources already is becoming intense in Asia, the question is: What factors can escalate this competition to overt conflict? Open conflict will surface only when an idea is translated into action to benefit one country at the expense of a riparian neighbor. But for any serious conflict to arise, the transboundary effects will need to tangibly hurt the lower-riparian state. The lower-riparian state also must have the capability to respond to any action damaging to its interests. But if the power situation is heavily tilted in favor of the upper riparian, the affected downriver country will be able to do little more than try to use the tools of diplomacy to protest. International law, after all, remains weak on concrete remedies for internationally wrongful acts—including cessation of unjust actions, restitution, guarantees of nonrepetition, and reparations—despite the International Law Commission's 2001 articles on state responsibility.[1] The tools of diplomacy, however, can be cogently employed by a weaker state to help spotlight a wrong and internationally embarrass the other side.

The establishment of subregional agreements governing transnational rivers and aquifers holds the key everywhere to building water security through mutually beneficial but environmentally sustainable cooperation. Building such agreements is never an easy task, given the complex physical, geopolitical, and economic factors usually at play, which include mismatched levels of economic development and the unilateral harnessing of shared waters by one or more co-riparian states. Conflict, admittedly, has still been avoided in most cases. Yet the future is unlikely to be guided by the past, in view of the fact that the demand for water is growing fast in the face of resource depletion and degradation. The past does show, however, that the one factor that can help check the escalation of water disputes into overt conflict is the institution of basin or subbasin agreements—by either fostering cooperative relations or at least contributing to conflict mitigation.

Basin agreements that are structurally dynamic—with independent monitoring, evaluation, dispute resolution, and flexible allocation powers—and place as much focus on water quality as on quantity are best suited to foster long-term integrated water management; they can actually ensure durable inter-riparian collaboration, even as they evolve in response to changing hydrological and anthropogenic conditions in the basin. No transnational basin in Asia can claim to have such an agreement. But the current absence of *any* water-sharing or cooperative-management framework in many Asian transboundary basins is hardly a comforting scenario. In truth, institution building is needed in Asia more than in any other continent, especially to develop guiding principles and norms on shared waters. The country best placed to play a leadership role to help develop cooperative water-related mechanisms is China, the geographical hub of the continent that shares land borders with fourteen countries. Add to this picture its control over Asia's water repository, the Tibetan Plateau. China is a common factor in more than a dozen crucial river basins in Asia that lack institutionalized cooperation and management among all co-riparian states.

China's policy, while advocating multilateralism in global affairs, has long been to keep all disputes with its neighbors on a bilateral basis by eschewing the multilateral path—a strategy seen by smaller states, like those in the Mekong River basin, as an attempt to "divide and conquer." But as the disputes over the islands in the South China Sea have shown, this approach may actually be bringing other claimants together in opposition to Chinese policy and making them turn to the United States for security assurances. A similar scenario could unfold with respect to interstate water disputes involving China. In fact, even though it favors bilateral initiatives over multilateral institutions on water, China has not shown enthusiasm for meaningful bilateral action. Take the Sino-Indian relationship, where water has increasingly become the new political divide and source of distrust. When President Hu Jintao visited New Delhi in late 2006, China and India agreed to set up a joint expert-level mechanism on interstate river waters. But this modest initiative for mere "interaction and cooperation" on hydrological data has not shown much promise, as Beijing has reduced it to a pro forma exercise carried out once a year at a relatively junior level. The central issue bedeviling multiple transboundary basins in Asia is that Chinese upstream projects remain wrapped in secrecy in spite of their direct bearing on cross-border flows. China, moreover, remains opposed to joining legally binding water-sharing arrangements on a bilateral or multilateral basis.

China already has significant financial, trade, and political leverage over most of its neighbors, which are in no position to openly challenge its interests. In fact, its trade muscles and political power are so strong that concerns about its approach or direction are usually expressed by other nations only in coded terms, such as "emerging strategic environment" and "need for transparency." But now a rapidly rising China is also gaining water-related clout in its neighborhood through its upstream projects on international rivers. Its asymmetric control over the transboundary flows of international rivers, with the aid of upstream dams, barrages, and other water diversion schemes, is set to become an issue of greater interstate concern in the coming years. After all, the growing Chinese power to control the most-critical natural resource could impel co-riparian states to be on good behavior and help underpin China's regional hegemony.

Indeed, what gives greater comfort to Beijing in its pursuit of such a unilateralist strategy is the fact that the formation of a counterbalancing Asian coalition of lower-riparian states just does not seem conceivable. The reason is simple: Several of the countries that receive river waters from China have their own water and other disputes with each other. In fact, China's closest allies or client states in Asia—North Korea, Pakistan, and Burma—also share a water relationship with it.

The pressing threat to the integrity of the Tibetan Plateau's freshwater ecosystems posed by Chinese megaprojects and human-made environmental change, however, is a subject of growing international concern. It is likely to propel some downriver states—independently and in partnership—to seek an international recognition of Tibet's waters as a common resource whose protection demands concrete safeguards, including appropriate Chinese assurances to refrain from actions that threaten natural flows, water quality, and resource sustainability. China's increasing riparian and territorial assertiveness is expected to also prompt a number of regional actors to work together to form a web of interlocking partnerships intended to impose discreet limits on the exercise of Chinese power. Indeed, some Asian countries already have started building security cooperation on a bilateral basis, thereby laying the groundwork for such a potential web.

These bilateral deals and partnerships, although not intended to contain China, represent a palpable shift in the Asian diplomatic landscape, with a new emphasis on mutually beneficial security cooperation and a quiet desire to positively shape China's behavior so that it does not go against the self-touted gospel of its "peaceful rise." The probability of a peaceful Chinese trajectory will actually grow if China rises in an Asia where other important actors are working closely together and enjoying productive relations with Beijing. Influencing China's riparian conduct, however, may prove more challenging than influencing its foreign policy. Even so, only genuine basin cooperation in an institutional framework—based on international norms of fair utilization and doing no harm to co-riparian states—can help Asia meet its water challenges and shore up regionwide peace, stability, and economic growth. The protection of the shared water resources of the Tibetan Plateau will need to be the focal point of such cooperation.

The political obstacles in Asia, admittedly, extend beyond China. With several Asian nations jockeying to control water resources, even as they demand transparency and the sharing of information about their neighbors' hydroengineering projects, the sharpening water competition threatens to provoke greater tensions and conflict. Still, given China's unique riparian position and role, it will not be possible to transform the Asian competition into cooperation without its active participation in different subregional water-sharing and cooperative-management mechanisms. To play an institution-building role on water, China will need to overcome its allergy to terms like "internationally shared water resources" and drop its opposition to entering into legally binding accords or joining multilateral institutions. To cite one example, China needs to go from being a "dialogue partner" to being a member of the Mekong River Commission so that it can work with its co-riparian states on a holistic water-management plan for the mutual benefit of all the basin states. Beijing ought to draw the right lessons from the international basin arrangements successfully operating in the world, although no agreement is free of challenges or complaints by one party or more.

However, given the large number of transboundary basins in Asia that have no interstate institutional mechanism of any kind on water sharing and cooperation, institution-building efforts must extend more broadly. Priority needs to be accorded to the establishment of water institutions that can facilitate basinwide cooperation to help sustainably optimize and manage resources. The equitable sharing of basin resources within and across national borders usually centers on difficult choices. But in the long run it pays to make the right choice.

The role of both state and nonstate actors is important in conflict avoidance. Aid donors, civil society, multilateral institutions, and intergovernmental organizations, besides governments, have an important function to play to help mitigate the Asian water competition and avert conflicts. The World Bank, for example, has done a commendable job in actively assisting with intercountry water arrangements, as in the Indus basin, and in helping to develop basin-specific plans, such as the Mekong Regional Water Resources Assistance Strategy (MWRAS). But it also has played a questionable role in promoting interbasin water-transfer schemes that are hardly environmentally sound, including China's gigantic South–North Water Transfer Project. In fact, in partnership with the Asian Development Bank, the World Bank helped the Mekong River Commission to incorporate large-scale water infrastructure projects into the ambitious MWRAS, evoking sharp criticism from environmental groups. The building of major new dams for hydropower, irrigation, and other water diversion was made part of MWRAS. International lending institutions, however, have been compelled by public pressure to become more sensitive to the need to consult not only with governments but also with representatives of communities likely to be affected by multilaterally funded projects.

Given the pressing Asian challenges, the establishment of the Asia-Pacific Water Forum (APWF) in 2006 has represented a small but significant step in the right direction to help identify and adopt cooperative water solutions in the region.[2] The APWF, which is supported by the Asian Development Bank, offers a platform for the region's water resources ministers and other officials to discuss and formulate joint strategies, and to learn about new techniques and practices of water conservation, efficiency, and management. Many of the water-related challenges the Asia-Pacific countries face are similar—from the need to improve public access to safe drinking water and sanitation to ensuring the protection and ecological restoration of drainage basins.[3]

As part of its aim to encourage more collaborative efforts in the region, the APWF has been organizing an Asia-Pacific Water Summit every three years. This summit is designed to create a greater awareness of water challenges by targeting top decision-makers beyond the water sector, including the heads of governments and ministers of finance and planning, as well as leaders from the private sector, provincial governments, and civil society.

Initiatives of this kind, by spotlighting key challenges in the conservation and holistic management of water resources and by providing a platform to jointly search for solutions, can help raise the profile of water as a strategic issue that deserves a higher priority in policymaking. In the competition to increasingly tap river and aquifer resources, it is often forgotten that watercourses not only serve as sources of supply but also perform critical ecological functions that can be seriously impaired through an overexploitation of resources. Such initiatives, more importantly, can help encourage the building of collaborative subregional approaches and, in the process, spur preventive diplomacy. After all, it is easier to prevent conflicts from arising than to stem them once they have flared up. Joint water projects between two or more co-riparian states are an important means of building cooperation and mutual trust.

A Better Way Forward

In an era of growing constraints on augmenting the supply of the most essential resource—water—Asian countries must seek sustainable, cost-effective solutions through collaborative efforts that extend beyond national borders. Competing demands for scarce water resources pose economic, social, and political threats that can be contained only through forward-looking policies. Such policies, as well as the promotion of greater interstate and intrastate water collaboration, depend on linking stakeholders together, collecting reliable data on water resources, and enunciating specific, measurable, attainable, realistic, and timely—SMART—goals.

Bilateral and multilateral initiatives are necessary to assist in the collection and dissemination of trusted data on river and aquifer resources, especially waters that are shared across national frontiers. Given the ease with which basic facts are distorted and water nationalism is kindled in an interstate context, the compilation of high-quality objective data, garnered through transnational efforts, can by itself serve as a conflict-avoidance mechanism. Asia's varied political systems and cultures, by fostering official opacity on specifics related to water quality and quantity, have impeded regional transparency on water-related issues. The collection and sharing of reliable facts and figures should thus serve as the building blocks for interstate (and even intrastate) cooperation.[4] Dependable data, in any event, are critical to economically rational policymaking and to promote efficient resource allocation and utilization.

More broadly, strategic frictions over water and other natural resources can be stemmed only by building shared Asian interests to safeguard supplies, boost resource conservation and efficiency, and tap nonconventional sources, including rainwater capture and storage, water recycling, the treatment of brackish water, and desalination. Developing such common interests and goals can serve as the basis for a cooperative approach to sustainably manage water resources, safeguard sea lanes of communication, and increase water and energy efficiency. Such wider cooperation can also help to regulate the competition to buy energy and mineral assets in distant lands and to moderate the need to hedge against risks of supply disruption. To underpin a two-way relationship, a region's states ought to invest in each other's water and energy infrastructures, given that water is essential to produce energy, and energy is indispensable for the provision of water.

Transparency must encompass engineering projects on international rivers and aquifers. Peacefully managing intercountry water competition in Asia calls for transparency on national projects that carry potential transboundary implications. It demands a binding commitment not to reroute the natural flow of any river or to diminish cross-border water supplies—either through upstream river projects or the overexploitation of aquifers straddling political frontiers. And it demands the formation of a basinwide community, functioning on the basis of institutional mechanisms and well-defined rules. Upstream states on international rivers have a duty to ensure that transboundary flows stay at predictable levels despite any hydropower or other waterworks that they may undertake. Without such elements in place, it will be difficult to mitigate geopolitical competition over water resources, let alone pursue cooperative and environmentally friendly water-management strategies.

More fundamentally, without improved regional and domestic hydropolitics, greater interstate and intrastate disputes are likely to arise in Asia in the coming years. Growing populations, an increasing demand for food and energy, the spread of water-intensive industries, and rising consumption and standards of living have all increased pressures on water quality and quantity. Add to this picture the uneven distribution and availability of water in Asia, which is expected to get worse. The stoking of political tensions over the resources of transnational aquifers (such as al-Disi on the Arabian Peninsula) and rivers like the Mekong, Salween, Brahmaputra, Indus, Jordan, Tigris-Euphrates, Syr Darya, Amu Darya, Irtysh-Illy, and Amur is a testament to the potential for water conflict in Asia. The specter of more-intense competition and conflict has made better hydropolitics and greater interstate cooperation a must.

The first imperative is to build Asian norms over shared transnational basin resources, using as a guide the codification of the principles of customary water law by the United Nations Convention on the Non-Navigational Uses of International Watercourses, even though this convention's entry into force is still not within sight. A second necessity is to set up truly inclusive river basin organizations and other cooperative mechanisms to manage and moderate water competition. Clearly, the way to forestall or control water disputes in Asia is to build basin arrangements involving all riparian neighbors. If a dominant riparian refuses to join, such institutional arrangements can hardly be effective. The successful interstate basin agreements in the world involve all important riparian states and are centered on transparency, information sharing, an equitable distribution of benefits, dispute settlement, pollution control, joint projects, and a mutual commitment to refrain from any projects that would materially diminish transboundary flows.

River basin organizations can help create interlocking institutional constraints that effectively limit the exercise of arbitrary power by a dominant riparian. To be effective, a river basin organization must function independently of the leading riparian power, yet be able to serve that state's interests. Just the way hegemonic self-restraint demands an international system in which "rules, rights and protections are widely agreed upon, highly institutionalized and generally observed," riparian self-restraint demands rules-based basin communities in which powerful states will find it in their own interest to pursue restraint and eschew actions that undercut established goals.[5] No agreement, however, can rein in a dominant but scofflaw riparian that accepts rules when it suits its interest but flouts them when it does not want to be restrained. That is a risk inherent in any institutionalized multilateral arrangement.

Yet another imperative in Asia is the adoption of holistic and integrated planning at the regional, national, provincial, and local levels so as to put the accent on water efficiency, conservation, environmental protection, rainwater capture, and water recycling. Considering that improvements in the efficiency of water use in agriculture, energy, and industry have remained constant at 1 percent or less a year for two decades, efforts to secure greater gains in water efficiency need to become a policy priority for Asian nations so that they can reduce their water footprints and, in the process, ensure that their future economic growth and environmental sustainability are not compromised.[6] Greater investments also are needed to upgrade and maintain the water-supply infrastructure, given that losses from leaky distribution in Asia, according to the Asian Development Bank, total up to 29 billion cubic meters of treated water a year, valued conservatively at $9 billion.

More important, if water is not to become the major new battleground between countries, much greater interstate cooperation in an institutional framework must occur in Asia than what we have seen thus far. In a continent where water resources are widely shared among countries, the idea of absolute water security (like the notion of absolute national security) is a nonstarter. Collaborative interstate efforts, if pursued genuinely, can serve as an important means to build water security and broader national security by helping to sustainably shield the region's water future.

Despite its rich history, ancient cultures, and an ongoing economic renaissance, Asia is the only continent other than Africa where regional integration has yet to take hold. In this respect, Asia's political and cultural diversity has acted as a barrier to collaboration and integration. Consequently, Asia lacks institutions to avert or manage conflict, even as greater prosperity and rising nationalism are stoking territorial and resource disputes. Yet given the fact that it now is a key factor in instigating global geopolitical change, Asia needs to be better integrated, with institutionalized collaboration on shared resources a burning need. The intercountry rivalries over water actually test Asia's ability to manage its resource problems.

More broadly, it was a mistake to believe that greater economic interdependence by itself would improve regional or global geopolitics. As Asia demonstrates, trade in today's market-driven world is not constrained by political differences. This is why even rival states boast rapidly growing trade even when their political ties may

be languishing. Asia also shows that booming trade is not a guarantee of modera-
tion or restraint between states. The greater stridency in territorial and maritime
disputes between countries locked in economic interdependence serves as one such
example. Another case in point is the aggressive resource-related competition
between states whose trade with each other is large and flourishing. What all this
underscores is that rapidly expanding trade is no measure of progress in bilateral
relations and that better politics is as important as better economics. Unless
estranged neighbors fix their political relations, economics alone will not be enough
to create goodwill or stabilize their relationship.

This reality, in turn, calls for greater Asian openness on strategic doctrines,
military expenditures, and resource-related strategies, as well as building cooperative approaches on shared concerns. In keeping with Asia's growing role in world
affairs, Asian states need to pursue policies that break free from history and are
pragmatic and forward-looking. At a time when various strategies are being played
out on the grand Asian geopolitical chessboard, including the concurrent pursuit of
hedging, balancing, and bandwagoning, the imperative for building Asian power
stability cannot be underestimated. Rather than be the scene of a twenty-first-
century cold war, Asia can chart a stable future for itself through shared security
and prosperity. The greatest need today is to improve Asian geopolitics through
institutional mechanisms and cooperative political approaches.

If the equation between two co-riparian states is characterized by a trust deficit
and tense or wobbly political relations, even a good water-sharing agreement
between them will not prove satisfactory or enduring. But if the politics is good, a
water arrangement, even if tentative, may present itself as a symbol of successful
bilateral cooperation. In this light, if water wars are to be averted in Asia, shared
basin resources need to be protected and prudently managed in a cooperative and
collaborative spirit.

In an era of shifting power equations and rapid change, the central challenge in
Asia with respect to freshwater resources is to find ways to minimize competition
and maximize avenues for reciprocally beneficial cooperation extending to conservation, efficiency, environmental protection, and the tapping of nonconventional
sources. With its multitude of interstate basins, Asia cannot continue to prosper
without building political and technological partnerships on water to help stabilize
inter-riparian relations, encourage greater water efficiency, promote environmental
sustainability, take on practicable conservation strategies, and invest in clean-water
know-how. If Asian states are to address their water challenges, they will need
to embrace good practices on the strategic planning and management of water
resources.[7]

The optimal but sustainable utilization of water resources will be possible to
achieve not by shying away from institutionalized bilateral and multilateral cooperation but by seeking to tackle contentious issues in a practical, forward-thinking
way. There needs to be an Asian norm against causing appreciable harm to a
riparian neighbor by way of diminished transboundary flows, pollution, or other

means. Cooperation needs to proceed on the basis that each state located along an international waterway has the right to reasonable and equitable utilization of the basin resources, but without qualitatively or quantitatively altering transboundary flows in such a way as to harm the downstream natural and human environments. After all, there can be no rights without responsibilities. To preempt conflict and resolve existing disputes, Asian nations must involve themselves in institution-building efforts to efficiently and sustainably manage transnational freshwater resources. In the absence of such institutionalization, peace would be the casualty in Asia, and water would become a treacherous new battleground.

Appendix A: Interstate Freshwater Agreements in Asia since the Start of the Decolonization Process

Date	River Basin	Signatories	Accord
May 4, 1948	Indus	Pakistan, India	Interdominion agreement on the canal water dispute between East and West Punjab
September 7, 1950	Helmand	Afghanistan, Iran	Terms of reference of the Helmand River Delta Commission
June 4, 1953	Yarmouk	Jordan, Syria	Agreement on utilization of the Yarmouk waters
April 25, 1954	Kosi/Ganges	Nepal, India	Agreement on the Kosi Project
August 18, 1956	Amur	China, USSR	Agreement between USSR and China on joint research operations to determine the natural resources of the Amur River basin
August 11, 1957	Aras, Atrak	USSR, Iran	Agreement for joint utilization of the frontier sections of the Aras and Atrak rivers for irrigation and hydropower
October 31, 1957	Mekong	Cambodia, Laos, Thailand, Vietnam	Statute of the Committee for Coordination of Investigations of the Lower Mekong Basin
December 4, 1959	Gandak	Nepal, India	Agreement between Nepal and India on the Gandak Irrigation and Power Project
September 19, 1960	Indus	India, Pakistan, World Bank	Indus Waters Treaty partitions rivers between India, Pakistan
August 9, 1965	Jahore, Tebrau, Scudai	Malaysia, Singapore	Separation Agreement, also known as the Independence of Singapore Agreement, guarantees continuation of the 1961 and 1962 water accords between Malaysia's Johor State government and Singapore City Council
December 19, 1966	Kosi	Nepal, India	Revised agreement concerning the Kosi Project
November 24, 1972	Ganges-Brahmaputra-Meghna	Bangladesh, India	Statute of the Indo-Bangladesh Joint Rivers Commission
January 31, 1975	Mekong	Khmer (Cambodia), Laos, Thailand, Vietnam	Joint declaration of principles for utilization of the waters of the Lower Mekong Basin
April 18, 1975	Ganges	Bangladesh, India	Provisional conclusion of a treaty on the division of the Ganges River waters
December 26, 1975	Tigris-Euphrates-Shatt al Arab	Iran, Iraq	Agreement on the use of frontier watercourses
November 5, 1977	Ganges	Bangladesh, India	Agreement on sharing of the Ganges waters at Farakka and on augmenting transboundary flows
January 5, 1978	Mekong	Laos, Thailand, Vietnam	Declaration concerning the Interim Committee for Coordination of Investigation of the Lower Mekong Basin
April 7, 1978	Kosi	India, Nepal	Agreement on the renovation and extension of Chandra Canal, Pumped Canal, and distribution of the Western Kosi Canal
October 7, 1982	Ganges	Bangladesh, India	Memorandum of understanding on the sharing of Ganges waters at Farakka Barrage
July 20, 1983	Teesta	Bangladesh, India	Agreement on the *ad hoc* sharing of the Teesta River waters
June 28, 1988	Malaysian water exports	Malaysia, Singapore	Memorandum of understanding between the two countries' prime ministers on water and gas
April 17, 1989	Euphrates	Iraq, Syria	Joint minutes concerning the provisional division of Euphrates waters
August 27, 1992	Ob, Irrysh, Ishim, Tobol, Ural	Kazakhstan, Russia	Agreement on the use and protection of transboundary waters

Appendix A: (Continued)

Date	Signatories	River Basin	Accord
March 26, 1993	Kazakhstan, Kyrgyzstan, Tajikistan, Turkmenistan, Uzbekistan	Amu Darya, Aral Sea, Syr Darya	Agreement on joint activities to help address the Aral Sea crisis
April 29, 1994	China, Mongolia	Bor Nor Lake, Bulgan, Halaha, Kerulen	Agreement on the protection and utilization of transboundary waters
September 20, 1994	Lebanon, Syria	Al-Asi/Orontes	Bilateral agreement on the division of the waters of the Al-Asi River (Orontes)
October 26, 1994	Israel, Jordan	Jordan River, freshwater springs, saline springs	Bilateral peace treaty, with an Annex II titled, "Water and Related Matters"
February 11, 1995	Russia, Mongolia	Amur, Har Us Nur, Jenissei, Lake Baikal, Lake Ubsa-Nur, Onon, Pu Lun T'o, Selenga	Agreement on the protection and use of transboundary waters
March 3, 1995	Kazakhstan, Kyrgyzstan, Tajikistan, Turkmenistan, Uzbekistan	Amu Darya, Aral Sea, Syr Darya	Resolution of the heads of states of Central Asia on the work of the Executive Committee of the Interstate Council for the Aral Sea (ICAS) on implementation of the action-plan
April 5, 1995	Cambodia, Laos, Thailand, Vietnam	Mekong	Agreement on cooperation for the sustainable development of the Mekong River Basin
September 28, 1995	Israel, Palestine Liberation Organization	Groundwater	Israeli-Palestinian Interim Agreement on the West Bank and the Gaza Strip, including on supply and management of water resources and establishment of a Joint Water Committee
February 12, 1996	India, Nepal	Mahakali	Treaty on the integrated development of the Mahakali River, including the Sarada Barrage, Tanakpur Barrage, and Pancheshwar Project
December 12, 1996	India, Bangladesh	Ganges	30-year treaty on sharing of the Ganges River waters
November 10, 1997	Russia, China	Transboundary rivers	Agreement on principles of joint economic use of several islands and adjacent water areas of transboundary rivers
March 17, 1998	Kazakhstan, Kyrgyzstan, Uzbekistan	Syr Darya	Agreement on the use of water and energy resources of the Sry Darya Basin, along with a separate accord on the reservoirs of the Naryn-Syr Darya cascade
May 7, 1999	Kazakhstan, Kyrgyzstan, Tajikistan, Uzbekistan	Syr Darya	Protocol on inserting amendments and addenda in the agreement on the use of resources of the Syr Darya
January 21, 2000	Kazakhstan, Kyrgyzstan	Talas	Agreement on the utilization of the water facilities on the Chu and Talas rivers
August 15, 2000	Singapore, Malaysia	Water exports	Agreed items on water and other issues between Malaysian Prime Minister Mahathir Mohamed and Singaporean Senior Minister Lee Kuan Yew at their "4-Eye" meeting at Putrajaya
April 20, 2002	Syria, Lebanon	Al-Kaber Al-Janoubi	Agreement on sharing the Great Southern River Basin water and building a dam jointly

Appendix B: Web Links to Key Asian Water Treaties

The Indus Waters Treaty, 1960; location of the text: World Bank, www.worldbank
.org/indus.

Agreement on Cooperation for the Sustainable Development of the Mekong River
Basin, 1995, location of the text: Mekong River Commission, www.mrcme
kong.org.

Annex II on "Water and Related Matters" in the Treaty of Peace between the State
of Israel and the Hashemite Kingdom of Jordan, 1994; location of the text:
Government of Israel, Ministry of Foreign Affairs, http://bit.ly/afYao2.

Treaty between the Government of the People's Republic of Bangladesh and the
Government of the Republic of India on the Sharing of the Ganga/Ganges
Waters at Farakka, 1996; location of the text: Government of Bangladesh, www
.jrcb.gov.bd/attachment/Gganges_Water_Sharing_treaty,1996.pdf.

Notes

Chapter 1

1. See A. K. Biswas, ed., *Asian International Waters: From Ganges-Brahmaputra to Mekong* (Bombay: Oxford University Press, 1996); United Nations Environment Program, *Freshwater under Threat: South Asia* (Nairobi: United Nations Environment Program, 2009); Ashok Swain, *Managing Water Conflict: Asia, Africa and the Middle East* (London: Routledge, 2004); World Wide Fund for Nature, *World's Top 10 Rivers at Risk* (Gland, Switzerland: WWF International, 2007); Michael A. Gheleta, "Sustaining the Giant Dragon: Rational Use and Protection of China's Water Resources in the Twenty-First Century," *Colorado Journal of International Environmental Law and Policy* 9, no. 2 (1998): 221–83; Thi Dieu Nguyen, *The Mekong River and the Struggle for Indochina: Water, War, and Peace* (Westport, CT: Praeger, 1999); Fred Pearce, *When the Rivers Run Dry: What Happens When Our Water Runs Out?* (Bodelva, UK: Eden Project Books, 2006); Diane Raines Ward, *Water Wars: Drought, Flood, Folly and the Politics of Thirst* (New York: Riverhead, 2002); Vandana Shiva, *Water Wars: Privatization, Pollution and Profit* (Cambridge, MA: South End Press, 2002); Arun P. Elhance, *Hydropolitics in the Third World: Conflict and Cooperation in International River Basins* (Washington, DC: US Institute for Peace Press, 1999); Iwao Kobori and Michael H. Glantz, eds., *Central Eurasian Water Crisis: Caspian, Aral, and Dead Seas* (Tokyo: United Nations University Press, 1998); David Michel and Amit Pandya, eds., *Troubled Waters: Climate Change, Hydropolitics, and Transboundary Resources* (Washington, DC: Henry L. Stimson Center, 2009); E. W. Sievers, "Transboundary Jurisdiction and Watercourse Law: China, Kazakhstan, and the Irtysh," *Texas International Law Journal* 37, no. 1 (2002): 1–42; and Peter Bosshard, "China Dams the World," *World Policy Journal*, Winter 2009–10, 43–51.

2. United Nations Environment Program, *Global Environment Outlook 2000* (Nairobi: United Nations Environment Program, 1999), chap. 2, "Asia and the Pacific: Freshwater."

3. Food and Agriculture Organization of the United Nations (FAO), Aquastat online table, "Freshwater Availability: Precipitation and Internal Renewable Water Resources (IRWR)."

4. United Nations, *The State of the Environment in Asia and the Pacific 2005* (Bangkok: United Nations Economic and Social Commission for Asia and the Pacific, 2006): 57–58.

5. FAO, "Coping with Water: Q&A with FAO Director-General Dr. Jacques Diouf," FAO, Rome, March 22, 2007. Also see United Nations, *Water in a Changing World*, United Nations World Water Development Report (Colombella, Italy: United Nations World Water Assessment Program, 2009); Jill Boberg, *Liquid Assets: How Demographic Changes and Water Development Policies Affect Freshwater Resources* (Santa Monica, CA: RAND Corporation, 2005); and Daniel Wild, Carl-Johan Francke, Pierin Menzli, and Urs Schön, *Water: A Market of the Future* (Zurich: Sustainable Asset Management, 2007).

6. Igor A. Shiklomanov, *World's Water Resources and Their Use* (Paris: International Hydrological Program, UNESCO, 1999); M. Falkenmark and M. Lannerstad, "Consumptive

Water Use to Feed Humanity: Curing a Blind Spot," *Hydrology and Earth System Sciences* 9 (2005): 15–28; H. Yang, P. Reichert, K. Abbaspour, and A. J. B. Zehnder, "A Water Resources Threshold and Its Implications for Food Security," *Environmental Science and Technology* 37, no. 14 (2003): 3048–54; Peter H. Gleick, "Basic Water Requirements for Human Activities: Meeting Basic Needs," *Water International* 21, no. 2 (1996): 83–92; and A. J. B. Zehnder, H. Yang, and R. Schertenleib, "Water Issues: The Need for Actions at Different Levels," *Aquatic Sciences* 65 (2003): 1–20.

7. Malin Falkenmark, "Global Water Issues Confronting Humanity," *Journal of Peace Research* 27, no. 2 (May 1990): 177–90; M. Falkenmark, J. Lundqvist, and C. Widstrand, "Macro-Scale Water Scarcity Requires Micro-Scale Approaches: Aspects of Vulnerability in Semi-Arid Development," *Natural Resources Forum* 13, no. 4 (November 1989): 258–67; Malin Falkenmark, "The Massive Water Scarcity Now Threatening Africa—Why Isn't It Being Addressed?" *Ambio* 8, no. 2 (1989): 112–18.

8. UN-Water, "Coping with Water Scarcity: A Strategic Issue and Priority for System-Wide Action," United Nations, New York, August 2006, 2.

9. United Nations Development Program, *Human Development Report 2006: Beyond Scarcity—Power, Poverty and the Global Water Crisis* (New York: United Nations Development Program, 2007), 12.

10. Steven Ferrey, *Environmental Law: Examples & Explanations* (New York: Aspen Publishers), 297.

11. E.g., the losses in India average as much as 40 percent in large cities and can be even higher in smaller cities and towns. See Alliance to Save Energy, *Watergy: Energy and Water Efficiency in Water Supply and Wastewater Treatment—Cost-Effective Savings of Water and Energy* (Washington, DC: Alliance to Save Energy, 2007).

12. See, e.g., Michael Schuman, *The Miracle: The Epic Story of Asia's Quest for Wealth* (New York: Harper Business, 2009).

13. See Michael T. Klare, *Resource Wars: The New Landscape of Global Conflict* (New York: Holt Paperbacks, 2002); Peter M. Vitousek, Harold A. Mooney, Jane Lubchenco, and Jerry M. Melillo, "Human Domination of Earth's Ecosystems," *Science* 277, no. 5325 (July 25, 1997): 494–99; Peter H. Gleick, "Water and Conflict: Freshwater Resources and International Security," *International Security* 18, no. 1 (Summer 1993): 77–192; M. Falkenmark and M. Lannerstad, "Consumptive Water Use to Feed Humanity: Curing a Blind Spot," *Hydrology and Earth System Sciences* 9 (2005): 15–21; and Ismail Serageldin, "Water: Conflicts Set to Arise within as Well as between States," *Nature* 459, no. 7244 (May 14, 2009): 163.

14. United Nations Population Division, *The World at Six Billion* (New York: United Nations, 2000); and United Nations Population Division, Department of Economic and Social Affairs, *World Population Prospects: The 2008 Revision* (New York: United Nations, 2009). In its definition of Asia, the UN includes all of Asia, excluding the part in the Russian Federation but including central and southwest Asia, the Caspian Sea Basin, and the countries of the Persian Gulf and beyond, such as Turkey, Bahrain, Qatar, Israel, and Saudi Arabia.

15. Although some Asian countries—like Japan, South Korea, China, and Singapore—are experiencing or set to experience declining populations, others—like Pakistan, Bangladesh, Nepal, and the Philippines—continue to maintain high birthrates. The majority of Asia's population growth over the next two decades is projected to come from South Asia.

16. For details, see J. A. Allan, "Virtual Water: A Strategic Resource—Global Solutions to Regional Deficits," *Groundwater* 36, no. 4 (July 1998): 545–46; William J. Cosgrove and Frank R. Rijsberman, *Making Water Everybody's Business* (London: Earthscan, 2000); A. Y. Hoekstra and P. Q. Hung, "Virtual Water Trade: A Quantification of Virtual Water Flows between Nations in Relation to International Crop Trade," Value of Water Research Report 11 (Delft: UNESCO Institute for Water Education, 2002); D. Wichelns, "The Role of 'Virtual Water' in Efforts to Achieve Food Security and other National Goals, with an Example from

Egypt," *Agricultural Water Management* 49, no. 2 (July 17, 2001): 131–51; and Daniel Zimmer and Daniel Renault, "Virtual Water in Food Production and Global Trade: Review of Methodological Issues and Preliminary Results," in *Virtual Water Trade*, Proceedings of the Expert Meeting held December 12–13, 2002, at Delft, edited by A. Y. Hoekstra (Delft: UNESCO Institute for Water Education, 2003).

17. United Nations Environment Program, *Challenges to International Waters: Regional Assessments in a Global Perspective* (Nairobi: United Nations Environment Program, 2006), 8.

18. United Nations, "Water without Borders," Backgrounder, Water for Life 2005–2015 project (New York: United Nations, n.d.), 1.

19. Joel E. Cohen, Christopher Small, Andrew Mellinger, John Gallup, and Jeffrey Sachs, "Estimates of Coastal Populations," *Science* 278, no. 5341 (November 14, 1997): 1209–13.

20. World Water Forum, "Asia-Pacific Regional Document," March 16–22, 2006, available at www.worldwatercouncil.org.

21. A report by the Asian Development Bank says Southeast Asia will be among the regions in the world worst affected by the rise in sea levels. The rise could force the sprawling archipelago of Indonesia to redraw its sea boundaries. Asian Development Bank, *The Economics of Climate Change in Southeast Asia: A Regional Review* (Manila: Asian Development Bank, April 2009).

22. United Nations secretary-general Ban Ki-moon, "Message to the Inaugural Asia-Pacific Water Summit in Beppu, Japan, December 3, 2007."

23. Water Resources Group (Barilla Group, Coca-Cola Company, International Finance Corporation, McKinsey & Company, Nestlé S.A., New Holland Agriculture, SABMiller PLC, Standard Chartered Bank, and Syngenta AG), *Charting Our Water Future* (New York: 2030 Water Resources Group, 2009), 6; J. Martínez Beltrán and S. Koo-Oshima, *Water Desalination for Agricultural Applications*, Land and Water Discussion Paper 5 (Rome: FAO, 2004), v.

24. United Nations, *State of the Environment in Asia and the Pacific 2005*, 57.

25. Asia Society, ed., *Asia's Next Challenge: Securing the Region's Water Future* (New York: Asia Society, 2009), 9.

26. Mahabub Hossain, "Asian Population Growth Is Overtaking Rice Output," *International Herald Tribune*, March 18, 1994.

27. United Nations Economic and Social Commission for Asia and the Pacific, *Sustainable Agriculture and Food Security in Asia and the Pacific* (Bangkok: United Nations Economic and Social Commission for Asia and the Pacific, 2009), 65, www.unescap.org/65/documents/Theme-Study/st-escap-2535.pdf.

28. Hong Yang, Yuan Zhou, and Junguo Liu, "Land and Water Requirements of Biofuel and Implications for Food Supply and the Environment in China," *Energy Policy* 37, no. 5 (May 2009): 1876–85.

29. United Nations Economic and Social Commission for Asia and the Pacific, *Sustainable Agriculture and Food Security in Asia and the Pacific*.

30. Robert Glennon, "Our Water Supply, Down the Drain," *Washington Post*, August 23, 2009.

31. See United Nations Development Program, *Human Development Report 2007–2008: Fighting Climate Change—Human Solidarity in a Divided World* (New York: United Nations Development Program, 2008).

32. International Water Management Institute and FAO, *Revitalizing Asia's Irrigation: To Sustainably Meet Tomorrow's Food Needs* (Colombo: International Water Management Institute, 2009), 10.

33. FAO, *Irrigation in Asia in Figures* (Rome: FAO, 1999), 9.

34. It was through his novel *Kim*, first published in 1901 by Macmillan, that Rudyard Kipling popularized the term "Great Game." The novel is about the story of an orphan boy groomed by the British secret service to go "far and far into the North, playing the Great

Game." Rudyard Kipling, *Kim*, edited with an introduction and notes by Edward S. Said (London: Penguin Classics, 1987).

35. FAOSTAT data, available at: http://faostat.fao.org/.

36. United Nations Economic and Social Commission for Asia and the Pacific, *Sustainable Agriculture and Food Security in Asia and the Pacific*, figure III-2, 63.

37. Ibid.

38. US National Intelligence Council, *Global Trends 2025: A Transformed World* (Washington, DC: US National Intelligence Council, 2008), x.

39. Gunnar Myrdal, *Asian Drama: An Inquiry into the Poverty of Nations* (New York: Pantheon, 1968).

40. Niall Ferguson, *The War of the World: Twentieth-Century Conflict and the Descent of the West* (New York: Penguin Press, 2006), xviii.

41. Haruhiko Kuroda, president, Asian Development Bank, "The Financial Crisis and Its Impact on Asia," speech to a Conference in Montreal, June 9, 2008.

42. Ibid.

43. See Joseph Nye, *The Future of Power* (New York: PublicAffairs, 2011).

44. Jaswant Singh, "The Great Game's New Players," Project Syndicate column, September 24, 2010.

45. Martin Fackler, "Japan Goes from Dynamic to Disheartened," *New York Times*, October 16, 2010.

46. A richer China and India, however, will not make the United States poorer. Because the number of Chinese and Indians together is 8.5 times greater than the number of Americans, average living standards in China and India are likely to lag behind America's indefinitely. According to projections by Goldman Sachs, average American incomes will still be twice as large as Chinese incomes in 2050.

47. Angus Maddison, *The World Economy: A Millennial Perspective* (Paris: Organization for Economic Cooperation and Development, 2001).

48. Kishore Mahbubani, *The New Asian Hemisphere: The Irresistible Shift of Global Power to the East* (New York: PublicAffairs, 2008).

49. Jeffrey D. Sachs, "Welcome to the Asian Century by 2050: China and Maybe India Will Overtake the US Economy in Size," *Fortune Magazine*, January 12, 2004.

50. US Department of Defense, *Military and Security Developments Involving the People's Republic of China 2010*, Report to Congress Pursuant to the National Defense Authorization Act for Fiscal Year 2010 (Washington, DC: Office of the Secretary of Defense, 2010), 24.

51. "How China Must Counter US Containment Strategy," *Qiu Shi Journal*, December 10, 2010, www.qstheory.cn/lg/zl/201012/t20101210_59023.htm. *Qiu Shi Journal* is an important ideological and theoretical organ that seeks to guide the whole Communist Party and the country.

52. China has staked its claim to an area in Bhutan's north and to the strategic Dolam Plateau, located at the Bhutan–Tibet–India tri-junction. The Dolam Plateau, located in western Bhutan, has been the target of increasing Chinese military incursions, according to Bhutanese and Indian officials.

53. Intergovernmental Panel on Climate Change, *Climate Change 2007: Impacts, Adaptation and Vulnerability*, Working Group II Contribution to the Fourth Assessment Report of the Intergovernmental Panel on Climate Change (New York: Cambridge University Press, 2007).

54. Ivo J. H. Bozon, Warren J. Campbell, and Mats Lindstrand, "Global Trends in Energy," *McKinsey Quarterly*, no. 1 (2007): 48.

55. Walter W. Immerzeel, Ludovicus P. H. van Beek, and Marc F. P. Bierkens, "Climate Change Will Affect the Asian Water Towers," *Science* 328, no. 5983 (June 11, 2010): 1382–85, DOI: 10.1126/science.1183188.

56. T. P. Barnett, J. C. Adam, and D. P. Lettenmaier, "Potential Impacts of a Warming Climate on Water Availability in Snow-Dominated Regions," *Nature* 438 (November 17, 2005): 306.

57. Johannes Linn, "Water-Energy Links in Central Asia: A Long-Term Opportunity and Challenge," Brookings Institution, Washington, June 30, 2008; Agence France-Press, "Uzbekistan, Tajikistan at Odds over Mega-Dam Plan," February 4, 2010; EurasiaNet, "Fergana Valley: Relations Cooling, Uzbek-Kyrgyz Border Growing Increasingly Violent," March 9, 2010.

58. United Nations, *State of the Environment in Asia and the Pacific 2005*, 57–58.

59. The Antarctica ice cap contains about 70 percent of the planet's freshwater and about 90 percent of its ice. Although it had long been assumed that except for some hardy penguins, Antarctica had virtually no life, scientists in recent years have discovered that this harsh and barren continent is "the kingdom of microbes, of tiny bacteria and other microscopic organisms that in some Antarctic regions eke out a bare existence, and in others are almost flourishing. They are extremely small, but one Antarctic researcher has calculated that the mass of living cells in Antarctica equals or exceeds all the living creatures in the freshwater lakes, rivers and streams elsewhere on earth." Marc Kaufman, "Antarctica Shelters Abundant Microbial Life in Water Miles below the Icy Surface," *Washington Post*, March 23, 2010.

60. FAO, Aquastat online table, "Freshwater Availability."

61. Ibid.

62. Ibid. Also see United Nations, *The State of the Environment in Asia and the Pacific 2000* (Bangkok: United Nations Economic and Social Commission for Asia and the Pacific, 2001), part II of "Executive Summary," 20; and FAO, *Review of World Water Resources by Country* (Rome: FAO's Aquastat Program, 2003), "Summary of World Water Resources."

63. United Nations, *State of the Environment in Asia and the Pacific 2005*, chap. 3, "Environmental Sustainability under Threat," 57.

64. Asia is made up of the following countries: Afghanistan, Armenia, Azerbaijan, Bahrain, Bangladesh, Bhutan, Brunei Darussalam, Burma, Cambodia, China, Georgia, India, Indonesia, Iran, Iraq, Israel, Japan, Jordan, Kazakhstan, Kuwait, Kyrgyzstan, Laos, Lebanon, Malaysia, the Maldives, Mongolia, Nepal, North Korea, Oman, Pakistan, Palestinian Territories, Papua New Guinea, the Philippines, Qatar, Saudi Arabia, Singapore, South Korea, Sri Lanka, Syria, Tajikistan, Thailand, Timor-Leste, Turkey, Turkmenistan, United Arab Emirates, Uzbekistan, Vietnam, and Yemen.

65. FAO, Aquastat Online Database, 2010.

66. Ibid.

67. World Bank, *World Development Indicators 2009* (Washington, DC: World Bank 2009); United Nations, *State of the Environment in Asia and the Pacific 2000*; FAO, Aquastat Online Database.

68. FAO, Aquastat Online Database.

69. See, e.g., I. A. Shiklomanov, *Comprehensive Assessment of the Freshwater Resources and Water Availability in the World: Assessment of Water Resources and Water Availability in the World* (Geneva: World Meteorological Organization, 1997).

70. FAO, Aquastat online table, "Freshwater Availability."

71. Kyrgyzstan and Tajikistan are water-rich states, yet their excessively high water withdrawals for agriculture as a percentage of total renewable water resources have put them in the high-risk category because such rates of resource extraction are simply unsustainable.

72. FAO, Aquastat Online Database.

73. Ibid. Also see United Nations, *State of the Environment in Asia and the Pacific 2000*, "Executive Summary."

74. Vitousek et al., "Human Domination of Earth's Ecosystems," 497.

75. Aiguo Dai, Taotao Qian, Kevin E. Trenberth, and John D. Milliman, "Changes in Continental Freshwater Discharge from 1948 to 2004," *Journal of Climate*, May 15, 2009.

76. Kang Juan, "Water Project Leads to Mass Relocation," *Global Times*, February 24, 2010; Hu Jiahai, deputy director of the migration bureau of the Wanzhou District of Chongqing Province, cited in Wang Huazhong, "Dam Forces Relocations of 300,000 More," *China Daily*, January 21, 2010.

77. Mara Hvistendahl, "China's Three Gorges Dam: An Environmental Catastrophe?" *Scientific American*, March 25, 2008.

78. Wang, "Dam Forces Relocations of 300,000 More."

79. FAO, Aquastat online table, "Freshwater Availability."

80. Ibid. Also see International Water Management Institute and FAO, *Revitalizing Asia's Irrigation*, 5, 9.

81. International Water Management Institute and FAO, *Revitalizing Asia's Irrigation*, 5, 9.

82. Although the 2030 Water Resources Group puts the global average of water withdrawal for agriculture at 71 percent, the FAO figure is 70 percent.

83. FAOSTAT data, available at http://faostat.fao.org/.

84. FAO, Aquastat online data.

85. Food and Agriculture Organization, *Water at a Glance*, www.fao.org/nr/water/art/2007/glance/facts.html.

86. David Molden, ed., *Water for Food, Water for Life, A Comprehensive Assessment of Water Management in Agriculture* (London: Earthscan, 2007); Organization for Economic Cooperation and Development, *Sustainable Management of Water Resources in Agriculture* (Paris: Organization for Economic Cooperation and Development, 2010); FAOSTAT data.

87. International Water Management Institute and FAO, *Revitalizing Asia's Irrigation*; FAO, *Water at a Glance*.

88. Kenneth F. Kiple and Kriemhild Coneé Ornelas, eds., *The Cambridge World History of Food* (Cambridge: Cambridge University Press, 2000), part II: "Staple Foods—Economic and Biological Importance of Rice."

89. United Nations Conference on Trade and Development, Online Commodities Database, www.unctad.org/infocomm/comm_docs/documents.htm.

90. Naomichi Ishige, "The Dietary Culture of Asia," translated by Thomas A. Steele, Asia Society, New York, September 3, 2008.

91. See Asian Development Bank, *A Study of Rural Asia: An Overview beyond the Green Revolution* (Manila: Asian Development Bank, 2000).

92. FAOSTAT data, available at http://faostat.fao.org/.

93. Pakistan Ministry of Water and Power, *Pakistan Water Sector Strategy*, Detailed Strategy Formulation, vol. 4 (Islamabad: Ministry of Water and Power, 2002), 7.

94. FAO, Aquastat online database; Paul Harrison and Fred Pearce, *AAAS Atlas of Population & Environment* (Washington, DC: American Association for the Advancement of Science, 2007), "Part 2—Natural Resources: Introduction."

95. Pakistan Ministry of Water and Power, *Pakistan Water Sector Strategy*, 31–33.

96. FAOSTAT data; International Water Management Institute and FAO, *Revitalizing Asia's Irrigation*.

97. Kang Juan, "Water Project Leads to Mass Relocation."

98. Jing Ma, Arjen Y. Hoekstra, Hao Wang, Ashok K. Chapagain, and Dangxian Wang, "Virtual versus Real Water Transfers within China," *Philosophical Transactions of the Royal Society*, no. 361 (2006): 835, 841–42.

99. FAO, Aquastat Online Database.

100. International Water Management Institute and FAO, *Revitalizing Asia's Irrigation*, 6.

101. Water Resources Group, *Charting Our Water Future*, 58.

102. Shams-ul Mulk, "Pakistan's Water Economy, the Indus River System and Its Development Infrastructure and the Relentless Struggle for Sustainability," in *Running on Empty: Pakistan's Water Crisis*, edited by Michael Kugelman and Robert M. Hathaway (Washington, DC: Woodrow Wilson International Center for Scholars, 2009), 68.

103. United Nations Economic and Social Commission for Asia and the Pacific, *Sustainable Agriculture and Food Security in Asia and the Pacific*, 62.

104. International Water Management Institute and FAO, *Revitalizing Asia's Irrigation*, 9.

105. Jim Yardley, "Beneath Booming Cities, China's Future Is Drying Up," *New York Times*, September 28, 2007.

106. World Bank, *China: Country Water Resources Assistance Strategy* (Washington, DC: World Bank, 2002), 4.

107. Pakistan Ministry of Water and Power, *Pakistan Water Sector Strategy*, 14, 82–110.

108. See World Bank, *Deep Wells and Prudence: Towards Pragmatic Action for Addressing Groundwater Overexploitation in India* (Washington, DC: World Bank, 2010).

109. Planning Commission of India, *Report of the Expert Group on "Groundwater Management and Ownership"* (New Delhi: Planning Commission of India, 2007), 4–14.

110. World Bank, *Deep Wells and Prudence*.

111. Matthew Rodell, Isabella Velicogna, and James S. Famiglietti, "Satellite-Based Estimates of Groundwater Depletion in India," *Nature*, no. 460 (August 20, 2009): 999–1002.

112. One reason for the sharp drop in water tables in parts of India is that some states have for decades promoted irrigated agriculture by subsidizing electricity, thereby facilitating reckless groundwater extraction.

113. World Bank, *Deep Wells and Prudence*, 1–18.

114. Royal Embassy of Saudi Arabia, London, "Agricultural Achievements," www.mofa .gov.sa/Detail.asp?InNewsItemID = 24496.

115. A. R. al-Nuaim, K. al-Rubeaan, Y. al-Mazrou, O. al-Attas, N. al-Daghari, and T. Khoja, "High Prevalence of Overweight and Obesity in Saudi Arabia," *International Journal of Obesity and Related Metabolic Disorders* 20 (June 1996): 547–52; Mohsen A. F. El-Hazmi, A. S. Warsy, A. R. Al-Swailem, A. M. Al-Swailem, and R. Sulaimani, "Diabetes Mellitus as a Health Problem in Saudi Arabia," *Eastern Mediterranean Health Journal* 4, issue 1 (1998): 58–67; J. S. Al-Malki, M. H. Al-Jaser, and A. S. Warsy, "Overweight and Obesity in Saudi Females of Childbearing Age," *International Journal of Obesity* 27 (2003): 134–139; and W. Y. Al-Saeed, K. M. Al-Dawood, I. A. Bukhari, and A. Bahnassy, "Prevalence and Socioeconomic Risk Factors of Obesity among Urban Female Students in Al-Khobar City, Eastern Saudi Arabia," *Obesity Reviews* 8, no. 2 (2203): 93–99.

116. Asian Development Bank, *Asian Water Development Outlook 2007* (Manila: Asian Development Bank, 2007), 4.

117. United Nations, *State of the Environment in Asia and the Pacific 2005*, 58–60.

118. Kelly D. Alley, *On the Banks of the Ganga: When Wastewater Meets a Sacred River* (Ann Arbor, Michigan: The University of Michigan Press, 2002).

119. See Asian Development Bank, *Emerging Asia: Changes and Challenges* (Manila: Asian Development Bank, 1997).

120. United Nations Economic and Social Commission for Asia and the Pacific, *Sustainable Agriculture and Food Security in Asia and the Pacific*, 63.

121. Asian Development Bank, *Asian Water Development Outlook 2007*, 8.

122. United Nations, *State of the Environment in Asia and the Pacific 2005*, 62.

123. In some areas in Bangladesh, the level of arsenic in the drinking water is in excess of 1 part per 1,000—far higher than the safe limit. The World Health Organization guidelines set the maximum level of arsenic in drinking water at 10 parts per billion. See World Health Organization, *Guidelines for Drinking-Water Quality, Volume 1: Recommendations*, 3rd ed. (Paris: World Health Organization, 2006).

124. Tom W. Gebel, "Arsenic and Drinking Water Contamination," *Science* 283, issue 5407 (1999): 1455.

125. According to the US Environmental Protection Agency, arsenic contamination can also result from runoff from orchards along with runoff from glass and electronic production wastes.

126. A. H. Welch and K. G. Stollenwerk, eds., *Arsenic in Groundwater: Geochemistry and Occurrence* (Boston: Kluwer Academic Publishers, 2003); D. K. Nordstrom, "Worldwide Occurrences of Arsenic in Groundwater," *Science* 296, no. 5576 (2002): 2143–45.

127. D. K. Nordstrom, "An Overview of Arsenic Mass-Poisoning in Bangladesh and West Bengal, India," in *Minor Elements 2000: Processing and Environmental Aspects of As, Sb, Se, Te and Bi*, edited by C. Young (Littleton, CO: Society for Mining, Metallurgy, and Exploration, 2000), 21–30.

128. Arsenicosis, or chronic arsenic poisoning from drinking water, can result in myriad symptoms and diseases, including skin cancer, lung cancer, cancer of the kidney and bladder, jaundice, cirrhosis, peripheral vascular disease, Raynaud's syndrome, blackfoot disease (a type of gangrene), anemia, and a thickening of the skin. It is caused by drinking arsenic-tainted water over an extended period. According to the World Health Organization, "The symptoms and signs that arsenic causes appear to differ between individuals, population groups and geographic areas. Thus, there is no universal definition of the disease caused by arsenic. This complicates the assessment of the burden on health of arsenic. Similarly, there is no method to identify those cases of internal cancer that were caused by arsenic from cancers induced by other factors." The World Health Organization, however, believes that "long-term exposure to arsenic via drinking water causes cancer of the skin, lungs, urinary bladder, and kidney, as well as other skin changes such as pigmentation changes and thickening (hyperkeratosis)." See World Health Organization, *Guidelines for Drinking-Water Quality*, 114–21.

129. Allan H. Smith, Elena O. Lingas, and Mahfuzar Rahman, "Contamination of Drinking Water by Arsenic in Bangladesh: A Public Health Emergency," *Bulletin of the World Health Organization* 78, no. 9 (2000): 1093–1103.

130. Fluoride is a desirable substance, helping to prevent or reduce dental decay and strengthen bones. Too little fluoride causes tooth decay and brittle bones. That is why fluoride is added to city water during treatment, if the fluoride level is low. But too much fluoride is toxic. Unless such water is treated, it leads to fluorosis, a condition characterized by severe anemia, stiff joints, painful and restricted movement, mottled teeth, and kidney failure. See World Health Organization, *Fluorides and Oral Health*, Report of a WHO Expert Committee on Oral Health Status and Fluoride Use, WHO Technical Report 846 (Geneva: World Health Organization, 1994).

131. "Groundwater in 33% of India Undrinkable—Iron, Fluoride, Salinity, Arsenic beyond Tolerance Levels in Many Districts: Government," *Times of India*, March 12, 2010.

132. A. Y. Hoekstra and A. K. Chapagain, *Globalization of Water: Sharing the Planet's Freshwater Resources* (Oxford: Blackwell, 2008); "Water Saving by Trade," Water Footprint Network, Enschede, the Netherlands, www.waterfootprint.org/index.php?page=files/ Water-saving-by-tra de; FAO, *Water Resources of the Near-East Region: A Review* (Rome: FAO, 1997).

133. International Water Management Institute and FAO, *Revitalizing Asia's Irrigation*, 24–38.

134. Water Resources Group, *Charting Our Water Future*, 12.

135. Intergovernmental Panel on Climate Change, *Climate Change 2007: Impacts, Adaptation and Vulnerability*, Working Group II Contribution to the Fourth Assessment Report of the Intergovernmental Panel on Climate Change (New York: Cambridge University Press, 2007), chap. 10, section 10.5.2, "Hydrology and Water Resources."

136. Harrison and Pearce, *AAAS Atlas of Population & Environment*, "Part 2—Natural Resources: Introduction."

Chapter 2

1. Cited by Joseph Nevins, "Resource Conflicts in a New World Order," *Geopolitics* 9, no. 1 (March 2004): 258. For a discussion of potential water wars, see Steven Solomon, *Water: The Epic Struggle for Wealth, Power and Civilization* (New York: HarperCollins, 2010); Diane Raines Ward, *Water Wars: Drought, Flood, Folly and the Politics of Thirst* (Darby, PA: Diane Publishing, 2002); Vandana Shiva, *Water Wars: Privatization, Pollution and Profit* (Cambridge, MA: South End Press, 2002); Fred Pearce, *When the Rivers Run Dry: Water—The Defining Crisis of the Twenty-First Century* (Boston: Beacon Press, 2007); and Marq de Villiers, *Water Wars: Is the World's Water Running Out?* (London: Weidenfeld & Nicolson, 1999).

2. Environmental News Service, "Water Wars Forecast If Solutions Not Found," January 1, 1999.

3. US National Intelligence Council, *Global Trends 2025: A Transformed World* (Washington, DC: National Intelligence Council, 2008), 66–67.

4. Ibid., 82.

5. Food and Agriculture Organization of the United Nations (FAO), *Irrigation in Asia in Figures*, Water Report 18 (Rome: FAO, 1999), 108.

6. Jian Xie, with Andres Liebenthal, Jeremy J. Warford, John A. Dixon, Manchuan Wang, Shiji Gao, Shuilin Wang, Yong Jiang, and Zhong Ma, *Addressing China's Water Scarcity: A Synthesis of Recommendations for Selected Water Resource Management Issues* (Washington, DC: World Bank, 2009), 8.

7. See United Nations Development Program (UNDP), *Human Development Report 2006: Beyond Scarcity—Power, Poverty and the Global Water Crisis* (New York: UNDP, 2007).

8. Ma Jun, *China's Water Crisis*, translated by Nancy Yang Liu and Lawrence R. Sullivan (Norwalk, CT: Eastbridge, 2004).

9. FAO, *Country Fact-Sheet: China*, www.fao.org/nr/water/Aquastat/data/factsheets/Aquastat_fact_sheet_cpr_en.pdf.

10. Jian Xie et al., *Addressing China's Water Scarcity*.

11. Robyn Meredith, *The Elephant and the Dragon: The Rise of India and China and What It Means for All of Us* (New York: W. W. Norton, 2007), 9–14.

12. See Peter Engardio, ed., *Chindia: How China and India Are Revolutionizing Global Business* (New York: McGraw-Hill, 2006); Jagdish N. Sheth, *Chindia Rising: How China and India Will Benefit Your Business* (New York: McGraw-Hill, 2008); and Jairam Ramesh, *Making Sense of Chindia: Reflections on China and India* (New Delhi: India Research Press, 2006).

13. Paul Kennedy, "A Bigger Nation Isn't Always Better," *New York Times*, April 18, 2008.

14. Charles Darwin, *The Origins of Species*, edited with an introduction and notes by Gillian Beer, Oxford World's Classics (Oxford: Oxford University Press, 1996), 68.

15. See, e.g., Clyde V. Prestowitz Jr., *Trading Places: How We Allowed Japan to Take the Lead* (New York: Basic Books, 1988).

16. Francis Fukuyama, "The End of History?" *The National Interest*, Summer 1989. Fukuyama was deputy director of the State Department's policy planning staff when this essay was published.

17. US secretary of state Hillary Clinton, "Remarks on Internet Freedom," speech at the Newseum, Washington, January 21, 2010, www.state.gov/secretary/rm/2010/01/135519.htm.

18. Stefan Halper, *The Beijing Consensus: How China's Authoritarian Model Will Dominate the Twenty-First Century* (New York: Basic Books, 2010); Ian Bremmer, *The End of the Free Market: Who Wins the War between States and Corporations?* (New York: Portfolio, 2010).

19. United Nations, *The State of the Environment in Asia and the Pacific 2005* (Bangkok: United Nations Economic and Social Commission for Asia and the Pacific, 2006), 63.

20. William R. Cline, *Global Warming and Agriculture: Impact Estimates by Country* (Washington, DC: Center for Global Development and Peterson Institute for International Economics, 2007), chap. 5, p. 49.

21. United Nations, *World Population Prospects: The 2006 Revision* (New York: Population Division, Department of Economic and Social Affairs, United Nations, 2007), 2.

22. Kapil Narula and Upmanu Lall, "Water Security Challenges in India," in *Asia's Next Challenge: Securing the Region's Water Future*, edited by Asia Society (New York: Asia Society, 2009), 21; FAO, Aquastat online data.

23. FAO, Aquastat online data, available at http://faostat.fao.org.

24. Chinese official Zhu Guangyao quoted in "Great River Theft," *South China Morning Post*, July 15, 2007.

25. Paul M. Kennedy, *The Rise and Fall of the Great Powers: Economic Change and Military Conflict from 1500 to 2000* (New York: Random House, 1990).

26. *Foreign Policy* journal and Fund for Peace, *The Failed States Index 2010* (Washington, DC: Fund for Peace, 2010), www.foreignpolicy.com/articles/2010/06/21/2010_failed_states_index_interactive_map_and_rankings.

27. Until a few years ago, Singapore was importing half its water supply. See Diane Segal, "Singapore's Water Trade with Malaysia and Alternatives," John F. Kennedy School of Government, Harvard University, 6; and Valerie Chew, "Singapore-Malaysia Water Agreements," National Library Board, Singapore, June 18, 2006. But with the expansion of nonconventional sources of supply, the imports came down to 40 percent in 2009.

28. United Nations Economic and Social Commission for Asia and the Pacific, *Guidebook to Water Resources, Use and Management in Asia and the Pacific, Vol. 1: Water Resources and Water Use*, Water Resources Series No. 74 (Bangkok: United Nations Economic and Social Commission for Asia and the Pacific, 1995), 305.

29. As part of the 1965 Separation Agreement, the two existing water accords were reconfirmed by the governments of Malaysia and Singapore and deposited with the United Nations.

30. Singapore Ministry of Foreign Affairs, "Singapore and Malaysia: Frequently Asked Questions," n.d.

31. Joey Long, "Desecuritizing the Water Issue in Singapore-Malaysia Relations," *Contemporary Southeast Asia* 23, no. 3 (December 2001): 504–32.

32. See, e.g., Tim Huxley, *Defending the Lion City: The Armed Forces of Singapore* (Crows Nest, Australia: Allen & Unwin, 2000); C. G. Kwa, ed., *Beyond Vulnerability: Water in Singapore–Malaysia Relations* (Singapore: Institute of Defense and Strategic Studies, 2002); and Y. C. Kog, *Natural Resource Management and Environmental Security in Southeast Asia: A Case Study of Clean Water Supplies in Singapore*, Working Paper 15 (Singapore: Institute of Defense and Strategic Studies, 2001).

33. Lee Kuan Yew, *From Third World to First: The Singapore Story 1965–2000*, Memoirs of Lee Kuan Yew, vol. 2 (Singapore: Straits Times Press and Times Media, 2000), 276.

34. Water Resources Group (Barilla Group, Coca-Cola Company, International Finance Corporation, McKinsey & Company, Nestlé S.A., New Holland Agriculture, SABMiller PLC, Standard Chartered Bank, and Syngenta AG), *Charting Our Water Future* (New York: 2030 Water Resources Group, 2009), 124.

35. FAO, *General Summary for the Countries of the Former Soviet Union*, Aquastat Online Data.

36. Jian Xie et al., *Addressing China's Water Scarcity*.

37. Cited by Scott Moore, "Climate Change, Water and China's National Interest," *China Security*, 5, no. 3 (2009); and "Funds Flow into Water Industry," *The Standard* (Hong Kong), May 14, 2007.

38. Judith Shapiro, *Mao's War against Nature: Politics and the Environment in Revolutionary China* (Cambridge: Cambridge University Press, 2001). Also see Robert P. Weller and Peter K. Bol, "From Heaven-and-Earth to Nature: Chinese Concepts of the Environment and Their Influence on Policy Implementation," in *Energizing China*, edited by Michael B. McElroy, Chris P. Nielsen, and Peter Lydon (Cambridge, MA: Harvard University Press, 1998); and Todd M. Johnson, Liu Feng, and Richard Newfarmer, *Clear Water, Blue Skies: China's Environment in the New Century* (Washington, DC: World Bank, 1997).

39. Yang Jisheng, *Tombstone* (Mùbēi), in Mandarin, vols. 1 and 2 (Hong Kong, 2008). The book has not been translated into English thus far. It has been banned in mainland China.

40. Brook Larmer, "Bitter Waters: Can China Save the Yellow—Its Mother River?" *National Geographic*, May 2008.

41. Peter M. Vitousek, Harold A. Mooney, Jane Lubchenco, and Jerry M. Melillo, "Human Domination of Earth's Ecosystems," *Science* 277, no. 5325 (July 25, 1997): 494–99.

42. Michael Gorbachev, "People: Water Rights," introductory article by Guest Editor Mikhail Gorbachev, *Civilization* (the magazine of the US Library of Congress), October–November 2000.

43. CNN, "Water, Water Everywhere—But Will There Be Enough to Drink?" January 3, 2000.

44. See Shui Fu, "A Profile of Dams in China," in *The River Dragon Has Come! The Three Gorges Dam and the Fate of China's Yangtze River and Its People*, edited by John G. Thibodeau and Philip Williams, and translated by Ming Yi (Armonk, NY: M. E. Sharpe, 1998).

45. Jiyu Chen, "Dams, Effect on Coasts," in *Encyclopedia of Coastal Science*, edited by Maurice L. Schwartz, vol. 24, Encyclopedia of Earth Sciences Series (Berlin: Springer, 2005).

46. Founded in 1928, the International Commission on Large Dams (ICOLD) is a nongovernmental international organization that serves as a forum for engineers, geologists, and scientists from governmental and private bodies, companies, universities, and laboratories to exchange their ideas and experience in dam engineering. The World Commission on Dams has adopted the ICOLD definition and reported that there are more than 45,000 large dams worldwide.

47. FAO, *Country Fact-Sheet: China*, 2010, Aquastat online data.

48. Peter Bosshard, "China's Overseas Dam Builders: From Rogue Players to Responsible Actors?" *Asia-Pacific Journal,* April 26, 2010.

49. Kristen McDonald, Peter Bosshard, and Nicole Brewer, "Exporting Dams: China's Hydropower Industry Goes Global, *Journal of Environmental Management* 90, supplement 3 (July 2009): S301.

50. Human Rights Watch, *World Report 2008: Sudan* (New York: Human Rights Watch, 2008).

51. Voice of America, "Bomb Blasts Hit Burma Dam Project," April 17, 2010, www1 .voanews.com/english/news/asia/Bomb-Blasts-Hit-Burma-Dam-Proj ect-91243989. html.

52. "The Burmese Villagers Who Face a Flood of Discontent and Displacement," *Irish Times*, June 19, 2010.

53. India has made several protests to China and Pakistan over the series of new dams under construction by Chinese firms in Pakistan-administered Kashmir. After China signed an accord with Pakistan in August 2009 to build the Bunji Dam in the Gilgit-Baltistan region, India's External Affairs Ministry announced: "The government of India lodged a protest against the construction of the project located in a part of Jammu and Kashmir under the illegal occupation of Pakistan." The protests, however, have fallen on deaf ears. Indian foreign secretary Nirupama Rao admitted in May 2010 that China had disregarded repeatedly expressed Indian concerns over Chinese hydro projects in Pakistan-held Kashmir.

54. Selig Harrison, "China's Discreet Hold on Pakistan's Northern Borderlands," *International Herald Tribune*, August 26, 2010. The Chinese Foreign Ministry, reacting to the revelations, said on September 2, 2010: "'The story that China has deployed its military in a northern part of Pakistan is totally groundless and out of ulterior motive." It did not, however, deny specifically that Chinese troops were helping build major infrastructure and strategic projects in the Gilgit-Baltistan region.

55. The use of convict laborers by Chinese companies has been reported in countries ranging from Sri Lanka and the Maldives in the Indian Ocean to Africa. Such a practice impacts international humanitarian law and trade and investment norms, besides potentially imperiling the security of local communities. Brahma Chellaney, "China's Newest Export: Convicts," *The Guardian* (London), July 29, 2010; Brahma Chellaney, "China's Latest Export Innovation? Send Your Convicts Overseas," *Washington Times*, July 6, 2010; and Brahma Chellaney, "Exporting Convicts Stains China's Reputation," *Globe and Mail* (Toronto), August 3, 2010. Richard Behar, an award-winning American investigative journalist, wrote: "In Zambia, an immigration consultant told me she has processed paperwork for hundreds of Chinese prisoners." Richard Behar, "China's New Oil Supplier," *Fast Company*, June 1, 2008. Citing China's road construction in the African country of Benin, Roberta Cohen, deputy assistant secretary of state for human rights in the Jimmy Carter administration, wrote in 1991 that "the Chinese not only export goods made by prison labor, but they export prison workers too. . . . Each year, thousands of Chinese laborers are sent to Africa and other third-world countries to build roads and work on construction projects." Roberta Cohen, "China Has Used Prison Labor in Africa," letter to the editor, *New York Times*, May 11, 1991.

56. Chinese Ministry of Commerce, official statement of August 10, 2010, denying unspecified "foreign media reports" on use of Chinese prison labor at Chinese-run overseas projects; and Xinhua, "Ministry Rejects Report on China Convicts Sent Abroad to Labor," August 10, 2010. The general denial merely cited China's national regulations, even though Beijing has been accused of failing to enforce its own laws.

57. Norwegian Nobel Committee, "The Nobel Peace Prize 2010: Liu Xiaobo," October 8, 2010, http://nobelprize.org/nobel_prizes/peace/laureates/2010/press.html.

58. Roy Walmsley, *World Prison Population List—Eighth Edition* (London: International Centre for Prison Studies, King's College, 2009), 1, 4.

59. Gulag labor in China has long produced goods for exports. Countless numbers of detainees have died in the labor camps. In fact, China is the only important power with a still-thriving system of labor camps. See Philip F. Williams and Yenna Wu, *The Great Wall of Confinement: The Chinese Prison Camp through Contemporary Fiction and Reportage* (Berkeley: University of California Press, 2004); Jean-Louis Margolin, "China: A Long March into Night," in *The Black Book of Communism: Crimes, Terror, Repression*, edited by Stephane Courtois, Nicolas Werth, Jean-Louis Panne, Andrzej Paczkowski, Karel Bartosek, and Jean-Louis Margolin and translated by Jonathan Murphy and Mark Kramer (Cambridge, MA: Harvard University Press, 1999), 463–546; Hongda Harry Wu, *Laogai: The Chinese Gulag* (Boulder, CO: Westview Press, 1992); Orville Schell, "Capitalist Slavery in China," *New York Times*, April 27, 1991; and Jung Chang and Jon Halliday, *Mao: The Unknown Story* (London: Jonathan Cape, 2005).

60. Amnesty International, *Death Sentences and Executions in 2009* (London: Amnesty International, 2010).

61. E.g., in Angola the *Wall Street Journal* reported that the majority of the workforce on a number of projects was Chinese. One specific example is the 505-kilometer Mocamedes Railway project in southern Angola, which employs 160 Chinese workers and 60 Angolans. Benoit Faucon and Sherry Su, "Hostility toward Workers Cools Angola–China Relationship," *Wall Street Journal*, August 10, 2010.

62. Meredith, *Elephant and the Dragon*, 179.

63. Dennis Pamlin and Long Baijin, *Re-Think China's Outward Investment Flows* (Gland, Switzerland: World Wide Fund for Nature, 2007), 19–21.

64. Peter Bosshard, "China Dams the World," *World Policy Journal*, Winter 2009–10), 44.

65. Jim Yardley, "China Banks on Hydropower to Cut Emissions, but at Huge Human Cost," *New York Times*, November 18, 2007.

66. Peter Bosshard, "China Dams the World," 44–45.

67. McDonald, Bosshard, and Brewer, "Exporting Dams," S301.

68. Bates Gill and James Reilly, "The Tenuous Hold of China Inc. in Africa," *Washington Quarterly* 30, no. 3 (Summer 2007): 40.

69. McDonald, Bosshard, and Brewer, "Exporting Dams," S299.

70. Bosshard, "China Dams the World," 45.

71. Wang Huazhong, "Dam Forces Relocations of 300,000 More," *China Daily*, January 21, 2010.

72. Chen, "Dams, Effect on Coasts."

73. "Experts Warn China's Water Supply May Well Run Dry," *South China Morning Post*, September 1, 2003.

74. Geremie R. Barmé, *Shades of Mao: The Posthumous Cult of the Great Leader* (Armonk, NY: M. E. Sharpe, 1996), 54.

75. Gavan McCormack, "Water Margins: Competing Paradigms in China," *Critical Asian Studies* 33, no. 1 (March 2001): 29–30.

76. See J. Denis Summers-Smith, *In Search of Sparrows*, illustrated by Euan Dunn (London: T. & A. D. Poyser, 1992).

77. Tim Luard, "China Follows Mao with Mass Cull," BBC News, January 6, 2004, http://news.bbc.co.uk/2/hi/asia-pacific/3371659.stm.

78. The forcible relocation of people on a mass scale began as soon as the Three Gorges project began. See Human Rights Watch, *The Three Gorges Dam in China: Forced Resettlement, Suppression of Dissent and Labor Rights Concerns* (New York: Human Rights Watch, 1995).

79. HydroChina Corporation, "Map of Planned Dams," www.hydrochina.com.cn/zgsd/images/ziyuan_b.gif.

80. Meredith, *Elephant and the Dragon*, 20.

81. Cheng Li, *China's Leaders: The New Generation* (Lanham, MD: Rowman & Littlefield, 2001), 35.

82. Chinese president Jiang Zemin, "Speech Marking Yangtze Damming for Three Gorges Project," November 8, 1997, text released by Embassy of the People's Republic of China, Washington, www.china-embassy.org/eng/zt/sxgc/t36514.htm.

83. Cited by Damien Mcelroy, "China Planning Nuclear Blasts to Build Giant Hydro Project," *The Telegraph* (London), October 22, 2000.

84. Claude Arpi, "Diverting the Brahmaputra: Declaration of War?," Rediff.com, October 23, 2003, www.rediff.com/news/2003/oct/27spec.htm.

85. Vaclav Smil, "Finding Mutual Interests in Nature," *Far Eastern Economic Review* 172, no. 8 (October 2009): 44.

86. Darrin Magee, "Powershed Politics: Yunnan Hydropower Under Great Western Development," *China Quarterly*, no. 185 (March 2006): 25.

87. Jim Yardley, "Choking on Growth, Part II: Water and China's Future," *New York Times*, September 28, 2007.

88. Kenneth Pomeranz, "Water Shortages, Mega-Projects and Environmental Politics in China, India, and Southeast Asia," *Asia-Pacific Journal*, July 27, 2009, www.japanfocus.org/Kenneth-Pomeranz/3195; also published in *New Left Review*: Kenneth Pomeranz, "The

Great Himalayan Watershed: Agrarian Crisis, Mega-Dams and the Environment," *New Left Review*, July–August 2009, 5–39.

89. Tan Yingzi, "Yellow River Dams on Verge of Collapse," *China Daily*, June 19, 2009, www.chinadaily.com.cn/china/2009-06/19/content_8301942.htm.

90. Ibid.

91. Keith Bradsher, "China's Energy Use Threatens Goals on Warming," *New York Times*, May 6, 2010.

92. Shixiong Cao, "Why Large-Scale Afforestation Efforts in China Have Failed to Solve the Desertification Problem," *Environmental Science & Technology*, March 15, 2008, 1827.

93. He Bochuan, *China on the Edge: The Crisis of Ecology and Development* [Shan'ao shang de Zhongguo], translated by Jenny Holdaway, Guo Jian-sheng, Susan Brick, Hu Si-gang, and Charles Wong (San Francisco: China Books and Periodicals, 1991).

94. Yardley, "Choking on Growth, Part II: Water and China's Future."

95. Shaozhong Kang, Xiaoling Su, Ling Tong, Jianhua Zhang, Lu Zhang, and W. J. Davies, "A Warning from an Ancient Oasis: Intensive Human Activities Are Leading to Potential Ecological and Social Catastrophe," *International Journal of Sustainable Development and World Ecology* 15, no. 5 (October 2008): 440–47.

96. Probe International, *Beijing's Water Crisis: 1949–2008 Olympics* (Toronto: Probe International, 2008).

97. Yan Weijue, "Beijing's Water Shortage Worsens as SNWD Project Delayed," *China Daily*, June 28, 2010.

98. Joseph Kahn and Jim Yardley, "Choking on Growth, Part I: As China Roars, Pollution Reaches Deadly Extremes," *New York Times*, August 26, 2007.

99. The 2007 survey by the Yellow River Conservancy Committee was cited in "One-Third of China's Yellow River Polluted," Associated Press, November 25, 2008.

100. Emma Graham-Harrison, "China's Water Pollution Level Higher Than Estimated in 2007," *Washington Post*, February 10, 2010.

101. Agence France-Press, Beijing-datelined dispatch, December 30, 2005. Also see Maria Burke, "Managing China's Water Resources," *Environmental Science & Technology*, May 1, 2000, 219–21.

102. See Asian Development Bank, Japan Bank for International Cooperation, and World Bank, *Connecting East Asia: A New Framework for Infrastructure* (Washington, DC: World Bank, 2005).

103. For an account of the origins of China's environmental and water crisis, see Vaclav Smil, *China's Environmental Crisis: An Inquiry into the Limits of National Development* (Armonk, NY: M. E. Sharpe, 1993); Elizabeth C. Economy, *The River Runs Black: The Environmental Challenge to China's Future* (Ithaca, NY: Cornell University Press, 2005); and Shapiro, *Mao's War against Nature.*

104. Cited by Larmer, "Bitter Waters."

105. Planning Commission of India, *Report of the Steering Committee on Water Resources for Eleventh Five-Year Plan 2007–2012* (New Delhi: Planning Commission, 2007), 3.

106. United Nations, *State of the Environment in Asia and the Pacific 2005*, 58–59.

107. Water Resources Group, *Charting Our Water Future*, 10.

108. The full text of the amended Inter-State River Water Disputes Act is available at the website of the Indian Ministry of Water Resources, http://wrmin.nic.in/index3.asp?subsublink id = 377&langid = 1&sslid = 385.

109. The territorial division of rivers was a proposal tabled by the World Bank, which rejected the idea of building India-Pakistan interdependence and sought to ensure that each party enjoyed relative independence to develop the resources of rivers allotted to it. Niranjan D. Gulhati, *Indus Waters Treaty: An Exercise in International Mediation* (Bombay: Allied Publishers, 1973), 139. Also see, Aloys Arthur Michel, *The Indus Rivers: A Study of the Effects of*

Partition (New Haven, CT: Yale University Press, 1967); and G. T. Keith Pitman, "The Role of the World Bank in Enhancing Cooperation and Resolving Conflict on International Watercourses: The Case of the Indus Basin," in *International Watercourse: Enhancing Cooperation and Managing Conflict*, World Bank Technical Paper 414, edited by Salman M. A. Salman and Laurence Boisson de Chazournes (Washington, DC: World Bank,1998).

110. Salman M. A. Salman and Kishor Uprety, *Conflict and Cooperation on South Asia's International Rivers: A Legal Perspective* (London: Kluwer Law International, 2002), 61.

111. The principles of customary international water law were codified in The Helsinki Rules on the Uses of the Waters of International Rivers, adopted by the International Law Association at Helsinki in August 1966. The Helsinki Rules, in turn, shaped the provisions of the Convention on the Law of the Non-Navigational Uses of International Watercourses, which was adopted by the United Nations General Assembly on May 21, 1997.

112. Gulhati, *Indus Waters Treaty*, 149.

113. See, e.g., John Briscoe and R. P. S. Malik, *India's Water Economy: Bracing for a Turbulent Future* (New York: Oxford University Press, 2006).

114. Water Resources Group, *Charting Our Water Future*, 10, 54–56.

115. Planning Commission of India, *Report of the Expert Group on Groundwater Management and Ownership* (New Delhi: Planning Commission, 2007), 1.

116. FAO, *Country Profile: Pakistan*, www.fao.org/nr/water/Aquastat/countries/pakistan/index.stm; Pakistan Ministry of Water and Power, *Pakistan Water Sector Strategy*, Detailed Strategy Formulation, Volume 4 (Islamabad: Ministry of Water and Power, 2002), 82.

117. Water Resources Group, *Charting Our Water Future*, 56.

118. National Water Policy, as adopted by the National Water Resources Council on April 1, 2002, official text, www.nih.ernet.in/belgaum/NWP.html.

119. Prime Minister Atal Bihari Vajpayee, Speech to the Fifth Meeting of the National Water Resources Council in New Delhi, April 1, 2002, official transcript released by the Prime Minister's Office.

120. Narula and Lall, "Water Security Challenges in India," 22.

121. Water Resources Group, *Charting Our Water Future*, 106, 114.

122. Cited by Payal Sampat, *Groundwater Shock: The Polluting of the World's Major Freshwater Stores* (Washington, DC: Worldwatch Institute, 1999).

123. *The Times of India*, March 12, 2010.

124. UN-Water, *Water in a Changing World: The United Nations World Water Development Report 3* (Paris and London: UNESCO and Earthscan, 2009), 36.

125. World Commission on Dams, "Dams and Water: Global Statistics," online data, available at www.dams.org/global/.

126. Government of India, *Report of the Working Group on Water Resources for the Eleventh Five-Year Plan 2007–2012* (New Delhi: Ministry of Water Resources, 2006), 8.

127. M. Falkenmarkand and M. Lannerstad, "Consumptive Water Use to Feed Humanity—Curing a Blind Spot," *Hydrology and Earth System Sciences* 9, nos. 1–2 (2005): 25–26.

128. Government of India, *Report of the Working Group on Water Resources for the Eleventh Five-Year Plan 2007–2012*, 12.

129. Yuanhua Li, "Strategies for Coping with Water Scarcity in China," presentation by the deputy director-general of the Department of Rural Water Management, Ministry of Water Resources, China, at UN-Water meeting in Stockholm, August 23, 2006, www.unwater.org/downloads/wwwYuananhua.pdf.

130. Lester R. Brown, "Melting Mountain Glaciers Will Shrink Grain Harvests in China and India," Earth Policy Institute, March 20, 2008.

131. *Food Price Watch* (World Bank), May 2010, 1.

132. Paul Harrison and Fred Pearce, *AAAS Atlas of Population & Environment* (Washington, DC: American Association for the Advancement of Science, 2007), "Part 2—Natural Resources: Foodcrops."

133. Falkenmarkand and Lannerstad, "Consumptive Water Use to Feed Humanity," 26.

134. Shilong Piao, Philippe Ciais, Yao Huang, Zehao Shen, Shushi Peng, Junsheng Li, Liping Zhou, Hongyan Liu, Yuecun Ma, Yihui Ding, Pierre Friedlingstein, Chunzhen Liu, Kun Tan, Yongqiang Yu, Tianyi Zhang, and Jingyun Fang, "The Impacts of Climate Change on Water Resources and Agriculture in China," *Nature* 467 (September 2, 2010): 43–51, DOI: 10.1038/nature09364.

135. Sandra Postel, "But Who Will Export Tomorrow's Virtual Water?" *Seed Magazine*, May 14, 2009.

136. William J. Cosgrove and Frank R. Rijsberman, *World Water Vision: Making Water Everybody's Business* (London: Earthscan, 2000), xxi.

137. Mark W. Rosegrant, Ximing Cai, and Sarah A. Cline, *Global Water Outlook to 2025: Averting an Impending Crisis*, Food Policy Report (Washington, DC: International Food Policy Research Institute, 2002), 72.

138. H. G. Rees and D. N. Collins, "An Assessment of the Impacts of Deglaciation on the Water Resources of the Himalaya," in *Snow and Glacier Aspects of Water Resources Management in the Himalayas*, Final Technical Report (Wallingford, UK: Center for Ecology and Hydrology, Natural Environment Research Council, 2004).

139. Shilong Piao et al., "Impacts of Climate Change."

140. FAO, *World Water Resources by Country*, Aquastat Online Database, 2010.

141. Water Resources Group, *Charting Our Water Future*, 10.

142. Jennifer L. Turner, "Water Conflicts: Catalyzing Change in China," in *Asia's Next Challenge: Securing the Region's Water Future*, edited by Asia Society (New York: Asia Society, 2009), 27.

143. World Bank, *China: Country Water Resources Assistance Strategy*, 11.

144. Briscoe and Malik, *India's Water Economy*, 1.

145. Water Resources Group, *Charting Our Water Future*, 56.

146. FAO, *Country Factsheet: India* and *Country Factsheet: China*, June 2010.

147. Narula and Lall, "Water Security Challenges in India," 21.

148. The middle class in China is projected to grow from 4 percent of the population in 2005 to 56 percent in 2030, in the fastest such expansion in modern world history.

149. India has the highest arable land in the world as a percentage of the total national land area, with slightly more than 50 percent of the country's geographic area considered arable.

150. See Ashok Swain, *Managing Water Conflict: Asia, Africa and the Middle East* (London: Routledge, 2004); A. K. Biswas, ed., *Asian International Waters: From Ganges-Brahmaputra to Mekong* (Bombay: Oxford University Press, 1996); Arun P. Elhance, *Hydropolitics in the Third World: Conflict and Cooperation in International River Basins* (Washington, DC: US Institute of Peace, 1999); and Anthony Turton and Roland Henwood, eds., *Hydropolitics in the Developing World* (Pretoria: African Water Issues Research Unit, 2002).

151. Gwyn Rees, ed., *Hindu Kush-Himalayan FRIEND 2000–2003* (Paris: International Hydrological Program of UNESCO, 2004), ix.

152. FAO, *General Summary for the Countries of the Former Soviet Union*, 2010, Aquastat Online Data.

153. Michael Renner, *Water Challenges in Central-South Asia*, Noref Policy Brief 4 (Oslo: Norwegian Peacebuilding Center, 2009), 2.

Chapter 3

1. Zhang Bai-ping, Chen Xiao-dong, Li Bao-lin, and Yao Yong-hui, "Biodiversity and Conservation in the Tibetan Plateau," *Journal of Geographical Sciences* 12, no. 2 (April 2002): 135.

2. See Tatum S. Simonson, Yingzhong Yang, Chad D. Huff, Haixia Yun, Ga Qin, David J. Witherspoon, Zhenzhong Bai, Felipe R. Lorenzo, Jinchuan Xing, Lynn B. Jorde, Josef T. Prchal, and RiLi Ge, "Genetic Evidence for High-Altitude Adaptation in Tibet," *Science*, May 13, 2010, DOI: 10.1126/science.1189406; Cynthia M. Beall, Gianpiero L. Cavalleri, Libin Deng, Robert C. Elston, Yang Gao, Jo Knight, Chaohua Li, Jiang Chuan Li, Yu Liang, Mark McCormack, Hugh E. Montgomery, Hao Pan, Peter A. Robbins, Kevin V. Shianna, Siu Cheung Tam, Ngodrop Tsering, Krishna R. Veeramah, Wei Wang, Puchung Wangdui, Michael E. Weale, Yaomin Xu, Zhe Xu, Ling Yang, M. Justin Zaman, Changqing Zeng, Li Zhang, Xianglong Zhang, Pingcuo Zhaxi, and Yong Tang Zheng, "Natural Selection on *EPAS1 (HIF2α)* Associated with Low Hemoglobin Concentration in Tibetan Highlanders," *Proceedings of the National Academy of Sciences* (PNAS) 107, no. 25 (June 22, 2010): 11459–464; and Xin Yi, Yu Liang, Emilia Huerta-Sanchez, Xin Jin, Zha Xi Ping Cuo, John E. Pool, Xun Xu, Hui Jiang, Nicolas Vinckenbosch, Thorfinn Sand Korneliussen, Hancheng Zheng, Tao Liu, Weiming He, Kui Li, Ruibang Luo, Xifang Nie, Honglong Wu, Meiru Zhao, Hongzhi Cao, Jing Zou, Ying Shan, Shuzheng Li, Qi Yang, Asan, Peixiang Ni, Geng Tian, Junming Xu, Xiao Liu, Tao Jiang, Renhua Wu, Guangyu Zhou, Meifang Tang, Junjie Qin, Tong Wang, Shuijian Feng, Guohong Li, Huasang, Jiangbai Luosang, Wei Wang, Fang Chen, Yading Wang, Xiaoguang Zheng, Zhuo Li, Zhuoma Bianba, Ge Yang, Xinping Wang, Shuhui Tang, Guoyi Gao, Yong Chen, Zhen Luo, Lamu Gusang, Zheng Cao, Qinghui Zhang, Weihan Ouyang, Xiaoli Ren, Huiqing Liang, Huisong Zheng, Yebo Huang, Jingxiang Li, Lars Bolund, Karsten Kristiansen, Yingrui Li, Yong Zhang, Xiuqing Zhang, Ruiqiang Li, Songgang Li, Huanming Yang, Rasmus Nielsen, Jun Wang, and Jian Wang, "Sequencing of 50 Human Exomes Reveals Adaptation to High Altitudes," *Science* 329, no. 5987 (July 2, 2010): 75–78.

3. Xuefeng Cui, Hans-F. Graf, Baerbel Langmann, Wen Chen, and Ronghui Huang, "Hydrological Impacts of Deforestation on the Southeast Tibetan Plateau," *Earth Interactions* 11, no. 15 (September 2007): 1–18.

4. Hong Xie, Jiansheng Ye, Xiuming Liu, and Chongyi E., "Warming and Drying Trends on the Tibetan Plateau," *Theoretical and Applied Climatology* (September 2009): DOI: 10.1007/s00704-009-0215-9.

5. Daniel Viviroli, Hans H. Dürr, Bruno Messerli, Michel Meybeck, and Rolf Weingartner, "Mountains of the World, Water Towers for Humanity: Typology, Mapping and Global Significance," *Water Resources Research* 43, no. W07447 (July 28, 2007): DOI: 10.1029/2006WR005653.

6. Rolf Weingartner, Daniel Viviroli, and Greg Greenwood, "Mountain Waters in a Changing World," in *Global Change and Sustainable Development in Mountain Regions*, Proceedings of the COST Strategic Workshop, Alpine Space—Man & Environment Volume 7, edited by R. Jandl, A. Borsdorf, H. van Miegroet, R. Lackner and R. Psenner (Innsbruck: Innsbruck University Press, 2009).

7. Based on 2010 estimates of the United Nations' Population Information Network or on figures in United Nations, *World Population Prospects: The 2008 Revision* (New York: United Nations Population Division, Department of Economic and Social Affairs, 2009).

8. A megadelta is defined as having an area of more than 10,000 square kilometers.

9. R. V. Cruz, H. Harasawa, M. Lal, S. Wu, Y. Anokhin, B. Punsalmaa, Y. Honda, M. Jafari, C. Li, and N. Huu Ninh, "Asia," in *Climate Change 2007: Impacts, Adaptation and Vulnerability. Contribution of Working Group II to the Fourth Assessment Report of the Intergovernmental Panel on Climate Change*, edited by M. L. Parry, O. F. Canziani, J. P. Palutikof, P. J. van der Linden, and C. E. Hanson (Cambridge: Cambridge University Press, 2007), chap. 10, section 10.6.1, "Mega-Deltas in Asia."

10. Walter Immerzeel, Jetse Stoorvogelb, and John Antlec, "Can Payments for Ecosystem Services Secure the Water Tower of Tibet?" *Agricultural Systems* 96, issues 1–3 (March 2008): 52–63.

11. Cruz et al., "Asia," 469–506.

12. Walter W. Immerzeel, Ludovicus P. H. van Beek, and Marc F. P. Bierkens, "Climate Change Will Affect the Asian Water Towers," *Science* 328, no. 5983 (June 11, 2010): 1382–85, DOI: 10.1126/science.1183188.

13. World Wide Fund for Nature, *World's Top 10 Rivers at Risk* (Gland, Switzerland: WWF International, 2007), 4.

14. D. G. Hahn and S. Manabe, "The Role of Mountains in the South Asian Monsoon Circulation," *Journal of the Atmospheric Sciences* 32 (1975): 1515–41; H. H. Hsu and X. Liu, "Relationship between the Tibetan Plateau Heating and East Asian Summer Monsoon Rainfall," *Geophysical Research Letters* 30 (2003): 2066, DOI: 10.1029/2003GL017909; B. Wang, ed., *The Asian Monsoon* (Berlin and New York: Springer Verlag and Praxis Publishing, 2006).

15. A. M. Duan and G. X. Wu, "Role of the Tibetan Plateau Thermal Forcing in the Summer Climate Patterns over Subtropical Asia," *Climate Dynamics* 24, no. 7/8 (June 2005): 793–807; Tomonori Sato and Fujio Kimura, "How Does the Tibetan Plateau Affect the Transition of Indian Monsoon Rainfall?" *Monthly Weather Review* 135, no. 5 (2007): 2006–15.

16. Rashid Hassan, Robert Scholes, and Neville Ash, eds., *Ecosystems and Human Well-Being: Current State and Trends, Volume 1, Millennium Ecosystem Assessment* (Washington, DC: Island Press, 2005), chap. 24, "Mountain Systems," 686.

17. Conservational International, "The Himalaya Hotspot" (Arlington, VA: Conservation International, 2007).

18. Paul Harrison and Fred Pearce, *AAAS Atlas of Population & Environment* (Washington, DC: American Association for the Advancement of Science, 2007), "Part 2—Ecosystems: Mountains."

19. Guodong Cheng and Tonghua Wu, "Responses of Permafrost to Climate Change and Their Environmental Significance, Qinghai-Tibet Plateau," *Journal of Geophysical Research* 112 (2007): DOI: 10.1029/2006JF000631.

20. Baolai Wang and Hugh M. French, "Climate Controls and High-Altitude Permafrost: Qinghai-Xizang (Tibet) Plateau, China," *Permafrost and Periglacial Processes* 5, no. 2 (August 2006): 87–100.

21. Xinhua, "Environment of 'Roof of the World' under Threat," May 16, 2005, posted by the Chinese Ministry of Water Resources on its website, www.mwr.gov.cn/english/.

22. If all types of glaciers are counted, the figure jumps to 36,793, according to official Chinese statistics. See Y. Ding, S. Liu, J. Li, and D. Shangguan, "The Retreat of Glaciers in Response to Recent Climate Warming in Western China," *Annals of Glaciology* 43, no. 1 (2006): 97–105; Cruz et al., "Asia."

23. Food and Agriculture Organization of the United Nations, *Irrigation in Asia in Figures* (Rome: Food and Agriculture Organization of the United Nations, 1999), 93.

24. Intergovernmental Panel on Climate Change, *Climate Change 2007: The Physical Science Basis. Contribution of Working Group I to the Fourth Assessment Report of the Intergovernmental Panel on Climate Change*, edited by S. Solomon, D. Qin, M. Manning, Z. Chen, M. Marquis, K. B. Averyt, M. Tignor, and H. L. Miller (Cambridge: Cambridge University Press, 2007), 235–336.

25. Hong Xie et al., "Warming and Drying Trends on the Tibetan Plateau."

26. T. P. Barnett, J. C. Adam, and D. P. Lettenmaier, "Potential Impacts of a Warming Climate on Water Availability in Snow-Dominated Regions," *Nature* 438 (November 17, 2005): 306.

27. Immerzeel, van Beek, and Bierkens, "Climate Change Will Affect the Asian Water Towers," 1384–85.

28. See Per Kvaerne, *The Bon Religion of Tibet: The Iconography of a Living Tradition* (Boston: Shambala, 2001).

29. Charles Allen, *A Mountain in Tibet: The Search for Mount Kailash and the Sources of the Great Rivers of Asia* (London: Abacus, 2003), 25–26; Robert Thurman and Tad Wise, *Circling the Sacred Mountain: A Spiritual Adventure through the Himalayas* (New York: Bantam Books, 1999), 3–4.

30. The Irrawaddy River, Burma's largest river and most important commercial waterway, originates as small streams on the Tibetan Plateau. The main Irrawaddy is formed by the confluence of the N'Mai and Mali rivers, which draw waters from the Himalayan-range glaciers. Before the confluence in Kachin state, the N'Mai and the Mali are joined by smaller streams from the Tibetan Plateau.

31. One stem of River Manas originates in Tibet's Mount Zholchen and enters India's Arunachal Pradesh State at the Bumla Pass.

32. A. M. Anders, G. H. Roe, B. Hallet, D. R. Montgomery, N. J. Finnegan, and J. Putkonen, "Spatial Patterns of Precipitation and Topography in the Himalayas," in *Tectonics, Climate and Landscape Evolution*, Geological Society of America Special Paper 398, edited by S. D. Willett, N. Hovius, M.T. Brandon, and D. M. Fisher (Boulder, CO: Geological Society of America, 2006), 39–53.

33. Mianping Zheng, *An Introduction to Saline Lakes on the Qinghai-Tibet Plateau* (Berlin: Springer, 1997), 55.

34. Chinese Ministry of Water Resources, "Water Resources in China," Ministry of Water Resources, n.d., Beijing, available at www.mwr.gov.cn/.

35. Gavan McCormack, "Water Margins: Competing Paradigms in China," *Critical Asian Studies* 33, no. 1 (March 2001): 5–8.

36. Patrick T. Hughes, "Environmental Degradation in the Tibetan Autonomous Region," Inventory of Conflict and Environment Case Study (Washington, DC: American University, 2006).

37. Elizabeth C. Economy, *The River Runs Black: The Environmental Challenge to China's Future* (Ithaca, NY: Cornell University Press, 2005), 27–58.

38. Ben Hillman, "Development with Tibetan Characteristics," *Wall Street Journal*, January 31, 2010.

39. See Tsering Shakya, *The Dragon in the Land of Snows: A History of Modern Tibet since 1947* (New York: Columbia University Press, 1999); James Millward, *Beyond the Pass: Economy, Ethnicity, and Empire in Qing Central Asia, 1759–1864* (Stanford, CA: Stanford University Press, 1998); Peter Perdue, *China Marches West: The Qing Conquest of Central Eurasia* (Cambridge, MA: Belknap Press, 2005); Melvyn C. Goldstein, *The Snow Lion and the Dragon: China, Tibet, and the Dalai Lama* (Berkeley: University of California Press, 1999); and Diane Wolff, *Tibet Unconquered: An Epic Struggle for Freedom* (New York: Palgrave Macmillan, 2010).

40. Information Office of the State Council of the People's Republic of China, *Tibet—Its Ownership and Human Rights Situation*, White Paper (Beijing: People's Republic of China, 1992), preamble to Part I, "Ownership of Tibet."

41. The October 2009 session of the UNESCO Intergovernmental Committee for the Safeguarding of Intangible Cultural Heritage acceded to the Chinese request, taking Kyrgyzstan by surprise.

42. Warren W. Smith Jr., *Tibetan Nation: A History of Tibetan Nationalism and Sino-Tibetan Relations* (Boulder, CO: Westview Press, 1996), 83–100.

43. Michael C. van Walt van Praag, *The Status of Tibet: History, Rights, and Prospects in International Law* (Boulder, CO: Westview Press, 1987), 7.

44. Smith, *Tibetan Nation*, 83–100.

45. For China's entry into the Korean War, see Richard W. Stewart, *The Korean War: The Chinese Intervention November 3, 1950–January 24, 1951* (Washington, DC: US Army Center of Military History, 2003).

46. They are the Aba Tibetan-Qiang Autonomous Prefecture, the Ganzi Tibetan Autonomous Prefecture, and the Mili Tibetan Autonomous County in Sichuan Province. More recently, Chongqing Province was carved out of Sichuan.

47. The Tibetan areas in Gansu Province are the Tianzu Tibetan Autonomous County and the Gannan Tibetan Autonomous Prefecture.

48. This Tibetan area in Yunnan has been named the Dechen Tibetan Autonomous Prefecture.

49. See, e.g., Walt van Praag, *Status of Tibet*; and Smith, *Tibetan Nation*.

50. Xinhua, "Weather Keeps Heating Up in Tibet," *China Daily*, July 23, 2007.

51. Xinhua, "Tibet Has Second Highest Temperature in 37 Years in 2007," *China View*, February 28, 2008.

52. The IPCC's response to the so-called glacier-gate scandal stated, "The Chair, Vice-Chairs and Co-chairs of the IPCC regret the poor application of well-established IPCC procedures in this instance. This episode demonstrates that the quality of the assessment depends on absolute adherence to the IPCC standards, including thorough review of 'the quality and validity of each source before incorporating results from the source into an IPCC Report.'" Intergovernmental Panel on Climate Change, *IPCC Statement on the Melting of Himalayan Glaciers* (Geneva: Intergovernmental Panel on Climate Change, 2010).

53. Tandong Yao, Youqing Wang, Shiying Liu, Jianchen Pu, Yongping Shen, and Anxin Lu, "Recent Glacial Retreat in High Asia in China and Its Impact on Water Resource in Northwest China," *Science in China, Series D: Earth Sciences* 47, no. 12 (December, 2004): 1065.

54. Cited in the Chinese Communist Party's mouthpiece, *People's Daily*, January 5, 2007.

55. Chinese Academy of Sciences, *China Glacier Inventory* (Lanzhou: World Data Center for Glaciology and Geocryology, Lanzhou Institute of Glaciology and Geocryology, 2004).

56. See Richard Louis Edmonds, *Patterns of China's Lost Harmony* (London: Taylor & Francis, 2007), chap. 5, "Desertification, Grassland Degradation, Water Shortages and Salinization-Alkalisation."

57. John Studley, *Hearing a Different Drummer: A New Paradigm for the 'Keepers of the Forest'* (London: International Institute for Environment and Development, 2007), 37.

58. Xuefeng Cui and Hans-F. Graf, "Recent Land Cover Changes on the Tibetan Plateau: A Review," *Climate Change* 94, nos. 1–2 (May 2009): 47.

59. "Known Nuclear Tests Worldwide, 1945–1993," *Bulletin of the Atomic Scientists*, May–June 1994, 62; "China Increases Test Total before Treaty," *Jane's Defense Weekly*, April 8, 1995, 3; Robert S. Norris, "French and Chinese Nuclear Weapon Testing," *Security Dialogue*, March 1996, 49.

60. Xinhua, July 19, 1995. The report described the site in Haibei as a "20-square-meter dump for radioactive pollutants."

61. US Defense Intelligence Agency, *People's Republic of China: Nuclear Weapons Employment—Policy and Strategy* (Washington, DC: US Defense Intelligence Agency, 1972), "Annex E: Nuclear Weapons Research and Development Production and Related Facilities," www.fas.org/irp/dia/product/prc_72/app_e.htm.

62. The Tibetan government in exile has identified one site near the Kokonor Complex, two in the Tsaidam basin, and a fourth at Delingha—all in Tibet's traditional region. Central Tibetan Administration, "Militarization and Regional Peace" (Dharamsala: Department of Information and International Relations, Central Tibetan Administration, 1996). The site near the Kokonor Complex, according to the US Defense Intelligence Agency, involved building three vaults in a ridge. US Defense Intelligence Agency, *People's Republic of China*.

63. Michael Zhao and Orville Schell, "Tibet: Plateau in Peril," *World Policy Journal* 25, no. 3 (Fall 2008): 171.

64. Wang and French, "Climate Controls and High-Altitude Permafrost," 87–100.

65. Cheng and Wu, "Responses of Permafrost to Climate Change."

66. The China–Tibet railway network is designed not only to aid mineral exploitation but also to strengthen China's hold on Tibet and augment its rapid military-deployment capability. Beijing is considering taking the Tibet railroad to Kathmandu, Nepal's capital, and also establishing a rail link with Pakistan through the Karakoram Range.

67. United Nations Environment Program, *Global Environment Outlook: Environment for Development* (Nairobi: United Nations Environment Program, 2007). Also see United Nations Environment Program, *Dead Planet, Living Planet: Biodiversity and Ecosystem Restoration for Sustainable Development* (Nairobi: United Nations Environment Program, 2010).

68. Abrahm Lustgarten, "Will Global Warming Melt the Permafrost Supporting the China–Tibet Railway?" *Scientific American*, July 21, 2009.

69. Zhao and Schell, "Tibet: Plateau in Peril," 176.

70. Xinhua, "Environment of 'Roof of the World' under Threat."

71. The estimate by Dondui Namgyi, director of the Tibet Mining Bureau, was about the mineral wealth in the so-called Tibet Autonomous Region, not in the entire Tibetan Plateau. *China's Tibet* magazine 6, no. 5 (December 1995).

72. Xinhua, "Tibet to Step Up Exploitation of Mineral Resources," *China Daily*, March 13, 2010.

73. Even as Japanese officials and international rare-earth industry executives reported that China halted exports to Japan of raw rare earths following the fishing-boat incident, Beijing claimed it had imposed no ban on export of rare earths. Indeed, after the Sino-Japanese spat over the incident ended, Premier Wen Jiabao declared: "China is not using rare earth as a bargaining chip." However, the Chinese action in continuing to block shipments weeks after the boat captain's release jolted Japan, which now is considering becoming a rare-earths recycling center and is working with Mongolia and India to develop new rare-earth mines. US secretary of state Hillary Clinton described the suspension of exports as "a wake-up call" for countries dependent on rare-earth imports from China.

74. Central Tibetan Administration, *Guidelines for International Development Projects and Sustainable Development in Tibet* (Dharamsala: Central Tibetan Administration, 2004), www.-tibet.net/en/index.php?id=223&rmenuid=11.

75. Data in the 2007 bulletin of the Chinese Ministry of Land and Resources cited in "China Discovers 208 Mineral-Resource Deposits in 2007," China Mining Association, April 22, 2008, www.chinamining.org/News/2008–04–22/1208830137d13143.html.

76. Jianchu Xu, R. Edward Grumbine, Arun Shrestha, Mats Eriksson, Xuefei Yang, Yun Wang, and Andreas Wilkes, "The Melting Himalayas: Cascading Effects of Climate Change on Water, Biodiversity, and Livelihoods," *Conservation Biology* 23, no. 3 (2009): 526.

77. Studley, *Hearing a Different Drummer*, 27.

78. The Natural Forests Conservation Program was launched to reverse a half century of reckless forest exploitation across China that had spawned "disastrous consequences, including degradation of forests and landscapes, loss of biodiversity, unacceptable levels of soil erosion, and catastrophic flooding." Peichang Zhang, Guofan Shao, Guang Zhao, Dennis C. Le Master, George R. Parker, John B. Dunning Jr., and Qinglin Li, "China's Forest Policy for the 21st Century," *Science* 288, no. 5474 (June 23, 2000): 2135–36.

79. Jiyuan Liu, Hanqin Tian, Mingliang Liu, Dafang Zhuang, Jerry M. Melillo, and Zengxiang Zhang, "China's Changing Landscape during the 1990s: Large-Scale Land Transformations Estimated with Satellite Data," *Geophysical Research Letters* 35 (2005): DOI: 10.1029/2004GL021649.

80. Xuefeng Cui et al., "Hydrological Impacts of Deforestation," 1–18.

81. Georg Miehe, Sabine Miehe, Katja Koch, and Martin Will, "Sacred Forests in Tibet," *Mountain Research and Development* 23, no. 4 (November 2003): 324–28.

82. Daniel Winkler, "Major Threats to Tibetan Forest Ecosystems and Strategies for Forest Biodiversity Conservation," in *Proceedings of WWF China Program International Workshop, "Tibet's Biodiversity: Conservation and Management, Lhasa, September 1998"* (Beijing: China Forestry Publishing House, 1999), 62–67.

83. Zhang Bai-ping et al., "Biodiversity and Conservation in the Tibetan Plateau," 135.

84. Christa Kletter and Monika Kriechbaum, eds., *Tibetan Medicinal Plants* (Stuttgart: Medpharm Scientific Publishers, 2001).

85. Yanchun Liu, Zhiling Dao, Chunyan Yang, Yitao Liu, and Chunlin Long, "Medicinal Plants Used by Tibetans in Shangri-La, Yunnan, China," *Journal of Ethnobiology and Ethnomedicine* 5, no. 15 (2009): DOI: 10.1186/1746-4269-5-15.

86. China Tibet Online, "Rare Birds in Tibet," China–Tibet People, http://chinatibet.people.com.cn/6796797.html.

87. Robert L. Fleming Jr., Dorje Tsering, and Liu Wulin, *Across the Tibetan Plateau: Ecosystems, Wildlife, and Conservation* (New York: W. W. Norton, 2006), chap. 1.

88. George B. Schaller, *Wildlife of the Tibetan Steppe* (Chicago: University of Chicago Press, 2000), 330–32.

89. In April 2000, at their meeting in Gigiri, Kenya, CITES parties passed a resolution titled "Conservation of and Control of Trade in the Tibetan Antelope," with the aim of eliminating the continuing commercial trade in Tibetan antelope parts and derivatives, especially *shahtoosh*. For the official text of the resolution, see www.cites.org/eng/res/all/11/E11–08R13.pdf.

90. Economy, *River Runs Black*, 153; Schaller, *Wildlife of the Tibetan Steppe*, 41–79.

91. George B. Schaller, *The Last Panda* (Chicago: University of Chicago Press, 1994), xv.

92. See, e.g., Loa Iok-sin, "Tibet Activists Don Panda Costumes at Taipei Zoo," *Taipei Times*, February 8, 2009, www.taipeitimes.com/News/world/archives/2009/02/08/2003435598.

93. The ban has reduced but not eliminated the production, sale, and use of tiger and leopard medicines. TRAFFIC International, *The State of Wildlife Trade in China: Information on the Trade in Wild Animals and Plants in China 2006* (Beijing: TRAFFIC East Asia–China Program, 2006), 4.

94. Second World Water Forum, "Ministerial Declaration of The Hague on Water Security in the 21st Century," The Hague, March 22, 2000, www.waternunc.com/gb/secwwf12.htm.

95. See, e.g., Orville Schell, *Virtual Tibet: Searching for Shangri-La from the Himalayas to Hollywood* (New York: Metropolitan Books, 2000).

96. Xiaodong Liu and Baode Chen, "Climatic Warming in the Tibetan Plateau during Recent Decades," *International Journal of Climatology* 20, issue 14 (2000): 1729–42.

97. China Meteorological Administration chief Zheng Guoguang, quoted by Xinhua, "Met Chief: Tibet Challenged by Global Warming," May 6, 2009.

98. K. Rikiishi and H. Nakasato, "Height Dependence of the Tendency for Reduction in Seasonal Snow Cover in the Himalayas and the Tibetan Plateau Region," *Annals of Glaciology* 43, no. 1 (2006): 369–77.

99. T. Yao, J. Pu, A. Lu, Y. Wang, and W. Yu, "Recent Glacial Retreat and Its Impact on the Hydrological Processes on the Tibetan Plateau, China, and Surrounding Regions," *Arctic, Antarctic, and Alpine Research* 39 (2007): 642–50; Cruz et al., "Asia."

100. John Bolton, the former US ambassador to the United Nations, "Where People Matter: Navigating the Labyrinth of Human Security," Speech at Lewis and Clark College's Forty-Sixth Annual International Affairs Symposium, April 7, 2008.

101. Jiahua Zhang, Fengmei Yao, Lingyun Zheng, and Limin Yang, "Evaluation of Grassland Dynamics in the Northern Tibet Plateau of China Using Remote Sensing and Climate Data," *Sensors* 7 (2007): 3312–28.

102. Xinhua, "Environment of 'Roof of the World' under Threat."

103. Johan Rockström, W. Steffen, K. Noone, Å. Persson, F. S. Chapin, III, E. Lambin, T. M. Lenton, M. Scheffer, C. Folke, H. Schellnhuber, B. Nykvist, C. A. De Wit, T. Hughes, S. van der Leeuw, H. Rodhe, S. Sörlin, P. K. Snyder, R. Costanza, U. Svedin, M. Falkenmark, L. Karlberg, R. W. Corell, V. J. Fabry, J. Hansen, B. Walker, D. Liverman, K. Richardson, P. Crutzen, and J. Foley, "Planetary Boundaries: Exploring the Safe Operating Space for Humanity," *Ecology & Society* 14, no. 2 (2009).

104. UN-Water, *Water: A Shared Responsibility*, United Nations World Water Development Report 2 (New York: United Nations, 2006), 136.

105. Cruz et al., "Asia," chap. 10, section 10.6.1, "Mega-Deltas in Asia."

106. Ibid.

107. World Wide Fund for Nature, *World's Top 10 Rivers at Risk*, 25–26.

108. Orville Schell, "The Thaw at the Roof of the World," *New York Times*, September 26, 2009.

109. Environment and Development Desk, Department of Information and International Relations, Central Tibetan Administration, *Tibet 2000: Environment and Development Issues* (Dharamsala: Central Tibetan Administration, April 26, 2000), 19.

110. Wang Weiluo, "Water Resources and the China-India Strategic Partnership," *China Rights Forum*, no. 1 (2006), translated from the original article posted on the China Information Center website, www.observechina.net/info/artshow.asp?ID=37736&ad=1/10/2006.

111. HydroChina Corporation, "Map of Planned Dams," 2010, www.hydrochina.com.cn/zgsd/images/ziyuan_b.gif.

112. HydroChina Corporation, "Core Business," www.hydrochina.com.cn/English/pages/Business/Business.jsp.

113. Zhang Xiwen, "Lhasa, Land of the Gods," *China Today*, December 2008.

114. BBC, "Flash Floods Hit Northeast India," July 6, 2004, http://news.bbc.co.uk/2/hi/south_asia/3868633.stm.

115. Wang, "Water Resources and the Sino-Indian Strategic Partnership."

116. Shishir Gupta, "Made in China," *India Today*, June 25, 2001.

117. Darrin Magee, "Powershed Politics: Yunnan Hydropower under Great Western Development," *China Quarterly*, no. 185 (March 2006): 23–41.

118. Li Ling, *Xizang Zhi Shui Jiu Zhongguo: Da Xi Xian Zai Zao Zhongguo Zhan Lue Nei Mu Xiang Lu* (Tibet's Waters Will Save China), in Mandarin (Beijing: Zhongguo chang'an chu ban she, 2005), book sponsored by the Ministry of Water Resources.

119. "Taming the Floodwaters: The High Heritage Price of Massive Hydraulic Projects," *China Heritage Newsletter*, no. 1 (March 2005).

120. Ibid.

121. Kang Juan, "Water Project Leads to Mass Relocation," *Global Times*, February 24, 2010.

122. Xinhua, December 15, 2008.

123. BBC News, "Delays Block China's Giant Water Scheme," February 8, 2009.

124. Water-Technology.net, "South-to-North Water Diversion Project, China," www.water-technology.net/projects/south_north/.

125. According to Chinese officials, the central route has been designed to transfer 13 to 14 billion cubic meters of water per year. "Delay of the Water Diversion Project Leaves Beijing Thirsty," *People's Daily Online*, June 29, 2010.

126. Michael Bristow, "Delays Block China's Giant Water Scheme," BBC News, February 9, 2009.

127. Water-Technology.net, "South-to-North Water Diversion Project."

128. Vaclav Smil, "Finding Mutual Interests in Nature," *Far Eastern Economic Review* 172, no. 8 (October 2009): 45.

129. "Experts Warn China's Water Supply May Well Run Dry," *South China Morning Post*, September 1, 2003.

130. "Pollution Hinders South-to-North Water Diversion," *China Daily*, July 6, 2010.

131. Julian L. Wong, "The Food–Energy–Water Nexus: An Integrated Approach to Understanding China's Resource Challenges," *Harvard Asia Quarterly*, Spring 2010, 15.

Chapter 4

1. Science Museums of China, "Yarlung Tsangpo Great Canyon" (Beijing: Computer Network Information Center of the Chinese Academy of Sciences, n.d.).

2. Zhang Jimin, *The Yarlung Tsangpo Great Canyon: The Last Secret World* (Beijing: Foreign Languages Press, 2006); Todd Balf, *The Last River: The Tragic Race for Shangri-la* (New York: Three Rivers Press, 2001); Peter Heller, *Hell or High Water: Surviving Tibet's Tsangpo River* (Emmaus, PA: Rodale Books, 2004).

3. Science Museums of China, "Yarlung Tsangpo Great Canyon."

4. Food and Agriculture Organization (FAO) of the United Nations, *Country Summary Fact-Sheet on Bangladesh*, June 15, 2010, Aquastat online database.

5. HydroChina Corporation, "Map of Planned Dams," 2010, www.hydrochina.com.cn/zgsd/images/ziyuan_b.gif.

6. Ryan Hodum, *Conflict over the Brahmaputra River between China and India*, ICE Case Study 205 (Washington, DC: Inventory of Conflict & Environment, 2007).

7. The growth in water use in China will alone account for 40 percent of the additional industrial demand for water worldwide. Although China's industrial water demand in 2030 is projected at 265 billion cubic meters, its water withdrawals for agriculture are likely to be 420 billion cubic meters. 2030 Water Resources Group (Barilla Group, Coca-Cola Company, International Finance Corporation, McKinsey & Company, Nestlé S.A., New Holland Agriculture, SABMiller PLC, Standard Chartered Bank, and Syngenta AG), *Charting Our Water Future* (New York: 2030 Water Resources Group, 2009), 6.

8. Gyurme Dorje, *Tibet Handbook with Bhutan* (Bath, UK: Footprint Travel Guides, 1999), 408.

9. Heller, *Hell or High Water*, 2.

10. *Lost Horizon* was published by Pocket Books as one of the world's first paperbacks, and the novel is best remembered for inventing Shangri-La.

11. For a discussion on *neri* mountains and the esoteric and popular traditions of ritual that have evolved around them, see Toni Huber, *The Cult of Pure Crystal Mountain: Popular Pilgrimage and Visionary Landscape in Southeast Tibet* (New York: Oxford University Press, 1999).

12. John Studley, *Hearing a Different Drummer: A New Paradigm for the 'Keepers of the Forest'* (London: International Institute for Environment and Development, 2007), 34–35.

13. Ian Baker, *The Heart of the World: A Journey to the Last Secret Place* (London: Penguin Press, 2004), xix.

14. Tenzin Gyatso (Fourteenth Dalai Lama of Tibet), "Introduction," in *Heart of the World*, by Baker, 1–2.

15. See Michael McRae, *The Siege of Shangri-La: The Quest for Tibet's Sacred Hidden Paradise* (New York: Broadway Books, 2002).

16. Karunakar Gupta, "The McMahon Line 1911–45: The British Legacy," *China Quarterly*, no. 47 (July–September 1971): 526–27.

17. Kenneth Cox, ed., *Frank Kingdon Ward's Riddle of the Tsangpo Gorges: Retracing the Epic Journey of 1924–25 in South-East Tibet* (Suffolk, UK: Antique Collectors' Club, 2001).

18. See Baker, *Heart of the World*.

19. Zhang Wenjing, "Nyingchi, the Natural Beauty, the Beauty of Nature," *China's Tibet Magazine*, March 2008.

20. Baker, *Heart of the World*, xx.

21. *People's Daily*, September 1, 2007.

22. Xin Dingding, "Tibet Railway Extension under Construction," *China Daily*, September 27, 2010.

23. "China Strives to Protect Virgin Forests on Qinghai-Tibet Plateau," *People's Daily Online*, June 25, 2010.

24. Heller, *Hell or High Water*, 2.

25. Shemin Ge, Mian Liu, Ning Lu, Jonathan W. Godt, and Gang Luo, "Did the Zipingpu Reservoir Trigger the 2008 Wenchuan Earthquake?" *Geophysical Research Letters*, 36 (2009): DOI: 10.1029/2009GL040349. Also see Richard Kerr and Richard Stone, "A Human Trigger for the Great Quake of Sichuan," *Science*, 323, no. 5912 (January 16, 2009); Sharon La Franiere, "Possible Link between Dam and China Quake," *New York Times*, February 6, 2009; and Jordan Lite, "Great China Earthquake May Have Been Man-Made," *Scientific American*, February 3, 2009.

26. According to Fan Xiao, the chief engineer, there have been other "cases in which a water reservoir has triggered an earthquake." Another Chinese expert, Lei Xinglin, of the China Earthquake Administration, said that the Zipingpu dam "clearly affected the local seismicity and it is worthwhile to study the role it played in triggering the earthquake further." Malcolm Moore, "Chinese Earthquake May Have Been Manmade, Say Scientists," *The Telegraph* (London), February 2, 2009.

27. The construction actually began in 1986 but was suspended in response to protests by the Panchen Lama and some international organizations. But soon after the Panchen Lama passed away in January 1989, work was resumed. The Panchen Lama, who spent fifteen years in detention up to the late 1970s, died at the age of fifty-one at the ancient Tashi Lhunpo Monastery in the city of Shigatse, five days after he gave a speech describing the Tibetans' suffering under Chinese rule. His death was followed by the Tiananmen Square massacre in Beijing about five months later. In that setting, overriding international concerns, the Chinese government pushed ahead and completed the project. See Michael Buckley, *Tibet* (Chalfont St. Peter, UK: Bradt Travel Guides, 2006), 176.

28. See "Chinese Draw Their Power from Tibet's Sacred Lake: A Hydroelectric Project on the Yamdrok Tso Threatens Ecological Disaster Next Century," *The Independent* (London), July 20, 1993.

29. Tashi Tsering, *Megoe Tso: The Damming of Tibet's Sacred Lake* (Oakland: Tibet Justice Center, April 2005).

30. The announcement was published in the official *Sichuan Daily*, November 8, 2006.

31. Huber, *Cult of Pure Crystal Mountain*, 219.

32. See Mara Hvistendahl, "China's Three Gorges Dam: An Environmental Catastrophe?" *Scientific American*, March 25, 2008.

33. C. A. Chen, "The Three Gorges Dam: Reducing the Upwelling and Thus Productivity in the East China Sea," *Geophysical Research Letters* 27, no. 3 (2000): 381–83.

34. Associated Press, "China to Build 20 Hydro Dams on the Yangtze River," April 21, 2009.

35. Kevin Rafferty, "China's Disturbing Dam Plan," *Japan Times*, July 14, 2010.

36. See, e.g., Thomas L. Sims and Jonathan James Schiff, "The Great Western Development Strategy," *China Business Review*, November 1, 2000; and Darrin Magee, "Powershed Politics: Yunnan Hydropower under Great Western Development," *China Quarterly*, no. 185 (March 2006).

37. Cited by Matthew D. Moneyhon, "China's Great Western Development Project in Xinjiang: Economic Palliative or Political Trojan Horse?" *Denver Journal of International Law and Policy* 31, no. 3 (Summer 2003).

38. Environment and Development Desk, Department of Information and International Relations, Central Tibetan Administration, *Tibet: A Human Development and Environment Report* (Dharamsala: Central Tibetan Administration, 2007), 127–28.

39. *Southern Weekend* (Guangzhou), "Controversial Plan to Tap Tibetan Waters," August 8, 2006; translated into English by and available at www.china.org.cn.

40. The survey team was accompanied by a China Central Television crew, which provided regular coverage to national television viewers on the scientists' investigations. Held between May 18 and June 22, 1999, the survey involved experts from the Chinese Academy of Sciences, the State Development Planning Commission (the forerunner to the National Development and Reform Commission), and the ministries of water resources, railways, forestry, and land resources.

41. Li Ling, *Xizang Zhi Shui Jiu Zhongguo: Da Xi Xian Zai Zao Zhongguo Zhan Lue Nei Mu Xiang Lu* (Tibet's Waters Will Save China), in Mandarin (Beijing: Zhongguo chang'an chu ban she, 2005).

42. "China to Conduct Feasibility Study on Hydropower Project in Tibet," *People's Daily*, July 17, 2003.

43. Ibid.

44. Set up in 2002 by the State Council, the China Hydropower Engineering Consulting Group Corporation's main functions include the following: "To study the issues concerning the power sector; to put forward suggestions on policies and legislation; to make industrial analysis and participate in formulating development plans for the industry; and to be in charge of the management of legal consulting for the industry and enterprises."

45. James Johnston, "The Great River Theft," *South China Morning Post*, July 15, 2007.

46. Reuters, August 1, 2006.

47. *Southern Weekend*, "Controversial Plan to Tap Tibetan Waters."

48. Craig Simons, "In China, a Water Plan Smacks of Mao," Cox News Service, http://web.archive.org/web/20070911233235/http://www.coxwashington.com/hp/content/reporters/stories/2006/09/10/BC_CHINA_WATER10_COX.html.

49. Chinese Ministry of Water Resources, *A General Introduction to Rivers in China* (Beijing: Ministry of Water Resources, 2004).

50. Li Jing, "India Questions Chinese Projects over Shared River," *China Daily*, May 11, 2010.

51. Wang Jiaji, Gao Jixi, and Shu Jianmen, "Modification of Agriculture Landscape in Three-River Area in Xizang," *Chinese Geographical Science* 9, no. 2 (June 1999): DOI: 10.1007/BF02791361.

52. "Gezhouba Wins 1.14b Yuan Hydropower Contract," *China Daily*, March 4, 2009; Changan Xu, *Zangmu Shuidianzhan Haigong Jianshe Shou Zou Daxing Shuidianzhan Chang Xizang Zhi* (Groundbreaking of the Zangmu Dam Marks the Beginning of Large-Scale Construction of Dams in Tibet), in Mandarin, Xinhua, September 29, 2010.

53. Xinhua, "Road to Link Tibet's Last Road-Less County," China Tibet Information Center, December 2004, http://en.tibettour.com.cn/geography/200412006816102549.htm.

54. China now has high-altitude airports in Tibet at Lhasa, Shigatse, Chamdo, Ngari, and Nyangtri. In addition, it is building the world's highest airport at an altitude of 4,436 meters in the northern Tibetan area of Nagchu.

55. Vaclav Smil, "Finding Mutual Interests in Nature," *Far Eastern Economic Review*, 172, no. 8 (October 2009): 46.

56. John Horgan, "Peaceful Nuclear Explosions: China's Interest in This Technology May Scuttle a Test-Ban Treaty," *Scientific American*, June 1996, 14–15.

57. See Scott Kirsch, *Proving Grounds: Project Plowshare and the Unrealized Dream of Nuclear Earthmoving* (New Brunswick, NJ: Rutgers University Press, 2005).

58. Mllo D. Nordyke, "The Soviet Program for Peaceful Uses of Nuclear Explosions," *Science & Global Security* 7, no. 1 (1988): 1–17.

59. For a review of China's PNE proposal, see Horgan, "Peaceful Nuclear Explosions."

60. Smil, "Finding Mutual Interests in Nature," 44.

61. M. D. Nordyke, "A Review of Soviet Data on the Peaceful Uses of Nuclear Explosions," *Annals of Nuclear Energy* 2 (1975): 657–73; Nordyke, "Soviet Program for Peaceful Uses of Nuclear Explosions."

62. Nordyke, "Review of Soviet Data on the Peaceful Uses of Nuclear Explosions."

63. US Department of Energy, "A Chronology of Ploughshare Program Milestones, including Proposed Tests and Projects Concluded" (US Department of Energy, Nevada Operations Office, Office of Public Affairs and Information, n.d.), 14–15, www.atomictraveler.com/PlowshareProgram.pdf.

64. Jozef Goldblat and David Cox, *Nuclear Weapon Tests: Prohibition or Limitation* (New York: Oxford University Press, 1988), 65–66.

65. Statement by the Chinese Delegation on "Peaceful Use of Nuclear Energy and Peaceful Nuclear Explosion" at Working Group II of the Nuclear Test Ban Ad Hoc Committee, Conference on Disarmament, Geneva, March 9, 1995, www.nti.org/db/china/engdocs/ctbt0395.htm.

66. See David Fairhall, "Nuclear Blasts to Irrigate Desert," *The Guardian*, May 15,1996; Kyodo, "Experts Propose Nuclear Blasts to Dig Underground Canal," April 20, 1996; and Patrick Tyler, "Chinese Seek Atom Option to Fend Off Asteroids," *New York Times*, April 27, 1996, 4.

67. United Nations, *Final Report of Main Committee III of the 1995 NPT Review and Extension Conference, May 5, 1995*, Document NPT/CONF.1995/MC.III/1 (New York: United Nations, 1995). The final report of Main Committee III constituted part of the "Final Document" of the NPT Review and Extension Conference.

68. This is what the Chinese ambassador placed on the record: "I would like to explain the position of the Chinese Government on some major issues in the CTBT negotiations. First, scope and peaceful nuclear explosions. No arms control or disarmament treaty should hinder the scientific and economic development of its States parties. This is a universally accepted principle. As a technology with enormous potential, PNEs, if used properly, can play a dynamic role in promoting the economic development of some countries. This is of special significance for China—a populous country with a large territory but relatively scarce natural resources. We cannot agree to ban a promising technology just for the sake of banning nuclear-weapon test explosions. As the saying goes, the baby should not be thrown out with the bath water—a simple wisdom. China's original intention in raising the issue of PNEs remains unchanged. The concerns that PNEs are not easily distinguishable from nuclear explosions for military purposes, and that they may have an adverse effect on the environment, are fully shared by us. However, we do not think these problems are insurmountable. Although we still need to be convinced by the various counter-arguments, we also recognize the fact that the CTBT negotiations have reached their final stage, and in order to facilitate the conclusion of the Treaty within the timeframe as planned, the Chinese delegation is now ready to go along with a temporary ban on PNEs. China can agree to a Treaty provision that the possibility of permitting the conduct of PNEs shall be considered by the review conference of the States parties. If all the States parties agree to permit the conduct of PNEs by consensus, the conference of the States parties shall immediately commence its work with a view to agreeing on arrangements for the possible approval and conduct of such explosions. The arrangements shall preclude any military benefits and shall be consistent with the obligations of States under other international agreements." Statement by Sha Zukang, Chinese ambassador to the Conference on Disarmament, Geneva, June 6, 1996, United Nations Document CD/PV.737.

69. Comprehensive Test Ban Treaty, full text, www.ctbto.org/the-treaty/treaty-text/.

70. The London *Telegraph* said China would "attract international opprobrium" if it implemented plans to use nuclear-explosive devices for tunneling. Damien Mcelroy, "China Planning Nuclear Blasts to Build Giant Hydro Project," *The Telegraph*, October 22, 2000.

71. German state-owned television ZDF, *Die Welt* program, January 7, 1998.

72. Tashi Tsering, "Hydo Logic: Water for Human Development" (Oakland: Tibet Justice Center, 2002), 23.

73. Arthur Thomas, "Diverting the Brahmaputra: Start of the Water Wars?" *On Line Opinion* (Australia), May 2, 2008.

74. Jaswant Singh, *Speech in Rajya Sabha, Upper House of Parliament, March 19, 2008*, Official Transcript (New Delhi: Rajya Sabha Secretariat, 2008).

75. Arthur Waldron, "The Soviet Disease Spreads to China," *Far Eastern Economic Review* 172, no. 8 (October 2009): 27.

76. Chinese Water Resources Minister Wang Shucheng said the cost of transferring water from Tibet to the Yellow River could add up to 20 yuan per cubic meter, much higher than the 3 yuan per cubic meter it would cost to conserve water using various technologies. Reuters, "Official Says Tibet Water Diversion Not Feasible," October 24, 2006.

77. "China Taps Tibetan Waters," *International Herald Tribune, August 1, 2006.*

78. Cited in Brook Larmer, "Bitter Waters: Can China Save the Yellow—Its Mother River," *National Geographic*, May 2008.

79. "Ex-Water Chief: China Won't Divert World's Highest River to Thirsty North," Xinhua, March 25, 2009. "It is unnecessary, unfeasible and unscientific to include the Yarlung Tsangpo river in the western route of the massive project," Wang Shucheng said at a 2009 Beijing seminar coorganized by the China Institute for International Strategic Studies and the Hong Kong–based Michael Eric Bosman Hotung Foundation.

80. Simons, "In China, a Water Plan Smacks of Mao."

81. *Southern Weekend*, "Controversial Plan to Tap Tibetan Waters."

82. The doubters had warned the South–North project was too costly and gigantic, and was unlikely to mitigate water woes in the North. One critic was Xu Qianqing, a former no. 2 engineer at the ministry of water resources, who said that the price of water to be transferred under the project was likely to be "too high for users to accept."

83. E.g., referring to Zangmu Dam, Indian foreign minister S. M. Krishna said in Parliament on April 22, 2010: "It is a fact that when we met in Beijing, the question of the power station did come up. The Chinese foreign minister assured me that there would be no water storage at the dam and it would not in any way have an impact on downstream areas."

84. John G. Thibodeau and Philip B. Williams, "Preface," in *The River Dragon Has Come! The Three Gorges Dam and the Fate of China's Yangtze River and Its People*, by Dai Qing, translated by Ming Yi (Armonk, NY: M. E. Sharpe, 1998), ix–xiii.

85. Smil, "Finding Mutual Interests in Nature," 45.

86. Zha Daojiong, "Dangerous Myths: Making the Case for Water Diplomacy," in *Foresight Conference Reader: India* (Berlin: Foresight, 2010), www.foresightproject.net/publications/readers/article.asp?p = 558 4&d = 2119.

87. Jeremy Page, "Millions Live in Fear That China Aims to Steal Their River," *The Times* (London), November 20, 2006.

88. Johnston, "Great River Theft."

89. The Himalayan states have drawn up ambitious plans to build numerous new dams, although many of them are intended to be small, run-of-the-river projects. As one report has put it, "Recent years have seen a renewed push for building dams in the Himalayas. . . . This dam-building activity will fundamentally transform the landscape, ecology and economy of the region and will have far-reaching impacts all the way down to the river deltas." Shripad

Dharmadhikary, *Mountains of Concrete: Dam Building in the Himalayas* (Berkeley, CA: International Rivers, 2008), 3.

90. *Southern Weekend*, "Controversial Plan to Tap Tibetan Waters."

91. Walter W. Immerzeel, Ludovicus P. H. van Beek, and Marc F. P. Bierkens, "Climate Change Will Affect the Asian Water Towers," *Science* 328, no. 5983 (June 11, 2010): 1384–85.

92. FAO, *Country Profile: Bangladesh*, 2010, Aquastat online database.

93. Asit K. Biswas and Juha I. Uitto, eds., *Sustainable Development of the Ganges-Brahmaputra-Meghna Basins* (Tokyo: United Nations University Press, 2001).

94. The Sundarbans provide habitats for a wide range of endangered species. See Johanna L. Ostling, David R. Butler, and Richard W. Dixon, "The Biogeomorphology of Mangroves and Their Role in Natural Hazards Mitigation," *Geography Compass* 3, no. 5 (September 2009): 1607–24; and Laskar Muqsudur Rahman, "The Sundarbans: A Unique Wilderness of the World," *USDA Forest Service Proceedings*, RMRS-P-15-VOL-2 (2000): 143–48.

95. FAO, *Country Profile: Bangladesh*.

96. Government of Bangladesh, Master Plan Organization, *National Water Plan Summary Report* (Dhaka: Ministry of Water Resources, 1986); Government of Bangladesh, Master Plan Organization, *The Groundwater Resource and Its Availability for Development*, Technical Report 5, National Water Plan Phase I (Dhaka: Ministry of Water Resources, 1987).

97. FAO, *Country Profile: Bangladesh*.

98. Ibid.

99. Bangladesh's total renewable water resources aggregate 1,210.64 km^3 per year.

100. FAO, *Country Summary Fact-Sheet on India*, June 15, 2010, Aquastat online database.

101. FAO, *Country Summary Fact-Sheet on Bangladesh*.

102. Ibid.

103. See, e.g., Q. K. Ahmad, ed., *Bangladesh Water Vision 2025: Towards a Sustainable Water World* (Dhaka: Bangladesh Water Partnership and Global Water Partnership, 2000).

104. FAO, *Country Profile: Bangladesh*.

105. Ashim Das Gupta, Mukund Singh Babela, Xavier Alberta,and Ole Mark, "Water Sector of Bangladesh in the Context of Integrated Water Resources Management: A Review," *International Journal of Water Resources Development* 21, no. 2 (June 2005): 385–98.

106. Allan H. Smith, Elena O. Lingas, and Mahfuzar Rahman, "Contamination of Drinking Water by Arsenic in Bangladesh: A Public Health Emergency," *Bulletin of the World Health Organization* 78, no. 9 (2000): 1093.

107. Salinity in the southwestern Ganges basin in Bangladesh ranges from 10 percent during the monsoons to 40 percent in the dry season. See Ahmad, *Bangladesh Water Vision 2025*.

108. Annex 1 of the Treaty Between the Government of the Republic of India and the Government of the People's Republic of Bangladesh on Sharing of the Ganga/Ganges Water at Farakka, signed on December 12, 2006 in New Delhi.

109. Martin Walker, "The Most Dangerous Place," United Press International, May 14, 2007, www.upi.com/Business_News/Security-Industry/2007/05/14/Walkers-World-The-most-dangerous-place/UPI-87261179157455/

110. FAO, *Country Summary Fact-Sheets on Bangladesh, Pakistan and Myanmar (Burma)*, June 15, 2010, Aquastat online database.

111. Central Water Commission, *Water Data Complete Book 2005* (New Delhi: Central Water Commission, Ministry of Water Resources, 2005), table 1.3.

112. Damarla Balaguravaiah and Acharya N.G. Ranga, "India," in *Impact of Land Utilization Systems on Agricultural Productivity*, edited by Asian Productivity Organization (Tokyo: Asian Productivity Organization, 2003), 162.

113. FAO, *Country Profile: India*, 2010, Aquastat online database.

114. FAO, *Irrigation in Asia in Figures* (Rome: FAO, 1999), 93.

115. US Department of Defense, *Military and Security Developments involving the People's Republic of China 2010*, Report to Congress Pursuant to the National Defense Authorization Act for Fiscal Year 2010 (Washington, DC: Office of the Secretary of Defense, 2010), 38.

116. Government of Arunachal Pradesh, *Arunachal Pradesh State Industrial Policy 2008* (Itanagar, India: Department of Industries, Government of Arunachal Pradesh, 2008), 1.

117. Indian Prime Minister Manmohan Singh, Speech of January 31, 2008, at Itanagar, capital of Arunachal Pradesh, Prime Minister's Office, official transcript, http://pmindia .nic.in/prelease/pcontent.asp?id=717.

118. Charles Bell, *Tibet Past and Present* (Oxford: Clarendon Press, 1924), 149.

119. Melvyn C. Goldstein, *A History of Modern Tibet 1913–1951: The Demise of the Lamaist State* (Berkeley: University of California Press, 1989), 68–80, 832–41.

120. People's Republic of China, *Tibet: Its Ownership and Human Rights Situation*, White Paper (Beijing: Information Office of the State Council of the People's Republic of China, 1992), part II, "Origins of So-Called Tibetan Independence."

121. Interview on October 22, 2009, by e-mail with Ambassador Ranjit Sethi, an Indian diplomat who has present at that meeting and has since retired.

122. The Indian national security adviser, quoted by the *Straits Times* of Singapore as saying in an interview: "What is important is that areas of convergence are increasing. But areas of divergence remain. Tawang, in Arunachal Pradesh state, remains the most important. Till that is settled whatever else we may do, it is difficult to say we have crossed the Rubicon." *Straits Times*, August 12, 2008.

123. FAO, *Irrigation in Asia in Figures*, 82.

124. What is known as the Panchsheel Treaty is the Agreement between the Republic of India and the People's Republic of China on Trade and Intercourse between Tibet Region of China and India, signed on April 29, 1954, in Beijing; ratified August 17, 1954.

125. Item nos. 1 and 2 in the "Notes Exchanged" concurrently with the Agreement between the Republic of India and the People's Republic of China on Trade and Intercourse between Tibet Region of China and India.

126. Jiyu Chen, "Dams, Effect on Coasts," in *Encyclopedia of Coastal Science*, edited by Maurice L. Schwartz, vol. 24 of Encyclopedia of Earth Sciences Series (Berlin: Springer, 2005).

127. *Selected Works of Jawaharlal Nehru,* series 2, vol. 12 (New Delhi: Jawaharlal Nehru Memorial Fund), 410–11.

128. Address to the Nation on All India Radio, October 22, 1962, in *Jawaharlal Nehru's Speeches, September 1957–April 1963*, vol. 4 (New Delhi: Ministry of Information and Broadcasting, 1964), 226–30.

129. Declaration on Principles for Relations and Comprehensive Cooperation between the Republic of India and the People's Republic of China, signed on June 23, 2003, in Beijing by Atal Bihari Vajpayee, prime minister of the Republic of India, and Wen Jiabao, premier of the State Council of the People's Republic of China.

130. Four separate "sources" of international law are spelled out in the Statute of the International Court of Justice. The Statute's Article 38 (1) reads: "The Court, whose function is to decide in accordance with international law such disputes as are submitted to it, shall apply: (a) international conventions, whether general or particular, establishing rules expressly recognized by contesting States; (b) international custom, as evidence of a general practice accepted as law; (c) the general principles of law recognized by civilized nations; (d) . . . judicial decisions and the teachings of the most highly qualified publicists of the various nations, as subsidiary means for the determination of rules of law."

131. In the words of one UNESCO report, "International custom is a legal rule that has evolved from the practice of states, usually in the absence of formal agreements (although agreements may contain rules of customary law). To become binding, customary law must

be the subject of a general widespread practice that demonstrates the rule is considered by states to be a 'law' that governs their activities. The evidence of customary law (state practice) can be found in the form of agreements, statutes and decrees, diplomatic correspondence, statements of states' representatives in international organizations and conferences, and so forth." UNESCO, *Water Security and Peace: A Synthesis of Studies Prepared Under the PCCP-Water for Peace Process*, compiled by William J. Cosgrove (Paris: UNESCO, 2003), 26.

132. The Convention on the Law of the Non-Navigational Uses of International Watercourses, Adopted by the General Assembly of the United Nations on May 21, 1997. The Convention is not yet in force.

133. Britain came full circle in 2008 when it removed Tibet's suzerainty status and accepted Chinese sovereignty over Tibet. See the written Ministerial Statement on Tibet by the British secretary of state for foreign and Commonwealth affairs, David Miliband, in Parliament, October 29, 2008, available at www.parliament.uk.

134. The US Tibet Policy Act, e.g., supports talks between the Dalai Lama and the Chinese government, as well as respect for Tibetans' human rights and religious, linguistic, and cultural heritage.

135. For an overview, see David H. Getches, *Water Law in a Nutshell* (Buffalo: West Information Publishing Group, 1997); and Dan A. Tarlock, *Law of Water Rights and Resources* (New York: Clark Boardman Callaghan, 1988).

136. Article IV of the Indus Waters Treaty.

137. The Helsinki Rules on the Uses of the Waters of International Rivers, adopted by the International Law Association at its conference held at Helsinki in August 1966.

138. Article V of the Helsinki Rules identifies the following factor—"the past utilization of the waters of the basin, including in particular existing utilization"—among eleven factors. It goes on to say: "The weight to be given to each factor is to be determined by its importance in comparison with that of other relevant factors. In determining what is reasonable and equitable share, all relevant factors are to be considered together and a conclusion reached on the basis of the whole."

139. Asian-African Legal Consultative Committee, *Report of the Fourteenth Session Held at New Delhi, January 10–18, 1973* (New Delhi: Asian-African Legal Consultative Committee, 1973), 7–14, 339–40; Arthur Watts, *The International Law Commission 1949–1998*, Volume Two: The Treaties, Part 2 (Oxford: Oxford University Press, 2000), 1359.

140. Article 6 of the Convention on the Law of the Non-Navigational Uses of International Watercourses.

141. UNESCO, *Water Security and Peace*, 29.

142. Li Ling, *Xizang Zhi Shui Jiu Zhongguo*.

143. Uttam Kumar Sinha, "Tibet's Watershed Problem: Water is China's New Weapon," *Washington Post*, June 14, 2010.

144. K. R. Bolton, "Rivalry over Water Resources as a Potential Cause of Conflict in Asia," *Journal of Social, Political and Economic Studies* 35, no. 1 (Spring 2010): 24.

145. Indian External Affairs Minister S. M. Krishna, Statement in Parliament, July 9, 2009, Ministry of External Affairs, New Delhi.

146. Asian Development Bank, "ADB to Help India's Arunachal Pradesh Combat Floods, Erosion," news release, October 16, 2008.

147. Indian environment minister Jairam Ramesh made those comments while addressing the Foreign Correspondents' Club in Beijing in May 2010. See Ananth Krishnan, "On Rivers and Glaciers, India, China Walk on Thin Ice," *The Hindu*, May 10, 2010; and Li Jing, "India Questions Chinese Projects on Shared Rivers," *Global Times*, May 11, 2010.

148. FAO, *General Summary Asia: Water Resources*, 2010, Aquastat online database.

149. Tan Yingzi, "Yellow River Dams on Verge of Collapse," *China Daily*, June 19, 2009, www.chinadaily.com.cn/china/2009-06/19/content_8301942.htm.

150. Ibid.

151. Vijay P. Singh, V. P. Singh, and Nayan Sharma, *The Brahmaputra Basin Water Resources* (Berlin: Springer, 2004).

152. Johnston, "Great River Theft."

153. *People's Daily*, "Indian Hegemony Continues to Harm Relations with Neighbors," editorial, October 14, 2009.

154. Chinese Ministry of Foreign Affairs, Statement on India, Beijing, October 13, 2009.

155. Šalman M. A. Salman, "The Helsinki Rules, the UN Watercourses Convention and the Berlin Rules: Perspectives on International Water Law," *Water Resources Development* 23, no. 4 (December 2007): 627–28.

156. Wen Jiabao, "Working Together for New Glories of the Oriental Civilization," speech by the Chinese premier at the Indian Council of World Affairs, New Delhi, December 16, 2010, www.icwa.in/pdfs/Chinapm_Lecture.pdf.

157. Thomas, "Diverting the Brahmaputra."

158. Bolton, "Rivalry over Water Resources as a Potential Cause of Conflict in Asia," 43–44.

159. David Axe, "War Is Boring: China Dam Project Stokes Regional Tensions," *World Politics Review*, April 28, 2010.

160. Stanley A. Weiss, "Rivals and Partners," *International Herald Tribune*, January 9, 2010.

161. Peter Sawyer, "Obama's State Department: Putting Water Front and Center," Pulitzer Center for Crisis Reporting, March 18, 2010.

162. Marc Reisner, *Cadillac Desert: The American West and Its Disappearing Water* (New York: Penguin Books, 1993); Patrick McCully, *Silenced Rivers: The Ecology and Politics of Large Dams* (London: Zed Books, 1997).

Chapter 5

1. United Nations, Economic and Social Council, "Emerging Challenges and Trends in Water Resources Management," Note by the Secretariat, July 19, 2010, prepared for the Ministerial Conference on Environment and Development in Asia and the Pacific at Astana, Kazakhstan, September 27–October 2, 2010, Document E/ESCAP/MCED(6)/5, 9–10. The document uses the term "conflict" to refer "not only to armed conflict but to all water-related disputes that have necessitated mediation. Whether violent or not, these disputes have threatened the stability of the socioeconomic development process."

2. Pal Tamas contends that "a water conflict as a natural resource control issue or a redistribution conflict around water is hardly ever isolated from a sort of framing encased by other conflicts." Pal Tamas, *Water Resource Scarcity and Conflict: Review of Applicable Indicators and Systems of Reference* (Paris: UNESCO, 2003), 2.

3. Steven Solomon, "Drowning Today, Parched Tomorrow," *New York Times*, August 15, 2010.

4. The Bangladeshi government says the war killed 3 million people. The number of estimated women raped has ranged from 200,000 to 400,000, depending on the source. But accepting "even the lowest set of figures for Bangladesh forces a horrifying comparison—the 1992–95 Bosnian war saw one-tenth the number of rapes as did the Bangladesh war." Nilanjana S. Roy, "The Female Factor: Bangladesh's War Toll on Women Still Undiscussed," *New York Times*, August 24, 2010.

5. Food and Agriculture Organization of the United Nations (FAO), Aquastat Online Database, www.fao.org/nr/water/Aquastat/main/index.stm.

6. United Nations Economic and Social Commission for Asia and the Pacific (ESCAP), *Statistical Yearbook for Asia and the Pacific 2009* (Bangkok: ESCAP, 2010), chap. 11, "Access to Water and Sanitation."

7. United Nations, Economic and Social Council, "Emerging Challenges and Trends in Water Resources Management," 2.

8. China's Water Resources and Hydropower Planning and Design General Institute, Presentation at the ESCAP Ad Hoc Expert Group Meeting on Water-Use Efficiency Planning, Bangkok, October 26–28, 2004.

9. United Nations, *The State of the Environment in Asia and the Pacific 2005* (Bangkok: ESCAP, 2006), 63.

10. The figure averages 84 percent in Asia's most-populous southern, eastern, and southeastern regions. But the figure drops slightly to 81 percent when other parts of Asia are included. FAO, "General Summary Asia: Water Resources," 2010, www.fao.org/nr/water/Aquastat/dbase/index.stm.

11. Ibid.

12. T. P. Barnett, J. C. Adam, and D. P. Lettenmaier, "Potential Impacts of a Warming Climate on Water Availability in Snow-Dominated Regions," *Nature* 438 (November 17, 2005): 303–9.

13. International Commission on Large Dams, "Intranet," online data; World Commission on Dams, "Dams and Water: Global Statistics," online data.

14. United Nations, *State of the Environment in Asia and the Pacific 2005*, 69.

15. Rashid Hassan, Robert Scholes, and Neville Ash, eds., *Ecosystems and Human Well-Being: Current State and Trends, Volume 1, Millennium Ecosystem Assessment* (Washington, DC: Island Press, 2005), chap. 24, "Mountain Systems," 697.

16. United Nations Environment Program (UNEP), *Environmental Degradation Triggering Tensions and Conflict in Sudan* (Nairobi: UNEP, 2007).

17. Shira B. Yoffe, Greg Fiske, Mark Giordano, Meredith Giordano, Kelli Larson, Kerstin Stahl. and Aaron T. Wolf, "Geography of International Water Conflict and Cooperation: Data Sets and Applications," *Water Resources Research* 40, no. 5 (2004): 3.

18. Michael Schwirtz and Ellen Barry, "Russia Weighs Pleas to Step in as Uzbeks Flee Kyrgyzstan," *New York Times*, June 14, 2010.

19. Kang Juan, "Water Project Leads to Mass Relocation," *Global Times* (Beijing), February 24, 2010.

20. United Nations, *State of the Environment in Asia and the Pacific 2005*, 62.

21. ABC News, "Aid Agency Probes Sri Lankan Massacre," August 7, 2006, www.abc.net.au/news/stories/2006/08/07/1708668.htm.

22. See Sayed Askar Mousavi, *The Hazaras of Afghanistan: An Historical, Cultural, Economic and Political Study* (New York: Palgrave Macmillan, 1997); and Alessandro Monsutti, *War and Migration: Social Networks and Economic Strategies of the Hazaras of Afghanistan*, translated by Patrick Camiller (New York: Routledge, 2005).

23. For the genesis of Baluch nationalism, see Martin Axmann, *Back to the Future: The Khanate of Kalat and the Genesis of Baluch Nationalism 1915–1955* (New York: Oxford University Press, 2008).

24. The Baluch insurrection is linked to Baluchistan's forcible annexation by Pakistan soon after Pakistan was carved out of India as a homeland for Muslims of the subcontinent. Decades of economic and political marginalization have aided the insurgency. See Carlotta Gall, "Another Insurgency Gains in Pakistan," *New York Times*, July 12, 2009.

25. The Gwadar port was inaugurated on March 20, 2007, by then Pakistani military ruler, General Pervez Musharraf, setting the stage for Gwadar's expansion into an energy-transport hub and naval base. The Gwadar port's first phase was completed by China ahead of schedule. During Chinese president Hu Jintao's visit to Islamabad in November 2006, one of the documents unveiled was titled "Transfer of Completion Certification of Gwadar Port (Phase I) between the People's Republic of China and the Islamic Republic of Pakistan."

That certification revealed that China built the port on a turnkey basis. It had pledged more than $1 billion in grants and loan guarantees for the multiphase Gwadar project.

26. For an overview, see Tim Dyson, Robert Cassen, and Leela Visaria, eds., *Twenty-First Century India: Population, Economy, Human Development and the Environment* (New Delhi: Oxford University Press, 2004); and Ramaswamy R. Iyer, *Water: Perspectives, Issues, Concerns* (New Delhi: Sage, 2003).

27. Indian prime minister Manmohan Singh, "Address to the Nation," June 24, 2004, official transcript, www.pmindia.nic.in/speech/content.asp.

28. United Nations, Economic and Social Council, "Emerging Challenges and Trends in Water Resources Management," 10.

29. Common Minimum Program of the United Progressive Alliance government, May 27, 2004, full text, http://bit.ly/bZYQ7w.

30. "Five Farmers Killed over Water," *Hindustan Times*, June 14, 2005.

31. The *Hirakud* reservoir is built across River Mahanadi about 15 kilometers upstream of the town of Sambalpur in the state of Orissa.

32. Cauvery Water Disputes Tribunal, *The Report of the Cauvery Water Disputes Tribunal with the Decision* (New Delhi: Water Resources Ministry, 2007), http://wrmin.nic.in/index3 .asp?sslid=393&subsublinkid=376&langid=1.

33. Ramaswamy R. Iyer, "Cauvery Dispute: Time for Closure," *The Hindu*, February 9, 2010.

34. For the details, see P. B. Anand, *Water and Identity: An Analysis of the Cauvery River Water Dispute*, BCID Research Paper 3 (Bradford, UK: Bradford Center for International Development, University of Bradford, 2004); and S. Guhan, *The Cauvery River Dispute: Towards Conciliation* (Madras: Frontline Publications, 1993). On the political economy of irrigation, see David Mosse, *The Rule of Water: Statecraft. Ecology, and Collective Action in South India* (New Delhi: Oxford University Press, 2003).

35. See Ramaswamy I. Iyer, ed., *Water and the Laws in India* (New Delhi: Sage, 2009); Michael R. Anderson, "Individual Rights to Environmental Protection in India," in *Human Rights Approaches to Environmental Protection*, edited by Alan Boyle and Michael R. Anderson (Oxford: Oxford University Press, 1996); Satyajit Singh, *Taming the Waters: The Political Economy of Large Dams in India* (New Delhi: Oxford University Press, 1997); and John Briscoe and R. P. S. Malik, *India's Water Economy: Bracing for a Turbulent Future* (New York: Oxford University Press, 2006).

36. Jack D. Ives, *Himalayan Perceptions: Environmental Change and the Well-Being of Mountain Peoples* (New York: Routledge, 2004), 194.

37. For a short history of this dispute and the safety aspects, see Indian Ministry of Water Resources, *Mullaperiyar Dam Issue* (New Delhi: Ministry of Water Resources, 2008), http:// mowr.gov.in/index3.asp?subsublinkid=751&langid=1&sslid=733.

38. A Kerala State government committee headed by the additional chief secretary reported in March 2010 that the Coca-Cola Company had caused damages worth the equivalent of $47.5 million to public health, agriculture, and water resources by overwithdrawal of groundwater and by passing off its sludge as manure to farmers in Plachimada, in the Palakkad District of Kerala. It said that cadmium, lead, and chromium had been detected in the sludge, affecting the health of the local people. The Coca-Cola Company also has faced popular protests elsewhere in India—including in Mehdiganj (Uttar Pradesh State), Kala Dera (Rajasthan State), Thane (Maharashtra), and Sivaganga (Tamil Nadu)—for allegedly extracting large quantities of local water resources and creating water shortages and contamination.

39. Rick Johnson, "Water Use in Industries of the Future: Steel Industry," paper prepared for the Industrial Technologies Program, Office of Energy Efficiency and Renewable

Energy, US Department of Energy, July 2003, www.ana.gov.br/Destaque/d179-docs/Publica coesEspecificas/Metalurg ia/Steel_water_use.pdf.

40. In a short, seventy-six-page book published in 1999, Arundhati Roy presented an emotive case against dam building in India. Arundhati Roy, *The Greater Common Good* (Mumbai: India Book Distributor, 1999). Roy earned fame by winning Britain's prestigious Booker Prize in 1997 for her novel *The God of Small Things* (New York: Random House, 1997).

41. Environmental concerns apparently influenced the federal government's decision in March 2010 not to start work on the long-approved 381-megawatt Bhairon Ghati and 480-megawatt Pala Maneri hydropower projects in the rugged northern state of Uttarakhand. The decision, however, triggered a strong protest by the state government, which demanded that federal authorities arrange to supply equivalent amount of electricity to Uttarakhand from other sources. That decision was followed by the abandonment in August 2010 of the 600-megawatt Loharinag Pala hydropower project, also in Uttarakhand. The Loharinag Pala project was dumped on environmental grounds after local Hindu leaders mounted protests, saying a free-flowing Bhagirathi River was essential to feed the Ganges, considered sacred by the Hindus.

42. "The Bends in Our Rivers," *Hindustan Times*, August 27, 2010.

43. India's harvested irrigated crop area is estimated at 77 million hectares, of which 31 percent grows wheat; 29 percent, rice; 2 percent, maize; 7 percent, oil palm; 6 percent, vegetables and fruits; and 5 percent, sugarcane.

44. Rahul Gandhi, News Conference in Chennai, September 10, 2009, transcript of selected remarks released by Congress Party.

45. Indian water resources minister P. K. Bansal, statement in the Lok Sabha (ruling lower house) of Parliament, December 2, 2009, Lok Sabha Secretariat, New Delhi.

46. Commission for Integrated Water Resource Development, *Integrated Water Resource Development: A Plan for Action*, vol. 1 (New Delhi: Commission for Integrated Water Resource Development, Ministry of Water Resources, 1999); National Water Development Agency, Indian Ministry of Water Resources, "The Need," http://nwda.gov.in/index2.asp?sublinkid = 46&langid = 1.

47. National Water Development Agency, "The Need."

48. See J. Gupta and P. Van der Zaag, "Inter-Basin Water Transfers and Integrated Water Resources Management: Where Engineering, Science and Politics Interlock," *Physics and Chemistry of the Earth* 33 (2008): 28–40.

49. Kelly Alley, "The Making of a River Linking Plan in India: Suppressed Science and Spheres of Expert Debate," *India Review* 3, no. 3 (July 2004): 210–38; M. Feroze Ahmed, Qazi Kholiquzzaman Ahmad, and Mohammad Khalequzzaman, eds., *Regional Cooperation on Transboundary Rivers: Impact of the Indian River Linking Project*, compilation of papers of the International Conference on Regional Cooperation on Transboundary Rivers: Impact of the Indian River Linking Project (Dhaka: Mati ar Manush, 2004).

50. The tribunal estimated the number to be relocated would be "6,147 families spread over 158 villages in Madhya Pradesh, and 456 families spread over 27 villages in Maharashtra." When the World Bank in 1985 approved the eligibility of the project to receive $450 million in loans, it estimated the scheme would displace 67,000 people. NGO activists, however, claim that the number of people actually forced to relocate is more than 200,000. Indian courts and tribunals have held that the affected people must receive equivalent land in compensation for the land they lost to the project, plus monetary compensation for relocating. Narmada Water Dispute Tribunal, *Final Order and Decision of the Tribunal*, December 12, 1979, www.sscac.gov.in/NWDT.pdf.

51. According to a report in *The Guardian* (London), the Narmada Bachao Andolan (NBA) is "funded by the EDF," or the Environmental Defense Fund, which is based in New

York. Kirk Leech, "The Narmada Dam-Busters Are Wrong," *The Guardian*, March 3, 2009. On July 10, 2007, India's Supreme Court dismissed a petition filed by the National Council for Civil Liberties, a Gujarat-based NGO, alleging that the NBA and its leader, Medha Patkar, received foreign funds in violation of India's 1976 Foreign Contribution (Regulation) Act, or FCRA. The Court relied on a government inquiry that showed that there had been "no specific instance of any violation of FCRA."

52. Asian Development Bank, *Asian Water Development Outlook 2007* (Manila: Asian Development Bank, 2007), 6.

53. Jim Yardley, "As Games Begin, India Hopes to Save Its Pride," *New York Times*, October 2, 2010.

54. Indian prime minister Atal Bihari Vajpayee, speech to the Fifth Meeting of the National Water Resources Council in New Delhi, April 1, 2002, official transcript released by the Prime Minister's Office, New Delhi. With water being a provincial-level subject in India, the national water policy released by the Vajpayee government in 2002 did not translate into a national action plan to build water security.

55. The name "Pakistan" emerged from "Pakstan"—an acronym for Punjab, Afghan borderlands (North-West Frontier Province), Kashmir, Sind, and Baluchistan that was coined in 1933 by a hard-line Muslim nationalist, Choudhary Rahmat Ali.

56. Hilary Synnott, "How to Help Pakistan," *Survival* 52, no. 1 (February–March 2010), 17.

57. Michael Kugelman and Robert M. Hathaway, eds., *Running on Empty: Pakistan's Water Crisis* (Washington, DC: Woodrow Wilson International Center for Scholars, 2009); and Kaiser Bengali, ed., *The Politics of Managing Water* (Islamabad and New York: Sustainable Development Policy Institute and Oxford University Press, 2003).

58. Ministry of Food, Agriculture, and Livestock, Government of Pakistan, *Agriculture Statistics of Pakistan* (Islamabad: Government of Pakistan, 2008); FAO, *Summary Fact-Sheet Pakistan*, 2010, Aquastat Online Database.

59. Pakistan Ministry of Water and Power, *Pakistan Water Sector Strategy*, Detailed Strategy Formulation, vol. 4 (Islamabad: Ministry of Water and Power, 2002), 11.

60. World Bank, *Pakistan Country Water Resources Assistance Strategy: Water Economy— Running Dry*, Report 34081-PK (Washington, DC: World Bank, 2005).

61. Shahid Javed Burki, "Pakistan's Aid-Addicted Economy Needs Reform," *Japan Times*, July 29, 2010.

62. Daanish Mustafa and James L. Wescoat Jr., "Development of Flood Hazards Policy in the Indus River Basin of Pakistan, 1947–1996," *Water International* 22, no. 4 (December 1997): 238–44.

63. World Bank, *Pakistan Country Water Resources Assistance Strategy*, 109–10.

64. Asianics Agro Development International, "Tarbela Dam and Related Aspects of the Indus River Basin, Pakistan," World Commission on Dams Case Study, 105ff.

65. J. W. Kijne and M. Kuper, "Salinity and Sodicity in Pakistan's Punjab: A Threat to Sustainability of Irrigated Agriculture?" *Water Resources Development* 11, no. 1 (March 1995): 73–86.

66. For an overview of the sodic-soil problem in the world, see Malcolm E. Sumner and Rajendra Naidu, eds., *Sodic Soils: Distribution, Properties, Management, and Environmental Consequences* (New York: Oxford University Press, 1999).

67. Pakistan Ministry of Water and Power, *Pakistan Water Sector Strategy*, 65.

68. Ibid., 67.

69. In April 2009, Waqar Ahmed Khan, the federal minister of investment, revealed that Pakistan was holding talks with Saudi Arabia, the United Arab Emirates, Bahrain, and other Arab states interested in Pakistan's offer to lease or sell 1 million acres of farmland. See Reuters, "Investors Eye Global Agricultural Sector for Boost," June 21, 2009; Mohammed

Arifeen, "Foreign Investment in Farmlands Mainly in Underdeveloped Countries," *The News*, October 19, 2009; Razi Syed, "PARC against Leasing Land to Foreign Investors," *Daily Times*, September 16, 2009.

70. FAO, *Summary Fact-Sheets on Pakistan, India and the United States*, 2010 (based on 2008 figures), Aquastat Online Database, www.fao.org/nr/water/Aquastat/countries/index.stm.

71. World Bank, *Pakistan Country Water Resources Assistance Strategy*, viii–ix.

72. Estimates for 2010 by the Population Division of the Department of Economic and Social Affairs of the United Nations Secretariat, *World Population Prospects: The 2008 Revision* (New York, United Nations, 2009), available at http://esa.un.org/unpp.

73. Based on a statement of the chairman of the Pakistan Water and Power Development Authority, Shakil Durrani, quoted in "Per Capita Water Availability Down: Drip and Sprinkler Irrigation Urged to Overcome Shortage," *Dawn*, March 23, 2010.

74. United Nations Population Division, *World Population Prospects*.

75. Pew Forum on Religion & Public Life, *The Future of the Global Muslim Population: Projections for 2010–2030* (Washington, DC: Pew Research Center, 2011); United Nations Population Division, *World Population Prospects*.

76. Pew Forum on Religion & Public Life, *Future of the Global Muslim Population*, executive summary.

77. Griffith Feeney and Iqbal Alam, "New Estimates and Projections of Population Growth in Pakistan," *Population and Development Review* 29, no. 3 (September 2003): 483–92.

78. Woodrow Wilson International Center for Scholars, "Defusing the Bomb: Overcoming Pakistan's Population Challenge," summary of the event organized in Washington, June 9, 2010, www.wilsoncenter.org/index.cfm?fuseaction=events.event_summary&event_id=620365.

79. World Bank, *World Development Indicators*, online data, April 2010; Stanley A. Weiss, "Help Us or We Leave," *International Herald Tribune*, May 28, 2009. Total fertility rate is an estimate of the number of children an average woman is likely to have during her reproductive years.

80. Population Division, Department of Economic and Social Affairs, United Nations, *World Population Prospects: The 2006 Revision* (New York: United Nations, 2007), xii.

81. Pakistan Ministry of Water and Power, *Pakistan Water Sector Strategy*, 7.

82. John Kerry, "Pakistan Needs Our Support," *Washington Times*, January 23, 2009.

83. The Pakistani government's 2005 estimate of national literacy rate was 47 percent. Pakistan has become more unequal than ever before, as shown by the United Nations Development Program's annual *Human Development Reports*, which measure inequality on the basis of the "gini index" instead of the "gini coefficient."

84. Griff Witte, "Poor Schooling Slows Anti-Terrorism Effort in Pakistan," *Washington Post*, January 17, 2010.

85. Pew Global Attitudes Project, *America's Image Remains Poor: Concern about Extremist Threat Slips in Pakistan* (Washington, DC: Pew Research Center, 2010).

86. E.g., one person was killed and three were wounded in a water-related riot in the southern port city of Eden in August 2009. "Yemen's Capital Running Out of Water," *Washington Times*, November 15, 2009.

87. Judith Evans, "Yemen Could Become First Nation to Run Out of Water," *The Times* (London), October 21, 2009.

88. Republic of Yemen, *National Water Strategy and Implementation Plan* (Sanaa: Ministry of Water and Environment, 2005); Qahtan Yehya A. M. Al-Asbahi, "Water Resources Information in Yemen," paper presented to International Work Session on Water Statistics, organized by United Nations Intersecretariat Working Group on Environment Statistics, Vienna, June 20–22, 2005, 2.

89. Sabrina Tavernise and Waqar Gillani, "Frustrated Strivers in Pakistan Turn to Jihad," *New York Times*, February 28, 2010.

90. Woodrow Wilson International Center for Scholars, "Defusing the Bomb."

91. Pakistan's public schools, with more than 20 million students, count for far more than the madrassas, which still educate only about 1.5 million.

92. Pew Forum on Religion & Public Life, *Future of the Global Muslim Population*.

93. Pakistan Ministry of Water and Power, *Pakistan Water Sector Strategy*, 7.

94. Khaleeq Kiani, "WB Calls for Overhauling of 1991 Indus Water Accord," *Dawn*, March 24, 2005.

95. Pakistan Ministry of Water and Power, *Pakistan Water Sector Strategy*, 18.

96. Ibid., 21–22.

97. Indus Waters Treaty, Annexure E, "Storage of Waters by India on the Western Rivers," treaty signed in Karachi on September 19, 1960.

98. Pakistani foreign minister Shah Mahmood Qureshi, news conference in Islamabad, April 30, 2010.

99. After Pakistan–India armed conflict in the Rann of Kutch in April 1965, an international arbitral tribunal was established with the help of the United Nations secretary-general. The tribunal in February 1968 awarded approximately 10 percent of the disputed territory to Pakistan—an award bitterly resented in India, which believed it had a solid case for sovereignty over the entire Rann of Kutch. India, however, has come to live with that award. For details of the award, see J. Gillis Wetter, "The Rann of Kutch Arbitration," *American Journal of International Law* 65, no. 2 (April 1971): 346–57.

100. Alice Albinia, *Empires of the Indus: The Story of a River* (New York: W. W. Norton, 2010), 284–309.

101. Patrick McCully, "And the Walls Came Tumbling Down," *World Rivers Review*, June 2005, www.internationalrivers.org/node/1464.

102. The slice ceded under the 1963 Sino-Pakistan Frontier Agreement comprised mainly the Shaksgam Valley, which is surrounded by snow-capped Karakoram mountains.

103. Human Rights Watch, "With Friends Like These . . .," September 20, 2006.

104. Zulfiqar Halepoto, "Diamer-Bhasha Dam: Risks and Controversies," *Dawn*, November 17, 2008.

105. World Wide Fund for Nature, *World's Top 10 Rivers at Risk* (Gland, Switzerland: WWF International, 2007), 25. Also see Azra Meadows and Peter S. Meadows, eds., *The Indus River: Biodiversity, Resources, Humankind* (Karachi: Oxford University Press, 1999).

106. Mustafa Talpur, "A Sorry Tale," *The News on Sunday*, June 22, 2008.

107. Simi Kamal, "Pakistan's Water Challenges: Entitlement, Access, Efficiency, and Equity," in *Running on Empty*, ed. Kugelman and Hathaway.

108. See, e.g., Kaiser Bengali, ed., *The Politics of Managing Water* (Karachi: Oxford University Press, 2003).

109. See Walter W. Immerzeel, Ludovicus P. H. van Beek, and Marc F. P. Bierkens, "Climate Change Will Affect the Asian Water Towers," *Science* 328, no. 5983 (June 11, 2010): 1382–85, DOI: 10.1126/science.1183188.

110. World Bank, *Pakistan Country Water Resources Assistance Strategy*, ix.

111. Steven Solomon, *Water: The Epic Struggle for Wealth, Power, and Civilization* (New York: HarperCollins, 2010), 18.

112. The annual Failed States Index—prepared jointly by *Foreign Policy* journal and the independent Washington-based group Fund for Peace—focuses on the comparative vulnerabilities and weaknesses of various countries that carry the risk of state failure. See *The Failed States Index 2010* (Washington, DC: Fund for Peace and Foreign Policy, 2010), www.foreignpolicy.com/articles/2010/06/21/2010_failed_states_index_interactive_map_and_rankings.

113. FAO, *Summary Fact-Sheet Pakistan*.

114. *The News* (Pakistan), September 27, 2010.

115. S. Akbar Zaidi, *Pakistan's Roller-Coaster Economy: Tax Evasion Stifles Growth*, Policy Brief 88 (Washington, DC: Carnegie Endowment for International Peace, 2010), 10.

116. UNEP, "Freshwater and Industry: Facts and Figures," *UNEP Industry and Environment* 27, no. 1 (January–March 2004); Jiyu Chen, "Dams, Effect on Coasts," in *Encyclopedia of Coastal Science*, edited by Maurice L. Schwartz, vol. 24 of Encyclopedia of Earth Sciences Series (Berlin: Springer, 2005).

117. Mara Hvistendahl, "China's Three Gorges Dam: An Environmental Catastrophe?" *Scientific American*, March 25, 2008.

118. Howard W. French, "Letter from China: Dichotomies Endure, But the Pressure Builds," *International Herald Tribune*, January 18, 2008.

119. United Nations, Economic and Social Council, "Emerging Challenges and Trends in Water Resources Management," 10. Also see ESCAP, *Sustainable Agriculture and Food Security in Asia and the Pacific* (Bangkok: ESCAP, 2009), 63.

120. Center for Strategic and International Studies and Sandia National Laboratories, *Global Water Future: Addressing Our Global Water Future* (Washington, DC: Center for Strategic and International Studies and Sandia National Laboratories, 2005), 40.

121. Jennifer L. Turner, "Water Conflicts: Catalyzing Change in China," in *Asia's Next Challenge: Securing the Region's Water Future*, edited by Asia Society (New York: Asia Society, 2009), 28.

122. See, e.g., Sociology Institute, Chinese Academy of Social Sciences, *Society of China: Analysis and Forecast 2010* (Beijing: Chinese Academy of Social Sciences, 2009).

123. According to the newspaper, "The country is facing mounting pressure during its social transition, including frequent attacks on vulnerable groups, aggravating pollution, serious corruption, inequality of distribution, and a widening income gap." *Global Times*, August 23, 2010.

124. Shan Guangnai, "Mass Incidents in 2009," *Southern Weekend*, February 3, 2010.

125. Malcolm Moore, "China's Middle Class Rise Up in Environmental Protest," *The Telegraph* (London), November 23, 2009.

126. John Garnaut, "China Insider Sees Revolution Brewing," *Sydney Morning Herald*, February 27, 2010, www.smh.com.au/world/china-insider-sees-revolution-brewing-201002 26-p92d.html.

127. Yu Jianrong, "The Unbearable Cost," *Caixin*, January 19, 2011, http://english.caing .com/2011-01-19/100218601.html.

128. Wang Huazhong, "Dam Forces Relocations of 300,000 More," *China Daily*, January 21, 2010.

129. Kang Juan, "Water Project Leads to Mass Relocation."

130. The official *People's Daily* quoted Zhang Jiyao, the director of the South–North Water Diversion Project office, as making the comment in an interview with it. *People's Daily*, July 29, 2010.

131. Kristen McDonald, Peter Bosshard, and Nicole Brewer, "Exporting Dams: China's Hydropower Industry Goes Global," *Journal of Environmental Management* 90, supplement 3 (July 2009): S301.

132. Wang Yahua, "River Governance Structure in China: A Study of Water Quantity/ Quality Management Regime," paper presented to inaugural meeting of World Citizens Assembly on Water, Kuala Lumpur, October 27–29, 2005, 2–5.

133. "Experts Warn China's Water Supply May Well Run Dry," *South China Morning Post*, September 1, 2003.

134. World Bank, *China: Country Water Resources Assistance Strategy* (Washington, DC: World Bank, 2002), 12.

135. Turner, "Water Conflicts," 27.

136. The highest population density is 17,289 inhabitants per square kilometer in Seoul, which now boasts 23 million residents, making it by some counts the second-largest metropolitan area in the world.

137. Based on figures of Ministry of Construction and Transportation, Republic of Korea, and FAO's Aquastat Online Database (2010).

138. FAO, Aquastat Online Database.

139. Shu Jae-myung, *Water Resources Prospect for the 21st Century* (Seoul: Korea Water Resources Corporation, Ministry of Construction and Transportation, 1993); Lee Yun-sik, *A Report on Long-Term Comprehensive Plan of Water Resources, 1991–2011* (Seoul: Korea Water Resources Corporation, Ministry of Construction and Transportation, 1990); FAO, *Summary Fact-Sheet Republic of Korea*, 2010, Aquastat Online Database.

140. Lee Hyo-sik, "Four-River Refurbishment Project Receives Legal Boost," *Korea Times*, January 18, 2011.

141. Food and Fertilizer Technology Center for the Asian and Pacific Region, *Major Agricultural Statistics 2008* (Taipei: Food and Fertilizer Technology Center, 2009), www.ag net.org/situationer/stats/.

142. The term "fertigation" is a fusion of "fertilization" and "irrigation," with the most common nutrient applied by fertigation being nitrogen. When combined with an efficient irrigation system, both nutrients and water can be manipulated and managed to obtain the optimal yield of production from a given quantity of these inputs.

143. World Bank, *Pakistan Country Water Resources Assistance Strategy*, xiv.

144. Water Footprint Network, "Water Saving by Trade," www.waterfootprint.org/index .php?page=files/Water-saving-by-tra de.

145. United Nations, *State of the Environment in Asia and the Pacific 2005*, 65; Water Footprint Network, "Water Saving by Trade."

Chapter 6

1. Intergovernmental Panel on Climate Change (IPCC), *Climate Change 2007: Impacts, Adaptation and Vulnerability*, Working Group II Contribution to the Fourth Assessment Report of the IPCC (New York: Cambridge University Press, 2007), chapter 10, "Asia, Executive Summary," www.ipcc.ch/publications_and_data/ar4/wg2/en/ch10s10-es.html.

2. Ibid., "Executive Summary" and section 10.4, "Hydrology and Water Resources."

3. Jianchu Xu, R. Edward Grumbine, Arun Shrestha, Mats Eriksson, Xuefei Yang, Yun Wang, and Andreas Wilkes, "The Melting Himalayas: Cascading Effects of Climate Change on Water, Biodiversity, and Livelihoods," *Conservation Biology* 23, no. 3 (2009): 520–30.

4. Food and Agriculture Organization of the United Nations (FAO), *Background on Water and Wastewater in the State of Kuwait* (Rome: FAO, 2005), 2–8.

5. "Turkmenistan," in *Irrigation in the Near East Region in Figures*, edited by FAO (Rome: FAO, 2007); FAO, Aquastat Online Database, 2010.

6. United Nations, *The State of the Environment in Asia and the Pacific 2005* (Bangkok: United Nations Economic and Social Commission for Asia and the Pacific, 2006), 62.

7. FAO, *Review of Water Resources Statistics by Country*, 2010, Aquastat Online Database.

8. FAO, *Country Factsheet China* and *Country Factsheet India*, 2010, Aquastat Online Database.

9. Yuanhua Li, "Strategies for Coping with Water Scarcity in China," presentation by deputy director-general of Department of Rural Water Management, Ministry of Water Resources, China, at UN-Water meeting in Stockholm, August 23, 2006, www.unwater.org/ downloads/wwwYuananhua.pdf.

10. Todd M. Johnson, Liu Feng, and Richard Newfarmer, *Clear Water, Blue Skies: China's Environment in the New Century* (Washington, DC: World Bank, 1997), section on "Water: Preserving Scarce Resources."

11. Cited in "World Bank Presses China to Take Action to Prevent Water Shortages," *US Water News Online*, June 2001, www.uswaternews.com/archives/arcglobal/1worban6.html.

12. James E. Nickum, "Is China Living on the Water Margin?" *China Quarterly*, no. 156 (Special Issue: China's Environment), December 1998, 880.

13. FAO, "General Summary Asia: Water Resources," Aquastat Online Database.

14. Ibid.

15. See Peter C. Perdue, *China Marches West: The Qing Conquest of Central Eurasia* (Cambridge, MA: Belknap Press, 2010); and James A. Millward, *Eurasian Crossroads: A History of Xinjiang* (New York: Columbia University Press, 2007).

16. Dilnur Aji and Akihiko Kondoh, "The Study on the Dynamic Change of Water Resources in Xinjiang by Using GIS," *Journal of Japan Society of Hydrology & Water Resources* 19, no. 4 (2006): 280–91; Shen Yuling and Lein Haakon, "Land and Water Resources Management Problems in Xinjiang Uygur Autonomous Region, China," *Norwegian Journal of Geography* 59, no. 3 (September 2005): 237–45.

17. Liu Yongbo and Chen Yaning, "Impact of Population Growth and Land-Use Change on Water Resources and Ecosystems of the Arid Tarim River Basin in Western China," *International Journal of Sustainable Development and World Ecology* 13, no. 4 (August 2006): 295–305.

18. The 1963 Sino-Pakistan Frontier Agreement states that the transfer of the Pakistani slice of Kashmir to China would be subject to "the settlement of the Kashmir dispute between Pakistan and India," as if China is not a party to the Kashmir dispute. Article 6 of the Sino-Pakistan Frontier Agreement reads: "The two parties have agreed that after the settlement of the Kashmir dispute between Pakistan and India, the sovereign authority concerned will reopen negotiations with the Government of the People's Republic of China on the boundary as described in Article 2 of the present agreement, so as to sign a formal boundary treaty to replace the present agreement, provided that in the event of the sovereign authority being Pakistan, the provisions of the present agreement and of the aforesaid protocol shall be maintained in the formal boundary treaty to be signed between the People's Republic of China and Pakistan."

19. Dean Cheng and Lisa Curtis, "China's Indian Provocations Part of Broader Trend," Heritage Foundation, September 9, 2010, www.heritage.org/Research/Reports/2010/09/Chinas-Indian-Provocations-Part-of-Broader-Trend.

20. FAO, Aquastat Online Data, 2010.

21. Ibid.

22. Eugenia Ferragina and Francesca Greco, "The Disi Project: An Internal/External Analysis," *Water International* 33, no. 4 (2008): 451–63; Greg Shapland, *Rivers of Discord: International Water Disputes in the Middle East* (London: C. Hurst & Company, 1997), 148–50.

23. See World Bank, *Climate Change, Irrigation, and Israeli Agriculture: Will Warming Be Harmful?* Policy Research Working Paper 4135 (Washington, DC: World Bank, 2007).

24. The plan is named after its author, Eric Johnston, a special adviser to then–US president Dwight D. Eisenhower. Negotiations lasted from 1953 to 1955 and, with Johnston playing a key role, a "Unified Plan" was negotiated, assigning the following quotas to the four riparians: Lebanon, 35 million cubic meters (MCM) per year; Syria 132, MCM; Israel, 400 MCM; and Jordan, 720 MCM—with 505 MCM for the East Bank and 215 MCM for the West Bank. See Sharif S. Elmusa, "Toward a Unified Management Regime in the Jordan Basin: The Johnston Plan Revisited," in *Transformations of Middle Eastern Natural Environments: Legacies and Lessons*, edited by Jeff Albert, Magnus Bernhardsson, and Roger Kenna (New Haven, CT: Yale University Press, 1998).

25. *Israel-Jordan Peace Treaty Annex II: Water and Related Matters.*

26. The Declaration of Principles (DOP) signed by Israeli prime minister Yitzhak Rabin and Palestine Liberation Organization chairman Yasser Arafat on September 13, 1993, incorporated a two-phase timetable. During the first five-year "interim" or "transitional" period,

Israel would incrementally withdraw from Palestinian centers in the West Bank and Gaza Strip, transferring administrative powers to an elected Palestinian Authority. In the second phase, the "permanent" or "final status" negotiations were to begin. According to the timetable, the "final status" negotiations were to begin no later than the start of the third year of the interim period, or May 1996, and conclude by the end of the interim period, or May 1999. Those deadlines, however, fell by the wayside.

27. See Peter Rogers and Peter Lydon, eds., *Water in the Arab World: Perspectives and Prognoses* (Cambridge, MA: Harvard University Press, 1995); Elisha Kally with Gideon Fishelson, *Water and Peace: Water Resources and the Arab-Israeli Peace Process* (Westport, CT: Praeger, 1993); Arnon Soffer, *Rivers of Fire: The Conflict over Water in the Middle East* (Lanham, MD: Rowman & Littlefield, 1999); Miriam R. Lowi, *Water and Power: The Politics of a Scarce Resource in the Jordan River Basin* (Cambridge: Cambridge University Press, 1995); Aaron T. Wolf, *Hydropolitics along the Jordan River: Scarce Water and Its Impact on the Arab-Israeli Conflict* (New York: United Nations University Press, 1995); Sandra Postel, *Last Oasis: Facing Water Scarcity* (New York: W. W. Norton, 1997); and Green Cross Italia, "Water for Peace: The Jordan River Basin" (n.d.), www.greencrossitalia.it/ita/acqua/wfp/jordan_wfp_001.htm.

28. International Commission on Large Dams, *World Register of Dams* (Paris: International Commission on Large Dams, 2003); International Journal of Hydropower and Dams, *1998 World Atlas and Industry Guide* (Guilford: Aqua-Media International, 1998).

29. FAO, *China: Survey 2010*, table 6, and "Country Profile: Democratic People's Republic of Korea," Aquastat Online Database.

30. See, e.g., Edward Cody, "China Gives No Ground in Spats over History," *Washington Post*, September 22, 2004.

31. US Department of Defense, *Military and Security Developments involving the People's Republic of China 2010*, Report to Congress Pursuant to the National Defense Authorization Act for Fiscal Year 2010 (Washington, DC: Office of the Secretary of Defense, 2010), 24.

32. David Shambaugh, "When Giants Meet," *New York Times*, June 16, 2009.

33. Five once-disputed islands in the Amur—Popov, Savelyev, Evrasikha, Nizhne-Petrovskiy, and Lugovskoy—total 3,000 square kilometers of territory. Also in dispute were Tarbarov and Bolshoy Ussuriyskiy islands, located in a 30-kilometer section of the boundary at the Amur-Ussuri confluence, and Bolshoy Island, situated in the Argun River's upper reaches.

34. Andrew E. Kramer, "China's Hunger Fuels Exports in Remote Russia," *New York Times*, June 9, 2010.

35. Eric W. Seivers, "Transboundary Jurisdiction and Watercourse Law: China, Kazakhstan and the Irtysh," *Texas International Law Journal* 37, no. 1 (2002): 1–2.

36. Marat Yermukanov, "China Obstructs River Management Talks with Kazakhstan," *Eurasia Daily Monitor* (Jamestown Foundation) 3, issue 34 (February 17, 2006) .

37. Seivers, "Transboundary Jurisdiction and Watercourse Law," 1–42.

38. Temirbolat Bakhytjan, "Water Dispute Threatens Central Asian Stability," Institute for War & Peace Reporting, RCA Issue 4, February 21, 2005.

39. Sergei Blagov, "Russia Wary of Possible Water Dispute with China," *Eurasia Daily Monitor* 2, issue 178 (September 25, 2005).

40. Frédéric Lasserre, "The Amur River Border: Once a Symbol of Conflict, Could It Turn into a Water Resource Stake?" *Cybergeo*, April 27, 2007, http://cybergeo.revues.org/index4141.html.

41. Xie Liangbing and Chen Yong, "Making Up for Lost Time: China's Hydropower Push," *Economic Observer*, January 4, 2011, www.eeo.com.cn/ens/Industry/2011/01/24/192214.shtml.

42. UNESCO World Heritage Committee, "Three Parallel Rivers of Yunnan Protected Areas," Decision 28 COM 15B.9, 2004, http://whc.unesco.org/en/decisions/181.

43. UNESCO World Heritage Committee, "Three Parallel Rivers of Yunnan Protected Areas," Decision 29 COM 7B.7, 2005, http://whc.unesco.org/en/decisions/362.

44. UNESCO World Heritage Committee, "Three Parallel Rivers of Yunnan Protected Areas," Decision 30 COM 7B.11, 2006, http://whc.unesco.org/en/decisions/1094, and Decision 31 COM 7B.15, 2007, http://whc.unesco.org/en/decisions/1396.

45. Reuters, "Chinese Province Hopes to Build Dams Despite Concerns," March 6, 2008.

46. Jin Zhu, "Nu Jiang Hydro Project Back on Agenda," *China Daily*, February 1, 2011; Jonathan Watts, "China's Big Hydro Wins Permission for 21.3-GW Dam in World Heritage Site," *The Guardian*, February 1, 2011.

47. Transboundary Freshwater Dispute Database, Oregon State University, "Case Study of Transboundary Dispute Resolution: Salween River," available at www.transboundarywaters.orst.edu/

48. Thomas Fuller, "Dams and Development Threaten the Mekong," *New York Times*, December 17, 2009.

49. Vitoon Viriyasakultorn, "The Mekong River Commission," in *Asia's Next Challenge: Securing the Region's Water Future*, edited by Asia Society (New York: Asia Society, 2009), 16.

50. Thomas Fuller, "Countries Blame China, Not Nature, for Water Shortage," *New York Times*, April 1, 2010.

51. Jamil Anderlini and Tim Johnston, "China Dam Plans Raise Mekong Fears," *Financial Times*, March 31, 2010.

52. Richard P. Cronin, "Destructive Mekong Dams: Critical Need for Transparency," RSIS Commentary 21, 2007, S. Rajaratnam School of International Studies, Nanyang Technological University, Singapore.

53. United Nations Environment Program and Asian Institute of Technology, *Freshwater Under Threat Southeast Asia: Vulnerability Assessment of Freshwater Resources to Environmental Change—Mekong River Basin* (Nairobi, Kenya: United Nations Environment Program, 2009), 13.

54. For a detailed account, see Ma Jun, *China's Water Crisis*, translated by Nancy Yang Liu and Lawrence R. Sullivan (Norwalk, CT: Eastbridge, 2004), first published in 1999.

55. Viriyasakultorn, "Mekong River Commission," 17.

56. Richard Cronin, "Mekong Dams and the Perils of Peace," *Survival* 51, issue 6 (December 2009): 149.

57. The Mekong River Commission (MRC) has a three-tiered organizational structure: A ministerial council, a joint committee, and a secretariat that is responsible for MRC's technical and administrative functions. The MRC has sought to promote subregional cooperation on resource management challenges related to water, hydropower development, biodiversity, forestry, agricultural productivity, and fisheries.

58. Geoffrey Gunn and Brian McCartan, "Chinese Dams and the Great Mekong Floods of 2008," *Asia-Pacific Journal*, August 31, 2008.

59. Cronin, "Mekong Dams and the Perils of Peace," 154.

60. Agreement on Cooperation for the Sustainable Development of the Mekong River Basin, signed April 5, 1995, in Chieng Rai, Thailand.

61. Calum MacLeod, "China's New Dam Seen as a Water Hog," *USA Today*, April 22, 2010.

62. Michael Richardson, "Dams in China Turn the Mekong into a River of Discord," *YaleGlobal*, July 16, 2009.

63. Lawi Weng, "Chinese Dams Accused of Flooding the Region," *The Irrawaddy*, November 14, 2008.

64. Mekong River Commission, press statement, August 25, 2008.

65. Denis Gray, "Mekong's Woes," *The Star* (Malaysia), December 10, 2002.

66. IPCC, *Climate Change 2007: Impacts, Adaptation and Vulnerability*, chap. 6: "Coastal Systems and Low-Lying Areas," 327.

67. Ibid., chap. 5, box 5.3.

68. Carmen Revenga, Jake Brunner, Norbert Henninger, Ken Kassem, and Richard Payne, *Pilot Analysis of Global Ecosystems: Freshwater Systems* (Washington, DC: World Resources Institute, 2000), 15–24.

69. Shi Lishan, a deputy director in China's National Energy Administration, quoted in "Nu Jiang Hydro Project Back on Agenda," *China Daily*, February 1, 2011.

70. See Judith Shapiro, *Mao's War against Nature: Politics and the Environment in Revolutionary China* (Cambridge: Cambridge University Press, 2001), chap. 1, "Population and Dams"; and Robert Louis Edmonds, ed., *Managing the Chinese Environment* (Oxford: Oxford University Press, 2000).

71. Jehangir Pocha, "Water Crisis Looming for China, Officials Warn," *Boston Globe*, January 2, 2004.

72. Vaclav Smil, *China's Environmental Crisis: An Inquiry into the Limits of National Development* (Armonk, NY: M. E. Sharpe, 1993), xv–xix; Changhua Wu, Crescencia Maurer, Yi Wang, Shouzheng Xue, and Devra Lee Davis, "Water Pollution and Human Health in China," *Environmental Health Perspectives* 107, no. 4 (April 1999).

73. Tan Yingzi, "Yellow River Dams on Verge of Collapse," *China Daily*, June 19, 2009.

74. As one writer has put it, "The proliferation of factories, farms and cities—all products of China's spectacular economic boom—is sucking the Yellow River dry. What water remains is being poisoned." Brook Larmer, "Bitter Waters: Can China Save the Yellow—Its Mother River?" *National Geographic*, May 2008.

75. US National Intelligence Council, *Global Trends 2025: A Transformed World* (Washington, DC: National Intelligence Council, 2008), www.dni.gov/nic/PDF_2025/2025_Global_Trends_Final_Report.pdf.

76. Tevfik Emin Kor, "Tigris-Euphrates River Dispute," Case Study by the Inventory of Conflict & Environment (Washington, DC: American University, 1997), www1.american.edu/TED/ice/tigris.htm.

77. Evelyn Goh, *China in the Mekong River Basin: The Regional Security Implications of Resource Development on the Lancang Jiang*, Issue 69 (Singapore: Institute of Defense and Strategic Studies, Nanyang Technological University, 2004). According to Goh, the power asymmetry between China and the lower Mekong states ensures that the water disputes will not flare into armed conflict; nevertheless they exacerbate Southeast Asian concerns about China's self-touted peaceful rise. Evelyn Goh, *Developing the Mekong: Regionalism and Regional Security in China-Southeast Asian Relations*, Adelphi Paper 387 (London: International Institute of Strategic Studies, 2007).

78. Aquastat Online Database, 2010.

79. FAO, *Review of World Water Resources by Country* (Rome: FAO's Aquastat Program, 2003), 63.

80. "Water Dispute May Trigger Indo-Pak War: Assef," *The Nation* (Pakistan), January 3, 2010, available at http://ow.ly/SivD.

81. Gwynne Dyer, *Climate Wars* (Toronto: Random House Canada, 2008).

82. FAO, *Review of World Water Resources by Country*, 65.

83. For an account of the protracted dispute over the Farakka Barrage, see Ben Crow with Alan Lindquist and David Wilson, *Sharing the Ganges: The Politics and Technology of River Development* (New Delhi: Sage, 1995).

84. Treaty between the Government of the Republic of India and the Government of the People's Republic of Bangladesh on Sharing of the Ganga/Ganges Water at Farakka, signed on December 12, 2006, in New Delhi.

85. Salman M. A. Salman and Kishor Uprety, *Conflict and Cooperation on South Asia's International Rivers: A Legal Perspective* (London: Kluwer Law International, 2002), 175.

86. Ishtiaq Hossain, "Bangladesh–India Relations: The Ganges Water-Sharing Treaty and Beyond," *Asian Affairs* 25, no. 3 (Fall 1998): 131–32.

87. Article XII of the India-Bangladesh Ganges Water-Sharing Treaty.

88. Article VII of the India-Bangladesh Ganges Water-Sharing Treaty.

89. A. Nishat and I. M. Faisal, "An Assessment of the Institutional Mechanisms for Water Negotiations in the Ganges-Brahmaputra-Meghna System," *International Negotiation* 5, no. 2 (2000): 289–310.

90. FAO, *Country Profile: Bangladesh*, 2010, Aquastat online database.

91. Stanley A. Weiss, "The Untapped Might of the Himalayas," *International Herald Tribune*, May 11, 2005.

92. Indian deputy national security adviser Satish Chandra, "Water in Global Security," speech to the twentieth international workshop on "Toward Global Security: New Strategies, Technologies and Alliances," Moscow, June 27–30, 2003, www.csdr.org/moscow03/chandra.htm.

93. For an overview of water resources development in Nepal, see Ministry of Irrigation, *Water Resources Strategy* (Kathmandu: Ministry of Irrigation, 2002); Dipak Gyawali, *Water in Nepal* (Kathmandu: Himal Books, 2001); and A. R. Rao and T. Prasad, "Water Resources Development of the Indo-Nepal Region," *International Journal of Water Resources Development* 10, no. 2 (1994): 157–73.

94. Hydropower made up 655 megawatts of the 714 megawatts of installed electricity-generating capacity in 2010 in Nepal. Ministry of Finance, *Economic Survey of Fiscal Year 2009–2010* (Kathmandu: Government of Nepal, 2010).

95. FAO, *Irrigation in Asia in Figures* (Rome: FAO, 1999), 177.

96. Ibid.

97. Dams and Development Project, United Nations Environment Program, *Mahakali River* (Nairobi: United Nations Environment Program, n.d.).

98. Treaty between His Majesty's Government of Nepal and the Government of India concerning the Integrated Development of the Mahakali Barrage, including Sarada Barrage, Tanakpur Barrage and Pancheshwar Project, signed February 12, 1996, in New Delhi, entered into force on June 5, 1997.

99. H. D. S. Greenway, "Hopes for Bhutan," *International Herald Tribune*, July 2, 2008.

100. FAO, *Summary Fact-Sheet on Bhutan*, Aquastat Online Database, 2010.

101. World Bank, *Bhutan: Development in a Himalayan Kingdom*, Report 4307-BHU (Washington, DC: World Bank, 1983); FAO, Aquastat Online Database.

102. King Jigme Singye Wangchuck, remarks at news conference in New Delhi, September 18, 2003, official transcript released by Royal Bhutanese Government.

103. Water Resources Group (Barilla Group, Coca-Cola Company, International Finance Corporation, McKinsey & Company, Nestlé S.A., New Holland Agriculture, SABMiller PLC, Standard Chartered Bank, and Syngenta AG), *Charting Our Water Future* (New York: 2030 Water Resources Group, 2009), 56.

104. Niranjan D. Gulhati, *Indus Waters Treaty: An Exercise in International Mediation* (Bombay: *Allied* Publishers, 1973), 139; Ramaswamy R. Iyer, "Indus Treaty: A Different View," *Economic and Political Weekly* 11, no. 29 (July 16, 2005): 3144.

105. Article XII(3) and Article XII(4) of the 1960 Indus Waters Treaty.

106. Fred Pearce, "Water War," *New Scientist* 174, no. 2343 (May 18, 2002): 18.

107. Jeremy Kahn, "The Next Al-Qaeda?" *Newsweek*, March 8, 2010.

108. Hilary Synnott, "Closing Argument: After the Flood," *Survival* 52, no. 5 (October–November 2010): 254. In his study on Pakistan, Synnott says the army has used Islam and the Kashmir issue to sustain its political clout, often with disastrous consequences for the

security of Pakistan and the wider world. Hilary Synnott, *Transforming Pakistan: Ways Out of Instability*, Adelphi Paper 406 (London: International Institute of Strategic Studies, 2009).

109. US assistant secretary of state for South and Central Asia Robert Blake, interview with the Press Trust of India, Washington, May 8, 2010.

110. Article III(2) and Annexures C and D of the Indus Waters Treaty.

111. The Indus Waters Treaty: The Baglihar Hydroelectric Plant, "Expert Determination on Points of Difference Referred by the Government of Pakistan under the Provisions of the Indus Waters Treaty," full text of the neutral expert's report, http://siteresources.worldbank .org/SOUTHASIAEXT/Resources/223546-1171996340255/BagliharSummary.pdf.

112. The full stipulation in the 1969 Vienna Convention on the Law of Treaties reads: *Article 62: Fundamental change of circumstances:* 1. A fundamental change of circumstances which has occurred with regard to those existing at the time of the conclusion of a treaty, and which was not foreseen by the parties, may not be invoked as a ground for terminating or withdrawing from the treaty unless: (*a*) the existence of those circumstances constituted an essential basis of the consent of the parties to be bound by the treaty; and (*b*) the effect of the change is radically to transform the extent of obligations still to be performed under the treaty. 2. A fundamental change of circumstances may not be invoked as a ground for terminating or withdrawing from a treaty: (*a*) if the treaty establishes a boundary; or (*b*) if the fundamental change is the result of a breach by the party invoking it either of an obligation under the treaty or of any other international obligation owed to any other party to the treaty. 3. If, under the foregoing paragraphs, a party may invoke a fundamental change of circumstances as a ground for terminating or withdrawing from a treaty it may also invoke the change as a ground for suspending the operation of the treaty.

113. Leaders of different political parties in India's Jammu and Kashmir have long contended that the long-term resource needs of their state were ignored by the federal government while concluding the Indus treaty with Pakistan—a view "shared largely by the intellectual, media and public circles in Jammu and Kashmir." K. Warikoo, "Indus Waters Treaty: View from Kashmir," *Himalayan and Central Asian Studies* 9, no. 3 (July–September 2005): 3–4.

114. Only 2,696 megawatts of hydropower-generating capacity has been built thus far in the Indian state of Jammu and Kashmir, as against the proven reserves of 18,653 megawatts.

115. David E. Lilienthal, "Another Korea in the Making?" *Colliers*, August 4, *1951*.

116. Lieutenant General Hameed Gul claimed that India has built sixty-two dams on the western rivers of the Indus system. Mamoona Ali Kazmi, "India's Hydro-Atrocities," *Daily Mail*, February 20, 2009. Also see "Jihadist Polemic Holds Clues to Mission Bombing," *The Hindu*, July 10, 2008. For its part, Hafiz Mohammad Saeed, the founder of the terrorist group Lashkar-e-Taiba, charged India with "water terrorism" by constructing "illegal dams" and diverting waters away from Pakistan, saying the Pakistani government must prepare the nation to counter the "Indian aggression." He organized a public rally of militants on March 7, 2010, where a resolution was passed declaring, "If India continues with its water terrorism, Pakistan must keep open the option of using force." The rallyists carried placards that read "Water or War," "Water Flows or Else Blood Flows," "Indian Water Bomb," and "Liberate Kashmir to Secure Water." *The Times of India,* March 8, 2010.

117. Lydia Polgreen and Sabrina Tavernise, "Water Dispute Raises Tension between India and Pakistanis," *New York Times*, July 20, 2010.

118. Usman Ahmad, "Baglihar Dam," Inventory of Conflict and Environment Case Studies 168 (Washington, DC: American University, 2006).

119. Paragraph 14 of Annexure D and Paragraph 18 of Annexure E to the Indus Waters Treaty.

120. India is permitted to build a maximum of 2.1 billion cubic meters (m^3) of storage on the Chenab, 1.86 billion m^3 on the Jhelum, and 0.49 billion m^3 on the main Indus stream.

Indus Waters Treaty's Annexure E, which is headlined "Storage of Waters by India on the Western Rivers."

121. Steven Solomon, "Drowning Today, Parched Tomorrow," *New York Times*, August 15, 2010.

122. US Senate, *Avoiding Water Wars: Water Scarcity and Central Asia's Growing Importance for Stability in Afghanistan and Pakistan*, Majority Staff Report Prepared for the Use of the Committee on Foreign Relations (Washington, DC: US Government Printing Office, 2011), 9. The report actually bristled with other basic inaccuracies, including asserting that the Indus treaty "quantifies the amount of water both countries will receive from these rivers" and confusing the western rivers with the eastern rivers with regard to hydropower stipulations.

123. "Along the Indus River, Saber Rattling over Water Security," *Science* 328 (June 4, 2010): 1226–27.

124. Pearce, "Water War," 18.

125. Walter W. Immerzeel, Ludovicus P. H. van Beek, and Marc F. P. Bierkens, "Climate Change Will Affect the Asian Water Towers," *Science* 328, no. 5983 (June 11, 2010): 1382–85, DOI: 10.1126/science.1183188.

126. F. J. Fowler, "Some Problems of Water Distribution between East and West Punjab," *Geographical Review* 40, no. 4 (October 1950): 589–91.

127. Article VIII of the 1909 Treaty Relating to Boundary Waters between the United States and Canada, official text, www.ijc.org/rel/agree/water.html.

128. See Article VIII of the Indus Waters Treaty, "Permanent Indus Commission."

129. Article VIII(4)(a) of the Indus Waters Treaty.

130. The United States-Canada Great Lakes Water Quality Agreement of 1978, as amended by the protocol signed November 18, 1987.

131. "Case Study—The International Joint Commission: Canada and the United States of America," Institute for Water and Watersheds, Oregon State University, October 2002, www.transboundarywaters.orst.edu/research/case_studies/Documents/ijc.html.

132. For the details, see the website of the US section of the International Boundary and Water Commission, United States, and Mexico, www.ibwc.state.gov/home.html.

133. Center for Strategic and International Studies, University of Texas at Austin, and Autonomous Technological Institute of Mexico, *US-Mexico Transboundary Water Management: The Case of the Rio Grande/Rio Bravo*, Report of the US-Mexico Binational Council (Washington, DC: Center for Strategic and International Studies, 2003), 11.

134. Article VIII(4)(d) and Article VIII(7) of the Indus Waters Treaty.

135. Article VII(1) of the Indus Waters Treaty.

Chapter 7

1. The International Law Commission (ILC), created by the United Nations to focus on specific international legal issues, adopted and submitted to the UN General Assembly in 2001 the draft articles under the title *Responsibility of States for Internationally Wrongful Acts*. ILC, "Responsibility of States for Internationally Wrongful Acts," in *Yearbook of the International Law Commission*, vol. 2, part two (New York: ILC, 2001). The draft articles, detailing internationally wrongful acts and possible countermeasures and penalties, were "welcomed" by the United Nations General Assembly on December 12, 2001, through a resolution. The resolution merely stated that the General Assembly "*takes note* of the articles on responsibility of states for internationally wrongful acts, presented by the International Law Commission, the text of which is annexed to the present resolution, and *commends them to the attention of governments without prejudice to the question of their future adoption or other appropriate action*" (emphasis added). For the full text of the resolution, see www.lcil.cam.ac.uk/Media/ILCSR/

A_56_83(e).pdf. The ILC articles are general in character and the possibility of convening a conference to help conclude an international convention on this subject remains distant. See a book on this topic by an ILC member, James Crawford, *The International Law Commission's Articles on State Responsibility: Introduction, Text and Commentaries* (Cambridge: Cambridge University Press, 2002).

2. The decision to create the Asia-Pacific Water Forum was incorporated in the "Joint Declaration" issued by the water resources ministers of the Asia-Pacific region during the Fourth World Water Forum meeting in Mexico City on March 21, 2006. The Declaration stated: "During the regional process leading up to the 4th World Water Forum, it became clear that several water-related issues and challenges were common across the entire Asia-Pacific region. Furthermore, with the increased interactions in the implementation of follow-up activities to the 3rd World Water Forum held in Kyoto in March 2003, stakeholders in the region quickly recognized that the region's diversity was not an obstacle but rather an asset to the identification and adoption of solutions to specific water issues. Based upon this common understanding, we will establish a new network, the Asia-Pacific Water Forum, to work in complete solidarity to identify and adopt solutions to water issues in the region."

3. With two-thirds of the world's poor living on the Asian continent, the water divide in Asia is revealing. Some 400 million residents lack access to safe drinking water and an estimated 1.9 billion lack basic sanitation in the Asia-Pacific. See Asia-Pacific Water Ministers' Forum, "Water Security: Challenges and Solutions for the Asia-Pacific," June 28, 2010.

4. See Asian Development Bank and Asia-Pacific Water Forum, *Asian Water Development Outlook 2007: Achieving Water Security for Asia* (Manila: Asian Development Bank, 2007).

5. G. John Ikenberry, *After Victory: Institutions, Strategic Restraint, and the Rebuilding of Order after Major Wars* (Princeton, NJ: Princeton University Press, 2001), 36.

6. Arjun Thapan, special senior adviser (infrastructure and water) for the Asian Development Bank, Opening Remarks to the Conference "Water: Crisis and Choices—ADB and Partners Conference 2010," Manila, October 11, 2010.

7. See United Nations Economic and Social Commission for Asia and the Pacific, *Good Practices on Strategic Planning and Management of Water Resources in Asia and the Pacific* (New York: United Nations Economic and Social Commission for Asia and the Pacific, 2005).

About the Author

Brahma Chellaney is a professor at the independent Centre for Policy Research in New Delhi and a member of the board of governors of the National Book Trust of India. He has served as a member of the Policy Advisory Group headed by the foreign minister of India. Before that, he was an adviser to India's National Security Council, serving as convener of the External Security Group of the National Security Advisory Board. As a specialist on international security issues, he has held appointments at Harvard University, the Brookings Institution, the Paul H. Nitze School of Advanced International Studies at Johns Hopkins University, and the Australian National University. His scholarly articles have appeared in numerous journals, including *International Security*, *Orbis*, and *Survival*. His opinion articles have appeared in *The Guardian*, *International Herald Tribune*, *Wall Street Journal*, *New York Times*, *Financial Times*, *Times of India*, *Hindustan Times*, *Economic Times*, and *Japan Times*. He is the author of five previous books, including *Asian Juggernaut: The Rise of China, India, and Japan* (HarperCollins, 2010).

Index

Figures, maps, notes, and tables are indicated with f, m, n, and t following the page number.

China (*continued*)
method in, 161–65; and regional power
balance, 17, 18–19, 21–22, 299; securitization of water resources, 49, 50–51;
storage capacity, 89; territorial conflicts,
2, 22–23, 177–80, 180*m,* 249, 250, 318*n*52;
Tibetan rivers as water source for, 98,
102–03; US relations with, 18; water
resources in, 9, 16, 29, 48, 51–52, 199. *See
also specific regions and hydroengineering
projects*
China–Brazil Earth Resources Satellite
(CBERS), 127
China Central Television, 340*n*40
China Daily on construction quality of dams,
72
China Gezhouba Group, 64
China Glacier Inventory (Chinese Academy
of Sciences), 112
China Hydropower Engineering Consulting
Group Corporation, 155, 340*n*44
China Natural Science Foundation, 115
China on the Edge (He Bochuan), 73
China Southern Power Grid Corporation,
256
China's Water Crisis (Ma Jun), 51, 67
China–Tibet railroad, 115–16, 117, 118, 148,
160, 335*n*66
Chinese Academy of Engineering Sciences,
161
Chinese Academy of Sciences, 100, 112, 114,
340*n*40
Chinese Communist Party: engineers in
leadership of, 69–71; 167; and Great
South–North Water Transfer Project,
135–36
chiru antelope, 124, 336*n*89
Chokle Namgyel Mountains, 117
Chongqing Province (China), 334*n*46
Chonji Lake, 255
Chukha Project, 286
CITES (Convention on the International
Trade in Endangered Species of Wild
Fauna and Flora), 124, 336*n*89
civil society, 204, 209–10, 304
climate change, effects of, 4, 10, 12–13,
24–25; on Asian water resources, 24, 88,
90, 101, 112, 243; and food security,

87–88, 173–74, 243; on glaciers, 101, 112;
and hydropower, 243–44, 274–75; on
Brahmaputra and Indus rivers, 101, 170,
226–27, 287, 294; on Ganges and
Mekong deltas, 272; and intercountry
water conflicts, 90, 287; and intrastate
water conflicts, 199; in Southeast Asia,
317*n*21; on Tibetan Plateau, 126–27, 176,
201
Climate Wars (Dyer), 278
Clinton, Hillary, 53, 335*n*73
cloud-seeding program, 275
coal-burning power plants, 72
Coastal Aquifer (Israel), 251
Coca-Cola Company, 209, 348*n*38
Cohen, Roberta, 326*n*55
Colca Canyon, 142
Cold War, end of, 19–20
"Colorado Doctrine," 187
Colorado River, 197
Common Minimum Program (India), 207
communist parties, economic growth's effect
on, 20
compensation for forced relocation, 232
Comprehensive Test Ban Treaty (CTBT),
161, 164, 192, 341*n*68
Conference on Disarmament (UN), 162–63
consumption growth, 11
continental land under irrigation, 31
continental water availability, 26–27, 26*t*
Convention on the International Trade in
Endangered Species of Wild Fauna and
Flora (CITES), 124, 336*n*89
Convention on the Non-Navigational Uses
of International Watercourses (UN), 185,
188, 306, 329*n*111
convict laborers, 63, 66, 326*n*55, 326*n*59
copper, 117, 118; Brahmaputra River
pollution from mining of, 148
corn production: in Asia as a whole, 31, 241;
and biofuels, 14; in China, 40, 84, 85, 87,
246; and food security, 31, 84–86, 86*t*; in
India, 85, 86*t*, 349*n*43; in Indonesia, 86*t*;
and irrigation, 37, 241; in Pakistan, 215
costs of fragmented approach, 75–84
cotton production: in China, 246; and irrigation, 36; irrigation needs for, 93, 241;
in Pakistan, 36, 215, 227; in ex-Soviet
Central Asia, 36, 67, 93